A Companion to
African American Literature

Blackwell Companions to Literature and Culture

This series offers comprehensive, newly written surveys of key periods and movements and certain major authors, in English literary culture and history. Extensive volumes provide new perspectives and positions on contexts and on canonical and post-canonical texts, orientating the beginning student in new fields of study and providing the experienced undergraduate and new graduate with current and new directions, as pioneered and developed by leading scholars in the field.

Published Recently

64. *A Companion to Twentieth-Century United States Fiction*	Edited by David Seed
65. *A Companion to Tudor Literature*	Edited by Kent Cartwright
66. *A Companion to Crime Fiction*	Edited by Charles Rzepka and Lee Horsley
67. *A Companion to Medieval Poetry*	Edited by Corinne Saunders
68. *A New Companion to English Renaissance Literature and Culture*	Edited by Michael Hattaway
69. *A Companion to the American Short Story*	Edited by Alfred Bendixen and James Nagel
70. *A Companion to American Literature and Culture*	Edited by Paul Lauter
71. *A Companion to African American Literature*	Edited by Gene Jarrett
72. *A Companion to Irish Literature*	Edited by Julia M. Wright
73. *A Companion to Romantic Poetry*	Edited by Charles Mahoney
74. *A Companion to the Literature and Culture of the American West*	Edited by Nicolas S. Witschi
75. *A Companion to Sensation Fiction*	Edited by Pamela K. Gilbert
76. *A Companion to Comparative Literature*	Edited by Ali Behdad and Dominic Thomas
77. *A Companion to Poetic Genre*	Edited by Erik Martiny
78. *A Companion to American Literary Studies*	Edited by Caroline F. Levander and Robert S. Levine
79. *A New Companion to the Gothic*	Edited by David Punter
80. *A Companion to the American Novel*	Edited by Alfred Bendixen
81. *A Companion to Literature, Film, and Adaptation*	Edited by Deborah Cartmell
82. *A Companion to George Eliot*	Edited by Amanda Anderson and Harry E. Shaw
83. *A Companion to Creative Writing*	Edited by Graeme Harper

A COMPANION TO AFRICAN AMERICAN LITERATURE

EDITED BY

GENE ANDREW JARRETT

WILEY-BLACKWELL

A John Wiley & Sons, Ltd., Publication

This paperback edition first published 2013

Edition history: Blackwell Publishing Ltd (hardback, 2010)

Blackwell Publishing was acquired by John Wiley & Sons in February 2007. Blackwell's publishing program has been merged with Wiley's global Scientific, Technical, and Medical business to form Wiley-Blackwell.

Registered Office
John Wiley & Sons Ltd, The Atrium, Southern Gate, Chichester, West Sussex, PO19 8SQ, UK

Editorial Offices
350 Main Street, Malden, MA 02148-5020, USA
9600 Garsington Road, Oxford, OX4 2DQ, UK
The Atrium, Southern Gate, Chichester, West Sussex, PO19 8SQ, UK

For details of our global editorial offices, for customer services, and for information about how to apply for permission to reuse the copyright material in this book please see our website at www.wiley.com/wiley-blackwell.

Library of Congress Cataloging-in-Publication Data

A companion to African American literature / edited by Gene Andrew Jarrett.
p. cm. – (Blackwell companions to literature and culture)
Includes bibliographical references and index.
ISBN 978-1-4051-8862-3 (cloth) – ISBN 978-1-118-43878-7 (pbk.)
1. American literature–African American authors. 2. African Americans–Intellectual life. 3. African Americans in literature. I. Jarrett, Gene Andrew, 1975-
PS153.N5C57 2010
810.9′896073–dc22

2009050302

A catalogue record for this book is available from the British Library.

Cover image: Lois Mailou Jones, *Jeanne, Martiniquaise*, 1938, oil on canvas. Photograph © 2010 Museum of Fine Arts, Boston, Gift of the Lois Mailou Jones Pierre-Noel Trust, 2006.1440.
Cover design by Richard Boxall Design Associates

Set in 11 on 13 pt Garamond 3 by Toppan Best-set Premedia Limited
Printed in Malaysia by Ho Printing (M) Sdn Bhd

1 2013

Contents

Notes on Contributors

Joanna Brooks is the author of *American Lazarus: Religion and the Rise of African-American and Native American Literatures* (2003), winner of the MLA William Sanders Scarborough Award, as well as editor of *The Collected Writings of Samson Occom: Literature and Leadership in Eighteenth-Century Native America* (2006). She is Associate Professor of English and Comparative Literature at San Diego State University.

Glenda R. Carpio is Professor of African and African American Studies and English at Harvard University, and the author of *Laughing Fit to Kill: Black Humor in the Fictions of Slavery* (2008). She is currently working on a book tentatively entitled *Ambivalent Alliances: Black and Latina/o Fiction in the Americas*, which includes a chapter on Junot Diaz's novel *The Brief Wondrous Life of Oscar Wao*. Professor Carpio started her teaching career in Compton, California, where she taught 8th-grade English and 4th grade through the Teach for America program. She recently received Harvard University's Abramson Award for Excellence and Sensitivity in Undergraduate Teaching.

Vincent Carretta, Professor of English at the University of Maryland, specializes in eighteenth-century transatlantic historical and literary studies. He has recently held fellowships from the John Simon Guggenheim Memorial Foundation, the Library Company of Philadelphia, the John Carter Brown Library, the Massachusetts Historical Society, the University of London, the W.E.B. Du Bois Institute for Afro-American Research at Harvard University, and the School of Historical Studies at the Institute for Advanced Studies, Princeton. Author of more than 100 articles and reviews, Carretta has also written and edited 11 books, most recently *Equiano, the African: Biography of a Self-Made Man* (2005) and (with Ty M. Reese) *Philip Quaque, Correspondence* (2010). His current project is a biography of Phillis Wheatley.

Theresa Delgadillo is Assistant Professor of Comparative Studies at The Ohio State University. Her research centers on twentieth- and twenty-first-century literature, visual culture, and music. Her research and teaching interests are interdisciplinary and include mestizaje, diaspora, cross-cultural and multiethnic contexts, intersectionality, performance, memory, nationalisms, gender, spirituality, and religion. Her monograph *Spiritual Mestizaje in Contemporary Chicana Narrative: Race, Religion, Gender, and (Trans)Nation* is forthcoming.

Michael J. Drexler is Associate Professor of English at Bucknell University in Lewisburg, PA. He is editor of Leonora Sansay's novels *Secret History* and *Laura* (2007) and, with Ed White, of the collection *Beyond Douglass: New Perspectives on Early African-American Literature* (2008). His current project, also co-authored with Ed White, is entitled *The Traumatic Colonel: The Burr of American Literature*, a portion of which recently appeared in *Early American Literature*.

Madhu Dubey is a Professor of English and African American Studies at the University of Illinois–Chicago. She is the author of *Black Women Novelists and the Nationalist Aesthetic* (1994) and *Signs and Cities: Black Literary Postmodernism* (2003), as well as essays on twentieth-century African American literature published in journals such as *African American Review*, *American Literary History*, *The Black Scholar*, *differences*, *New Formations*, and *Signs*. Her areas of research interest include African American literary and cultural studies, feminist theory, postmodernism, and science fiction.

Frances Smith Foster is Charles Howard Candler Professor of English and Women's Studies at Emory University. She has authored or edited 14 books, the most recent of which are *Love and Marriage in Early African America: An Anthology* (2008), *Still Brave: The Evolution of Black Women's Studies* (2009), and *'Til Death or Distance Do Us Part: Love and Marriage in African America* (2009).

Guy Mark Foster has published essays in numerous journals and anthologies, including *The African American Review*, *Empowerment versus Oppression: 21st Century Views of Popular Romance Novels*, *Souls: A Critical Journal of Black Culture, Politics, and Society*, as well as *The New Queer Aesthetic on Television: Essays on Recent Programming*, among others. His current book project, *Waking up with the Enemy: Critical Readings of Interracial Desire in Postwar African American Texts,* is forthcoming. He teaches both African American literature and Gay and Lesbian Studies at Bowdoin College in Brunswick, Maine.

Michelle Yvonne Gordon is Assistant Professor of English at the University of Southern California in Los Angeles. Her work on black writing and Chicago has appeared in *African American Review*, and she is currently working on a manuscript about the Chicago Renaissance and the Black Arts Movement.

Philip Gould is Professor of English at Brown University. His recent work involves eighteenth-century transatlantic literatures and cultures, particularly of this period's writing of the black Atlantic. He is the author of *Barbaric Traffic: Commerce and*

Antislavery in the 18th-Century Atlantic World (2003). His current book project examines the literature of the American Revolution through loyalist perspectives.

Kim D. Green is a PhD Candidate in the Department of English at Emory University, and she expects to earn her PhD in the spring of 2010. She studies African American and African Canadian literatures. Her awards include the Emory Diversity Fellowship (2004–9), Social Science Research Council Travel and Research Grants (2004–8), and a Mellon Travel and Research Grant (2009–10).

Gene Andrew Jarrett is Associate Professor of English and former Acting Director of African American Studies at Boston University. He is the author of *Deans and Truants: Race and Realism in African American Literature* (2007), and the editor or co-editor of *The Complete Stories of Paul Laurence Dunbar* (2006), *African American Literature beyond Race: An Alternative Reader* (2006), *A Long Way from Home* by Claude McKay (2007), *The New Negro: Readings on Race, Representation, and African American Culture, 1892–1938* (2007), and *The Collected Novels of Paul Laurence Dunbar* (2009). He has just completed a book on the politics of African American literature from Thomas Jefferson to Barack Obama, and is now writing a biography of Paul Laurence Dunbar.

Arlene R. Keizer is Associate Professor of English and African American Studies and Director of the PhD Program in Culture and Theory at the University of California, Irvine. She is the author of *Black Subjects: Identity Formation in the Contemporary Narrative of Slavery* (2004), as well as essays and articles in a range of journals including *African American Review*, *American Literature*, and *PMLA*. Her current work deals with black feminist postmodernism in literature, performance, and visual art; African American literature and psychoanalytic theory and practice; and the intersections between memory and theory.

Maurice S. Lee is Associate Professor of English at Boston University. He is the author of *Slavery, Philosophy, and American Literature, 1830–1860* (2005) and the editor of *The Cambridge Companion to Frederick Douglass* (2009). His work has appeared in such journals as *American Literature*, *PMLA*, *African American Review*, and *Raritan*. He is currently writing a book on chance, skepticism, and nineteenth-century American literature.

Keith D. Leonard is Associate Professor and Chair of the Department of Literature at American University in Washington DC. He is the author of *Fettered Genius: The African American Bardic Poet from Slavery to Civil Rights* (2006), co-editor of a special issue of *Callaloo* on the future of African American studies, and has published essays and reviews on such writers as Yusef Komunyakaa and Michael Harper.

Robert S. Levine is Professor of English and Distinguished Scholar-Teacher at the University of Maryland. He is the author of *Conspiracy and Romance* (1989), *Martin Delany, Frederick Douglass, and the Politics of Representative Identity* (1997), and *Dislocating Race and Nation* (2008); and the editor of a number of volumes, including *Martin R. Delany: A Documentary Reader* (2003), *The Norton Anthology of American Literature,*

1820–1865 (2007), and (with Samuel Otter) *Frederick Douglass and Herman Melville: Essays in Relation* (2008).

Tyler Mabry is a graduate student in English at the University of Texas at Austin. He is completing a dissertation on nineteenth-century African American poetry.

William J. Maxwell is Associate Professor of English and African American Studies at Washington University in St. Louis. He is the author of the award-winning book *New Negro, Old Left: African American Writing and Communism between the Wars* (1999) and the editor of Claude McKay's *Complete Poems* (2004; 2008). He is now completing a book, *F.B. Eyes: How J. Edgar Hoover's Ghostreaders Framed African American Literature*. He is a contributing editor of *American Literary History* and the book-review editor of *African American Review*.

Shirley Moody-Turner, Assistant Professor of English at Penn State University, specializes in African American literature and race and folklore studies. Her article, "Anna Julia Cooper, Charles Chesnutt and the Hampton Folklore Society – Constructing a Black Folk Aesthetic through Folklore and Memory," was published in *New Essays on the African American Novel* (2008), and she has articles on Cooper forthcoming in *African American Review*. Currently, she is working on her monograph, *Conjuring the Color Line: Folklore, Fiction, and Race in the Jim Crow Era*, which explores the complex relationships between representations of folklore and US racial and national identity formations.

Marlon B. Ross is Professor of English and African American Studies at the University of Virginia. The winner of John Simon Guggenheim and Lilly Endowment fellowships, he is the author of *Manning the Race: Reforming Black Men in the Jim Crow Era* (2004) and *Contours of Masculine Desire: Romanticism and the Rise of Women's Poetry* (1989), as well as various articles and essays on nineteenth-century British literature, twentieth-century African American culture, race theory, and gender and queer studies.

Cherene Sherrard-Johnson is Associate Professor of English at the University of Wisconsin–Madison where she teaches nineteenth- and twentieth-century American and African American literature, cultural studies, and feminist theory. She is the author of *Portraits of the New Negro Woman: Visual and Literary Culture in the Harlem Renaissance* (2007) and the editor of a new, annotated edition of Jessie Redmon Fauset's novel: *Comedy: American Style* (2009). She is currently writing a biography of Dorothy West.

James Sidbury is Professor of History at the University of Texas at Austin. He studies race, slavery and the cultures of the enslaved in the Anglophone Atlantic world during the seventeenth, eighteenth and nineteenth centuries. He is the author of *Ploughshares into Swords: Race, Rebellion, and Identity in Gabriel's Virginia, 1730–1810* (1997) and *Becoming African in America: Race and Nation in the Early Black Atlantic* (2007). He is currently at work on a study of patterns of race formation for Native Americans, African Americans, and European Americans during the era of the American Revolution.

James Edward Smethurst is Associate Professor of Afro-American Studies at the University of Massachusetts Amherst. He is the author of *The New Red Negro: The Literary Left and African American Poetry, 1930–1946* (1999) and *The Black Arts Movement: Literary Nationalism in the 1960s and 1970s* (2005), winner of the Organization of American Historians' James A. Rawley Prize. He is also the co-editor of *Left of the Color Line: Race, Radicalism and Twentieth-Century Literature of the United States* (2003) and *Radicalism in the South since Reconstruction* (2006).

Robin V. Smiles earned a doctorate in English from the University of Maryland. Her dissertation, "Romance, Race and Resistance in Best-Selling African American Narrative," critically examines popular romantic fiction by African American writers and argues for its inclusion in the canons and curricula of African American literary study. She has published articles on popular literature in mainstream publications such as *Black Issues in Higher Education* and recently published an essay on teaching popular literature in *Engaging Tradition, Making It New: Essays on Teaching Recent African American Literature* (2008).

Michelle Ann Stephens is Associate Professor of English at Colgate University and the author of *Black Empire: The Masculine Global Imaginary of Caribbean Intellectuals in the United States, 1914 to 1962* (2005). She is a member of the editorial collective of the *Radical History Review* and co-edited the special issue "Reconceptualizations of the African Diaspora" (January 2009). She is currently working on a book entitled *Black Acts: Race, Masculinity, and Performance in the New World*, featuring discussions of the performers Bert Williams, Paul Robeson, Harry Belafonte, and Bob Marley.

Mark Christian Thompson is Associate Professor of English, at Johns Hopkins University. His work explores the interrelatedness of African American expressive culture and European thought, often finding problematic, at times undesirable yet nevertheless existent, confluences between the two. In so doing, he uses a wide array of critical approaches, including historicism, political theory, psychoanalysis and deconstructive practices. As well as having published numerous essays, he is the author of *Black Fascisms: African-American Literature and Culture between the Wars* (2007). Thompson has taught courses in nineteenth- and twentieth-century African American literature; critical theory; and European modernism. He received his PhD in Comparative Literature from New York University in 2001, where his studies primarily focused on German Idealism and contemporary French philosophy.

Jeffrey Allen Tucker is Associate Professor in the Department of English and former Director of the Frederick Douglass Institute for African and African American Studies at the University of Rochester. He is the author of *A Sense of Wonder: Samuel R. Delany, Race, Difference, and Identity* (2004), co-editor of *Race Consciousness: African-American*

Studies for the New Century (1997), and author of articles on Octavia E. Butler and Colson Whitehead. His current research is on the life and work of John A. Williams.

Ed White is Associate Professor of English at the University of Florida. He is the author of *The Backcountry and the City: Colonization and Conflict in Early America* (2005), and has published essays in *Early American Literature*, *American Literature*, *American Quarterly*, and *American Literary History*. He is more recently the co-editor, with Michael Drexler, of *Beyond Douglass: New Perspectives on Early African-American Literature* (2008), and the editor of Hugh Henry Brackenridge's early novel *Modern Chivalry* (2009).

Andreá N. Williams is Assistant Professor of English at The Ohio State University, where she specializes in African American and American literature. She is a co-editor of the collection *North Carolina Slave Narratives* (2003). She currently is completing a book that examines social class divisions in postbellum African American fiction.

Ivy G. Wilson teaches comparative literatures of the black diaspora and US literary studies with a particular emphasis on African American culture, at Northwestern University where he is Assistant Professor. His books include *At the Dusk of Dawn: Selected Poetry and Prose of Albery Allson Whitman* (2009) and *Specters of Democracy: Blackness and the Aesthetics of Nationalism* (forthcoming).

Introduction

Gene Andrew Jarrett

The Blackwell *Companion to African American Literature* studies the canons and traditions of African American literature, even as it unsettles their major assumptions and representations. On the one hand, this collection of essays, written by today's preeminent and rising scholars, examines most of the well-known texts, contexts, genres, forms, themes, authors, and interpretations of the literature authored by the African diaspora in America. Ever since the eighteenth century, this literature has consistently incorporated forms ranging from orature, the written word, and song, to dance, jazz, and film, effectively demonstrating its versatility as a medium of African American cultural expression. The literature has constantly documented the struggles of African Americans with race and (anti-black) racism, African heritage and Euro-American influence, slavery and freedom, constitutional enfranchisement and educational progress, political agency and social assimilation, as well as the specters of history and modernity. Finally, African Americans have also regularly wrestled with the critical and commercial expectations that guided, compromised, or contradicted their own agendas as creative writers or as proclaimed agents of social change. On the other hand, the essays in this collection also interrogate why these formal, thematic, and commercial patterns have come to determine what we consider to be the best or most emblematic texts of African American literary history. The essays attempt to describe African American authors in international terms, not merely in national terms. They seek to interpret the literature as containing diverse, not predetermined, portrayals of African American experiences. They intend to reveal the complexities and contradictions of African American literature, not merely its coherence and consistency across history. They even endeavor to broaden conceptions of the literature beyond one race or ethnicity, or beyond the notions of race and ethnicity entirely, to consider how African American writers have grappled primarily with other social factors of human identity and relationships, including gender, sexuality, culture, class, politics, and ideology. By paying equal attention to the patterns and problems of African American literary history, this collection hopes to represent a landmark achievement in academic literary studies.

Of course, previous books of scholarship have been published with lengths and ranges equal to, if not greater than, those of this *Companion*, while fleshing out to a comparable degree the theoretical and historical dimensions of African American literature. However, these books have been mostly encyclopedias, a genre of academic writing that is not without its own set of limitations. Indeed, this *Companion* distinguishes itself from two chief competitors that have been in circulation for quite some time – namely, Gale Research Company's multivolume biographical encyclopedia of African American writers and Oxford University Press's companion to African American literature.[1] Though covering an equivalent scope of history and issues, the Gale and Oxford textbooks differ remarkably. Subtitled "dictionary of literary biography," the Gale volumes provide entries in alphabetical order on writers who lived during particular historical periods. The Oxford book also provides entries in alphabetical order, but they might include not only biographies of African American writers, but also descriptions of literary works, intellectual movements, and relevant social, cultural, and political issues. These huge books have been wonderful contributions to the historical and ongoing arguments that African American literature is a subject of legitimate scholarly inquiry, and that information about this literature deserves broad and continual distribution to academic and mainstream readers alike. What the Gale and Oxford books gain in encyclopedic detail and organization, however, they lose in highlighting the ideas on literature and history that contemporary scholars have been addressing in sustained, sophisticated, and cutting-edge ways. Each essay featured in this *Companion* thus approximates the textual length and analytic depth of an article published in an academic journal. At the same time, the whole collection of essays and their appended bibliographies offer the breadth of information that one would find in an encyclopedia. The combined presentation of advanced scholarship and vast information distinguishing this *Companion* aims to provide a clear, accessible, and comprehensive account of African American literature, while challenging the very assumptions that undergraduates, graduate students, and academic teachers have long held about it.

Although the history of Africans and their descendants on American soil can go as far back as the seventeenth century, the practical chronology of this *Companion* starts in the mid-eighteenth century, when the inaugural publications of African American literature appeared in 1746 with Lucy Terry Prince's poem "Bars Fight" and in 1760 with Briton Hammon's spiritual autobiography, *A Narrative of the Most Uncommon Sufferings and Surprizing Deliverance of Briton Hammon, a Negro Man*. The subsequent essays divide into three main sections – not according to the customary calendar of when centuries begin and end, but according to those specific historical events or periods that have had a discernible impact on the direction of African American literature.

Part I, "The Literatures of Africa, Middle Passage, Slavery, and Freedom," opens with a cluster of essays on the early American period, when our relatively recent term of "African American literature" fails to capture not only the native and ideological complexity of eighteenth-century authors but also the formal and thematic diversity of their literature. According to the first essay by Vincent Carretta, that term is fraught with contradiction, neglecting that English-speaking authors of African descent, such as Hammon, David George, Boston King, George Liele, James Albert Ukawsaw Gronniosaw, John Marrant, Olaudah Equiano, and Phillis Wheatley, were more transatlantic or international than exclusively New World or national in their identities. In addition to the enforced movement occasioned by the intercontinental slave trade, the voluntary travels of the authors across and around the Atlantic shaped their conceptions of "Africa" and "America." James Sidbury elaborates Carretta's thesis by providing historical background on the rise of plantation slavery in the British American colonies between the mid-seventeenth century and the late eighteenth century. Coupled with the provisional self-definition of Africans and their descendants during this period, the social effacement of slavery made African identity interchangeable with such New World terms as "Negro" and "black." However, Africa still remained a distinct trope for authors of African descent – including the aforementioned Gronniosaw, Equiano, and Wheatley, but also Venture Smith and John Jea. The trope suggested an imaginative reorientation to the traumas of the past, the struggles of the present, and the promises of the future, even as the material experiences of Africa itself continued to dissipate as a personal or collective reference point at the dawn of the nineteenth century.

Frances Smith Foster and Kim D. Green help usher the *Companion* into a more focused discussion on how authors of African descent in the early national period pivoted toward establishing an identifiably African American tradition of literary writing. In their analyses of some of the authors listed above alongside Jupiter Hammon (unrelated to Briton Hammon), Jarena Lee, and David Walker, Foster and Green examine the creole languages and religious dimensions of early African American literature. Particularly, the concepts of "ports" and "pulpits" characterize the dual means by which African American writers had expressed religious doctrine and demonstrated their own salvation, and by which their readers entered into religious or spiritual fellowship (as in a conventional church) with them and with cooperating communities of readers. Nonetheless, early African American literature had employed the two concepts in the service of antislavery and anticolonial discourse, a subject that Joanna Brooks and Tyler Mabry expound on. In their essay, Brooks and Mabry paint in broader historical strokes the fact that many early African American writers, such as (Briton and Jupiter) Hammon, Wheatley, Marrant, Equiano, King, Smith, and Prince Hall, belonged to Boston- and Philadelphia-based religious networks of Anglo-Protestantism. From here, the scholars connect the struggles of these writers against racial discrimination and oppression with their literary uses of certain rhetorical forms and religious themes, as well as with their cultural and commercial strategies to publish and circulate the literature within religious networks.

As persuasive as the argument for the multilingual and religious origins of African American literature may be, we must acknowledge yet another potential origin, according to Michael J. Drexler and Ed White: the 1801 constitution disseminated by Toussaint L'Ouverture, the leader of a slave revolt on the French colony of

Saint-Domingue, declaring the transition of this island toward national independence. They suggest that this document turned out to be one of the most widely read in early America, even though authored by an English-speaking African descendant. In debates over the origins of African American literature, Drexler and White argue, we must account for the specific text and context of Toussaint's critique of the Anglo-Saxon universalist claims to social and political morality that had underwritten Western Enlightenment rationality.

Part I also includes a second cluster of essays concentrating mostly on the antebellum years, or roughly from the early 1830s, when American antislavery societies were being founded, through the early 1860s, the period of the Civil War. Philip Gould elucidates the economic sophistication of antebellum antislavery literature, such as those written by William Wells Brown, Harriet Jacobs, Henry Bibb, William Grimes, Solomon Northrup, and Frederick Douglass, whose critique of slave capitalism anticipated the anxieties of white, bourgeois, and Protestant readers who were experiencing the modernization of the North. Maurice S. Lee shifts our attention to the renascence of African American literature in the 1850s – in which participated some of the slave-narrative authors mentioned by Gould, but also such novelists as Brown, Frank J. Webb, Harriet Wilson, and Martin Delany. During the decade, this literature evolved across multiple genres, ranging from the slave narrative and the novel to drama and poetry, buoyed, in part, by the special coalescence of ideological, economic, and political forces as slavery became increasingly untenable and as the country began to brace for the Civil War.

In the mid-nineteenth century, nationalism was one of the great ideological forces that African American writers had claimed as their own and had concomitantly expressed in literature. In short, it was the basis of what Robert S. Levine calls African American literary nationalism. Sown in the early part of the nineteenth century, the seeds of literary nationalism blossomed into the antebellum era, inviting present-day study not because of the clarity of its compelling argument for a black nation within a US nation. Rather, nationalism – which intrigued David Walker and Martin Delany, most notably – demands new explanations of its sometimes conflicting, sometimes compatible, set of biological, cultural, political, and spiritual doctrines. That diverse set of ideologies complicates the one-to-one relationship between racial nationalism, on the one hand, and African American literature, on the other. Finally, Ivy G. Wilson reminds us that poetry, not only the prose that Lee and Levine mostly discuss, had been a literary form of historical significance. For example, he examines the poems of James Monroe Whitfield and James Madison Bell, as well as their publications in periodicals, to limn the broader relationship between, say, African American readers and what Wilson calls an emergent "print nationalism."

The essays in Part II, entitled "New Negro Aesthetics, Culture, and Politics," turn squarely toward the era ranging from 1865, the end of the Civil War, to around 1940, when World War Two was just underway. Beginning in the postbellum nineteenth century, Marlon B. Ross conducts an erudite analysis of the discourses of racial uplift vis-à-vis the "New Negro," particularly as they accompanied the political movement of most African Americans from slavery to freedom, through Southern "Reconstruction" in the 1870s, through the rise of Jim Crow segregation in the 1880s, through the renaissance of African American intellectual and artistic culture culminating in the 1920s, and even extending into the next couple of decades. For the purpose of this volume, the most discernible registers of New Negro discourse lay in the aesthetic, cultural, and political negotiation of African American communities with national modernity, which was signified by the increasing constellation of urban centers and the advancing technologies of cultural representation, to name but two examples. Within Ross's rubric, my own essay argues that certain African American writers of the postbellum period used dialect not merely to demonstrate class and intellectual divisions within and among social groups, but also to deliver subtle moral and political messages that elevated the sensibilities of whites on race and racism. Andreá N. Williams studies the generic development of African American literary realism within this context of cultural and political change. She discerns the imprints of political agency in how certain African American writers, such as Charles W. Chesnutt, Pauline Hopkins, Sutton Griggs, and Paul Laurence Dunbar, refused to deny the political and historical exigencies that happened to bear on the aesthetics of literary representation. Shirley Moody-Turner takes a similar line in her essay, but she emphasizes the historical relationship between folklore and African American literature, such as in the way Chesnutt, Hopkins, and Dunbar envisioned folklore as a key feature of African American communities, political discourses, and cultural genealogies.

The next cluster of essays in Part II deal mainly with the manifestations of New Negro ideology in the first half of the twentieth century. Michelle Ann Stephens acknowledges, as Marlon B. Ross does, the long history of New Negro thought. Nonetheless, she cites the 1920s as the climax of this history, when Harlem, in particular, became an epicenter of an artistic, cultural, and intellectual efflorescence whose repercussions could be felt as far away as western Europe. The movement was led by Alain Locke, the so-called dean of the New Negro Renaissance, and featured Zora Neale Hurston, Langston Hughes, and Claude McKay. Although typically described as a New Negro Renaissance in Harlem – or the Harlem Renaissance, in short – Stephens suggests that we need a transnational or international understanding of the movement, in which not only Harlem but other parts of the United States, as well as parts of Europe, Africa, and the Caribbean, all convened diasporic formations of black identity and consciousness. Cherene Sherrard-Johnson, who likewise appreciates transnational valences, focuses on their refractions through both visual and literary media. She points to a number of illustrators, including Aaron Douglas, Winold Reiss, and Miguel Covarrubias, who collaborated with writers. Conversely, she points to a number of writers, including Hurston, Jean Toomer, and Jessie Redmon Fauset, who worked with illustrators. Such alternately intraracial, interracial, and international relationships indicate that, between World Wars One and Two, the particular dimensions of literary artistry were more complex than we may have initially imagined.

Far less cordial than the collaborations mentioned by Sherrard-Johnson was the mutual detestation between Marcus Garvey and W.E.B. Du Bois, according to Mark

Christian Thompson. Writing in the 1920s, both men disagreed on the political value of aesthetic beauty. Whereas Du Bois believed that art could serve as a doctrinal means of promulgating the rights of blacks while specifically countering white hegemonic discourse, Garvey believed that art should serve as a rhetorical means of appreciating black cultural autonomy and accomplishment irrespective of this discourse. Even less respectful than this antagonism between Garvey and Du Bois, furthermore, was the Federal Bureau of Investigation's surveillance of African American writers in the age of modernism. More to the point, William J. Maxwell argues that the secret investigations of Hughes, McKay, Richard Wright, Gwendolyn Bennett, Sterling Brown, Georgia Douglas Johnson, J.A. Rogers, George Schuyler, and Walter White, among many others, by the FBI – then directed by J. Edgar Hoover and staffed with surreptitious literary critics – could have inspired the very literary imagination that has come to typify some of their works as modernist.

The final part of this *Companion*, entitled "Reforming the Canon, Tradition, and Criticism of African American Literature," deals with the contemporary period, which ranges from around 1940 to the present. In this age, the criticism of African American literature continued to evolve, and, by the rise of Black Studies departments across the United States in the 1970s and 1980s, it had become a cornerstone of African American canons and literary traditions in academic curricula. Put another way, part of the intellectual development and academic institutionalization of African American literary studies derived from a heightened awareness among African American critics and writers of the principles, stakes, and repercussions of previous movements. For example, Michelle Yvonne Gordon differentiates the (African American) Chicago Renaissance – born in Chicago's South Side and emblematic of African American artistic activity between the mid-1930s and the mid-1950s – from the Harlem Renaissance. Although numerous artistic forms emerged under the auspices of both movements, the literary avatars of the Chicago Renaissance including Wright, Gwendolyn Brooks, Margaret Walker, Frank Marshall Davis, Willard Motley, and William Attaway, were renowned for their expertise with social or documentary realism. Several attended to the cultural, environmental, and psychological circumstances of Chicago itself, and not infrequently incorporated a host of material, ideological, and political themes, ranging from plebeianism and proletarianism to the Popular Front and the Communist Party. Most important, the literary celebration of these themes was an antidote to the eventual bankruptcy, both literal and conceptual, of the New Negro Renaissance in the 1920s, even though, in fairness, the writers of the Chicago Renaissance owed some of their inspiration and creativity to the accomplishments of the earlier movement.

Jazz, one of the musical forms that Chicago, among other cities, founded in the early twentieth century, developed during the period of the Chicago Renaissance as an aesthetic bedrock of African American literature. Keith D. Leonard describes the literary traits of jazz – such as cultural hybridity, thematic complexity, and discursive improvisation – in works by Hughes and Ralph Ellison, to name but two. The literary works attest to the musical interface between, on the one hand, the rhythms of dissident African cultures and, on the other, the harmonies and instrumentation of imperial European cultures. The Black Arts Movement of the 1960s and 1970s was another renaissance that appreciated the aesthetic and performative intersections of literature and music. But whereas the New Negro and Chicago Renaissances openly acknowledged the interracial or intercultural hybridity of African American literary forms, the proponents of the Black Arts Movement, including Amiri Baraka, Larry Neal, Sonia Sanchez, Jayne Cortez, Haki Madhubuti, and Nikki Giovanni, insisted that black political power, racial pride, and cultural authenticity exist independent of the mainstream, or predominantly white, influences of North America and Europe. The Black Arts and fellow Civil Rights Movements helped crystallize the cultural and political terms in which African American writers defined themselves and the experiences of others within their racial or ethnic communities.

African Americans writing during and in the wake of these movements, however, also may have grappled with the cultural and political implications of reading and writing the past, the present, and the future. According to Glenda R. Carpio, humorous forms, such as satire, parody, tragicomedy, and "signifying," have long been crucial to the ways that African American writers portrayed their communities while critiquing racism. Contemporary writers, like Ishmael Reed, Charles Johnson, Suzan-Lori Parks, Colson Whitehead, and Paul Beatty, have exploited the ability of humor to unsettle the assumptions of race and racism that have hamstrung discourses of African American identity and humanity. For Madhu Dubey, the neo-slave narrative, a genre of literature about slavery and freedom emerging especially since the 1970s, and featuring the likes of Reed, Johnson, and Sherley Anne Williams, among others, is another strategy by which contemporary African American writers have interpreted the history of racial-political struggle. For Robin V. Smiles, within the past two decades, Terry McMillan, Connie Briscoe, Tina McElroy Ansa, Bebe Moore Campbell, and other African American women writers have developed a special genre of popular fiction that likewise enables them to realize the history of racial-political struggle. The genre also helps the authors record the persistence, permutations, and complications of this struggle in the post-Civil Rights era, in terms of such topics as urban development, suburban migration, upward socioeconomic mobility, academic education, business professionalization, and romantic relationships within African American communities. Finally, for Jeffrey Allen Tucker, science fiction has become a form by which certain African American writers, Samuel Delany and Octavia Butler, above all, have overcome the monopolistic representations of human experience in African American canons and literary traditions. The writers have designed alternative representations of racial humanity and non-human species; global territoriality and cosmic extra-territoriality; temporality and a-temporality – indeed, representations that disrupt our prominent categories of identity, including but not limited to race and ethnicity, gender and sexuality, class and culture.

The final three essays in the volume show that the methodologies used to read scholarly texts are as important as the methods used to read literary texts. In other words, reading African American literature requires understanding the scholarly conversations that have already taken place or are still ongoing. For example, Theresa

Delgadillo calls for a more comparative approach to African American literature. She urges us to address the manifestations of the African diaspora not only in the American South, Northeast, and Midwest, but also in the broader Americas, including the Pacific Northwest, the Californian Southwest, Latin America, and the Caribbean. Expanding the geographic frame of African American literary studies can reveal the interstices and influences between and among the literary communities, cultures, experiences, and histories of the African diaspora. Guy Mark Foster argues for rethinking the relationship between African American literature and Queer Studies. Using the scholarship on James Baldwin as a main source for his examples, Foster exposes the consistent inability of Queer Studies scholars to account for race, along with ethnicity, class, and nation, in their same-sex or desire-based definitions of sexuality. Foster's critique opens the door to a more sophisticated and evenhanded reassessment of the literary, political, and sexual lives of Baldwin and of African American writers generally. Finally, Arlene R. Keizer sheds light on the increasing popularity and utility of psychoanalytic theory for African American literary studies. Keizer's refreshing meta-critical readings aim to identify the longer history in which African American writers engaged this theory, while indicating what the future may hold for this exciting new field of academic study.

To be sure, this *Companion* is not without its limitations. This brief introduction can only attempt to capture the nuances of the following essays, and many topics merely skimmed in the essays are important enough to deserve extended treatment. At this juncture, however, the goal of this book is not to tell a definitive scholarly story, but rather a provisional one that anticipates future corrections, elaborations, refinements, and extensions. Future editions of the Blackwell *Companion to African American Literature* – along with future publications of books similar to or emerging from it – would be the sign of not only the unwavering advancement of the study of African American literature, but also the unflagging appreciation of the literature itself.

Note

1 The first is the multivolume set published by Gale Research Company, and edited by Trudier Harris and Thadious M. Davis, *Afro-American Fiction Writers after 1955* (1984), *Afro-American Poets since 1955* (1985), *Afro-American Writers, 1940–1955* (1988), *Afro-American Writers after 1955: Dramatists and Prose Writers* (1985), *Afro-American Writers before the Harlem Renaissance* (1986), and *Afro-American Writers from the Harlem Renaissance to 1940* (1987). The second is published by Oxford University Press, and edited by William L. Andrews, Frances Smith Foster, and Harris, *The Oxford Companion to African American Literature*, which appeared in 1997 and 2001 in complete and concise formats, respectively. Note that I cite these books as opposed to the more general and widely available encyclopedias of African American culture and history, which Gale and Oxford have also published, along with Macmillan Reference Books.

Part I
The Literatures of Africa, Middle Passage, Slavery, and Freedom: The Early and Antebellum Periods, c.1750–1865

1

Back to the Future: Eighteenth-Century Transatlantic Black Authors

Vincent Carretta

Writing a chapter for the Blackwell *Companion to African American Literature* on eighteenth-century authors who in retrospect are seen as pioneers in the development of that literature immediately poses the problems of literary authorship, national definition, and ethnic categorization. For example, how does one define "author" in this context? The term "author" here subsumes both the subject and primary source of the published account. The author may or may not also have been the *writer*. When the *subject* and *writer* differed, the *writer* was a white amanuensis, who transcribed and edited the *author*'s oral account, and published it as an as-told-to tale. Whenever a black author speaks through a white writer, separating their voices is always challenging and may be impossible. The original author may have had a very different agenda in relating his or her narrative than the writer had in publishing it. Different agendas may help account for what can strike contemporary readers familiar with post-1800 writings by authors of African descent as the surprising absence in some pre-1800 texts of commentary on the transatlantic slave trade or the institution of slavery.

The anachronistic term "African American" is not a category capacious enough to cover eighteenth-century English-speaking authors of African descent. Most of the eighteenth-century authors now considered pioneers of African American literature would have been very surprised to find themselves classified as such. How should one categorize authors of sub-Saharan African birth or descent like David George (1743?–1810) and Boston King (1760?–1802), who were born into slavery in what would become the United States, emancipated themselves by joining the British forces as black Loyalists during the American Revolution, were evacuated to Canada by the defeated British, and who chose to move from there to settle in Africa? Or George Liele (1751?–1825), who fled from Lowcountry South Carolina as a black Loyalist to Jamaica at the end of the war? Or James Albert Ukawsaw Gronniosaw (1705?–1775), John Marrant (1755–1791), and Olaudah Equiano (1745?–1797), who, whether born in America or Africa, ultimately chose to live and die in England as African Britons?

Or Phillis Wheatley (1753?–1784), who published in London the first book by an author of African descent, decided to become an African American, and lived only the last year of her life as a subject of the United States government?

Many of the authors would have been most surprised to find themselves now considered African *American*. They fled the country that denied them full citizenship to live in Britain, where, as the case of Ignatius Sancho (1729?–1780) demonstrates, the only bar to voting rights was the same property qualification whites had to meet; or in Sierra Leone, where they were self-governing; or even in Jamaica, where the extraordinary case of Francis Williams (1697?–1762) shows that status could supersede ethnicity in a British slave society. Down the road, we might have to turn to a consistently lower-case use of "white" and "black." Only in the last decades of the century did people forcibly removed from Africa to undergo the Middle Passage and enslavement in the New World come to accept and gradually appropriate the trans- and supra-national social and political identity of "African" initially imposed on them by Europeans who sought to deracinate them. The indigenous people of Africa did not identify themselves as "African": they saw themselves as Ashanti, Fante, Yoruba, or any one of a number of other ethnic groups with differing cultures, languages, religions, and political systems. Victims of the Middle Passage and their descendants increasingly styled themselves "Sons of Africa," even if they had never been there. The transatlantic slave trade during the eighteenth century in effect created an *African* identity in the Americas for the millions of enslaved people who suffered the social death of the various ethnic identities they had while living in Africa.

The eighteenth-century African diaspora was not restricted to people who were forcibly extracted from Africa by Europeans, usually by means of African entrepreneurs, and taken to the Americas. Diasporic authors of the Black Atlantic also moved from one continent to another, and back and forth in many directions as they redefined themselves several times over. For some, the Middle Passage even led back to Africa. Paradoxically, the category "African," originally used by Europeans to erase ethnic identities, and later embraced by those upon whom it had been imposed, now enables us to discuss the range of identities available before 1800 to people of African descent. Elaborating our definitions of "African," "transatlantic," "diasporan," and "American" enables us to appreciate ways that eighteenth-century texts anticipate those in the following centuries, without judging the achievements of the earlier works by the standards and expectations of later periods.

The solution to the categorical problem may lie in two fields that take us back to the future in the ways we conceive of the first generation of Black Atlantic authors. The recent expansion of the purview of African American literary studies to include English-speaking authors in the Western hemisphere beyond the territorial limits of the United States, and the development of African diasporan historical and literary studies mark a return to the eighteenth-century conceptual framework that encompassed works authored by people of sub-Saharan African descent. In both modern fields of study, authors are included by virtue of line of descent from a shared continental source, no matter how many generations removed, as well as by complexion.

A more capaciously defined transatlantic diasporan approach emphasizes the role that crossing the ocean played in the conception, production, distribution, and reception of eighteenth-century Anglophone literature by people of African descent, and in the ways those authors identified themselves and were identified by others.

Attempting to trace the beginning of a canon or tradition to one text is risky, but transatlantic Anglophone-African studies offers a leading candidate, a date, and a cause in Briton Hammon's spiritual autobiography, *A Narrative of the Most Uncommon Sufferings and Surprizing Deliverance of Briton Hammon, a Negro Man*, published in Boston in July 1760. The transatlantic evangelical Christian movement known as the Great Awakening began in England in the 1730s and spread throughout Britain and its colonies during the following three decades. Led by John Wesley and George Whitefield, both Methodists within the Anglican Church of England, the Great Awakening provided the means, motive, and opportunity for the apparently sudden appearance of Hammon's *Narrative*. The evangelicals took religion to the people, rather than waiting for the people to come to church, and they saw all levels of society, including slaves, as having a potential share in salvation. The evangelicals actively proselytized throughout the British colonies, making little distinction between blacks and whites as potential converts, and preaching the spiritual equality of all believers. Unlike Presbyterians and non-Methodist Anglicans, evangelicals were relatively equalitarian in their assignment of leadership roles: they did not require advanced levels of literacy and education. The evangelicals approved of the emotional appeal and expression of faith, and the immediacy of the born-again experience. The emphasis by Protestant Christianity in general, and the Great Awakening in particular, on direct knowledge of the Bible was the primary motive for gaining literacy. Protestantism encouraged self-examination by the faithful, and the writing of spiritual autobiographies, both to monitor one's own spiritual development, and to serve as a model for the belief and behavior of others. Consequently, virtually all the early publications in prose by people of African descent took the form of spiritual autobiographies that trace the transition from pagan beliefs to the Christianity shared with the authors' British and colonial readers. White as well as black spiritual autobiographers commonly contrasted some form of physical captivity with spiritual freedom. Because evangelicalism was often perceived as critical of, if not hostile to, slavery, the long-standing belief that conversion to Christianity merited emancipation from slavery frequently underlies the emphasis on religion in the inspired black-authored religious narratives. The belief was so widespread that colonial statutes eventually denied its validity.

Briton Hammon's 14-page *Narrative* illustrates many of the complexities found in early Black Atlantic writing. Like many later black works, his narrative is about captivity, liberation, and restoration. And like many contemporaneous authors, at least at some point in his life he implicitly condoned the institution of slavery, albeit not for himself. Prior to 1800, slavery was usually accepted as a long-familiar part of the social and economic hierarchy. All recorded history, including the Bible, recognized the existence of slavery. Although some people called for the amelioration of the conditions of the enslaved, very few people imagined that slavery could, or perhaps even should, be eradicated. Had Briton Hammon not been identified in the title of his *Narrative* as "a Negro," nothing in his work would have assured us of his ethnic and social status. Presumably irrelevant to his narrative, that status is significant rhetorically solely because it demonstrates that the Gospel is designed for everyone, and that the ways of God can be justified to all people, regardless of complexion or status. Hammon's *Narrative* is clearly intended to be exemplary for whites as well as blacks, freemen as well as slaves.

With the permission of his "master" (which could mean either owner or employer), Major-General John Winslow, Hammon sailed in 1747 from Plymouth, Massachusetts, to Jamaica and Central America to harvest logwood for making dye. He was soon captured by Caribbean Indians, and subsequently rescued from them by a Spanish captain who took him to Cuba. There, Hammon lived with the governor until he was imprisoned for more than four years for refusing to be drafted into the Spanish navy. Hammon finally escaped from Cuba by gaining passage on an English ship, whose captain refused to "deliver up any *Englishman* under *English* Colours" (emphasis in original) to the pursuing Spaniards. Hammon joined several Royal Naval vessels as a cook after he reached England. When he was discharged in London he engaged to join a slave ship sailing to Guinea, but before he was to depart for Africa he learned of a vessel bound for Boston. He quickly changed his plans and signed on the voyage to Massachusetts as a cook. Once aboard, he was providentially reunited with his former "master," Winslow.

Although Briton Hammon's *Narrative* was probably not known by any later eighteenth-century authors of African descent, most likely because it was not published outside of Boston, it was the first of a succession of pre-1800 transatlantic spiritual autobiographies that culminated in Olaudah Equiano's *The Interesting Narrative of the Life of Olaudah Equiano, or Gustavus Vassa, the African. Written by Himself* (London, 1789). Even most black-authored as-told-to criminal, or execution, narratives, such as *Sketches of the Life of Joseph Mountain, a Negro, Who Was Executed at New-Haven, on the 20th Day of October, 1790, For a Rape, Committed on the 26th Day of May Last* (New Haven, 1790), are formally spiritual autobiographies. Like Hammon, Mountain is, according to *Sketches*, a transatlantic figure who at one point served in the British Royal Navy, but unlike Hammon, Mountain is a picaro who pursues his criminal career in England and the United States. Neither Hammon's *Narrative* nor Mountain's *Sketches* criticizes either the transatlantic slave trade or the institution of slavery. The stories did, however, give public voices to people of African descent, even if only indirectly, and to a geographically restricted audience.

The first transatlantic African autobiographer to gain an international reputation through the transatlantic distribution of his as-told-to tale was James Albert Ukawsaw Gronniosaw. His *A Narrative of the Most Remarkable Particulars in the Life of James Albert Ukawsaw Gronniosaw, an African Prince, as Related by Himself* was initially published in Bath, England, in 1772. Dedicated to the Countess of Huntingdon, Whitefield's patron, Gronniosaw's *Narrative* appeared in at least ten editions in England and

America by 1800, as well as in a Welsh translation (1779) and serial publication in the *American Moral and Sentimental Magazine* in New York (1797). Although Hammon's 1760 *Narrative* was undeniably the first publication by a transatlantic black author, the 1772 publication of Gronniosaw's *Narrative* arguably marks the beginning of the Anglophone canon of autobiographies authored by former slaves of African descent.

Known to later authors, Gronniosaw's spiritual autobiography introduced to the canon the framing comments by a white amanuensis, as well as the story of the Middle Passage, from Africa to North America via Barbados in his case. Gronniosaw's text also introduced the trope of the talking book: when an enslaved author mistakenly believes that a white person observed reading a book is engaged in an actual conversation with the book, he or she appreciates the need to become literate to also be able to "talk" to books, especially the Bible. John Marrant, Quobna Ottobah Cugoano, and Olaudah Equiano later elaborated the trope as they increasingly appropriated the Bible for the Black Atlantic canon. For example, Cugoano speaks as if he is an Old Testament prophet, and Equiano emphasizes the primary generic status of his *Interesting Narrative* as a spiritual autobiography by initially introducing himself to his readers with a frontispiece in which he extends an open Bible to them.

Gronniosaw's tale is more color-conscious than Hammon's, and less color-conscious than nineteenth-century slave narratives. Gronniosaw attributes his mistreatment during the Middle Passage to his complexion. When he moves to England as a free man and marries a white woman there, however, the only objection raised is to his marrying a poor widow. Gronniosaw's primary interest is in demonstrating the trials and tribulations a true believer faced anywhere in the world. Like Hammon's *Narrative*, Gronniosaw's does not address the abolition of either the transatlantic slave trade or slavery.

More complicated in its treatment of slavery is the as-told-to *A Narrative of the Lord's Wonderful Dealings with John Marrant, a Black (Now Going to Preach the Gospel in Nova-Scotia), Born in New York, in North America. Taken down from his own Relation*, first published in London in 1785. Unlike Gronniosaw's *Narrative*, Marrant's is a captivity narrative rather than a slave narrative because he was born free in New York and taken first to Spanish Florida and then South Carolina as a child. He experienced his spiritual rebirth when he heard Whitefield preach in Charleston. In response to his family's opposition to his new faith, Marrant wandered into the wilderness, depending upon God to feed and protect him. An Indian hunter brought him to a Cherokee town, where he was condemned to a painful death. His life was saved, however, by the miraculous conversion of the executioner. He tells us that during the American Revolution he was impressed into the British Royal Navy as a musician. Naval records, however, do not support his claims. Other records suggest that he may himself have been an owner of slaves in South Carolina. Following the war, he went to Britain, where he was ordained as a Methodist minister before being sent to Nova Scotia as a missionary.

At least in the fourth edition (1785), the "Preface" by his amanuensis/editor, Reverend William Aldridge, and a concluding affidavit from Marrant's English landlord attesting to his character and Christianity frame the *Narrative* proper. Only the fourth edition claims to have been "PRINTED FOR THE AUTHOR." Absent the phrase "a Black" in the title in all editions, and a reference only in the fourth edition to Marrant as "the free Carpenter," nothing in Aldridge's "Preface" or the *Narrative* itself – as in Hammon's *Narrative* – indicates that Marrant was of African descent. Not surprisingly, then, we find his ethnicity explicitly referred to within the *Narrative* only in the edition Marrant claims to have published himself. The fourth edition is also the only one that portrays Marrant interacting with slaves. He gives them religious instruction despite the objections of their owners, one of whom is the prototype of the excessively cruel white female slave owner who frequently reappears in subsequent slave narratives. Every edition of Marrant's *Narrative* carefully avoids making an emancipationist attack on the institution of slavery, perhaps because the text was mediated by an amanuensis, and ultimately patronized by the Countess of Huntingdon, who owned slaves in Georgia. Indeed, the ameliorationist message of the two paragraphs added to the fourth edition argues that Christianity will render slaves more docile and obedient. Marrant's actions and writings after the publication of his *Narrative* expressed a more hostile attitude toward slavery, and a more active resistance toward oppressive whites only after he moved from South Carolina to England following the American Revolution, and only when his words were published without the mediation of a white amanuensis. Publication of the narratives of Gronniosaw and Marrant marked the beginning of the tradition of Black Atlantic authorship, in which later authors were aware of their predecessors. For example, Cugoano acknowledges the works of "Ukawsaw Groniosaw [*sic*], an African prince," and "A. Morrant [*sic*] in America" in his polemical prose work *Thoughts and Sentiments on the Evil and Wicked Traffic of the Slavery and Commerce of the Human Species* (London, 1787).

Marrant was the first of several black Loyalists to produce transatlantic spiritual autobiographies by evangelical preachers. George Liele and David George each saw his own as-told-to "Account" published in *The Baptist Annual Register, for 1790, 1791, 1792, and Part of 1793* in London in 1793, and distributed simultaneously in New York, Philadelphia, Boston, Richmond, Savannah, and Charleston. "The Memoirs of the Life of Boston King, a Black Preacher. Written by Himself" was published in *The Methodist Magazine* (London, 1798). George and King, both former slaves, were evacuated by the British to Nova Scotia at the end of the American Revolution. They subsequently accepted a British offer to be brought to Sierra Leone to resettle in Africa. Liele was evacuated to Jamaica at the end of the Revolution. Although the ethnicity Liele and George share is foregrounded in their narratives far more prominently than in earlier Black Atlantic authors, the transatlantic slave trade goes unmentioned, and slavery is treated from an ameliorationist perspective. Their "Accounts" could be distributed in the slave societies of the Deep South because they explicitly reassure readers that Christianity poses no threat to the culture of slavery. Converted slaves, we are told, will be more productive, not freer, workers. King, on the other hand, exerting far more agency in the autobiography "Written by Himself," condemns, albeit only briefly, both the transatlantic slave trade and slavery.

Equiano's *The Interesting Narrative of the Life of Olaudah Equiano, the African. Written by Himself* (London, 1789) is far more complex than the works of Hammon, Gronniosaw, Marrant, Liele, and George. A remarkable achievement, it is very difficult, if not impossible, to classify in terms of its genre. Among other things, it is a spiritual autobiography, captivity narrative, travel book, adventure tale, rags-to-riches saga, economic treatise, apologia, testimony, and slave narrative. If Equiano was born in South Carolina, as his baptismal and naval records say, rather than in Africa, as he claims, *The Interesting Narrative* is also, in part, historical fiction. Equiano's control over the writing, production, and distribution of his autobiography throughout Britain probably helps account for why he was able and willing to address the issues of abolition of the slave trade and the institution of slavery more forthrightly than many of his predecessors and contemporaries. Equiano's pre-publication advertisements for the book and supervision of the publication and distribution of his autobiography make him an important figure in the history of book publishing. *The Interesting Narrative* was an international bestseller during Equiano's lifetime, with editions and translations published without his permission in Holland (1790), New York (1791), Germany (1792), and Russia (1794), in addition to the nine English, Irish, and Scottish editions, whose publication he supervised between 1789 and 1794. Explicitly an attack on the transatlantic slave trade, *The Interesting Narrative* is also implicitly an assault on slavery. Equiano constructs his argument so as to compel his readers to conclude that slavery must be ended. At various times in *The Interesting Narrative*, Equiano comes very close to crossing the line between amelioration and emancipation. For example, as he closes his account of his life as a slave in Georgia, South Carolina, and the West Indies, he likens himself to Moses, and quotes Beelzebub from John Milton's *Paradise Lost* positively. He leads his readers to conclude that slave rebellions are unavoidable and justified, only to step back rhetorically to promote an ameliorationist solution: "By changing your conduct, and treating your slaves as men, every cause of fear would be banished. They would be faithful, honest, intelligent and vigorous; and peace, prosperity, and happiness would attend you." In 1788, Equiano published in newspapers his overtly emancipationist positions in reviews of pro-slavery books, and an argument in favor of interracial marriage.

According to his autobiography, Equiano was born in 1745 in what is now Southeastern Nigeria. There, he says, he was enslaved at the age of 11, and sold to English slave traders who took him on the Middle Passage to the West Indies. He tells us that within a few days he was taken to Virginia and sold to a local planter. After about a month in Virginia he was bought by Michael Henry Pascal, an officer in the British Royal Navy. Pascal renamed him Gustavus Vassa. Equiano saw military action with Pascal during the Seven Years War. Pascal shocked Equiano by refusing to free him at the end of the conflict in 1762. Instead he sold him into the horrors of West Indian slavery. A clever businessman, Equiano managed to save enough money to buy his own freedom in 1766. Once free, Equiano set off on voyages of commerce and adventure to North America, the Mediterranean, the West Indies, and the North Pole. In Central America he helped purchase and supervise slaves on a plantation. Returning to London in 1777, he became concerned with spiritual and social reform. He converted to Methodism and later became an outspoken opponent of the slave trade, first in his letters to newspapers and then in his autobiography. Equiano became increasingly involved with efforts to help his fellow blacks in London, with the drive to abolish the transatlantic African slave trade, and with the project to resettle the black poor in Sierra Leone. Unfortunately, he was fired from his administrative position in the Sierra Leone settlement project just before his trip to Africa. One of the reasons he published his autobiography was to show that his behavior was ultimately vindicated. In 1792, Equiano married an Englishwoman, with whom he had two daughters. Thanks largely to profits from his publications, when Equiano died on March 31, 1797 he was probably the wealthiest, and certainly the most famous, person of African descent in the English-speaking world. He had achieved the economic and social status he sought throughout his life.

The Interesting Narrative is universally accepted as the fundamental text in the genre of the slave narrative. Equiano offered his own life as a model for others to follow. Equiano's personal conversions and transformations from enslaved to free, pagan to Christian, and pro-slavery to abolitionist, anticipated the changes he hoped to make in his readers, as well as the transformation he called for in the relationship between Britain and Africa. *The Interesting Narrative* was immediately recognized as a remarkable achievement, earning the praise of Mary Wollstonecraft and other reviewers. Part of the book's great popularity can be attributed to the timing of its initial publication at the height of the movement in Britain to abolish the slave trade. *The Interesting Narrative* offered the first account from the victim's point of view of slavery in Africa, the West Indies, North America, and Britain, as well as of the Middle Passage. His first reviewers quickly acknowledged the significance of the first-hand perspective of *The Interesting Narrative*, which greatly influenced the development of the nineteenth-century African American slave narrative.

Equiano was arguably the quintessential transatlantic African. He was ideally positioned to construct an identity for himself. He defined himself as much by movement as by place. Indeed, he spent as much of his life on water as in any place on land. Even while he was enslaved, the education and skills he acquired with the Royal Navy rendered him too valuable to his owners to be used for the dangerous and back-breaking labor most slaves endured. Service at sea on royal naval and commercial vessels gave him an extraordinary vantage point from which to observe the world around him. His social and geographical mobility exposed him to all kinds of people and levels of Atlantic society. Although the convincing account of Africa Equiano offers to his readers may have been derived from the experiences of others he tells us he listened to during his many travels in the Caribbean, North America, and Britain, his genius lies in his ability to have created and marketed a voice that for over two centuries has spoken for millions of his fellow diasporan Africans. Fittingly, Equiano was the first Black Atlantic author to call himself "the African."

By the end of the eighteenth century a tradition of accounts by authors of African descent had been sufficiently established to enable subsequent authors to subvert it.

As the wording of its title implies, *A Narrative of the Life and Adventures of Venture Smith, a Native of Africa: But Resident above Sixty Years in the United States of America. Related by Himself* (New London, CT, 1798) seems clearly indebted to the slave narrative tradition established before 1798. But in the work itself, the author appears to acknowledge that tradition by intentionally deviating from it. For example, Smith's *Narrative* is not an "abolitionist" text in either the pre-1808 or post-1808 sense. It apparently was not designed to participate in the international campaign to abolish the transatlantic slave trade, accomplished in both Britain and the United States in 1808. Nor does it seem to have anticipated later texts aimed at the abolition of the institution of slavery. On the other hand, Venture's willingness to resist slavery physically, his refusal to wait for emancipation in the afterlife, and his skepticism about Christianity anticipate significant aspects of nineteenth-century slave narratives exemplified by Frederick Douglass's *Narrative of the Life of Frederick Douglass, an American Slave. Written by Himself* (Boston, 1845).

One third of Smith's *Narrative* is devoted to his early life in Africa; another to his difficult life as a slave in Connecticut; and the last third to his economic success against great odds as a free black in New York and Connecticut. Smith's *Narrative* virtually erases his experience on the Middle Passage aboard the slave ship that brought him from Africa to the Americas, an absence particularly telling in the last decade of the eighteenth century, when opposition to the horrific conditions of the transatlantic slave trade received tremendous attention in the press on both sides of the Atlantic. Less than ten years after the reception of Equiano's *Narrative* demonstrated the market for, and the rhetorical power of, a first-hand victim's account of the Middle Passage, Venture recalled his transatlantic voyage as simply "an ordinary passage, except great mortality by the small pox." The author of Venture Smith's *Narrative* apparently intentionally avoided engaging in the international debate over the transatlantic slave trade. Nor is Smith represented as objecting to slavery as an institution. Unlike Cugoano, King, and Equiano, Smith appears to see slavery as bad for individuals, especially himself and members of his family, without attacking the system of slavery directly in his *Narrative*.

Unlike earlier narratives, Venture Smith's life in Africa and America is remarkably religion-free. His only reference to his African religion is to an implicitly monotheistic "Almighty protector," but unlike other contemporaneous authors of African descent he draws neither parallels nor contrasts between his original African faith and Christianity. Venture's explicit references to religion in America undermine his editor's prefatory characterization of the United States as "this Christian country." For Gronniosaw, alienated from his family and society in his African homeland by his intimations of monotheism, once he reaches America, European religious values quickly supersede those of benighted Africa. For Equiano, who devotes nearly one sixth of his *Interesting Narrative* to an account of life in Africa, many African cultural, political, and religious values prefigure the superior ones he finds in the European-American world. For Smith, however, African ethical values retain their superiority to American. Whereas Gronniosaw and Equiano contrast true Christianity with the hypocritical versions that most whites embrace, Smith apparently discovers all professed Christians to be hypocrites. Unlike the accounts of Gronniosaw, Marrant, Liele, George, and King, or those by Cugoano and Equiano, Smith's is pointedly not a providential conversion narrative. In effect, Venture Smith's unspiritual autobiography subverts the tradition to which it is indebted.

Paralleling the development of Black Atlantic autobiographies was the development of a transatlantic belletristic African canon represented by Francis Williams, Ignatius Sancho, and Phillis Wheatley. Williams was born to free black parents in Jamaica at the end of the seventeenth century. His father, a wealthy merchant and plantation owner, sent him in 1721 to London to be trained in the law. Three years later he was back in Jamaica, having inherited his father's estate and slaves. Williams' wealth and power were so great that in Jamaica he had the legal status of a free white man: no black could legally testify against him; he could sue whites; he could legally physically defend himself against whites; and he was the only free black who had the right to wear a sword. He died in 1762, leaving a greatly reduced estate, which included 15 slaves. His sole surviving poem is a Latin ode.

According to the biography that prefaces his posthumously published *Letters of the Late Ignatius Sancho, an African* (London, 1782), Sancho was born on the Middle Passage from Africa to the Spanish West Indies. At the age of two he was brought to England and given to three unmarried sisters. They renamed him Sancho because they thought he resembled the fictional Don Quixote's pudgy squire. He fortunately came to the attention of the Duke of Montagu, who was so impressed by his intelligence that he contributed books to his education. When the duke died, Sancho fled from his owners to the duke's widow, who took him into her employ as her butler. Her heir helped Sancho establish himself as a grocer. Sancho's financial independence as a male householder in Westminster qualified him to become the only eighteenth-century person of African descent known to have voted in Parliamentary elections in 1774 and 1780. Many of his letters discuss public affairs, and he published newspaper essays, serious and comic, under both his own name and the pseudonym "Africanus," in which he expresses his allegiance to the monarchy and his support for the British in the war against the rebellious Americans led by "General Washingtub" (November 5, 1777). Sancho's constant concern for his friends and his country enabled him to keep his own problems in perspective. He uses humor to avoid sounding self-indulgent even when talking of discrimination, illness, political disappointment, and death. Sancho gained widespread celebrity when one of his letters appeared in the posthumously published *Letters* (London, 1775) of Laurence Sterne. Sancho had initiated a correspondence with Sterne on July 21, 1766 when he encouraged him to continue writing to alleviate the oppression of Sancho's fellow Africans. The first African to be given an obituary in the British press, Sancho died on December 14, 1780 from complications associated with the gout.

Destined to become the first published woman of African descent, as well as the first black transatlantic international celebrity, Phillis Wheatley was born around 1753 in West Africa, probably between present-day Gambia and Ghana. She was brought to Boston as a slave in 1761. Encouraged by her mistress, who used her as a domestic servant, Phillis quickly became literate and began writing poetry that soon found its way into Boston newspapers. She gained transatlantic recognition with her 1770 funeral elegy on the death of Whitefield, addressed to his English patron, the Countess of Huntingdon. It was published in both Boston and London in 1771. Phillis had written enough poems by 1772 to enable her to try to capitalize on her growing reputation by producing a book of previously published and new works. Unable to find a publisher in Boston, her mistress successfully sought a London publisher and Huntingdon's patronage. Phillis spent several weeks in London with her owner's son in 1773. She returned to Boston before the publication of her book, *Poems on Various Subjects: Religious and Moral*, to nurse her ailing mistress, probably in exchange for a promise of manumission if she agreed to do so. Once there, she was soon freed, "at the desire of my friends in England." Wheatley's last years were marked by personal and financial loss. In 1778 she married John Peters, a free black who subsequently changed occupations frequently and was often in debt. They reportedly had three children, who all died young. Phillis failed to find a publisher for her proposed second volume of poetry, which was to include some of her transatlantic correspondence. Phillis Wheatley Peters died in poverty in Boston on December 5, 1784, and was reportedly buried with her youngest child in an unmarked grave three days later.

Poems on Various Subjects: Religious and Moral amply demonstrates her talents in various forms of verse, such as hymns, elegies, translations, philosophical poems, tales, and epyllions (short epics). Perhaps in part because of Huntingdon's patronage and protection, Wheatley's *Poems* was widely and generally favorably reviewed in British literary magazines, many of which included examples from the collection. Wheatley benefited from the growing transatlantic interest during the later eighteenth century in temporally, geographically, socially, and ethnically exotic sources of sentiment and literature. For example, after reproducing the text of "To Maecenas," the anonymous writer in the British *Critical Review* (September 1773) remarks, "[t]here are several lines in this piece, which would be no discredit to an English poet. The whole is indeed extraordinary, considered as the production of a young Negro, who was, but a few years since, an illiterate barbarian." The American Benjamin Rush praises Wheatley's achievements as a woman and a person of African descent in *An Address to the Inhabitants of the British Settlement in America, upon Slave-Keeping* (Boston, 1773), although he mistakes her status and how long she had been in America: "[t]here is now in the town of Boston a Free Negro Girl, about 18 years of age, who has been but 9 [*sic*] years in the country, whose singular genius and accomplishments are such as not only do honor to her sex, but to human nature. Several of her poems have been printed, and read with pleasure by the public." In France, a 1774 letter from Voltaire to Baron Constant de Rebecque states that Wheatley's very fine English verse disproves Bernard Le Bovier de Fontenelle's contention that no black poets exist. Political considerations also affected literary judgments. Several British commentators shared the opinion expressed anonymously in the *Monthly Review* (December 1773): "[w]e are much concerned to find that this ingenious young woman is yet a slave. The people of Boston boast themselves chiefly on their principles of liberty. One such act as the purchase of her freedom, would, in our opinion, have done them more honour than hanging a thousand trees with ribbons and emblems."

Sancho considered Wheatley's return to Boston as a slave a tragic move. He never met her, even though some of the places she visited while in London were within blocks of his home, and he never learned of her manumission. Establishing himself as the first Black Atlantic critic, Sancho wrote on January 27, 1778 to the Quaker Jabez Fisher of Philadelphia to thank him for the gift of a copy of Wheatley's *Poems*:

> Phyllis's poems do credit to nature – and put art – merely as art – to the blush. – It reflects nothing either to the glory or generosity of her master – if she is still his slave – except he glories in the *low vanity* of having in his wanton power a mind animated by Heaven – a genius superior to himself – the list of splendid – titled – learned names, in confirmation of her being the real authoress. – alas! shews how very poor the acquisition of wealth and knowledge are – without generosity – feeling – and humanity. – These good great folks – all know – and perhaps admired – nay, praised Genius in bondage – and then, like the Priests and the Levites in sacred writ, passed by – not one good Samaritan amongst them.

Neither the anonymous writer in the *Monthly Review* nor Sancho knew that Wheatley's trip to London had not only transformed her literary identity, but also offered her the opportunity to transform her legal, social, and political identities.

Williams, Sancho, and Wheatley posthumously became major figures in the transatlantic debate over slavery during the last quarter of the eighteenth century because both sides in the debate agreed that only equally human authors were capable of producing imaginative literature. For Thomas Jefferson and his pro-slavery contemporaries, African heritage subsumed any national or ethnic claims of identity. Jefferson could not conceive of people of African descent as being American or British. They were always and everywhere African because of their complexion. To justify slavery in the face of mounting transatlantic opposition, Jefferson felt compelled in his *Notes on the State of Virginia* (London, 1787) to reject claims for the literary achievements of anyone of African descent on either side of the Atlantic. In doing so Jefferson ironically acknowledges the existence of a canon of Black Atlantic authors:

> Religion indeed has produced a Phyllis Whately [*sic*]; but it could not produce a poet. The compositions published under her name are beneath the dignity of criticism ... Ignatius Sancho has approached nearer to merit in composition; yet his letters do more honour to the heart than to the head. They breathe the purest effusions of friendship and general philanthropy, and show how great a degree of the latter may be compounded with strong religious zeal. He is often happy in the turn of his compliments, and his stile is easy and familiar ... But his imagination is wild and extravagant, escapes incessantly from every restraint of reason and taste, and, in the course of its vagaries, leaves

a tract of thought as incoherent and eccentric, as is the course of a meteor through the sky. His subjects should often have led him to a process of sober reasoning: yet we find him always substituting sentiment for demonstration. Upon the whole, though we admit him to the first place among those of his own colour who have presented themselves to the public judgment, yet when we compare him with the writers of the race among whom he lived, and particularly with the epistolary class, in which he has taken his own stand, we are compelled to enroll him at the bottom of the column.

Defenders of the humanity of people of African descent were quick to respond. In *The Capacity of Negroes for Religious and Moral Improvement Considered* (London, 1789), Richard Nisbet notes, "The Letters of Ignatius Sancho; the Latin compositions of Francis Williams; and the more natural and ingenious productions of Phillis Wheatley … each of these has already furnished a publick and ample testimony of, at least, as considerable a portion of mental ability, as falls to the lot of mankind in general." And William Dickson challenges their detractors in *Letters on Slavery* (London, 1789): "To the Latin Ode of Francis Williams … , poetical pieces of Phillis Wheatley, and the letters of Ignatius Sancho, we appeal for specimens of *African literature*. – Have their calumniators obliged the literary world with any such specimens?"

Protest literature was not restricted to white opponents of the transatlantic slave trade and slavery, as the works of Cugoano, Equiano, and King demonstrate. Significantly, they all wrote as free men exercising their agency in the composition of their texts unmediated by white editors. Freedom also allowed women to speak more freely. Wheatley's antislavery stance became more overt in her poetry and correspondence after she was manumitted. For example, in the poem "On the Death of General Wooster," included in a July 15, 1778 letter to Wooster's widow, Mary, Wheatley exclaims,

But how, presumptuous shall we hope to find
Divine acceptance with th' Almighty mind –
While yet (O deed ungenerous!) they disgrace
And hold in bondage Afric's blameless race?

Similarly, in the as-told-to "Petition of an African Slave to the Legislature of Massachusetts," published in *The American Museum* (Philadelphia, 1787), Belinda briefly recounts her kidnapping from an idyllic Africa into North American slavery before appealing for compensation from the seized estate of her former Loyalist owner to enable her to enjoy "that freedom, which the Almighty Father intended for all the human race."

Whether it is Wheatley identifying herself with "Afric's blameless race," Belinda and Cugoano considering themselves "Africans," or Equiano proclaiming himself "the African," eighteenth-century authors of African descent saw their identities as transatlantic in ways that anticipate more recent transnational approaches to the writings of the Black Atlantic.

Bibliography

Carretta Vincent, ed. *Unchained Voices: An Anthology of Black Authors in the English-Speaking World of the Eighteenth Century*. Lexington: University Press of Kentucky, 1996; revised and expanded edition, 2004.

Carretta, Vincent and Philip Gould, ed. *"Genius in Bondage": Literature of the Early Black Atlantic*. Lexington: University Press of Kentucky, 2001.

Cugoano, Quobna Ottobah. *Thoughts and Sentiments on the Evil of Slavery and Other Writings*. Ed. Vincent Carretta. New York: Penguin Putnam, 1999.

Daggett, David. *Sketches of the Life of Joseph Mountain, a Negro, Who Was Executed at New-Haven, on the 20th Day of October, 1790, For a Rape, Committed on the 26th Day of May Last*. New Haven: T. & S. Green, 1790. Online at Documenting the American South, University of North Carolina Online: http://docsouth.unc.edu/neh/mountain/mountain.html.

Dickson, William. *Letters on Slavery*. London: 1789.

Equiano, Olaudah. *The Interesting Narrative and Other Writings*. Ed. Vincent Carretta. New York: Penguin, 1995; revised and expanded edition, 2003.

Gilroy, Paul. *The Black Atlantic: Modernity and Double Consciousness*. Cambridge, MA: Harvard University Press, 1993.

Gould, Eliga H. *The Persistence of Empire: British Political Culture in the Age of the American Revolution*. Chapel Hill: University of North Carolina Press, 2000.

Gronniosaw, James Albert Ukawsaw. *A Narrative of the Most Remarkable Particulars in the Life of James Albert Ukawsaw Gronniosaw, an African Prince, as Related by Himself*. Bath: 1772.

Hammon, Briton. *Narrative of the Most Uncommon Sufferings and Surprizing Deliverance of Briton Hammon, a Negro Man*. Boston, MA: 1760.

Jefferson, Thomas. *Notes on the State of Virginia*. London: 1787.

Klooster, Wim and Alfred Padula, ed. *The Atlantic World: Essays on Slavery, Migration, and Imagination*. New York: Prentice Hall, 2004.

Marrant, John. *A Narrative of the Lord's Wonderful Dealings with John Marrant, a Black*. London: 1785.

Nisbet, Richard. *The Capacity of Negroes for Religious and Moral Improvement Considered*. London: 1789.

Rush, Benjamin. *An Address to the Inhabitants of the British Settlement in America, upon Slave-Keeping*. Boston: 1773.

Sancho, Ignatius. *Letters of the Late Ignatius Sancho, an African*. Ed. Vincent Carretta. New York: Penguin Putnam, 1998.

Smith, Venture. *A Narrative of the Life and Adventures of Venture, a Native of Africa: But Resident above Sixty Years in the United States of America. Related by Himself*. New London, CT: 1798.

Walvin, James. *Making the Black Atlantic: Britain and the African Diaspora*. London & New York: Cassell, 2000.

Wheatley, Phillis. *Complete Writings*. Ed. Vincent Carretta. New York: Penguin Putnam, 2001.

2

Africa in Early African American Literature

James Sidbury

Before the 1760s, there were many black people in English letters, but there were no prominent black producers of English letters.[1] Shakespeare's *Othello* had been succeeded by heroic, comic, and tragic figures on the stage; Aphra Behn's *Oroonoko* opened the door to numerous enslaved black characters in fiction; less elite literary genres were peopled by countless black men, women, and children playing a variety of roles in English life. Both elite and popular graphic art brought even more black bodies into English society and Anglophone culture.[2] Blacks could be found as princes, jesters, victims, heroes, criminals, slaves, and loyal retainers in English culture. Nonetheless, the complex of oppressive forces arrayed against the hundreds of thousands of black people who actually lived in the British Empire blocked their access to literacy and to the kinds of learning necessary to produce an accomplished writer.

By the second half of the eighteenth century some things had begun to change. Increasing numbers of creoles among those enslaved by Britons, including many native English-speakers, lowered the linguistic hurdle faced by aspiring Anglophone writers. More importantly, doubts about the morality of slavery intensified among white Britons, leading some to attempt to ameliorate slavery while others offered encouragement and material support to individual slaves they perceived to have special talents. A vogue for black servants within British aristocratic households further increased the number of blacks with access to formal education. These combined changes never began to provide reliable opportunity to talented black people caught up in the machinery of British slavery. The vast majority of the victims of Atlantic slavery were sold into miserable lives on Caribbean sugar islands where their masters worked them to death. The changes did, however, produce conditions in which a small and extraordinary group of people who combined relative good fortune with unusual ability managed to overcome the persistent structures of oppression that they faced, and author texts that found their way into print in Anglo-America and England.[3] A number began to publish as self-styled African authors.

They faced a daunting cultural landscape. Between 1650 and 1800 plantation slavery emerged and then flourished in many of Britain's American colonies. Britons in England and America used the term "Africans" interchangeably with "Negroes" and "blacks" to refer to the people they purchased and imported into the Americas, as well as to the American-born (or creole) descendants of those victims of the slave trade. The intensification of the Atlantic slave trade, the increasing economic and cultural integration of plantation America into European society, and the growing currency of Western notions of human progress helped produce a conventional image of Africa as a primitive and pagan place. African people, according to this view, existed outside of the narrative of Western progress, and Africa remained an "unexplored" and dangerous place.[4]

Black authors were not the only ones to challenge this image, but they were among the most important. People like Ignatius Sancho, James Albert Ukawsaw Gronniosaw, Quobna Ottobah Cugoano, and Olaudah Equiano or Gustavus Vassa in England, as well as Phillis Wheatley, Venture Smith, and John Jea in North America, published texts, often autobiographical, in which they referred to childhoods in Africa or laid claim to African heritages.[5] They did not succumb to prevailing views of Africa, but neither could they fully escape the negative connotations associated with the continent, in part because they worked within Western literary and cultural traditions. Transforming terms so laden with connotations of primitivism and savagery into potential sources of pride required these authors to re-place Africa within the eighteenth century's grand narrative of human history.[6]

Because virtually all of the authors who gained access to print during the eighteenth and early nineteenth centuries were committed Christians – Venture Smith might be the exception that proves the rule – their accounts of Africa were shaped by their understandings of its place in the Bible and in God's plan. Different writers used biblical tropes in different ways, but the common reliance on scripture underscores the degree to which the Africa that appeared in early African American and Afro-British writing was influenced by the Africa – or Africas – that had evolved in Western culture over the previous millennia.

Those Africas were not all the same. In different black authors' hands Africa could be a diabolic place from which to escape, a trope for a fallen paradise, an outside space from which to offer dispassionate advice, a repository of past glories, or a projected home. Through the early years of the nineteenth century, whatever meaning or combination of meanings different authors associated with the continent, Africa was almost always portrayed as calling forth the missionary efforts of the peoples of its diaspora. Whether its past was glorious or blighted, its promise rested in the hands of those who would bring scriptural "truth" and "civilization" to its backward peoples. That began to change, however, with the rise of the American Colonization Society: beginning in the 1820s, black authored texts evinced a growing uneasiness about the meaning of the continent and its peoples for black Americans.

The first two important black writers to revise received beliefs about Africa and Africans were Ignatius Sancho and Phillis Wheatley. Both rose from slavery to literary prominence, the first in London and the second in Boston. Sancho achieved fame as a letter writer and Wheatley as a poet. Each quickly became an emblem of the potential of black people in the eyes of whites arguing for or against slavery. Neither wrote much about Africa or the peoples who lived there. Sancho could not have given a first-hand account if, as he claimed, he was born on a slaver, and Wheatley, according to an oral tradition passed down in the white Wheatley family, lacked "any remembrance of the place of her nativity, or of her parents, excepting the simple circumstance that her mother *poured out water before the sun at his rising*."[7] Still, each produced a single extended portrayal of the continent, and each rooted that portrayal in Western literary conventions of tropical plenty that reached back to the Garden of Eden: Sancho referred to a land "blessed with the most fertile and luxuriant soil" (Sancho 131), while Wheatley used explicit biblical imagery when she described "pleasing Gambia" whose "soils spontaneous" produced such "exhaustless stores" as to convince observers that "Eden blooms again" (Wheatley 87). The poem contrasts Africa's natural abundance with the cultured and elevated British virtues that had bred a scientist like Newton and a poet like Pope. Wheatley's unlettered Africa, in both its natural riches and cultural poverty, was as rooted in Western letters (as opposed to indigenous African societies) as was her civilized England (Bruce 58–9; Shuffleton 184–5; Barker chapter 1).

In keeping with these roots in English culture, Africa was a fallen Garden, not a remembered paradise. Sancho noted the continent's natural bounty but quickly turned to a diabolical alliance between "the Christians' abominable traffic for slaves" and "the horrid cruelty and treachery of the petty kings" of Africa (131). Their conspiracy explained how God's intended blessing had transformed this garden of earthly delight into the home of "poor wretched natives." Similarly, in "On being brought from AFRICA to AMERICA," Wheatley claimed that " 'Twas mercy brought" her to Christian America from the "*Pagan* land" of her birth (13). Wheatley and Sancho, like Britons more generally, understood Africa to be a place of natural bounty, but also a place whose divine and natural gifts had been so overshadowed by the sins of men as to have been transformed into false gifts. Both the visions of bounty and the condemnations of sinful behavior were conventional aspects of the image of Africa then current among whites in England and North America. These "African" authors did emphasize, however, Christian Britons' participation in the sins that had caused man's fall from the original Garden.

These passages describing Africa play minor roles in either author's body of work. They served, however, to open one path through which an image of Africa rooted in biblical and other Western literary traditions entered black discourses on the African while acting as conduits through which early Western notions of exotic Africa entered this nascent black Anglophone tradition. These passages also help make sense of aspects of the later discourse on African identity that were absent from the work and legacies of Sancho and Wheatley. One of the most important of these involved the two authors' portrayals of themselves as "African" persons. Africans must be placed in quotation marks precisely because Wheatley and Sancho very rarely referred to residents of Africa – the people who might first come to modern minds thinking of Africans. In addition to the brief references mentioned above, Wheatley included an often-quoted, explicitly imagined allusion to her African father in one poem, and Sancho's letters include a couple of references to individuals born in Africa. But neither displayed much interest in or knowledge of the residents of Africa in their published work (Wheatley 40; Sancho 60, 200–1).

Instead, when Sancho or Wheatley claimed to be African in a letter or poem, they were usually asserting outsider status. Sancho sometimes made such claims as part of an ironic effort to underscore his disinterestedness when attempting to exercise the political prerogatives of an insider: twice when writing to newspapers about public policy he signed his letters "AFRICANUS." He used similar rhetorical strategies in more private letters, spicing his complaints about governmental actions with comments about what "a poor starving Negroe" had to do with "politics? – aye, or poets and painters?" (86) Elsewhere, he insisted that even "a poor, thick-lipped son of Afric" had the right and ability to pass judgment on events (216). Similarly, Wheatley attempted to shame deists for the lack of faith represented by their belief in a rational universe when she asked whether "Ethiopians must be employ'd" to show them the error of their ways (72). In another poem she took on the rhetorical stance of "the Afric muse" to offer a widower respite from grief (61). And then, in a more complicated invocation of the outsider's voice that allowed Wheatley to advocate antislavery in the guise of a less controversial plea, she argued for American liberty in the face of British oppression by insisting that the power of "Liberty" could make "strong the weak / And (wond'rous instinct) Ethiopians speak" (75).

The rhetorical stance of the "African" was that of an outsider with judgment unsullied by self-interest or prejudice. These claims to disinterestedness often gained strength by ironically acknowledging prejudice against black people (e.g., Wheatley's poem to the deists and Sancho's "poor starving Negroe"), for neither Sancho nor Wheatley left evidence of taking seriously any claim that they lacked moral or intellectual authority to speak on public or private issues. Much that they contributed to the emerging black discourse on African identity rests, in fact, on their insistence that they could speak to those issues as *Africans*, and that being African afforded them a valuably different perspective. It was, however, Africa's place outside world events, or world history, that lay behind the "African's" rhetorical claim to disinterestedness.

The senses of allegiance to Africa and African-ness that Sancho and Wheatley expressed reached back only to the moment of enslavement. While neither author was conscious of beginning a discursive tradition – such as a black Atlantic discourse on Africa or African identity – each did seek, at least implicitly, to situate an African identity within the immediate settings in which they lived, and within the broader Anglophone Atlantic culture of which they were a part. That identity was rooted in history and in literature, but the historical roots were much shallower than the literary ones. When Sancho spoke of blackamoors and Othello or Wheatley of Ethiopians and of the Afro-Roman poet Terence, each consciously tapped into longstanding Western traditions that looked to Africa as the home of an exotic difference that helped make England "English," Europe "European," and Western Christendom "civilized."[8] Neither Wheatley nor Sancho accepted these literary/cultural traditions uncritically; like most creative writers they revised and played off of them, sometimes to great effect.

Being "African" also meant something else in their texts. For if each referred most consistently to literature (or cultural history), each left evidence of an allegiance to Africa and "Africans" that found its roots in social history, though even here the relevant history was of the peoples of the diaspora rather than the continent. When Wheatley or Sancho referred to their black "brethren," or to a black "nation," or when they decried the evils that their "fellow blacks" suffered, or when they sought the alleviation of that suffering, they implicitly claimed to share as "Africans" in the oppression faced by those suffering on slavers or under plantation slavery. Africans were implicitly people of the diaspora with a real but vaguely defined relationship to the continent or the peoples who lived there.

Other authors, some of whom had spent more time in Africa than Wheatley and Sancho, and some of whom were influenced by the growing importance of the movement to abolish the Atlantic slave trade, offered more detailed descriptions of Africa. Their portrayals were not devoid of the sentiment one might expect to find in childhood memories, but neither were they fond reminiscences. Like Sancho and Wheatley, they judged African "paganism" harshly. Many tied it to the participation of indigenous African leaders in the Atlantic trade, a reminder that many authors had been enslaved in Africa as well as having grown up there. Africa in their hands became a place of promise and of threat, but the promise was tied less to the cultures or societies that existed on the continent than to a projected Christian transformation that would create a new and better place.

The earliest text that foreshadows this portrayal of the continent is *A Narrative of the Most Remarkable Particulars in the Life of James Albert Ukawsaw Gronniosaw, An African Prince* (1774). Gronniosaw reported having been born to a royal family "in the city of Bournou" in Africa and told the story of his journey from his inland home to a slave-trading city on the Gold Coast, and from there to Barbados before being sold to a Dutch-speaking New York master (Gronniosaw 34). In New York he converted to Christianity and received freedom. He remained close to his former owners, but when the last of them died, he took to sea, eventually reaching Europe. Gronniosaw first settled in England, and then traveled to Holland in search of former religious associates of his American master, before finally returning to England to start a family and continue his pursuit of salvation. At the end of his account, Gronniosaw described himself and his wife as "Pilgrims … travelling through many difficulties towards our HEAVENLY HOME, and … waiting patiently" to be delivered "out of the evils of this present world" (53).

The adult Gronniosaw founded his story of enslavement on his intuition, while still a young boy in Africa, of the inadequacy of animist religion, as well as on his conviction that there must be a single god. Africa, for Gronniosaw, was a place to escape: even as a child he began to perceive religious "Truth," and God favored him by guiding him into Christian lands. He portrayed Bournou as so spiritually deluded that he could have found neither salvation nor happiness had he remained there. When, in the text, he was saved from execution by being sold into Atlantic slavery, he explicitly celebrated the "miracles" that the "ALMIGHTY was pleased to work" for him, and he was grateful not just for his life, but because the Captain of a slaver chose to buy him (34–8). Africa, in Gronniosaw's narrative, offered nothing, because living there provided no pathway to true religion.

The coincidental similarity between Wheatley's poetic expression of gratitude for being saved from "Pagan" Africa and Gronniosaw's invocation of providence to explain his sale into Atlantic slavery highlights a problem faced by Christian writers coming to grips with the perceived absence of true religion in Africa. During the last three decades of the eighteenth century, a group of authors embraced Africa in ways that Wheatley and Gronniosaw had not, but they did so within an equally devout Christian framework. Many were devotees of the evangelical Huntingdon Methodist Connexion – the religious group with which George Whitefield, as well as Wheatley and Gronniosaw, had been affiliated. Almost all were evangelical Protestants of some kind. They shared the conviction that the absence of Christianity in Africa marred the continent, but rather than seeing it as a fatal flaw that doomed its residents, they began to portray Africa as a promising site for evangelical work. In short, Africa became a potential destination for pious black Africans rather than a diabolical space from which they needed to escape. As a result it became a concrete place, and one ripe for religious and commercial transformation.

The most influential figure in this new portrayal of Africa was the most influential figure in early Anglophone black literature – Olaudah Equiano or Gustavus Vassa. Scholar Vincent Carretta's recent archival discoveries have cast doubt on Equiano/Vassa's birthplace, but nonetheless in the *Interesting Narrative of the Life of Olaudah Equiano, or Gustavus Vassa, the African, Written by Himself*, Equiano/Vassa reports having been born in an Igbo town called Essaka. Kidnapped as a young child, he told of being transported to the coast of Africa and sold into Atlantic slavery. His narrative includes the longest account of West Africa in early black Anglophone literature.

He begins with a detailed ethnographic description of Essaka, which, along with the account of his "true" conversion to Christianity, is one of the narrative's most fully realized set pieces. He explicitly and repeatedly compares Essaka with ancient Israel, setting the stage for the Christian transformation of the continent that he will project later in the *Interesting Narrative*. The people of Essaka "practiced circumcision like the Jews," used "purifications and washings … on the same occasions … as the Jews" (Equiano 41), and governed themselves through "chiefs or judges" just as had "the Israelites in their primitive state" (44).[9] Equiano went beyond arguing by analogy that the Igbo were *like* the ancient Hebrews, endorsing the claim that black Africans descended from "Afer and Afra, the descendants of Abraham by Keturah his wife" (44).[10] Portraying the Igbo, and by extension the other peoples of sub-Saharan Africa, in this way contributed to the antislavery agenda of the narrative. As children of

Abraham, these Igbo chosen people could scarcely be thought unworthy of legal protection, especially once they accepted the "true" word of Christ.[11] It also incorporated modern Africa into sacred history.

Equiano/Vassa elaborated on this image of Igboland through his representation of the relationship between the village of his birth and his later life. He did not summarize this relationship in a single sentence or paragraph; instead, he presented it implicitly through his description of Essaka. By alternating between first- and third-person descriptions of Essaka ("our language" but "Their mode of marriage" [Equiano 32–3]), Equiano inserts both the voice of an Igbo (Olaudah Equiano) and that of a Christian African of the diaspora (Gustavus Vassa, the African) into the *Interesting Narrative*. This permits the author to portray Africa both as a land in which people continue to live under the old dispensation, and as a promising place waiting to be transformed through evangelical activism. *The Interesting Narrative* told the story of Equiano/Vassa's efforts in that regard. After purchasing his liberation from American slavery, he eventually moved to London where he petitioned for an end to the slave trade, took part in Granville Sharp's initial attempt to found an evangelical and anti-slavery colony at Sierra Leone, and promoted Africa's economic development (Equiano 226).[12]

An initial step in projecting a history of commercial development onto Africa involved stories of the African slave trade, and Equiano/Vassa was not alone in telling stories that highlighted the problems with market relations in Africa. Those who had been born on the continent of Africa had to confront and make sense of having been enslaved by people Europeans called "Africans." The moment of enslavement stands in their texts as the epitome of the unjust and illegitimate market that had to be eradicated if Africa was to be transformed.[13]

This does not mean that these authors portrayed their native societies as characterized by illegitimate market cultures. Instead each described his enslavement in ways that showed the local traditional market relations of his village to have been perverted or infringed upon in some way by trade with Europe and the Americas. Equiano, for example, described the traditional markets that he reported having frequented with his mother, markets that included what he believed to be a more legitimate trade in enslaved people: the "strictest account" was taken, he said, of the "manner of procuring" slaves, and only those who were "prisoners of war, or … had been convicted of kidnapping, or adultery" or other heinous crimes were "suffered to pass" (Equiano 37). The people of his native village enslaved prisoners of war, but Equiano insisted that slavery in Essaka differed fundamentally from American slavery: "with us they" did "no more work than other members of the community," their material lives resembled those of free people, and they could own property (40).[14]

Many black authors illustrated the trade's unjust effects by portraying themselves as having been illegitimately enslaved. Equiano and Cugoano both reported having been kidnapped by marauding bandits; Gronniosaw was sold after joining a merchant traveling to the coast; Smith and his village fell victim to a "numerous army … instigated by some white nation" that attacked his people, killed and tortured his father, and took young Smith himself "and the women prisoners" (373). They reported being brutally transported from their homes to the coast in response to market forces that pulled them into the Atlantic world. Whether victims of brutal armies, unscrupulous merchants, or evil bandits, each of these men portrayed an Africa in which the forces of international commerce had transformed men into monsters who cheated and stole without concern for right or wrong in their efforts to feed European and American demand. Ending the slave trade promised to usher in a new era and to create a transformed "Africa."

Quobna Ottobah Cugoano offered the most elaborate vision of the future transformation of Africa. If "noble Britons" ended the slave trade and began to deal with West Africans "in a friendly manner," then learning and commerce would transform the coast, enabling Africans to "imitate their noble British friends" by improving their lands, and engaging in international trade. Africa "would become a kind of first ornament to Great-Britain," and Africans would emerge as fully equal participants in the West's narrative of universal history (172–3).

Such a transformation would end the iniquitous traffic in human beings, and, by integrating Africa into the market, it would raise its peoples out of primitivism. Just as the masters of several early black authors had, by granting them the privilege of self purchase, permitted them to transform themselves from object to subject, so Britain, by fostering the commercial development of Africa, would permit the peoples there and in the diaspora – "Africans" – to transform themselves into a nation and to take their proper place on the stage of world history. The individual elements of this commercial vision reflected conventional if advanced European social theory, but Equiano/Vassa and Cugoano were the first to use it to project a transformed and new African people.[15]

Given London's status as the cultural metropole of the eighteenth-century English-speaking world, it is unsurprising that many of these early narratives of black American life were produced by men who had moved to England and published there. Blacks who remained in the Americas also acquired greater access to print, but sustained narratives of the sort written by Equiano/Vassa did not become common in the United States until the antebellum era. Black author/activists found their way into print, but they were more likely to do so through sermons or speeches that were printed as pamphlets. In these brief, occasional works they developed and elaborated on the earlier black portrayals of Africa.

One key trope remained: Africa as a place corrupted by the combination of European intervention and the greed of indigenous rulers. A relatively early example can be found in two "Charges" that Prince Hall, the Bostonian who founded African Freemasonry, delivered to his followers, the first in 1792 and the next in 1797.[16] In these published speeches he outlined African Freemasons' responsibilities to one another and to society while reminding them of their glorious histories as both Masons and Africans. Not surprisingly this entailed a discussion of Africa, but he did not spend much time on the contemporary state of the continent. Instead he sought to unpack the biblical and secular histories of African people, uncovering African compassion in Bible stories and African prominence in classical history. The Africa of Hall's first Charge had enjoyed prominence and importance for millennia prior to the Atlantic slave trade. Hall's second Charge (1797) continued to present the history of Africans, while linking African Masons' ancient illustrious past to the contemporary world of the late eighteenth century (Wesley 110–19).

The links Hall drew became the basis for his interpretation of Africa's modern difficulties. Whites often saw the contemporary state of the continent as a sign of Africans' innate inferiority, but Hall saw it as evidence of the inevitability of historical change and the certainty that current conditions would not remain unchanged forever.[17] In a complicated juxtaposition, he praised black Bostonians for their patience in the face of day-to-day racism, but then invoked the threat of violent revolution by encouraging them to recall what their "African brethren" had done six years earlier "in the French West-Indies." He made sense of the struggle that was then becoming the Haitian Revolution in explicitly biblical terms: "Thus doth Ethiopia begin to stretch forth her hand, from a sink of slavery to freedom and equality" (Wesley 115).[18] Hall's choice of an increasingly autonomous black polity in Saint-Domingue, rather than the civilizing project centered at Sierra Leone, as the site of the initial fulfillment of the Psalmist's prophecy, shows that for some black Americans "Africa" was becoming less a specific continent than a metaphor for space controlled by civilizing black leaders.

Hall's embrace of Africa as metaphor was part of a claim to a broad diasporic and trans-temporal unity. All blacks were brothers, whether the church fathers of the late classical period, the Ethiopians of the Bible, the revolutionaries of Saint-Domingue, or the "African kings and princes" who destroyed their "peaceable kingdoms" to participate in the slave trade. As brothers, all could accomplish much so long as they feared and obeyed God. All should love and respect their fellow man. In this regard, Hall's vision was universalist: "give the right hand of affection and fellowship to whom it justly belongs; let their colour and complexion be what it will."[19] But until African Masons, and by extension all African people, embraced their fellow men and stopped the oppression of slavery and the slave trade, suffering would continue, and Africa would remain aspiration rather than reality.

The transatlantic antislavery movement's first climactic triumphs – the British and American decisions to outlaw the Atlantic slave trade by 1808 – stimulated a steady stream of celebratory black-authored speeches and sermons that extended these themes in their discussions of the current and projected future state of the slave trading coast of Africa. Absalom Jones, an important religious and political leader of Philadelphia's free black community and the pastor of St. Thomas African Episcopal Church, delivered the first important speech of this sort. On January 1, 1808, the day the trade to the United States was legally ended, Jones preached on Exodus 3: 7–8:

> And the Lord said, I have surely seen the affliction of my people, which are in Egypt, and have heard their cry by reason of their task-masters; for I know their sorrows; and I am come down to deliver them out of the land of the Egyptians. (Jones 335)

As Jones explicated this text and explained its relevance to the spiritual and secular lives of his listeners, he portrayed the ties that bound his listeners to one another, and he encoded assertions that Africans were God's Chosen in Old Testament citations. When he addressed his "brethren," he referred to the "nations from which most of us have descended" as well as the "country in which some of us were born." The "affliction of our countrymen" arose out of the wars that whites had "fomented among the different tribes of the Africans," the horrors of the Middle Passage, and the abuses suffered by those held in American slavery. Having tied Africa and the Americas together through the trials their black populations had shared, Jones returned to the theme of a chosen people. He celebrated the willingness of "Jehovah" to hear his people and to answer their prayers by coming "*down to deliver* our suffering countrymen from the hands of their oppressors" (original emphasis). Because God "*came down*" to the United States in 1788 – presumably because its Constitution empowered Congress to close the trade – to Great Britain in 1807, and again to the United States in 1807, the "land of our ancestors" would no longer suffer at British or American hands (Jones 338).[20] His listeners should pray to God to complete "his begun goodness to our brethren in Africa" by convincing the rest of Europe's nations to abolish the trade. Jones also insisted that listeners recognize their own engagement with Africa by acknowledging "publickly and privately … that an African slave, ready to perish, was our father or our grandfather." Though Jones did not spell out a causal link, this acknowledgment might somehow allow a Joseph to "rise up" among black Americans, as the original Joseph had arisen in biblical times and become "the instrument of feeding the African nations with the bread of life."[21] Africa, for Jones, was a suffering lost homeland in need of religious and secular salvation – a salvation that black Americans could provide.

Daniel Coker, the founder of the African Methodist Episcopal movement in Baltimore, echoed this theme in *A Dialogue between a Virginian and an African Minister* (1810). *Dialogue* takes place when a fictional Virginia slaveholder wanders into an "African minister's" office to contest the supposedly "strange opinion" that the legislature should "enact a law, for the emancipation of our slaves" (Coker 4–5). The fictional minister overcomes the slaveholder's attempts to rest defenses of the peculiar institution on natural law, practical reality, and biblical sanction, and forces the Virginian to face the gross inhumanity of both the slave trade and the treatment of slaves within the United States. Coker presents a learned compendium of standard early nineteenth-century arguments against slavery that takes the form of a fantasy in which slaveholders could be convinced to free their chattel through a straightforward appeal to justice and reason.

Coker's African minister initially tries to obscure the role of indigenous Africans in the Atlantic slave trade when he argues that masters lack legitimate title to their slaves, because that title reached back "many years" to an unspecified moment when people were "by law converted into property." No legislature, he insists, could ever have the right to effect such a conversion. The argument assumes that this generalized slave is a creole – a man enslaved by the laws of an American polity rather than an African-born man enslaved in the Old World (Coker 6–7). The Virginian barges through the door that the African minister has opened, pointing out that it was not "the legislature [that] made them slaves … for the Africans enslave one another," and whites only purchase people already "reduced to slavery." Coker's minister responds by insisting that Africa was the victim, rather than the creator, of Atlantic slavery. It was Europeans who encouraged the wars in which "Africans" enslaved each other, and then rewarded the victors. These were not, in fact, true wars: the Africans were "thieves," not warriors, meaning that slave traders were receivers of stolen goods rather than purchasers of legitimately acquired commodities. This rhetorical move destroys slaveholders' title to their chattel, while casting a different light on African responsibility for the trade. Who, the minister asks, is more at fault under these circumstances, the "civilized European or the untutored African?" (Coker 9–11). This may have been effective as a debating point – it works within the fictional dialogue – but it does so by portraying Africa as a land of unsophisticated dupes, as a land where the international norms governing commerce do not hold sway. Only through instruction by more civilized and sophisticated people schooled in the ways of the West would the peoples of Africa be able to assume true responsibility for themselves and their continent.[22]

While Coker's dialogue was not specifically tied to the end of the slave trade, it and Jones' Sermon of Thanksgiving were the two most important among a group of texts celebrating the end of the trade that appeared between 1808 and 1820. These published speeches had often been delivered at one of the self-styled African churches that became so prominent in the Northern United States at this time, but many of these orators distanced themselves from the continent in subtle ways.[23] This gentle estrangement from Africa and its residents came through most clearly when speakers incorporated the history of Africa into the story of the slave trade. With remarkable consistency they portrayed Africans as having been something akin to natural man living in prelapsarian innocence prior to the arrival of European traders on the coast, a vision that historian Wilson Jeremiah Moses has strikingly labeled Afrotopia. One orator, William Hamilton, described the "country of our forefathers" as a "paradise … of ease and pleasure" (Porter 35). Another, Peter Williams, Jr., presented the "state of our forefathers" as one of "simplicity, innocence, and contentment" (Porter 346). Henry Sipkins argued that Africa in "its primitive state" had been a land of "innocent inhabitants … unacquainted with the concerns of a busy life" (Porter 366–7). George Lawrence portrayed residents of "our mother country" as having been a people whose "employments were innocent, neither did they seek evil, contented in the enjoyments of their native sports; they sued not for the blood of their fellow men; they arose in the morning with cheerfulness before their God, and bowed down their heads at night, fully sensible of his goodness" (Porter 376–7). Early Africa was, in these talks, a true garden of earthly delights, but it was also a place outside of history.[24]

With the arrival of Europeans, however, as George Lawrence writes, "the scene changes." White traders introduced greed to stimulate war. They raised "accursed demagogues" above the people and allowed the "baneful deed of avaricious power" to "pierce the hearts of our ancestors" (Porter 377). Not only were countless innocent people dragged across the ocean in slavery, but the land itself was pillaged, leaving a vicious wasteland in its place. The crimes done to Africa and its residents by white slave traders in league with European nation states and American buyers were inhuman and their effects heartrending. The end of the Atlantic slave trade presumably promised a new era, but it is difficult to know whether that would have meant a return to innocence or a turn to "civilization," because these speakers spent little time on any projected transformation of life in Africa that might result from the end of the slave trade.[25] This is especially striking given the attention to exactly that question present in the discussions of Africa and African identity authored by Equiano, Cugoano, and others. Unlike these earlier authors who had linked the transformative effects that "true" religion and legitimate trade would have on the "dark" continent, later celebrants of outlawing the Atlantic trade largely ignored Africa's future.

This inattention does not mean that the speakers were either unaware of or hostile to the project of transformation that others were pursuing.[26] Relative inattention to transforming Africa may have been strategic. Given the central role of white reformers in ending the slave trade, there was good reason for black orators to highlight American events, universal equality and interracial cooperation rather than kinship with Africans. Speakers moved quickly from stories of Africa's victimization to the horrors of slavery in the Americas, and then to their real subject – the legislative victory over the forces of greed, oppression, and sin. They projected a future in which the implicitly white public would begin to recognize that the apostles of racial inequality were mistaken, in which prominent white allies like Anthony Benezet, Thomas Clarkson, John Jay, Benjamin Rush, and William Wilberforce would multiply and justice would be achieved. They called on black people to live upright lives that would earn the continuing support of old allies and win new ones. The logic of this situation led most speakers, however complicated their personal opinions on their "African" heritage may have been, to present a relatively simple narrative that situated black Americans less in the land of their ancestors than in that of their birth. Their Africa was a continent victimized by European greed, but it was also more a part of African Americans' past than of their present or future.

This turn away from Africa in African American letters during the 1810s represented some combination of a strategic political decision, a reflection of the fading importance of Africa for Northern free blacks as a result of the closing of the Atlantic slave trade, and the complicated social and economic forces that determined what kinds of black authored texts were published and thus survived. The founding of the American Colonization Society (ACS) in 1816, a white-dominated organization dedicated to the emigration of free black Americans from the United States to the colony of Liberia in West Africa, exacerbated this trend by providing a decisive push away from Africa for African Americans. Most black Americans considered the ACS a stalking horse for slaveholding interests. Many came to believe that whites labeled blacks "African" in order to strengthen slavery by deporting free blacks and by cementing the association of dark skin with both slavery and savagery (Sidbury, *Becoming African in America* chapters 6–7).

Africa receded in black-authored publications as black people throughout the North rallied to reject both the ACS and any expression of interest in black emigration to Africa. Authors – often speakers, since most of these texts are published orations – developed something close to a formula in which they combined varying elements to attack the ACS and its program. Blacks, they pointed out, had been born in the United States and had fought beside whites for the new nation's independence in 1776 and in 1812. Black labor had made the United States prosperous. Then, these orators argued, when more and more black people were winning their freedom and demanding the equal treatment to which they were entitled, the ACS was founded by false friends serving the interests of the slave South. White colonizationists hid behind a veil of false benevolence by claiming to be interested in the welfare of Africa and of black victims of American racism, but, in truth, they sought to remove free black people in order to shackle the enslaved more securely.[27]

Those black authors who contested this narrative did not try to revive earlier projections of a rising Africa, though there is evidence that this vision persisted among many of the first two cohorts of settlers sent out by the ACS (Sidbury, *Becoming African in America* chapters 6–7). Published authors looked instead to the practical, contrasting the challenges faced by free black people in the United States and those faced by emigrants to Liberia.[28] The case of John B. Russwurm, the most prominent person to move to early Liberia, is instructive in this regard. Russwurm was the son of a white Virginia merchant who was living in Jamaica and a Jamaican woman of African descent. When his father returned to the United States in 1807, he sent his eight-year-old mixed race son to Quebec to attend secondary school.[29] Russwurm then went to Bowdoin College, becoming one of the first African Americans to earn a college degree, and delivering an address at his graduation on "The Condition and Prospects of Hayti." After college he moved to New York City where, in 1827, he signed on as junior editor to Samuel E. Cornish on *Freedom's Journal*, the first black newspaper published in the United States. In the absence of a reference to Africa in its title as well as in much of its editorial content, *Freedom's Journal* embodied the decline in public black discussions of African identity during the 1820s. It began as an explicitly anti-colonization newspaper, and the editors invoked a particularly powerful icon of freedom in nineteenth-century black American culture when they proudly declared that the Constitution of the United States would be their "polar star" as they sought to give voice to "FIVE HUNDRED THOUSAND FREE PEOPLE OF COLOUR."[30] The paper voiced free black Americans' determination to find a place as equal citizens in the United States.

The editors pledged to keep their "columns … open to a temperate discussion" of a wide range of topics and lived up to that promise. They published articles by supporters and critics of the ACS as well as news about events affecting black people throughout the world.[31] In fact, though the editors did not claim to be Africans, they showed particular interest in Africa. *Freedom's Journal* published extensively on Africa and on colonization in both Sierra Leone and Liberia, but the visions of colonization that were debated in its columns were just that – visions of colonization, rather than discussions of emigrationist projects designed to transform a continent.

Freedom's Journal ceased when Russwurm stepped down as editor after two years, and just before doing so he announced a change of heart regarding the ACS and Liberia. His "views [had] materially altered," and he offered an extended explanation of his new position that stretched across three issues.[32] He explained that he had come to think that "citizenship in this country" was a chimera and to believe that the widespread suspicions of the ACS among black Americans were based on prejudice. Russwurm argued, both explicitly and implicitly, that Liberia and colonization offered black people the broadest scope for individual advancement and the greatest opportunity to claim their basic human rights – that, in a very real sense, Liberia offered blacks their best chance to live as Americans. He offered a brief bow to the importance of serving as "pioneers of civilization and Heralds of the Cross" to an "unexplored quarter of our globe," but the weight of his argument rested on the claim that blacks faced a brighter prospect in Liberia than in the United States. Russwurm was less interested in transforming Africa than in building a Liberia that would offer basic human rights to oppressed black Americans, and thus offer him and many other talented black people their rightful chance to live satisfying lives.

Russwurm's old colleague, Samuel Cornish, took exactly the opposite stance regarding emigration to Africa, but he based his rejection of the continent on a different reading of the same variables. This became clear when he declared: "Let us and our friends unite, in baptizing the term '*Colored American*,' and henceforth let us be written of, preached of, and prayed for as such. It is the true term, and one which is above reproach." And why was it above reproach? In part because it lacked the negative connotations of other terms ("*Negroes, Africans,* and *blacks*"), but also, presumably, because it embodied the belief that Cornish had long held: that blacks "should some day possess in" their "native-land, *a perfect equality, in all respects*, with" their "white brethren."[33] Russwurm went to Africa not because he disagreed with Cornish on this point and hoped to transform Africans into a single people who would rise to assume their place among the nations of the world, but because he despaired of America recognizing blacks' claims to the rights Cornish asserted and hoped to build a nation in Africa where black Americans could claim those rights.

The degree to which Africa moved to the background in these discussions can be seen in the most famously radical text produced by a black American during this period. In 1829 and 1830 David Walker published his *Appeal to the Coloured Citizens of the World*, revealing in its title the rise of the language of colored Americanism, while showing in its content that such language did not reflect a rejection of Africa. Walker used examples stretching from scripture, to classical history, to the contemporary world to show how grievously blacks suffered under American slavery. When making that argument, he usually referred to "coloured people," but he forthrightly proclaimed himself "one of the oppressed, degraded and wretched sons of Africa," and on several occasions he discussed African history (Walker 74–5). Sometimes this was done in analogies to black American history – the great African General Hannibal might have defeated Rome had his people not been "disunited, as the coloured people are now, in the United States of America" (22). At other times, he confronted whites with their crimes in Africa in language that tied black Americans directly to the continent of their forebears: "have you not … entered among us, and learnt us the art of throat-cutting" so that we would "make slaves for you and your children?" (Walker 44). At still other times, he called forth racial pride, discussing the "sons of Africa or of Ham, among whom learning originated" (20). Notwithstanding Walker's engagement with the same kinds of classical and historical sources that had informed Prince Hall's construction of the history of African Freemasons, one of the main thrusts of his *Appeal* is a refutation of the claims and program of the American Colonization Society. As the historian Peter Hinks has shown, David Walker wielded his radical pen to demand that whites cease denying "coloured Americans" the American rights that were properly theirs. Walker sought to rally blacks to claim the United States as their home, not to organize emigrants to travel to Freetown or Monrovia in order to build a diasporic nation. Africa, in Walker's *Appeal*, becomes a trope whose meanings shift in response to the immediate rhetorical demands of the text.

Walker's multivalent invocation of Africa – sometimes as location, sometimes as heritage – reinforces the multiple and changing ways that early black writers invoked Africa as place and as trope. The absence of a single fixed meaning does not indicate, however, that "Africa" was a free-floating signifier. While different authors evinced a greater or lesser interest in the actual continent and the peoples who lived there, all who invoked Africa did so in a cultural context that slotted Africa into a primitive and pre-Christian position as a place that remained outside of Western history. This could and did lead writers to render it as an Edenic place in the past that had been left behind. It could and did lead other writers to render it as a pagan place that provided a promising field for evangelical endeavor and commercial transformation. It did not offer a way for early black writers to present Africa as the source of admirable and "authentic" indigenous culture(s) that offered an attractive alternative to the West.

Notes

1 This essay draws on material from my *Becoming African in America: Race and Nation in the Early Black Atlantic*.

2 See Vaughan, Wheeler, Aravamudan, Boulukos, Krise, and Molineux, "The Peripheries Within" and "Hogarth's Fashionable Slaves."

3 See Eltis; Thomas C. Brown; Molineux, "Peripheries Within," chapters 8 and 9; Aravamudan, chapters 1 and 2; and Carretta and Gould.

4 For early understandings of racial difference, see Curtin, Jordan (especially chapters 1 and 6); Appiah, and Kathleen M. Brown, chapter 1. Essays by David Brion Davis, Emily C. Bartels, Alden T. Vaughan and Virginia Mason Vaughan, and Benjamin Braude in a special issue on race of *The William and Mary Quarterly*, 3rd ser., 54 (January 1997) testify to the complexity of medieval and early modern Western understandings of Africa

and race. For race, Christianity, and the Enlightenment, see Kidd, especially chapter 4. Adeleke, Introduction and chapter 1, provides a concise review of much secondary literature. Eze includes a useful selection of edited primary texts on "racial" thought from Linnaeus to Hegel. For an overview, see Hannaford chapters 6–8.

5 The literature on early black writing is large and growing. For an introduction to it, see Bruce, Andrews (chapters 1 and 2), and Gates.

6 Woodard, chapter 4, explores this issue in a reading of Equiano/Vassa.

7 Odell 10; original emphasis. Margaretta Matilda Odell descended from the Wheatleys and wrote the "memoir" that preceded Wheatley's poems.

8 For the meanings of Africans for British culture during the seventeenth and eighteenth centuries, see Molineux, "Peripheries Within"; and Barker (chapters 1 and 2).

9 Being identified with Jews was no unalloyed good in eighteenth-century Europe, but identifying with ancient Israel was different, and its advantages were greatest among dissenting communities, many of which were inclined to see themselves as the "new Israel." See Manuel, "Israel in the Christian Enlightenment" 107–10, 119, 122, and *The Broken Staff* 168–9, 179. I develop these points more fully in "From Igbo Israeli to African Christian."

10 Cugoano makes a similar though more contingent claim: "and some think that Africa got its name from the King of Lybia marrying a daughter of Aphra, one of the descendants of Abraham, by Keturah" (33).

11 Equiano also explicitly equated the Igbo with the Greeks, the secular "fathers" of "civilized" European society (Equiano 242n44; 167–8).

12 For the basic story of the "Black Poor" and Sharp's Province of Freedom, see Braidwood, West, and Pybus chapter 7 and 139–44. For antislavery thinkers' commercial vision for Africa, see Christopher Leslie Brown (especially chapter 5), and Gould.

13 They wrote as the slave trade was increasingly coming to be seen as an illegitimate form of commerce in "enlightened" Anglo-American thought. See Gould, Bender, Christopher Leslie Brown, Davis (especially chapters 1, 2, 5, and 8), and Drescher chapters 1–4. The experience of having been sold also served as the base from which Equiano entered the literary marketplace to resell his life, this time as text (see Sidbury, "Early Slave Narratives").

14 Cugoano states that "some of the Africans in my country keep slaves, … but those which they keep are well fed, and good care taken of them" (150).

15 For this critique in eighteenth-century Anglo-American culture more generally, see Gould and Meek. Pocock discusses these issues in the context of eighteenth-century history writers.

16 Brooks (chapter 4) sees a transformation in Hall's politics during the five years separating the petition discussed above and Hall's first Charge. For Hall's life, see Wesley; for the "Charges" themselves, see Wesley 55–61, 110–19.

17 For a French contemporary who used African history to make a similar argument, see Volney.

18 Hall combined this support for revolution with loyalty to established order: "My brethren, let us pay all due respect to all whom God hath put in places of honor over us: do justly and be faithful to them that hire you, and treat them with that respect they may deserve; but worship no man. Worship God, this much is your duty as christians and as masons" (Wesley 117).

19 For Hall's notes on important Africans from classical history, see *Letters and Sermons by Prince Hall*, 1787–1802, Prince Hall Records by H.V.B. Voorhis, 1950, made from negative film at Boston Grand Lodge, Boston Grand Masonic Lodge Library. Much of the film is illegible because of apparent water damage to the originals.

20 Jones claimed inaccurately that the Constitution stopped "the trade in our African fellowmen" in 1808.

21 For Joseph in black antislavery writing, see Richards 221–35 and Saillant 87.

22 Coker would end his life as a missionary trying to bring Christianity and "civilization"

to Africa (Sidbury, *Becoming African in America* 173).

23 For the rise of African churches, see Sidbury, *Becoming African in America* chapters 5 and 6. The distancing could include signing as a "descendant of Africa" rather than as an "African" and other similar moves. Of seven speeches commemorating the end of the slave trade collected in Porter 34–5, 337–8, 345, 366, 375 ("descendants"), 391 ("our parents"), four authors are listed on the title page without a racial identifier (Absalom Jones, Joseph Sydney, George Lawrence, and Russell Parrott), and three are listed as "Descendant of Africa" (Peter Williams, Jr., Henry Sipkins, and William Hamilton). They may, of course, have been introduced differently when they spoke; only the published versions survive.

24 Bruce Dain alludes to Edenic portrayals of Africa by black orators (117). Dain says Equiano portrays Africa similarly (50), but this conflates Eden with what Equiano calls the "Israel of the Patriarchs."

25 Two partial exceptions strengthen the case, for they focus on what will no longer happen in Africa rather than on a progressive transformation: Henry Sipkins, "An Oration on the Abolition of the Slave Trade: Delivered in the African Church, in the City of New York, January 2, 1809," in Porter 372 ("No longer shall the shores of Africa be drenched with human gore. No longer shall its inhabitants be torn from their native soil; no longer shall they be brought on cruel shipboard, weighed down in chains … ."); Peter Williams, Jr. "An Oration on the Abolition of the Slave Trade: Delivered in The African Church, in the City of New York, January 1, 1808," in Porter 349 ("Rejoice, Oh! Africans! No longer shall tyranny, war, and injustice, with irresistible sway, desolate your native country").

26 For example, Peter Williams, Jr.'s "Oration on the Abolition of the Slave Trade" followed this pattern, but he participated in Paul Cuffe's efforts to effect just such a transformation. For most of these speaker/authors, one or two short published addresses constitute the only evidence of what they thought.

27 The black rejection of the ACS became a stepping stone toward embracing what came to be known as Garrisonian immediate abolitionism. For excellent accounts of this process throughout the North, see Miller chapter 3, and Horton and Horton chapter 8. For more detailed accounts of Philadelphia, see Nash chapters 6 and 7, and Winch, *A Gentleman of Color* chapters 8–10, and *Philadelphia's Black Elite* chapters 2–5. William Lloyd Garrison himself was the first to synthesize this narrative in *Thoughts on African Colonization* (1832).

28 This included both supporters of emigration and disgruntled emigrants to Liberia who returned and described the colony there in negative terms. See, for example, *News from Africa* (1832) and *Examination of Mr. Thomas C. Brown* (1834).

29 See Brewer, Beyan chapter 1, and Huberich 437–9.

30 *Freedom's Journal*, March 16, 1827.

31 For the fullest treatments of the newspaper, see Bacon and Gross. Gross is harsh toward Russwurm. For other recent discussions of *Freedom's Journal*, see McHenry chapter 2, especially 88–102, Horton and Horton chapters 7–8, and Cooper 605–9.

32 *Freedom's Journal*, February 14, 21 and 28, 1829. Russwurm told the Colonization Society of his new opinion and began seeking a position in Liberia (Russwurm to Gurley, New York, January 26, 1829, American Colonization Society Papers, microfilm, ser. 1, vol. 13, reel 5).

33 *The Colored American*, March 4, 1837 ("reproach") and May 13, 1837 ("brethren"), Box 3, Miscellaneous American Letters and Papers, Schomburg Center, New York Public Library.

Bibliography

Adeleke, Tunde. *Unafrican Americans: Nineteenth-Century Black Nationalists and the Civilizing Mission*. Lexington: University Press of Kentucky, 1998.

Andrews, William L. *To Tell a Free Story: The First Century of Afro-American Autobiography*. Urbana: University of Illinois Press, 1986.

Appiah, Kwame Anthony. *In My Father's House: Africa and the Philosophy of Culture*. Oxford & New York: Oxford University Press, 1992.

Aravamudan, Srinivas. *Tropicopolitans: Colonialism and Agency*. Durham, NC: Duke University Press, 1999.

Bacon, Jacqueline. *"Freedom's Journal": The First African American Newspaper*. Lanham: Lexington Books, 2007.

Barker, Anthony J. *The African Link: British Attitudes to the Negro in the Era of the Atlantic Slave Trade, 1550–1807*. London: F. Cass, 1978.

Bender, Thomas, ed. *The Antislavery Debate: Capitalism and Abolitionism as a Problem in Historical Interpretation*. Berkeley: University of California Press, 1992.

Beyan, Amos J. *African American Settlements in West Africa: John Brown Russwurm and the American Civilizing Efforts*. New York: Palgrave Macmillan, 2005.

Boulukos, George Eleftherios. "The Grateful Slave: Representations of Slave Plantation Reform in the British Novel, 1720–1805." PhD diss. University of Texas, Austin, 1998.

Braidwood, Stephen J. *Black Poor and White Philanthropists: London's Blacks and the Foundation of the Sierra Leone Settlement, 1786–1791*. Liverpool: Liverpool University Press, 1994.

Brewer, William M. "John B. Russwurm." *Journal of Negro History* 13 (1928): 413–22.

Brooks, Joanna. *American Lazarus: Religion and the Rise of African-American and Native American Literatures*. New York & Oxford: Oxford University Press, 2003.

Brown, Christopher Leslie. *Moral Capital: Foundations of British Abolitionism*. Chapel Hill: University of North Carolina Press, 2006.

Brown, Kathleen M. *Good Wives, Nasty Wenches and Anxious Patriarchs: Gender, Race, and Power in Colonial Virginia*. Chapel Hill: University of North Carolina Press, 1996.

Brown, Thomas. C. *Examination of Mr. Thomas C. Brown, a free Colored Citizen of S. Carolina, as to the Actual State of Things in Liberia in the Years 1833 and 1834*. New York: S.W. Benedict and Co., 1834.

Bruce, Dickson D., Jr. *The Origins of African American Literature*. Charlottesville: University of Virginia Press, 2001.

Carretta, Vincent. *Equiano, the African: Biography of a Self-Made Man*. Athens: University of Georgia Press, 2005.

Carretta, Vincent, and Philip Gould, ed. *Genius in Bondage: Literature of the Early Black Atlantic*. Lexington: University Press of Kentucky, 2001.

Coker, Daniel. *A Dialogue between a Virginian and an African Minister, Written by the Rev. Daniel Coker, a Descendant of Africa … Minister of the African Methodist Episcopal Church in Baltimore*. Baltimore: Benjamin Edes for Joseph James, 1810.

Cooper, Frederick. "Elevating the Race: The Social Thought of Black Leaders, 1827–1850." *American Quarterly* 24 (1972): 604–25.

Cugoano, Quobna Ottobah. *Thoughts and Sentiments on the Evil of Slavery*, ed. Vincent Carretta. New York: Penguin, 1999.

Curtin, Philip D. *The Image of Africa: British Ideas and Actions, 1780–1850*. Madison: University of Wisconsin Press, 1964.

Dain, Bruce. *A Hideous Monster of the Mind: American Race Theory in the Early Republic*. Cambridge, MA: Harvard University Press, 2002.

Davis, David Brion. *The Problem of Slavery in the Age of Revolution, 1770–1823*. Ithaca, NY: Cornell University Press, 1975.

Drescher, Seymour. *Capitalism and Antislavery: British Mobilization in Comparative Perspective*. Oxford & New York: Oxford University Press, 1986.

Eltis, David. *The Rise of African Slavery in the Americas*. Cambridge: Cambridge University Press, 2000.

Equiano, Olaudah. *The Interesting Narrative and Other Writings*, ed. Vincent Carretta. New York: Penguin, 1995.

Eze, Emmanuel Chukwudy, ed. *Race and the Enlightenment: A Reader*. Malden: Blackwell, 1997.

Garrison, William Lloyd. *Thoughts on African Colonization*. 1832. Rpt. New York: Arno, 1969.

Gates, Henry Louis, Jr. *The Signifying Monkey: A Theory of African-American Literary Criticism*. Oxford & New York: Oxford University Press, 1988.

Gould, Philip. *Barbaric Traffic: Commerce and Antislavery in the Eighteenth-Century Atlantic World*. Cambridge, MA: Harvard University Press, 2003.

Gronniosaw, James Albert Ukawsaw. *A Narrative of the Most Remarkable Particulars in the Life of James Albert Ukawsaw Gronniosaw, An African Prince*. 1774. In Vincent Carretta, ed. *Unchained Voices: An Anthology of Black Authors in the English-Speaking World of the 18th Century*. Lexington: University Press of Kentucky, 1996.

Gross, Bella. "Freedom's Journal and the Rights of All." *Journal of Negro History* 17 (1932): 241–86.

Hannaford, Ivan. *Race: The History of an Idea in the West*. Washington, DC: Woodrow Wilson Center Press, 1996.

Hinks, Peter P. *To Awaken My Afflicted Brethren: David Walker and the Problem of Antebellum Slave Resistance*. University Park: Pennsylvania State Press, 1997.

Horton, James Oliver, and Lois E. Horton. *In Hope of Liberty: Culture, Community and Protest among Northern Free Blacks, 1700–1860*. New York: Oxford University Press, 1997.

Huberich, Charles Henry. *The Political and Legislative History of Liberia*, 2 vols. New York: Central, 1947.

Jones, Absalom. "A Thanksgiving Sermon, Preached January 1, 1808, in St. Thomas's, or the African Episcopal, Church, Philadelphia: on Account of the Abolition of the African Slave Trade." In Dorothy Porter, ed. *Early Negro Writing, 1760–1837*. Boston, MA: Beacon, 1971. 335–42.

Jordan, Winthrop D. *White over Black: American Attitudes toward the Negro, 1550–1812*. Chapel Hill: University of North Carolina Press, 1968.

Kidd, Colin. *The Forging of Races: Race and Scripture in the Protestant Atlantic World, 1600–2000*. Cambridge: Cambridge University Press, 2006.

Krise, Thomas H., ed. *Caribbeana: An Anthology of English Literature of the West Indies, 1657–1777*. Chicago: University of Chicago Press, 1999.

Manuel, Frank E. *The Broken Staff: Judaism through Christian Eyes*. Cambridge, MA: Harvard University Press, 1992.

Manuel, Frank E. "Israel in the Christian Enlightenment." In *The Changing of the Gods*. Hanover, NH: University Press of New England, 1983.

Maryland State Colonization Society. *News from Africa. A Collection of Facts, relating to the Colony in Liberia, for the information of the Free People of Colour in Maryland*. Baltimore: J.D. Toy, 1832.

McHenry, Elizabeth. *Forgotten Readers: Recovering the Lost History of African American Literary Societies*. Durham, NC: Duke University Press, 2002.

Meek, Ronald L. *Social Science and the Ignoble Savage*. Cambridge: Cambridge University Press, 1976.

Miller, Floyd J. *The Search for a Black Nationality: Black Emigration and Colonization, 1786–1863*. Urbana: University of Illinois Press, 1975.

Molineux, Catherine. "Hogarth's Fashionable Slaves: Moral Corruption in Eighteenth-Century London." *English Literary History* 72 (2005): 495–520.

Molineux, Catherine. "The Peripheries Within: Race, Slavery, and Empire in Early Modern England." PhD diss. The Johns Hopkins University, 2005.

Moses, Wilson Jeremiah. *Afrotopia: The Roots of African American Popular History*. Cambridge: Cambridge University Press, 1998.

Nash, Gary B. *Forging Freedom: The Formation of Philadelphia's Black Community, 1720–1840*. Cambridge, MA: Harvard University Press, 1988.

Odell, Margaretta Matilda. *Memoir and Poems of Phillis Wheatley*. Boston, MA: Wright, 1834.

Pocock, J.G.A. *Barbarism and Religion: Barbarians, Savages and Empires*. Cambridge: Cambridge University Press, 2005.

Porter, Dorothy, ed. *Early Negro Writing, 1760–1837*. Boston, MA: Beacon, 1971.

Pybus, Cassandra. *Epic Journeys of Freedom: Runaway Slaves of the American Revolution and Their Global Quest for Liberty*. Boston, MA: Beacon, 2006.

Richards, Phillip. "The 'Joseph Story' as Slave Narrative: On Genesis and Exodus as Prototypes for Early Black Anglophone Writing." In Vincent Wimbush, ed. *African Americans and*

The Bible: Sacred Texts and Social Textures. New York: Continuum, 2001.

Russwurm, John B. "The Condition and Prospects of Hayti," ed. Philip S. Foner. *Journal of Negro History* 54 (1969): 393–7.

Saillant, John. *Black Puritan, Black Republican: The Life and Thought of Lemuel Haynes, 1753–1833*. New York & Oxford: Oxford University Press, 2003.

Sancho, Ignatius. *Letters of the Late Ignatius Sancho, an African*, ed. Vincent Carretta. New York: Penguin, 1998.

Shuffleton, Frank. "On Her Own Footing: Phillis Wheatley in Freedom." In Vincent Carretta and Philip Gould, ed. *Genius in Bondage: Literature of the Early Black Atlantic*. Lexington: University Press of Kentucky, 2001.

Sidbury, James. *Becoming African in America: Race and Nation in the Early Black Atlantic*. Oxford: Oxford University Press, 2007.

Sidbury, James. "Early Slave Narratives and the Culture of the Atlantic Market." In Eliga H. Gould and Peter S. Onuf, ed. *Empire and Nation: The American Revolution and the Atlantic World*. Baltimore: Johns Hopkins University Press, 2005. 79–106.

Sidbury, James. "From Igbo Israeli to African Christian: The Emergence of Racial Identity in Olaudah Equiano's *Interesting Narrative*." In Stephan Palmié, ed. *Africas of the Americas: Beyond the Search for Origins in the Study of Afro-Atlantic Religions*. Leiden: Brill, 2008.

Smith, Venture. *A Narrative of the Life and Adventures of Venture, A Native of Africa: But resident above sixty years in the United States of America*. 1798. In Vincent Carretta, ed. *Unchained Voices: An Anthology of Black Authors in the English-Speaking World of the 18th Century*. Lexington: University Press of Kentucky, 1996.

Vaughan, Virginia Mason. *Performing Blackness on English Stages, 1500–1800*. Cambridge: Cambridge University Press, 2005.

Volney, C. F. *The Ruins, or, Meditation on the Revolutions of Empires and the Law of Nature*. Rpt. Baltimore: Black Classic Press, 1991.

Walker, David. *David Walker's Appeal to the Coloured Citizens of the World*, ed. Peter P. Hinks. University Park: Pennsylvania State University Press, 2000.

Wesley, Charles H. *Prince Hall: Life and Legacy*, 2nd edn. Washington, DC: United Supreme Council, Southern Jurisdiction, Prince Hall Affiliation, 1983.

West, Richard. *Back to Africa: A History of Sierra Leone and Liberia*. London: Cape, 1970.

Wheatley, Phillis. *Complete Writings*. Ed. Vincent Carretta. New York: Penguin, 2001.

Wheeler, Roxann. *The Complexion of Race: Categories of Difference in Eighteenth-Century British Culture*. Philadelphia: University of Pennsylvania Press, 2000.

Winch, Julie. *A Gentleman of Color: The Life of James Forten*. Oxford & New York: Oxford University Press, 2002.

Winch, Julie. *Philadelphia's Black Elite: Activism, Accommodation, and the Struggle for Autonomy, 1787–1848*. Philadelphia: Temple University Press, 1988.

Woodard, Helena. *African-British Writings in the Eighteenth Century: The Politics of Race and Reason*. Westport, CT: Greenwood, 1999.

3
Ports of Call, Pulpits of Consultation: Rethinking the Origins of African American Literature

Frances Smith Foster and Kim D. Green

As our title implies, we are offering an alternative to traditional understandings of the origins of African American literature. We challenge a prevailing assumption that there is but one origin and that oral literature begat written literature. We suggest that histories of oral literature and written literature overlap, sometimes merge, but ultimately are not the same. Oral literature, that which the *Norton Anthology of African American Literature* regards as the "vernacular," is generally a "mass" or "popular" literature (Pearce). Folklore is a primary example. Such literature may have formed in the imagination of an individual, but it was adopted and adapted by others until any original author and any authoritative text were, if remembered, not relevant. Oral literature allows, invites, maybe even requires embellishments and revisions. Oral literature tends to be popular literature because it is truly of the people, for the people, by the people. It is not a lesser form of creative expression; but its rules and its purposes generally are not the same as written literature. Oral literature sometimes serves as a source or foundation for written literature. Literary scholars and literature anthologies might include folklore in their purview but their sources are oral recitations rendered in writing. Written literature, on the other hand, begins as text. A written text may have nearly identical intentions as oral literature; but it is a part of print culture, and, as such, written literature requires techniques and engenders expectations that are not identical to those of oral literature. The writing may or may not be intended as *belles-lettres*, which prioritizes aesthetics and form over function. The choice to write, however, is also a choice to create an object with an origin that can be traced to an individual or an established source. Our first thought for reexamination, then, may seem simply common sense or it may seem academic. We believe, however, that it is not said or written often enough: There is no one origin of African American literature.

Our genesis story focuses upon written literature. It includes writings by African Americans that are directed to or even mediated by people with cultural traditions that do not have African or even American origins, but it privileges literature published by African Americans for African Americans and generally about African Americans. Foundational to our understanding of how African American print culture developed are ideas promulgated by scholars such as Elizabeth McHenry and Michael Gomez. We refer particularly to McHenry's discussions of print culture as "technological tools" and Gomez's explanations of processes by which people from diverse cultures and of various ethnicities became Africans and then African Americans.

Our origin story comes from our own archival research, but it also builds upon that of other scholars in several disciplines who are rediscovering texts relevant to revising historical narratives of how African America developed within and against other American cultures. Research on literacy, literature, aesthetics, and authorship in early African America by scholars such as Jacqueline Jones Royster and Janet Duitsman Cornelius helps our rethinking and revisions of African American literary history. Joanna Brooks, Tiya Miles, and John Saillant are among those who have guided us in forging new understandings of the roles of religion and the influences of Native American and other ethnic groups. Marion DeCosta-Willis and Sylviane Diouf remind us that our unthinking equation of "African American literature" with the literature written in English ignores a lot of literature produced in America by people of African descent. Such scholars compel us to enlarge and complicate literary histories – especially those that privilege antislavery slave narratives as the sole or most legitimate interest of writers before the Civil War.

Our genesis narrative for written African American literature recognizes that African America is, and always has been, polyglot. While this essay focuses upon literature written in or translated into English, we affirm that early African Americans were multicultural and, perhaps more so than today, multilingual. Some writers, who had been educated in the art, aesthetics, and aspirations of their native cultures, communicated via words used according to aesthetic norms derived from Arabic, Spanish, French, Dutch, and other non-English languages. While most extant texts are written in English and bear stylistic and theoretical similarities to British and American literatures, these writings are not generally derivative or imitative of Euro-American and Western cultural conventions. Since the cultural constructions of race deny voice and render presence invisible, even if a writer of known African heritage writes of the most mundane topics in the most traditional ways, that writer adds color to established literary traditions. However, we need not rely upon abstract technicalities. Close textual analyses within cultural contexts tend to show that early African American writers adapted or adopted English literary conventions for African American purposes, including petitions, protests, and explanations directed to readers who were not necessarily African American. Equally, if not more important, the writers used literature to forge a strong and purposeful African America from diverse African cultures. We argue that African American literary production was (and remains) artful, diverse, complicated, sometimes contradictory, occasionally esoteric, and almost always intended to sustain faith, encourage hope, and provoke change. Our inescapable conclusion is that the best-known and most often repeated ideas about how African American literature began, where, when, and by whom are not entirely accurate.

Our "rethinking" is best understood in the context of conventional wisdom about African American literary production before the twentieth century; so, we begin with a brief summary. Anthologies and literary histories of African America imply or define oral literature as antecedent to written literature. Most categorize texts as either "authentic" or "inauthentic." They recognize "authentic" literature because it focuses upon "the" African American experience, as represented by the "vernacular" or obviously emerging from folk culture. "Authentic" African American literature deplores slavery, resists racism, and genuflects to the gods of ancient Africa. Except for Brer Rabbit tales, the dozens, and similar didactic or confrontational genres, "authentic" literature is instructive, motivational, and mimetic. "Inauthentic" literature, so the theory goes, portrays racial ambivalence, Anglophilic aspirations, and insufficient subversion or protest of values routinely attributed to American mainstream culture. Often this literature is judged effete, derivative, and focused more on the aesthetic or spiritual than on the pragmatic and material.

Two twentieth-century cultural moments ideally represent prevailing ideas about the origins of African American literature. The "New Negro Movement" or the "Harlem Renaissance" exemplifies the first half of the twentieth century. The Black Arts Movement or the "Second Black Renaissance" illustrates the second half. Terms for these literary eras vary but each is imagined as defining moments and as "rebirths." Before a "New Negro" came an old one. If there is a "movement," there is change from one place to another. The artists and observers of both periods focused more on what was happening (or what they wanted to happen) than on what had happened before.

Both the New Negro proponents of the 1920s and the Black Arts spokespeople half century later placed their "now" as positive contrast with a "then," but it is fair to say that each group recognized political and social advantages to claiming a lengthy tradition of written literature. They readily reminded readers that Americans of African descent had been publishing literature for at least as long as Americans of European descent. They claimed Olaudah Equiano as a founder of African American slave narrative tradition, even though his sojourn in the United States and the amount of space he gives to those experiences are brief and his politics closer to imperialism or colonization than to abolitionism. They commended Phillis Wheatley for being one of the first women in the New World to publish a volume of poetry, even though they thought her poetry derivative and colorless. They debated whether Frederick Douglass's "The Heroic Slave" (1853) or William Wells Brown's *Clotel* (1853) was the first published prose fiction, while ignoring or downplaying the religious and assimilationist politics of both texts. In neither era were pre-twentieth-century creative license, aesthetic experiments, complicated racial politics, and class distinctions deemed worthy of serious consideration. The consensus was that the quality of the various "firsts" is less praiseworthy than the fact of their existence.

The conclusion in William Stanley Braithwaite's essay, "The Negro in American Literature," is a typical example.

> The Negro as a creator in American literature is of comparatively recent importance. All that was accomplished between Phyllis [*sic*] Wheatley and Paul Laurence Dunbar, considered by critical standards, is negligible, and of historical interest only. Historically it is a great tribute to the race to have produced Phyllis Wheatley, not only the slave poetess in eighteen century Colonial America, but to know she was as good, if not a better, poetess than Ann Bradstreet whom literary historians give the honor of being the first person of her sex to win fame as a poet in America. (36)

Braithwaite's essay was published in Alain Locke's edited collection of essays, stories, poetry, and visual art, *The New Negro: An Interpretation.* Locke's selections examine "self expression and the forces and motives of self-determination" that characterize the "New Negro." The anthology aimed, Locke says, "to document the New Negro, culturally and socially, – to register the transformations in the inner and outer life of the Negro in America that have so significantly taken place in the last few years" (ix). *The New Negro* focused on literature that heralded the social transition of people trying to escape racial stereotypes and proscriptions. Less interested in the details of what came before and ignoring the ideas and ideals of those who were not aspiring to cultural change, the writers in this collection and those influenced by it announced a new beginning of African American culture and art. Vernon Loggins' *The Negro Author: His Development in America to 1900* (1921) and Benjamin B. Brawley's *The Negro in Literature and Art in the United States* (1929) are early examples of the literary histories written during that time and in this vein.

Writers and critics in the second half of the twentieth century cautiously acknowledged earlier African American literature. They paid homage to the Harlem Renaissance by reprinting what they considered to be its canonical text, *The New Negro*. The preface to the 1986 edition of Locke's anthology shows continued distinctions between folk and literary, authentic and inauthentic now augmented by "good" and "bad" literature:

> Under the oppressive conditions of slavery in the United States the only channels of artistic expression open to the Negro were in song, graceful movement, and poetic speech. More sophisticated forms did not emerge, with minor exception, until the late 19th Century, notably with Dunbar in poetry and Chesnutt in fiction. And the real flowering of aesthetic expression among Negroes did not begin until the decade of the twenties, aptly characterized as the period of "The Negro Renaissance. (n.p.)

The most vocal proponents of the Black Arts Movement were less charitable, however. They advocated African American literature as a tool to dismantle the old and build the new. In 1966, Leroi Jones (soon to be renamed Amiri Baraka) published a manifesto entitled "The Myth of Negro Literature" that blasted the past with these words:

> The mediocrity of what has been called "Negro Literature" is one of the most loosely held secrets of American culture. From Phillis Wheatley to Charles Chesnutt, to the present generation of American Negro writers, the only recognizable accretion of

> tradition readily attributable to the black producer of a formal literature in this country, with a few notable exceptions, has been of an almost agonizing mediocrity. (Jones 105)

These writers tended to blame this mediocrity upon the black middle class and others who embraced literary aesthetics attributed to Euro-Americans. Jones, who abdicated his own made-in-the-USA, middle-class status by changing his name shortly thereafter to Imamu Amiri Baraka, declared that

> There are a great many reasons for the spectacular vapidity of the American Negro's accomplishment in other formal, serious art forms ... but one of the most persistent and aggravating reasons for the absence of achievement among serious Negro artists, except in Negro music, is that in most cases the Negroes who found themselves in the position to pursue some art, especially the art of literature, have been members of the Negro middle class, a group that has always gone out of its way to cultivate *any* mediocrity, as long as that mediocrity was guaranteed to prove to America, and recently to the world at large, that they were not really who they were, i.e., Negroes. (Jones 106)

In 1968, Baraka teamed up with Larry Neal to publish *Black Fire* (1968). Part anthology, part literary history, part manifesto, *Black Fire* is fairly typical of the perceptive and provocative publications that influenced the Black Studies Movement.[1] Black Arts writers asserted that most, if not all, previous literary productions were pleas for sympathy and petitions for acceptance written primarily for the benefit of people who were not African American. They proposed to create a new literature that looked to African cultures for inspiration and the urban North jungles for reality. They found it useful to cite the existence of writers such as Phillis Wheatley, Paul Laurence Dunbar, and Countee Cullen as evidence of a literate cultural past. They extolled the stridency of writers such as Frederick Douglass, Sojourner Truth, W.E.B. Du Bois, and Marcus Garvey with carefully culled examples while overlooking obvious aspects of their lives and their literature in order to prove that the literature of struggle was rooted in the past. For example, consider the essays promoted by Hoyt Fuller in "Towards a Black Aesthetic" (1968) or Addison Gayle, Jr. in *The Black Aesthetic* (1971).

Not all the scholars in the 1970s were as radical or essentialist as Baraka, Neal, Fuller, and Gayle, but almost all agreed with their assessments of literature before the 1900s. They, too, acknowledge the "firsts" in each genre or era, but, they, too, privileged more recent and politically acceptable writings and writers. Pre-twentieth-century writings got short shrift, partly because most spokespersons and teachers knew very little about the earlier literature, and partly because what they knew embarrassed – or irritated – them. Those students of the 1970s who deliberately set out to reassess pre-twentieth-century writings were primarily attracted to autobiographical writings. Scholarly works such as *Witnessing Slavery* (1975), *The Slave's Narrative* (1985), *Slavery and the Literary Imagination* (1989), and *To Tell a Free Story* (1986) promoted the personal narratives by enslaved and formerly enslaved writers as the *ur*-genre, and the archetypal movement of African American literature to be from slave South to free North. Though they were fine contributions, such works did not start at the beginning. Moreover, they omitted much, if not all, of the literature published prior to the Civil War.

Thus, we title our essay "Ports of Call, Pulpits of Consultation" to represent a relationship between content and intent, and to establish some useful tangible associations as we suggest an alternative history based on themes of mobility and community that figure prominently in words written by Americans of African descent prior to the Civil War. On the one hand, *ports* exist because of mobility; they are places of entry and exit, and function as temporary sites of interaction between transients and residents. At the same time, *ports* represent refuge, rest from journeys completed, sites of stability before venturing forth again, and permanent change for those who remain. *Ports* are places of contact, transportation, and transition. In this essay, we adopt the multiple meanings of this word, especially those of movement, contact, and change. On the other hand, from *pulpits* come pronouncements on universal and unchanging truths. They are the symbolic furniture of institutionalization and community, the platforms from which ideals and methods for change, transformation, and tolerance are preached. *Pulpits* are sites from which individuals and groups seek answers, interpretations, and inspiration. Literal pulpits are also important. A number of authors under discussion were deeply involved with religious institutions and because most of the periodicals and presses were also affiliated with these institutions.

John Marrant, Richard Allen, and Jarena Lee, for example, were ministers who preached social gospel from pulpits in churches, on camp grounds, and in private homes. *Pulpits* may evoke ideas of oral literature, and, of course, the sermons and speeches were often first spoken into being. Before or after the speeches and sermons, however, their notes and manuscripts circulated as well, printed sometimes as broadsides, pamphlets, or books. Some early African American writers were neither particularly religious nor formally recognized as ministers, but they, too, mounted the lectern, stood on street corners, or sat in parlors to argue, debate, analyze, inform, and please audiences. Finally, *pulpit* can mean the lecture halls, living rooms, and metaphorical, if not actual, soapboxes from which ideas and ideals are presented. The front porch of Abijah and Lucy Terry Prince, for example, was a pulpit where folks were entertained and enlightened by recitations, music, and poetry.

Of the people of African ancestry who gathered at the Princes' home and probably elsewhere to share their creative and intellectual talents, literary history has recorded only the names of Lucy Terry Prince and her daughter, Druexa. Of the prose and poetry attributed to the Prince women, only about a dozen lines of one poem by Lucy Terry Prince, "Bars Fight," are extant. But these lines, about a 1746 massacre in Deerfield, Massachusetts, are frequently printed in anthologies, and likewise hailed by scholars, as the first poem by a known African American author, and thus as the first example of "written" literature. This conventional description tends to ignore the value of "Bars Fight" as an exceptional proof of the direct merger of oral and written literatures.

Evidence that Lucy Terry Prince actually *wrote* the poem is weak. Certainly, she was capable of composing the original ballad. Scholars such as Sidney Kaplan, David Proper, and Gretchen Holbrook Gerzina agree that she had a reputation as a talented wordsmith and that she could "mesmerize" an audience. Stories that she argued a property dispute before the Vermont Supreme Court and debated for hours with the Williams College Board of Trustees about admitting her son as a student are legends that grew undoubtedly from her frequent willingness to employ formidable rhetorical skills in various pulpits. Though no one else has been suggested as the author of "Bar's Fight," we cannot be certain that the poem, as written, is completely her invention. The version we celebrate was published in 1854 on the front page of the *Springfield Daily Republican* decades after Lucy Terry died in 1821. For that matter, we are not yet certain that Lucy Terry could even write. Again, it is possible, maybe even probable, that she could, but the actual evidence of Lucy Terry's literacy is scant. David Proper points to a "cryptic" reference in a letter written by Clarissa Ashley that seems to speak of Lucy Terry's method of writing.[2] Proper and Gerzina suggest that since Lucy's husband, Abijah Prince, purchased *The Secretary's Guide, or Young Man's Companion*, it is likely that the couple was literate.

Regardless of the details, the life and writings of Lucy Terry Prince reflect one way in which mobility and community were significant to early African American authors and their works of literature. Indeed, Lucy Terry Prince was a person who knew ports as well as pulpits. Possibly she was born in Africa. If not, she was the daughter of African immigrants. When she was four years old she came to live in the frontier town of Deerfield, Massachusetts as a slave to Ebenezer Wells. Her freedom and her marriage to Abijah Prince occurred about the same time. The couple moved to Guilford, Vermont, owned land, and built a home there. When Abijah Prince died years later, Lucy Terry Prince moved intrastate to Sunderland. Nonetheless, Guilford remained one of her ports. Until her death, she traveled at least annually the 60 or so miles between Guilford and Sunderland to visit Abijah's grave. According to historians, the Princes' Deerfield, Massachusetts home was more than a refuge for them and the six children they reared. It was also a place where their friends and neighbors gathered to talk, listen, and learn. It was both a port and a pulpit.

A self-ordained minister, Jupiter Hammon probably preached from a physical pulpit. Unlike Lucy Terry Prince, Jupiter Hammon's life and writings have been well enough documented that he is (thus far) accepted as the first African American to write *and* publish his own work (Ransom 9). Of the four poems and four prose pieces he is known to have written, the texts of all but one, *An Essay on the Ten Virgins*, are extant (Ransom 11). Scholars note that Jupiter Hammon received a better formal education than the average colonist, slave or free, and that he had access to Henry Lloyd's library (Ransom 13). By taking a closer look at his literary work, replete with biblical allusions and quotations and with contexts for the political history of emancipation, we can see that he took advantage of his educational opportunities to derive the metaphors of pulpits and ports as part of his search for religious refuge and release.

In his earliest extant poem, "An Evening Thought" (1760), for example, Hammon uses biblical verses to unify religious principles for various peoples and nations. Indicating an urgency of seeking shelter in Christianity, his speaker says:

> Now is the Day, excepted [*sic*] Time;
> The Day of Salvation;
> Increase your Faith, do not repine:
> Awake ye every Nation. (Hammon 53–6)

From this poetic pulpit, a message of direct address to "every Nation," a wide and diverse audience, is an effort to move readers from their own various places to the port of salvation. Another poem, one of Hammon's best known, is addressed to Phillis Wheatley. Its full title, "An Address to Miss Phillis Wheatly [*sic*], Ethiopian Poetess, in Boston, who came from Africa at eight years of age, and soon became acquainted with the gospel of Jesus Christ," is replete with implications of port and pulpit alike. Written in 1778, the poem connects a man from Long Island, New York to a woman in the port city of Boston, Massachusetts whose previous journey to England her volume of poetry, *Poems on Various Subjects, Religious and Moral* (1773), had already assured her fame. The poem links the experiences of Hammon and Wheatley with those of an ancient people once enslaved on the African continent. The poem's references to "the raging main," and "thousands tossed by the sea" as well as "thousands mov'd to distant shore / And others left behind" highlight dangerous journeys, migration, and refuge. Like a sermon, the verse explicitly makes Jesus Christ a sheltering, welcoming port, redeeming kidnapping by attributing it to Divine Providence's rescue from a "distant," "heathen" shore. In this poem, the journey and all of the trials Wheatley endured are worth the safety and refuge she has found as a Christian convert. However, the poem also implies that Wheatley's life and writings are influential, and warns her to be an especially careful role model. Hammon's poem is intertextual call and response to other literary works. Jupiter Hammon signs himself as author and amanuensis, writing, he says, on behalf of a group of African Americans in Long Island. With "Address to Miss Phillis Wheatly," and with other works such as his essay, "Address to the Negroes in the State of New-York," which identifies the "Members of the African Society, in the City of New York" as among the intended audience, Hammon exemplifies writers who intended their texts to carry consultation and consolation to and from many ports. His work represents others that provide opportunities for readers to contemplate the symbiosis of real and metaphorical ports and pulpits in early African American literature.

In 1760, the same year that Jupiter Hammon of Long Island, New York, wrote "An Evening's Thought," Briton Hammon of Marshfield, Massachusetts, published a memoir, *A Narrative of the Uncommon Sufferings and Surpizing Deliverance of Briton Hammon, a Negro Man*. These men shared a common surname and both were enslaved in colonial New England, but there is no evidence that they knew one another. Briton Hammon's narrative shows the centrality of movement – voluntary and involuntary, in and out of literal ports – across the New and Old Worlds. The narrative begins in 1747, after Hammon's master had permitted him to leave Marshfield and go to Plymouth, Massachusetts to look for work. Hammon found a job as a sailor but on the return trip from Jamaica, Native American pirates apprehended the ship near the Florida Cape and made Briton Hammon prisoner. During the 13 years chronicled by his narrative, Briton Hammon travels to ports that ranged from the Caribbean Islands to the British Isles and beyond before he returned to Boston.

Briton Hammon's 1760 *Narrative* and the 1785 *Narrative of the Life of John Marrant, of New York, in North America* are both often found in collections of the genre known as "Indian Captivity Narratives." As such, they bridge African American and Euro-American literatures about bondage and freedom, abandonment, abduction, escape, and reconciliation. But they are also quintessential examples of an early African American literature of importation, deportation, and other forms of travel, exploration, and transition. Marrant's title, which identifies him as being "Of New York, in North America," suggests that he expected his writing to reach ports so distant the readers would not know the location of New York. The first lines of his memoir further promote ideas of ports of call and pulpits of consultation: "I, John Marrant, born June 15th, 1755, in New York, in North-America, wish these gracious dealings of the Lord with me to be published, in hopes they may be useful to others, to encourage the fearful, to confirm the wavering, and to refresh the hearts of true believer."

When we consider writings by John Marrant, Briton Hammon, Jupiter Hammon, and Lucy Terry Prince, we find that ports of call and pulpits of consultation are more useful and inclusive than the popular idea that flight from slavery to freedom is the original structure of African American autobiographical writing. They accommodate paradigms for more discerning compendia, interpretations, and analyses of extant texts than those that have emerged from anachronistic or exclusive political expectations. This approach solves the aforementioned problem that plagued theorists of the New Negro and the Black Arts Movements who have ignored or marginalized a large segment of literary production; dated the emergence of written literature in African America about two generations later than the data shows; and wrestled with, the literature has recognized, persistent examples of what might be considered as apolitical or as neither antislavery nor Afro-centric.

For scholars who try to establish "firsts" and "earliest," our approach moves the earliest slave narrative back a full generation – from 1760 to 1734 when *Some Memoirs of the Life of Job* tells the story of Ayuba Suleiman Diallo, renamed after captivity as Job ben Solomon. Focusing on travel and communicative among communities facilitates our incorporation of marginalized or ignored writings, while placing the better known stories of slavery and freedom in a more inclusive context. For example, Diallo's story has significant similarities to *The Interesting Narrative of the Life of Olaudah Equiano* (1789). Diallo, like Equiano, was kidnapped and enslaved, moved to England and tried to return to Africa. Though Equiano did not succeed in his attempt, perhaps it was Diallo's success that encouraged Equiano to try. The circular, international journeys of Briton Hammon, Ayuba Suleiman Diallo, and others place later works

– such as Olaudah Equiano's – in a context that displaces the conventional idea of the journey from slavery to freedom as the earliest theme in African American literature. The journeys challenge us to rethink the role of fugitive slave narratives in the origins of the black autobiographical tradition.

Beginning with the idea of ports and pulpits requires us to reconsider the multiple significances of religion, region, and labor. Phillis Wheatley was brought from Senegambia and enslaved in Boston. Like Jupiter Hammon, she found port and pulpit in literacy and literature. Her oeuvre is full of allusions and paraphrases of the Christian Bible, along with Greek and Roman mythologies, that represent her pulpit for ideas and her meditations on past and present events. Not only were the Afro-Roman playwright Terence, the Hebrew boy-soldier David, and the curious but incautious Greek Icarus travelers of heroic deeds with whom Phillis identified; their stories were also ports, so to speak, where she could visit and mediate her position as an enslaved African American woman. The following stanza from to "To Mæcenas" demonstrates Wheatley's imaginative travel and her recognition of literature as a port, highlighting the movement of Terence's name and his Muse-inspired words from "age to age" through the port of literature:

> The happier *Terence* all the choir inspir'd
> His soul replenish'd, and his bosom fir'd;
> But say, ye *Muses*, why this partial grace,
> To one alone of *Afric's* sable race;
> From age to age transmitting thus his name
> With the first glory in the rolls of fame?

Like the travels of others, Wheatley's were not simply mental or spiritual, though such ports indeed offer not only shelter but also transcendence. Her writings were traveling pulpits from which she could communicate her versions of reality and her visions of hope and change. Wheatley published her first poem in a Rhode Island newspaper in 1767. She arranged the publication of her book, *Poems on Various Subjects, Religious and Moral*, in 1773, when she traveled to England. She wrote on themes of physical and spiritual mobility in early works such as "On Being Brought from Africa to America," and in later ones such as "Oceans," a recently discovered poem presumed written on her return from England to America. Clearly, Phillis Wheatley's conversion to Christianity was sincere; however, like many African descendent people, Wheatley's spirituality retained firm roots in Islam and paganism. Hers was one extreme of Afro-Protestantism. Richard Allen's writings place him on a continuum that is more moderate, but equally significant.

Again, Richard Allen knew many ports. Born into slavery in the Germantown area of Philadelphia in 1760, the same year in which Jupiter Hammon and Briton Hammon wrote and published their texts, Allen and his family were later sold to a plantation outside of Dover, Delaware, where he lived until he was about 20 years old. Allen and his enslaver were converted to Christianity from the pulpits of The Methodist Society. The slaveholder's newfound religion convinced him that slavery was unchristian, and gave Allen an opportunity to buy his freedom. By 1786, Allen owned himself. For several years, Allen traveled as an itinerant minister, preaching the gospel according to the Great Awakening concepts. With Absalom Jones and others, Allen organized an African American exodus from segregated Methodist churches and established a Philadelphia branch of the African Union Society. Allen wrote hymns and songs to relieve and to inspire wandering, troubled souls and published, in 1801, *A Collection of Spiritual Songs and Hymns, Selected from Various Authors*. From enslaved Christian convert to itinerant Methodist minister to co-founder and first bishop of the African Methodist Episcopal Church, Allen personified ports and pulpits. These themes informed his many published broadsides and pamphlets, as well as his memoir published posthumously in 1836, *The Life, Experiences, and Gospel Labours of the Rt. Rev. Richard Allen*.

Richard Allen's writings were metaphorical ports and pulpits that helped foster the intellectual and physical movement of others. He contributed to *Freedom's Journal*, a periodical forum for debates about such issues as colonization or, as we might say, whether and under what conditions one should seek shelter in the United States or set sail for other, more hospitable ports. With his wife Sarah, Allen operated a station on the railroad for 30 years, giving shelter and refuge to fugitive and travelers alike. One sojourner, Jarena Lee, required Allen to confront sexism in the Afro-Protestant Church. While serving as Lee's spiritual advisor, he first resisted, then allowed, her requests for official authority to preach, making her the first known female formally authorized to preach in that denomination. Not only did Sarah Allen provide a place for Lee's children to stay when Lee ventured abroad, but she was the first person to purchase Lee's *Life and Religious Experience of Jarena Lee* (1836).

Like Richard Allen and others, Jarena Lee believed that Christianity was a viable port of various capacities and that she was called to find shelter and succor in the kindness of strangers and in the words of the gospels. Like Allen and Marrant, Lee had an itinerant ministry that took her to many ports of call. Although she had been born free in New Jersey, like such enslaved foremothers as Lucy Terry Prince and Phillis Wheatley, Jarena Lee well knew the particular problems and privileges that sexism made for women who claimed pulpit authority. She, too, was undaunted and continued to transport her religious principles and women's rights messages. For example, although church officials did not support her book's questioning of gender roles, Jarena Lee used book sales, generated during preaching tours, to raise money for her church in Philadelphia. This decision shows Lee's dedication to religious uplift and women's rights.

David Walker, Jarena Lee's contemporary, also valued movement. Walker's *Appeal in Four Articles; … to the Coloured Citizens of the World, but in Particular, and Very Expressly, to those of the United States of America, Written in Boston, State of Massachusetts* (1829) recalls writings of John Marrant's and other early African American writers who knew many ports and assumed that their words would reach and succor strangers as well as those among whom they themselves sojourned. Walker, like Jarena Lee and Richard Allen, wrote to expand the audience for his words. Walker had a shop near the docks and conventional wisdom has it that he outfitted sailors not only with clothing and supplies but also with copies of his *Appeal*, which they delivered to others. Walker's distribution system for his writings was perhaps more covert than that of others, but it is also typical of the marketing and distribution system that many African American writers developed. As they traveled, they sold copies of their writings, while other travelers served as salespersons and agents for writers. Walker, like Lee and Allen, did not submit to the oppressive forces that attempted to hinder the changes and challenges their words intended to inspire. Rather, these literary forbearers recognized the power of their words, spoken and written. Just as this recognition of literary power continued to move through David Walker, it has traveled to and through contemporary African American writers. This recognition is one of the many links between the past and the present in the African American literary tradition, and one illustration of the importance of contemplating beginnings of African American literature in a more critical way.

Although unified thematically, the range and complexity of the topics and purposes of the works covered in this essay alone are testaments to the necessity of revising approaches to early African American literature. Recently rediscovered documents from antebellum African America provide impetus for reconsiderations of beginnings of African American literature. These rediscovered documents introduce "new" writers, "new" texts, and multiple perspectives that encourage more accurate information about early African American literary culture while enriching and informing our knowledge of currently canonized writers and their work.

The origin story we sketch here is a revision of conventional wisdom about the genesis of African American literature. It begins by assuming that African American written literature began as deliberate syntheses of the real and the ideal, infused and promulgated by writers' travels and religions. It recognizes that literature often served and still serves as a port through which and a pulpit from which writers give voice to African America. Ours is not intended to replace other stories. It does rethink implications of earlier literary histories in light of new discoveries that, we hope, will inspire other re-visioned narratives of African American literature. The process of reconsideration and its products are essential for more accurate ideas of African American literary history particularly and of global literary development generally.

Notes

1 Other examples are Hoyt Fuller's and Gayle's *The Black Aesthetic* and George Kent's *Blackness and the Adventure of Western Culture.*

2 Proper does not offer detail about the level of Clarissa Ashley's acquaintance with Lucy Terry.

Bibliography

Allen, Richard. *The Life, Experience, and Gospel Labors of the Rt. Rev. Richard Allen* (1836). In J.E. Wideman, ed. *My Soul Has Grown Deep*. Philadelphia: Running Press, 2001. 22–36.

Andrews, William L. *To Tell a Free Story: The First Century of Afro-American Autobiography, 1760–1865*. Urbana: University of Illinois Press, 1986.

Bigsby, C.W.E., ed. *The Second Black Renaissance: Essays in Black Literature*. Westport, CT: Greenwood, 1980.

Braithwaite, W.S. "The Negro in American Literature." In Alain Locke, ed. *The New Negro: An Interpretation*. New York: Boni, 1925.

Brawley, Benjamin. *The Negro in Literature and Art in the United States*. New York: Duffield, 1918.

Cornelius, Janet Duitsman. *"When I Can Read My Title Clear": Literacy, Slavery, and Religion in the Antebellum South*. Columbia: University of South Carolina Press, 1991.

Davis, C.T. and Henry Louis Gates, Jr., ed. *The Slave's Narrative*. New York: Oxford University Press, 1985.

Diouf, Sylviane Anna. *Servants of Allah: African Muslim Encounters in the Americas*. New York: New York University Press, 1998.

Equiano, Olaudah. *The Interesting Narrative of the Life of Olaudah Equiano* (1789). In Werner Sollors, ed. *The Interesting Narrative of the Life of Olaudah Equiano, or Gustavas Vassa, the African/ Written By Himself: Contexts, Criticism*. New York: Norton, 2000. 2–178.

Foster, F.S. *Witnessing Slavery: The Development of Ante-bellum Slave Narratives*. Westport, CT: Greenwood, 1979.

Fuller, H. "Towards a Black Aesthetic" (1968). In A. Mitchell, ed. *Within the Circle: An Anthology of African American Literary Criticism from the Harlem Renaissance to the Present*. Durham, NC: Duke University Press, 1994. 199–206.

Gayle, Addison, Jr. *The Black Aesthetic*. Garden City: Doubleday, 1971.

Gerzina, G.H. *Mr. and Mrs. Prince: How an Extraordinary Eighteenth-Century Family Moved out of Slavery and into Legend*. New York: Amistad, 2008.

Gomez, M. *Exchanging Our Country Marks: The Transformation of African Identities in the Colonial and Antebellum South*. Chapel Hill: University of North Carolina Press, 1998.

Hammon, B. *A Narrative of the Sufferings and Deliverance of Briton Hammon* (1760). In W.E. Washburn, ed. *The Garland Library of Narratives of North American Indian Captives*. New York: Garland, 1978. 1–14.

Hammon, Jupiter. "An Evening Thought." In S.A. Ransom, ed. *America's First Negro Poet: The Complete Works of Jupiter Hammon of Long Island*. New York: Kennikat, 1983. 104–18.

Jones, LeRoi. *Home: Social Essays*. New York: William Morrow, 1966.

Kaplan, S. and E. N. Kaplan. *The Black Presence in the Era of the American Revolution*. Amherst: University of Massachusetts Press, 1989.

Lee, J. *Religious Experience and Journal of Mrs. Jarena Lee* (1836). In J.E. Wideman, ed. *My Soul Has Grown Deep*. Philadelphia: Running Press, 2001. 83–186.

Lewis, D. L. *When Harlem Was in Vogue*. New York: Penguin, 1997.

Locke, Alain. *The New Negro (1925)*. Salem, NH: Ayer, 1986.

Loggins, V. *The Negro Author: His Development in America to 1900*. Port Washington, NY: Kennikat, 1959. (Originally issued as thesis in 1921.)

Marrant, J. *A Narrative of the Life of John Marrant, of New York, in North America (1785)*. Leeds: Davies, 1810. [Microfiche.]

McDowell, Deborah. E. and Arnold Rampersad, ed. *Slavery and the Literary Imagination*. Baltimore: Johns Hopkins University Press, 1989.

McHenry, Elizabeth. *Forgotten Readers: Recovering the Lost History of African American Literary Societies*. Durham, NC: Duke University Press, 2002.

Neal, L. and A. Baraka. *Black Fire*. New York: William Morrow, 1968.

Pearce, R. H. *Historicism Once More: Problems and Occasions for the American Scholar*. Princeton: Princeton University Press, 1969.

Proper, D. R. *Lucy Terry Prince: Singer of History*. Deerfield, MA: Pocumtuck Valley Memorial Association, 1997.

Ransom, S.A. *America's First Negro Poet: The Complete Works of Jupiter Hammon of Long Island*. New York: Kennikat, 1983.

Solomon, Job ben. *Some Memoirs of the Life of Job* (1734). In P.D. Curtin, ed., *African Remembered: Narratives by West Africans from the Era of the Slave Trade*. Madison: University of Wisconsin Press, 1968. 17–59.

Thompson, J. E. *Dudley Randall, Broadside Press, and the Black Arts Movement in Detroit, 1960–1995*. Jefferson, NC: McFarland, 1999.

Walker, D. *Appeal in Four Articles; Together with a Preamble to the Coloured Citizens of the World, but in Particular, and Very Expressly, to those of the United States of America, Written in Boston, State of Massachusetts (1829)*. Rpt. S. Wilentz, ed. New York: Hill and Wang, 1995.

Watson, S. *The Harlem Renaissance: Hub of African American Culture, 1920–1930*. New York: Pantheon, 1995.

Wheatley, P. *Poems on Various Subjects, Religious and Moral (1773)*. Rpt. Julian D. Mason, ed. Chapel Hill: University of North Carolina Press, 1989.

4

The Constitution of Toussaint: Another Origin of African American Literature

Michael J. Drexler and Ed White

In the summer of 1801, Toussaint L'Ouverture, the rebel leader of the slave revolt on the French colony of Saint-Domingue, promulgated a constitution that signaled the quasi-independence of the island. By January of 1804, Haiti would become the second independent republic in the Western hemisphere, the culmination of the first anti-colonial insurgency carried out by former slaves. The 1801 Constitution has generally been overshadowed in the history books – in the rare cases that the Haitian Revolution garners any attention in histories of the early US – by the story of Toussaint's ascendancy, his arrest and deportation to France, and the rise of his successor, Jean-Jacques Dessalines. But as a document of the age of revolutions, the 1801 Constitution, known as Toussaint's Constitution, deserves to stand alongside The Declaration of Independence, The Declaration of the Rights of Man and the Citizen, and the US Constitution as a signal text. Our interest here, however, is to make a perhaps more modest claim, but one that could have significant repercussions for the study of early African American literature. Our claim will be that, following its dissemination throughout the US in the fall of 1801, Toussaint's Constitution became the most widely read piece of literature authored by an African American and may have remained so until the publication of *Narrative of the Life of Frederick Douglass* in 1845.[1]

Several caveats might be immediately raised to such a suggestion. Most obviously, the text was neither written in, nor published in, nor even ostensibly about the United States. What's more, not only was Toussaint not from, in, or of the United States, he was not the author of "his" constitution in any traditional sense. How, then, does a work prepared in the West Indies by a committee of mostly white planters warrant consideration as an important African American text? We would note that similar analogous objections have been raised, together or in isolation, about any number of African American writings. Phillis Wheatley's first book of poetry had to be published in London because neither sufficient subscribers nor willing printers could be found for a North American edition. Despite the popularity and impressively wide dissemination of her elegy on the death of George Whitefield (1771), Wheatley's book would not be published in the United States until after her death.[2] Olaudah Equiano's *Interesting Narrative* is now considered a crucial text of an Atlantic, not to mention US, literary canon, not because he visited Pennsylvania or Georgia, nor even because he may have been born in the Carolinas. As Vincent Carretta argues, Equiano wrote of himself, and appealed to those of African descent, as "citizens of the world" at a moment when "trans- or supra-national identities" partly indicated that "national identities were denied them" (Carretta 2008: 99). Likewise, simpler models of authorship have been problematized by African American studies, such that few would dismiss the narratives of Venture Smith and Sojourner Truth, for example, due to the major roles of their amanuenses, Elisha Niles and Olive Gilbert. As we will see, Toussaint's Constitution should also be viewed as a text dictated to amanuenses, in this case the assembly committee strictly directed by the General. All of these examples demonstrate the necessary reconceptualization of textual and authorial classification demanded by African American writing. Texts written or published outside of the United States are often so precisely because of institutional or cultural hostility, and these difficult conditions in turn necessitate broader understandings of authorship and spatial identity or self-affiliation.[3]

Each of these critiques informs our view that Toussaint's Constitution joins, if not inaugurates, a tradition in African American letters of holding white social and political morality to account for its more abstract and universalizing strands. The appearance of the 1801 Constitution represents a strategic inversion of foundational documents and principles of the West. From Equiano, who leveraged the golden rule to castigate "nominal Christians," to Jones and Allen's appeal for civic recognition, and to the redirection of the US Constitution and the Declaration of Independence in David Walker's *Appeal* and Douglass's Fourth of July oration, Toussaint's Constitution ought to take a place as a most powerful example. It offers students of African American literature both a powerful articulation of Black agency in letters as well as an unprecedented archive of responses from white audiences in the US. One might reasonably consider the committee that drafted the constitution as Toussaint's collective amanuensis, albeit under very different conditions than one normally encounters with, say, a fugitive slave narrative. Certainly, too, the 1801 Constitution exemplifies one possible and important manifestation of paranational identity germane to the US context, articulating as it did a Revolutionary state determined to protect those of African descent from chattel slave status.

It is difficult to assess the impact of Toussaint's Constitution among the some 900,000 black residents of the United States in 1801. It is certainly plausible that both slaves and free people of color may have identified more with the emergent black republic of Haiti than with the US republic, which held them in bondage. Gabriel Prosser's slave rebellion in Virginia in 1800 suggests a possible earlier awareness of events in Saint-Domingue, as do the nineteenth century's numerous plans for relocation to and colonization of Haiti. If African American poetry can trace its roots to Wheatley, the protest tradition in African American letters ought to extend back from

James Forten, David Walker, Henry Highland Garnet, Martin Delany, and others to the actions and words of Toussaint. Certainly William Wells Brown suggested as much in the first, 1863 edition of *The Black Man, His Antecedents, His Genius*, which included extensive profiles of six Haitians (Toussaint, Dessalines, Henri Christophe, Andre Rigaud, Alexandre Petion, and Jean Pierre Boyer).

What is notable about the 1801 Constitution, however, is that it profoundly intervened in the political self-awareness of the white citizenry and elite as well. Indeed, it arguably challenged the US understanding of revolution and race more than any work prior to (or even including) Douglass's "What to a Slave is the Fourth of July?" or William Wells Brown's *Clotel*. We get some sense of the text's remarkable impact from its migration through US newspapers, Federalist and Republican alike. The first reports about the Constitution appeared as early as August 3, 1801, in *The Baltimore American*. About a week later, it appeared in the national Democratic Republican standard-bearer, *The National Intelligencer*, as well as the chief Federalist organ, the *Gazette of the United States*. Within months, it had appeared in at least 24 newspapers from Virginia, Maryland, and the District of Columbia, northward to Philadelphia, New Jersey, New York, Connecticut, Massachusetts, and even into New Hampshire, Vermont, and the territory of Maine. Such a proliferation dwarfs, for instance, the readership of Equiano's narrative, the first American edition of which ran but 336 copies, with no second edition until 1829.

Before we return to the circulation and reception of the Constitution, let us turn to a description of what we consider to be the text at issue. We do not isolate just the text of the 1801 Constitution itself as the critical text, as it typically appeared as one component within a textual cluster. In this larger grouping, four texts seem particularly important. The first of these reports on events of April 6, 1801 – the 17th Germinal in the French Revolutionary calendar – when Toussaint ordered the preparation of a new form of government. In this text, of just under 800 words, Toussaint appoints a committee of eight deputies – two each from the four departments – and orders it to prepare "a constitution suited to [the] climate, soil, culture, trade, and to the manners" of the inhabitants of the "Island of St. Domingo." The second text, running just under 4,000 words, is a full translation of the Constitution itself. There appears to have been only one translation, appearing first in the *National Intelligencer* before its extensive circulation. No indication is given of its translator. The third text, of just over 3,500 words and sometimes appearing in two installments, describes the formal acceptance and promulgation of the Constitution on July 7, 1801 (19th Messidor). This textual sequence begins with Toussaint's arrival at Cape-François and his formal reception; a speech (just over 1,100 words) by the president of the central assembly, Citizen Borgella; an answer from Toussaint (just over 650 words) accepting the new constitution and calling on the citizens of the island to honor the new system; a concluding speech again by Borgella (just over 1,000 words); and a quick summary of the closing ceremonies. Finally, a fourth text (of slightly more than 800 words) sometimes appeared proximate to the above texts: the "Character of the Celebrated Black General, *Toussaint L'Ouverture*." The three auxiliary segments – the Germinal convocation, the Messidor promulgation, and the character sketch – were essential to the reception of the Constitution itself, and they should be considered part of the larger textual apparatus, just as prefaces, notes, testaments, and accounts of speeches or meetings are essential parts of later fugitive slave narratives.

What, then, is this text? One should first note that it does contain some of the organizational features of the US Constitution and would therefore have been readily identifiable as belonging to the same "family" of texts. Titles 7 through 9, for example, outline St. Domingo's legislative, executive, and judicial branches, albeit with important distinctions. Most notably, power is concentrated in the executive branch – here forcefully equated with the "Government" itself – and, at the moment of the Constitution's enactment, the supreme executive, "the Governor," is Toussaint. Indeed, not only is Toussaint named in the text six times, but his "firmness, activity, indefatigable zeal, and … rare virtues" earn him the office until "the melancholy event of his decease," at which point his successor will have been named by Toussaint himself.[4] As for the governor's powers, he oversees the military (§ 34), "proposes laws," even those that change the constitution (§ 36), "promulgates" them (§ 34), and "exacts the observation" of all laws and obligations (§ 35). In these points, the constitution codifies its own creation: it exists because it has been called forth and then promulgated by Toussaint. Toussaint is furthermore granted the duties and powers of overseeing finances (§ 38), monitoring and censoring "all writings designed for the press" (§ 39), and suppressing any "conspiracy" against the state (§ 40). With this tremendous, individual concentration of power, the responsibilities of the legislature and the tribunals are definitively subordinated to the governor. The assembly, for instance, "votes the adoption or the rejection of laws which are proposed by the Governor" (§ 24). They are further granted the power of providing opinions on existing laws (§24) and of managing the details of the national budget (§ 26). Tribunals shall exist in three tiers: those of "first demand," then of "appeal," and finally of "cassation" or annulment (§§ 44–5). But "special tribunals" organized by the Governor shall oversee all military infractions, as well as "all robberies and thefts," as well as "house-breaking," "assassinations, murders, incendiaries, rapes, conspiracies and rebellions" (§ 47). Furthermore, Titles 10 through 12 extend the power of the governor over local or "municipal" government, the armed forces, and the basic financial matters of the island. Toussaint is granted the authority to nominate all "members of the municipal administration" (§ 49), to control with total authority the armed forces (§ 52), and to appoint a commission of three to "regulate and examine accounts of the receipts and expences of the colony" (§ 62).

The hegemonic hermeneutic of the US Constitution makes many readers today read Toussaint's Constitution cynically. The US text implied a series of beliefs about politics and human nature, laboriously expounded in accounts of Florentine political thought, early modern British history, and principles of the Scottish Enlightenment. Whereas the US Constitution, therefore, enacted theories of collective power and private property, the 1801 Saint-Domingue text concentrates power in the hands of an autocrat and, read through the same US hermeneutic, seems a power grab. It would be more productive to see Toussaint's governmental apparatus enacting a different hermeneutic, one based not on political principles inflected by a theory of human nature and commerce, but on a particular local history and a state of society that might be called ethnographic. Indeed, this latter foundation becomes clear when we consider the stunning departures of the 1801 text from that of 1789. For Toussaint's Constitution's opening segments detail St. Domingo's territorial extent (Title 1), its "Inhabitants" (Title 2), its religion and morals (Titles 3 and 4), "Men in Society" (Title 5), and its "Agriculture and Commerce" (Title 6). As even these headings indicate, it would have been difficult not to see the parallels between the 1801 Constitution and the older colonial genre of the ethnography, which structured its analyses of the indigenous other within a similar progression from region and demographics, to morality and religion, and then economy. The insertion of these elements – associated in the turn-of-the-century US with non-white peoples – demonstrated a competing hermeneutic with an unusual defamiliarizing potential.

What is more, this ethnographic strand was peculiarly accentuated by its association with the slave code. The latter, from the memorable moment of the Barbados code of 1661, demonstrated a transmutation of ethnographic genres, taking a descriptive analytic frequently tooled to penetration and mastery and rendering it a supervisory code for better management and domination. This may be the most remarkable aspect of the 1801 Constitution, which can be read as a revolutionary, emancipatory answer to the French *Code Noir*, accepting its strictures and structures to emphasize its repudiation. Article 2 of Louis XIV's well-known 1685 code enjoined that "All slaves that shall be in our islands shall be baptized and instructed in the Roman, Catholic, and Apostolic Faith," while subsequent articles outlined the rules for marriage, bastardy, and ownership. Article 6 of the 1801 text echoes its predecessor – "The Catholic, Apostolic and Roman religion, is the only one publicly professed" – while subsequent articles elevate marriage, ban divorce, and declare the need to address illegitimate children. This is the slave code rewritten for ex-slaves – an antislavery code in which abolition is emphatically announced at the outset. Section 3 declares "Slaves are not permitted in this territory; servitude is forever abolished – All men born here, live and die freemen and Frenchmen." As abstract as this principle is, the overall context of the document shows that this revolutionary assertion must be understood as a moral and practical resistance to a specific history of slavery. So Toussaint's Constitution challenges its more abstract counterpart to the North, so uneasy with historical and sociological details as to veil these realities with euphemisms like "Persons as any of the States now existing shall think proper to admit" through "Importation" (Article 1, § 9) or the "Person held to Service or Labour in one State … escaping into another" (Article 4, § 2). From this perspective, the details of Title 8, "General dispositions," display not odd particularities inappropriate to political theory, but a particular historical consciousness that wants to reward innovations in agricultural technology (§ 70), punish the arbitrary seizure of persons (§ 65), and monitor local "associations inimical to public order" (§ 67). When Section 76 proclaims "that every citizen owes his services to the country that has given him birth, and to the soil that nourishes him, to the maintenance of liberty, and the equal divisions of property, whenever the law calls him to defend them," it is also insisting that allegiance and service to the state have a very particular meaning at a crucial point in the Revolution. This is a constitution assuming crisis, not stasis.

One should already be able to anticipate the impact of the 1801 text on a US readership, for whom the constitution may have seemed less a poor cynical imitation than a stunning historical and social revelation about the 1789 US Constitution. Yet, before turning to the 1801 Constitution in its US context, we must outline a final important generic strain to the textual complex – the characterological romance in the portrait of Toussaint himself. As we have indicated, the institutional-ethnographic text of the constitution itself was consistently presented in the US press with auxiliary texts that developed a necessary narrative frame confirming the label of "Toussaint's Constitution." These texts operated on several levels.

The simplest narrative is that of the constitutional ceremonies, summarized above: Toussaint greets the eight members of the assembly (seven of whom were white, one "mulatto," and all former slave owners); he demands that they draft a constitution "consult[ing] past events to avoid their repetition"; he warns them against "publish[ing] any of the legislative acts you may think proper to make" before receiving Toussaint's approval. After the constitution has been drafted, Citizen (Bernard) Borgella, the head of the assembly, greets Toussaint in a public ceremony of tremendous pomp and circumstance: "The croud was immense … There existed the most profound silence." Borgella delivers two long speeches, and Toussaint one, somewhat shorter. In fact, the text of Borgella's longer speech concludes noting that Toussaint offered yet another speech, "which being little more than a reiteration of the sentiments of the orator who preceded him, it would be superfluous to give a translation of."

On another level, these declamations offer a situational explanation of the new constitution. Toussaint and especially Borgella summarized details of colonial history, the Revolution in France (including Bonaparte's return to France from Egypt), the difficult relations between the two realms, and the struggle for order in the island. It is clear that the concern, in these speeches, is the legitimation of the constitutional enterprise itself, since, despite all assertions of fidelity to France, the "unfortunate colony" has suffered from the "perverse influence" of "the Metropolis." This more broadly colonial narrative confirms and reinforces the ethnographic elements of the constitution summarized above. For a major problem of governance heretofore was the old French constitution, in which a "multiplicity of wheelworks" had "run afoul of each other … giv[ing] rise to popular cabals, diversity of opinion, and public Calamities." In short, it was the mechanical differentiation of structures that had provoked first "the Spirit of Party," as devious politicians had known how to "interpret [laws] according to their interests"; conflict, anarchy, and disorder had followed. These catastrophes had been averted by the actions of Toussaint, who, at every moment of seemingly terminal chaos, had risen "like a phoenix from the ashes." He had "take[n] charge of the rein of an abandoned colony," suppressing unrest, unifying the regions, and even "conquer[ing] inveterate prejudices," replacing them with "the most tender fraternity." The new constitution would enact in writing the heroic achievements of Toussaint himself, specifically addressing the demands of the immediate colonial situation:

> [Toussaint] announces to you that the time of convulsions is past; he demonstrates the necessity of giving you laws of convenience; and adopting this constant maxim, that laws are conventions established by men, to conform themselves to, for the regulation of the order of society. He makes you conceive that it is with them as it is with the production of the earth, that every country has its manners, its statutes, as well as its appropriate fruits.

Inspired by and modeled upon Toussaint, this new text thus answered those "circumstances which present themselves but once during a long series of ages, to fix the destiny of mankind" – not embody timeless principles, as the US Constitution might have it. Finally, the Messidor speeches made clear the pressing demands of the near future: the need for new planters, unification of the island, property regulation, and reestablishment of the plantation system.

Thus the texts of convocation and promulgation had both told the story of the constitution as a kind of textual analogue or extension of Toussaint: he had requested, assessed, endorsed, and proclaimed it; his action was demanded and affirmed within it; and its internal logic and propositions reflected those of his behavior in resisting French interference. He was even cast as the local counterpart to "the re-edifying genius" of Bonaparte, who had restored order and unity to France. It is not surprising, then, that these texts were at times accompanied by the "Character of the Celebrated Black General *Toussaint L'Ouverture*." This short text describes the "extraordinary man" in terms of his intelligence, achievements, gratitude, and humanity, but above all his practicality. It mentions his childhood education in France,[5] his rise to military leadership, and his attempts to restore economic order. The key anecdote, however, concerns the request by the British General Thomas Maitland, who requested the favor of the restoration of twelve planters to their estates. Upon their return, Toussaint "clapped them in prison," but within days had them brought to a church in which he preached a sermon of reconciliation:

> "We were for a while Spaniards, (the blacks fled to the Spanish protection, in the beginning of the troubles), but we were missed. We were born Frenchmen, and now we are Frenchmen again. These twelve men have also been missed. They were born Frenchmen. For a time they have been British; but now they have returned, and are Frenchmen again. Let us embrace." Here Toussaint embraced them, and reconciled his followers – He restored them to their estates, and gave them negroes as servants.

The episode exemplifies a pragmatism consistent with the ethnographic formulations of the other texts, and in contrast to which patriotic affiliations are fickle and relatively meaningless. Even as the sketch affirms Toussaint's service to the French Republic, it likewise stresses that same republic's incompetence and antagonism toward Toussaint. Insisting that Toussaint is *not* concerned with amassing power for its own sake – he "did not treat as an independent prince as some of the papers have said" – the sketch presents him as the most practical of figures, ultimately concerned with restoring "commerce and prosperity." Thus the character sketch simultaneously emphasizes Toussaint's self-effacing qualities and his heroic actions, such that he becomes the paradigmatic republican.

Such was the textual aggregate that arrived in the United States in August of 1801, with a remarkable circulation through newspapers. If the constitutional text appeared in at least 24 papers, the promulgation texts appeared in at least 22, the character sketch in at least 17, and the convocation texts in at least five. Newspapers printing these texts ranged across much of the United States: at least seven papers in Connecticut, 14 in Massachusetts, four in New Hampshire, two in Maine, one in Rhode Island, four in Vermont, two in New Jersey, nine in New York, and five in Pennsylvania. The text even appeared in some of the Southern states: in at least three papers in the District of Columbia, two in Maryland, one in Virginia, and three in South Carolina.[6] Though the character sketch appears in papers as early as June 11 (*The American Intelligencer* of Massachusetts), most of the texts appeared in sequential issues of newspapers from August into December.

The impact of the text was surely related to the fractious political context it entered. The conflicts and turmoil of the Federalist era are well known, but three dimensions of that moment – all relevant to the reception of Toussaint's Constitution – may be briefly rehearsed here. Most obvious was the emergence of political parties from the mid-1790s onward. The split had numerous causes, consequences, and manifestations, including an increasingly partisan press and the growing association of the competing factions with Britain (the Federalists) and France (the Democratic-Republics). Several other dimensions are particularly germane to Toussaint's Constitution, including the increasing formulation of partisan difference in terms of constitutional hermeneutics – for instance, in the 1792 debates over the "general welfare" clause, prompted by Alexander Hamilton's 1791 "Report on the Subject of Manufactures." Also important was President Washington's 1794 attack on the Democratic-Republican societies, widely associated with the so-called Whiskey Insurrection, the largest domestic insurrection in US history prior to the Civil War. Washington's Message to the Third Congress, in November of 1794, explained his oversight, as "Commander-in-Chief of the Militia," of the expedition to suppress the insurrection, while condemning "certain self-created societies" that incited opposition to the state. Four years later, the Kentucky and Virginia Resolutions further highlighted constitutional disagreements, raising the specter of the dissolution of the union in responding to the Adams administration's Alien and Sedition Acts. The 1800 election could justly seem like a referendum on (among other things) the interpretation of the US Constitution. Within the first year of Jefferson's administration assault on the lame-duck Sixth Congress's Judiciary Act was anticipated; Republicans of various stripes would target judges and the very notion of the separate judiciary. In these and other conflicts, basic components of the constitutional order and its interpretation were challenged: individual freedoms had uncertain foundations, as did the separation of powers; "self-created societies" seemed a threat to the constitutional order, which apparently did not extend far enough, yet efforts to centralize power had provoked a major domestic insurrection and the first signs of a state secession movement.

During this period, too, political conflicts were increasingly codified in terms of the cult of personality. This characterological fixation had long been a feature of North American political culture, with Washington emerging as an iconic figure before even the Declaration of Independence. But a new wave of character-oriented politics emerged in the 1790s, which is the moment when we see the emergence of that constellation we today know as "the Founding Fathers." "Washington" and "Franklin" were slightly reconfigured from their earlier formulations, as each was appropriated or condemned by a party culture, and as each became the subject of biographical sketches or edited collections of writing. When the actual persons conveniently died (Franklin in 1790, Washington in 1799), they were increasingly lionized and vilified: Washington as the federalist leader holding together the country or betraying the Revolution, Franklin as the true voice of democracy or the hidden seed of revolutionary licentiousness. At the same time, the cults of "Hamilton" and "Jefferson" rapidly took shape, codifying the major figures of the succeeding generation. Both were subjects of much characterological writing from the mid-1790s through the Jefferson administration, in works like John Wood's 1801/1802 *History of the Adams Administration*, not to mention a host of pamphlets and newspaper pieces. Other figures were significant in this emerging constellation as well – Thomas Paine, who arrived back in the US in 1801; Aaron Burr, who emerged as an intriguing foil for both Jefferson (after the 1800 electoral tie) and Hamilton (whom he was to kill); and Adams and Madison, among others. Our point, however, is that these figures had become a symbolic system for thinking about political conflicts, just at the moment that Toussaint's Constitution arrived in the US.

Finally and relatedly, US political definitions became increasingly regionalized, specifically around the question of race. This was particularly true with the 1800 election, in which New England was solidly Federalist against the Democratic-Republican South and mid-Atlantic, these divisions reflecting the candidates' regional associations. The Kentucky and Virginia Resolutions demonstrated a regional resistance to the Adams administration that would be answered, during the Jefferson administration, by hints of a New England secession movement. This regional differentiation was thus understood in terms of competing views of the constitution; what the Northern emphasis on a stronger government promoting commerce and naval protection, and the Southern stress on state authority and agricultural production revealed was the different economic lifestyles of the regions. The difference was in a basic sense a racial one, as was evident in the Northern discourse about Jefferson's election as the "Negro President" – that is, elected because of the three-fifths representation clause – not to mention the eventual conflicts over the 1807 Act Prohibiting Importation of Slaves. Furthermore, the regional–racial divide was manifest in the construction of cultic political figures, above all with news of Jefferson's relationship with Sally Hemings, the insinuation that Hamilton was a "creole bastard," the celebration of Washington as benevolent slave owner, or the concomitant sense of Franklin as an abolitionist. In such a climate, the New England writer William Jenks could pen, in 1808, an alternative future history, *Memoir of the Northern Kingdom*, in which a Napoleonic, French-speaking, slave-owning South was imagined at odds with a Britain-affiliated, English-speaking North of commercial and yeoman prosperity.

Each of these dimensions of US political life would contribute to the disruptive power of Toussaint's Constitution. The appearance of the US Constitution and the election of George Washington as the first president had encouraged an elaborate *ex post facto* mythology of an orderly revolution and its aftermath. But subsequent events seriously undermined this sense. The Constitution was the subject of deep interpretative controversy. As the Massachusetts Regulation seemed to find a more forceful avatar in the Whiskey Rebellion, the 1789 text suddenly seemed sparse, unable to regulate states or even local political associations. The unified myth of Toussaint as the great Revolutionary general was suddenly fragmented: either he was the strong man holding together a disintegrating nation, or he was the tool of the old authorities, fostering a newly repressive system of control. The US, in this context, was increasingly understood in terms of an economic divide that informed most legislative and diplomatic battles. In such a context, events in France and Saint-Domingue were semiotically charged, seeming to offer a foil for events at home.

The Revolution in Saint-Domingue was also understood through these emerging perspectives. Early accounts of the Revolution, following the massive slave uprising of 1791, were informed by the arrival of French creole refugees fleeing for their lives. Unsurprisingly, these accounts were filled with graphic descriptions of rapacious brutality committed against the white ruling class. As news of black-against-white violence increased, Northern states moved to limit slavery, explore various schemes of gradual emancipation, and ban the slave trade. Southerners by contrast began a vigorous defense of their slave-based economies and moved to limit the importation of slaves from the West Indies, fearing that population would bring a rebellious culture to domestic plantations. By the end of the decade, however, a more accommodating view of the Revolution in Saint-Domingue was taking shape. In the wake of Francophobia and the condemnation of French Revolutionary "excess," Federalist merchants successfully appealed to Congress to consider ways to limit French control over the West Indian carrying trade. What had once seemed a portent of a broadening race war now signaled an irresistible opportunity: to sever French colonial holdings from imperial France, while thwarting long-term French plans to revive ambitions in the Mississippi valley. In 1799, the Federalist-dominated Congress passed what became known as the Toussaint Clause, which allowed trade to continue with French West Indian islands while restricting trade with France. The clause was the first move by the US to recognize the *de facto* economic independence of Saint-Domingue and endorse the legislation's eponymous partner, a black general and former slave. Commercial self-interest for the moment trumped race. But Jefferson's inauguration in

1801 ultimately destroyed any friendly relationship between Haiti and the US, which would refuse formally to recognize the Caribbean state until after the American Civil War. To be sure, trade policy changed little prior to 1806, when legislation to prohibit direct mercantile trade with the island was sought and implemented. And Jefferson's ambivalence toward Haiti was inflected by his own plans for westward expansion. The official administration position was that Bonaparte would ideally maintain control of the island, but it was quickly understood that Saint-Domingue would be the base for a renewed French presence in Louisiana, just as it was understood that only Toussaint could make possible the Louisiana Purchase.

In this divided context, in which US political conflicts were refracted through events in the Caribbean, Toussaint's Constitution emerged as a profoundly catalytic text. As we have suggested, the reception of the text was deeply partisan and bi-vocal. To be sure, few newspapers from the early republican period included editorial commentary in their formats, but this is not to say that opinion-driven content was absent. Opinion pieces, propaganda, or rumor-mongering proliferated through reproduced letters from unnamed correspondents, commentary on articles in rival papers, and the strategic organization of articles within tight-margined pages. Most partisan papers also featured parodies and satires alongside reports of events both foreign and domestic. It is to such ancillary commentary that we now turn, to illustrate at least two competing inflections that emerged.

Federalist newspapers – the most likely to reprint the Toussaint cluster, at a rate of about five to one – were most inclined to place the texts in a positive light. After the passage of the Toussaint Clause in 1799, Federalist papers fairly consistently defended trade with Saint-Domingue against Republican opposition, regularly voiced for example in the Democratic-Republican *Aurora* of Philadelphia. But with the new constitution, the broader political ramifications became evident through the placement of other key storylines.

Discovering "The Character of the Celebrated Black General," for example, printed alongside attacks on Jefferson and Thomas Paine was not uncommon. Writers juxtaposed Paine with hagiographic portraits of George Washington that, like other biographical sketches proliferating since his death, featured the former president's moral and religious virtues.[7] Jefferson made himself an easy target by association when he decided to allow Paine, that international Revolutionary and Christian apostate, to return to the US from France aboard a US navy vessel. Federalists viewed Jeffersonian support for Paine as an endorsement of the radical anti-religious views espoused in *The Age of Reason*, as well as a quiet approval of Paine's criticisms of Washington.[8] To cite another example, the August 4, 1801 *Independent Gazetteer* (Worcester, MA) published a defense of Washington and Adams, singling out the Alien and Sedition Acts for special praise, while attacking the hypocrisy of Jacobins, democrats, whigs, and other mock republicans.[9] But we might most usefully illustrate the Federalist response with reference to a fascinating piece appearing alongside the promulgation text from Saint-Domingue in the August 13 *Gazette of the United States* in Philadelphia. The editors leave no doubt about the relevant context for the excerpt:

[The following outlines of a Constitution, framed after the model of modern systems of government, are extracted from a work lately published and entitled, "*My Uncle Thomas*:" *a Romance. From the French of Pegault Lebrun*. It will be observed that *My Uncle Thomas* is to *make* the Constitution, and then the people are to *obey* it. This is doubtless the natural and necessary result of persuading the people at large that they are able to govern themselves, and of flattering them with titles of sovereignty till they have wearied themselves out with their own commotions and are glad to gain tranquility by a quiet submission to the constitution of an *Uncle Thomas*, an Uncle *Buonaparte*, an Uncle *Gallatin*, or any body else who will be at the trouble of taking the burthen off their own shoulders. The basis of this excellent Constitution is: *"We are all free and equal* – but you shall obey me; because – I will have it so"*]

* That is, "all Republicans, all Federalists."

EXTRACT.

"You Uncle! You make a Constitution!
"S'death, why not as well as another?
"I fear it will not answer.
"Well, then, I will make a second.
"Which will be no better.
"Then I will try a third.
"Which will not last longer than the other.
"After meditating *two hours* he produced the following:

Rights of Man – "Every man has a right to live in plenty, and without doing any thing for his livelihood.

Of the Government – "General *Thomas* having been proclaimed Grand Regulator, shall regulate and misregulate just as he pleases.

Civil and Criminal Code – "As the only difference among men consists in one wanting what another possesses, no man shall have any exclusive possessions of his own.
"As Magistrates are useless where there are no disputes, there shall be no Magistrates among us.
"As there can be no occasion for prisoners, or goalers, or attornies, or hangmen, where there are no Magistrates, there shall be neither hangmen, attornies, goaler or prisoner.
"We have thus got rid, in a moment, of what has embarrassed the whole world from the earliest period.

Of the Finances – "There shall be established, in extraordinary cases only, a *general* and *voluntary tax*.

Upon Breathing – "My tax is purely voluntary, for those who do not chuse to breath will have no occasion to pay any thing." &c. &c.

> The same humourous writer observes:
> "Vanity and self-love transform us into strange creatures. There is no man, however low his condition, but thinks himself superior to every one else. I have no doubt but my shoe-black would accept the office of first Consul. All I hope is that it will not be offered to him."
>
> Can Americans *rationally* hope so of their shoe-blacks?

As the text itself admitted, the source here was a 1795 comic romance, Pigault-Lebrun's *Mon Oncle Thomas*.[10] Now the continuum of anti-Jacobin satire is extended to include the US context, with Uncle Thomas referring to Jefferson, as is made clear by the reference to Gallatin and the well-known citation ("all Republicans, all Federalists") from the 1801 inaugural address. Uncle Thomas's constitution becomes a weapon of irrationality and political domination, deliberately denying the social or ethnographic realities of commercial society. Magistrates imply conflicts – so let us do away with magistrates.

What is perhaps most notable about this satire, though, is how close it veers to the Saint-Domingue text. Toussaint's Constitution might fit the imperious model presented here, from the above dictation to the final reference to the plebeian, perhaps even racialized, figure of the shoe-black – a seeming commentary on the ex-slave-turned-general. But the *Gazette*'s treatment of the Caribbean constitution is consistently positive, revealing several important contrasts. Most obviously, Jeffersonian rule implies a potentially radical constitutional hermeneutic whereby political principles ignore or dominate social realities, thereby reflecting the dangerously idealistic character of the ruler. But Toussaint's Constitution seems to be read very differently, such as a properly Federalist text well adapted to existing conditions and emergencies, rather than to the promotion of abstract principles. Of course, such a reading necessitates the repression of Article 3: "Slaves are not permitted in this territory; servitude is forever abolished – All men born here, live and die freemen and Frenchmen." But perhaps as importantly, it necessitated the repression of Toussaint's race as a factor, and a transference of his blackness to Jefferson. Both gestures – deradicalization and reracialization – were necessary for the celebration of Toussaint as counter-Revolutionary, well discussed by Larry Tise. In Tise's view, the Federalists turned to Toussaint as antidote for both the new administration's republican enthusiasm and the Federalist losses in 1800. Conceived as a counter-Revolutionary, Toussaint had successfully reinstituted the rights of property, established a state religion, and re-elevated economic elites: he instated himself as ruler for life with the right to appoint his successor. This is the Toussaint of "The Character of the Celebrated Black General," in which the imperative "to restore the planters, and revive the trade" displaces Toussaint's race, mentioned only in the title and the first paragraph.

We may contrast this configuration with that implicit in the Democratic-Republican press. Few Toussaint texts appeared in those papers, but they were printed in the national partisan journals, like William Duane's *Aurora General Advertiser.* An earlier opponent of the Toussaint Clause, Duane remained contemptuous of Toussaint, so much so that the *Aurora* was one of the few papers to dedicate space for what might today be called an editorial.[11] His response to the promulgation of the constitution began with a principled objection to its anti-republican articles, but ended with a race-conscious warning to his compatriots in the Southern states. "[W]e are among those who deny the competency and question the legality of the authorities assumed by the extravagant organization which has lately been set up in St. Domingo," Duane wrote, launching an attack on Toussaint's character and executive authority. "In the new system of what is called a constitution, we see nothing to respect, nothing to admire, and much to excite abhorrence and disgust." Rather, the constitution was "a spurious mimicry" of its French antecedent, "a new made monster … a despotism of the worst kind, formed in the worst manner, conceived in treachery and masked by hypocrisy." The constitution is furthermore "a bitter and malignant satire on free government," foremost because it instates Toussaint governor for life.

Despite the ideological republicanism that drives the first half of Duane's response, the matters of race and slavery are not far away. The 1801 Constitution "ought to suggest to the union the necessity of providing every possible means of security," he continues, advocating liberal naturalization policies to encourage white emigration to the Southern states. Toussaint's constitution may "concentrate the force, ignorance, and superstition, in the great body of the unfortunate and injured descendants of Africa, and capacitate them for mischief – and it may spread some day the storm of retaliating destruction upon the heads of the whites, who may be … extirpated … *woe to the countries in its neighbourhood.*" The argument here essentially inverts the Federalist configuration, which maintained that a constitution must pragmatically respect the social order. By contrast, Duane sees Toussaint's Constitution bracketing true republicanism to serve the aberration of a slave society achieving emancipation. Like the Federalist position, however, the onus of this relationship between constitutional and ethnographic orders is placed upon the character of Toussaint, who is implicitly associated with Washington in an adjacent article entitled "TORYISM called FEDERALISM." This piece condemns Federalist editors for assaulting the republican values of the American Revolution, "while frequently the same editors in the same papers eulogize *Washington* as the greatest and best of men."

This split partisan response to the Toussaint texts reveals a fundamental parallax, by which we mean a different perspectival orientation due to a change in the position of the observer. In the Federalist configuration, the character of Toussaint (and one might say republicanism) worked to subordinate constitutionality to ethnography, and emerged as an ideal: a heroic military leader fashioned in the model of Washington, but even more lastingly effective than the latter in having more correctly fashioned his constitution. Such a figure could be contrasted with Jefferson or Paine, Francophile republicans signaling the worst excesses of French jacobinism. Toussaint's republicanism was Washingtonian Federalism, rejuvenated overseas, but such a fantasy required the suppression of the racial realities of Toussaint's actual achievement. Toussaint was a black *Washington*. For the Democratic-Republicans, however, Toussaint was a *black* Washington. Cynically devaluing republicanism, his agenda was the concentration of power: his obviously authoritarian constitution revealed the Federalist hermeneutic seeking to amass and concentrate power at the expense of the states and the decent associations of white people, who were destined to become *de facto* slaves. This Federalist elitism, serving mercantile interests and undermining those of the plantation economy, could only mean, eventually, rule by violent slaves, state religion, and an essentially monarchical executive. Republicans openly associated Toussaint with fears of racial warfare and widespread social instability; Federalists envisioned a figure superseding political anarchy, and reestablishing the unification of culture and government. In each instance, Toussaint elevated political conflicts to a far-reaching political fantasy: paranoid race war in the one instance, authoritarian narcissism in the other.

In the US context, the reception of Toussaint's Constitution was, thus, fantastically revealing. Its circulation and that of the auxiliary texts we have identified elicited a partisanly bi-vocal response, one that split upon nothing less than contrary fantasies about the future of the republican experiment in the US, if not also in the Americas. Most significantly, these reactions to Toussaint's Constitution disclose a pattern that would continue up to and through the Civil War: despite Constitutional compromises designed to postpone reckoning with US slavery, race would symptomatically emerge and define disputes about signal issues of the nation's future.

Considered from another perspective, however, Toussaint's Constitution joins, if not inaugurates, a tradition in African American letters of holding white social and political morality to account for its more abstract and universalizing strands. The appearance of the 1801 Constitution represents a strategic inversion of foundational documents and principles of the West. From Equiano, who leveraged the golden rule to castigate "nominal Christians," to Jones and Allen's appeal for civic recognition, and to the redirection of the US Constitution and the Declaration of Independence in David Walker's *Appeal* and Douglass's Fourth of July oration, Toussaint's Constitution ought to take a place as a most powerful example. It offers students of African American literature both a powerful articulation of black agency in letters as well as an unprecedented archive of responses from white audiences in the US.

Notes

1 The first American edition of Olaudah Equiano's *Interesting Narrative* (1791) had subscription orders numbering only 336 copies. There were two later reprints that precede Douglass's *Autobiography*, the first in 1829 and another in 1837.

2 The 1786 edition was an unchanged reissue of the first edition of 1773. It was sold out of the shop of Benjamin Crukshank in Philadelphia.

3 We pass over here another, but perhaps the weakest, possible objection to consideration of Toussaint's Constitution: that it was written in French. At a moment that sees a collection like Werner Sollors and Marc Shell's *The Multilingual Anthology of American*

Literature: A Reader of Original Texts with English Translations, not to mention common inclusion of French and Spanish texts in US literature anthologies, this criticism does not seem to warrant much attention.

4 Toussaint's name appears in Title 6 § 16, Title 8 §§ 28, 30 (twice), and 31, and Title 13 § 77. His signature concludes the text.

5 Almost certainly apocryphal.

6 Our numbers are based on searches of the Readex Newspaper Database, and of several papers not included in that database, like Philadelphia's *Aurora*; we assume that the text appeared in more papers than we have listed.

7 We note, too, the publication of Mason Locke Weems' *The Life of Washington* in 1800, which continued through nine editions in the first decade of the nineteenth century.

8 Paine's critical letter to Washington, written in 1796, was widely reprinted following the announcement of Paine's return.

9 Reprinted from *The Gazette of the United States*, May 7, 1801. Here, the piece gets reactivated by the appearance of Toussaint's Constitution.

10 The original is slightly edited, and the passage about the shoe-blacks appears much earlier in the original text.

11 *Aurora General Advertiser*, August 17, 1801.

Bibliography

Carretta, Vincent. "Early African-American Literature?" In Michael J. Drexler and Ed White, ed. *Beyond Douglass: New Perspectives on Early African-American Literature*. Lewisburg: Bucknell University Press, 2008. 91–106.

L'Ouverture, Toussaint. *The Haitian Revolution*. Introduction by Jean-Bertrand Aristide. New York: Verso, 2008.

Tise, Larry E. *The American Counterrevolution: A Retreat from Liberty, 1783–1800*. Mechanicsburg: Stackpole Books, 1998.

5
Religion in Early African American Literature

Joanna Brooks and Tyler Mabry

In May 2008, archeologists working in Annapolis, Maryland, unearthed from a seventeenth-century street gutter one of the oldest artifacts of African religious life in America: a clay bundle full of lead shot, bent copper pins, and iron nails, wrapped in cloth or leather, and topped with a stone axe head, an implement often associated with the Yoruba deity Shango. Once a major port of entry for enslaved Africans, the city of Annapolis is full of such treasures; at other Annapolis dig sites, archeologists had unearthed caches of hoodoo artifacts hidden in walls and buried in cellar floors to attract favorable spirits and repel unfavorable ones. But what was especially remarkable about this clay bundle, which experts date to the turn of the eighteenth century, was not only its antiquity, but its placement out on the street, in public space, where it was visible to whites and blacks alike. This bundle reveals that traditional African religion was an acknowledged and familiar part of the public sphere in early America.

The Annapolis bundle in many respects exemplifies four things we have learned about the complexity, transatlanticism, energy, and publicity of black religious life in early America. First, we know that early African American religious life was highly diverse. Africans brought to North America by the slave trade hailed from Senegambia, Sierra Leone, the Gold Coast, the Bight of Benin, the Bight of Biafra, as well as some central and East African territories. They spoke Akan, Guan, Ga, Adangbe, Ewe, Aja, Fon, Wolof, as well as Arabic and Swahili. Many observed traditional spiritual practices situated in specific landscapes and belonging to matrifocal clans. Non-elite captive Africans were often fluent in several languages and spiritual lexicons as a result of their forced transportation from one community and household to another. Others were highly literate practitioners of Islam, which had made its way through trade routes into sub-Saharan Africa sometime after the ninth century. Some had been exposed to the Christianity imported to West Africa by Portuguese, Dutch, English, and Spanish colonists. Christianity was especially influential in the African kingdom of Kongo, whose chief ruler had been baptized in the late fifteenth century. This original diversity of belief and practice was only compounded after forced migration to the Americas and other points around the Atlantic world.

Second, we know that early African American religious life (like early American religious life in general) was deeply and dynamically transatlantic in character. Whereas scholars such as E. Franklin Frazier once argued that the violence of the slave trade and enslavement ruined the continuity of traditional African religious practices, we now know that many Africans in America and their African American descendants attempted to continue traditional West African practices and developed New World African religious forms such as vodun, hoodoo, and lucuba. African Muslims also continued their daily prayers and fast observances after their arrival in the Americas. Other Africans and African Americans engaged in religious and spiritual exchange with other peoples they encountered in the Atlantic world. Black Muslims, Christians, and indigenous faith practitioners moved throughout the Atlantic world as free and unfree. Some exchanged traditional spiritual practices with European and Euro-American pagans and indigenous Americans. Enslaved black Muslims encountered in southern Europe existing Muslim communities. Black Christians took part in the Protestant Reformation, the Radical Reformation, the Inquisition, and other transatlantic religious movements originating from the Catholic and Protestant capitals of Europe. Some became Anglicans, Catholics, Moravians, Congregationalists, Baptists, Quakers, Shakers, Methodists, or Presbyterians. In turn, exposure to African worldviews and faith practices shaped the spiritual lives of Euro-American colonists and gave new force and direction to transatlantic religious movements such as the Great Awakening. A few black Christian men and women such as the Moravian Rebecca Protten even relocated to Europe, where they became influential figures in religious movements. The religious world inhabited by black people in the seventeenth and eighteenth centuries was one shaped by the circulation of ideas, beliefs, practices, and institutions among whites, blacks, and indigenous peoples around the Atlantic littoral.

Third, we know that rather than being simply conscripted into new religious affiliations in North America, black people exercised creative and adaptive agency in renewing their own spiritual lives. Some adapted West African practices to American contexts, or blended them with variants of Catholicism, or infused evangelical Christianity with their own traditions of spiritual expression. Some joined radically marginal faith communities as an expression of disdain for the violence of colonial culture. Some converted to and then decisively separated from mainline European-American denominations, while others helped increase denominational diversity within black communities, creating opportunities for robust theological discussion and differentiation among African Americans. Black preachers retooled Christian theologies to grapple with the radical discontinuities and dangers of black life in a violent imperial world, while black worshippers developed New World African religious rituals like the ring shout that affirmed a spiritual solidarity transcending their diverse origins. Black churches became places where black people first practiced institutional self-governance in North America and reconstructed a sense of common identity and belonging.

Finally, we know that African American religious life did not take place only in the secreted confines of hush arbors or slave quarters. Black religious practices were a visible part of daily public life, and they contributed to the shaping of a distinctively black public sphere. The Annapolis bundle suggests that in cities with large African populations, traditional African spiritual practices were conducted in public, at least until the middle of the eighteenth century. Black mutual aid and burial societies conducted tradition-tinged rituals at gravesites and in cemeteries throughout the British North American colonies. During the Great Awakening of the 1740s and 1750s, African American revivalists swooned, sang, and prophesied at large outdoor revivals in the North and in small rural churches in the South. Male and female black itinerants took to the open roads to evangelize, while black Masonic lodges staged elaborate formal processions through the streets of cities such as Boston. African Americans also founded their own churches and built their own church buildings in places rural and urban, from George Liele and the Baptists of Silver Bluff, South Carolina, in 1773 to Richard Allen and the African Methodist Episcopals of Philadelphia in 1794.

Given its shaping force in early African American community life, it is not surprising that religion played an equally formative role in the beginnings of written African American literature. As this essay will show, almost all of the first black writers of the eighteenth and early nineteenth centuries were deeply situated within religious networks, wrote about religious themes and concerns, and relied upon religious institutions and audiences to publish and promote their texts. What is striking in light of the robust diversity and dynamism of early African American religious life, however, is the fact that most of these first writers belonged to a tight circuit of Anglophone Protestant religious institutions concentrated around Boston and Philadelphia. A few Arabic-language letters and a life narrative written by Ayuba Suleyman Diallo, or Job ben Solomon (1701–1773), a Senegambian Muslim kidnapped into slavery in Maryland, do survive from the 1730s. We also have Arabic-language letters and manuscripts (some citing Koranic scholars) and an 1831 Arabic-language autobiography written by Omar Ibn Said (1770?–1864), a Senegambian enslaved in North Carolina, as well as a few German and Dutch-language letters by the Caribbean-born African Moravian missionary Rebecca Protten (1718–1780). Still, most of the surviving early African American literary archive composed by authors like Briton Hammon, Phillis Wheatley, John Marrant, Prince Hall, Jupiter Hammon, Olaudah Equiano, Boston King, and Venture Smith is Northern and Protestant in character. As literary historian Frances Smith Foster has observed, "Early African American print culture … is virtually synonymous with the Afro-Protestant Press" (715). It is important to recognize the profound impact of black Protestantism on early African American literature. At the same time, it is important to remember that black Protestant print culture reflects only one segment of early African American society. Just as there is a profound asymmetry between the slim surviving archive of early black writing and the hundreds of thousands of black people who built early America, there is an equally profound asymmetry between the Protestant character of this archive and the diversity of early African American spirituality.

Understanding the particular power of Protestantism in shaping an African American literary tradition, it is helpful to think about the contexts and specific histories through which the black church and black print culture came into being. Let us imagine first the spiritual ecology of early African America, a social-spiritual landscape shaped by historical experiences of the slave trade and chattel slavery. Especially in the seventeenth and early eighteenth centuries, black communities in America faced tremendous instability as they attempted to absorb wave after wave of newly arrived saltwater Africans or to cope with the division and separation of tentative family units by the internal slave trade. Individual African Americans grappled with the consequences of what Orlando Patterson has called "social death," or alienation from natal physical, spiritual, and social landscapes. If the mercantile logic of the slave trade had converted them into exchangeable individual commodities, their struggle was to reclaim themselves from this profound alienation. Compounding this struggle was the disruption of traditional funeral practices that ensured the soul's safe homegoing to the ancestors as well as the continuity of community life. Forced transportation to a New World also meant the loss of specific bodies of spiritual knowledge rooted in African ecologies, as well as familiar ritual calendars structured around seasonal cycles and days consecrated for the worship of particular ancestors (Smallwood 133–4). Historian Stephanie Smallwood catalogs the spiritual needs of these earliest black communities: "to reassert some kind of healthy relationship to ancestors; to manage death; to produce social networks, communities, and relations of kinship; to address the imbalance of power between black and white; to stake a claim to their bodies to counter the plantation economy's claim to ownership" (190). Facing radical social discontinuities and dislocations from the protections of traditional spiritual life, African Americans built new religious communities out of shared experiences of disruption and alienation.

No Protestant movement spoke more clearly to the sacred potential of disruptive change than the Great Awakening, a wave of revivalistic evangelism and enthusiasm that swept through the Atlantic Protestant world in the 1740s and 1750s. The brand of Christianity preached by Great Awakening evangelists such as George Whitefield and John Wesley centered on individual experiences of radical spiritual change: a sudden conversion, a massive change of heart, that utterly transformed the life of the believer. At great outdoor revivals and in tiny rural churches, diverse American peoples, dislocated from their original ancestral contexts, performed for each other the radicalizing power of the Holy Spirit, some shouting, some swooning, some silently taken by powerful feelings, some enacting the death of the old creature and rebirth in Christ. It is, we think, no historical accident that not until the middle of the eighteenth century, during and after the Great Awakening, that large numbers of African Americans came to adopt Christianity. Perhaps African Americans recognized something in these performances of death and life, this sacralization of discontinuity, that spoke to their own collective condition of dislocation and alienation. Thousands attended the revivals and affiliated with evangelistic religious movements that offered new forms of kinship with brothers and sisters who had also been born again.

One of the evangelistic movements that proved most attractive to African Americans was Methodism, a religious society founded by John and George Wesley in the 1730s. John Wesley first brought Methodism to America in 1736, when he traveled to Savannah, Georgia, as an Anglican missionary with orders to proselytize Native communities. In 1737, he visited a South Carolina plantation where he visited with a young Barbados-born slave named "Nanny," whose master had denied her even a rudimentary religious education. Inspired to take up the cause of promoting black religious literacy, Wesley extended to African American communities a system of classes, circuits, and conferences that constituted the infrastructural basis of the "Methodist Society" he had founded in England with his brother George as a supplement to institutional Anglicanism. During the Great Awakening, Methodist circuit riders visited black communities, and African American worshippers attended Methodist society classes and camp meetings. When American Methodist societies separated from Anglicanism after the Revolutionary War, the new Methodist Churches and circuit riders made even deeper inroads among African Americans. Phenomenal numbers of African American converts helped increase Methodist Church membership from 1,000 in 1770 to 250,000 in 1820.

Many African Americans also participated in the interdenominational revival movement led by celebrity English evangelist George Whitefield, a member of the England-based Huntingdon Connection. Founded by Lady Selina, the Countess of Huntingdon, the Huntingdon Connection sponsored a cohort of itinerant Calvinist preachers to preach around the Anglo-Atlantic world. Their message focused on the necessity of the conversion experience, or the "New Birth," to the faith of the Christian believer. Whitefield himself made six highly successful and widely publicized preaching tours of the American colonies from October 1739 until his death in Newburyport, Massachusetts, in September 1770. During his travels, he interacted with most of the black Atlantic writers of the eighteenth century. Especially celebrated was his theatrical preaching style, remembered here by Olaudah Equiano:

> I saw this pious man exhorting the people with the greatest fervour and earnestness, and sweating as much as I ever did while in slavery on Montserrat beach. I was very much struck and impressed with this; I thought it strange I had never seen divines exert themselves in this manner before, and was no longer at a loss to account for the thin congregations they preached to. (132)

The transatlantic networks established by the Huntingdon Connection supported the movements and publications of early black writers like Phillis Wheatley and John Marrant, who was ordained as a Huntingdon Connection preacher in England in 1785.

As attractive as these eighteenth-century evangelical movements proved to black Christians, none were uniformly progressive on issues of slavery and race, none developed a systematic theological analysis of race and racism, and none provided a totally safe haven from the experiences of racism. The Huntingdon Connection, for example, ordained black preachers like Marrant and David Margate who were vocal in their commitments to black freedom, and George Whitefield often expressed affection and concern for the African Americans who attended his revivals. In his *Letter to the Inhabitants of Maryland, Virginia, North and South-Carolina, Concerning Their Negroes* (1740), Whitefield argued that white supremacy had no basis in theology: "Think you, your children are in any way better by nature than the poor negroes? No! In no wise! Blacks are just as much, and no more, conceived and born in sin, as white men are; and both, if born and bred up here, I am persuaded, are naturally capable of the same improvement" (15). Still, Whitefield and the Connection lobbied Parliament to permit slaveholding in the colony of Georgia, and when Whitefield established an orphanage after the legalization of slavery in Georgia in 1750, he bought dozens of slaves to staff it. Methodism founder John Wesley published "Thoughts upon Slavery" (1774), a condemnation of the slave trade and slaveholding. Many Methodist circuit riders and society leaders shared Wesley's antislavery views. But the Methodist church never adopted a formal antislavery stance (as the Society of Friends, or Quakers, had in 1776). After the War of American Independence, the Methodist Church retreated from some of the more aggressive antislavery stances held by its early leaders, and it also refused ordination to black circuit riders and society leaders like Richard Allen, Harry Hosier, Moses Wilkinson, Boston King, Jarena Lee, and Zilpha Elaw. Customs of segregated seating in many local Methodist churches spurred black members to walk out on congregations in Baltimore (1787), Philadelphia (1792), Wilmington, Delaware (1805), and Charleston (1817). Indeed, although the evangelical revivals of the eighteenth century probably created moments of unprecedented spiritual intimacy between black and white people, they did not substantially change racial dynamics within established religious institutions.

Racism within established churches, an internal drive towards self-governance, and a desire to create a black-centered public sphere spurred African Americans to establish their religious institutions in the late eighteenth and early nineteenth centuries. They did so, historians Patrick Rael and Frances Smith Foster have argued, not as a simple imitation or revision of white religious ideals, but rather as an expression of longstanding spiritual needs, moral visions, and goals originating within black communities. In the South, black Baptists like Andrew Bryan and George Liele established isolated all-black congregations; in the North, black Protestants like Richard Allen, Absalom Jones, and Prince Hall organized entirely new denominations such as the African Methodist Episcopal (AME) and African Methodist Episcopal Zion (AME Zion) churches as well as black Masonic lodges. Allen, Jones, Hall, and other early black Protestant community leaders were especially skilled at adopting and adapting the principles and models of mainline denominations and putting them to work in black communities. The infrastructure and energy of the black church became an engine of political organization. Indeed, as Frances Smith Foster observes, "When American slavery was legal, the Afro-Protestant Church was the only institution, the only consistent site for any African American activity, whether it be the Negro Convention Movement or debates over colonization, schools and libraries, insurance or investment clubs, funerals, dances, weddings, or holiday celebrations" (717–18).

Protestant churches and religious networks were also the only consistent site for black print culture activity in the late eighteenth and early nineteenth centuries. This is not only a reflection of the organizational power of the black church in early America, but of specific Protestant theological principles as well. From its beginnings in fifteenth- and sixteenth-century Europe, Protestantism emphasized literacy. It was crucial that lay believers could read and (thanks to the invention of the printing press) sometimes even own their own Bibles. Reading afforded them unmediated access to the Word of God. Specifically, individual acts of scripture reading and engagement with the Word were at the heart of the Protestant movement. Teaching literacy was considered a form of ministry in Protestant churches, a critical (though not essential) element of spiritual formation. Many Protestant organizations also devoted institutional resources to the publication and distribution of sermons and other devotional material. The Bible and other religious literature then served as a tremendous wellspring of ideas and images – such as Moses leading the people of Israel out of slavery; the death and resurrection of Lazarus; and the trials of Shadrach, Meshach, and Abednego in the fiery furnace – that enabled African American writers and readers to imagine and accept their own spiritual concerns, while scripting their own stories of individual and collective redemption. For all of these reasons, telling the story of early African American literature is impossible without acknowledging the formative force of religion.

For example, Jupiter Hammon, the first African American to publish poetry, was born a slave on the Lloyd estate in Long Island. Having acquired a basic education alongside the other children on the estate, Hammon immersed himself in the Bible and the Methodist hymnal. He developed a local reputation as a preacher, delivering sermons and religious orations to audiences both black and white. Over his lifetime, Hammon published four poems and four prose pieces, beginning with "An Evening Thought," a broadside poem published in 1760. His writings are preacherly in theme; they consistently urge repentance from sin and proclaim salvation through Christ. Hammon's religious convictions inflect his choice of poetic form as well as his choice of subject matter: he wrote all of his poetry in ballad stanza, the standard verse pattern of evangelical hymnody. Hammon's writings, while concerned primarily with the universal imperatives of penitence and salvation, articulate the idea of a distinct black community, express support for the abolition of slavery, and make a theological case for racial equality. Hammon's first prose publication, the homiletic discourse "A Winter Piece" (1782), begins by addressing a heterogeneous audience, but soon turns to his countrymen: "my Brethren for whom this discourse is designed." He starts by urging them to seek repentance and Christian salvation, but soon addresses the issue of slavery. "Many of us," Hammon acknowledges, "are seeking a temporal freedom, and I wish you may obtain it." Resigning the matter to divine providence, Hammon cautions that "all power in heaven and on earth belongs to God" and urges his audience more urgently to seek "that freedom that tendeth to eternal life." In his most widely reprinted publication, "An Address to the Negroes in the State of New-York" (1787), Hammon also encourages his fellow blacks in their desire for freedom, stating that "liberty is a great thing, and worth seeking for, if we can get it honestly." Hammon nevertheless admonishes slaves to be dutiful and obedient, but goes on to puncture racist thinking by observing that all souls are equal before God: "[t]here are but two places where all go after death, white and black, rich and poor; those places are Heaven and Hell." Hammon concludes by exhorting free blacks to improve their spiritual condition by studying the Bible and by living "quiet and peaceable lives in all Godliness and honesty." In "An Address to Miss Phillis Wheatley" (1778), Hammon celebrates the life of Wheatley, also a black poet, and rejoices in the providence that brought her safely through the perilous Middle Passage:

> While thousand tossed by the sea,
> And others settled down,
> God's tender mercies set thee free,
> From dangers that come down.

Although Hammon does not expect to meet Wheatley in his lifetime, he recognizes her membership in a spiritual community which will be united in heaven:

> Dear Phillis, seek for heaven's joys,
> Where we do hope to meet.

Hammon's poem is a fitting tribute to Wheatley, whose poetry continually imagines just such a heavenly restoration of the fellowship of believers.

Wheatley herself was about six or seven years of age when she was taken from West Africa and brought to the American colonies aboard the slave-trading schooner *Phillis*. She arrived in Boston in 1761 and was purchased by Susannah Wheatley, wife of prominent Boston merchant John Wheatley. Under the tutelage of Susannah's daughter Mary, Phillis proved a precocious student, studying English and classical poetry, history, and the Bible. Wheatley began composing poetry around the age of 12 and established her literary fame in 1770 with the publication of a poem on the death of celebrated itinerant minister George Whitefield. This poem, published as a broadside and later as a pamphlet, made Wheatley's reputation on both sides of the Atlantic, and she soon initiated attempts to publish a volume of poetry, eventually securing a publisher in London for her *Poems on Various Subjects* (1773).

Wheatley forged her own authoritative poetic persona by taking on the voice of a Christian exhorter or minister in many of her poems, echoing the role African Americans first played as community exhorters during the Great Awakening. She first tries on this exhortatory role in her eulogy for George Whitefield. "Take him ye wretched, for your only good, / Take him, ye starving sinners, for your food," she begins the third stanza of the poem, achieving her own commanding voice by ventriloquizing the deceased minister in his appeals to white and black listeners to accept the saving grace of Jesus Christ. Wheatley used this exhortatory voice again in poems such as "To the University of Cambridge, in New-England," commanding the privileged young white male pupils at Harvard University to reconsider the loftiness of their learned ambitions in light of the "immense perdition" of sin that threatened their souls. Wheatley also adroitly deployed her numerous personal connections to a vibrant transatlantic network of evangelicals and religious activists in her efforts to publish and promote her writing. John and Susannah Wheatley were committed members of Boston's New South Congregationalist Church, and Phillis – herself a member of the Old South Congregationalist Church – met many of the itinerant ministers and religious organizers who visited the Wheatley household, including the Mohegan Presbyterian minister Samson Occom, to whom she addressed a 1774 letter (published in major New England newspapers) frankly critical of the philosophical contradictions of American slaveholding. Wheatley's most influential contact in the evangelical community was the Countess of Huntingdon, founder and patroness of the Huntingdon Connection. Wheatley dedicated her first published volume, *Poems on Various Subjects, Religious and Moral*, to the Countess, who accepted the dedication on the sole condition that the book include a portrait of Wheatley. Wheatley had hoped to meet the Countess personally in the course of her 1773 trip to London, but Susannah's failing health obliged Phillis to return to Boston before such a meeting could take place.

Back in the colonies, one of Wheatley's closest friends and supporters was Obour Tanner, an African American woman from Newport, Rhode Island. Tanner and Wheatley conducted an extensive correspondence in which they offered one another spiritual encouragement and coordinated the sale and distribution of Wheatley's book. The First Congregationalist Church in Newport, of which Tanner was a member, was a thriving center of evangelical activity and independent African American religious organization, home to an "Ethiopian Society" and an African American Sunday School which met in the home of Sarah Osbourne. Such organizations, comprised substantially of evangelical women, provided a sympathetic community and a print market for Wheatley's poetry. Not coincidentally, Newport placed the largest single order for Wheatley's published volume.

At the same historical moment that Phillis Wheatley was navigating the local and transatlantic circuits of Christianity, Olaudah Equiano arrived in London after having survived an often brutal enslavement in North America and the Caribbean as well as many near-death encounters during a subsequent term of service with the Royal Navy. Achieving for the first time in his life a modicum of physical stability with a new job as a hairdresser and an independent life in London, Equiano turned his mind to religious matters, investigating spiritual paths as divergent as Quakerism, Anglicanism, Judaism, and Roman Catholicism. Indeed, the entire second half of Equiano's life story, *An Interesting Narrative* (1789), constitutes a spiritual autobiography detailing his agonizing, extended search for fellowship, communion, and spiritual relief. A turning point in Equiano's spiritual life came in 1773, when, after dreaming of a vision of the Last Judgment and becoming convinced that only grace, and not his own human efforts, could win him true spiritual freedom, Equiano found a spiritual home among the evangelical Methodists of London. Invited to a Methodist "love feast" – a four-hour social gathering centered around spiritual nourishment rather than meat and drink – Equiano embarked on a path of self-examination and repentance that led eventually to his entering into communion at a Dissenting Anglican chapel in Westminster in 1774. The connections he developed with people of faith – Anglicans, Methodists, Quakers, and others – proved critical both to the completion and publication of his autobiography in 1789, his efforts to improve the condition of London's black poor, and the campaign to abolish the British slave trade, which achieved its goal in 1807.

The networks of evangelical Methodism that had offered institutional support to Wheatley, Tanner, and Equiano intersected with the life and work of John Marrant, an itinerant preacher who was also one of the most prolific writers of the early Black Atlantic. The publication that brought the young preacher his initial literary celebrity – *A Narrative of the Lord's Wonderful Dealings with John Marrant, a Black (Now Going to Preach the Gospel in Nova-Scotia)* (1785) – is a conversion and captivity narrative transcribed from Marrant's own remarks on ordination. In the *Narrative*, Marrant describes the events of his early life and ministry: Spirit-struck and converted to Christianity after hearing Whitefield preach at a Charlestown revival, Marrant fled his family home and wandered into the wilderness, where he was taken captive by Cherokees. Upon preaching the gospel to his captors, Marrant was released – the first of many providential deliverances he experienced as he continued to wander and preach to Indians and plantation blacks. In the *Narrative*, Marrant ascribes his deliverance from one peril after another to the divine providence of God, and concludes by relating his impressment into the British Navy, his hospitalization in London, and his subsequent ordination and commission by the Huntingdon Connection.

After the events detailed in the *Narrative*, Marrant sailed for Nova Scotia, charged by the Huntingdon Connection with the task of evangelizing the fledgling Loyalist communities of Nova Scotia. After the War of Independence, over 3,000 blacks migrated to Nova Scotia, having accepted the British offer of emancipation to any blacks who joined the Loyalist side. Many of the black Loyalists formed independent settlements, including Birchtown, the largest of these separatist communities, where Marrant chose to center his ministry. Marrant's *Journal* (1790), which documents his itinerancy in Nova Scotia, remains the most complete black-authored account of evangelicalism and religious community-formation in the eighteenth century. As the *Journal* demonstrates, Marrant came to Nova Scotia mobilizing Old Testament sermon texts to declare himself a prophet called to minister to black Loyalists as a chosen, gathered people, on the model of ancient Israel. He preached a specially developed Calvinism emphasizing regeneration within covenant communities, with oppressed blacks as special witnesses to God's power. The biblical references in the *Journal* narrate God's providential design for black people, thereby placing the trials and tribulations of Marrant (including his own struggles and victories over hunger, cold, fatigue, sickness, and danger) and his audience in the providential narrative. Although Marrant spent only two years at Birchtown and was forced to make his way back to London when funding dried up from the Huntingdon Connection, he developed a compelling early Black Atlantic brand of Christianity that used the day-to-day struggles of freedom-seeking black people as a testimony of God's power to regenerate and resurrect His chosen people.

As his *Journal* records, Marrant had a number of rivals in his efforts to preach the Connection's brand of Calvinistic Methodism. Although Marrant was the first, and at that time the only, black man with institutionally authorized pastoral authority, he found himself in competition with an astonishing array of talented and fiercely convicted black lay preachers who were themselves ministering to the people of Nova Scotia and struggling to win converts to their own particular theologies and congregations. One of Marrant's fiercest rivals was Moses Wilkinson, a blind and crippled ex-slave from Virginia who preached the theology of the Wesleyan Methodists. Wilkinson won a number of converts to the Methodist Society, notably Violet King and Boston King, who became a preacher himself after his conversion. But Wilkinson and King, despite their energetic ministries, were denied ordination by the Methodist Episcopal Church, and officially acknowledged only as pastoral assistants. Another prominent black preacher in Nova Scotia was David George, a Baptist, who had led a congregation in Silver Bluff, South Carolina, prior to joining the Loyalist migration. Boston King and David George both published important life narratives: *Memoirs of the Life of Boston King* (serialized in the *Methodist Magazine* in 1798) and *An Account of the Life of Mr. David George, from Sierra Leone in Africa* (1793). King and George both relate their conversion experiences and describe their ministry in Nova Scotia. Crucially, each of these narratives also provides an account of the Sierra Leone migration. In 1792, a contingent of black Nova Scotians emigrated to Sierra Leone with the goal of founding a free black nation in Africa. Twelve hundred free blacks, including all of Marrant's Huntingdon congregation and many members of Wilkinson's and King's pastorates, undertook the emigration. The Sierra Leone project was fraught with complications and difficulties from the beginning, however. Settlers struggled with malaria, experienced tense relationships with both the indigenous blacks and the white traders in the region, and met indifference from the English backers who viewed the settlement strictly as a commercial enterprise. King and George publicized and documented the difficulties and abuses suffered by the Loyalist emigrants.

Marrant himself, however, left Nova Scotia before the Sierra Leone migration. In 1789, physically worn and financially strapped, Marrant departed for Boston. Although he found himself, in the words of his *Journal*, "in a strange country knowing nobody," he had letters from the Countess of Huntingdon and contacts in Boston's religious community, and he soon formed ties within the city's pioneering black self-help and religious societies. Especially important was the relationship Marrant developed with Prince Hall, who was himself a path-breaking figure in both the social organization and the early literature of the Black Atlantic. In 1775, 15 years before Marrant's arrival in Boston, Prince Hall had founded the first African Lodge of Freemasons. The African Lodge offered a rare space in which blacks could openly exercise political authority, write their own history, and establish independent spiritual and cultural traditions. Prince Hall proceeded to charter lodges in many other cities as well, instituting a flourishing network of black Masonic societies. A tireless organizer and advocate, he produced a substantial body of writings in the course of his public career, including petitions, orations, letters to the editor, and letters to private citizens and public officials. When Marrant, shortly after his arrival in Boston, met Prince Hall, the two men were already well known both as print celebrities and as organizers committed to the development of socially and spiritually independent black communities. In short order, Marrant joined the African Lodge, Hall appointed him chaplain, and the two men established a collaborative relationship.

In 1789, in his new role as lodge chaplain, Marrant delivered the featured sermon at the festival of John the Baptist, an important Masonic holiday. This sermon, a collaborative effort between Marrant and Hall, offered a bold interpretation of biblical history and a sweeping vision of a transhistorical, transatlantic black community. It was published in Boston in September 1789. The central portion of the sermon – the part probably written by Hall – details the Masonic proof of anciency, emphasizing contributions of Africans and blacks. Marrant also launches a critical intervention into Euro-American efforts to use the Bible as a basis for rationalizing race slavery and racial prejudice. Theologians of racial prejudice often attempted to trace the origins of racial difference in the human species to the ancient story of Cain and Abel, linking blackness to the "mark" God placed on Cain for murdering his brother, or to the curse God placed on Ham, son of Noah, for humiliating his father. Marrant presents an alternative narrative describing racism as a degenerate condition resulting from the Fall, recentering the history of civilization and locating the Garden of Eden in Africa, and celebrating Ham's descendants' work on Solomon's temple.

Even after Marrant's return to London in 1790 and his death in 1791, Prince Hall continued to develop and articulate the visionary theology of Marrant's *Sermon*, particularly in two addresses delivered to the community of black freemasons. The first of these was the 1792 *Charge Delivered to the Brethren of the AFRICAN LODGE*, which describes itself as a continuation of the work begun by Marrant's 1789 *Sermon*. Recollecting Psalm 68's promise that Ethiopia would "stretch her hands to God," Marrant advises a forward-looking, prophetic vision, and urges his members to "make a beginning." In a second address, the *Charge delivered to the African Lodge, June 24, 1797, at Menotomy*, Hall builds on both Marrant's *Sermon* and his own earlier *Charge*, positioning black Americans as the inheritors of a scriptural narrative of suffering and redemption.

Hundreds of miles south of Boston, African Americans in Philadelphia were also developing their own modes of critical response to the racism of dominant Christian denominations. One fall Sunday in 1792, during services at Philadelphia's St. George Episcopal Church, white elders forcibly removed free African Americans, including

Richard Allen, Absalom Jones, and a number of other black worshippers, from pews customarily designated for white worshippers and instructed them to take their seats in a segregated gallery. Representing a decisive split for many black parishioners, the incident inspired groundwork for the African Church of Philadelphia. In August of the following year, shortly after the completion of the African Church building, the city of Philadelphia was laid low by yellow fever. The epidemic created a public health crisis that mushroomed into a near-obliteration of the city, which then contained some 55,000 individuals. Of this total, 4,000 to 5,000 perished from the fever, and 20,000 more fled for the countryside. The mayor and the municipal College of Physicians, under the erroneous belief that black people were naturally immune to the yellow fever, called upon the city's African American population to shoulder the dangerous public health work of nursing fever victims and burying the dead. Working in conjunction with the African Society, Richard Allen and Absalom Jones responded to this call for public health volunteers, organizing nursing and grave-digging corps. Jones and Allen jointly wrote a pointed history of the black community's experience during this epidemic, published as *A Narrative of the Proceedings of the Black People, During the Late Awful Calamity in Philadelphia, in the Year 1793: And a Refutation of Some Censures, Thrown upon them in some late Publications*. Jones's and Allen's *Narrative* is a seminal work, the first historical account of African American community life. By reporting on the collective black experience during Philadelphia's fever season, Jones and Allen disprove the notion of black immunity and refute popular portrayals of African Americans as incompetents and criminals – the "censures" of the title. But more than a "refutation" of the flawed official literature, their "Narrative" offers testimony to the spiritual fortitude of a covenanted black community and establishes a record of that community's providential triumph over the forces of death. Allen and Jones use the Old Testament story of Shadrach, Meshach, and Abednego – who, by divine intervention, survived being thrown into the "burning fiery furnace" (Daniel 3: 1, 6) – as narrative architecture for staging the story of how black Philadelphians miraculously survived the yellow fever epidemic. Allen also wrote and collected 54 hymns for *A Collection of Spiritual Songs and Hymns* (1801), a pocket-sized hymnbook designed specifically to celebrate the legacy of overcoming and overturning sacralized in the theology of African American Protestant churches.

A few African American writers found a vocation and a voice within the established church rather than in separatist movements. One such figure was the itinerant New Light minister Lemuel Haynes, who acquired a robust theological and literary education in the evangelical household of David Rose, reading extensively from the Bible and from the writings of Isaac Watts and George Whitefield. In 1775, Haynes left Granville to join the Continental Army during the Revolution, but returned to the Rose farm after the war to live and work while undertaking a study of classical languages. After the war, Haynes returned to Granville and embarked on a long and distinguished pastoral career, serving various New England churches as a licensed preacher and then as an ordained New Light minister. He wrote over 5,500 sermons over the course of his career. In sermons such as "Liberty Further Extended" (1776) and "Universal Salvation" (1805), Haynes developed a distinctive theology drawn from New Light and New Divinity principles, a theology emphasizing the crucial importance of liberty to spiritual and moral development. Like Prince Hall, he accepted a version of dispensationalist theology that found some meaning in the historical affliction of black people but rejected colonizationist agendas that aimed to relocate African Americans to the African continent.

From its beginnings in the eighteenth century, the profound influence of black Protestantism reached into nineteenth-century African American literature and well beyond. Black churches served as central organizational nodes for the conception, development, publication, and distribution of an early nineteenth-century African American literature focused not merely on belletrism or aesthetic refinement but also on moral improvement, political organization, and history-keeping. We see this impulse in the wealth of convention minutes and political addresses by individuals such as Maria Stewart, David Walker, and Henry Highland Garnet. Black itinerants like Jarena Lee and Zipha Elaw and church leaders like Richard Allen also composed from their spiritual journeys crucial documents of black life, hope, and consciousness. Even the basic formula of the conversion narrative, a genre honed by early black writers like Ukawsaw Gronniosaw and John Marrant, provided fundamental elements of the architecture of the nineteenth-century slave narrative in its politicized retelling of the movement from slavery to freedom, darkness to light, perdition to redemption. This account of black Protestantism and black print culture documents only one (albeit a particularly influential) strand of black religious life and expression. Still, we can see in these intertwined histories of faith and writing a testament to the continuing power of spirituality in African life around the Atlantic world in the age of slavery. We look forward to continuing research that is uncovering new documents of the vitality of Catholic, Muslim, and other faiths in the struggle for black freedom in the Americas.

BIBLIOGRAPHY

Austin, Allan. *African Muslims in Antebellum America: Transatlantic Stories and Spiritual Struggles*. New York: Routledge, 1997.

Brooks, Joanna. *American Lazarus: Religion and the Rise of African-American and Native American Literatures*. New York: Oxford University Press, 2003.

Brooks, Joanna and John Saillant, ed. *Face Zion Forward: First Writers of the Black Atlantic, 1785–1797*. Boston: Northeastern University Press, 2001.

Carretta, Vincent. *Equiano, the African: Biography of a Self-Made Man*. Athens: University of Georgia Press, 2005.

Diouf, Sylviane. *Servants of Allah: African Muslims Enslaved in the Americas*. New York: New York University Press, 1998.

Equiano, Olaudah. *The Interesting Narrative and Other Writings*. Ed. Vincent Carretta. New York: Penguin, 1995.

Foster, Frances Smith. "A Narrative of the Interesting Origins and (Somewhat) Surprising Devlopments of African-American Print Culture." *American Literary History* 17.4 (2005): 714–40.

Gomez, Michael. *Exchanging our Country Marks: The Transformation of African Identities in the Colonial and Antebellum South*. Chapel Hill: University of North Carolina Press, 1998.

Hammon, Jupiter. *An address to Miss Phillis Wheatley, Ethiopian poetess*. Hartford: n.p., 1778.

Hammon, Jupiter. *An address to the Negroes in the state of New-York, by Jupiter Hammon, servant of John Lloyd, Jun, Esq; of the manor of Queen's Village, Long-Island*. New York: Carroll and Patterson, 1787.

Marrant, John. *A Journal of the Rev. John Marrant, From August the 18th, 1785, to the 16th of March, 1790. To which are added Two Sermons; One Preached on Ragged Island on Sabbath Day, the 27th Day of October 1787; the Other at Boston in New England, On Thursday, the 24th of June, 1789*. London: Printed for the Author, 1790. Reprinted in *"Face Zion Forward": First Writers of the Black Atlantic, 1785–1798*. Ed. Joanna Brooks and John Saillant. Boston, MA: Northeastern University Press, 2002. 93–160.

Patterson, Orlando. *Slavery and Social Death: A Comparative Study*. Cambridge, MA: Harvard University Press, 1982.

Raboteau, Alfred. *Slave Religion: The Invisible Institution in the Antebellum South*. New York: Oxford University Press, 1980.

Rael, Patrick. *Black Identity and Black Protest in the Antebellum North*. Chapel Hill: University of North Carolina Press, 2002.

Saillant, John. *Black Puritan, Black Republican: The Life and Thought of Lemuel Haynes, 1753–1833*. New York: Oxford University Press, 2003.

Sensbach, Jon. *Rebecca's Revival: Creating Black Christianity in the Atlantic World*. Cambridge, MA: Harvard University Press, 2005.

Smallwood, Stephanie. *Saltwater Slavery: A Middle Passage from Africa to American Diaspora*. Cambridge, MA: Harvard University Press, 2007.

Sobel, Mechal. *The World They Made Together: Black and White Values in Eighteenth-Century Virginia*. Princeton: Princeton University Press, 1987.

Whitefield, George. *Three Letters from the Rev. Mr. G. Whitefield*. Philadelphia: B. Franklin, 1740.

6
The Economies of the Slave Narrative

Philip Gould

Antebellum antislavery literature set itself in full force against the brutalities of slave capitalism. The reduction of human beings to chattel slaves, and the self-evident immorality and abundant ironies that sprung from this central fact, most often provided the foundation of the antislavery position in the slave narratives, political orations, sermons, sketches, novels, and newspaper pieces published in the decades preceding the Civil War. Antebellum antislavery did not invent this critique – but it did refine and proliferate it. Nineteenth-century readers of antislavery literature, particularly the slave narrative, became familiar, for example, with the powerful literary trope of the slave auction. A major convention of the slave narrative, this scene, where the African American family is mercilessly separated, is premised on the affective reality of the racial family.

The convention of the slave auction, moreover, juxtaposes sentimental human value with the financial value of slave capitalism. William Wells Brown's famous antislavery novel, *Clotel; or, The President's Daughter* (1853) provides a fine example of this strategy. At the moment the heroine Clotel mounts the auction block, the auctioneer heartlessly begins the bidding of this prize possession, hectoring potential buyers with her exceptional value: she is "Real Albino" and "very intelligent." Clotel eventually brings $1,200 on the open market. The fact that the novel gives an exact, numerical value is significant, for it translates human beauty and virtue into the terms of cold, hard cash. This translation is as brutal as it is indispensable to the overall effect of antislavery literature. For slave capitalism's register of value, the $1,200 provides the touchstone for measuring that system's horrific reduction of human beings to exchangeable goods. *Clotel* pursues the point by following the scene of economic exchange with one of emotional wreckage. Bidding farewell to her mother and sisters, "the slave-girl stood with tears in her eyes." Tears in effect make tangible the argument for black humanity. They are all the more powerful in light of the preceding scene of capitalist exchange. As it turns out, "commodities" can feel. Indeed one might say that the scene's affective power depends upon a particular narrative sequence: first, the capitalist exchange of money for human beings, and then the sentimental exchange of feeling among family members experiencing loss, one to which the reader's feelings succumb as well.

Even this brief reading of one antislavery novel begins to suggest the literary value that antislavery writing procured from its critique of slavery as an economic institution. As the abolition movement gained momentum during the antebellum era, antislavery literature engaged the economics of slave capitalism with increasing sophistication. We should recognize that its overall critique of the plantation system took place during a time of economic modernization in the North. In other words, the major audience the slave narrative wished to reach – white, bourgeois, and Protestant – was itself greatly affected by important social and economic changes taking place in the Northern United States. There is much evidence that the antebellum slave narrative was particularly sensitive to these changes and often appealed to its Northern readers on their own terms. The genre's critique of plantation slavery mobilizes and (in some instances) redeploys the key subjects of nineteenth-century commercial capitalism: the nature of property and property rights, the sources of economic value, free (as opposed to slave) labor, and the costs and profits associated with any business venture.

As I discuss below, many of these ideas have intellectual and philosophical origins in early modern political and economic philosophy, particularly contract theory (focusing on the nature of rights in a social order) and political economy (focusing on the nation's management of wealth and trade). I focus on the seminal writings of John Locke and Adam Smith, who directly addressed the subject of chattel slavery, in light of their general concerns with the nature of rights and the value of labor and property. These subjects were important in antebellum US culture and to the slave narrative genre as well. The philosophical contexts for antebellum antislavery writing are not meant to reduce African American writing to the Anglo-American Enlightenment. But the writings and ideas of seminal thinkers like Locke and Smith did have a long afterlife, so to speak, in nineteenth-century America. What this essay calls the "economies" of the slave narrative represents the convergence of traditional Enlightenment ideas about natural rights and economic value with capitalist developments in antebellum America. As a literary genre highly self-conscious about (though not subservient to) its audience, the slave narrative engages a host of resonant economic issues – the nature of liberty and slavery, labor and property – as part of its overall critique of antebellum slave capitalism. From their vantage on the disenfranchised periphery of American society, African American writers marshaled and redeployed these discourses in ways that effectively reached Northern audiences while also subtly adjusting and even undermining their racial and cultural attitudes.

Locke, Liberty, and Property

Early modern social contract theory turned on the fundamental distinction between the states of liberty and slavery, a distinction that antislavery writers later would utilize to great effect. This was especially true for early nineteenth-century black writers who were arguing against slavery in a post-Revolutionary era that had virtually canonized the political ideas of John Locke. First published in 1690, with numerous editions and translations immediately following, the *Two Treatises* immediately became a standard reference point for British and Continental (and later British American) commentators on natural rights and political contract theory. (One might recall that, in the 1770s, Locke's Second Treatise of Government was published by itself in Revolutionary America, not in England.) At least prima facie, much in the *Two Treatises of Government* argues vehemently against slavery. Locke believes that slavery "was so vile and miserable an Estate of Man" that no real Englishman could argue in favor of it. Slavery would appear to violate the principle of natural rights in general and the identity of the individual subject in particular.

In large part, that identity derives from the capacity of the individual subject to mix his labor with the land. The First Treatise defines "Justice," for example, as a social condition that "gives every Man a Title to the product of his honest Industry" (sec. 42). The distinction that the Second Treatise carefully makes between the "state of war" and the "state of nature" is crucial to defining – and theoretically containing – slavery. Locke shrewdly removes slavery from the social contract by first theoretically abstracting it from the state of nature: "So that he who makes an attempt to enslave me, thereby puts himself into a State of War with me" (279). By consigning slavery to the state of war, Locke preserves the sanctity of natural rights, and, in this way, allows society an important loophole. The individual who has committed so heinous an act that he has forfeited his life to another (or, for example, has been captured as a war combatant) may choose to delay death by submitting himself to slavery. When that state of slavery becomes intolerable, he may "draw on himself the Death he desires."

Yet the above position on slavery raises a number of concerns. First, the relations among consent, enslavement, and natural law are somewhat murky. If consent is the touchstone for the liberal subject, he still cannot willingly enslave himself to another person. Arguing that the individual, "not having the Power of his own Life, cannot, by Compact, or his own Consent, enslave himself to any one, nor put himself under the Absolute, Arbitrary Power of another, to take away his life when he pleases" (284). Natural law forbids it. You cannot give away an ideal (life) that you do not actually "possess." Life, after all, was given to you. Yet, Locke's loophole allowing an individual, who is either captured in war or guilty of a terrible crime, to legitimately enslave himself suggests a curious paradox: you cannot commit yourself to bondage unless you somehow deserve it. If slavery, moreover, is a kind of "state of War continued, then we might reasonably wonder about the stability of such a society (formed by consensual compact) that is constantly presented with the prospect of violence, subjection, and suicide. These issues are not all that surprising in light of Locke's own shady relations with England's expanding commercial empire, which depended significantly on the African slave trade and slave labor in its West Indian colonies. Locke invested in the Royal African Company, for example, an institution that justified its practices in large part by arguing (as did Locke) that African slaves were nothing more than war captives who would have been put to death anyway. He also helped to draft the Fundamental Constitutions of Carolina (1669), legalizing chattel slavery in this new American colony.

Another concern compounded these tensions in Locke's position on slavery – namely, the interpretations later proslavery writers gave to the meaning of "property." As many intellectual historians have noted, Locke's seminal ideas about property rights did not immediately lend themselves to strictly antislavery positions in eighteenth- and nineteenth-century America. In fact, just the opposite was true. Less dependent on biblical justifications and theological rigor, "modern" rationales for the institutions of slavery gradually drifted away from the traditional view that chattel slavery was merely extension of the human enslavement to sin. Its modern cornerstone focused on the natural right to one's property – a right, in other words, that no form of positive law could eradicate. Anchored safely in the core thinking of contract theory, nineteenth-century proslavery thought (as evident in the infamous decision in 1857 of the proslavery Taney Court decision of the Dred Scott case) erased the distinction between human subjects and tangible property. One might say that early antislavery writing meant to reconstruct that distinction, but doing so was not at all simple, for it demanded particular rhetorical strategies to reformulate property rights while distinguishing between persons and property.

Early black writers were sensitive to the terms of contemporary proslavery and antislavery debates. While lacking the rhetorical sophistication of later writers like Frederick Douglass and Harriet Jacobs, this early writing nevertheless skillfully deploys basic Enlightenment ideas about the nature of rights and individual identity. This is apparent, for example, in James Forten's famous *Letters from a Man of Color* (1813), a work protesting recent Pennsylvania legislation meant to reduce the state's black population. "Many of us," Forten complained, "are men of property, for the security of which, we have hitherto looked to the laws of our blessed state, but should this become a law, our property is jeopardized, since the same power which can expose to sale an unfortunate fellow creature, can wrest from him those estates, which years of honest industry have accumulated" (2).

Yet early black writers also were capable of challenging the identification of the human subject with material possession. A contemporary of Forten's, for example, Daniel Coker, who was minister of the African Methodist Episcopal Church in Baltimore, published an important polemical piece, *A Dialogue between a Virginian and an African Minister* (1810). The *Dialogue* attacks the proslavery position based on a strict (and one might say skewed) interpretation of property rights by having the Minister explain the problem to the Virginian in this way: Africans were unjustly converted from men into property by human laws that violated "the law of humanity, common sense, reason, and conscience." He goes on: "But the question is concerning the liberty of a man. The man himself claims it as his own property … [and] by the common laws of justice and humanity, it is still his own" (6). The kind of language Coker employs makes good use of Enlightenment principles that would have been persuasive at the time. Yet, one can see that while Coker argues his case, the very concept of liberty slips back into something one possesses materially like any other form of property.

The antebellum slave narrative addresses this ethical dissonance by resorting to rhetorical techniques that heighten the absurdity of equating persons with property. Sometimes a deadpan tone actually amplifies the moral ironies imbedded within proslavery ideology. At the beginning of *Incidents in the Life of a Slave Girl* (1861), for example, Harriet Jacobs (writing as "Linda Brent") focuses on the history of her grandmother:

> She was a little girl when she was captured and sold to a keeper of a large hotel. I have often heard her tell how hard she fared during childhood. But as she grew older she evinced so much intelligence, and was so faithful, that her master and mistress could not help seeing it was for their interest to take care of such a valuable piece of property. (5)

Much of the work's (and, indeed, the genre's) thematic concerns are implicitly yet boldly apparent in the narrator's laconic delivery: the selfishness of slave owners, the loss of African American agency (sentimentalized in the figure of the child), and the immorality of a capitalist system that commodifies the values of intelligence and loyalty in this way.

The slave narrative generally pursues this last theme to mock the slave's "exchange value" – the dollar amount, in other words, the slave will bring on the open market. As the above discussion of *Clotel* begins to suggest, the slave auction was usually the place where the ethical ironies of slave capitalism were thrown into bold relief. The separation of the family becomes the chief rhetorical device that dislodges moral and sentimental value from exchange value. One might even say that the slave narrative "capitalizes" on this juxtaposition. Sometimes its language presses the point mercilessly, as though the repetition of exempla compounds the crime. In *The Life and Adventures of Henry Bibb, an American Slave* (1849), for example, the narrative ends with an indictment of the hypocrisy of slave-owning Christians, particularly the Southern clergy:

> During my life in slavery I have been sold by professors of religion several times. In 1836 "Bro." Albert G. Sibley of Bedford, Kentucky, sold me for $850. In 1839 "Bro" John Sibbley; and in the same year he sold me to "Bro." Gatewood of Bedford, for $850. In 1839 "Bro." Gatewood sold me to Madison Garrison, a slave trader … at a depreciated price because I was a runaway. In the same year he sold me with my family to "Bro." Whitfield, in the city of New Orleans, for $1200. (203)

While some slave narrators like Bibb exposed the hypocrisy of Christian slaveholding in this way, others took a more shrewdly pragmatic approach to the ethical problem of exchange value. Some played the game of slave capitalism on its own terms as a way of manipulating the limited possibilities of "freedom" within this system. This is certainly true of *The Life of William Grimes, the Runaway Slave* (1825), an autobiography that does not follow the structural and thematic conventions of the antebellum slave narrative. Grimes knows how to manipulate his exchange value and seek the interstices of freedom, even as he plays the game of making himself property. Refusing to eat and "pretending to be sick all the time," Grimes forces his antagonistic master to either sell or lose him, "which would grieve him as much as it would to lose a fine horse of the same value" (203). Once sold, he becomes a carriage driver, a role that cannot help but suggest that, at least temporarily, he has become a master of sorts – the driver and (at least not completely) the driven. The same is true, moreover, for Bibb, who actually collaborates with his new owners – a bunch of dissipated "sportsmen" – who agree to sell him to another master, divide the profits, and then show him the best way to escape to Canada. "They advised me to act very stupid in language and thought, but in business I must be spry; and that I must persuade men to buy me, and promise them that I would be smart" (149). If Bibb plays the stereotypical role that slave society already has made for him, he nevertheless emphasizes that he remains loyal to his new master, a Native American, and flees only after his master's death. While manipulating the system of the slave trade, then, Bibb simultaneously implies his moral stature to the reader, presenting his worth, one might say, on two different yet related registers of value.

Economy, Labor, and Value

The antebellum slave narrative's project of distinguishing between persons and property was commensurate with one of its other major critiques of slave capitalism: the injustice and inefficiency of slave labor. In the antebellum period, the very subject of labor resonated profoundly with both white and black audiences of antislavery literature. As the US economy became increasingly capitalized (some have even referred to the era as one characterized by "the market revolution"), the principle of free labor became increasingly associated with the autonomy of the individual subject, especially the male subject, whose capacities for hard work and individual initiative made him prosperous and fit for modern American public life. Such a normative view of US masculine citizenship had deep philosophical roots in a Lockean tradition founded on the principle that one claims possession of property (and makes it "private property") only by "mixing," as Locke puts it, one's labor with the land. In the *Two Treatises*, this kind of labor represents the crucial moment when the individual subject really becomes a viable public entity, someone, in other words, who exists publicly and will have to be reckoned with in the social contract.

Time and again, antebellum slave narrators lament the brutality of the work on the Southern plantation, including the endless hours, back-breaking work, and impoverished conditions of a labor regime monitored more often than not by a barbaric overseer. But they also bemoan the fact they have been deprived of their "natural" right to the profits of their labor. This is an issue as much moral as material, a crisis as much of identity as of wages lost; for those natural rights are tied intimately to their status *as* human beings. To amplify their complaints, moreover, slave narrators sometimes crafted creative rhetorical appeals to the principle of free labor, even merging secular and sacred discourses. Just as Locke in the *Two Treatises* had invoked biblical passages to justify the right to property as something natural – something founded metaphysically – some slave narrators like Henry Bibb saw the advantages of such a rhetorical approach. Alluding (as had Locke) to Genesis 3: 19, Bibb knew his white Protestant audiences well when he complained: "And who had a better right to eat the fruits of my own hard earnings than myself? Many a long summer's day have I toiled with my wife and other slaves, cultivating his father's fields, and gathering in his harvest, under the scorching rays of the sun, without half enough to eat" (194). Since he is "working without wages," he cannot be guilty of the crime of theft: "For while the slave is regarded as property, how can he steal from his master?" (195).

These writers focused not only on the injustice but also the viability of slave labor on the plantation. One problem easily segued to the next: after exposing the brutality of life on the plantation, slave narrators extended and redirected the subject to consider its profitability. They showed the lack of economic efficiency on the plantation and highlighted the overall theme of waste and mismanagement. One should recognize that every time the slave narrative recounts the ways slaves subtly circumvent the plantation's labor regime – such as stealing from a garden, courting on the sly, evading work at a master's expense, or even attempting to escape – the authors are suggesting not only the important (yet qualified) power slaves retained for themselves, but also the overall inefficiency of this mode of production.

The antebellum slave narrative did not really invent this argument. In the late eighteenth century, British and British American antislavery reformers like Thomas Clarkson and Anthony Benezet had suggested that free trade and free labor would make the British Empire (and West African societies) wealthier. Perhaps the most famous expression in eighteenth-century political economy of the advantages of free labor over slave labor is Adam Smith's *Wealth of Nations* (1776). Smith argues vehemently against the idea that slave labor is naturally cost-efficient and therefore profitable to the West Indian plantations that were making the British Empire rich by the export economies of coffee, sugar, and other staples. Smith offers an alternative analysis that portrays slave labor as unenlightened and unprofitable, a product of custom and tradition that ultimately undermines the public welfare. Considering the economic practices of early modern societies, Smith puts it this way: "The fund destined for replacing or repairing, if I may say so, the wear and tear of the slave is commonly managed by a negligent master or careless overseer. That destined for performing the same office with regard to the free man, is managed by the free man himself" (81). Turning to the seaports of British North America as the example of this principle of "frugality," he argues that the "liberal reward for labor" in free societies is both the effect of increasing wealth and the cause of population growth.

We should not be too sanguine, however, about the slave narrative's place in this kind of Enlightenment philosophical tradition. For just as often as not, the slave narrative ends up showing, unwittingly or not, the brutal rationality of the plantation regime. Put another way, the genre's narrative intention to unveil the horrors of plantation life, for purposes of appealing sentimentally to readers, often produces the image of a perfectly conceived slave labor regime based on the systematic implementation of abuse and terror. The slave labor system works according to its own brutal, rational logic. In *Twelve Years a Slave*, for example, Solomon Northrup impugns the inhumanity of the plantation's overseer, but just as readily suggests that this makes sound economic sense: "The requisite qualifications in an overseer are utter heartlessness, brutality and cruelty. It is his business to produce large crops, and that is accomplished, no matter what amount of suffering it may have cost" (170).

Twelve Years a Slave is one of the most detailed slave narratives we have of the agricultural methods and practices of the production of cotton and sugar. Northrup's first experience as part of the slave labor regime producing cotton further suggests the rationality at the foundation of this system. In *Wealth of Nations*, Smith has argued that "[a] person who can acquire no property, can have no other interest but to eat as much, and to labour as little as possible. Whatever work he does beyond what is sufficient to purchase his own maintenance, can be squeezed out of him by violence only, and not by any interest of his own." But in *Twelve Years a Slave*, Northrup offers a distinctive (though not altogether opposing) perspective on slave labor:

> No matter how fatigued and weary [the slave] may be – no matter how much he longs for sleep and rest – a slave never approaches the gin house with his basket of cotton but with fear. If it falls short in weight – if he has not performed the full task appointed to him, he knows he must suffer. And if he has exceeded it by ten or twenty pounds, in all probability his master will measure the next day's task accordingly. So, whether he has too little or too much, his approach to the gin-house is always with fear and trembling. (126)

The passage represents the slave narrative's larger critique of the overall dehumanization of slave capitalism. Nineteenth-century readers would have been attuned to its critique of the individual subject's loss of agency. Not only is the slave laborer deprived of wages, a regime of fear regulates his work and maintains a prescribed level of production. Some people like Smith, or like even a Northern reader of the mercantile middle class, might have pointed out that the slave labor system is not geared to maximize production levels, since slaves will not bring in as much cotton as possible. But Northrup here makes a case for the profitability of violence and coercion.

As he recounted his experience as a slave worker on the docks of Fells Point Baltimore, Frederick Douglass significantly expanded the scope and ramifications of such a critique. In this case, Douglass was interested not only in the violence and terror of the slave labor regime but also the insidious, sweeping power of slave capitalism to in effect "enslave" white laborers to its larger racial and ideological project. Whereas his earlier *Narrative of the Life of Frederick Douglass, an American Slave* (1845) portrays the terrible beating he took at the hands of Irish immigrant laborers, *My Bondage and My Freedom* (1855) offers a far more probing analysis of the dynamics of race, class, and capitalism in antebellum America. One passage is worth quoting at some length:

> The slaveholders, with a craftiness peculiar to themselves, by encouraging the enmity of the poor, laboring white man against the blacks, succeeds in making the said white man almost as much a slave as the black slave himself. The difference between the white slave, and the black slave, is this: the latter belongs to one slaveholder, and the former belongs to all the slaveholders, collectively. The white slave has taken from him, by indirection, what the black slave has taken from him, directly, and without ceremony. Both are plundered, and by the same plunderers. The slave is robbed, by his master, of all his earnings, above what is required for his bare physical necessities; and the white man is robbed by the slave system of the just results of his labor, because he is flung into competition with a class of laborers who work without wages ... At present, the slaveholders blind them to this competition, by keeping alive their racial prejudice against the slaves. (179–80)

Sounding almost like a Marxist social critic, Douglass argues the historical inevitability of white workers, someday soon, awaking enslaved to an entire system that nurtures racial hatred only to mystify social conflict. Read in light of *Wealth of Nations*, Douglass here resists the Smithian argument that slave labor is inherently unprofitable (though his writing elsewhere does make that argument as a way of debunking Southern laziness).

This important section of *My Bondage and My Freedom* adheres rigorously to the importance of free labor, which is, indeed, inseparable from the theme of identity at the heart of the slave narrative genre. Readers often overlook the fact, for example, that Douglass's famous definition of slavery in this chapter – "To make a contented slave, you must make a thoughtless one. It is necessary to darken his moral and mental vision" – comes on the heels of his own newfound status as a wage earner and the psychological empowerment that such status confers on the individual subject. "The reader will observe that I was now of some pecuniary value to my master. During the busy season, I was bringing six and seven dollars per week." Such value further catalyzes the enslaved protagonist's newfound sense of his worth – both material and moral – and leads to his escape to the North.

All of this raises the issue of how we go about defining the slave narrative genre. One might say that the genre's prevailing economic themes – the distinction between property and humanity, and yet the importance of "free" labor in acquiring property to reassert individual identity – manage, ultimately, to push at the boundaries of genre itself. The slave narrative's definition, however, inevitably rests on a more fundamental question of what constitutes "slavery." If we think of this broad concept, as many slave narrators did, in terms of the loss of the "fruits" of their labor, then the boundaries among genres in African American writing at this time begin to soften. Exhibit A in this regard might be what was once thought the first African American novel (published in the US), Harriet Wilson's *Our Nig; or, Sketches from the Life of a Free Black* (1859). This work, though not strictly a slave narrative, understands enslavement in terms of the power one exerts over one's labor. Indeed, the protagonist, Frado, is "free" in name only, and the novel goes to great lengths to destabilize an abstract concept that is not grounded in the realities of work. We see Frado constantly engaged in hard, physical labor on the farm and in the house, an indentured servant of sorts. "She was shown how it was always to be done, and in no other way; any departure from this rule to be punished by a whipping" (29). This is contrasted with her situation at the end of the novel, where the desire for "self-improvement" and the uplift myth (that would come to dominate postbellum discourses of "free" African Americans) converge in the symbol of Frado's "needle": her self-employment as a seamstress that at least points the way to her economic independence.

Bourgeois Morals and Manners

What I have been identifying as the major economic themes of the slave narrative provided these writers more than simply the means to critique the institutions and practices of slave capitalism. The subjects of property and labor easily became the literary medium of a form of African American identity that does not neatly fit into the categories "radical" or "conservative." As the above passage from Douglass begins to show, the slave narrative was quite capable of recuperating African American humanity within the normative field of an emerging capitalist culture in antebellum America. Some slave narrators pressed this rhetorical tactic of self-representation to the point where the very terms of their individual identity look something like the American success story – the entrepreneurial figure whose hard work, calculation, and initiative made him suitable, one might say, as the new American hero. Such an autobiographical argument at once embraces and challenges dominant social norms. The argument also uncouples blackness from its traditional stereotypical associations with shiftlessness and dishonesty, and reinserts it squarely within the emerging norms of the bourgeois, masculine individual. As I show below, this exchange simultaneously foists those negative values back onto the figure of the Southern slaveholder.

There is perhaps no better example of this than "Narrative of the Life of William Wells Brown," a condensed version of his life story that prefaced the 1853 London edition of *Clotel*. Written in the third person, the "Narrative" is noteworthy for portraying its protagonist as an entrepreneurial capitalist who is able to first acquire capital through diligent work, and then manipulate the speculative financial markets to flourish as a businessman. Once Brown has escaped to Ohio, for example, he relishes the moment where his labor brings him his first "shilling": "and that shilling made me feel, indeed, as if I had considerable stock in hand" (64). Reiterating the importance of literacy to freedom, Brown avoids the local banks ("I would not trust them") and instead invests half his earnings for a spelling book, with a plan in mind to "convert" the two little boys of the household employing him into his "teachers."

Typically, slave literacy (as it is in Douglass and many others) emerges as a kind of possession earned from a combination of industry and initiative – the latter verging into deceit, though sanctified in large part by the unassailable virtue of being able to read for oneself.

The formation of the budding capitalist becomes the *telos* of this autobiography. The work reads like a literary descendant of the eighteenth-century autobiographies of Venture Smith and Benjamin Franklin, the latter of which had a long and rich nineteenth-century publishing life. One of its most interesting episodes recounts the ingenuity of its protagonist in handling the complex fiscal landscape leading up to the Panic of 1837, which resulted in large part from excessive speculating on Western lands. "At this time," Brown says, "money matters in the Western States were in a sad condition. Any person who could raise a small amount of money was permitted to establish a bank and allowed to issue notes for four times the sum raised" (67). Urged on by some of the townspeople to become a banker, probably as a kind of joke, Brown proclaims that, " 'it was no laughing matter, for from that moment I began to think seriously of becoming a banker.' " Brown can barely contain his excitement – and can hardly sleep – over his newfound role as finance capitalist. As the episode develops, it becomes a battle of wits set within the larger historical context of "wildcat" banking, worthless currencies, and land speculation. Jealous of an African American's success, some of the town's young men intentionally put a "run" on his little bank's "shinplasters," the privately printed paper currency that Brown is issuing as promissory notes. Rather than panic, and fail, Brown closes his shop, escapes, and consults a friend who gives him a quick lesson in the banking strategy of keeping his shinplasters in constant circulation. "'I immediately commenced putting into circulation the notes which I had just redeemed, and my efforts were crowned with … success'" (69). The final lesson of the semi-comic episode may be that African Americans have the ingenuity and industry to navigate the complexities of finance capitalism – that they too can compete in modern American life.

This bourgeois version of African American manhood stands in stark contrast to its necessary foil: the lazy and vicious Southern aristocrat presiding over his landed estate. The image of the dissipated slave owner was not an antebellum invention. It had been disseminated, rather, in a good deal of eighteenth-century British and British American antislavery writing, some of it highly satirical, some of it horrifically gothic, that meant to expose the moral failings of the West Indian planter. A curious mixture of aristocratic hauteur and savage violence, this eighteenth-century portrait informs Smith's argument in *Wealth of Nations* that slavery continued to exist as a labor regime not out of financial necessity but out of some deeper and darker propensity in human nature for power. "The pride of man makes him love to domineer, and nothing mortifies him so much as to be obliged to condescend to persuade his inferiors. Wherever the law allows it, and the nature of the work can afford it, therefore, he will generally prefer the service of slaves to that of freemen" (238). The argument is thoroughly Protestant insofar as it attributes persistent irrational practices to innate depravity. For Smith and other Scottish moral philosophers, though, human reason and social progress would eventually overcome the residues of barbarity.

The antebellum slave narrative generally converts this kind of argument into both cause and effect of plantation slave capitalism. The stock image of the Southern planter focuses first and foremost on his inability to control one's passions, including images of uncontrollable appetites for food, sexual gratification, monetary wealth, land, or social and racial power. (Later liberal theorists such as Isaiah Berlin would call "positive liberty" the ability to control one's passions and hence not be enslaved by them.) This certainly underlies, for example, Harriet Jacobs's characterization of Linda's master, "Dr. Flint," an archetypal villain who is as much a gourmand as a sexual predator. In this same vein, *My Bondage and My Freedom* debunks the very ideal of aristocratic status by turning it into a kind of physical and psychological pathology. Why would any thinking human being, Douglass muses, identify himself an aristocrat like the great Colonel Lloyd:

> This immense wealth; this gilded splendor; this profusion of luxury; this exemption from toil; this life of ease; this sea of plenty; aye, what of it all? … The poor slave, on his hard, pine plank, but scantily covered with his thin blanket, sleeps more soundly than the feverish voluptuary who reclines upon his feather bed and downy pillow. Food, to the indolent lounger, is poison, not sustenance. (52–3)

In conclusion, if we think of the slave narrative as putting forth its own versions of an "economy" of living – a normative view of bourgeois life based on private property, free labor, and individual initiative – then the genre looks to be part of a larger antebellum reform literature meditating upon and often reformulating these subjects during the decades leading up to the Civil War. What is a book like *Walden* (1854), for example, but a treatise on the nature of property and labor, and on the costs and benefits arising from a new, radical "economy" of living? The antebellum slave narrative may be less a metaphysical project than Henry David Thoreau's book of self-reformation (whose opening chapter is entitled "Economy"). Nevertheless, the slave narrative engages such issues as the property we possess, the labor that goes into it, and the free, individual subject enjoying the fruits of that relation. No less than a work like *Walden*, contemporary works like *My Bondage and My Freedom* and *Incidents in the Life of a Slave Girl* operated in part as meditations on political economy, and offered both prescriptions and proscriptions for economic management within a particular – and unique – set of historical and racial contexts.

To this end, one of the principal objectives of the slave narrative is to repossess in racial ways the category of a "free" individual subject capable of thriving in modern society. Slave narrators like Bibb and Brown were uncompromising about the importance of free labor to a modern, civilized society, and about the capacity of African Americans to exhibit the virtues of hard work, thrift, and enterprising initiative, virtues that enhanced their narrative authority while making the larger argument (against the one Harriet Beecher Stowe offers, for example, at the conclusion to her 1852 novel, *Uncle Tom's Cabin*) for the ability of free African Americans to someday thrive in an American society finally purged of both slavery and racial prejudice. This theme was directly related, moreover, to the literary personae and narrative authority these writers forged for themselves. Slave narrators like Douglass and Northrup exerted narrative authority partly by writing as observant, often prescient, commentators on the plantation economy. By surveying the dynamics of plantation life, and later contrasting them with the bourgeois values of industry and property ownership, they not only exposed the brutality of slavery but inserted themselves, sometimes easily, sometimes tensely, into the cultural and ideological nexus of American middle-class life. They also created a place for themselves at once narrative, ideological, and racial. That place became the ground on which to stand with some assurance, and from which to proceed to critique the very culture that they were embracing.

Bibliography

Berlin, Isaiah. "Two Concepts of Liberty." *Four Essays on Liberty*. Oxford: Oxford University Press, 1969. 118–72.

Bibb, Henry. *The Life and Adventures of Henry Bibb, an American Slave*. Madison: University of Wisconsin Press, 2001.

Brown, William Wells. "Narrative of the Life of William Wells Brown." 1853. *Clotel: Or, the President's Daughter: A Narrative of Slave Life in the United States*. Ed. Robert S. Levine. Boston, MA: Bedford/St. Martin's, 2000.

Coker, Daniel. *A Dialogue between a Virginian and an African Minister*. Baltimore: Benjamin Edes, 1810.

Davis, David Brion. *The Problem of Slavery in Western Culture*. Ithaca, NY: Cornell University Press, 1966.

Douglass, Frederick. *My Bondage and My Freedom*. New York: Modern Library, 2003.

Forten, James. *Letters from a Man of Color*. Philadelphia: no pub., 1813.

Kloppenberg, James. *The Virtues of Liberalism*. New York: Oxford University Press, 1998.

Locke, John. *Two Treatises of Government*. Cambridge: Cambridge University Press, 1988.

Northrup, Solomon. *Twelve Years a Slave*. Baton Rouge: Louisiana State University Press, 1996.

Sellers, Charles. *The Market Revolution: Jacksonian America, 1815–1861*. New York: Oxford University Press, 1991.

Shapiro, Ian. *The Evolution of Rights in Liberal Theory*. Cambridge: Cambridge University Press, 1986.

Smith, Adam. *An Inquiry into the Nature and Causes of the Wealth of Nations*. Oxford: Oxford University Press, 1998.

Tully, James. *An Approach to Political Philosophy: Locke in Contexts*. Cambridge: Cambridge University Press, 1993.

Wilson, Harriet. *Our Nig; or, Sketches from the Life of a Free Black*. New York: Random House, 1983.

7

The 1850s: The First Renaissance of Black Letters

Maurice S. Lee

Well before African American literature established itself as an academic subject, literary critics of the early twentieth century founded a field that came to be known as the American Renaissance. Focusing on white male authors from the North writing before the Civil War, American Renaissance scholars were especially committed to texts from the 1850s – Nathaniel Hawthorne's *The Scarlet Letter* (1850), Herman Melville's *Moby-Dick* (1851), Henry David Thoreau's *Walden* (1854), Walt Whitman's *Leaves of Grass* (1855), and to a lesser extent Ralph Waldo Emerson's later essays such as "Fate" (1860) and "Illusions" (1860). The demographic exclusivity of the American Renaissance began eroding toward the end of the twentieth century, though the 1850s remained a locus of critical attention. Emily Dickinson, who began her poetry in the late 1850s, made her way into the canon, while Harriet Beecher Stowe's work – most notably, *Uncle Tom's Cabin* (1852) – rose to prominence in the late 1970s. Around the same time, African American literature gained increasing recognition; and it is no coincidence that the 1850s proved to be a fertile period in the field.

As the term "renaissance" suggests, the 1850s renaissance of black letters is marked by both unprecedented creativity and continuities with established traditions. A number of achievements characterize the decade, including the evolution of the slave narrative form, the rise of the African American novel, and the flourishing of African American intellectuals in the black press and beyond. These developments are not limited to the 1850s and have no single explanation, though a set of related factors constitute a crucial dynamic of the period: as the slavery conflict came to dominate United States thought and culture, African American writers were encouraged by increasing political, economic, and artistic support, even as they were acutely disappointed by the continued presence and spread of chattel bondage.

In many ways, proslavery forces gained ground in the 1850s. Much of the territory ceded to the United States as a result of the Mexican-American War (1846–1848) was considered open to slavery. The Fugitive Slave Law of 1850 made it easier for masters to reclaim escaped slaves from the North. The Kansas-Nebraska Act of 1854 opened new territories to the possibility of chattel bondage; and in its 1857 Dred Scott decision, the Supreme Court ruled that African Americans had no legal standing under the Constitution. Throughout the decade, free Northern blacks endured discrimination, displacement by white immigrants, and the rise of racist pseudo-sciences espousing black inferiority. In hindsight, we know that slavery was coming to an end, but at the time it seemed to many ascendant.

African American authors and their allies responded to such challenges. Long marginalized, the antislavery movement became a formidable transatlantic force that supported many black abolitionist writers, while advances in literacy, print technology, and distribution made it easier for them to publish on a range of cultural and intellectual topics. The travels and emigration of American-born blacks also led to innovative writings. Perhaps most importantly, African American writers of the 1850s participated in energizing dialogues – within the black community, with white authors, and across generic, ideological, and national lines. Like the concurrent American Renaissance and the New Negro (or Harlem) Renaissance about 70 years later, African American letters from the 1850s is a field of concentrated literary achievement and densely interwoven plots. As if in anticipation of the Civil War, black writers of the era staged a revolution.

Transforming the Slave Narrative

Slave narratives from the 1850s adopt, adapt, and depart from the conventions of a mature literary form. Eighteenth-century slave narratives by such authors as Briton Hammon, John Marrant, James Albert Ukawsaw Gronniosaw, and Olaudah Equiano are wonderfully difficult to categorize. They participate in diverse artistic traditions – African myth and oral culture, political tracts, captivity stories, picaresque novels, and Christian conversion narratives. They also range across the Atlantic world and express an array of ideological positions, even regarding chattel bondage. Slave narratives throughout the nineteenth century remain productively heterogeneous, but by the 1850s the genre is more established and intertextually complex.

Generalizations are never entirely accurate, but the autobiographies of ex-slaves in the 1840s and 1850s often share common traits. Recurring scenes include whippings and murders, the breaking up of slave families, the spectacle of the auction block, and the breathless flight to freedom. Slave narratives also tend to focus on similar thematic interests, such as the painful acquisition of knowledge, the search for spiritual regeneration, the power and limitations of language, and the ongoing construction of personal identity within embattled communities. Narratives usually adopt an unvarnished style (some more strategically than others), though they also deploy stylized abolitionist rhetoric that, along with proslavery discourse, had become somewhat formalized by the 1850s. As they vindicate their intelligence, invoke democratic principles, and appeal to the sympathies of their Christian readers, ex-slaves shared patterns of allusion to the Bible, the Declaration of Independence, and antislavery poetry. They also cited other slave narratives directly and indirectly, indicating – as Frances Smith Foster has shown – that authors and readers self-consciously participated in an established literary tradition.

One reason for the coalescing of slave narratives is that United States slavery had become less dynamic by the 1850s. Escaped slaves did move outside the United States, particularly after the Fugitive Slave Law; and the westward expansion of the nation included the uprooting of slaves. Conditions of enslavement in America did differ depending on master, region, and type of labor. That said, legislation in slaveholding states increasingly regulated chattel bondage, while the outlawing of the international slave trade and the abolition of slavery in the Northern United States, Europe, and most of the Caribbean made the experience of slavery in America more localized than in the eighteenth century. Moreover, slave narratives by the 1850s had become something of an industry – written for a growing antislavery audience in the United States and Britain, marketed through speaking tours and the burgeoning abolitionist press, spurred by the popularity of earlier efforts such as Frederick Douglass's 1845 narrative and William Wells Brown's 1847 autobiography. As William Andrews has argued, the late 1840s brought slave narratives international visibility, while the next decade witnessed an explosion of production, popularity, and innovation. One can define the genre in various ways, but roughly as many American slave narratives first appeared in the 1850s as in the preceding 90 years. Some of these texts are available in modern print editions, and many are accessible through the University of North Carolina's website, *Documenting the American South* (http://docsouth.unc.edu).

The institutionalization of slave narratives in the 1850s raises some critical challenges. As with most autobiographies, ideological biases and financial interests can undermine authenticity. This is particularly true of slave narrators, almost all of whom had pressing political and economic motives and often relied on white editors and (in some cases) amanuenses committed to abolitionism. Hardly free from prejudice, proslavery critics tried to discredit slave narratives; and it remains difficult today to distinguish truth from fiction, skillful rhetoric from literary license.

Generic conventions further complicate matters. As Douglass suggests in his second autobiography, *My Bondage and My Freedom* (1855), ex-slaves felt pressured to tailor their stories to audience expectations. (In Douglass's case, he was asked to be less eloquent so that his listeners would believe he had actually been a slave.) Along similar lines, the increasingly graphic violence of slave narratives suggests a desire to shock and even titillate readers grown jaded with the genre. That Josiah Henson, author of an 1849 narrative, repackaged himself in 1858 as the model for Uncle Tom after the success of Stowe's novel shows how aggressively some slave narrators courted success in the literary marketplace. Generally speaking, slave narrators at least superficially accommodate their largely white readers, who were mostly antislavery women. Many present themselves as suffering Christians dependent on white sympathy. Few focus on racial oppression in the North, let alone within the antislavery movement. Most avoid or carefully qualify support for violent revolt and black nationalism. Even slave narratives published in Britain are wary of attacking America too fiercely.

Yet as much as the maturation of the slave narrative form leads to some predictable plotting and language, as well as conventional ideology, it also offers opportunities for literary distinction. John Brown's *Slave Life in Georgia* (1854) and John Thompson's *The Life of John Thompson* (1856) can be taken as relatively traditional narratives against which to measure departures from the norm – some of them explicit, some more subversive, all marked by sophisticated storytelling. Conveying the unpredictability of slave life, Henry Bibb's *Narrative of the Life and Adventures* (1849) describes Bibb's servitude under a professional gambler, a respected deacon, and a Cherokee master (among others). Upon reaching the North after numerous attempts, Bibb takes a startling risk – returning to his home state of Kentucky in the hope of freeing his wife. Henry "Box" Brown mails himself to freedom, as recounted in his 1849 narrative; and in *Running a Thousand Miles to Freedom* (1860), William and Ellen Craft recount how William posed as the slave of his lighter skinned wife, who passed as a white male invalid. Solomon Northrup in *Twelve Years a Slave* (1853) is more a victim than a manipulator of social identity. As a free New Yorker kidnapped and sold into bondage, Northrup's experience is especially disorienting, and his release is more of a return to identity than the dawning of a new life. All of these texts are open to literary and ideological analysis, though of particular interest are slave narratives that quarrel with the slave narrative genre itself, that self-consciously question how ex-slaves can tell a free story in – and out of – America.

Published ten years after his wildly successful *Narrative of the Life of Frederick Douglass* (1845), Douglass's *My Bondage and My Freedom* simultaneously evinces and moves beyond his mastery of the slave narrative form. After publishing his *Narrative*, Douglass traveled through Britain, where he established an international reputation. Upon returning to the United States, he began his own newspaper, became increasingly militant, and broke with his mentor William Lloyd Garrison and the American Anti-slavery Society, which had sponsored his first book. As Eric Sundquist has emphasized, *My Bondage and My Freedom* is about escaping Southern slavery *and* fighting for justice in the North; and though almost all moments from the *Narrative* remain, they take on additional meanings. In *My Bondage*, when Douglass imagines the death of his beloved grandmother, he explicitly quotes a passage from the *Narrative*, thus deploying the affective power of the scene while distancing his more mature self from its highly wrought sentimentality. Something similar happens when Douglass comments on his celebrated fight with the slave-breaker Covey: "Well, my dear reader, this battle with Mr. Covey, – undignified as it was, and as I fear my narration of it is – was the turning point in my '*life as a slave*'" (286). Eloquent, cultivated, passionate yet objective, and prefaced by the image of a well dressed Douglass, *My Bondage and My Freedom* is both a slave narrative and the memoir of a great public figure.

Fittingly, *My Bondage* features an introduction not by Garrison, Douglass's white mentor who wrote one for the *Narrative*, but rather by James McCune Smith, a black intellectual colleague and friend. Also appropriate is the book's lengthy appendix, which contains examples of Douglass's journalism and oratory, including his widely reprinted speech, "What to the Slave is the Fourth of July?" (1852). Such materials make clear that the slave narrative is but one of Douglass's modes of expression. In fact, he also wrote some poetry in the 1850s and published one of the first African American short stories, "The Heroic Slave" (1853).

Whereas *My Bondage and My Freedom* presents Douglass as an accomplished representative man, *The Narrative of Sojourner Truth* (1850) offers a counter example. Written in the third person by the white abolitionist Olive Gilbert, to whom Truth told her life story, Truth's *Narrative* describes the trials of a powerful speaker who was illiterate, folksy, and passionately committed to motherhood, feminism, and Christian spirituality. Truth's story does not take the form or describe the experiences of a typical slave narrative. She was born a slave in New York in 1797 and grew up speaking Dutch. In 1827, the state abolished slavery, though Truth had already "escaped" from her master by refusing to work for him and finding employment in a neighboring village. Truth suffered greatly under slavery, including beatings, separations from her family, and what are most likely sexual assaults that Gilbert passes over for "motives of delicacy" (18). Truth also found resources that most Southern slaves lacked – the support of antislavery whites in her vicinity, integrated religious organizations, even recourse to the legal system (with the help of a lawyer, she brings back her son who was illegally sold into slavery in Alabama). Unlike Douglass, who insists on his own self-authorship, Truth's illiteracy complicates questions of authenticity. Gilbert periodically interjects her own commentary and mutes the radical elements of Truth's religious seeking. But whether we see Gilbert as an obscuring presence, a protective shield, a fellow worker, or some combination thereof, the voice and personality of Truth show forth much more than in the over-determined article Stowe wrote on Truth in 1863. Fiercely protective of her rights and family while advocating – and sometimes struggling to maintain – a balance between Christian outrage and sympathy, Truth's *Narrative* expands a reader's sense of American slavery and how it might be rendered and read.

The first slave narrative written by an African American woman herself is Harriet Jacobs's *Incidents in the Life of a Slave Girl*, not published until 1861, though largely written by 1857. The book touches on public events such as Nat Turner's Rebellion in 1831 and the Fugitive Slave Law, but it is more centrally a family story told against the backdrop of a political struggle. *Incidents* is a morally complicated and powerfully ironic text. Jacobs writes in an intimate first-person voice, but her name does not appear on the title page and she uses the pseudonym Linda Brent throughout the book, in part because of the sexual trauma at the heart of her experience. To save herself from her lecherous master, Brent becomes the mistress of a less objectionable slaveholder with whom she has two children, a severely coerced choice that her grandmother condemns and that falls outside the ethical pale of Jacobs's imagined readership. Brent eventually decides to escape, not initially by running away, but by hiding in her grandmother's garret where she stays for almost seven years, watching her children through a gimlet hole and hoping that their father will fulfill his promise to free them (which he never does). Like the ghostly black women who haunt gothic plots in Charlotte Brontë's *Jane Eyre* (1847), Stowe's *Uncle Tom's Cabin*, and (as we shall see) Hannah Crafts's *The Bondwoman's Narrative* (c.1853–1861), Brent exercises psychological power from her marginalized position. Moreover, like an ideal reader of *Incidents* itself, Brent is a domestic witness to slavery who ultimately intervenes in events, modeling both the power and the limits of abolitionist sentimentality.

Even when Jacobs hews closer to slave narrative conventions – when she describes Brent's escape to the North and her struggles to reunite her family – *Incidents in the Life of a Slave Girl* remains a resistant text. Brent's children are both motives for freedom and beloved links to her past oppression, simultaneously signs of her humanity and her history of enslavement. *Incidents* can be read as an ambivalent attempt to explain Brent's difficult choices – to her grandmother, her daughter, her largely white readership, and also to Jacobs herself. The book pays some tribute to moral delicacy, yet Jacobs does not repress her liaison nor does she ultimately apologize for it. As Dana Nelson has argued, she uses the sentimental language of affect, sympathy, and family while also showing that standards of sexual purity and marriage are not equally available to all. Defending her autonomy and denying that even sympathetic readers can entirely know the feelings of a slave, Jacobs demonstrates that breaking conventions can release original powers.

While antebellum slave narratives tend to be less international than their eighteenth-century forerunners, they offer important transatlantic perspectives of a different sort. After slavery was abolished in most of the British Empire by the 1830s, the British antislavery movement turned its energies to the United States, publishing texts by American-born blacks, sponsoring their speaking tours in Britain, and contributing to such enterprises as Douglass's newspapers. In a brief chapter concerning her 10 months in England, which she visits as a nanny, Jacobs makes two common abolitionist points: blacks are treated more humanely in Britain than in America; and poor laborers in England, contra proslavery claims, are better off than United States slaves. This kind of transatlantic shaming involves, as Elisa Tamarkin has shown, broader questions of cultural capital and national identity. It is also complicated by a shift in black abolitionism in the 1850s.

Racist colonization schemes had long advocated removing African Americans beyond the borders of the United States; but after such dispiriting setbacks as the Fugitive Slave Law and Dred Scott decision, some black Americans looked for better conditions in Canada, Britain, the Caribbean, Central America, and West Africa. African American emigrationists of the 1850s included Henry Highland Garnet (later US minister to Liberia), Alexander Crummell (Cambridge-educated minister and missionary in Liberia), James Theodore Holly (leader of a group of black settlers to Haiti in 1861), and Martin Delany (who lived for a time in Canada and traveled to Liberia and the Niger Valley region in search of land for black settlements).

Samuel Ringgold Ward's *Autobiography of a Fugitive Slave* (1855) exemplifies how some later slave narrators make a return to the genre's eighteenth-century transnational roots (or as Paul Gilroy has emphasized, *routes*). Ward was a Maryland slave until his parents escaped to New Jersey with some help from Garnet. Educated in New York, he became a minister and abolitionist before leaving the United States in 1853. As described in his *Autobiography*, Ward tires of "the ever-present, ever-crushing Negro-hate" of the North (28). He also fears rendition under the Fugitive Slave Law, especially after helping a captured slave breakout of a New York courthouse. Ward thus leaves the United States, moving through various black settlements in Canada (Dawn and Buxton, as well as cities with large black communities such as Chatham and Toronto). He describes each locale with sociological care, not ignoring the struggles of Canadian blacks, but giving a more positive assessment than Austin Steward's *Twenty-Two Years a Slave, and Forty Years a Freeman* (1857). Ward then travels as an antislavery speaker through Britain, where he publishes his *Autobiography*, a book whose views on race and racism are intensely comparative. Ward measures the treatment of blacks in America against conditions in Canada, England, Ireland, Cuba, Brazil, and Dutch Guiana. He also compares the relative status of Africans, Irish, Poles, and Jews. Ward's critique is international but retains a sense for an American audience, as when he contrasts the Fugitive Slave Law to both the Declaration of Independence and the Magna Carta. A descendant of Africa and born in America, he published his *Autobiography* in London with a title page that reads, "Samuel Ringgold Ward, Toronto." Soon after that, he moved to Jamaica where he lived for the remaining 11 years of his life.

Unlike Ward, the escaped slave William Wells Brown returns to the United States after traveling abroad. *The American Fugitive in Europe*, published in Boston in 1855, is a curious text in at least two ways: it shows Brown's relish for new experiences; and its generic heterogeneity is compellingly strange. The book is an expanded version of Brown's *Three Years in Europe*, published in London in 1852. It starts with a "Memoir" drawn from Brown's popular *Narrative of William W. Brown* (1847), though the section is written in a third-person voice by a British journalist, thus simultaneously acknowledging and resisting Brown's roots in the slave narrative form. Switching to the first person, the rest of the book often feels more like a middle-class travel narrative than the autobiography of an ex-slave. Guidebooks in hand, Brown visits palaces and museums while attending the 1849 Peace Conference in Paris. Later, he travels through England and Scotland, paying particular attention to London's 1851 World's Fair and the historic homes of great authors. As one of the first African American novelists (see below), Brown has a sharp eye for telling details and an excellent ear for everyday speech. So focused is he on his European touring that it is possible to forget that he is an American ex-slave. Or as Brown himself writes near the end of the book, "I had begun to fancy myself an Englishman by habit, if not by birth" (303).

And yet, as its very title suggests, *The American Fugitive in Europe* does not leave United States slavery behind. Brown discusses an array of authors partly through the lens of racial politics. For instance, he praises the abolitionist John Greenleaf Whittier, condemns the racist Thomas Carlyle, and to some extent excuses Lord Byron's licentiousness because of his liberal views. Brown also notices the power of *Uncle Tom's Cabin*, appreciates the story of William and Ellen Craft (living in England at the time), praises Crummell (whom he visits), and cites the African American poet James Whitfield as an example of a literary genius stifled by racial oppression. Brown quotes Emerson regarding literary nationalism, suggesting how *The American Fugitive in Europe* – for all its cosmopolitan leanings – also calls for an American literature that includes African Americans authors. At the same time, Brown remains ambivalent about his own affiliations. He is fascinated by Joseph Jenkins, an ex-slave who was born in Africa, successively owned by nine masters, and currently living in London as a tract distributor, street sweeper, preacher, and actor (playing Othello). A precursor to James Weldon Johnson's Ex-colored Man and Ralph Ellison's Rinehart in the twentieth century, Jenkins has a fluid identity that gives him freedom and power. But just when Brown seems ready to cut himself loose from his American moorings, he decides to return to the United States to fight for abolitionism. The racism that greets him when he returns is a shock to both Brown and the reader: after all the pleasant excursions and aesthetic reflections, political imperatives remain. Brown is committed to abolitionism, but his mixed feelings toward his country are suggested by the facts that he leaves his daughters in school in England and later considers moving to Haiti.

The Rise of the African American Novel

As the slave narrative evolved in the 1850s, the African American novel began its long rise. Only a handful of known examples antedate the Civil War, and as a group they invite definitional questions about provenance, genre, and primacy. William Wells Brown's *Clotel, or the President's Daughter* (1853) is generally regarded as the first African American novel, though the text is quite hybrid, was first published in London, and was later issued in three revised versions. Frank J. Webb's *The Garies and Their Friends* (1857) is more stable in terms of genre and textual history, though it too was published in London where Webb was living before moving to France and Jamaica for 10 years before returning to the United States. *The Bondwoman's Narrative* was not published until 2002, after Henry Louis Gates, Jr. acquired the manuscript and found evidence that its author, Hannah Crafts, was in all likelihood African American. Another long-neglected book, Harriet Wilson's *Our Nig or, Sketches from the Life of a Free Black* (1859), was not authenticated as an African American text until 1982, and some scholars consider the book less a novel than a non-fictional work. Martin Delany's *Blake, or the Huts of America* was serialized between 1859 and 1862, but the final chapters of the novel seem to be missing, if indeed they were written at all. Without a firmly established literary lineage and, for many writers, reliable publishing opportunities, African American novels before the Civil War reflect the conditions of a nascent tradition.

This is not to say that the first generation of black American novelists had no models to work from and against. The French writer Alexandre Dumas, born in 1802, was recognized as an accomplished novelist of African descent. Among white authors, the abolitionist and novelist Lydia Maria Child edited Jacobs's *Incidents*, helped *Our Nig* find a publisher, and also influenced Wells Brown. Crafts echoes Charlotte and Emily Brontë, Charles Dickens, Hawthorne, and Sir Walter Scott, while Webb conjures a deep history of the novel when a character refers knowingly to "'virtue rewarded'" (305). Novels such as Gustave de Beaumont's *Marie* (1835) and Richard Hildreth's *The Slave* (1840) focused on American slavery, though, more than any other novel, *Uncle Tom's Cabin* helped shape antebellum African American fiction. Stowe's work was in some ways inspiring, showing that an abolitionist novel could be politically effective and financially rewarding. Still, many black writers objected to Stowe's racial caricatures, seeming support for colonization, and indirect knowledge of chattel bondage (often drawn from American slave narratives that Stowe did not initially credit). Like *Uncle Tom's Cabin*, African American novels of the 1850s deploy slave narrative conventions, though – as Carla Peterson has argued – they tend to exhibit a broader range of political and aesthetic expressions. Variously influenced, historically grounded, and not always concerned with formal unity, early African American novels contain a multitude of voices.

In this regard, few novels demonstrate as much heterogeneity as *Clotel* (1853). As in *The American Fugitive in Europe*, Brown prefaces his novel with a version of his 1847 slave narrative; and the novel itself draws on lengthy quotations from newspaper pieces, proslavery sermons, legal documents, and a host of literary sources, including British romantic poetry, Child's story "The Quadroons" (1842), and Thomas Jefferson's writings. John Ernest argues that such materials encourage readers to think like historians, to encounter evidence firsthand so as to resist ideological bias. The novel opens with a traditional abolitionist scene in which Clotel is separated from her mother and sister during a slave auction. That Clotel is beautiful and nearly white announces the controversial topics of passing and miscegenation. Moreover, by making Clotel a daughter of Jefferson, Brown dramatizes the hypocrisy of United States freedom and the intimate role of blacks in American history.

More theoretically, debates on a Mississippi plantation assert the philosophical, political, legal, and religious claims of blacks, though Brown's novel remains predominantly committed to stories that cross the color line. A slave turns out to be a white German immigrant illegally sold into bondage. Clotel's sister, Althesa, is married to a white man who treats her and their two daughters well. Clotel herself and her white lover live happily together and have a daughter, Mary; and Clotel later passes for a white man in a manner inspired by the Crafts. Yet if Brown dismantles racial dualisms and envisions a nation of mixed-race families, he also shows how overbearing the power of racism and slavery is. Althesa's husband dies and the daughters are sold as concubines, though they die before they can be violated. Clotel's lover marries a vindictive white woman, who uses Mary as a servant out of spite. Brown calls attention to social distinctions between light-skinned and dark-skinned blacks, especially when Clotel, along with Althesa and her daughters, become tragic mulatto figures. Having returned to Virginia to free Mary, Clotel drowns herself in sight of the White House rather than be recaptured. Only Mary survives with a chance for happiness, and that is overseas. After the death of her French husband, she reencounters the fugitive slave rebel George, a manly hero in the model of Stowe's George Harris and Douglass's Madison Washington (from "The Heroic Slave"), except that George in Brown's novel is passing as a white man in England. Their sentimental reunion offers some hope, though Brown reminds his readers that Mary and George cannot return to America except as fugitives. With its many inserted documents, multiple characters and plot strands, and ambivalent perspectives on racial mixing and nationality, *Clotel* is less a portrait of an individual psyche than a panorama of a culture torn by slavery, less a traditional slave narrative than a novel in the rough.

More than *Clotel*, *The Bondwoman's Narrative* reads like a conventional nineteenth-century novel. Crafts does draw on the slave narrative form: the narrator, Hannah, describes her journey from bondage to freedom, and much of the story seems based on what Crafts in her preface calls "plain unvarnished truth" (3). Yet the book's politics are decidedly turbulent when compared to slave autobiographies of the time. Hannah is loyal to her kind mistress, who turns out to be a tragic mulatto; and as if to denigrate the majority of slaves, Hannah decides to escape only when her new master tries to pair her with a brutal field hand. Such departures from abolitionist orthodoxy may help to explain why *The Bondwoman's Narrative* went unpublished during a time in which black writers depended on the antislavery press, a possibility strengthened by the fact that the novel is so accomplished. Crafts's style, plotting, and patterns of allusion – as well as the contents of her (probable) master's library – suggest a knowledge of sentimental and gothic traditions, which Crafts sets in animating tension. Seemingly nurturing domestic spaces conceal or are penetrated by the horrors of slavery. The benevolent feelings of sentimentality slide into the sensationalism of gothic haunting, violence, and sexual danger. Unlike *Incidents in the Life of a Slave Girl*, sentimentalism finally wins out when Hannah is reunited with her mother, marries, and becomes a teacher in the North.

Webb's *The Garies and Their Friends* has a more vexed relationship with sentimentality. On the one hand, Webb dwells on the conventional threat that racism poses to domestic values. On the other hand, *The Garies and Their Friends* is original in its extensive critique of Northern racism, focus on black economic uplift, and attention to aesthetics. Born and raised in Philadelphia with connections to the prestigious Forten family, Webb witnessed both the possibilities and challenges of African American upward mobility. After his business failed in 1854, Webb traveled with his wife Mary to England, where she gave dramatic readings (including excerpts from Henry Wadsworth Longfellow's popular poem *Hiawatha* [1855] and a piece written for her by Stowe, who also provided a prefatory letter for *The Garies and Their Friends*). Webb published his novel in London, where it sold moderately well, though it remained largely unnoticed in America, perhaps because it, like *The Bondwoman's Narrative*, does not always conform to abolitionist conventions. The Georgia plantation where the story begins is a relatively pleasant place, and the master Clarence Garie actually fulfills his promise to marry Emily, his nearly white slave. The problems start when they move to Philadelphia and encounter an array of racist practices – social exclusion, educational segregation, job discrimination, and mob violence. By explicitly discussing miscegenation and black militancy, Webb takes up topics often submerged in abolitionist discourse. He also condemns passing with a psychological depth that anticipates the work of Charles Chesnutt, James Weldon Johnson, and Nella Larsen. Webb's depiction of Northern racism has the structural insights of sociological analysis, while his rich physical descriptions, sophisticated tonal shifts, and attention to the role of aesthetics in black life opens the novel to diverse modes of literary analysis. For these and other reasons, *The Garies and Their Friends* may have more in common with postbellum novels than with antebellum antislavery fiction.

Our Nig also focuses on racism in the North, though its plainer style and economic perspective differ from *The Garies and Their Friends*. Like Jacobs, Wilson uses a pseudonym to tell her story, though she does so in a third-person voice that occasionally slips into the first person. *Our Nig* describes the trials of Frado, born to a black father and white mother and sent to work as an indentured servant for a white New England family. The willful Frado suffers under the cruel Mrs. Bellmont and her daughter but also receives some protection from whites who help her toward Christian conversion. Wilson draws on sentimental traditions and quotes liberally from popular poets of the time, though – as Xiomara Santamarina emphasizes – *Our Nig* is less concerned with demonstrating the literary accomplishments of blacks and more committed to exposing the interrelations of economic and racial oppression. Insisting on the value of physical labor, Wilson follows Sojourner Truth in cutting against the middle-class values of so many abolitionists, white and black. Frado even takes up with and is abandoned by an abolitionist lecturer-conman who pretends to be a fugitive slave. Realistically portraying Frado's struggles as a member of the black working poor, Wilson begins and ends by asking her "colored brethren" to support her literary work (287).

Whereas *Clotel* at the start of the 1850s concludes with transatlantic possibilities, *Blake* at the end of the decade imagines a cisatlantic plot. Wilson J. Moses and Robert S. Levine have shown that Martin Delany's international black separatism was well established by the time he wrote *Blake*. In *The Condition, Elevation, Emigration, and Destiny of the Colored People of the United States* (1852), he attacks racism within the antislavery movement and advocates emigration to Central America. In 1859, he traveled to West Africa to secure land for a potential black settlement, a trip later described in his *Official Report of the Niger Valley Exploring Party* (1861). As early as 1849, when some Southerners advocated annexing Cuba as a slave state, Delany encouraged Cuban slaves to establish a black government and spark hemispheric emancipation.

Blake envisions such a possibility. Serialized between 1859 and 1862 in *The Weekly Anglo-African* (and also *The Anglo-African Magazine*), the novel focuses on Henrico

Blacus (also called Henry Blake), a free West Indian sailor kidnapped and enslaved in Louisiana. Blake escapes and travels through the United States organizing a shadowy slave rebellion. He then sails to Cuba to free his wife and joins a plot to overthrow the slaveholding Spanish government, making *Blake* both an abolitionist and an anti-colonial novel. Delany plays somewhat loosely with chronology and Cuban culture, though he bases his fiction on historical facts, most notably in his portrayal of Placido, the Cuban poet and political rebel who was executed in 1844. What we have of *Blake* ends before the revolution, but signs of upheaval are everywhere. The last available line is spoken by a Nat Turner figure: "Woe be unto those devils of whites, I say!" (313). Formally, *Blake* is not particularly original, but it is as ideologically radical as anything in the period. Delany embraces violent rebellion and the birth of a black nation, not in Liberia (the preferred choice of most colonizationists), but rather on an island just off the United States from whence a broader revolution might spread.

The African American Press

Slave narratives and novels may rightfully dominate the study of antebellum black literature, if only because scholars tend to prefer long works written by identifiable authors in traditional literary forms such as fiction and autobiography. Writings in the African American press before the Civil War are by contrast often anonymous, ephemeral, journalistic, and difficult to mobilize in overarching arguments. Meredith McGill has shown that this was generally true for most antebellum newspapers and magazines, which borrowed heavily from each other (and transatlantic sources) while covering a vast range of subjects. It is difficult to conceptualize, let alone trace, the sprawling networks of antebellum print culture, though this does not diminish – and, indeed, attests to – the important role that the black press played in the 1850s renaissance of black letters.

As the historians Frankie Hutton, Penelope Bullock, and Armistead Pride have shown, African Americans sporadically edited newspapers and magazines beginning in the late 1820s, though the decade before the Civil War saw the emergence of more stable enterprises. These included Louis Putnam's *Colored Man's Journal* (1851–1861), W.J.C. Pennington's *The Aliened American* (1852–1856), the AME Church's *The Christian Recorder* (1852–1860), and Mary Shadd Cary and Samuel Ringgold Ward's *The Provincial Freeman* (published in Canada from 1853–1857). Led by Bishop Daniel Payne, the AME Church's *Repository of Religion and Literature and of Science and Art* (1858–1863) was especially committed to intellectual topics, as was Thomas Hamilton and James McCune Smith's *The Anglo-African Magazine* (1859–1860). Most prominently, Douglass edited the *North Star* (1847–1851), later renamed *Frederick Douglass's Paper* (1851–1859) and then transformed into *Douglass' Monthly* (1859–1860). Driven by increasing literacy rates, technological advances, antislavery activism, and (as Elizabeth McHenry has emphasized) organizational structures within the black community such as churches, fraternities, vigilance committees, national conventions, and literary societies, the black press achieved new reach and sophistication during the 1850s.

Frances Smith Foster has pointed out that any generalizations about the African American press require some qualification. African American editors and writers were particularly dedicated to abolitionism and racial equality, though they also wrote on science, art, religion, entertainment, fashion, and travel. Middle-class sensibilities emphasized Christian morals, economic uplift, and conventional gender roles, though there were also plenty of exceptions: humorists undermined social pretensions; laborers asserted their class consciousness; women such as Cary, Mary Bibb, Frances Ellen Watkins Harper, and Charlotte Forten Grimké entered the public sphere. Articles were local and global, original and reprinted. Publications tended to be based around urban centers, though they also appeared on the frontier (for instance, *Mirror of the Times* and *The Pacific Appeal* were published in San Francisco). It is difficult to define the African American press precisely, for black editors often collaborated with whites and relied on subscriptions and donations from white readers, while many African American writers published in the white press (and not only in antislavery organs). Most importantly, even as it sought to convince a racist nation of black capabilities, the African American press also focused on issues within the freeman community. As McCune Smith wrote for *Frederick Douglass's Paper* in an 1852 sketch, "The Black News-Vender," African American writers and readers avidly participated in "the Republic of Letters" (190).

The African American press of the 1850s supported African American literature in a number of ways. Most basically, it provided a relatively open venue for beginning and established writers. If the white antislavery press such as Garrison's *Liberator* and the *National Anti-slavery Standard* tended to present a unified abolitionist front focused solely on the issue of slavery, the African American press was more likely to air dissent and voice more radical opinions. Editors tended to be more comfortable with militancy, black nationalism, and critiques of Northern racism. It is not surprising that *Blake* was serialized in the African American press, or that when Delany asked Garrison to help him publish the novel in book form, nothing came of the request. It also makes sense that William Wells Brown published *Miralda, or the Beautiful Quadroon* (1860–1861), a more radical version of *Clotel*, in the *Weekly Anglo-African*. More than white abolitionist outlets, the African American press addressed an array of cultural and intellectual topics, further providing black writers opportunities for creative expression. Author of *America and Other Poems* (1853), James Whitfield published his verse in the African American press. So too did Harper, whose *Poems on Miscellaneous Subjects* appeared in 1854, and whose early short story, "The Two Offers" (1859), came out in the *Anglo-African Magazine*, which also published *Blake*.

Not only did African American newspapers and magazines host a range of writings by black Americans, they also dramatically broadened and linked communities of readers and authors. As letters to the editor make clear, the African American press reached a transnational, multiracial, variously educated, and ideologically diverse audience. It also served as a real and virtual community for antebellum

African American intellectuals. Douglass's sustained work as an editor suggests how interwoven such relationships were. He co-edited the *North Star* with Delany in an office just below a reading room where Jacobs worked (and may have begun *Incidents in the Life of a Slave Girl*). Douglass also published Wells Brown's letters from Europe, along with works from such writers as Whitfield, Harper, Forten, and William Nell (whose landmark history, *Colored Patriots of the American Revolution*, appeared in 1855). In the pages of his paper, Douglass feuded with Ward (over emigration), Garnet (over violent resistance), Delany (over *Uncle Tom's Cabin*), and Truth (over religious views). Douglass also employed McCune Smith as a correspondent and asked him to write the introduction to *My Bondage and My Freedom*. In doing so, Douglass joined forces with the preeminent African American intellectual of the period.

As John Stauffer has shown, Smith powerfully exemplifies the sophistication of the African American press. Born in New York City, Smith attended the same high school as Crummell, Ward, and Garnet. He later earned three degrees from Glasgow University, returned to New York as a prominent physician, and published in an array of disciplines. In his work for *Frederick Douglass's Paper* and *The Anglo-African Magazine*, Smith wrote articles on Nicaragua and the West Indies, the Hungarian and Haitian revolutions, Jefferson's theories of race, the medical condition of prostitutes, and the accomplishments of the chess champion Paul Morphy (whom Smith suspected was part black). Smith's learning is everywhere apparent – in his multilingual allusions, cultivated prose, and references to science, art, and history. His review of *Moby-Dick* is one of the first to read the novel as a political allegory; and of particular interest is "Heads of the Colored People" (1852–1853), a series of sketches describing different classes of African Americans, including not only inventors and teachers, but also bootblacks and laundresses. Partly a satire on racial sciences such as phrenology, partly an exercise in sociological types, partly a literary work in the tradition of Dickens, and partly an occasion to ruminate on everything from class and race to cosmology and the African American press itself, the wildly experimental "Heads of the Colored People" retains Smith's distinctive voice as it moves restlessly between genres and narratives.

One of Smith's sketches, "The Editor" (1853), can serve as a conclusion that highlights the struggles and achievements of the African American press and the 1850s renaissance of black letters as a whole. Smith wrote (partly with Douglass in mind):

> In the transition state of colored-Americandom, the editor must be an amphibious animal, half orator, half editor; he must tear the fibres of his brain one way to adorn his columns for the inspection of the most fastidious and merciless newspaper critics in the world – I mean colored Americans; and then, he must tear the fibres of his brain another way, to coax, beg, or wheedle money enough out of chance audiences to print his paper and keep a coat on his back. (213)

The 1850s was indeed a transitional state for African American writers moving from the slave narrative to the novel, from decentralized print culture toward a more modern press, from three centuries of enslavement in America toward emancipation and a new set of struggles. Black writers of the decade were in many ways (as Smith puts it) "amphibious" in that they worked in multiple genres, often blurring categorical distinctions. Almost always under extreme financial pressure and lacking cultural capital, they were especially influenced – for better and worse – by rapidly changing conditions in the abolitionist movement and the publishing industry. They were also torn between various audiences – whites on both sides of the Atlantic and an increasingly connected and diverse black readership. As slave narrators, African American novelists, and African American intellectuals of the period show, great pressures combined with great hopes led to astonishing literary production in the decade before the Civil War.

Bibliography

Andrews, William L. "The 1850s: The First Afro-American Literary Renaissance." In *Literary Romanticism in America*. Ed. William L. Andrews. Baton Rouge: Louisiana State University Press, 1981. 38–60.

Andrews, William L. *To Tell a Free Story: The First Century of Afro-American Autobiography, 1760–1865*. Urbana: University of Illinois Press, 1986.

Brown, William Wells. *The American Fugitive in Europe: Sketches of Places and People Abroad*. New York: Negro Universities Press, 1969.

Bruce, Dickson D., Jr. *The Origins of African American Literature, 1680–1865*. Charlottesville: University Press of Virginia, 2001.

Bullock, Penelope L. *The Afro-American Periodical Press, 1838–1909*. Baton Rouge: Louisiana State University Press, 1981.

Crafts, Hannah. *The Bondwoman's Narrative*. Ed. Henry Louis Gates, Jr. New York: Warner Books, 2002.

Delany, Martin. *Blake, or the Huts of America*. Boston, MA: Beacon, 1970.

Douglass, Frederick. *Frederick Douglass: Autobiographies*. New York: Library of America, 1994.

Ernest, John. *Resistance and Reformation in Nineteenth-Century African-American Literature*. Jackson: University Press of Mississippi, 1995.

Foster, Frances Smith. "A Narrative of the Interesting Origins and (Sometimes) Surprising Developments of African-American Print Culture." *American Literary History* 17.4 (2005): 714–40.

Foster, Frances Smith. *Witnessing Slavery: The Development of Ante-bellum Slave Narratives, Second Edition*. Madison: University of Wisconsin Press, 1994.

Gates, Henry Louis, Jr. *Figures in Black: Words, Signs, and the "Racial" Self*. New York: Oxford University Press, 1987.

Gilbert, Olive with Sojourner Truth. *The Narrative of Sojourner Truth*. Ed. Margaret Washington. New York: Vintage Books, 1993.

Gilroy, Paul. *The Black Atlantic: Modernity and Double Consciousness*. Cambridge, MA: Harvard University Press, 1993.

Hutton, Frankie. *The Early Black Press in America, 1827–1860*. Westport, CT: Greenwood, 1993.

Levine, Robert S. *Martin Delany, Frederick Douglass, and the Politics of Representative Identity*. Chapel Hill: University of North Carolina Press, 1997.

McGill, Meredith. *American Literature and the Culture of Reprinting, 1834–1853*. Philadelphia: University of Pennsylvania Press. 2003.

McHenry, Elizabeth. *Forgotten Readers: Recovering the Lost History of African-American Literary Societies*. Durham, NC: Duke University Press, 2002.

Moses, Wilson J. *Afrotopia: The Roots of African American Popular History*. Cambridge: Cambridge University Press, 1998.

Nelson, Dana D. *The Word in Black and White: Reading "Race" in American Literature, 1638–1867*. New York: Oxford University Press, 1992.

Peterson, Carla L. *"Doers of the Word": African-American Women Speakers and Writers in the North (1830–1880)*. New York: Rutgers University Press, 1995.

Pride, Armistead and Clint Wilson. *A History of the Black Press*. Washington, DC: Howard University Press, 1997.

Santamarina, Xiomara. *Belabored Professions: Narratives of African American Working Womanhood*. Chapel Hill: University of North Carolina Press, 2005.

Smith, James McCune. *The Works of James McCune Smith: Black Intellectual and Abolitionist*. Ed. John Stauffer. Oxford: Oxford University Press, 2006.

Stauffer, John. *The Black Hearts of Men: Radical Abolitionists and the Transformation of Race*. Cambridge, MA: Harvard University Press, 2002.

Sundquist, Eric J. *To Wake the Nations: Race in the Making of American Literature*. Cambridge, MA: Harvard University Press, 1993.

Tamarkin, Elisa. *Anglophilia: Deference, Devotion, and Antebellum America*. Chicago: University of Chicago Press, 2008.

Ward, Samuel Ringgold. *Autobiography of a Fugitive Negro: His Anti-slavery Labors in the United States, Canada, and England*. New York: Arno Press and the *New York Times*, 1968.

Wilson, Harriet. *Our Nig; Or, Sketches from the Life of a Free Black*. In *Three Classic African-American Novels*. Ed. William L. Andrews. New York: Mentor Books, 1990. 285–365.

8

African American Literary Nationalism

Robert S. Levine

US literary nationalism has traditionally been understood as an effort by early national writers, editors, and cultural commentators to encourage the production of a distinctively "American" literature equal to or better than British literature. But a complicating issue in any simple story of US literary nationalism is the idea of the nation itself. Given the sectional divide on slavery, Northerners and Southerners had sometimes conflicting views on the goals and practices of literary nationalism. Black literary nationalism emerged in relation to US literary nationalism and shared some of its broad aspirations, but the complications of the latter pale in comparison to those of the former. For example, what is the "nation" in African American literary nationalism? Is it the US nation, the nation within a nation (e.g., the black community within the US nation), or an African diasporic black "nationality" unbounded by national borders? Whereas most American literary nationalists regarded the US nation as essentially white, for African American literary nationalists race was an additional complicating factor. For some, African American literary nationalism was about political and cultural notions of race, and for others biological or spiritual notions of race. Some African American literary nationalists linked themselves to the US nation and others thought about racial distinctiveness in terms of the mystical Ethiopianism of Psalms 68: 31: "Ethiopia shall soon stretch out her hands unto God." The essential point is that early national and antebellum African American literary nationalism had an uneasy and complex relation to race and nation (see Stuckey, Moses, and Glaude). The very complexities and tensions within African American literary nationalism helped to inspire African American literary production.

Before addressing these complexities head-on, however, it would be useful to consider what has become a familiar story of the "rise" of African American literary nationalism. As is well known, American literary nationalism took shape during the 1780s and 1790s and was re-energized by the War of 1812 and the founding in 1815 of the *North American Review*, which published a number of calls for a distinctively American literature. In traditional accounts, African American literary nationalism took its own distinct shape somewhat belatedly in 1827, the year that New York State abolished slavery, when William Whipper and John Russwurm founded the first African American newspaper, *Freedom's Journal*, in New York City. As announced in the opening issue, the goal of the newspaper was to provide African Americans with a much needed forum for literary and political expression, and the editors regularly featured essays on neglected black writers. An article on Phillis Wheatley in the "Original Communications" column of March 23, 1827, for instance, celebrated a poet "who by her writings has reflected honour upon our name, and character, and demonstrated to an unbelieving world that genius dwells not alone in skins of whitish hue." Similarly, in "The Surprising Influence of Prejudice," which appeared in the issue of May 18, 1827, the anonymous author surveyed the accomplishments of the many black writers – Wheatley, Francis Williams, Quobna Ottabah Cugoano, Olaudah Equiano, Ignatius Sancho, and Benjamin Banneker, among others – who had been able to achieve literary excellence despite whites' anti-black prejudices. The editors and their contributors asked readers to commit themselves to the project of establishing a great African American literature, even as they conceded the difficulties blacks faced in finding publishers and readers. In the December 19, 1828 issue of the newspaper, David Walker, a contributing editor and sales agent, pointed to "the disadvantages the people of Colour labor under, by the neglect of literature." Just as US Americans feared that they would be mocked by the British if they failed to produce a great literature, so Walker argued that blacks would be mocked by whites if they failed to display their capacity for literary achievement, insisting that it was precisely whites' "derision, violence, and oppression" that made it incumbent upon African Americans to work "for the acquirement of both literature and property."

As Walker's linking of literature and property might suggest, African American literary nationalism had much to do with the project of black elevation in the United States. Whipper in particular believed that blacks who were respected by whites would have a better chance of surviving and even prospering in US society. Aware of the odds against gaining that respect in the foreseeable future, black literary nationalists connected with *Freedom's Journal* and other antebellum African American newspapers additionally argued that literature would help blacks to strengthen their own community. Anticipating Benedict Anderson's influential claim about the connections between print and community, Whipper and Russwurm (and Walker as contributing editor and sales agent) maintained that *Freedom's Journal* would unite currently scattered and fragmented free blacks through the medium of print. As the editors stated in the inaugural issue of March 16, 1827: "It is our earnest wish to make our Journal a medium of intercourse between our brethren in the different states of this great confederacy." The stronger and more unified the black community, the editors believed, the better it could resist white oppression.

There was also much antislavery and antiracist writing in *Freedom's Journal* and other antebellum black newspapers, to the point that antislavery itself came to form a crucial (but hardly sole) component of black literary nationalism. As suggested by both the literary and uplift dimension of the newspaper, the editors of *Freedom's Journal* were not simply reaching out to black readers. They hoped as well that whites would see in the writings of African Americans like the poet-slave George Horton (the subject of a number of articles) the humanity of the enslaved and disenfranchised blacks. Again and again, the editors of antebellum black journals underscored the important role that such journals could play in demonstrating that blacks were just as capable as whites of producing worthy literature. The politics of demonstration, which became an important component of African American literary nationalism, thus served the interrelated purposes of black uplift and antislavery. While some black editors and writers were inspired by eighteenth-century notions of literary nationalism, which held that each nation or race had its own distinct gifts, the editors of *Freedom's Journal* (and most subsequent antebellum African American newspapers and journals) emphasized that black literary expression could best be understood in relation to established literary and cultural traditions, whether in the United States, England, Europe, the greater Americas, or Africa.

Despite the occasional references to Haiti and Africa, the editors of *Freedom's Journal*, at least in its first year of publication, remained intent on linking African American literary nationalism to their project of black elevation in the United States. But a debate that came to the fore in 1828 and 1829 issues of *Freedom's Journal* was whether the newspaper should be understood as US nationalist or African diasporic. For Whipper, the journal was intended to improve the condition of African Americans in the United States, and he remained committed to an African American literary nationalism that would help blacks to become a more vital force within the free North. Russwurm initially shared Whipper's US orientation, but the intractability of white racism led him to identify with black Africans over white Americans and ultimately to renounce his connections to the US nation. In late 1828 and 1829, Russwurm began to use the journal to advocate African American emigration to Liberia, even as Whipper held steady with his own project of black elevation in the United States. With the newspaper editors divided between themselves on the matter of race and nation, the newspaper folded in 1829.

Tensions between diasporic and national perspectives would remain central to African American literary nationalism. Nevertheless, it would be fair to say that most black nationalists of the antebellum period were primarily concerned with improving the lot of African Americans in the United States. Despite the dissolution of *Freedom's Journal*, African American newspapers and literary expression continued to be regarded as crucial to the cause of abolitionism and black uplift. At the annual black national conventions commencing in the early 1830s, there were regular discussions about the need to establish a national black newspaper or journal in order to further the project of black uplift. During the late 1830s and early 1840s, the New York-based *Colored American* served as such a forum for a limited number of readers. In 1847, Frederick Douglass established the *North Star*, which he hoped would become blacks' main literary and political forum and have a considerably larger national reach. Concerned that William Lloyd Garrison's antislavery newspaper, the *Liberator*, mainly conveyed the perspective of its white editor, Douglass argued that blacks needed to make their own arguments and demonstrate their own literary and editorial skills, though not necessarily as separatists. In an important statement of his own black literary nationalism, Douglass declared in the inaugural December 3, 1847 issue of the *North Star*:

> It is evident we must be our own representatives and advocates, not exclusively, but peculiarly – not distinct from, but in connection with our white friends. In the grand struggle for liberty and equality now waging, it is meet, right and essential that there should arise in our ranks authors and editors, as well as orators, for it is in these capacities that the most permanent good can be rendered to our cause.

An inevitable result of the African American literary nationalism linked to such newspapers as *Freedom's Journal*, the *Colored American*, and the *North Star* was precisely what Douglass envisioned: an upsurge of black literary production, particularly in the form of the essays, letters, and reportage best suited to these journals. Inspired by the black newspaper and convention movement, and the burgeoning abolitionism of the period, there was an upsurge of other forms of African American writing as well, such as the slave narrative. Douglass's 1845 *Narrative* was widely read in the Northeast and in Europe, and the popularity of slave narratives by Douglass, William Wells Brown, Josiah Henson, and many others, led the white minister Ephraim Peabody to declare in the July 1849 issue of the *Christian Examiner* that slave narratives were "among the most remarkable productions of the age, – remarkable as being pictures of slavery by the slave, … and not less remarkable as a vivid exhibition of the force and working of the native love of freedom in the individual mind."

Slave narratives and essays were hardly the only forms of literary achievement inspired by the African American literary nationalism of the antebellum period. There was also a rise in history, poetry, and religious writings, and an increase in the number of pamphlets addressing the condition of the free and enslaved blacks. Key works included Maria Stewart's *Productions of Mrs. Maria W. Stewart* (1835), Hosea Easton's *A Treatise on the Intellectual Character and Civil and Political Condition of the Colored People of the U. States* (1838), James Pennington's *Text Book of the Origin and History, &c. &c. of the Colored People* (1841), *The Poetical Works of George M. Horton* (1845), and Henry Highland Garnet's *The Past and Present Condition, and the Destiny of the Colored Race* (1848). The 1850s were a particularly important decade for African American writings, and thus for African American literary nationalism. William Wells Brown's *Clotel*, the first African American novel, was published in 1853, and Brown also published travel books, lectures, and a play during that decade. The 1850s saw the publication of several other significant African American novels, such as Frank J. Webb's *The Garies and Their Friends* (1857) and Harriet Wilson's *Our Nig* (1859); major volumes of poetry, such as James Whitfield's *America and Other Poems* (1853) and Frances Harper's *Poems on Miscellaneous Subjects* (1854); influential historical and political writings, such as Martin Delany's *The Condition, Elevation, Emigration and Destiny of the Colored People of the United States* (1852) and James Holly's *A Vindication of the Capacity of the Negro Race for Self-Government and Civilized Progress* (1857); along with such striking slave narratives (or autobiographies) as Douglass's *My Bondage and My Freedom* (1855) and Harriet Jacobs's *Incidents in the Life of a Slave Girl* (1861).

The relatively familiar story of black literary nationalism that I have been sketching in these opening pages provides a rather upbeat account of the rise of African American writing from the first African American newspaper to the glorious achievement of a "Literary Renaissance," as William Andrews has dubbed African American writing of the 1850s, with a bow to F.O. Matthiessen's *American Renaissance* (1941). But this story is not quite as optimistic as it might seem. Even as African American literary nationalists sought to demonstrate that blacks were just as capable as whites of producing great literature, and thus were the equals of whites, the Supreme Court of the United States nevertheless declared in its infamous 1857 Dred Scott decision that blacks were inferior to whites and could never become US citizens. In this respect, the work of African American literary nationalism remained unfinished up to the time of the Civil War.

The very concept of "unfinished" work conveys a sense of group purpose and goals, but it needs to be underscored that the project of African American literary nationalism was ultimately not as coherent or unified as some literary historians have presented it – or as I have been presenting it thus far. As Frances Smith Foster argues (in her essay with Kimberly Green in this volume and independently elsewhere), the notion that the 1827 inauguration of *Freedom's Journal* should be taken as the starting point for a history of African American literary nationalism is highly arbitrary and in crucial ways inaccurate. At the very least, she maintains, we need to push the starting point back several decades. The late eighteenth and early nineteenth century saw the rise of black reading societies (see McHenry), Masonic organizations, mutual aid societies, and black Methodist churches, and all of these institutions contributed to the production of African American writings, including black Masonic texts by Prince Hall and religious writings by Reverend Richard Allen, that are not normally regarded as integral to an African American literary renaissance of the 1850s. Viewed from this perspective, the 1817 founding of the African Methodist Episcopal Book Concern (the first known African American publishing house) was just as important as the founding of *Freedom's Journal*. Writings connected to the African Methodist Episcopal Church addressed issues seemingly disconnected from the antislavery and uplift agenda that would come to be central to *Freedom's Journal*, the *North Star*, and *Frederick Douglass' Paper*, and suggest a religious orientation for some expressions of African American literary nationalism.

When we look beyond the early black newspapers that were edited by black male leaders, African American literary nationalism begins to seem less political, less abolitionist, and more varied in terms of male and female voices. It also seems less about the politics of demonstration (with an emphasis on those texts produced to demonstrate blacks' humanity and capabilities to whites) than about the pragmatics of creating and sustaining black community (with an emphasis on those black texts written mostly for blacks). In her revisionary account, Foster maintains that pre-1827 African American print culture "originated from self-interest, from the desires of African

Americans to communicate their experiences and philosophies, to record the words and ideas most precious to their own psychic and spiritual (as well as physical or political) survival, and to create and to preserve their history for themselves and for others" (723). Crucial to Foster's conception here is multiplicity, the idea of a variety of "experiences and philosophies" which are conveyed to a variety of audiences, many of whom thought of the "nation" in relation to black family and religion. An account that begins with *Freedom's Journal* presents a seemingly monolithic or unbroken notion of the rise of African American literary nationalism (despite the fact that the editors of that journal were in conflict over the black nation), while an account that begins in the late eighteenth century offers varied ideas about the terms and goals of African American literary nationalism, and destabilizes the notion of what is "African American," "literary," and "nationalist." If we take Phillis Wheatley as an important progenitor of black literary nationalism, we would have to consider the work of such important, but still obscure, African American women poets and essay writers of the early nineteenth century as Ann Plato, Jarena Lee, and Rebecca Cox Jackson, who are not easily read in relation to the major works of the 1850s by Douglass, Delany, and others (see Bassard). And if we take Olaudah Equiano's *Interesting Narrative* (1789) as a foundational text for the popular African American slave narratives of the 1840s and 1850s, early national and antebellum African American writing begins to look more diasporic and global.

In short, we might focus our attention less on the "rise" of African American literary nationalism than on multiple traditions and debates within African American literary nationalism. By the late 1840s and 1850s, leading participants in those debates were Douglass and Delany, who offered very different perspectives on the nation, the racial, and the literary. Douglass attempted to link African American literary nationalism to the project of black uplift and antislavery in the United States, while Delany more insistently looked beyond the US nation to blacks of the Southern Americas and Africa. But before turning to this revealing cultural debate on black literary nationalism, it would be useful to consider the work of David Walker, which addressed competing or conflicting strains of African American literary nationalism in ways that look forward to the debates between Douglass and Delany. A concluding discussion of Maria Stewart will press us to consider other perspectives as well.

David Walker's *Appeal* (1829) is one of the great works of African American literary nationalism, drawing on the inspirational history of black churches and self-help organizations in the United States. As suggested by the book's full title, *David Walker's Appeal, in Four Articles, Together with a Preamble, to the Coloured Citizens of the World, but in Particular, Very Expressly, to Those of the United States of America*, Walker seeks to legitimate blacks' claims to a US national narrative while simultaneously making a transnational, community-creating appeal to blacks in the Americas and throughout the world. And yet more often than not, as signaled by his opening reference to "*My dearly beloved Brethren and Fellow Citizens*," Walker's concerns are centered on African Americans in the United States. Because there are dramatic moments when Walker sensationally calls for black violence against whites ("kill or be killed," he famously declares), we tend to forget that much of the short book is about black elevation in the United States, focusing on the various black institutions that have historically worked to sustain black community. As a participant in the early African American newspaper movement, Walker cites articles from *Freedom's Journal* and its successor, *The Rights of All*, to show how black newspapers have opposed the racist work of the white colonizationists. He also suggests how the circulation of black newspapers can create African American community by emphasizing his own success as he circulates from place to place, state to state, to pass along his message of black resistance and community (see Levine, *Dislocating Race*, chap. 2). But perhaps his most essential point is that blacks need to learn how to read and write in order to contest whites' efforts to limit their freedom and diminish their humanity. Responding to Thomas Jefferson's remarks in *Notes on the State of Virginia* (1787) on how (white) Roman slaves were able to become notable writers while American (black) slaves have failed to distinguish themselves in the same way, Walker asserts, "Every body who has read history, knows, that as soon as a slave among the Romans obtained his freedom, he could rise to the greatest eminence in the State." And he remarks that anyone who has read US laws knows that blacks do not have similar opportunities. The "heart-rending" results of such racist exclusions were on display, Walker notes, when he recently "examined school-boys and young men of colour in different parts of the country, in the most simple parts of Murray's English Grammar, and not more than one in thirty was able to give a correct answer to my interrogations." In the most basic ways imaginable, Walker suggests, black literary nationalism, and the project of black elevation itself, is dependent upon what could be called black *literacy* nationalism.

As intent as Walker is on the situation of blacks in the United States, he looks beyond the nation's borders in an effort to develop black pride and identity, presenting a diasporic vision of the linkages among "all … coloured people under Heaven." Specifically, he discusses African Americans' close ties to "our brethren" in Haiti, proclaiming that the relatively new nation is "the glory of the blacks and terror of tyrants." Still, it is worth emphasizing that, perhaps even despite itself, the *Appeal* is inspired by the liberatory potential of Jefferson's revolutionary US nationalism, and thus to some extent anticipates Douglass's great speech of 1852, "What to the Slave Is the Fourth of July?" Like Walker's own text, Douglass's speech is torn between an anger at the nation's (and Jefferson's) failure to live up to the ideals of the Declaration and a commitment to Jefferson's ideals. Walker suggests his own anger and admiration in the closing pages of the *Appeal*, where he reprints the portion of the Declaration of Independence that calls for revolution when a "long train of abuses and usurpation" is imposed upon "one people." With his final remarks on the Declaration, Walker brings the focus back to the situation of African Americans. Nevertheless, there remains an animating tension in his rhetorically canny *Appeal* between nationalistic notions of "our country" and transnational or diasporic notions of "[our] *enslaved brethren all over the world*." The unresolved conflicts between nationalism and transnationalism, US citizenry and colored "citizenry," that ultimately energize the *Appeal* would continue to inform the creatively resilient black literary nationalism of the nineteenth century.

Walker was found dead at his Boston home under suspicious circumstances in 1830, but his *Appeal* lived on in the culture through blacks' efforts to circulate it during the 1830s and 1840s. In 1848 it was republished as part of *Walker's Appeal, with a Brief Sketch of His Life. By Henry Highland Garnet. And also Garnet's Address to the Slaves of the United States of America*, and Douglass called attention to this text by reprinting Garnet's "A Brief Sketch of the Life and Character of David Walker" in the July 14, 1848 issue of the *North Star*. It is appropriate that Douglass printed Garnet's tribute to Walker. In the tradition of Cornish, Walker, and other African Americans interested in the black press, Douglass's own African American literary nationalism was for many years expressed through his editing and circulating of black newspapers, and there was much in the *North Star* and *Frederick Douglass' Paper* (and Douglass's autobiographies) about the importance of literacy to black uplift and black nationalist identity. There was also much about the importance of nurturing African American literary writers. In a column by "Dion" in the September 23, 1853 *Frederick Douglass' Paper*, the contributor laments that "while American literature is rapidly growing into universal appreciation, the name of no colored American has as yet been blazoned upon its rolls of heraldry," and insists that blacks' best hope for the emergence of such a figure is by supporting various literary associations and enterprises "among our people," especially newspapers.

Douglass himself regularly wrote about the crucial contributions that black authors, editors, and orators could make to the cause of black elevation. Thus it is one of the great ironies of his career that he spent nearly four years championing Harriet Beecher Stowe's *Uncle Tom's Cabin* (1852) in his newspaper. Whereas Martin Delany maintained in the April 29, 1853 *Frederick Douglass' Paper* that Stowe opportunistically "draughted on all of the best fugitive slave narratives" in order to publish a book that made her wealthy and furthered her desire to colonize the free blacks to Africa, Douglass saw Stowe as highly sympathetic to the cause of black elevation in the United States, and in the April 1, 1853 *Frederick Douglass' Paper* asserted in the mode of a non-exclusionary African American literary nationalist that the "the field" must be "open" to any writer "who is moved to do anything on our behalf." It should be emphasized that despite Douglass's championing of Stowe, he was capable of writing as diasporically as Delany. In his only work of fiction, the novella "The Heroic Slave" (1853), he celebrates the 1841 slave rebellion on the *Creole* led by Madison Washington, and in the novella's final scene depicts blacks of the Bahamas finding common cause with rebellious ex-slaves of the United States. In his writings on West Indies emancipation, particularly his 1857 "The Significance of Emancipation," and in his writings on Haiti in the months before the Civil War, Douglass similarly expressed a fraternal alliance with blacks of the Southern Americas.

Still, the debate between Douglass and Delany on the virtues of Stowe's *Uncle Tom's Cabin* emerged as a key moment in African American literary nationalism of the antebellum period (see Levine, *Martin Delany*, chap. 2). In a black national convention held in Rochester in 1853, Douglass called on participants to support *Frederick Douglass' Paper* as *the* national newspaper for African Americans; and as appropriate to a newspaper that had a large number of white subscribers, he advocated a literary nationalism of black uplift that resisted racial exclusivity. In the *Proceedings of the Colored National Convention*, published in *Frederick Douglass' Paper* and as a separate pamphlet, Douglass and his fellow participants conveyed a remarkably hopeful outlook for the possibility of social change in the United States, hailing Stowe's *Uncle Tom's Cabin* as a literary development that could only help the cause of black elevation, and was in its own way an important contribution to African American literary nationalism. The convention's resolution on Stowe's novel underscores that point, suggesting a very different perspective on literary nationalism from what had been enunciated at prior national black conventions: "Resolved. That we recognize in 'Uncle Tom's Cabin' a work plainly marked by the finger of God, lifting the veil of separation which has too long divided the sympathies of one class of the American people from another."

For Martin Delany and his supporters at the 1854 National Emigration of Colored People in Cleveland (which Delany himself had organized), such a view of African American writing in alliance with Stowe was willfully blind to the workings of white power. Convinced of blacks' racial distinctiveness and of the limits of the US nation, Delany and his fellow delegates set forth a view of black literary nationalism that was congruent with their advocacy of black emigration. It is worth emphasizing that the conference proceedings themselves, published in 1854 as *Proceedings of the National Emigration Convention of Colored People*, were presented as a crucial text in the development of such a literary nationalism, expressive of African Americans' true feelings: "Let every black person keep by him a copy of these Minutes, and hand them, in lieu of an argument, to his oppressor or well wisher, who may there read the living sentiments as they teemed from the black man's heart." A desire for a literature that conveys "the living sentiments as they teemed from the black man's heart" informs the report on black literary nationalism authored by the African American poet James Whitfield, whose 1853 *America*, dedicated to Martin Delany, can itself be taken as a key work of African American literary nationalism. Just as *America* has poems on black leaders and locales in the Southern Americas, Whitfield in his "Report on the Establishment of a Periodical, to Be the Organ of the Black and Colored Race on the American Continent," rejects the representativeness of *Frederick Douglass' Paper*, looks beyond the US nation to the Southern Americas, and imagines a diasporic racial connectiveness among peoples of color. His committee on publications calls for "a literary periodical, calculated to give a fair representation of the acquirements of the colored people," which would have "the ablest colored writers in both hemispheres … engaged as its regular contributors." In the tradition of *Freedom's Journal*, Whitfield declares that this new journal "would present to colored men of ability an inducement to write, which they do not now possess," elaborating "that a considerable portion of is patrons, as well as its contributors, will probably be from other countries." It would be fair to say that Whitfield, his committee, and the participants of the emigration convention regarded African American literary nationalism as a constituent of a larger black nationalism with only tangential connections to US literary nationalism.

Delany would shift back and forth on the question of black literary nationalism, at times embracing a global or diasporic vision of black cultural achievement, and at other times, particularly in the decade immediately after the Civil War, intent on keeping his focus on the situation of blacks in the United States. But at this 1854 convention he adopts a literary and political vision that is consistent with Whitfield's. In his 1854 "Political Destiny of the Colored Race on the American Continent," a speech presented over several hours to the Cleveland convention and published in the *Proceedings*, Delany provides acute political commentary on race relations in the United States and an eloquent pan-African vision of blacks' potentially regenerative role in the Americas. Celebrating blacks for their distinctiveness and difference, Delany proclaims: "The truth is, we are not identical with the Anglo-Saxon or any other race of the Caucasian or pure white type of the human family, and the sooner we know and acknowledge this truth, the better for ourselves and our posterity." Though he concedes that whites may have advantages in "mathematics, sculpture and architecture," and that with respect to the "arts and sciences" have made advances similar to their advances in other "enterprises," he ultimately sees blacks as more gifted in the arts, and he proclaims that "in languages, oratory, poetry, music, and painting, … there is no doubt but that the black race will yet instruct the world." In his 1852 *The Condition, Elevation, Emigration and Destiny of the Colored People of the World*, Delany makes similar claims about racial distinctiveness and potential literary achievement. In a chapter titled "Literary and Professional Colored Men and Woman," Delany presents African American literary nationalism, as Whitfield would in *Proceedings*, in a larger diasporic framework, focusing on the achievements of African American writers with emigrationist sympathies, such as Russwurm, Garnet, and Whitfield. Delany's interest in the Southern Americas culminated in his best known literary work, the serialized novel *Blake* (1859, 1861–1862), which imagines the possibility of a slave revolution throughout the Americas led by a black rebel with a political vision very much resembling Delany's own. The evidence suggests that Delany thought *Blake* could become the emigrationists' *Uncle Tom's Cabin*, but he was unable to find an interested New York publishing house and settled for serializing the novel in New York's *Weekly Anglo-African*.

Delany's and Whitfield's diasporic vision of black (literary) nationalism was shared by a number of other African Americans of the time. In his 1857 *A Vindication of the Capacity of the Negro Race*, James Holly similarly conceives of blacks in relation to the Southern Americas, imagining a black "nation" coming into its own with a base in Haiti: "A concentration and combination of the negro race, of the Western Hemisphere in Hayti, can produce just such a national development." Accordingly, he calls on African Americans to consider emigrating to the Southern Americas, "carrying with us such of the arts, sciences and genius of modern civilization, as we may gain from this hardy and enterprising Anglo-American race, in order to add to Haytian advancement." Here, African American literary nationalism is acknowledged as having important sources and inspirations in Western (or Anglo) traditions, which could then be put to the service of a larger diasporic literary nationalism in the Americas. William Wells Brown conveys a similarly diasporic account of black literary achievement in *The Black Man: His Antecedents, His Genius, and His Achievements* (1863), which he composed at a time when he was supporting Haitian emigration. In this book he celebrates the Cuban poet Placido, the French writer Alexandre Dumas, the Haitian emigrationist Holly, and the emigrationists Whitfield and Delany. He does have a short section on Douglass, but the overall book considers African American literary nationalism in the broadest possible national contexts. Nevertheless, as highlighted by the book's title, Brown shared much with Douglass, Delany, and Holly in neglecting the role that black women might play in the development of a black literary nationalism. Of the over 50 African American writers he considers, he mentions only three women: Phillis Wheatley, Frances Ellen Watkins (Harper), and Charlotte L. Forten.

Over the past several decades, the Schomburg Library of Nineteenth-Century Black Women Writers (published by Oxford University Press) has made available the remarkable literary and cultural work of African American women writers who were sometimes neglected in their own time. (For comprehensive studies of African American women writers, see Peterson and Santamarina.) Still, it is worth noting that most works by black women writers of the antebellum period did not self-consciously address African American literary nationalism, perhaps because most women were not in the public leadership roles that would have led them to make the sorts of pronouncements typical of Whipper, Douglass, and Delany. This is not to say that African American women failed to offer distinct pronouncements on black writing. Frances Ellen Watkins Harper concluded her 1854 *Poems* with a short essay, "The Colored People in America," in which she speaks of the importance of education and literacy, and extols the work of black newspaper editors as an example of blacks' ability to exert their literary influence in the United States: "We have papers edited by colored editors, which we may consider it an honor to possess, and a credit to sustain." African American women did work behind the scenes of a number of black newspapers, and in the late 1850s took on editorial roles in the newly formed *Christian Recorder*, which became a significant publishing outlet for African American women writers, serializing Julia C. Collins's novel, *The Curse of Caste; or the Slave Bride* (1865), along with three novels by Harper.

As Harper's essay suggests, the relative lack of public pronouncements does not mean that women were silent on the topic of African American literary nationalism, nor does it mean that they failed to assume important leadership roles in the culture. Women had a central place in educational and religious institutions, precisely the institutions that black male leaders argued were crucial to blacks' ability to achieve a broader rate of literacy and eventually a wider influence as writers. Of course, the act of publication itself could be taken as a commitment to African American literary nationalism. That is precisely the argument of Harriet Wilson, whose autobiographical *Our Nig; or, Sketches from the Life of a Free Black* (1859) is generally regarded as the first novel by an African American woman. In the preface and appendix, Wilson makes clear that she published her novel not only with the hope of gaining funds to help her ailing son, but also (in the manner of black newspaper editors) with the aim of creating a stronger sense of black community in the Northeast. As she remarks in the preface: "I sincerely appeal to my colored brethren universally for patronage, hoping they will not condemn this attempt by their sister to be erudite, but rally around me a faithful band of supporters and defenders." Along these same lines, Harriet Jacobs in *Incidents in the Life of a Slave Girl* (1861) remarks that black women writers are differently situated from white women writers, "whose purity has been sheltered from childhood," and that they therefore must rise to the occasion to tell sometimes uncomfortable and unhappy truths about "the evils of the world," even at the risk of alienating whites.

The African American woman writer, lecturer, and educator with the most sustained career during the pre-Civil War years is Maria Stewart, whose own work as a cultural worker intent on taking on "the evils of the world" was inspired by the black churches and educational institutions of the 1790s to the 1820s, the black newspaper movement of the late 1820s, and David Walker. In her 1831 "Religion and the Pure Principles of Morality," she praises "the most noble, fearless, and undaunted David Walker" as a presiding deity over her own black nationalist commitments. "Though David Walker sleeps," she remarks in her sermonic essay, "yet he lives, and his name shall be in everlasting remembrance." Marilyn Richardson observes that Stewart "drew from Walker's impassioned manifesto an ethic of resistance to physical and political oppression," but that she also "moved beyond Walker's influence … in insisting upon the right of women to take their place in the front ranks of black moral and political leadership" (19). In her most famous speech, "An Address, Delivered at the African Masonic Hall, Boston, Feb. 27, 1833," Stewart castigates black men for seemingly acquiescing to white supremacist culture, while again depicting Walker as a lone beacon of resistance: "But where is the man that has distinguished himself in these modern days by acting wholly in the defense of African rights and liberty? There was one, although he sleeps, his memory lives." And she calls on African Americans to commit themselves to precisely what Walker was arguing for in his *Appeal*: educational institutions that would contribute to the literacy of the rising generation of African Americans.

Among the ideas bequeathed by Walker to Stewart is the tension between a US nationalism and a diasporic concept of what Stewart refers to as the "sons and daughters of Africa" who had "sprung from [the] learned and enlightened nation" of Ethiopia. But the overall emphasis of her lectures and essays of the 1830s and beyond is on pursuing full rights of citizenship for blacks in the United States. Thus, like Walker, she links her black nationalist project to the egalitarian ideals that she asserts were articulated in the nation's founding documents. She remarks in her 1831 "Religion and the Pure Principles of Morality" that "according to the Constitution of these United States, he [God] hath made all men free and equal," and she sums up her political goals in her 1833 address to Boston's black Masons: "Let every man of color throughout the United States, who possesses the spirit and principles of a man, sign a petition to Congress, to abolish slavery in the District of Columbia, and grant you the rights and privileges of common free citizens." But even as she urged men to work publicly to challenge slavery and gain their political rights, Stewart increasingly focused her efforts on education and religion, publishing essays and fiction in the African Methodist Episcopal Church's *Repository of Religion and Literature and of Science and Art*. Eric Gardner argues that Stewart's writings in this periodical during the early 1860s advocated "a sense of domestic womanhood centering on a revision of republican motherhood and teaching and combined … with Afro-Protestant Evangelicalism and nascent black nationalism" (157) – precisely the emphases that Claudia Tate has located in traditions of black women's writing running from the 1850s to the turn of the century.

During the antebellum period, African American literary nationalism was about community and the pragmatics of survival. It was also about pride, consciousness, and connections of language to personhood. As I have been emphasizing throughout this essay, there was no single African American literary nationalism, for there was much conflict during this period on a number of vital issues connected to race and nation. These conflicts inspired and continued to inform much African American writing. By the late nineteenth century, African American women writers such as Anna Julia Cooper and Pauline Hopkins, in the tradition of Stewart, were boldly enunciating a gendered black literary nationalism, even as they remained conflicted about its very terms, with Hopkins in particular adopting an Ethiopianism that she may well have encountered in the writings of Walker and Stewart. The debates between Booker T. Washington and W.E.B. Du Bois at around the same time, the racial dynamism of the Harlem Renaissance, the cultural nationalism of the Black Arts movement of the 1960s, and many other crucial debates and developments in African American literary history clearly have sources in the debates of the pre-Civil War period on African American literary nationalism. In short, Walker and Stewart, Douglass and Delany, and a number of other black writers of the early national and antebellum period, some increasingly well known and some still invisible, all helped to identify and explore the tensions and conflicts that would remain central to African American literary traditions, however conceptualized and understood.

Bibliography

Anderson, Benedict. *Imagined Communities: Reflections on the Origin and Spread of Nationalism*. London: Verso, 1983.

Andrews, William L. "*My Bondage and My Freedom* and the American Literary Renaissance of the 1850s." In Andrews, ed., *Critical Essays on Frederick Douglass*. Boston, MA: G.K. Hall & Co., 1991. 133–47.

Bassard, Katherine Clay. *Spiritual Interrogations: Culture, Gender, and Community in Early African American Women's Writing*. Princeton: Princeton University Press, 1999.

Foster, Frances Smith. "A Narrative of the Interesting Origins and (Somewhat) Surprising Developments of African-American Print Culture." *American Literary History* 17.4 (2005): 714–40.

Gardner, Eric, ed. "Maria W. Stewart: Two Texts on Children and Christian Education." *PMLA* 123.1 (2008): 156–65.

Glaude, Eddie S., Jr. *Exodus! Religion, Race, and Nation in Early Nineteenth-Century Black America*. Chicago: University of Chicago Press, 2000.

Levine, Robert S. *Dislocating Race and Nation: Episodes in Nineteenth-Century American Literary Nationalism*. Chapel Hill: University of North Carolina Press, 2008.

Levine, Robert S. *Martin Delany, Frederick Douglass, and the Politics of Representative Identity*. Chapel Hill: University of North Carolina Press, 1997.

McHenry, Elizabeth. *Forgotten Readers: Recovering the Lost History of African American Literary Societies*. Durham, NC: Duke University Press, 2002.

Moses, Wilson Jeremiah, ed. *Classical Black Nationalism: From the American Revolution to Marcus Garvey*. New York: New York University Press, 1996.

Peterson, Carla L. *"Doers of the Word": African-American Women Speakers and Writers in the North (1830–1880)*. New York: Oxford University Press, 1995.

Richardson, Marilyn, ed. *Maria W. Stewart: America's First Black Woman Political Writers*. Bloomington: Indiana University Press, 1987.

Santamarina, Xiomara. *Belabored Professions: Narratives of African American Working Womanhood*. Chapel Hill: University of North Carolina Press, 2005.

Stuckey, Sterling. *Slave Culture: Nationalist Theory and the Foundations of Black America*. New York: Oxford University Press, 1988.

Tate, Claudia. *Domestic Allegories of Political Desire: The Black Heroine's Text at the Turn of the Century*. New York: Oxford University Press, 1992.

9
Periodicals, Print Culture, and African American Poetry

Ivy G. Wilson

In the summer of 1828, George Moses Horton published his poem "Slavery" in *Freedom's Journal*. A self-taught poet who lived most of his life as a slave in North Carolina, Horton used the poem to convey his own sense of indignation regarding chattel slavery. He concludes the poem with the dismal recognition that the grave alone may be the only place where "Oppression's voice is heard no more" (34). Horton's "Slavery" underscores how poetry was part of a larger discursive system of oratory, essays, and the slave narrative that constituted an African American politics.

As important as the antislavery theme of Horton's poem remains, equally important are the routes of its publication that disseminated it as an *objet d'art* and mode of social critique. Initially published on July 18, 1828, in *Freedom's Journal*, it was republished nearly six years later in William Lloyd Garrison's *Liberator* on March 29, 1834. Like Garrison's *Liberator*, *Freedom's Journal* was staunchly antislavery but, significantly, it was also the first newspaper owned and operated by African Americans appearing from 1827 to 1829 and edited principally by Samuel Cornish and John B. Russwurm as a weekly out of New York City. Horton's inclusion in the pages of *Freedom's Journal* intimates the reach of the periodical either as a vehicle through which Horton himself might have sought a readership in New York or as the extension of an African American weekly below the Mason-Dixon Line. Furthermore, the republication of "Slavery" in Garrison's *Liberator* in 1834 signals its dissemination to an audience composed primarily of black and white abolitionists.

The publication of Horton's poem raises a number of issues about periodicals, reading audiences, and print culture for African Americans in the nineteenth century. Reprinting was rampant during this time and exploited especially by African American writers, some of whom were public intellectuals seeking to garner the widest possible audience for their ideas and messages. Figures like Frederick Douglass, William Wells Brown, and Frances Ellen Watkins Harper all published or republished various literary works in such venues as newspapers, songbooks, and compendia. In the immediate sense, the African American publication of poems in periodicals offers an opportunity to consider the presentation and function of poetry in recurring print formats in comparison to single-authored volumes. In another sense, a reconsideration of poetry and periodicals offers an opportunity to reassess nineteenth-century African American literary production beyond the slave narrative.

Horton's experience needs to be understood within the larger patterns of circulation and print culture for nineteenth-century African American writers. By focusing on two poets, James Monroe Whitfield and James Madison Bell, this essay seeks to delineate the traffic in verse as a means to analyze the relationship between the black reading public and an emergent print nationalism. Whereas there has been scholarly work on the "traffic in poems" in the transatlantic context, our turn to black periodicals offers a different geography of black cultural production that moves from the Eastern seaboard to the West coast of the US.[1] Extending the claims of Elizabeth McHenry, examining periodicals helps to expose a spectrum of African American reading communities from the literary societies of densely populated urban centers to the more sparsely populated areas on the frontier and in the West. Investigating Whitfield and Bell discloses alternative archives of African American literature and illuminates a wider boundary of the black public sphere.[2] Such a focus would allow for an investigation of Harper's poetry, for example, which, by the end of slavery, had to take a different route for dissemination when the antislavery circuit dissolved. Negotiations with print culture, then, reveal as much about the larger discursive formations of African American thought as about an engagement with the typography within the space of the page itself.

"We wish to plead our own cause": Early African American Periodicals

In one of the sketches for a series that he wrote for the *Anglo-African Magazine* in 1859, William J. Wilson stages a scene where his fictive persona "Ethiop" engages in a tête-à-tête with a white patron to the gallery: "I was about to remark," he said, "that if your men had capacity they might write for our anti-slavery journals and other ably conducted magazines in the country, such as *Harpers'* or the *Atlantic Monthly*. It would be more creditable. You don't want a separate magazine and pen up your thoughts there." The fictional encounter between Ethiop and the white visitor illuminates a number of concerns about black periodicals. On the one hand, the patron's comments contain a subsumed critique of value, by which, if they had any "capacity," black writers might write for "more creditable" journals. On the other hand, his comments are decidedly political: black writers should not want to publish their ideas in "separate" magazines. But Ethiop counters that having "colored men" in the position of editors allows for a wider range of perspectives to be circulated, providing forums where black writers could more freely express their ideas. Indeed, in a meta-fictional sense, Wilson's sketches themselves are exactly the type of writing that might not readily find a place in periodicals edited by white Americans and are therefore an illustration of the need for expressly African American forums.

Between Phillis Wheatley and Paul Laurence Dunbar, periodicals were especially important venues through which African American poets disseminated their verse. The same issue of *Freedom's Journal* that featured Horton's poem, for example, included "The Knight's Farewell" by one "Arion." Composed of regularized stanzas written in hexameter, "The Knight's Farewell," in light of Horton's verse in the same poetry column and the newspaper itself, expresses an utter disinterest in slavery or blacks. A number of the early black periodicals regularly printed poetry and some featured dedicated poetry columns, such as the *Impartial Citizen*, a semi-weekly and then weekly paper founded by Samuel Ringgold Ward in Syracuse, New York, that ran from 1849 to 1856, and Thomas Hamilton's *The Weekly Anglo-African*, a companion to his *Anglo-African Magazine*, which, in its two-year run from 1859 to 1861, also published excerpted passages from books (Pride and Wilson, 47–9; Penn 119).

Although topics such as temperance, religion, and appearance were frequently discussed, slavery and black equality were the central focus of nearly every antebellum African American periodical.[3] When Douglass launched *The North Star* (1847–1851), he introduced the paper with a prospectus announcing his objective: "The object of *The North Star* will be to attack slavery in all its forms and aspects; advocate Universal Emancipation; exact the standard of public morality; promote the moral and intellectual improvement of the colored people; and to hasten the day of freedom to our three million enslaved fellow countrymen" (quoted in Bryan 19). Willis A. Hodges' *The Ram's Horn*, an abolitionist paper out of Williamsburgh, New York, ran for three years between 1847 to 1850, reaching a peak circulation of 2,500 (Penn 63–5). While every paper advocated the abolition of slavery, there was a wide divergence on whether African Americans should leave the US altogether or remain isolated in either insular, segregated communities and strive for integration. The *Alienated American* (1853–1854), based in Cleveland, Ohio, and Mary Ann Shadd's *Provincial Freeman* (1853–1857), published in Windsor, Ontario, Canada, championed integration. Henry Bibb argued for keeping black communities protected and isolated from whites in his paper, *Voice of the Fugitive*, while John B. Russwurm, in wresting control of *Freedom's Journal* from Samuel Cornish, turned the angle of the paper to one that decidedly advocated that blacks should leave the US for Africa.

While African Americans frequented the pages of white-edited periodicals such as Garrison's *Liberator*, black periodicals pressed the call for self-representation as an urgent if not necessary responsibility.[4] "We wish to plead our own cause," reads the editorial statement of *Freedom's Journal* – "Too long have others spoken for us. Too long has the publick been deceived by misrepresentations, in things which concern us dearly."[5] After *Freedom's Journal* and *The Rights of All*, Samuel Cornish became editor of the short-lived *The Weekly Advocate* (1837), where he stated in the first issue to his black readership that the paper was "their paper, in every sense of the word … devoted particularly to our own interests – conducted by ourselves, devoted to our moral, mental and political improvement."[6] And Hamilton made special note in the introductory issue of his *Anglo-African Magazine* that African American men and women would write all its articles.

If Douglass's periodicals commanded the largest readership, then the *Anglo-African Magazine* might be thought of as the most sophisticated antebellum nineteenth-century African American periodical. Running from 1859 to 1865, the *Anglo-African Magazine* was an illustrated paper that covered literature, poetry, art, science, and the topics of slavery and citizenship in editorial, political, and satirical essays. Published in New York City, it featured some of the most prominent African American intellectuals such as Martin Delany, James Theodore Holly, and James McCune Smith.

In pleading their own cause, poetry was an important aspect of the discourse regarding US black political subjectivity as well as a notable component of an aesthetic archive that sought to illustrate their humanity. The poetry featured in these periodicals was either original or reprinted. As reprints, they undergirded a particular ideological position or introduced African American readers to the classics. In the opening issue of the *Anglo-African Magazine*, Hamilton quotes from John Greenleaf Whittier's "Songs of Labor" (1850) and Elizabeth Barrett Browning's *Aurora Leigh* (1857) to support positions about the potential black contribution to the makings of the US in the areas of industry and aesthetics. Similarly, in his "Afric-American Picture Gallery" series for the magazine, William J. Wilson quotes Walter Scott, among others. All these writers were well versed in important contemporaneous poetry as well as the classical canon. More often than not, when these poems were quoted, they were almost always unidentified, perhaps a sign itself about the kinds of works assumed to be known by black reading audiences.

Equally important, these periodicals featured poetry from both established and unknown black writers. In the first year of the *Anglo-African Magazine*, for example, it ran Frances Ellen Watkins (Harper)'s "Gone to God" and "The Dying Fugitive" as well as Wilson's "The Coming Man" and "The Teacher and His Pupil"; it also circulated works from lesser-known figures including Grace A. Mapps's "Lines" and Reverend J. Sella Martin's "The Sentinel of Freedom." Perhaps the most remarkable understanding of poetry as a sign of the progress of the race and its future is that the very first editorial for the *Anglo-African*'s "Youth Department" highlighted poetry as its inaugural topic.

Lost in Translation: The Circulation of James Monroe Whitfield

No better example illustrates the importance of periodicals for poets and poetry than the literary career of James Monroe Whitfield. Whitfield was born to free blacks in 1822 and worked as a barber for the majority of his life but long aspired to be a poet exclusively. Douglass published a number of Whitfield's poems in *North Star* and *Frederick Douglass' Paper*, encouraging him to abandon manual labor for the *belles-lettres* of poetry. The first known poem published by Whitfield was entitled "Self-Reliance," which appeared in the *North Star* on December 14, 1849, followed the next week by one entitled "The North Star." Another six poems appeared in Douglass's periodicals between 1850 and 1852. In the antebellum period, he also published in Garrison's *Liberator* and Julia Griffith's collection *Autographs for Freedom* (1853), culminating with the appearance of his volume *America and Other Poems* in 1853 by the James S. Leavitt Company in Buffalo, New York.

One conspicuous aspect of Whitfield's poetry, as it appeared in Douglass's periodicals, is how little they concern race or slavery, intimating that the periodicals provided both political debate as well as aesthetic sites of black art. In "Self-Reliance," Whitfield depicts a man's conscience informed by Christianity; "To A— H—" is a paean to a noble figure whom even the gods admire; and "Ode to Music" finds Whitfield illuminating the aurality of nature. Whitfield's "Morning Song," a poem published after *America and Other Poems*, extends his interest in nature and the pastoral.

The placement of Whitfield's "Morning Song" in *Frederick Douglass' Paper* underscores the newspaper as a particular site of nineteenth-century African American sociality, one that outlines modes of consciousness ranging from specific political positions to aesthetic sensibilities. Subdivided into seven vertical columns, the page which features "Morning Song" includes classifieds for, among other things, a bank in Rochester, a watchmaker in New York City, and an offer to manage a clothing store in Brooklyn. The page also features a sketch "Cicely Hunt; or, The Lame Girl" (1853) from Fanny Fern, one of the most popular writers of the day, and a chapter from the serialized story *An Unsuccessful Enterprise* by an anonymous writer. Importantly, there is also a notice for the sale of Julia Griffith's *Autographs for Freedom* by the publisher Wanzer, Beardsley & Co. and a call for the National Emigration Convention of Colored Men to be held in Cleveland, Ohio, in August, 1854. Among the many names listed as delegates are Delany and Whitfield; Douglass, however, refused to enlist in the emigrationist movement, deciding that African Americans should remain in the US and fight for civil rights here rather than emigrate elsewhere.

Whitfield's position on emigration, which aligned him with Delany and James Theodore Holly, among others, alienated Douglass, and marked the decline of Whitfield's presence as a writer for Douglass's newspaper. In contrast to when Douglass urges his readers to purchase *America and Other Poems* in the Literary Notices section of the July 15, 1853 edition of his paper, Whitfield nearly vanishes from Douglass's pages. In a larger sense, the history of Whitfield in Douglass's periodicals illuminates a wider dilemma of how the reification of the volume per se obfuscates the depths of the African American archives and, in a meta-theoretical sense, delimits the very modes of critical inquiry that are used to examine nineteenth-century African American literature. In this regard, a perspective on the history of the book (which encourages a deeper understanding of print history), or a focus on the question of genre specifically, might yield new insights on the poems by Whitfield that are and are not

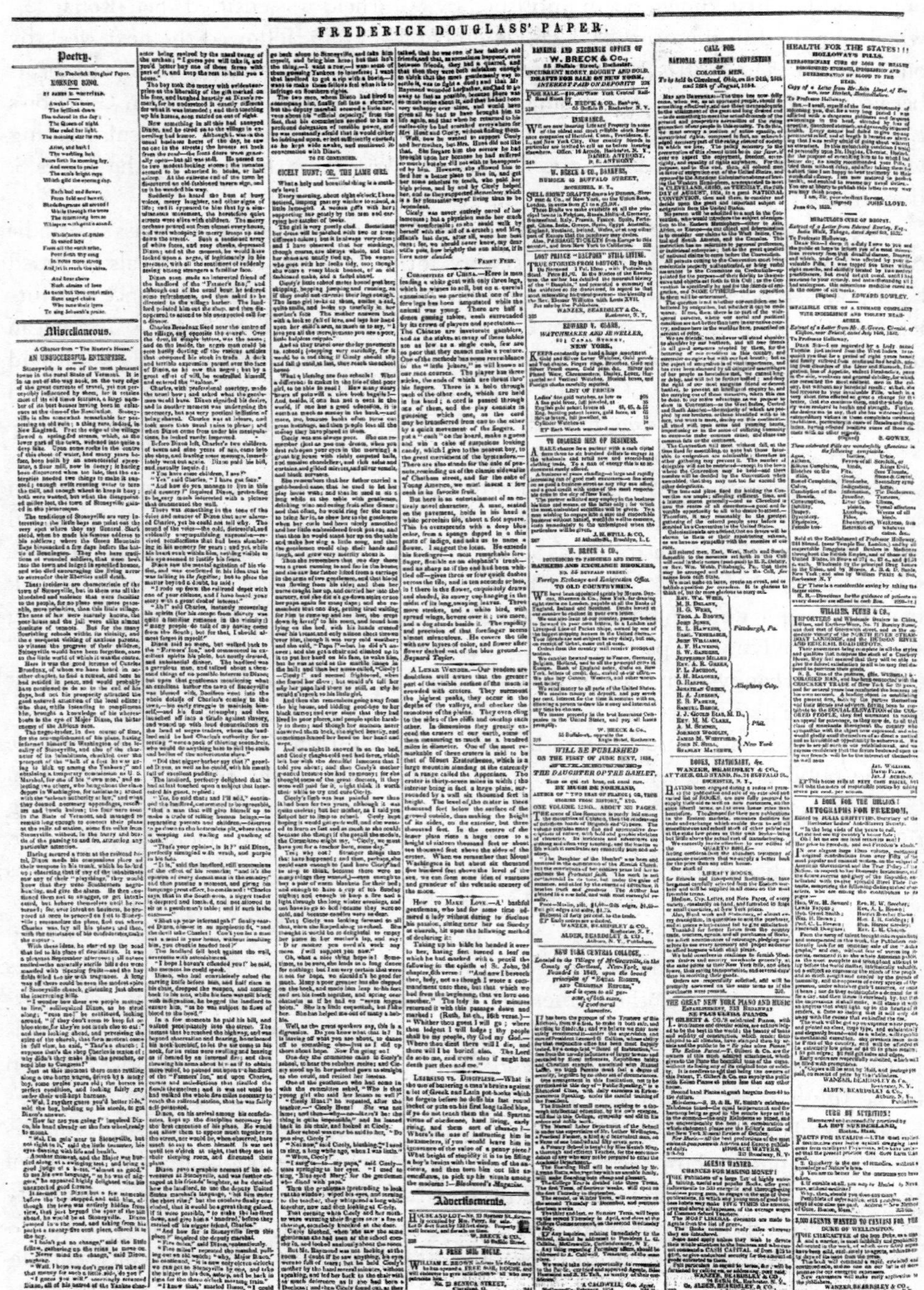

FREDERICK DOUGLASS' PAPER.

Figure 9.1 *Frederick Douglass' Paper*, July 28, 1854

included in *America and Other Poems*. A study of Whitfield's poetry, then, is as much about his verse as about such periodicals as *Frederick Douglass' Paper*, the *Pacific Appeal*, and, as it turns out, the *Anglo-African*.

In the opening years of the Civil War in 1861 and 1862, Martin Delany surreptitiously incorporated a number of poems by Whitfield, his friend and fellow black emigrationist, into *Blake; or the Huts of America*, a novel that first appeared serially in the *Anglo-African Magazine* and the *Weekly Anglo-African*.[7] As Eric J. Sundquist notes, Delany ventriloquizes a host of Whitfield's poems throughout his novel (Sundquist 203–4). In *Blake*, Whitfield's poem "Prayer of the Oppressed" is rendered through the mouth of the Cuban Placido, while other poems include "To Cinque," "Yes! Strike Again the Sounding String," and "How Long." The assimilation of Whitfield into Delany's story signals one discourse of political strategy.

By foregrounding the hemispheric perspective of Whitfield's antislavery position as an analytic lens, the circulation of Whitfield as a poet necessarily expands. "Prayer of the Oppressed" and "To Cinque" were initially published in Whitfield's 1853 volume but both "How Long" and "Yes! Strike Again the Sounding String" took more circuitous itineraries en route to Delany's *Blake*. "How Long" was originally published in the first iteration of Griffith's *Autographs for Freedom* which also featured poems by Harriet Beecher Stowe, John Greenleaf Whittier, and J.M. Eells. "Yes! Strike Again the Sounding String" was originally published in the March 15, 1850, issue of the *North Star*. After Whitfield included it in his volume, Douglass subsequently republished it in an advertisement for *America and Other Poems* in the July 15, 1853, issue of his newspaper. In the case of "How Long," the poem migrated from giftbook to volume to magazine; in the case of "Yes! Strike Again the Sounding String," the poem migrates from newspaper to volume to newspaper to magazine. In both instances, the poems migrated from the specific spatio-temporality of their initial publications only to be reset in a serialized novel and instantiated by their transformation from verse into performance.

Stylistically, the transfer of "To Cinque" and "Prayer of the Oppressed" to chapters 60 and 61 of *Blake*, respectively, illuminates the common elements between poetry, oratory, and song as part of a similar genealogy of cultural discourse in the mid-nineteenth century. When Placido utters words from Whitfield's "Prayer of the Oppressed" before the Grand Council in Cuba, he does so with a tone of noticeable authority and gravitas, almost as if it were a declamation – "At the signal of the Chief, the poet, stepping upon the elevation on which were seated the orchestra, amidst a deathlike silence of anxious listeners and fond admirers, read in a loud, impressive, and solemn manner" (Delany 259). As a performance, Whitfield's poem is transformed into a formal speech. By contrast, Whitfield's "To Cinque" is illustrated as a communal and extemporaneous performance in chapter 60: "Suddenly, as if by magic, the whole company simultaneously rose to their feet. With silent and suppressed demonstrations, men and women waved hand and handkerchief, Blake and Placido entering at the instant when the amateur orchestra, instrumental and vocal commenced in strains most impressive" (Delany 250). The transliteration of Whitfield's poetry into

The Weekly Anglo-Afri[can]

"MAN MUST BE FREE!—IF NOT THROUGH LAW, WHY THEN ABOVE THE LAW."

VOL. I. NO. 36. NEW YORK, APRIL 5, 1862.

The Weekly Anglo-African.

IS PUBLISHED EVERY SATURDAY BY ROBT. HAMILTON

BLAKE; OR THE HUTS OF AMERICA.

A Tale of the Mississippi Valley, the Southern United States and Cuba.

BY MARTIN R. DELANY.

PART II.

CHAPTER XXXIV.

CHAPTER XXXV.

ENTERTAINMENT AT CAROLUS BLACUS.

ARMY CORRESPONDENCE.

Figure 9.2 *The Weekly Anglo-African*, April 5, 1862. Features Chapter 35 of Martin Delany's serialized novel *Blake* with embedded lines from James Monroe Whitfield's poem "Yes! Strike Again the Sounding String"

Blake is a figurative act of transubstantiation, one where the discursive routes of its re-articulation in narrative form through the periodical format are symbolic of a proleptic collectivity that Delany hopes will encourage his reading audience to mobilize against chattel slavery. Although veiled as such, the presence of Whitfield in *Blake* marked his widest audience after his initial exposure in Douglass's newspapers. As the leading figure of his time, Douglass's newspapers commanded the largest readership of any African American periodical. For his part, Whitfield would never again hold the audience he enjoyed as part of the East Coast black intelligentsia.

California Dreaming: Periodicals, Poetry, and the West

While there is some evidence that Whitfield may have traveled to Central America between 1859 and 1861 in search of land for a black colony, he probably reemerged in California in the summer of 1862. On August 23, 1862, the *Pacific Appeal* acknowledged that, beginning on March 14, 1863, it had a correspondent under the initials "J.M.W.," and a "J.M. Whitfield" is listed in the "Our Contributors" column of the first page of the paper. As this correspondent articulated in an editorial for the *Pacific Appeal* in the August 9, 1862, issue, he was shifting from his emigrationist position toward championing black participation in the Union cause at the outset of the Civil War. He also continued writing as a poet, publishing "To A— Sketching from Nature" on May 23 of the following year. "To A— Sketching from Nature" was as much an opportunity to reflect on the transcendence of nature as a reflection that California itself might be the perfect embodiment of nature; an Eden where African Americans could start anew. As much as Whitfield's interaction with the *Pacific Appeal* reveals about his own shifting position as a writer, it can also help to illuminate the history of Northern California's African American communities in the years during and after the Civil War.

Although fewer than those on the East Coast, a number of African American periodicals existed in California. One of the most popular was the San Francisco-based *Mirror of the Times* (which ran from 1857 to 1862), founded by two African American businessmen, Mifflin W. Gibbs and James Townsend, and edited by William H. Newby. An entrepreneur who made a fortune in dry goods and land speculation, Gibbs was motivated to support the creation of a black periodical because there was little to no coverage of African Americans in the Northern California's white press (Lapp 101). In its pages, the weekly outlined how California, as a free state, was no paradise for African Americans and it encouraged its readers to confront the state's "Black Laws" that restricted the civil liberties of its black population. Later African American periodicals in the West included *Vindicator* (1888–1889) and *Western Outlook* (1894–1928).

Among these periodicals, the *Pacific Appeal* (1862–1880s) and the *Elevator* (1865–1899) remain among the most important. Subtitled "A Weekly Journal, devoted to the Interests of the People of Color," the *Pacific Appeal* was published by Peter

Anderson in San Francisco and edited by Philip A. Bell, one of the most prominent newspaper figures of the nineteenth century having worked with Charles B. Ray on *The Colored American* in the late 1830s and early 1840s. In the "Salutatory" section of the first issue, Bell acknowledges the tradition of his predecessors in the publishing industry including *Freedom's Journal*, *The Colored American*, *Frederick Douglass' Paper*, and the *Anglo-African*. "A Weekly Paper," wrote Bell, "is needed in California as much as in the Atlantic States: one which will be the exponent of our views and principles, our defense against calumny and oppression, and our representative among one of the recognized institutions of Civilization."[8] The *Pacific Appeal* would be preoccupied, Bell announced, with advocating equality before the law for African Americans and, in particular, with the repeal of laws which disallowed blacks from testifying in court cases in which a white person was a party.

In the inaugural issue of the *Pacific Appeal* on April 5, 1862, Bell appealed to California's black population to support the paper. "There are said to be six thousand Colored people in California, sufficient, if only one tenth subscribe, to support our paper; that proportion, say six hundred, we must have within six months, for the remaining four hundred, we must depend on our neighbors on the northern coast."[9] Bell's appeal to the 6,000 "Colored people" is an important indication of self-identification whereby "Colored" signaled a new beginning in the history of African Americans to the nation marked by the promise of both California and the Emancipation Proclamation. If we take the newspaper agents as representative of demography, the *Pacific Appeal* further outlines the broader presence of African Americans along the West Coast. Although based in San Francisco, the agents for the paper were concentrated across towns associated with gold speculation including Sacramento, Grass Valley, and Coloma in California, as well as Carson City in what was then Nevada Territory. In its early months, the paper had agents in a number of towns between San Francisco and the Eastern border of California and by 1864 it had an agent as far North as Victoria, British Columbia and as far South as Panama. While one might say that many of these African Americans relocated to California as part of the Gold Rush, many also hoped that they would be able to more fully enjoy their civil liberties as Americans in the new free state. The March 14, 1863, issue included a short note that "a number of lady contributors" would be announced, joining the ranks of those who regularly wrote for the paper. In addition, within the early months of the paper's beginning, a weekly San Francisco Literary Institute was continually announced in the advertisement section, first with James P. Dyer presiding and later with the poet James Madison Bell assuming responsibility.

A four-page weekly, the *Pacific Appeal* promoted poetry, regularly featuring it in a dedicated column. The poems cover a range of emotions from anticipation, loss, and hope to political critiques of the contemporary moment. Of the latter, W.H. Anderson's verse for the *Pacific Appeal* was insistently political, if not humorous. In one turn, the poet satirizes the Civil War by parodying Jefferson Davis and caricatures the slave trade in another. In "The Ship of State in Dixie's Land," Anderson depicts the US as a leaky ship made of "Calhoun wood" where "robber men" meet their "watery grave":

The wood is passed, both fore and aft:
Get in your boats and leave the craft;
We'll board old U.S.A. again,
And there forever will remain.

Now let them all return again
Beneath the stars and stripes the same;
The eagle then shall ever be
The emblem of our liberty.[10]

What is striking about the poem is not simply its sardonic tone but its political subtext that a veritable democracy might materialize only if Southern "robber men" and their accomplices in Faneuil Hall are capsized and metaphorically re-baptized before returning to a reconfigured US. The *Pacific Appeal* also featured a sketch on Phillis Wheatley, widely conceived as a prodigy and progenitor of the African American literary tradition. In the February 7, 1863, issue, the *Pacific Appeal* reprinted a short sketch of Wheatley from *American Female Poets*, closing the column with perhaps her best-known poem "On Being Brought from Africa to America" (1773) by incorporating (and misquoting) one of its most important and subversive couplets:

Remember, Christians, negroes, black as Cain,
May be refined, and join the angel train! (7–8)[11]

The presence of the Wheatley sketch in the *Pacific Appeal* evinces both the promise and the dangers of reprinting culture in African American periodicals as much as it signals, in a larger sense, the ways that that reprinting culture offers a different way to conceive the field of African American historiography.

The most prominent poet featured in the pages of the *Pacific Appeal* was James Madison Bell. Born in Ohio, Bell spent nearly the first 30 years of his life there before moving to Canada West, Ontario, from 1854 to 1860 and then to California for five years, between 1860 and 1865. While in Ontario, Bell became a friend of John Brown and supported Brown's assault on Harper's Ferry. Bell gained a reputation on the lecture circuit for his long verse-orations that detailed the history of African Americans, ranging from slavery and the Civil War to Emancipation and Reconstruction, in such works as "The Day and the War" (1864), "The Progress of Liberty" (1866), and "The Triumph of Liberty" (1870). Like his contemporary Albery Allson Whitman, he emulated popular British poets such as Alexander Pope, Walter Scott, and Alfred Tennyson, typically using iambic tetrameter, couplets, or simple, alternating rhymes.

The very parameters of the print format of the newspaper column in the *Pacific Appeal* prompted Bell to exert more control and authority over the style of his versification. He composed "Abolition of Slavery in D.C.," for example, composed in four octaves with varying lines of six to eight feet. In the poem, Bell praises the recent law outlawing slavery in Washington, DC and imagines the capitol synecdochically, as a part that could stand for the whole nation. Beyond the stylistic changes in his versification, writing for a newspaper also allowed Bell to consider themes different from those with which he was associated as a public speaker. For instance, his April 12, 1862, poem "Song," written in ballad stanzas of alternating lines of octameter and hexameter, is a romantic expression of love. In "Apostrophe to Time," the speaker is overwhelmed by the seeming infinity of time while awaiting salvation and redemption.

The most pronounced element of Bell's poetry, however, used an overwrought style to accentuate the political necessity of African Americans gaining civil liberties in the US and equal rights more broadly. This style was influenced by his position as an orator that sometimes impaired his poems with clichés and, as Joan R. Sherman notes, inundated them with a "monotonously regular iambic tetrameter" (Sherman 192). Typical of Bell's verse-oratory is "The Day and the War," part of which was published on January 2, 1864, after having been delivered only the day before as part of a ceremony celebrating the first anniversary of the Emancipation Proclamation. Taking place at Platt's Hall in San Francisco, the celebration was presided over by Philip A. Bell and included both a speech by W.H. Hall and a veritable declamation of Bell's poem. He took as his subject the Black Brigade of Cincinnati that, in 1862, had organized and volunteered to serve on behalf of the Union army.

In single combat. Ah! 'twas then
The Black Brigade proved they were men!
For ne'er did Swiss! or Russ! or knight!
   Against such fearful odds array'd,
With more persistent valor fight,
   Than did the Union Black Brigade!
...
   And thus they fought, and won a name—
None brighter on the scroll of Fame;
For out of one full corps of men,
But one remained unwounded, when
The dreadful fray had fully past—
And killed or wounded but the last![12]

Thematically, "The Day and the War" was not so different from similar poems – including W.H. Anderson's "A Song for the Volunteers of Massachusetts" (1863) – that valorized African American men who volunteered for war and, significantly, wore the uniform of a soldier as an emblem of their dedication to both the state and the idea of liberty. But the inclusion of "The Day and the War" excerpt illuminates the *Pacific Appeal* as a particular kind of social and performance text, one that nominally recreates and distills the event within the columns of its pages, marked, in this moment, by a note that Bell's poem was preceded by a band playing "Marching On!" and concluding with "Hail Columbia!" Importantly, where most of the poems for the *Pacific Appeal* were published on the last page, situated among advertisements and classifieds, "The Day and the War" excerpt is more specifically contextualized as political discourse per se by its placement immediately preceding a "Declaration of Sentiments" where its authors reiterate their claim for full citizenship. The sense of pride and euphoria encapsulated in "The Day and the War" bespoke different pieces by Bell and other poets as well, including the verse-oratories of "The Progress of Liberty," which celebrates the third anniversary of the Emancipation Proclamation and "The Triumph of Liberty," which heralds the Fifteenth Amendment that gave African Americans the right to vote.

Whereas Bell's "The Day and the War" was one of the longest poems (even when excerpted) in the *Pacific Appeal*, poetry would receive yet more space in the San Francisco *Elevator*, another black periodical, started by Philip A. Bell after he left the *Pacific Appeal*. Beyond what it suggests about a possible disagreement between Bell and his former employer Peter Anderson, the appearance of the *Elevator* might also suggest that the black community in the West and northern California was large or viable enough to support two periodicals. Taking "Equality before the Law" as its motto, Bell was keen to emphasize that the weekly journal would be an advocate of civil liberties – "Such are our general principles and objects, but we will have, in addition thereto, a special mission to fulfill; we will labor for the civil and political enfranchisement of the Colored people – not as a distinct and separate race, but as American citizens."[13] When Bell departed for the *Elevator*, it also signaled the return of James Whitfield to the public sphere as a periodical poet.

Whereas Whitfield's lengthiest poem had been "How Long," published 14 years earlier initially in *Autographs for Freedom*, his poetry for the *Elevator* was largely occasional. In 1867, he published "A Poem, Written for the Celebration of the Fourth Anniversary of President Lincoln's Emancipation Proclamation" for the San Francisco *Elevator*. Whitfield's "Fourth Anniversary" was a 400-line poem, written in iambic tetrameter and published in two parts on January 4 and 11. It was also published as a small volume under separate cover alongside Ezra R. Johnson's "Emancipation Oration." The poem outlined the history of the country from the beginning to the present moment beyond the Civil War. Rather than depict emancipation as simply the freeing of America's black subjects, Whitfield conceptualized the poem as an illustration of how the Emancipation Proclamation liberated the country writ large, freeing the idea of liberty from a slaveocracy which held it in bondage.

> One century and a half had flown
> When Freedom gained the first great fight;
> Defied the power of the throne,
> And bravely proved the people's might,
> When banded in a righteous cause,
> To overthrow oppressive laws.
> 'Twas then, when struggling at its birth,
> To take its proper place beside
> The other Nations of the earth,
> The rule of justice was applied;

And all mankind declared to be
Inheritors of Liberty;
With right to make their freedom known,
By choosing rulers of their own.
But when it came t' enforce the right,
Gained on the well-contested field,
Slavery's dark intrigues won the fight,
And made victorious Freedom yield. (113–30)

In this respect, Whitfield's poem intimates that slavery, by conscripting the US to an anachronistic temporality, disaggregated this nation from the teleology of modernity being ushered in by "The other Nations of the earth." In the poem, Whitfield enumerates, almost in the vein of one of Walt Whitman's catalogs, a litany of national and regional identities that comprise the US and have worked to preserve the Union and abolish slavery. In contrast to his position as recently as a decade earlier regarding the necessity of black emigration, Whitfield's message and tone here are more than nominally patriotic, a difference in perspective due as much perhaps to being on the other side of the Civil War as well as the other side of the country.

Whitfield continues underscoring progress as a theme in his last known published poem by accentuating the US as the apotheosis of the sign of the times. In an untitled poem for the *Elevator* appearing on May 6, 1870, Whitfield distills much of the "Fourth Anniversary" poem:

To lead the van of Freedom's march,
Till on the earth there shall remain,
Nowhere beneath the heaven's blue arch
A single slave to clank his chain;
Till all around, from east to west,
From north to south, on land and sea,
Like us, the nations shall be blest
With equal laws and liberty. (145–52)

Published in the midst of Radical Reconstruction, Whitfield's concluding lines intimate that only after the end of slavery could the US come to embody a "city upon a hill," as a model for the rest of the world to emulate. Here, Whitfield's poem moves beyond a national anthem into a kind of transcendent paean.

Between the Lines

In an editorial, "Afro-American Poets and Their Verse," for the *AME Church Review* in 1898, Katherine Davis Tillman reflected on some of the best-known poets through the nineteenth century, including Phillis Wheatley, Frances Harper, Albery Allson Whitman, and Paul Laurence Dunbar. Tillman believed, as had many others, that the mastery of poetry was an index of the progress of the race and proof that blacks would "be enabled to take [their] place among the nations of the earth" (Tillman 422).

> Any one who has been a close reader of the columns of our various race journals, has doubtless observed the poetical effusions which have so frequently adorned them. Verses good; verses bad; verses indifferent. Written in all styles of metre [*sic*]; and, in many instances, without the remotest idea of versification. Occasionally, a bit of genuine poetry has greeted our eyes and received a hearty welcome, because it was a production of our own, and, therefore, a herald of better days ahead. (421–2)

Periodicals were key venues for this work, as Tillman herself notes that both Harper and Cordelia Ray both recently contributed to the *Church Review*. In a more critical sense, Tillman's comments are a reminder of the necessity of not simply turning to the genre of poetry but reading between the lines of the periodical as a genre itself, as both a documentary sign of the times and as an aesthetic palimpsest. Furthermore, returning to the periodical offers one way of reconstructing the historical context in which a poem was published, a way often obfuscated by the assumed thematic continuity of the self-contained volume per se. In other words, these poems are correlated to the other texts embedded in the newspaper or magazine as much as they have an aesthetic relationship with other poems when they are collected in volumes.

Nineteenth-century magazines were the precursors to early-twentieth-century publications: the *Anglo-African* laid the groundwork for the Harlem Renaissance's *Fire!*, while *The Colored American* and *Frederick Douglass' Paper* did the same for the *Crisis* and *Opportunity*, in which some of the most modern important twentieth-century poets, including Langston Hughes, Claude McKay, and Countee Cullen, published their work. In "Black and Unknown Bards" (1922), one of his best-known poems, James Weldon Johnson laments the forgotten black poets of previous generations. Returning to the archives of periodicals promises not only to outline a wider panorama of nineteenth-century African American letters but also to recover many an unknown poet; a sentiment pronounced by Tillman's review as she concludes, "To the editors of Afro-American journals who have encouraged us to sing our trembling lays by giving them a place in their columns, we owe a debt of gratitude" (Tillman 428).

Notes

1 I invoke Meredith McGill's notion of the "traffic in poems" here. Although the distinction can be overly constructed, my emphasis here on verse is meant to allow for aspects such as oratory and rhetoric that undergird the phonetic structures of African American cultural production. See McGill.

2 Todd Vogel has noted that examining "the press gives us the chance to see writers forming and reforming ideologies, creating and recreating a public sphere, and staging and restaging race itself" (3).

3 Early African American periodicals, in this sense, differed from Benedict Anderson's claim that the rise of periodicals was intimately tied to the rise of the market place; rather than primarily being an appendage to a commercial economy, African American

periodicals were primarily political. See Anderson 33, 36.

4 Some white editors of abolitionist newspapers also felt that the antislavery movement could not support additional journals; see Ripley, Finkenbine, Hembree, and Yacovone 32.

5 *Freedom's Journal*, March 16, 1827.

6 *Weekly Advocate*, January 7, 1837.

7 Robert S. Levine has provided one of the most comprehensive outlines of the publication history of *Blake*; see Levine 179–80.

8 *Pacific Appeal*, April 5, 1862.

9 *Pacific Appeal*, April 5, 1862.

10 *Pacific Appeal*, May 16, 1863: 21–8.

11 The last lines of the poem should read "Remember, *Christians*, *Negroes*, black as *Cain*, / May be refin'd, and join th' angelic train." The syllabic configuration is slightly misaligned in the reprint and, importantly, the typographical absence of the italics alters the relationship between its visual demarcation and its subsumed political meaning.

12 *Pacific Appeal*, January 2, 1864.

13 *San Francisco Elevator*, December 6, 1867.

Bibliography

Anderson, Benedict. *Imagined Communities: Reflections on the Origin and Spread of Nationalism. 1983*. 2nd edn. New York: Verso, 1991.

Bryan, Carter R. "Negro Journalism before Emancipation." *Journalism Monographs* 25 (1969).

Delany, Martin. *Blake; or, the Huts of America. 1861–1862*. Rpt. Boston, MA: Beacon, 1970.

Lapp, Rudolph M. *Blacks in Gold Rush California*. New Haven: Yale University Press, 1995.

Levine, Robert S. *Martin Delany, Frederick Douglass, and the Politics of Representative Identity*. Chapel Hill: University of North Carolina Press, 1997.

McGill, Meredith, ed. *The Traffic in Poems: Nineteenth-Century Poetry and Transatlantic Exchange*. New Brunswick, NJ: Rutgers University Press, 2008.

McHenry, Elizabeth. *Forgotten Readers: Recovering the Lost History of African American Literary Societies*. Durham, NC: Duke University Press, 2002.

Penn, I. Garland. *The Afro-American Press and Its Editors*. Springfield, MA: Wiley, 1891.

Pride, Armistead S. and Clint C. Wilson II. *A History of the Black Press*. Washington, DC: Howard University Press, 1997.

Ripley, C. Peter, Roy E. Finkenbine, Michael F. Hembree, and Donald Yacovone, ed. *The Black Abolitionist Papers, volume III, The United States, 1830–1846*. Chapel Hill: University of North Carolina Press, 1991.

Sherman, Joan R. *African-American Poetry of the Nineteenth Century*. Urbana: University of Illinois Press, 1992.

Sundquist, Eric J. *To Wake the Nations: Race in the Making of American Literature*. Cambridge, MA: Belknap, 1993.

Tillman, Katherine Davis. "Afro-American Poets and Their Verse." *AME Church Review* 14.4 (1898): 421–8.

Vogel, Todd, ed. *The Black Press: New Literary and Historical Essays*. New Brunswick, NJ: Rutgers University Press, 2001.

Wilson, William J. "Afric-American Picture Gallery – Second Paper," *Anglo-African Magazine*, March 1859.

Part II

New Negro Aesthetics, Culture, and Politics: The Modern Period, 1865–c.1940

10
Racial Uplift and the Literature of the New Negro

Marlon B. Ross

Who merits the heroic epithet of "New Negro"? This question bubbles beneath many of the social, political, and cultural debates engaged not only among leading African American intellectuals and activists but also among ordinary working people from the emergence of Jim Crow segregation in the 1880s to the height of the Civil Rights Movement in the early 1960s. Although the phrase "New Negro" is rarely explicitly defined in the discussions where its name is deployed or its tenor self-evident, the term and its ideologically entangled meanings were at the center of various efforts to overcome white supremacy and its devastating effects. The term "New Negro" is usually not explicitly defined in the literature and other cultural products of the time where its provenance presides. This is partly because it names an identity whose power lies in its existential performance. A New Negro is what a New Negro does. A New Negro becomes one by behaving like one.

While New Negro identity was claimed in performance, paradoxically the existence of the idea of a New Negro could be effectively promulgated and modeled only by self-consciously constructing and disseminating a verbal and visual discourse on the New Negro. The problem for the advocates of New Negrodom is that there was very little agreement on how a New Negro should behave, and thus even less agreement on what a New Negro definitively is. All the individuals, informal groups, and formally constituted organizations who hail the term, in one form or another, agree about one matter: that the only way to defeat white supremacy is by raising up (or "uplifting") the race to its proper place in United States society and in global culture. Thus, the New Negro was the physical manifestation – the tangible subject/agent in the flesh, or at least the representation of such – emerging from the more abstract conceptual demand for racial uplift. In other words, uplift was the elusive theory whose practice was embodied in the presence of a New Negro image. If New Negro identity was embattled, it was most certainly because there was deep controversy, especially from the 1880s through the 1930s, over how to achieve racial uplift – in fact, over what exactly an uplifted race would look like.

Would it look like a race as separate from others as the fingers but joined to the national whole like the hand, in which the economic and industrial enterprise of New Negroes would redeem their place among the powerful and wealthy, as Booker T. Washington preached and enacted through his Tuskegee Machine and its myriad "Bookerite" enterprises? Diametrically opposed to this Bookerite New Negro in rhetoric, if not fully in practice, was the New Negro image promulgated by the National Association for the Advancement of Colored People (NAACP), since its founding in the 1910s. Would a raised race look like a group legally integrated into US society at every political, economic, and social level, but possibly retaining its biological distinctiveness as a cultural group, or would it be socially assimilated or biologically amalgamated into a single American race? Perhaps the most broadly popular New Negro image was fostered by the nationalist "Back to Africa" movement of the 1920s and 1930s – a mass grassroots movement whose success among the working poor garnered the contempt of virtually every competing ideology. Was an uplifted race one transported from the shores of the New World back to Africa to colonize a powerful new black nation, as was the nationalist plan of Marcus Garvey and his international Universal Negro Improvement Association (UNIA)? Against the Bookerite New Negro, the Garveyite nationalist New Negro, and the NAACP integrationist New Negro stood another competing version, the red New Negro. Would an uplifted race mean the radical emergence of a Negro nation carved out of the Black Belt South through communist consciousness-raising and revolution, as was advocated briefly by the "self-determination" doctrine of the Communist International during the late 1920s? Even among black communists, there was no single version of Negro renewal. According to Cyril V. Briggs, founder of the African Blood Brotherhood and its journal, the *Crusader*, the New Negro was the advance guard of pan-African communist revolution, nurtured by secret cells of Negro men who took blood oaths to protect and promote the race worldwide.

Across these varying political agendas, the claim to New Negro identity hinged on other factors – often less clearly articulated and more generally assumed. Did New Negro identity entail the privilege of belonging to a particular socioeconomic status, particularly as related to the degree of formal education, vocation, and standard of living? To be a New Negro, did one have to live not only in a particular way but also in a particular region or city, wherein the rural "Deep" South (the Black Belt) was frequently seen as the backwater habitat of the Old Negro, and the urban North (particularly uptown Manhattan and Southside Chicago) as the natural destiny and home of the genuine New Negro. This regionalist dimension of New Negro identity largely assumed that, wherever one started out or ended up, mobility itself was frequently taken as a necessity.

In addition to the class and regionalist dimensions, New Negro identity was shaped by assumptions of gender roles and sexual conduct. The New Negro is often implicitly gendered masculine and often presumes a heteronormative conduct of manly vocation and recreation, marital obligation, masterly leadership in civil governance, and devotion to fraternal organizations and rituals. The reality on the ground, however, was much more complicated and vexed. From the outset women emerged at the forefront of the New Negro enterprise, shaping not only its quotidian practice but also its intellectual, iconographic, and discursive frameworks. Likewise, despite the endeavor to manage a masculine norm of social and sexual conduct, the New Negro enterprise was haunted and riddled by persons who refused or resisted this gender/sexual norm, and whose central participation raised the concern among some leaders that, at its core, the New Negro identity may harbor a perverse racial complex that forebodes its own undoing within the dictates of normative US power as defined by heterosexual upper-class white men.

The concept of uplift, and its manifest imaging through the New Negro, cannot be separated from the putative failure of Reconstruction as a political casualty of white power's political and economic compromise. As white Redemptionists (of the Confederate cause) propagandized through circular reasoning, Reconstruction failed because it was doomed from the outset by an African racial nature that could not be "reconstructed": it failed because members of an inferior race were granted any degree of authority (in political governance, education, and economic enterprise) over white men. This view, which came to dominate in the US by the end of the nineteenth century, was propagated in every sphere of US life by white supremacists, who mounted a public campaign to reaffirm white power as naturally ordered, divinely ordained, and scientifically justified. When not attacking the Negro as a beastly inferior whose presence was a threat to democracy and civilization, Southern apologists were busy romanticizing the antebellum plantation culture of happy, docile, primitive slaves and beneficent, knowing, civilized slaveholders in fiction like that penned by Thomas Nelson Page and Joel Chandler Harris. In his novels, Thomas Dixon, Jr. constructs a fantastic history that casts freed Negroes in authority as naturally corrupt, sexually undisciplined agents of political chaos, brought under control by the glorious knights of the Ku Klux Klan – a narrative immortalized in the first feature film, *Birth of a Nation* (1915), by D.W. Griffith. These racial representations are intended to fix the identity of the Negro race as retrograde (tied permanently to slavery) and/or lagging (incapable of catching up with upper-class white men) by imaging the race as stupid, lazy, cowardly, pilfering, as humorously charming and loyal when properly governed by whites, and as savagely vicious and dangerous when left to their own devices. In case the illogic of these discourses might be exposed, or the blatant contradiction between the racial iconography and the reality of black persons might be too apparent, myriad forms of racial violence were perpetrated to enforce the imagery of racial backwardness.

Against such a barrage of racial invective parading as rational, scientific discourse, and in the midst of ongoing violations and lynchings, the appeal to a New Negro identity became the palpable counter-argument, the object-lesson for progressive racial conduct, and the vehicle through which a racial advance could be maneuvered. Even before the "failure" of Reconstruction, however, African Americans, writing during an era of chattel captivity, were setting the stage for the idea of the New Negro, even though the term itself was probably not used until the 1880s. In slave narratives, polemical texts, poetry, and novels, African Americans, emancipated and bound, began to image the notion of "freedom" and citizenship through the idea of the Negro's exceptional position for progressing democratic ideals and, in the process, advancing the race's capacity for self-governance and national and global citizenry.

One of the most formative figurations of this notion comes in *Narrative of the Life of Frederick Douglass, an American Slave* (1845). Throughout the narrative Douglass has illustrated (and modeled for his readers) how to resist the regimes of captivity. Climaxing the narrative with a hand-to-hand battle with the slave-master to whom he has been hired out, Mr. Covey, Douglass frames this violent encounter, in which he defeats Mr. Covey in the fight, as a turning point physically, psychologically, and spiritually. The turning point occurs – or is made by Douglass – when he refuses to be whipped and instead fights back to "whip" Mr. Covey. The turning point is dramatized as a temporal and spatial breakage, whereby even though he is the same person in the same place, he is now a new man in a psychically different register of time and space. Douglass writes:

> This battle with Mr. Covey was the turning-point in my career as a slave. It rekindled the few expiring embers of freedom, and revived within me a sense of my own manhood … It was a glorious resurrection, from the tomb of slavery, to the heaven of freedom. My long-crushed spirit rose, cowardice departed, bold defiance took its place; and I now resolved that, however long I might remain a slave in form, the day had passed forever when I could be a slave in fact. (74)

Referencing the Pauline experience of conversion into a new man, the Christological resurrection from the dead, as well as the apocalyptic vision of St. John in the Book of Revelation, Douglass creates an iconic moment that helps to define the ideal of racial renewal as a breaking/turning point in which the past (of slavery) is forever killed and buried, allowing the future (of freedom) to supplant it wholly as a personal and potentially collective scene of resurrection.

As Henry Louis Gates, Jr. points out, this idea of an absolute breakage from the past, clearly rhetorical and mythical, puts in motion the need for an iterative claim to racial renewal ("The Trope of the New Negro"). To signal New Negro progress, individuals must repeatedly distance and displace themselves from the common racial history (enslavement, Jim Crow oppression), while at the same time they must repeatedly and aggressively claim to be new selves constituting an ever-new race. Although particular to African American literature and culture, this rhetorical, mythical claim to the race's self-renewal also resonates intimately with larger US notions of radical self-making, such as those narratives figured through a move from rags to riches, immigrant to American, and the manifest destiny achieved by conquest of the Western frontier. In one of the most famous uses of chiasmus in American literature, Douglass prepares the conversion scene by intoning, "You have seen how a man was made a slave; you shall see how a slave was made a man" (62). As with many assertions of New Negroness, the progress (from slave to citizen) depends not only on a temporal/

spatial breakage but also on a violent territorial contest between (white) man and black (man) through which the African American claims the right to full humanity and citizenship by wresting from whiteness *his* right to manhood privilege.

Although this figure of slave-to-man conversion through a total break in identity can be seen in many slave narratives and polemical texts of the antebellum era, it by no means represents the sole formative embodiment of racial uplift through renewal. Phillis Wheatley's poem "To the Right Honourable William, Earl of Dartmouth" (1773), for instance, constructs a narrative of racial renewal without reference to such breakage. If her address is politely structured in epistolary form, with due reverence for the earl's high office, her subject of freedom for the American colonies, and thus for enslaved Africans, is subtly impolite. Even if Dartmouth were to prove sympathetic to the American complaints against the crown, Wheatley's epistle aggressively converts this sympathy into an attack on the crown as tyrannical:

> No more, *America*, in mournful strain
> Of wrongs, and grievance unredress'd complain,
> Which wanton *Tyranny* with lawless hand
> Had made, and with it meant t'enslave the land. (74, lines 15–19)

In the succeeding verse paragraph, Wheatley justifies her "love of Freedom" for the "common good" by narrating her own experience of being "snatch'd from *Afric's* fancy'd happy seat" (lines 20–4):

> Such, such my case. And I can then but pray
> Others may never feel tyrannic sway? (lines 30–1)

Ironically writing as though she is politely pleading the case on behalf of her masters (the rebelling colonials), she inserts at the very heart of the poem her own "grievance" as an "unredress'd" complaint. Using this more oblique, seemingly deferential strategy, Wheatley helps to initiate a different approach in racial uplift literature, as she returns to Africa as a collective and personal resource. Rather than a breakage from the past, she affirms an ongoing linkage with a previous condition, African nativity, as the basis for a free identity.

Wheatley's strategy of displaying great longsuffering sacrifice on behalf of others (the white American colonists, her masters) is also apparent in other slave narratives by men and women. In Harriet Jacobs's *Incidents in the Life of a Slave Girl* (1861), the narrator (fictionalized as Linda Brent) tells how she hid herself in a narrow garret, a virtual tomb, for almost seven years, venturing out and risking detection only to plead for the freedom of her children. When a fellow slave needs a hiding place, she shares this tomb-sized garret with her. As with Wheatley, there is no absolute breakage represented, even as Brent escapes from captive entombment to the putatively free North. Where we would expect such a triumphant breakage, instead we are repeatedly reminded of the tragic ties that bind her to her still-bound grandmother and other relatives and friends. She forces us to grasp the great economic burden and psychic cost of needing to purchase herself (or for a sympathetic racial patron to purchase her) to protect against recaptivity: "The more my mind had become enlightened, the more difficult it was for me to consider myself an article of property; and to pay money to those who had so grievously oppressed me seemed like taking from my sufferings the glory of triumph" (205). Brent's gradualist enlightenment, contrasted with Douglass's instant conversion, highlights the inescapable burden of racial distinction even within free society, as she discovers that "freedom" is a relative condition, at best. Even in the final paragraphs, as Brent exhilarates in her new free condition and that of her children, she reminds us of the cost that she bears within her new existence, a cost that entails a racially perverse relation to the heteronorm of white ladyhood: "Reader, my story ends with freedom; not in the usual way, with marriage … We are as free from the power of slaveholders as are the white people of the north; and though that, according to my ideas, is not saying a great deal, it is a vast improvement in *my* condition." Freedom from being held as property, it turns out, is not enough. Brent continues, "The dream of my life is not yet realized. I do not sit with my children in a home of my own home. I still long for a hearthstone of my own, however humble. I wish it for my children's sake far more than for my own" (207). Closing her story with a yearning that tempers the newness of her free identity, Jacobs foregrounds the absence of the normative US household as definitive of her vastly improved place, while emphasizing the immense difficulty in trying to break with the deprivation exacted through captivity, whose brutal exclusions continue to mark her racial estate even in the guise of her own "improvement."

In antebellum literature like Jacobs's, we can already detect a signal contradiction that helps to define the uplift literature of the Jim Crow era. Whereas "vast improvement" or uplift dictates a temporal scheme of piecemeal and laborious gradualness, the assertion of New Negroness implies a decided break or conversion, which often is imagined as the quickened mobility of picking up and moving elsewhere. If one is to stay put, then there are only two viable options: an accommodation to prevailing circumstances while trying to effect a painfully gradual uplift or violent revolution to effect a territorial takeover. For the emancipated narrator, the former is obviously not an option, since the narrator's identity relies on the individual defeat of slavery as a premonition of full, universal emancipation. In the slave narrative, the movement from captive to free territory is a stop-gap measure delaying (or prefiguring) the final violent collision between slave and free, insofar as the freedom of the individual can only be relative when others remain shackled, as Douglass repeatedly points out.

Despite the slave narrative's favoring of a territorial movement from slave to free, the notion of a bloody takeover from the masters is also necessarily a central dimension of abolitionist literature. Such an option is hinted at in Douglass's bloody duel with Mr. Covey, but it can be seen outright in David Walker's *Appeal to the Colored Citizens of the World*, an 1830 treatise aimed at inciting slave insurrection on the model of the Haitian Revolution, and in Martin Robison Delany's 1852 treatise *The Condition, Elevation, Emigration, and Destiny of the Colored People of the United States, Politically*

Considered, as well as in his serial novel *Blake, or the Huts of America* (1859–1862), which narrates a revolution to liberate all New World captives through the organization of a bi-gender elite advance guard conspiracy. Inspired by the revolutionary fervor of Toussaint L'Ouverture, Gabriel Prosser, Denmark Vesey, Nat Turner, and John Brown, as well as by the heroic daring of warring ex-slave liberators like Harriet Tubman, the firebrand revolutionary haunts uplift literature, though most frequently as a foil to the respectably uplifting New Negro and thus as a veiled warning to the white establishment, should they utterly reject the New Negro's reasonable interventions.

American Negroes had to do more than disconnect their identity from that of the preternatural slave as fashioned by the postbellum Redemptionists and plantation apologists; they also had to claim aggressively a racial identity allied with newness, modernity, mobility, progress, urbanity, and self-empowerment against the assault of racial invective and violence that defined their status as Negro. By confirming racial separation as the law of the land, the Supreme Court in its 1896 *Homer v. Plessy* decision placed all Negroes in the same tide, whether ebbing or rising. Unless they could pass for white, higher-status Negroes (those with education, income, and professional skills), they could not seek to enter into white society as an exceptional group distinct from the Old Negroes (those whose way of life was still dependent on domestic servitude, agricultural labor, and the oversight of white landlords and bosses). They had to sink or swim in a single tide. This ethic is best summed up by the New Negro slogan, "Lifting as we rise," as formulated by the National Association of Colored Women, founded in the same year as the *Plessy* decision by middle-class New Negro women such as Mary Church Terrell, Ida B. Wells-Barnett, and Frances E.W. Harper.

The colored women's club movement constituted one of the most visible and active faces of the New Negro enterprise. Shaping and shaped by the era of the New Woman (the period of agitation for and just after female suffrage, the 1880s to the 1920s), these women viewed the New Negro effort as a call to racial consolidation by bestowing a gender-specific obligation on women, particularly middle-class women of education, means, and professional talent. Even as these women adhered in some ways to prescribed gender roles, usually related to sexual respectability, they saw the New Negro/Woman identity as a fight against the kinds of sexual discrimination that attempted to exclude women from seats of power in civil and civic life. Educator Anna Julia Cooper's *A Voice from the South by a Black Woman of the South* (1892) captures this dynamic of racial consolidation expressed through African American women's specific gender obligation, advancing a racial tradition reaching back into captivity in which a less decided distinction was made between male and female intelligence, savvy, labor, strength, and leadership. In her treatise Cooper lays out a theory and program for uplift through a logic of representativeness, whereby every (New) Negro has a burden to represent the best of the race and the race at its best. Because such tutelage occurs most within the home, this places a special burden, and a special capacity, on the women of the race (see 30–1). Borrowing from the Christian notion of the mission, which had also been the impetus for much of the freedmen's school-building during

Reconstruction, Cooper contravenes the dominant Western notion that only a patriarch can represent (lead, speak for, govern) a race, instead insisting that women's missionary work embodies and authorizes their essential representativeness: "Only the Black Woman can say 'when and where I enter, in the quiet, undisputed dignity of my womanhood, without violence and without suing or special patronage, then and there the whole *Negro race enters with me*'" (31; original emphasis). The notion of this New Negro/Woman mission was both modeled and interrogated in African American women's fiction and autobiography at the turn into the twentieth century, as educators and activists like Pauline Hopkins, Harper, Wells-Barnett, and Terrell used narrative to explore the constraints and powers of New Negro Womanhood. In Harper's serialized novel *Trial and Triumph* (1888–9), for instance, she presents a mulatta teacher as a heroine, one whose Reconstruction-based educational work is impeded by emerging Jim Crow racial and sexual indignities. Rather than succumbing to despondency or fleeing, Harper's protagonist recommits herself to the uplift of the race in a Cooper-like Christian mission that entails personal sacrifice through spiritual conversion, transforming her feminine vulnerability into a womanly strength.

Although New Negro/Woman narratives shared social themes, formal structures, and political strategies with those written by New Negro men, the male writers more clearly exploited the tradition of Douglass's 1845 *Narrative*, as they used the achievement of manhood, often through violence, as the basis for their claim to New Negro identity. Douglass himself had established the pattern for transforming the slave narrative into the uplift autobiography in reshaping the story of his life to meet the circumstantial demands of the changing condition of the race. His 1881 book, *The Life and Times of Frederick Douglass* (revised 1892), moderated the power of the slave-to-man structure by elaborating the quotidian experience of his enslavement and updating and expanding the achievement of his career in the face of mounting Jim Crow discrimination. Whereas the 1845 narrative climaxes with his conversion into a man and quickly moves to closure with his escape and his call for general emancipation, the later autobiographies present his life *both* as an individual career of an exceptional man who achieves national prominence *and* as the representative experience of a committed race man. In a sense, Douglass represents his leadership within the (white) nation as a natural reward bestowed for his race leadership, his fathering of the race, and likewise his fathering of the race mirrors his own prospering stewardship of his personal estate. As an advisor to presidents, a marshal for the District of Columbia, and consul-general to Haiti, Douglass displays the advance of the race toward gradual national inclusion, even as his narrative retains the structure of a protest against the unfair obstacles increasingly placed in the way of the race's natural ascent.

The masculinizing form of the uplift autobiography is perfected in Booker T. Washington's 1901 masterpiece, *Up from Slavery*, which chronicles the great accommodationist's rise to become the Wizard of Tuskegee, the racial patriarch who serves as the black arbitrator for the white establishment. Based on the system of political patronage common at the time, Washington's "machine" achieved heretofore unparalleled (not even by Douglass) access to presidents, wealthy industrialists, and world leaders. Like Douglass's, Washington's autobiography charts his path from slavery to the pinnacle of becoming "head" of the Negro racial family, but the narrative structure of this uplift must be shifted to adjust for the rigorous racial protocols of Jim Crow, a shift that entails a curtailment of manly self-assertion and thus a demasculinization of the form, even while its virile structure of heroic ascent remains intact. Significantly, Washington accomplishes this accommodation by repressing any "natural" manly impulse toward violence against white men's oppression. In the first chapter, he quickly establishes this accommodation by picturing captivity as a "school of slavery" (16), asserting: "Ever since I have been old enough to think for myself, I have entertained the idea that, notwithstanding the cruel wrongs inflicted upon us, the black man got nearly as much out of slavery as the white man did" (17). Contrary to Douglass's use of violent resistance as a liberating rite of manhood, Washington repeatedly images the tenderness and fidelity of the enslaved. "This tenderness and sympathy on the part of those held in bondage," he writes, "was a result of their kindly and generous nature. In order to defend and protect the women and children who were left on the plantations when the white males went to war, the slaves would have laid down their lives" (13). In this way, Washington converts the white Southerners' violent hostility toward the Civil War and Reconstruction into a cross-racial alliance between the formerly enslaved and the former slave masters. The most vivid iconography of *Up from Slavery* captures Washington in matronly poses and acts, meticulously sweeping the floor to gain entry to Hampton Institute, preaching "the gospel of the toothbrush," instructing the Tuskegee students on how to make their beds properly, and extolling the virtues of domestic servitude as a nursery for the tutelage of thrift, discipline, and entrepreneurship. Critics such as the formidable W.E.B. Du Bois viscerally responded to this model of New Negro leadership by castigating not only its spoils machinery but also its unmanliness. In his highly influential attack included in *The Souls of Black Folk* (1903), Du Bois quips, "He insists on thrift and self-respect, but at the same time counsels a silent submission to civic inferiority such as is bound to sap the manhood of any race in the long run" (44–5).

Confronted with the gargantuan task of leading the effort to raise up millions of unlettered, impoverished former slaves and their children in the Black Belt, Washington rejected rhetorically and strategically the option of mass migration. As he phrases it in his famous 1895 Atlanta Exposition speech, "No race can prosper till it learns that there is as much dignity in tilling a field as in writing a poem. It is at the bottom of life we must begin, and not at the top" (220). He enjoins his bi-racial audience to "Cast down your buckets where you are" (220), an injunction that fits the race's economic needs to the larger economy of what was being called "the New South." By pegging the New Negro's uplift to the larger economic success of the New South, Washington wagered that economic self-interest and regard for entrepreneurship as monetary success were genuine, rather than superficial, American national values, ones that would in the long run ensure the progress of the Negro race. "In all things that are purely social we can be as separate as the fingers, yet as one as the hand in all things essential to mutual progress" (221–2). This Wizard's bargain, however, engaged the Tuskegee Machine in a delicate balancing act. On the one hand, the Bookerite advance of the race depended on the independent exercise of an entrepreneurial spirit, the accumulation of property, and the tangible display of material success as a visible sign of the race's worthiness. On the other hand, with every visible sign of material prosperity, the New Negro became a threat to the underlying logic of the Jim Crow regime, with its insistence on the natural inferiority of the group in exactly those spheres where Washington called for competence: independent-mindedness, intelligent entrepreneurship, and disciplinary self-governance.

This uneasy balance had to be maneuvered at every juncture and in every venue where the material success of the Bookerite New Negro was placed on display. It could be seen in the various compendia of New Negro achievement authored in the waning decades of the nineteenth century and the rising ones of the twentieth. From William Wells Brown's 1874 *The Rising Son; or, The Antecedents and Advancement of the Colored Race* to Carter G. Woodson's 1922 *The Negro in Our History*, individual achievement of exceptional Negroes was seen as incontrovertible evidence for the collective progress of the race. In addition to biographical compendia and great man/woman histories, New Negroes of this era produced a variety of race albums, which emphasized photographic displays alongside inspiring stories of New Negro achievement. The epitome of this trend can be seen in the 1900 volume *A New Negro for a New Century*, where the progress of the race is trumpeted and chronicled visually, as well as verbally. In the Bookerite volume, black men's honorable service in national warfare is foregrounded (along with the image of a decorated soldier in ceremonial military dress), and the race is depicted as an extended family: sturdy, respectable patriarchs paired with matronly virtuous women whose fit progeny will surely continue this long upward ascent. As Darwinian in its visual logic as the Negrophobes were in their race science, this focus on the material display of self-worth meant that every shiny new car, Queen-Anne-style house, four-story brick bank building, or well-managed farm and farmhouse could be corralled as evidence of the race's Darwinian fitness for advancing civilization.

If the literature of uplift sometimes repressed the Jim Crow violence that everywhere conditioned the experience of the race, many whites' fatal hostility toward the display of Negro ascent could not be so easily pushed aside for real-life New Negroes. Across the country in every region, riots were carried out against prosperous Negro communities. Although Washington had enjoined Black Belt Negroes to "cast down their buckets where you are," the larger Tuskegee enterprise also encouraged frontier settlement in the newly opened states of the West. In Greenwood, Oklahoma, for instance, African Americans set up a separate prosperous Bookerite town. When whites from nearby Tulsa attacked the town in 1921, black veterans armed themselves and fought back using their wartime experience. Against the Bookerite image of a tender people unable to be provoked, the interwar period brought to the fore myriad realities of New Negroes, many uniformed veterans, doing battle with the lynchers and rioters in an effort to protect their households, their lives, and their sense of manhood.

The emblem for this mode of New Negro militancy became Claude McKay's poem, "If We Must Die" (1919), which the Jamaican immigrant composed while he was working as a sleeping car porter. In deploying the sonnet form, McKay takes seriously the uplift mission of producing high literature as a sign of racial worthiness, but he turns the elite European form into a fierce battle-cry for racial self-defense. Like Douglass's violent turning point, the sonnet figures a speaker backed against a symbolic wall:

> Though far outnumbered let us show us brave,
> And for their thousand blows deal one deathblow!
> What though before us lies the open grave?
> Like men we'll face the murderous, cowardly pack,
> Pressed to the wall, dying, but fighting back!
>
> (See Johnson, *Book of American Negro Poetry*: 169, lines 10–14)

If Washington could ridicule writing a poem as paltry proof of fitness for a race scratching its way from the bottom, then McKay, who himself had journeyed to the US inspired by Washington's Tuskegee project, uses the sonnet to reply forcefully on two fronts: putting the lie to Washington's favoring of industrial education, while also squashing the sentimental representation of the New Negro man as a nonthreatening, tender, servile creature of the white man's economic making.

In the 1910s and 1920s especially, at the apex of lynching and genocidal violence against Negroes, the extinction of whom race science had clearly wrongly predicted, New Negro militancy emerged in a variety of literary and cultural forms. Perhaps the best promoter of this brand of New Negro identity was William Pickens, educator, NAACP recruiter, and champion of armed self-defense. In oratory, journalism, fiction, autobiography, and polemics, Pickens preaches the idea that the New Negro must present a militant front if the race is ever to achieve its manhood inheritance. In his treatise *The New Negro: His Political, Civil, and Mental Status* (1916), Pickens revamps the Bookerite New Negro compendium from a stable Victorian family romance into a Wild West contest among the races. Similarly, his 1923 *Bursting Bonds: The Autobiography of a New Negro* constructs the image of the New Negro as one who, tutored as much in the open West frontier as in the ivied halls of Yale, never backs down, always shoots from the hip, and risks his life in pursuit of racial justice and progress. Ironically, as a young man, Pickens had fashioned himself on the model of the Tuskegee Wizard, but by the time of Washington's death (in 1915), the power vacuum as "head" of the race had helped to release some of these militant impulses into public view. Like Wells-Barnett, who had also used journalism and autobiography to represent the New Negro as a hard-hitting, cool-tempered crusader for justice, Pickens skirted the line between NAACP organizational advocacy and a pioneering free-agency of individualist activism.

Another New Negro pioneer who skirted this line was Oscar Micheaux, the most prolific creator of "race films." In many ways, his moving pictures embodied the

Bookerite initiative of displaying respectable, educated, middle-class (and often light-skinned) people pursuing their American dreams as though Jim Crow strictures did not apply to them. Micheaux had attempted his own New Negro frontier experiment in South Dakota, and then reprised the experience in a semi-autobiographical narrative, *The Conquest: The Story of a Negro Pioneer* (1913); a novel, *The Homesteader* (1917); and a film of the same title (1919). Against this backdrop of Bookerite entrepreneurship and attention to the material display of success, Micheaux also represented the firebrand risk-taking of the post-Bookerite militant New Negro. His controversial 1919 film, *Within Our Gates*, frames a fiery reply to Griffith's vicious race-baiting in *Birth of a Nation*. Whereas Griffith had represented the Reconstruction mulatto as corrupt and lecherous, and his lower-class darker-skinned double as a raping beast, both in pursuit of elite white ladies, Micheaux reverses the tables to represent the Southern white elite as undisciplined, decadent rapists of colored womanhood, and likewise African American men as willing to sacrifice all in its protection. The climactic scene of the film depicts the horror of a lynching spectacle, and the degrading effects of savage atavism afflicting the whites who attend the spectacle.

With this sense of urgent militancy, uplift literature of the interwar period redoubles its focus on lynching and other acts of Jim Crow violence. The first two African American secretaries of the NAACP, James Weldon Johnson and Walter White, penned important uplift novels whose plots hinge on the New Negro response to such violence. In Johnson's *Autobiography of an Ex-Coloured Man* (1912, 1927), he takes the unusual step of constructing a mulatto protagonist who can pass for white (a form more familiar in the tragic mulatta heroine). Johnson's unnamed narrator fails at his attempt to become a New Negro when he witnesses a lynching. Passing into whiteness, he achieves all the privileges of a heteronormative dispensation – a white wife, white progeny, a successful job, a network of influential friends – but this accomplishment of the white man's patriarchal norm by passing as white leaves the narrator bereft of value and purpose: "I cannot repress the thought that, after all, I have chosen the lesser part, that I have sold my birthright for a mess of pottage" (211). As a cautious object lesson, Johnson's reverse New Negro makes it painfully apparent that, as the author explains in his 1930 New Negro history *Black Manhattan*, to abandon the race, represented in his novel as a desire for whiteness, is both to forego the "genius of the race" and also to miss out on an exciting, if difficult, experiment in heroic race building. Following Johnson's lead in using fiction to meditate on the nature of New Negro heroism, White's novel, *Fire in the Flint* (1924), depicts a veteran of World War One returning South to build a medical practice on a Bookerite model. Foiled at every turn by the irrational riotous hatred and violence of many of the white townspeople, including the rape of his sister and the murder of his brother, White's hero braves a lynching to give medical attention to a white woman. As the novel concludes with the kind of anti-black race riot that occurred throughout the early twentieth century, White seems to emphasize the hardnosed reality of white supremacy, a reality not easily quelled by even the most boosterish Bookerite determination or the most calculating NAACP policies of protest assembly, legislative lobbying, and legal adjudication.

Despite Washington's insistence on casting down in the bowels of the Deep South Black Belt, the rising tide of mass migration dictated that many African Americans, voting with their feet, felt that the only way to raise the tide was to move cityward and often northward. This migration was promoted intrepidly by a rash of black-owned newspapers, most prominently the Chicago *Defender*, whose editors pushed the migration in every issue. The *Defender*, as its name implies, saw its primary aim as the defense of the race through advocacy journalism, which included constant reporting on the racial violence afflicting the Jim Crowed South. If the *Defender*, against the tenor of its own Bookerite business practices, occasionally hyped the freedoms of the industrial North, and especially its home city of Chicago, it nonetheless served a purpose of informing its myriad Old Negro readers across the South by helping them to imagine a New Negro future for themselves elsewhere. Next to bloody stories about lynching and riots, black newspapers such as the *Defender* tracked and celebrated every accomplishment of Negro rising culture – literature, the arts, fashion, high society – as harboring a racial renaissance.

This cultural dimension of the New Negro enterprise was best captured and promoted in 1925 by Alain Locke's high-impact volume, *The New Negro*. In several erudite essays, Locke provided not only a manifesto but the most articulate theorization of the concept of a New Negro to date. His complex layering of the New Negro phenomenon was as much a report on the emerging renaissance as it was a call to racial uplift through cultural and artistic achievement. Locke saw this renaissance as being fostered by a variety of disparate social, historical, and psychological factors, and he identified the roots of this reawakening in a growing appreciation of the African "ancestral arts" (especially sculpture), already being rigorously appropriated by white modernist artists and art collectors; in the fast-paced urban jazz culture being forged by the working poor of mass migrants; and in the cosmopolitanism figured in his image of "the laboratory of great race-welding" (7) resulting from the jostle of international immigrants and internal migrants from every geographic and socioeconomic sphere. Locke's theory of the New Negro was a direct assault on the Bookerite version, making Washington seem like an Old Negro in New Negro costuming. Locke's Renaissance New Negro was to be iconoclastic, smashing the "idols of the tribe" by refusing "tutelage, even of the most interested and well-intentioned sort" (8). Locke's Renaissance New Negro also castigated the politically and violently militant version of socialists and communists, as Locke insists that "the present Negro is radical on race matters, conservative on others, in other words, a 'forced radical,' a social protestant rather than a genuine radical" (11). Even the NAACP New Negro comes in for a thrashing, as Locke writes, "The Sociologist, the Philanthropist, the Race-leader are not unaware of the New Negro, but they are at a loss to account for him. He simply cannot be swathed in their formulæ" (3). No longer "a perennial problem," the Renaissance New Negro evinces a "new psychology," a "new spirit"

(3), "a spiritual emancipation" (4), "a Spiritual Coming of Age" (16). Purging themselves of the patronizing sympathy, servile humor, and soft sentiment identified with the Old Negro as an Uncle Tom or Sambo (5), Renaissance New Negroes were unapologetically objective, scientific, self-disciplined, and self-reflective – in a word, *modern* – in their social outlook and cultural expression. This new attitude was expressed and displayed in the cosmopolitan high modernity of the aesthetics and substance of Locke's volume, including essays, short stories, plays, poems, portraiture, and sketching deemed the most avant-garde work being done, especially in the new "race capital" of Harlem (7).

Locke's volume seemed like both the harbinger and the epitome of a New Negro apocalypse based in the notion of art for culture's sake. That the volume coincided with and preceded a host of new literature, art work, choreographed dance, and composed music melding classical high culture with Negro folk expression seemed only to verify Locke's message. The volume was clearly respectable in intent, as it embraced essays by Du Bois (concluding the volume) as well as Washington's successor, Robert R. Moton; however, its impetus nonetheless raised the suspicions of those on the political left and right. The swelling tide of work by Locke's cohort only confirmed some suspicions that the aestheticization of the New Negro cause harbored its perversion. A year later, when the decadent white queer Harlem patron named Carl Van Vechten published his salacious novel *Nigger Heaven*, Du Bois and others went on the attack, with Du Bois soliciting essays on the question of how the Negro should be portrayed in art. Ironically, Van Vechten's novel presented itself as an exposé of the New Negro phenomenon in Harlem, but it did so by titillating its (white) readers with the seamier side of the Harlem underworld while also suggesting the failure of his New Negro protagonist (an aspiring writer) to rise to the occasion of race uplift by involving him, in the end, in a vulgar bar brawl. If the respectable New Negroes attacked Van Vechten and seemingly similar work by Negroes as morally venial, beneath this criticism was a more disconcerting suggestion: that the Renaissance notion itself was a sham minstrel show, in which literate urban Negroes put on the costumes of modernity while still harboring the primitive instincts of the Old plantation Negro.

Even more important than Van Vechten's exploitative exposé, some of Locke's putative disciples – Wallace Thurman, Langston Hughes, Zora Neale Hurston, Aaron Douglas, Richard Bruce (Nugent), Gwendolyn Bennett, and Arthur Huff Fauset – brought out the first (and only) issue of an iconoclastic journal *Fire!!* (1926). The issue contains a final commentary by Thurman defending Van Vechten (a subscribing patron of the new journal) and declaring independence for "the younger generation" of New Negroes. The bohemian flare of *Fire!!* is set by Thurman's Satanic Foreword, where he describes the periodical as "weaving vivid, hot designs upon an ebon bordered loom and satisfying pagan thirst for beauty unadorned … the flesh is sweet and real … the soul an inward flush of fire" (1). Along with Hughes' 1926 *Nation* essay, "The Negro Artist and the Racial Mountain," this volume became a manifesto of the bohemian New Negro, one who wanted to splinter social uplift from cultural progressiveness by calling into question the basis of racial uplift in conventional moral respectability. These artists would create art about whatever they wanted, in whatever form they deemed aesthetically fit, without regard to bourgeois norms.

That so many of these writers were publically or privately same-gender-loving, like Locke himself, only served to inflame Du Bois's fear that the New Negro was being hijacked and queered by the perversions of the "gutter." Intent on exploring the panoply of experiences in every sphere of Negro life, this "younger generation" wrote novels, plays, poetry, and autobiographies reflecting the lives of the working poor in all its richness and squalor, examined the problematic relations between the "dick-ties," or self-styled Negro elite, whom Hurston dubbed the Niggerati, and mercilessly satirized the bi-racial uplift efforts of the NAACP do-gooders. Hughes and others transfused literate poetry with oral and musical forms of the Negro "folk" (as they labeled those unlettered Negroes at the very bottom of US society). As they wrote fiction often showcasing empathetic portraits of the folk, writers like Jessie Fauset, Nella Larsen, Rudolph Fisher, Thurman, Hurston, McKay, and Hughes used the novel to examine unconventional social, sexual, and racial interactions across the classes, interactions that the previous generation of New Negroes preferred to leave unspoken. In his 1932 *roman à clef*, *Infants of the Spring*, focusing on "Niggerati Manor," Thurman fictionalized the activities and networks of the Harlem Renaissance itself, scrutinizing its quirks through a combination of fierce satire and tragic empathy. Such fictional treatments satirizing the middle class and highlighting the role of the folk gave heft and flavor to the controversial notion that the emerging Negro working class – with its labor unions, fraternal lodges, Back-to-Africa clubs, and other signs of cultural agency – was indeed the true New Negro.

Given the 1929 stock-market crash and the ensuing Depression, Thurman's novel served presciently as a swansong for the brief bohemian experiment. Ironically, such outrageously avant-garde cultural expression needed the patronage of the white wealthy, and as Hughes expressed in it in his 1940 autobiography, *The Big Sea*, the Depression made it certain that Harlem could no longer be quite "in vogue." When Harlem experienced a race riot in 1935, even Locke was forced to concede that the harsh racial brutalities of mass urban life could not be ignored (or lifted) by even the most brilliant art. By the time of Benjamin Brawley's magisterial 1937 artistic history, *The Negro Genius: A New Appraisal of the Achievement of the American Negro in Literature and the Fine Arts*, those writers and activists who had long been pushing the radical New Negro came into the limelight. Intellectuals like Du Bois, who had long flirted with socialism, sought ways to forge a pan-African agenda with revolutionary consciousness. Du Bois pursued this radical project in his 1928 fantasy novel, *Dark Princess*, which prophesies the symbolic marriage of the Orient and Africa as an anti-colonial romance embodied in the union of a son of African America and a princess from the Orient. He also pursued this project in his great 1935 revisionary history, *Black Reconstruction in America*, which brilliantly put to rest the Redemptionist propaganda of the Negro's corrupt role in Reconstruction and documented the period as laying the groundwork for a democratic, accountable public sphere. Other writers, such as Hughes, more overtly politicized their work, aiming it more squarely at the working poor, and experimenting with social and socialist realism in works like his 1930 novel *Not without Laughter*. Hughes's close friend, Arna Bontemps, published his 1936 historical novel on Gabriel Prosser's 1800 uprising, *Black Thunder*, bringing back into focus the firebrand New Negro as slave insurrectionist. With the white communist Jack Conroy, Bontemps published *They Seek a City* (1945), a portrait of the mass migration funded by Franklin D. Roosevelt's Works Progress Administration (WPA). New Marxist-influenced writers also came on the scene, revamping the New Negro through fictional representations that highlighted the intractable class structure of racial oppression. Whether flagrantly red or merely pink, working-class Negroes themselves were voicing their own claims to New Negrodom in union halls, letters to Negro newspapers, and occasionally in their own autobiographies. Angelo Herndon, a young coal-miner who became a leading communist organizer in Alabama, penned the autobiographical *Let Me Live* (1937) while serving a prison sentence for his political work. Radically revising the uplift memoir, Herndon returned to the Douglass-themed turning point of violent conversion, supplementing Douglass's vision of manhood freedom with communist consciousness, and tracking his own representative development through collective commitment to fundamental structural change. Most celebrated among these was the son of sharecroppers who fled North to Chicago, Richard Wright, who brought an edgier tone to New Negro protest in his blockbuster novel *Native Son* (1940), as well as in his WPA-funded work *12 Million Black Voices: A Folk History of the Negro in the United States* (1941), a collective portrait of the folk as energetic working-class agents of history, an image that starkly countered the boosterish Bookerite New Negro albums of 40 years earlier. Along with Wright, novelists like Ann Petry, William Attaway, and Chester Himes exploited social realism, naturalism, and Freudian psychoanalysis to uncover the psychological and social toll of racial and sexual oppression on the lives of everyday urban folk.

With the emergence of the nonviolent Civil Rights Movement after World War Two, however, the notion of the New Negro had begun to lose its resonance. Martin Luther King, Jr., the symbolic and organizational head of this new movement, still deployed the terminology of the New Negro, as he does in his 1958 book, *Stride toward Freedom*, a memoir of the 1955 Montgomery Bus Boycott:

> The members of the opposition had also revealed that they did not know the Negroes with whom they were dealing. They thought they were dealing with a group who could be cajoled or forced to do whatever the white man wanted them to do. They were not aware that they were dealing with Negroes who had been freed from fear. And so every move they made proved to be a mistake. It could not be otherwise, because their methods were geared to the "old Negro," and they were dealing with a "new Negro." (130)

In his 1963 book, *Why We Can't Wait*, justifying nonviolent direct action against a growing number of Black Power critics, King situates nonviolent direct action as the beneficiary, inheritance, and culmination of previous struggles of radical change from slave insurrections to the Black Muslims, and thus he posits the nonviolent movement as the teleological destiny of all those previous struggles: "For decades the long and winding trails led to dead ends" (33). As King was writing his apologia for nonviolent action, however, the very terms for renewing the Negro were experiencing a radical revision. The term "Negro" itself was falling into disfavor as the Black Power advocates sought to implode its usage as sheer anachronism, to be totally displaced with the term "Black." How ironic that for a century, African Americans had expended such intellectual, political, and cultural labor into revitalizing the notion of the Negro, only for the concept itself to become archaic, obsolete, reactionary, and irrelevant. By the 1960s the newest Negro was not a Negro at all, but a Black.

Bibliography

Cooper, Anna Julia. *A Voice from the South by a Black Woman of the South. 1892*. New York: Negro Universities Press, 1969.

Douglass, Frederick. *Narrative of the Life of Frederick Douglass, an American Slave. 1845*. Garden City: Doubleday, University of Virginia Library Digital Collections, 1993.

Du Bois, W.E.B. *The Souls of Black Folk*. Introduction by Donald B. Gibson. 1903. New York: Viking Penguin, 1989.

Foley, Barbara. *Spectres of 1919: Class and Nation in the Making of the New Negro*. Urbana: University of Illinois Press, 2003.

Gaines, Kevin K. *Uplifting the Race: Black Leadership, Politics, and Culture in the Twentieth Century*. Chapel Hill: University of North Carolina Press, 1996.

Gates, Henry Louis, Jr. "The Trope of the New Negro and the Reconstruction of the Image of the Black." *Representations* 24 (1988): 129–55.

Gates, Henry Louis, Jr. and Gene Andrew Jarrett, ed. *The New Negro: Readings on Race, Representation and African American Culture, 1892–1938*. Princeton: Princeton University Press, 2007.

Giddings, Paula. *When and Where I Enter: The Impact of Black Women on Race and Sex in America*. New York: Bantam Books, 1984.

Jacobs, Harriet. *Incidents in the Life of a Slave Girl*. Ed. L. Maria Child. 1861. Introduction and notes by Walter Teller. San Diego: Harvest/Harcourt Brace Jovanovich, 1973.

Johnson, James Weldon. *Black Manhattan. 1930*. Introduction by Sondra Kathryn Wilson. New York: Da Capo Press, 1991.

Johnson, James Weldon. *Autobiography of an Ex-Colored Man. 1912–1927*. Introduction by Henry Louis Gates. New York: Vintage/Random House, 1989.

Johnson, James Weldon, ed. *The Book of American Negro Poetry. 1922*. San Diego: Harvest/Harcourt Brace, 1969.

King, Martin Luther, Jr. *Stride toward Freedom. 1958*. New York: Harper & Row/Perennial Library, 1964.

King, Martin Luther, Jr. *Why We Can't Wait*. New York: Mentor/Penguin, 1964.

Locke, Alain. *The New Negro. 1925*. Introduction by Arnold Rampersad. New York: Atheneum, 1992.

Ross, Marlon B. *Manning the Race: Reforming Black Men in the Jim Crow Era*. New York: New York University Press, 2004.

Ross, Marlon B. "The New Negro Displayed: Self-Ownership, Proprietary Sites/Sights, and the Bonds/Bounds of Race." In *Claiming the Stones, Naming the Bones: Cultural Property and the Negotiation of National and Ethnic Identity*. Ed. Elazar Barkan and Ronald Bush. Los Angeles: Getty Research Institute, 2002. 259–301.

Thurman, Wallace. *Fire!!* 1.1 (1926).

Washington, Booker T. *A New Negro for a New Century*. Chicago: American Publishing House, 1900.

Washington, Booker T. *Up from Slavery. 1901*. New York: Viking Penguin, 1986.

Wheatley, Phillis. *The Collected Works of Phillis Wheatley*. Ed. John Shields. New York: Oxford University Press, 1988.

Wolters, Raymond. *The New Negro on Campus: Black College Rebellions of the 1920s*. Princeton: Princeton University Press, 1975.

11
The Dialect of New Negro Literature

Gene Andrew Jarrett

When Charles W. Chesnutt was first conceiving of "Mars Jeems Nightmare" – one of the seven stories he wrote between 1887 and 1897 that appeared in the *Atlantic Monthly*, *Overland Monthly*, and *Two Tales*, and that reappeared in *The Conjure Woman* (released in 1899) – he considered a different title: "De Noo Nigger." He confided this information in a letter, dated May 20, 1898, to Walter Hines Page, an editor of the *Atlantic Monthly*: "I have thought that a good title for the story would be 'De Noo Nigger,' but I don't care to dignify a doubtful word quite so much; it is all right for Julius [to use the phrase], but it might leave me under the suspicion of bad taste unless perchance the whole title's being in dialect should redeem it" (quoted in Sundquist 327–8). Chesnutt is referring to the word "nigger," which, if used in the title, would receive more attention than it deserved. After all, the story aims to show how the protagonist, Uncle Julius, an ingenious African American freeman, actually defies the profanity of "nigger." Nonetheless, Chesnutt's original "thought" is well taken: the trope of "de Noo Nigger" was indeed a reconstruction of the image of the black, but with a vernacular twist.[1] "Mars Jeems Nightmare," a story about how hoodoo turns a white master into a black slave and forces him to experience the painful fate of being a "noo nigger," ends up executing the advice that George Washington Cable provided Chesnutt in a September 25, 1889, letter: "You must remember that you are writing for white Americans and English," Cable stressed. "The greatest element of strength is to yield all the ground you honestly can to the possible prejudices of your reader" (quoted in Andrews 25). Put another way, the overt criticism of racial prejudice in white readers might not prove as polemically valuable or successful as the gambit of first indulging their racist sensibilities, then carefully disarming them of that racism. The fact that Cable is urging Chesnutt to put aside the ethical problem of being willingly complicit in expressions of racism is, of course, problematic. Nonetheless, Chesnutt internalizes Cable's recommendation enough to write *The Conjure Woman* mostly in black dialect, even as he also hopes to redeem Uncle Julius in the eyes of readers.

In this essay, I argue that certain African American writers, Chesnutt and Paul Laurence Dunbar above all, used dialect not merely to demonstrate class and intellectual divisions within and among social groups, but also to deliver subtle moral and political messages that elevated the sensibilities of whites on race and racism. Black dialect and racist iconography in antebellum minstrelsy not only inspired the mass appreciation of Anglo-American literature's so-called plantation tradition, which likewise utilized these protocols, but also set the stage for African American writers to exploit the protocols in counterintuitive ways on behalf of racial uplift. Since these writers often emphasized education and eloquence, the compromise between racial uplift, on the one hand, and minstrel imagery and discourse, on the other, explains one of the more ironic, if not paradoxical, features of African American literature at the turn into the twentieth century. However, as we later see in the case of Dunbar, the vogue for dialect had complicated as much as it had enhanced his poetics and polemics.

To categorize Chesnutt and Dunbar as racial uplift ideologues is to assert that they believed in the largely optimistic and romantic transition of African Americans from the "Old Negro" to the "New Negro" during the Civil War. At this time, their emancipation transformed them from chattel to citizen, from a state of political disenfranchisement to one of constitutional entitlement. Since then, African American writers and critics proceeded to interrogate the twin doctrines of white supremacy and anti-black racism in mainstream American culture. As varied as Chesnutt, Dunbar, Pauline Hopkins, Frances Ellen Watkins Harper, W.E.B. Du Bois, Booker T. Washington, James Weldon Johnson, Nella Larsen, and Alain Locke, these writers cooperated in the production of New Negro literature, which sought to prove that blacks, when represented as a race, could be uplifted in moral, intellectual, cultural, and economic ways. As Marlon B. Ross stresses in his essay for this Blackwell *Companion*, and as he and other authors have reiterated elsewhere, racial uplift was a source of inspiration and angst among generations of African American writers, but nonetheless it remains an important index to our understanding of African American literary history.[2]

Literary representations of the New Negro exhibited *character*. "Literary character," according to Elizabeth McHenry, "offered black Americans a way to refute widespread claims of their miserable, degraded position; examples of it, made visible at meetings of African American literary societies or through the pages of an African American newspaper, would counter assumptions of African inferiority with displays of black genius" (85). Literary character, Ross adds, belonged to a cultural iconography in which "[t]he energetic force of the black body is indicated in its very composition and stance – the serious countenance of the face, the concentrated intentness of the eyes, the upward bearing of the head, the alert posture of the limbs" (49). New Negro literature aimed to heighten the language and the refinement of all African Americans – whether light-skinned or dark-skinned, racially mixed or "authentic" – in order to suggest that they could assimilate to national "civilization."

The nineteenth-century black press was sometimes so preoccupied with racial uplift that they went so far as to dissuade African Americans from writing about themselves altogether. In the January 7, 1848, issue of *North Star*, Frederick Douglass tries to rally his readers around two causes: "we must do just what white men do," and "we must take our stand side by side with our white fellow countrymen, in all the trades, arts, profession[s] and callings of the day" (quoted in McHenry 116–17). A September 1894 article published in *Woman's Era*, titled "Negro Folk-Lore," reiterates this point by encouraging "the colored people [to] make all haste to drop those marks distinctly Negroid, to strive to write like a white man, dress like a white man, and talk like one, and so hasten on the day when they will be distinguished only as 'Americans'" (quoted in McHenry 235). Although published half a century apart, these two articles share at least three goals: first, to demonstrate that the literary sophistication of African Americans rivaled that of their Anglo-American counterparts; second, to prove the cultural and intellectual equality of these two groups; and third, to substantiate the political arguments for African American enfranchisement.

Despite the admirable argument for racial self-improvement, New Negro literature proved unpalatable to mainstream (and usually white) literary critics. They dismissed the relatively bourgeois and eloquent New Negro protagonists as unintelligible and unrealistic. Richard Watson Gilder and William Dean Howells, for example, disparaged Chesnutt's 1901 novel, *The Marrow of Tradition*, as "amorphous" and "artificial," respectively.[3] Criticism of this sort encoded a broader devaluation – again, mostly in mainstream critical circles – of the formal and thematic propriety of New Negro literature, a quality, according to Victoria Earle Matthews, that African American writers must maintain. In "The Value of Race Literature," an address she delivered at the First Conference of Colored Women of the United States in Boston on July 30, 1895, Matthews stresses that "Race Literature," her term for what we now call African American literature, must either contain the kind of "race matter" uplifting the African American experience or the kind of high aesthetics that may be deemed universal in appeal. When "developed," this literature will "compare favorably with many, but [also] will stand out pre-eminent [*sic*], not only in the limited history of colored people, but in the broader field of universal literature" (173). By dignifying the qualities of African Americans that tend to be "wrongly interpreted" and "often grossly exaggerated," Matthews held that Race Literature will "enlarge our scope, make us better known wherever real lasting culture exists, will undermine and *utterly drive out the traditional Negro in dialect*, – the subordinate, the servant as the type representing a race whose numbers are now far into the millions" (172, 173; my emphasis).

Matthews's condemnation of "the traditional Negro in dialect" reflects her concern with the dilemma of racial uplift ideologues and their literary representatives in American culture: the ongoing appreciation of the Old Negro and the disesteem of the New. *Dialect*, specifically, was a dominant verbal and orthographic metonym of the Old Negro, whose origins trace back to the 1820s, when American culture was anchored to what scholar George Fredrickson calls "romantic racialism," which "simply endorsed the 'child' stereotype of the most sentimental school of proslavery paternalists and plantation romancers" (101, 102). The cultural consequences of romantic racialism crystallized during Reconstruction in the 1870s and 1880s, when federal mandates tried to transform the antebellum "Old South" from Democratic sensibilities that once endorsed slavery and racial inequality into a "New South" in which Republican notions of free labor and racial equality prevailed. The progress in racial politics facilitated by Reconstruction, however, incited anti-black feeling among Anglo-American citizens, a feeling that the postbellum minstrel show refracted through black dialect and racist iconography. Ranging from African American uncles and mammies to "chillun'" dressing, talking, behaving, and thinking in inferior ways, the dialect of minstrelsy became a cultural phenomenon that alleged the utter simplicity of African Americans and thus the improbability of their uplift. The ascription of dialect to racial authenticity – such that it elicited critical acclaim for its "novelty," "curiosity," "genuine" quality, "bona fide" nature, essence "without artifice," as scholar Robert C. Toll has shown – was prerequisite to a mainstream appreciation of what was taken to be African American culture (201).

New Negro literature, needless to say, refused to incorporate the dialect of minstrelsy. For this reason, it could not compete in a commercial marketplace whose romantic racialism sustained minstrel dialect and iconography in American literary forms. Retrospectively described as the plantation tradition, this kind of literature came mainly from the pens of Anglo-American Southerners, including Thomas Dunn English, the brothers Sidney and Clifford Lanier, Irwin Russell, George Tucker, James Ewell Heath, Harriet Beecher Stowe, Francis Hopkinson Smith, Mark Twain, John Esten Cooke, John Pendleton Kennedy, William Gilmore Simms, and, above all, Joel Chandler Harris and Thomas Nelson Page (both of whom, incidentally, regarded Russell as a literary mentor). While the works of these authors are not entirely homogeneous, the scholar David W. Blight suggests that their choice of language, plot, characters, settings, symbols, and themes consistently romanticize the plantation societies and cultures of the Old South in order to communicate and alleviate national anxieties over sectional reunion between the South and the North. By the 1890s, literary audiences embraced the literary orthography of African American dialect as much as minstrel audiences had decades earlier.

The 1890s marked the literary prime of Chesnutt and Dunbar, two individuals who excelled more than any other African American contemporary in capitalizing on the sales of literary dialect. But these authors were equally adept at exploiting the potential for racial uplift within the form. As mentioned at the outset of this essay, Chesnutt and Cable corresponded in 1889 on using dialect to appeal to and then disarm racial prejudices. Actually, Chesnutt considered experimenting in this form about a decade earlier. According to his journal entry dated May 29, 1880, he wanted to write literature softer than the "trumpet tones" of New Negro literature. The softer tones, perhaps, could result in the moral uplift of white readers, by which the uplift of black citizens would be indirect:

> The object of my writings would be not so much the elevation of the colored people as *the elevation of the whites*, – for I consider the unjust spirit of caste which is so insidious

> as to pervade the whole nation, and so powerful as to subject a whole race and all connected with it to scorn and social ostracism – I consider this a barrier to the moral progress of the American people; and I would be one of the first to head a determined, organized crusade against it. … But the subtle almost indefinable feeling of repulsion toward the negro, which is common to most Americans – and easily enough accounted for – , cannot be stormed and taken by assault; the garrison will not capitulate: so their position must be mined, and we will find ourselves in their midst before they think it. (Quoted in Brodhead, *Journals* 139–40; my emphasis)

We should never forget that "Chesnutt was resolutely middle class," according to Eric Sundquist, "and the majority of his published fiction … reflects in some measure his genteel literary tastes." Indeed, Chesnutt's "color line" stories – best exemplified by his 1899 collection, *The Wife of His Youth and Other Stories of the Color-Line*, and his 1901 novel, *The Marrow of Tradition* – portray educated and eloquent African Americans. But Chesnutt also knew that his other book, *The Conjure Woman*, "reflects his concern that the rise of a black middle class could jeopardize racial cohesiveness in the very act of uplifting the race and sacrifice a distinctive strain of African-American art whose record lay in the oral narratives" (Sundquist 298). The development of dialect-speaking Uncle Julius, the protagonist of the conjure tales, makes sense in these terms, but I would still posit that Chesnutt never entirely relinquishes racial uplift as a literary strategy. Rather, he suggests that, while "the problem of the Twentieth Century is the problem of the color-line," as Du Bois stated in 1903, its solution requires as much the moral elevation of whites as it does the material elevation of blacks.

"Uncle" Julius McAdoo is a parody of Uncle Remus, the main character of Joel Chandler Harris's plantation books, including *Uncle Remus, His Songs and His Sayings: Folklore of the Old Plantation* (1880), *Nights with Uncle Remus: Myths and Legends of the Old Plantation* (1883), *Daddy Jake the Runaway, and Short Stories Told after Dark by "Uncle Remus"* (1889), and *Uncle Remus and His Friends: Old Plantation Stories, Songs, and Ballads* (1892). Since both protagonists resemble each another in age, behavior, vernacular, and dress, *The Conjure Woman* seems yet another example of minstrel realism. The book employs the well-known technique of frame narration to recreate the conversations between John and Annie, a white Northern married couple, and Uncle Julius, whom they hired as a coachman upon moving to central North Carolina and purchasing a vineyard there. John describes in formal English his own experiences in North Carolina; he proceeds to recount in Uncle Julius's dialect several stories about conjure in slave communities; then he (occasionally with Annie) concludes with assessments of the impact of these stories on their lives.

Of all the stories, "Mars Jeems's Nightmare" illustrates best how the minstrel gambit of dialect in *The Conjure Woman* enables Chesnutt to subvert the implications of minstrelsy and the plantation literary tradition. The story begins with John's disappointment with the irresponsibility and laziness of a newly hired stableman and gardener, Tom, whom Uncle Julius calls his grandson. John decides to fire Tom and apprise Uncle Julius, who, now saddened, heeds his employer's instruction to take an afternoon drive around the town. While waiting for water, they observe an acquaintance, Mr. McLean, excessively beating a horse into submission. Uncle Julius then proceeds to warn John and Annie that if the man continues to abuse his horse, he will suffer the nightmare of his own grandfather, Jeems McLean, a former master himself. Master Jeems so mistreated his slaves that he once exiled the girlfriend of one of his slaves, Solomon, because she was a distraction. Solomon then asked a local conjure woman, Aunt Peggy, to help him get her back – which she did by casting a spell that erased Master Jeems's memory and turned him into an African American slave on his own plantation. Ironically, Master Jeems's overseer hated this "brash" new slave: so rebellious, lazy, and impudent was the "noo nigger," "puttin' on airs, des lack he wuz a w'ite man," that the overseer whipped him innumerable times. Eventually, the conjure woman returned Master Jeems to his original body, but "dress' lack a po' w'ite man," disheveled by his "most'us bad dream, – fac', a reg'lar, nach'ul nightmare" (Chesnutt 61, 65, 66).

Amid this wending tale, the evidence of Chesnutt's critique of Joel Chandler Harris's stories is striking. According to Sundquist, "Mars Jeems's Nightmare" alludes to *Harris's* portrayal of Mars (or "master") Jeems, whom Uncle Remus, as a slave, both protects and serves. "Mars Jeems's Nightmare," Sundquist notes, "is an example of Chesnutt's signifying upon Harris" (327). There are as many levels of imitation and mediation in such African American literature as there were among African American minstrel performers, who, as Gavin Jones reminds us, created "protean genres" after the Civil War: "They encompassed whites denigrating blacks, blacks demeaning blacks because that was what whites wanted to hear, blacks signifying on whites through dialectical double meaning, blacks protesting to blacks about racial abuse, and blacks presenting a nonoffensive version of blackness to the middle classes, both black and white" (180). More to the point, Sundquist states that African Americans were performing "imitation with a vengeance" against the minstrel caricatures of their communities (286).

Around the time Chesnutt was publishing *The Conjure Woman* and grappling with the moral gambit of black dialect, Paul Laurence Dunbar had released four books of short stories – *Folks from Dixie* (1898), *The Strength of Gideon and Other Stories* (1900), *In Old Plantation Days* (1903), and *The Heart of Happy Hollow* (1904) – dealing with the same set of issues. *Folks from Dixie* and *The Strength of Gideon* are collections of short stories focusing on the antebellum trials and tribulations of African America. The books met the public expectation that African American literature should, at the very minimum, venture a realistic representation of African American life, and at its very best, appear to inscribe this representation within the cultural politics of minstrelsy. Both collections concentrate mostly on slaves of the Southern plantation or on African Americans trying to navigate the urban terrains and free societies of the Northeast.

Of all the stories in the first two collections – 12 and 20, respectively – the title story of *The Strength of Gideon* captures best how dialect can mediate the thematic contradiction in black political ideology between, on the one hand, the African

American accommodation of white privilege and, on the other, the assertion of racial independence. Gideon, a slave born into an antebellum society of African American religious faith, has developed unwavering commitments not only to his master but to his own wife and his race as well. But when the master asks Gideon to promise to help take care of the "women folks" on the plantation during the Civil War, the slave experiences a crisis of loyalty. Emancipation has inspired the slaves on the plantation, including Gideon's wife, to consider fleeing northward and securing their own freedom. In the face of this smoldering resistance to the status quo, Gideon demonstrates the "strength" to remain faithful to his promise. Implicit in this loyalty is Gideon's belief that the conditions of slavery, however problematic, have not yet proven so unbearable as to warrant his own flight. Presumably shared by most readers of *The Strength of Gideon*, Gideon's feelings might rationalize at least two ideas: first, certain African Americans desired to remain enslaved in order to fulfill their duties admirably; and second, the story, "The Strength of Gideon," counters the history of African American trauma during slavery. Of course, it could be argued, rather simply, that the story and the collection as a whole represent mostly fictional accounts. However, reviews of the book regarded the texts as realistic. And the obfuscation of history in the name of racial realism had long characterized the plantation tradition of Anglo-American literature.

"Viney's Free Papers," also in the 1900 collection, echoes "The Strength of Gideon." Viney is a slave who secures the manumission paperwork for his wife, who then threatens to leave him when he resists the idea of achieving freedom in the North. Many manumitted slaves were traveling to the North, but, Viney argued, if freedom could not be experienced in the South, where the slaves were born and reared, it should not be experienced at all. Again, an unshakable fidelity to the family heritage and social stability of slavery trumps the desire for freedom. This story is not new in African American literary history; Booker T. Washington's autobiography, *Up from Slavery* (1901), described slaves preferring to stay on the plantation rather than enjoying emancipation. The appearance of this kind of story in *The Strength of Gideon*, as opposed to the more revolutionary and volatile narratives of slave insurrection (such as Nat Turner's) in order to secure freedom, certainly could have impressed on readers in Dunbar's era a highly conciliatory, if unbalanced, picture of slave life. Subversive humor in the stories of *The Strength of Gideon*, of course, encourage readers knowledgeable of African American history to cast a doubtful eye on this entertaining picture of racial conciliation. But Dunbar's overt catering to accommodationist or gradualist sensibilities betrays the more honest stance he consistently held in his nonfictional essays about the importance of expeditious African American intellectual and cultural progress, or racial uplift.

Despite probably boosting the critical and commercial success of *The Strength of Gideon*, initial reviews of the book reduce its complexity. The reviews perpetuate the view that the volume is a formula of "plantation" stories and that Dunbar is a novice.[4] Almost all the reviews laud the book's realistic depictions of "the character, feeling and sentiment of the southern darkey." The "plantation tales show the Negro in his truest light – fervid, credulous, full of rich, unconscious humor; lazy sometimes, but capable of dog-like faithfulness." And the stories "are correct reflections of the Negro dialect and habits and thoughts of the southern darkey."[5] (The interspersion throughout the book of E.W. Kemble's caricatures of the African Americans featured in the stories certainly contributed to such impressions.)

A closer look at *The Strength of Gideon*, however, reveals that most of these reviews missed crucial indications of Dunbar's commitment to racial uplift, manifest in his subtle thematic resistance to pastoral and minstrel imagery. Several stories portray African American demonstrations of resilience and perseverance in the face of social and cultural difficulties. In "The Ingrate," a story recalling the centrality of literacy to securing freedom in the antebellum slave narrative, a boy teaches himself to read while serving as an accountant for his master. Eventually he runs away, and his literacy qualifies him for the position of Union army sergeant during the Civil War. "The Finish of Patsy Barnes" concerns a boy who learns to tend and ride racehorses in order to pay for the healthcare of his sick mother, despite the racism entrenched in the racing industry. Finally, "Silas Jackson" follows the journey of a Southern country boy to a faraway aristocratic resort where, through hard work and humility, he "refines" his interactive and verbal skills and ascends to a managerial position. He later volunteers as leading tenor of the hotel's quartet, which enables him to travel to Northern cities to perform, but eventually his singing talents decline and he returns to his Southern home to persevere as a field-worker. Of course, *The Strength of Gideon* includes the more conventional examples of New Negro literature. "One Man's Fortunes, "Mr. Cornelius Johnson, Office-Seeker," "A Mess of Pottage," and "A Council of State" are stories about educated African Americans struggling to understand US social, political, and legal strategies of racial uplift. Whether conventionally uplifting or less attuned to middle-class sensibilities, *The Strength of Gideon* is more politically active than early readers realized.

Published three years after *The Strength of Gideon*, his next book of short stories, *In Old Plantation Days*, scholars have said, bears a title capturing the generic limitations within which Dunbar wrote. Accordingly, the collection represents one of his "chief" contributions to the plantation tradition of American literature (Brawley 96; Revell 108). Indeed, the collection of 25 stories revisits several of the same formulaic literary strategies and themes that have entertained white readers of *Folks from Dixie* and *The Strength of Gideon*. But *In Old Plantation Days* differs from these collections in one respect: most of the stories are set on the plantation of Stuart Mordaunt, partially explaining Dunbar's selection of the volume's title. Like the white "frame narrator" of Chesnutt's *The Conjure Woman*, Mordaunt is a master often kindhearted and open-minded toward his family and slaves, and these traits help to nurture a plantation atmosphere in which blacks and whites generally get along, respect one another, and form a tight social unit. The general collegiality between whites and blacks, as well as masters and slaves, in such stories as "The Walls of Jericho" and "How Brother Parker Fell from Grace" subordinates the history of interracial tension to the possibilities of interracial conciliation. In this regard, Dunbar arguably plays into the hands of the plantation tradition, reinforcing contemporaneous and mostly white sensibilities of racism or racial prejudice. Whites end up serving the black moral, religious, and political interests that reinforce communal networks, but the whites do so, of course, within the peculiar institution of slavery, which is predicated on tearing down these networks.

Although both Chesnutt and Dunbar were quite successful writers of literary dialect, Dunbar was the most accomplished and embattled during his lifetime (which lasted from 1872 to 1906). By the time he died just short of his 34th birthday, he had published 14 books of poetry, four books of short stories, four novels, and numerous songs, dramatic works, short stories, poems, and essays in several American periodicals. Beginning in the mid-1890s, he became the first American author of African descent to be an international phenomenon. Fellow writers and critics alike anointed him the literary laureate of the black race, spurring the extraordinary commercial sales of his creative writings, and establishing the public terms by which other black writers of his era and thereafter were appreciated. Yet he also negotiated a personal crisis. Evidently, his creative loyalties were torn between, on the one hand, demonstrating his commitment to black political progress and, on the other, representing blacks as slaves and their language as dialect, which are what prominent literary critics and publishers expected of him and black writers in general.

Dunbar rose to fame in the early months of 1896, when James A. Herne returned to his hotel in Toledo, Ohio, the city where he was directing and performing in his most popular play to date, *Shore Acres*. The hotel clerk informed the preeminent actor and playwright that Dunbar had left him a gift. Indeed, after attending and enjoying *Shore Acres*, Dunbar decided to leave Herne a complimentary copy of his second and latest book, *Majors and Minors* (1896). Fortunately for the African American poet, Herne was well acquainted with the most authoritative literary reviewer, cultural critic, editor, and publisher at the time, the so-called Dean of American Letters, William Howells. After sending his appreciation to Dunbar, Herne passed *Majors and Minors* on to Howells, who decided to review the book in the June 27, 1896, issue of *Harper's Weekly*.

The book's frontispiece, an image of a dark-skinned Dunbar at age 18, convinced Howells of what kind of writing should appear in the book: dialect. When Howells encountered the book, he noticed an opening section, "Majors and Minors," comprising approximately 70 prayers, lyrics, odes, ballads, and sonnets, amounting to nearly 75 percent of the book's total poems. Displaying formal – or what Howells calls "literary" – English, most of the poems in this section employ and sometimes play with the conventional diction, rhyme schemes, and metrical structures of classical Western poetry. Some poems explore sublime and universal themes of art, love, loss, family, and nature, recalling the work of British Romantic poets such as Percy Bysshe Shelley, Lord Byron, John Keats, William Wordsworth, and Samuel Taylor Coleridge.

Several other poems counterbalance these universal narratives with specific racial and historical references to events, concepts, and figures, including poems on Frederick Douglass, on the legacy of Ethiopia, and on why blacks "wear the mask" to feign collective joy amid bouts of racial misery.

However, Howells gravitated not to Dunbar's formal verse but to his dialect. In his review of *Majors and Minors*, Howells suggests that in order to assure both critical acclaim and commercial success, the poet should dedicate himself to writing verses only in "black" dialect, similar to those filling the second and smaller section of *Majors and Minors*, titled "Humor and Dialect." For Dunbar is "most himself," Howells insists, when he writes in such informal or colloquial English. Howells subtly reiterates this assessment one month later in a letter to Ripley Hitchcock, then serving as literary editor and advisor at D. Appleton and Company, stating that "I believe a book of entirely *black* verse from [Dunbar] would succeed. My notice raised such interest." Dunbar's *de facto* standing as "Poet Laureate of the Negro Race," the highest distinction enjoyed by any African American author in the late nineteenth century, resulted from Howells's review of *Majors and Minors* and his validation of black dialect as a form of African American literature.

Howells's obsession with "entirely black verse," however, causes him to misrepresent certain "humor and dialect" verses as "black" and to misread their polemics. For example, a poem that Howells lauds in his review, "When Malindy Sings," focuses on a singer who captivates anyone who hears her.

> G'way an' quit dat noise, Miss Lucy—
>   Put dat music book away;
> What's de use to keep on tryin'?
>   Ef you practise twell you're gray,
> You cain't sta't no notes a-flyin'
>   Lak de ones dat rants and rings
> F'om de kitchen to be big woods
>   When Malindy sings.
>
> You ain't got de nachel o'gans
>   Fu' to make de soun' come right,
> You ain't got de tu'ns an' twistin's
>   Fu' to make it sweet an' light.
> Tell you one thing now, Miss Lucy,
>   An' I'm tellin' you fu' true,
> When hit comes to raal right singin',
>   'T ain't no easy thing to do.
>
> Easy 'nough fu' folks to hollah,
>   Lookin' at de lines an' dots,
> When dey ain't no one kin sence it,
>   An' de chune comes in, in spots;
> But fu' real melojous music,
>   Dat jes' strikes yo' hea't and clings,

Jes' you stan' an' listen wif me
   When Malindy sings.

Ain't you nevah hyeahd Malindy?
   Blessed soul, tek up de cross!
Look hyeah, ain't you jokin', honey?
   Well, you don't know whut you los'.
Y' ought to hyeah dat gal a-wa'blin',
   Robins, la'ks, an' all dem things,
Heish dey moufs an' hides dey faces
   When Malindy sings.

Fiddlin' man jes' stop his fiddlin',
   Lay his fiddle on de she'f;
Mockin'-bird quit tryin' to whistle,
   'Cause he jes' so shamed hisse'f.
Folks a-playin' on de banjo
   Draps dey fingahs on de strings—
Bless yo' soul – fu'gits to move em,
   When Malindy sings.

She jes' spreads huh mouf and hollahs,
   "Come to Jesus," twell you hyeah
Sinnahs' tremblin' steps and voices,
   Timid-lak a-drawin' neah;
Den she tu'ns to "Rock of Ages,"
   Simply to de cross she clings,
An' you fin' yo' teahs a-drappin'
   When Malindy sings.

Who dat says dat humble praises
   Wif de Master nevah counts?
Heish yo' mouf, I hyeah dat music,
   Ez hit rises up an' mounts—
Floatin' by de hills an' valleys,
   Way above dis buryin' sod,
Ez hit makes its way in glory
   To de very gates of God!

Oh, hit's sweetah dan de music
   Of an edicated band;
An' hit's dearah dan de battle's
   Song o' triumph in de lan'.
It seems holier dan evenin'
   When de solemn chu'ch bell rings,
Ez I sit an' ca'mly listen
   While Malindy sings.

Towsah, stop dat ba'kin', hyeah me!
  Mandy, mek dat chile keep still;
Don't you hyeah de echoes callin'
  F'om de valley to de hill?
Let me listen, I can hyeah it,
  Th'oo de bresh of angels' wings,
Sof' an' sweet, "Swing Low, Sweet Chariot,"
  Ez Malindy sings. (Dunbar, *Collected Poetry* 82–3)

Buried beneath the poem's dense dialect, sentimental aura, and minstrel imagery (such as the banjo player) is the reference to Malindy's song, "Swing Low, Sweet Chariot":

Chorus:

Swing low, sweet chariot,
Coming for to carry me home.
Swing low, sweet chariot,
Coming for to carry me home.

I looked over Jordan and what did I see,
Coming for to carry me home?
A band of angels coming after me,
Coming for to carry me home.

(*chorus*)

If you get there before I do,
Coming for to carry me home,
Tell all my friends I'm coming too,
Coming for to carry me home.

(*chorus*)

The brightest day that ever I saw,
Coming for to carry me home,
When Jesus washed my sins away,
Coming for to carry me home.

(*chorus*)

I'm sometimes up and sometimes down,
Coming for to carry me home,
But still my soul feels heavenly bound
Coming for to carry me home.

(*chorus*) (reprinted in Cooper 81–2)

This "Negro spiritual" was first sung by slaves and, for generations, passed down among blacks as a melody of religious hope and civil rights activism. In fact, the musical notation of it is included in the epigraph of chapter 12 (about Alexander Crummell, an African American missionary, teacher, and activist) in Du Bois's 1903 book, *The Souls of Black Folk*. Du Bois's is a hallmark study of the slave's "sorrow songs," still known by Dunbar and several fellow first-generation African Americans born after slavery. "Swing Low, Sweet Chariot," first composed by Wallis Willis, a freedman, just before the Civil War, casts black struggle as divine aspiration.

Ultimately, Howells's review generated much critical excitement over the implications of *Majors and Minors*, but not for the kind of polemics in "When Malindy Sings." The repercussions were immediate when the readers of *Harper's Weekly* learned that Dunbar represented the "Robert Burns of Negro Poetry," a poet who wrote with the authentic voice of his race. In the wake of Howells's review, various lay and intellectual communities read, discussed, or wrote about the review, appreciating Dunbar in a way analogous to the way in which advertisers and audiences appreciated African American minstrel performers. Periodicals such as *Woman's Era*, an African American periodical that hailed the importance of Howells's review to African American communities across the country, helped turn Dunbar into a racial phenomenon. Between September 1896 and May 1897, other reviewers of Dunbar's book echoed Howells. One reviewer regarded *Majors and Minors* a "remarkably hopeful production" and a "triumphant demonstration" of the potential of the black race for verbal rhyme and melody. Another believed that the book "was not great, but it had, in its dialect verse at least, a certain homeliness of sentiment which challenged attention" (quoted in Metcalf 127). Greater proof of Dunbar's phenomenal rise appeared in reviews of his next book of poems, *Lyrics of Lowly Life*. Printed between January 1897 and April 1898 in major US and British periodicals, the 10 reviews praised Dunbar's orthography of dialect as an accurate and authentic recreation of African American vernacular. The critics stated that the dialect poems were "on the whole, excellent"; examples of a Negro being "thoroughly spontaneous and natural"; "pure Negro songs"; "not overloaded … with ornaments of culture so heavy and costly that the slender thought can stagger beneath the weight"; expressions of "a certain homeliness of sentiment which challenged attention"; and, finally, contributions to his "becom[ing] an interesting phenomena. He is a full blood Negro" (quoted in Metcalf 127–9). These phrases characterizing Dunbar's dialect poems echo those phrases previously applied to black minstrel performance, and those phrases central to Howells's review of *Majors and Minors*.

Associating Dunbar with minstrel realism departs from twentieth-century debates over whether or not he sold out to inherently racist mainstream literary and publishing tastes. Currently, the most popular scholarly argument on this subject emphasizes Dunbar's disenchantment with Howells and American literary criticism, and shows that the poet was more polemical than his mainstream readers might have realized. Indeed, Dunbar held mixed feelings about Howells's review. Sixteen days after it appeared, Dunbar sent Howells a letter (July 13, 1896) stating that he had read the article and "felt its effect" (quoted in Howells, *Life in Letters* 67). Less than a year after thanking Howells, however, Dunbar lamented on October 22, 1896: "One critic says a thing and the rest hasten to say the same thing, in many instances using the identical words. I see now very clearly that Mr. Howells has done me irrevocable harm in the dictum he laid down regarding my dialect verse. I am afraid that it will even influence English criticism" ("Unpublished Letters" 73). Dunbar realized that Howells was little different from many of the audiences of minstrel shows. The Dean was one of many "intelligent people … unable to differentiate dialect as a philological branch from the burlesque of Negro minstrelsy" (Dunbar quoted in Flusche 52).

Dunbar's dialect poems were all along protesting against minstrel realism even as they seemed to be perpetuating it. This argument, made by such scholars as Joanne M. Braxton, Gavin Jones, Dickson D. Bruce, Marcellus Blount, Darwin Turner, John Keeling, and James A. Emanuel, recalls that that African American performers of minstrelsy imitated blackface minstrelsy with a vengeance against Old Negro stereotypes. The public misinterpretations of Dunbar's dialect poetry and black minstrelsy were also analogous: audiences tended to miss the protest of black minstrelsy, just as readers often failed to detect the protest of Dunbar and African American authors of dialect literature.

Dunbar's polemical interests are conceivable. The record shows that minstrel realism bothered Dunbar well before Howells catapulted him into literary prominence. To his wife of 43 days, Alice Ruth Moore, Dunbar sent a letter wondering if he and other African American writers were obligated to contest the plantation tradition.[6] Little did Dunbar know that, one year later, the critical and commercial success of *Majors and Minors* would conspire to help standardize dialect for African American literature. Dunbar's own rationale for writing dialect poetry contrasted with the public perception that its racial representations advanced the plantation tradition to the next, more authentic stage of minstrel realism. Consequently, Dunbar faced a dual battle early in his literary career: a war against minstrel realism and another against readers that pigeonholed his dialect poetry into this cultural genre – two wars that would preoccupy him until his death.

Notes

1 I am punning on the title of the essay by Gates, "The Trope of a New Negro and the Reconstruction of the Image of the Black."

2 Since the publication of Henry Louis Gates, Jr.'s landmark essay, "The Trope of a New Negro and the Reconstruction of the Image of the Black," the most notable examples of scholarship specifically about the New Negro include works by Wilson Moses, George Hutchinson, J. Martin Favor, William J. Maxwell, Rebecca Carroll, Anne Elizabeth Carroll, Martha Jane Nadell, Marlon B. Ross, and Gates and Gene Andrew Jarrett.

3 Gilder quoted in Wonham, "Curious Psychological" 55; Howells quoted in Wonham, "Writing Realism" 708.

4 For examples of such deprecations, see Brawley 96, 104; Revell 108, 113.

5 Reviewers quoted in Metcalf 136–8.

6 Dunbar to Moore, April 17, 1895 (reprinted in Martin and Primeau 428).

Bibliography

Anderson, Lisa. "From Blackface to 'Genuine Negroes': Nineteenth-Century Minstrelsy and the Icon of the 'Negro'." *Theatre Research International* 21.1 (1996): 17–23.

Andrews, William L., ed. *The Literary Career of Charles W. Chesnutt*. Baton Rouge: Louisiana State University Press, 1980.

Blight, David W. *Race and Reunion: The Civil War in American Memory*. Cambridge, MA: Belknap, 2001.

Brawley, Benjamin Griffith. *Paul Laurence Dunbar, Poet of His People*. Port Washington, NY: Kennikat, 1967.

Brodhead, Richard, ed. *The Journals of Charles W. Chesnutt*. Durham, NC: Duke University Press, 1993.

Carroll, Anne Elizabeth. *Word, Image, and the New Negro: Representation and Identity in the Harlem Renaissance*. Bloomington: Indiana University Press, 2005.

Carroll, Rebecca, ed. *Uncle Tom or New Negro: African Americans Reflect on Booker T. Washington and "Up from Slavery" 100 Years Later*. New York: Broadway Books/Harlem Moon, 2006.

Chesnutt, Charles W. *The Conjure Woman and Other Tales*. Durham, NC: Duke University Press, 1993.

Cooper, Michael L. *Slave Spirituals and the Jubilee Singers*. New York: Clarion, 2001.

Du Bois, W.E.B. *The Souls of Black Folk*. 1903. New York: Penguin, 1989.

Dunbar, Paul Laurence. *The Collected Poetry of Paul Laurence Dunbar*. Ed. Joanne M. Braxton. Charlottesville: University Press of Virginia, 1993.

Dunbar, Paul Laurence. *Majors and Minors*. Toledo, OH: Hadley & Hadley, 1896.

Dunbar, Paul Laurence. "Unpublished Letters of Paul Laurence Dunbar to a Friend." *Crisis* 20 (1920): 73–6.

Favor, J. Martin. *Authentic Blackness: The Folk in the New Negro Renaissance*. Durham, NC and London: Duke University Press, 1999.

Flusche, Michael. "Paul Laurence Dunbar and the Burden of Race." *Southern Humanities Review* 11.1 (1977): 49–61.

Fredrickson, George M. *The Black Image in the White Mind: The Debate on Afro-American Character and Destiny, 1817–1914*. New York: Harper & Row, 1972.

Gates, Henry Louis, Jr. "The Trope of a New Negro and the Reconstruction of the Image of the Black." *Representations* 24 (1988): 129–55.

Gates, Henry Louis, Jr. and Gene Andrew Jarrett. *The New Negro: Readings on Race, Representation, and African American Culture, 1892–1938*. Princeton: Princeton University Press, 2007.

Hutchinson, George. *The Harlem Renaissance in Black and White*. Cambridge, MA: Belknap, 1995.

Jarrett, Gene Andrew. *Deans and Truants: Race and Realism in African American Literature*. Philadelphia: University of Pennsylvania Press, 2007.

Jones, Gavin. *Strange Talk: The Politics of Dialect in Gilded Age America*. Berkeley and Los Angeles: University of California Press, 1999.

Martin, Herbert Woodward and Ronald Primeau, ed. *In His Own Voice: The Dramatic and Other Uncollected Works of Paul Laurence Dunbar*. Athens: Ohio University Press, 2002.

Matthews, Victoria Earle. "The Value of Race Literature." First Congress of Colored Women of the United States (July 30, 1895). *The Massachusetts Review* (1986): 169–85.

Maxwell, William J. *New Negro, Old Left: African-American Writing and Communism between the Wars*. New York: Columbia University Press, 1999.

McHenry, Elizabeth. *Forgotten Readers: Recovering the Lost History of African American Literary Societies*. Durham, NC: Duke University Press, 2002.

Metcalf, E.W. *Paul Laurence Dunbar: A Bibliography*. Metuchen, NJ: Scarecrow, 1975.

Moses, Wilson Jeremiah. *The Golden Age of Black Nationalism, 1850–1925*. New York: Oxford University Press, 1988.

Nadell, Martha Jane. *Enter the New Negroes: Images of Race in American Culture*. Cambridge, MA: Harvard University Press, 2004.

Nowatzki, Robert C. " 'Passing' in a White Genre: Charles W. Chesnutt's Negotiations of the Plantation Tradition in *The Conjure Woman*." *American Literary Realism* 27.2 (1995): 20–36.

Revell, Peter. *Paul Laurence Dunbar*. Boston, MA: Twayne, 1979.

Ross, Marlon B. *Manning the Race: Reforming Black Men in the Jim Crow Era*. New York: New York University Press, 2004.

Sundquist, Eric J. *To Wake the Nations: Race in the Making of American Literature*. Cambridge, MA: Belknap, 1993.

Toll, Robert C. *Blacking Up: The Minstrel Show in Nineteenth Century America*. New York: Oxford University Press, 1974.

Wonham, Henry B. "'The Curious Psychological Spectacle of a Mind Enslaved': Charles W. Chesnutt and Dialect Fiction." *Mississippi Quarterly* 51.1 (1997–8): 55–69.

Wonham, Henry B. "Writing Realism, Policing Consciousness: Howells and the Black Body." *American Literature* 67 (1995): 701–24.

12
African American Literary Realism, 1865–1914

Andreá N. Williams

> *I am going to refer briefly to some {literature}, and point out how in these writings the Negro has been used, then leave it to you whether or not there has been such a portrayal of his life and character as I have said true realism, and therefore true art, should give.*
>
> (Chesnutt, "The Negro in Books" 430)

In his retrospective survey "The Negro in Books" (1916), novelist Charles W. Chesnutt concludes that there have been few wholly realist fictions of African American life. Chesnutt reviews some of the most popular literature published in Europe and America to date, but notably, his assessment of the "Negro" or African American *in* books includes few books written *by* African Americans. On first glance, these findings would seem to concur with the pattern of most early studies of American realism. Throughout much of the twentieth century, scholarship on turn-of-the-century realism generally has excluded works by black writers, relegating to the category of romance the entire tradition of African American fiction and poetry between the Civil War and World War One.

However, in accounting for this apparent dearth, Chesnutt considers the extent to which the genre of realism accommodates (or not) the aesthetic, professional, and sociopolitical aims of African American writers. Delivering his speech as part of "The National Buy-a-Book Campaign in the Interest of Negro Literature," he proposes that African Americans seldom have written "true realism" because their literary efforts in that vein have not been rewarded with adequate publishing opportunities, substantial sales, or faithful audiences who appreciated complex portrayals of African Americans' realities. White audiences largely were uninterested in literature that challenged the racial status quo; meanwhile, African American readerships – who especially developed and consumed art through African American periodicals, such as the *Colored American Magazine* and *AME Church Review* – were comparatively small and possessed limited purchasing power. By noting that market demands and social conditions influenced how authors, white and black, chose to depict African Americans, Chesnutt's remarks implicitly raised questions such as: Whose reality determines the "real"? What are the limits of a realist approach to representation? How do race and realism influence each other? By troubling the meaning of "true realism," Chesnutt revealed that both truth and realism were largely a matter of perspective and preference.

Reflecting on the practice and limitations of literary realism, Chesnutt could use his own career as an example. At the height of his publishing in the 1890s, he successfully deployed realism in amusing short stories, gaining popularity in elite outlets such as the *Atlantic Monthly*. However, as he attempted to convey more overt political messages, pushing realism to expose bitter race relations in the segregated South, as in his novel *The Marrow of Tradition* (1901), he lost favor with white audiences. Critics judged *Marrow* as not only offering an unpalatable message, but also as veering into the terrain of romance, given the novel's coincidental plot developments, corrupt white characters, and noble black heroes. However, writing during the era now known as the nadir of black political and economic status, Chesnutt concluded that it seemed permissible and even necessary to offer a truthful depiction, tinged with a bit of exaggeration in favor of positive black representation:

> And indeed, from the standpoint of the Negro himself, a little idealism, a little romanticism, would not be at all out of place. An occasional black or brown hero, a little braver, a little wiser, a little richer perchance, a little more self-sacrificing than one could reasonably expect to meet often in real life; an occasional black or brown heroine – aside from the octoroon, who is always beautiful in books … would be something by way of example or inspiration. (436)

His quip highlights the tension between African American authors' awareness of form and their execution of it. While black writers recognized the period's literary trend towards realism, they also valued what appeared to be "a little idealism" in conveying their aims of racial progress. Since both realism and romance seemed ill fitted to express varied black experiences, black writers drew freely from both traditions, sometimes merging the aesthetic or ideological conventions of the two approaches to create a form more flexible for politically conscious art.

Noting that black authors during the period were less engaged with "mainstream" realism or, better yet, that they crafted their own forms of realism invites us to rethink both African American literary history and the category of realism itself. In the 1920s and 1930s, literary scholars such as Sterling Brown and Arthur P. Davis identified postbellum black literature exclusively with the romance tradition. According to these critics, African American literature guaranteed its own critical neglect and commercial failure by clinging to sentimentalism rather than embracing the timely move toward realism. During the mid-twentieth century, critics further judged postbellum black writers' experimentation with realism as feeble by comparison to Richard Wright's naturalist paradigm. Even meticulous literary histories, such as Dickson

Bruce's *Black American Writing from the Nadir* (1989), seldom have identified the presence of realism that permeates turn-of-the-century black poetry and fiction. Conversely, according to Bernard Bell's literary chronology in *The Afro-American Novel and Its Tradition* (1987), postbellum black authors produced "transitional texts" that bridge the shift from antebellum romances to a more forthright engagement with twentieth-century realism.

A revisionist literary history rightly may acknowledge the arbitrary distinction between genres. Categories such as "romance" or "realism" often share many of the same narrative premises or characteristics, and the boundaries between the genres remain porous and subjectively constructed, rather than fixed and self-evident. Throughout the nineteenth century, African American authors destabilized the boundaries that attempted to separate didactic literature from disinterested art, romance from realism. By recognizing the interplay of multiple genres in any single text, we can trace the influence of realism in the works of Chesnutt and his turn-of-the-century contemporaries.

The Emergence of African American Literary Realism

Though its definition remains contested, critics generally associate realism with these characteristics: detailed, realistic settings; an unobtrusive narrator (rather than one who intervenes in the story to address the reader directly); and a focus on characters' psychological development or interior lives. These attributes should not be taken as a definitive checklist, but rather as a guide for discerning the forms that realism sometimes took. Admittedly, many of the self-proclaimed practitioners of realism used the term inconsistently; other authors never referred to their writing as realist, though literary historians repeatedly have labeled it as such. The slipperiness of "realism" does not indicate its imprecision so much as its capaciousness, and this quality attracted diverse writers to appropriate realism for their own aesthetic and ideological agendas.

Considering realism in these looser terms has led some scholars to trace its chronological origins to a period before the Civil War, much earlier than the generally accepted era of postbellum high realism. As Augusta Rohrbach has argued, African American slave narratives – now sometimes called "freedom narratives" – provided ways of representing everyday life that may have shaped later realist literary approaches by black and white writers. In conventional eighteenth- and nineteenth-century slave narratives, a modest and unassuming narrator used specific details to offer an "unvarnished" depiction of ordinary life. Although the best-recognized slave narrators such as Frederick Douglass and Harriet Jacobs complicated this framework, the basic form's economical language, emphasis on the material body, and focus on commonplace experience would become trademarks of late nineteenth-century realism (Rohrbach xiv). Yet, in these real-life stories, readers also found all the makings of American fictional romance: heroes and villains, action and adventure, and sentiment. Ironically, then, the genre of slave narratives that aimed to present a verifiable "truth stranger than fiction," to use a common phrase of the time, in fact inspired fiction. For instance, in one of the first African American novels, *Clotel; or, the President's Daughter* (1853), the slave autobiographer-cum-novelist, William Wells Brown, blended realist details with a romanticized story of the title character's heroic escape from slavery. To qualify *Clotel* as an early black-authored realist text, however, immediately raises the categorical dilemmas this essay addresses.

As popularized in the 1880s, realism is less a category unified by narrative characteristics than an artistic approach driven by certain philosophies about representation and the function of art. First, realism takes up the question of the proper relationship between artistic representation and the material world. In the words of William Dean Howells, the "Dean of American Letters" who most avidly promoted literary realism in the United States, the strategy was "nothing more and nothing less than the truthful treatment of material" (96–7). Howells supplemented this definition, as did other critic-authors who subscribed to and deviated from it, but the phrase pithily registers the gist of the approach. Realist artists aimed to capture the beauty and ugliness of human motives, actions, and relations with as much accuracy and as little exaggeration as possible. As realists assumed, artists needed the freedom to describe life without the stifling conventions of genteel literature that seemed to prefer artifice to simple reality.

Realism was not simply a matter of mimetic representation, however. The genre's second concern – the one most consistent across the broad range of works possibly construed as realist – is that realism aimed not only to reflect social reality, but also to construct it (Kaplan 20). Realist authors promoted literature as a form of social interpretation that, at least indirectly, could impact human relations. By depicting "life as it is" rather than how it might be in an impossibly perfect world, realist fiction intended to encourage people to interact with one another honestly, without prejudice or pretensions to idealism.

Yet Howells's statement underestimates the way that the very concept of "truthful treatment of material" remained subjective and contestable. Representations offered as "authentic" could convey the embedded racial and class prejudices of a supposedly objective mediator. As Kenneth Warren has observed, by portraying social differences reproducible in fiction as "truth," literary realism tended to essentialize difference and exacerbate the distance between "black and white strangers" in the American social order. As language works to create reality, words on the pages of literature conjured up black Americans in the reader's imagination to stand in for the actual person. By reading realism, one could derive the thrill, disgust, or empathy of imaginatively encountering the racial or ethnic Other without risking actual or meaningful personal contact. This was the concern of Anna Julia Cooper, one disenchanted African American commentator who objected to Howells's depiction of a charismatic black church community in his novel *An Imperative Duty* (1891). Cooper charged, "Mr. Howells' point of view is precisely that of a white man who sees colored people at long range or only in certain capacities … He has not seen, and therefore cannot be convinced that there exists a quiet, self-respecting, dignified class [of black Americans]" (1988: 206, 207). Realist works that claimed to be based on the author's observation of unsavory aspects of African American life – superstition, unemployment, prostitution, gambling, criminality, and illiteracy – could be taken as evidence of all African Americans' supposed inferiority. In this regard, realism did not necessarily bridge the distance between the (white) reader and alienated subject, despite realist writers' well-meant intentions.

Sensing both realism's limitations and radical possibilities, African American writers such as Chesnutt, Pauline Hopkins, Sutton Griggs, and Paul Laurence Dunbar, among others, intended their literature not only to reflect social conditions with a near ethnologic accuracy, but also to contemplate (or, in some cases, examine and discard) possible solutions to race and gender relations. Between the Civil War and the Harlem Renaissance of the 1920s, African American authors utilized realist narrative strategies but seldom theorized realism as a formal literary school or movement. As black cultural arbiters examined literary trends – as Cooper does in her book, *A Voice from the South* (1892), Victoria Earle Matthews in her essay, "The Value of Race Literature" (1895), and Hopkins in the opening pages of her novel, *Contending Forces* (1900), to name a few – they seldom elucidated a clear distinction between the genres of realism and romance. Instead, when black commentators call for "realist" writing, they referred to literature that presents black Americans realistically, that is, unexaggerated by the writer's prejudice.

These motives led most black writers to produce what one scholar calls "racial realism," literature that aimed to offer authentic portrayals of black experience for the expressed purpose of producing material effects, such as counteracting anti-black public sentiment and showing blacks as fully deserving of civil equality with whites (Jarrett). Rather than being a subgenre of realism, racial realism is a literary phenomenon or imperative that energized black writers' experimentation in multiple forms of prose and poetry. When aiming to produce aesthetically pleasing, socially conscious literature, black writers blended romance and realism into several versions of African American literary realism: regionalism or local color writing, domestic realism, and naturalism. That these were some of the same labels that applied to white-authored realism indicates that black writers engaged the prevalent forms, even while departing from them to create a tradition of African American literature.

Local Color and Regionalism

Realism, as its advocates envisioned it, was a means toward democratizing both the literary market and the "real" world beyond books. A talented person could write realistically without having the education and leisure often associated with authors. As a result, local color or regionalist fiction, one subgenre of realism, opened the field of authorship to writers of color, working-class writers, and female authors who were sometimes on the fringe of mainstream literature. As Richard Brodhead notes, by inviting authors to represent faithfully the ethnic and geographic realities closest to them, "regionalism made the experience of the socially marginalized into a literary asset, and so made marginality itself a positive authorial advantage" (117). Chesnutt, Paul Laurence Dunbar, and Dunbar's one-time spouse, Alice Ruth Moore Dunbar (later Nelson) capitalized on this literary access to reach dual white and black audiences. Yet, while the mode offered an entry point into *belles-lettres*, African American writers often became constrained by regionalism's demand for the entertaining literary performance of blackness.

Local color literature had antebellum roots, but the style developed considerably in the postbellum era in response to a number of social changes. In a nation rent by the Civil War and reeling with increased migration, immigration, and US imperial expansion, local color literature focused on regional differences to project a unified nation strengthened by its internal differences (Kaplan 25). Local color offered a psychological valve for readers and writers to contain the threat of social unrest by describing more subtle (and less threatening) interactions across classes, locations, or races. Whether reading the poetic ditties of Midwestern life or Paul Laurence Dunbar's poems and tales of the plantation South, American audiences could appear to celebrate diversity in the United States, all the while masking the social and material inequality behind these depictions.

Alice Dunbar's short fiction set in Louisiana suggests how local color fiction had the potential to critique social inequalities, but, more often, left them in place. In "Anarchy Alley" (1895), an unnamed narrator guides an observer (ostensibly the reader) on a walking tour of a working-class New Orleans neighborhood. After inviting the observer to witness household arguments, labor strikes, and the imminent threat of violence and working-class discontent, the piece concludes by returning to the safety of a luxury hotel, "ending, with a sudden return to aristocracy, this stamping ground for anarchy" (63). Read in one way, the sketch suggests that while one can return to privilege, the encounter with difference ultimately unsettles the comfort of life as one has known it. The observer's position can never be voyeuristically "casual" or "idle," as the narrator misleadingly suggests at the story's beginning. As likely, however, Dunbar's readers were reassured that the threat of social class disorder was real, but contained – limited to the pages of literature rather than imposing in everyday life.

Dunbar's story illustrates the way in which regionalist approaches paradoxically demanded that authors or narrators provide authentic accounts, based on personal experience or observation, while remaining detached enough to offer indifferent depictions. The narrator thus served as cultural interpreter, mediating between the audience (an outside interloper) and the subject (an insider, authentic source of culture). To delineate between the outsider and insider, regionalist narratives often feature a frame story and inset tale. This structure textually represents the power struggle over who defines or represents the subject, whether the framing authority (figures associated with the North, technology, imperialism, education, and the masculine) or the native informant (figures associated with the South, nature, insularity, vernacular, and the feminine). For instance, in Chesnutt's conjure tales, John, a white Northern transplant, grants readers access to the inner story, told by Uncle Julius, a former slave. Although the erudite John appears to retain control of the story, the dialect-speaking raconteur Uncle Julius often bests his auditors for his own material gain. Chesnutt revises this framing structure over the model of his white counterparts, such as Joel Chandler Harris, who was then famous for recording the "Uncle Remus" tales of a kindly black man who narrates animal stories for his indulgent white auditors. Subverting the power dynamics of Harris's tales, Chesnutt's conjure tales encode messages of black rebellion or resistance. Furthermore, as the stories function on two levels – appearing to romanticize slavery while simultaneously critiquing that account through realism – Chesnutt exposes romance and realism as complicit in the literary construction of American racial discourse.

The appeal of Chesnutt's Uncle Julius tales, which combined the popularity of conjure and dialect, indicated how Gilded Age America was preoccupied with what Gavin Jones calls the "the cult of the vernacular." Readers and writers "sought the soul of America in the rugged, racy vernaculars of the past," but also feared that "dialect frustrated the ideology of national unity" by admitting that diverse English speakers did not conform to a shared linguistic standard (39). For instance, in his famous introduction to Paul Laurence Dunbar's volume *Lyrics of Lowly Life* (1896), Howells assessed that while Dunbar's poems in standard English were good, "several people might have written them [,] but I do not know any one else at present who could quite have written the dialect pieces." By emphasizing Dunbar's artistic skill of writing dialect, literary reviews of his writing and poetry readings risked interpreting vernacular as an essential trait of black identity.

While many white readers may have accepted such assumptions without question, this does not explain fully why many black writers and readers savored regionalist literature, despite how it fetishized variant idioms, cultural practices, and ethnic identities. One response is that through local color literature, African Americans strategically interpreted racial essentialism in order to valorize difference. As some interpreted it, African American speech patterns, religiosity, and folk traditions that usually were the target of ridicule in fact constituted the race's particular "gifts" or "soul" (to use W.E.B. Du Bois's term in his 1903 book, *The Souls of Black Folk*). By imputing positive value to such traits, writers could celebrate so-called black distinctiveness. Dialect shifted from being "a literary device used to deny creativity and intelligence in blacks," to being used "creatively by black people themselves" (Bruce 107). Dunbar was a star of black dialect writing, but he was part of a constellation of African Americans who wrote dozens of poetry volumes featuring dialect. Frances Ellen Watkins Harper's *Sketches of Southern Life* (1872) subtly introduced black vernacular into African American poetry through Aunt Chloe Fleet, an ex-slave speaker. By the 1890s, writers including James Corrothers, Daniel Webster Davis, and James Edwin Campbell exceeded Harper's model with more creative textual renderings of black speech.

In addition to exhibiting folk culture, African American authors sometimes turned local color conventions to more politicized uses. Poets Maggie Johnson,

Clara Thompson, Priscilla Jane Thompson, and Lizelia Moorer wrote both dialect and nondialect poetry depicting Southern life under segregation. What made their poems realist were the commonplace black speakers, "hard-working, somewhat frazzled men and women" with interiority and a human capacity for pleasure, pain, and rationality (Bennett 152). Likewise, poet and novelist James Corrothers often produced distasteful dialect poetry (which he later resented), but in his dialect poem, "An Indignation Dinner" (1915), the speaker explains that black neighbors have pilfered food from their white employers in retaliation for unfair economic exploitation. Signifying on the popular stereotype of the black chicken thief, the poem's speaker explains that his motives are "[*n*]*ot* beca'se we was dishonest, but *indignant*, sah. Dat's all" (l. 28).

Nevertheless, Corrothers, like Chesnutt and Dunbar, had misgivings about dialect writing and the local color tradition. Though authors could convey social critique through local color, the use of dialect may have misled readers to expect a humorous rather than critical representation. For instance, by conflating Southern roots with a black folk identity, local color writing could lead audiences to conclude that "All Coons Look Alike to Me," as one epithetic ragtime song of the era suggested. Since such a conclusion worked counter to African Americans' claims to respectability and individual merit, local color had limited utility for positive black representation.

Domestic Realism

Literary history often has focused on the rise of local color and other forms of realism during the Gilded Age, but these trends did not entirely supplant earlier literary styles, including the sentimental modes that they challenged. Epitomized in Harriet Beecher Stowe's *Uncle Tom's Cabin* (1852), the logic of sentimentalism emphasized virtues of self-sacrifice, restraint, and moral sensibility as one's source of power or influence. As individuals learn to sublimate their sexual desire or willfulness into service and duty, so the logic goes, they modeled how sympathy for others could mediate the differences between white and black, rich and poor, good and evil. Though dismissed by critics who considered the style effete, sentimental literature continued to flourish in the decades after the Civil War.

Among African American authors – especially the generation of African American female writers developing literary careers in the 1890s and 1900s – sentimentalism remained a significant mode for inciting reform in favor of black civil rights. Many texts in this tradition followed a formula: when faced with the dilemmas of overcoming poverty, choosing a marriage partner, or pursuing a career, the protagonist chooses the alternative that demands her sacrificial duty to the cause of racial uplift. What differentiates these texts from those that Nina Baym classifies as "women's fiction" is that while the white female protagonists exist as though outside of history, eventually able to transcend race, class, and gender conditions, the protagonists of what Claudia Tate has called African American "allegories of political desire" engage more directly the issues of race and racial tension that remained only implicit in most white-authored domestic writing. Though seemingly bound by their positionality, black female protagonists who ostensibly focused on domestic concerns – such as courtship, childrearing, or household management – conveyed the general desire of women for citizenship and influence beyond the so-called private sphere of the home.

Written in this vein, fiction by such authors as Harper, Amelia Johnson, Pauline Hopkins, and Katherine Tillman aptly might be called "domestic realism." While focusing on sentimental affect, the texts also offer a realist approach through objective narrators and concrete details. Readers witness this blend of sentimentalism and realism, situated in a domestic setting, in Katherine Tillman's serialized novella *Clancy Street* (1898–1899). The novella draws a nearly ethnographic depiction of black experiences in the urban South, detailing speech, clothing, eating habits, labor practices, and social patterns. Yet Tillman's local color often gives way to symbolism in keeping with sentimental narratives (Tate 181). Rather than revealing the psychology of Caroline Waters, the schoolgirl who dies as a result of nursing her feverish white employer, the narrator allows biblical scripture to stand in for further character development. The blend of plausible settings and circumstances, along with the sometime implausible outcomes and emotional excesses, attempted to inspire both the rational and sympathetic responses of readers toward the black working class.

Women were the primary contributors to this form, but gender does not account fully for the development of domestic realism. Like their female counterparts, black male writers also featured the formation of households or the (re)constitution of families as the centerpiece of politicized narratives. Sutton Griggs's first novel, *Imperium in Imperio* (1899), focused on dual male protagonists who vie for leadership of a proposed black separatist nation within the US. Yet, surmising that such a plot seemed fantastical and politically radical, even to his African American readers, Griggs focused his second novel, *Overshadowed* (1901), on the more commonplace trials of a black woman seeking employment, then marriage. Still offering a social critique, the novel pushes the boundaries of sentimental literature by juxtaposing the melodramatic qualities of fainting women and hidden identities alongside realistic depictions of lynching, incarceration, and black labor exploitation. In order to further blend realist impressions of American society with romance, domestic realism often focused on the theme of interracial intimacy and passing, showing how racially exclusionary customs and legislation disrupt the domesticity of African Americans, whether they live as black or attempt to pass as white. By examining the misrecognitions that happen when people superficially interpret identity, passing narratives aligned with realism's insight that human beings have limited understanding of their own psychologies or the motives of others.

Chesnutt's *The House behind the Cedars* (1900) offers a poignant example. When deciding whether to disclose her bi-racial heritage, Rena Walden asks her white lover George Tryon, "Would you love me … if I were Albert's nurse yonder?" As the two observe a light-complexioned African American nurse, Tryon focuses on her class status as laborer, while Rena obliquely intends to highlight that the woman is of

African American descent, as is she. As the couple's language fails to match up with its referent, the narrator highlights how "two intelligent persons should each attach a different meaning to so simple a form of words as Rena's question" (Chesnutt, *Stories, Novels, and Essays* 326). Passing functioned as both theme and narrative strategy, allowing such fictions to "pass" between the genres of sentimentalism and realism to interrogate fully racial stratifications (Fabi 73). By tracing the imperfect correspondence between "real" humans and the oversimplified labels and conditions applied to them, domestic realist narratives shored up the possibilities and difficulties of representing the material world through language (and categorical demands) always inadequate to the task.

Naturalism and African American Fiction

As with other versions of realism, naturalism may be identified more by its underlying philosophies than by any consistent set of aesthetic traits. Emerging in US literature in the 1890s, naturalism shared with realism an investment in detached reportage of everyday life, yet resisted realism's lingering bourgeois pretensions. Howells had called for the democratization of authorship and literary representations, but his own novels, such as *The Rise of Silas Lapham* (1885), tended to consider middle-class or newly moneyed people as "common" Americans. Meanwhile, naturalism frequently grappled with the nation's economic and technological changes by focusing on working-class people. To some observers, the period's capitalist expansion, mechanization, and scientific inquiry indicated the forward march of American civilization. According to naturalism, however, these modern changes caused the degradation of American individualism.

Bolstered by the claims of scientific determinism, naturalist literature revealed how individuals' social mobility, moral development, and daily interactions were controlled by biology or environment. Characters prone to lurid sexuality, alcoholism, disease, and violence showed evidence of human retrogression, as scientist Herbert Spencer theorized during the era. Given its way of reducing characters to psychological, economic, racial, or biological types, literary naturalism bears kinship to the romantic typology of virtues or vices. Whereas romantic fiction portrays the ideal, naturalist writing exposes the ideal as false, impossible, or radically perverted. By focusing on characters not usually featured in polite literature, except as the objects of middle-class charity and redemption, naturalism gained a reputation among some nineteenth-century critics for being a sordid, blunt literature that could have a negative moral effect on readers.

Perhaps for this latter reason, naturalist themes and approaches infrequently appear in nineteenth-century African American literature that aimed toward racial uplift. While naturalism suggests that a higher spiritual being, if existing at all, is indifferent to human motives and actions, African American writers continued to subscribe to a world governed by divine intervention and moral absolutes. Characters in black fiction seldom experience complete alienation that leaves them to the forces of fate or environment. This worldview especially is evident in the generally hopeful conclusion of African American narratives, such as Harper's *Iola Leroy* (1892), which concludes with the title character, a Sunday School teacher, inspiring former slaves to transform their impoverished Southern environment. In this regard, Harper and her literary colleagues resisted the secularism or religious skepticism implicit in naturalism.

Like naturalism, however, African American literature during this era does pursue scientific inquiry, especially with regard to human and social evolution. The stories of interracial family lineage written by Griggs, Hopkins, and Chesnutt addressed the latest theories of genetics and "survival of the fittest," sometimes manipulating racist scientific claims into the service of counter-racist narratives. In the preface to *Overshadowed* (1901), for example, Griggs surmised that in order to rival the Anglo-Saxon in wealth, intelligence, and character, "the nature of the Negro *must be fitted to the civilization*, thus necessitating the casting aside of all that he had evolved" (5). And yet, these authors' attitude toward the potency of biology is ambivalent and sometimes even contradictory. In Hopkins's serialized novel, *Of One Blood* (1902–1903), the villain Aubrey Livingston "knew that fickleness was in his blood" (476), yet his siblings try to transcend their heredity by behaving morally. For African American writers, subscribing wholly to naturalism risked reinforcing insidious views of race and human development. While white naturalist authors such as Jack London depicted the devolution of human beings to animal instinct, African Americans recovering from the negative legacy of slavery needed to offset the claims that equated blacks with beasts. Even in African American texts that suggested naturalism, their authors considered the counterbalancing effect of societal redemption, such as education, religion, and political engagement.

Between the Civil War and World War One, Paul Laurence Dunbar is the African American author who deployed naturalist approaches most frequently. Much of Dunbar's short fiction fitted within the plantation tradition vein of local color writing. But occasionally in his short stories, and more consistently in his four novels, Dunbar depicts social reality to show the limited will of characters to resist their destinies. One marker of naturalism in Dunbar's writing is the resistance to the hopeful narrative resolutions of African American fiction, as mentioned above. For instance, in Dunbar's short story "One Man's Fortunes" (1900), the narrator calls attention to romantic idealism to critique it. Though initially an optimistic jobseeker, the college-educated Bert Halliday becomes increasingly cynical in response to his limited job opportunities. He bitterly reflects, "We have been taught that merit wins. But I have learned that the adages, as well as the books and the formulas were made by and for others than us of the black race" (138). Alluding to the success guides, rags-to-riches novels, and autobiographies by self-made men published during the Gilded Age, Halliday suggests the need to reconcile the emphasis on individualism and work ethic with the dire economic realities faced by most post-Reconstruction blacks.

Dunbar's last novel, *The Sport of the Gods* (1902), goes further towards questioning the cultivation of African Americans in a racist US environment. In Dunbar's naturalist fiction, the forces of fate or nature often converge with or manifest as the force of racism. Thus, while the novel's title refers to the arbitrary control of gods over the lives of characters, the Hamiltons, an African American family, seem more controlled by the effects of a biased judicial system, as a white employer's false accusation of Berry Hamilton catalyzes the family's disintegration. As the Hamiltons move to the North, the so-called promised land of slave narratives and other tales of black upward mobility, the urban environment instead proves deleterious, luring each family member to abandon the simple values he or she learned in the South. At the end of *The Sport of the Gods*, the return of the Hamiltons to their Southern "home" represents neither progress nor loss, but an ironic stasis.

In both the short fiction and his novels, Dunbar displaces conventions of other genres – the hopeful quest novel and the jolly plantation tradition – to assert a more doubtful reality for African Americans lacking the benefit of political equality. Not until the literary era of the 1940s would naturalism become a vehicle of social protest for writers, including Ann Petry and Richard Wright, to depict the struggles of African Americans against racial restriction and economic determinism. At the turn of the century, however, Dunbar initiated this approach by indicating how "Nature" or environment conspires with stereotype and prejudice to conform individuals' lives to stagnancy.

Categorical Misfits and Realist Innovations

African American writers attempted to negotiate the terms by which they engaged the above-mentioned subgenres of realism, but they also experimented with realist strategies in ways that defied the categories of either black or white narrative traditions. After all, even the well-intended demands of racial realism, which posited that black writers could offer their authentic perspective to positive effect, could stifle black literary expression. One way that Dunbar, Chesnutt, Alice Dunbar Nelson, and Amelia Johnson complicated the expected correspondence between racial authenticity and authority was by writing fiction featuring white or racially indeterminate characters. By frustrating readers' tendencies to categorize characters by speech or color, the authors attempt to neutralize race, thereby highlighting other means of character identification, including region, psychological state, or social class.

Focusing on the economic reversals of presumably white Americans, such fictions as Chesnutt's *A Business Career* pursued realist themes in ways that critics are only now recovering. Published posthumously in the 1990s, *A Business Career* was driven by a romantic plot, but aligned with realist novels' frequent focus on the loss, gain, lack or overabundance of money (Simmons 26). However, such texts did not gain much attention during Chesnutt's lifetime, perhaps in part because they veered from the thematic focus on race and racism expected of African American authors. In keeping with Chesnutt's pronouncement in "The Negro in Books," his failed attempts to write about white people show how the segregated US literary market made it difficult for black writers to produce realism in ways that were not informed more overtly by the operations of race.

Meanwhile, W.E.B. Du Bois's early fiction certainly fell within the scope of racial realism. In a 1926 essay, "Criteria of Negro Art," he would reiterate the importance of this aesthetic principle by proposing that "all art is propaganda." Yet he also was preoccupied with using realism to plot the relation between economics, race, and psychology. Likened to Frank Norris's naturalist trilogy because of its economic determinism, Du Bois's novel, *The Quest of the Silver Fleece* (1911), strikingly engages Marxist analysis more so than prior African American fiction. As Michael Elliott has shown, literary realism and social science shared the compulsion to delineate the everyday practices of particular social groups (xiv). That Du Bois, one of the earliest trained black sociologists, also pursued creative writing exemplifies the trend Elliott describes. The lingering romantic tone and characterizations tempered Du Bois's naturalist approach, however. This hybridity appears in the opening pages of the novel. Claiming to be an objective observer, the author alerts readers that nothing exists in the text that "I have not seen or known." Yet the author aligns the novel with romantic "ideals" such as "the herald of Truth" (1911: 3). In one scholar's estimation, "[t]here is no evidence that Du Bois learned much from his predecessors in the field of the black novel" (Rampersad 116). Though, as Rampersad suggests, the novel attempts to break free from existing narrative taxonomies by blending romance with economic exposé, in doing so, the novel in fact contributes to a tradition of African American intertextuality.

James Weldon Johnson's *Autobiography of an Ex-Colored Man* (1912) took this generic experimentation further. In this novel, written in the guise of an autobiography (and first published anonymously), Johnson contributed to the realist tradition through attention to detail, the narrator's relative indifference to religion, and, most of all, the omission of a moralizing narrator guiding the reader's emotional response. In his psychological unrest over whether to live as white or black, the unnamed protagonist possesses greater interiority than earlier mixed-race characters. With a tone shifting between sociological reportage and first-person reflection, *Autobiography* incorporates the themes and approaches of several narrative traditions: the passing narrative; the slumming narrative, tracing a relatively privileged man's encounter with urban reality and modernity; the international travelogue; and the local color account. If, as some accounts argue, Johnson's novel qualifies as one of the first clearly realist African American novels (Boeckmann 175), then this reiterates the extent to which African American literary realism between the Civil War and World War One was marked by generic hybridity.

A brief survey of current American literature anthologies and literary criticism suggests that James Weldon Johnson, Dunbar, and Chesnutt increasingly are being canonized among American realists (Kinnamon). Through efforts to reformulate the canon of American realism, studies in the 1990s and the new millennium have begun to consider the confluence between race and realism. Yet by enrolling Dunbar and other selected writers into the ranks of Howellsian realism, scholars inadvertently have followed Howells's pattern by cordoning off a few authors as representative of and yet superior to other productions within the African American literary tradition. As Ryan Simmons argues, specifically with regards to Chesnutt, scholars must resist the lure of restoring individual black authors or texts to the supposedly aesthetically superior category of American realism. Instead, readers can question the cultural primacy of realism, as well as examine how writers of color who less frequently are associated with realism – such as Hopkins, Griggs, and Du Bois – contributed to its development rather than merely imitated its model (Simmons 2).

For African American authors between the Civil War and World War One, presenting complex African American realities demanded multiple hybridized forms of literary realism. When Chesnutt presented "The Negro in Books" in 1916, he recommended realism as an approach with which he had mixed success two decades earlier, though he hoped that realism held greater promise for subsequent black writers. As he concludes his speech, if authors wrote more realistically about black Americans and readers actually supported such endeavors, "true realism" would direct readers' cultural tastes and fuel the publishing market. More significantly, "true realism" potentially would "promote the interest of the race and of humanity" (Chesnutt 438). By attributing to literature no less than the power to promote racial advancement and human reform, Chesnutt expressed an essential tenet of African American literary realism at the turn of the twentieth century.

Bibliography

Ammons, Elizabeth. "Men of Color, Women, and Uppity Art at the Turn of the Century." In *American Realism and the Canon*. Ed. Tom Quirk and Gary Scharnhorst. Newark: University of Delaware Press, 1994. 22–33.

Bell, Bernard. *The Afro-American Novel and Its Tradition*. Amherst: University of Massachusetts Press, 1987.

Bennett, Paula Bernat. "Rewriting Dunbar: Realism, Black Women Poets, and the Genteel." In *Post-Bellum, Pre-Harlem: African American Literature and Culture, 1877–1919*. Ed. Barbara McCaskill and Caroline Gebhard. New York: New York University Press, 2006. 146–61.

Boeckmann, Cathy. *A Question of Character: Scientific Racism and the Genres of American Fiction, 1892–1912*. Tuscaloosa: University of Alabama Press, 2000.

Brodhead, Richard H. *Cultures of Letters: Scenes of Reading and Writing in Nineteenth-Century America*. Chicago: University of Chicago Press, 1993.

Brooks, Kristina. "Alice Dunbar-Nelson's Local Colors of Ethnicity, Class, and Place." *Multi-Ethnic Literature of the United States* 23.2 (1998): 3–26.

Bruce, Dickson D., Jr. *Black American Writing from the Nadir: The Evolution of a Literary Tradition, 1877–1915*. Baton Rouge: Louisiana State University Press, 1989.

Chesnutt, Charles W. "Negro in Books." In *Charles W. Chesnutt: Essays and Speeches*. Ed. Joseph R. McElrath, Robert C. Leitz, and Jesse S. Crisler. Palo Alto: Stanford University Press, 1999. 426–40.

Chesnutt, Charles W. *Stories, Novels, and Essays*. New York: Library of America, 2002.

Cooper, Anna Julia. *A Voice from the South*. New York: Oxford University Press, 1988.

Du Bois, W.E.B. *Quest of the Silver Fleece*. Chicago: A.C. McClurg & Co., 1911.

Dunbar, Alice [Moore]. *Violets and Other Tales*. Boston: Monthly Review, 1895.

Dunbar, Paul Laurence. "One Man's Fortune" (1900). In *The Complete Stories of Paul Laurence Dunbar*. Ed. Gene Andrew Jarrett and Thomas Lewis Morgan. Athens: Ohio University Press, 2005. 127–39.

Elliott, Michael A. *The Culture Concept: Writing and Difference in the Age of Realism*. Minneapolis: University of Minnesota Press, 2002.

Fabi, M. Giulia. *Passing and the Rise of the African American Novel*. Urbana: University of Illinois Press, 2001.

Gaines, Kevin K. *Uplifting the Race: Black Leadership, Politics, and Culture in the Twentieth Century*. Chapel Hill: University of North Carolina Press, 1996.

Gates, Henry Louis, Jr. and Gene Andrew Jarrett, ed. *The New Negro: Readings on Race, Representation, and African American Culture, 1892–1938*. Princeton: Princeton University Press, 2007.

Griggs, Sutton E. *Overshadowed*. 1901. Freeport, NY: Books for Libraries Press, 1971.

Hopkins, Pauline. *The Magazine Novels of Pauline Hopkins*. New York: Oxford University Press, 1988.

Howells, William Dean. "Palacio Valdés, Realism, and Effectism." 1889. In *Documents of American Realism and Naturalism*. Ed. Donald Pizer. Carbondale: Southern Illinois University Press, 1998. 91–8.

Jarrett, Gene Andrew. *Deans and Truants: Race and Realism in African American Literature*. Philadelphia: University of Pennsylvania Press, 2007.

Jones, Gavin. *Strange Talk: The Politics of Dialect Literature in Gilded Age America*. Berkeley: University of California Press, 1999.

Kaplan, Amy. *The Social Construction of American Realism*. Chicago: University of Chicago Press, 1988.

Kinnamon, Keneth. "Three Black Writers and the Anthologized Canon." In *American Realism and the Canon*. Ed. Tom Quirk and Gary Scharnhorst. Newark: University of Delaware Press, 1994. 143–53.

Rampersad, Arnold. *The Art and Imagination of W. E. B. Du Bois*. Cambridge, MA: Harvard University Press, 1976.

Rohrbach, Augusta. *Truth Stranger than Fiction: Race, Realism and the U.S. Literary Marketplace*. New York: Palgrave, 2002.

Simmons, Ryan. *Chesnutt and Realism: A Study of the Novels*. Tuscaloosa: University of Alabama Press, 2006.

Tate, Claudia. *Domestic Allegories of Political Desire: The Black Heroine's Text at the Turn of the Century*. New York: Oxford University Press, 1992.

Warren, Kenneth. *Black and White Strangers: Race and American Literary Realism*. Chicago: University of Chicago Press, 1993.

13
Folklore and African American Literature in the Post-Reconstruction Era

Shirley Moody-Turner

There is a long, deep, and inextricable relationship between folklore and African American literature. When Olaudah Equiano wrote *The Interesting Narrative of the Life of Olaudah Equiano or Gustavus Vassa, the African, Written by Himself*, published in 1789, African folklore provided the lens through which he interpreted the strangely savage Euro-American world he encountered. Almost two centuries later, Toni Morrison drew on African folklore, incorporating the folktale of the flying Africans to give meaning and form to her story of Milkman Dead's journey back into his past in her 1977 novel, *Song of Solomon*. In the intervening years, the relationship between folklore and African American literature has been inflected in myriad ways under constantly fluctuating conditions and circumstances. African American authors have incorporated folklore into their literary texts to voice communal identity, maintain traditional values, protest racial inequalities, express desires for self-definition, encode messages, pass on collective wisdom, and resist and subvert dominant power structures.

For many, however, folklore is a vague concept denoting the quaint songs and sayings of a remote people spatially and temporally isolated from "modern" society. For others, folklore carries a more sinister connotation, a product of colonial discourses of conquest that construct folklore in terms of race and in opposition to civilization. For others, still, folklore represents a valuable connection to community and tradition – the beliefs, practices, stories, and tales that have sustained and preserved group identity and history. While each of these concepts suggests another layer of complexity in defining this laden term, most contemporary folklorists agree that folklore is one mode through which groups, irrespective of race, class, gender, or region, communicate values, beliefs, attitudes, feelings, traditions, and histories. Folklorist Dan Ben-Amos has referred to folklore simply as "artistic communication in small groups," while Robert Baron and Nicholas Spitzer have argued that "while folklore is private and intimately shared by groups in informal settings, it is also the most public of activities when used by groups to symbolize their identity to themselves and others" (Ben-Amos 13; Baron and Spitzer 1–2). Edward Ives, on the other hand, has emphasized the importance of understanding folklore in context, asserting that all folkloric songs, performances, and works of art must be understood within the culture or subculture of which it is a part (*Joe Scott, the Woodman-Songmaker*). In African American culture, in particular, the concept of folklore cannot be separated from larger social, political, and cultural contexts.

In Enlightenment ideology, for instance, written literacy and the capacity to produce "literature" were seen as representative of the cognitive ability to reason and thus as a measurement of humanity, progress, and social status. To demonstrate their humanity within this inherently flawed system, early Anglo-African and African American writers, such as James Albert Ukawsaw Gronniosaw, Equiano, and Phillis Wheatley adopted and mastered literary conventions of the Western tradition, albeit usually with what Henry Louis Gates, Jr. has referred to as a "black difference." Indeed, despite the hegemony of Western literary traditions, African American literature cannot be understood apart from its roots in the parallel traditions emerging from black folklore. As stated by Trudier Harris, a folklore and literary studies scholar, "African American folklore is arguably the basis for most African-American literature" (2).

Authors from at least the nineteenth century through the present have commented on the importance of folklore in African American literature and culture. Perhaps one of the most thoughtful commentators on black folk traditions, Ralph Ellison explains that folklore

> describes those rites, manners, customs and so forth, which insure the good life, or destroy it; and it describes those boundaries of feeling, thought and action which that particular group has found to be the limitation of the human condition. It projects this wisdom in symbols which express the group's will to survive, it embodies those values by which the group lives and dies. These drawings may be crude but they are nonetheless profound in that they represent the group's attempt to humanize the world. (172)

As Ellison's statement reveals, the inclusion of black folklore in African American literary texts is not solely driven by aesthetic motives, but is almost always part of a larger social, cultural, and political conversation centered on issues of survival, representation, self-determination, and freedom. The post-Reconstruction era in particular offers a compelling example of African American authors' attempts to incorporate folklore into their literary works to advance both their aesthetic and social justice agendas.

In the late nineteenth century, black folklore was the terrain across which issues of racial identity, citizenship, and equality were debated. Representations of black folklore and images of the black folk were commonplace on the minstrel stage and in popular plantation tradition literature. These dominant cultural representations of black folk and folklore codified black racial distinctiveness through various depictions of what were ostensibly black folk customs and traditions. At the same time, the rise of the social sciences and learned societies, particularly anthropology and folklore studies, provided an academic language that supported the construction of racial difference in relation to folklore, culture, and customs. The concurrent reign of social Darwinism created a convenient hierarchical structure through which to rank these racially distinct customs and, by extension, the groups associated with them. When the American Folklore Society was founded in 1888, for example, "Negroes of the Southern States of the Union" were identified as one of the four marginal ethnic groups that required further study from the members of the learned society (Newell 6). American Folklore Society founder, William Wells Newell, believed that the folkloric study of African Americans would render a more complete picture of the earlier primitive and savage stages of human social and cultural development. Inseparable from the pervasive social Darwinism of the late nineteenth century, folklore studies participated in constructing a hierarchy based on an ideology of racial difference, becoming an integral part of the machinery that maintained Jim Crow segregation.

Throughout post-Reconstruction debates over segregation, it was variously argued, for instance, that legislation could do little to change the folkways, habits, social practices, or folk customs that inherently differentiated the races. Lawmakers and justices fell back on vague references, such as those to racially distinct customs and inherited folkways, in order to rationalize and proclaim an inability to remedy the natural separation and inequalities among the races. The combination of the popular images of black folklore, along with the scientific framework provided by the newly emerging field of folklore studies, supplied segregationists with a convenient apparatus for legitimizing a system of racial separation predicated on the premise that racial identity could be clearly demarcated, if not through physical appearance (as the visibly white Homer Plessy had shown it could not), then at least through what were ostensibly racially differentiated behaviors, i.e. folk customs. Justice Henry Brown's majority opinion in the 1896 case *Plessy v. Ferguson*, for example, illustrated an effort to link social behavior and racial identity as a way to provide the necessary markers of racial distinction. Brown argued, "legislation is powerless to eradicate racial instincts or to abolish distinctions based upon physical differences" and that "if one race be inferior to the other socially, the Constitution of the United States can not be expected to put them on the same plane." This idea was repeated through post-Reconstruction discourse. Most notably, in the Mississippi Supreme Court 1896 case *Ratliff v. Beale*, the court argued that blacks "had acquired or accentuated certain peculiarities of habit, of temperament, and character, which clearly distinguished it as a race from that of the whites." In explicating their opinion, the justices contended they were following the precedent set six years earlier by the Mississippi State Convention in separating blacks from whites, not because of the former's race or color, but on the basis of the differences in habits, customs, and characteristics that *naturally* existed among the races.

The supposed racially based differences to which the politicians and lawmakers referred were epitomized in the representations of black folklore across the stages of the wildly popular minstrel performances. Simply stated, blackface minstrelsy refers to the pervasive popular culture phenomenon in which white actors from about the

1830s onward darkened their faces and took to the stage performing parodies of black folklore and cultural traditions. In his landmark study, *Blacking Up*, Robert Toll explains that blackface minstrelsy evolved into a kind of "'national folklore' – a constellation of images, definitions, symbols and meanings that most white Americans could and did share" (Toll 271). What these images and symbols conveyed to white America was that blacks were at best a boisterous and lively source of popular fascination, and at worst a grotesque and inane object of collective cultural laughter. Even after blackface minstrelsy passed from white actors into the hands of black performers, the parameters for black representation on the minstrel stage were firmly established by white actors' portrayals. When black actors inherited the stage, they found themselves trapped within the confines of minstrel conventions and rewarded for their ability to personify the stereotypes conjured up by the white minstrel performers, providing audiences with visual and bodily evidence of supposedly degenerate black difference. A similar phenomenon occurred in the concurrent literary traditions. Plantation tradition fiction manipulated black folklore so that it could become a marker of less civilized behavior. Works in this genre were typically set in the so-called good ol' days before the Civil War. Captured in the writings of Joel Chandler Harris and Thomas Nelson Page, plantation tradition literature erased the realities of slavery and created an idealized past valorizing Southern patriarchy and supporting "romantic" or paternalistic racism.

Into this context, post-Reconstruction African American writers, such as Paul Laurence Dunbar, Pauline Hopkins, and Charles W. Chesnutt intervened. Dunbar, Hopkins, and Chesnutt, each acutely aware of the emerging social and political significance of black folklore, strategically employed folklore in their respective literary works as a way to assert a rich black folklore tradition while challenging the merciless caricaturing and exploitation of black folklore on the cultural and political fronts. In Dunbar's 1902 novel, *The Sport of the Gods*, on the one hand, masking and dissimilation provided a way to critique the dominant power structures that circumscribed the range of black cultural and literary representation. For Hopkins's *Of One Blood* (1902–1903), on the other hand, black folklore, particularly folk forms related to African spiritualism, offered a way to recover a black cultural lineage that extended back to Africa and demonstrated the heights of civilization that African societies had achieved long before Western imperialist designs had obfuscated such histories. Chesnutt's folklore-inspired 1899 collection of short stories, *The Conjure Woman*, transforms the principles of conjure and ritual to critique the conventions that defined the parameters of black representation, while utilizing folklore to offer an African American-centered way of perceiving reality.

In his poetry and prose, as well as in his personal writings and letters, Dunbar deftly demonstrates how to manipulate the mask. For Dunbar, masking provided a way to expose the ruptures and hypocrisies in the prevailing discourse about African Americans and equality while also connecting him to a long tradition of masking as both black folk practice and literary technique. In African American culture, as a result of slavery and segregation, African Americans historically have had to learn how to mask or hide their true feelings, realizing that laments of discontent, plans for freedom, or displays of self-assertion could all bring down swift retribution from white oppressors. Frederick Douglass depicted this quandary in his 1845 *Narrative of the Life of Frederick Douglass*, relating that a slave master disguised his identity and then asked one of the plantation's slaves whether or not he was treated well by the master. The slave stated that he was not, and upon returning to the plantation, the slave was sold to a Georgia slave trader. Such deceitful practices, Douglass explains, often compel slaves, if questioned by a stranger, to state that they are treated well.

From its most overt representation in "We Wear the Mask" to its more implicit appearance in "An Ante-Bellum Sermon," both poems published in 1896 in *Majors and Minors*, Dunbar continually reiterates the theme of masking the African American experience behind the face that "grins and lies." In "An Ante-Bellum Sermon," for example, he situates this masking technique within the context of a long tradition of African American dissimulation, demonstrating how biblical rhetoric was used to encode discussions of slavery and freedom within the black community. After relating Moses' escape from oppression in Egypt, the preacher facetiously reminds his audience, "I'm still a-preachin ancient / I ain't talkin' bout to-day," asserting, "I'm talkin' bout ouah freedom / In a Bibleistic way." Similarly, his poem "Goin' Back" appears to support the stereotypes perpetuated by the plantation tradition that an old black man, when seemingly betrayed by the North, would return South. There is slippage in the old man's story that calls into question the sincerity of his desire to return South, even as he declares it. He begins, for example, by noting that this is, "the same ol' tale that I have to tell." The poem then concludes with the advice, "don't mind the ol' man's tears, but say / It's joy, he's goin' back to-day." In Dunbar's 1902 novel, the theme and literary device of masking become central to the development of plot, the revelation of character, and Dunbar's biting critique of the plantation tradition literature.

Dunbar's *The Sport of the Gods* tells the story of Berry Hamilton, a butler who labored on the plantation of Maurice Oakley for 30 years prior to his emancipation from slavery. Once freed, Berry wanders helplessly, presumably during the subsequent Reconstruction period, before returning to his former master's plantation. Once returned to his "proper" place, likely Dunbar's allusion to the return of near-slavery conditions in the post-Reconstruction era, the text establishes parallel separate spheres in which both master and servant coexist, not only harmoniously, but in fact profitably, relating, "when the final upward tendency of his employer began his fortunes had increased in a like manner" (2). In this way the narrative provides an abbreviated reiteration of the "fictions" referred to in the opening lines of the text. As with much of Dunbar's poetry, however, the text simultaneously offers signs that it is retelling these monotonous fictions with a difference. Indeed, while the Oakleys and the Hamiltons maintain separate households, and supposedly advance equality, the narrator offers textual cues that suggest the inherent flaws of this system. The Hamiltons and Oakleys advance separately and "equally," only so long as the Hamiltons remain at a social and economic level far below and subservient to the Oakleys, content to receive the discarded things "handed down" from the Oakley household. When the Oakleys realize that 500 dollars has been stolen from their home, they immediately discard the fiction of the contented former slave and replace it with the narrative of the thieving, untrustworthy freed black. When Oakley summons the sheriff to question Berry about the theft of the money, they encounter a *Berry* who is still acting out the plantation fictions upon which he has created his world. He is still a plantation type who grins and laughs for the white audience:

> "Shall I question him," asked the officer, "or will you?"
>
> "I will. Berry you deposited five hundred dollars at the bank yesterday?"
>
> "Well, suh, Mistak Oakley," was the grinning reply. "ef you ain't the beatenes' man to fin' out things I evah seen." (23)

Unlike most blacks in the South during the nadir, Berry, who is at this point still a romantic construct of the plantation tradition, "seemed not to understand at all" what it meant to have the owner of the plantation, "his man," and an officer arrive at his house. Berry crumbles when he realizes that the system he has bought into works only so long as it suffers no disturbances, real or imagined. He is convicted of the crime and sentenced to ten years of hard labor. After finding their life in the South destroyed by the false accusation of theft (the money was stolen by the Oakleys' own half-brother), the rest of the Hamilton family set off for the North. Escaping the constructs that imprisoned them in the South, however, proves more difficult than simply following the trajectory of yet another narrative myth. The Hamiltons identify New York "as a place vague and far away, a city that like Heaven, to them had existed by faith alone. All the days of their lives they had heard of it, and it seemed to them the centre of all the glory, all the wealth, and all the freedom of the world. New York. It had an alluring sound" (43–4). The Hamiltons quickly discover that New York is as fraught with as many intricately manufactured snares as the South. Far from offering a reprieve from the fictional constructions that confined them in the South, the Hamiltons are again thrust into a world defined by the popular and literary conventions of the day.

After arriving in New York, Skaggs, a reporter for the novel's aptly named newspaper, *The Universe*, learns about the Hamiltons and takes it upon himself to assume responsibility for representing their story. While Dunbar initially presents him as the hero, he slowly unmasks the motives behind Skaggs's supposedly benevolent acts. When the Hamilton's youngest son, Joe, first meets Skaggs at the Banner Club, Skaggs is operating behind a mask akin to those associated with the African American tradition. He creates a narrative of his life which legitimizes his associating with the blacks at the club, or, in other words, he justifies his "slumming." Even as Skaggs attempts to employ the mask, however, the narrator peers behind it, explaining, "it was the same old story that the white who associates with negroes from volition usually tells to explain his taste," and then goes on to "tell the truth about the young reporter" (Dunbar 69). Captivated by the rag-time dancers, Skaggs further demonstrates his own inability to see behind the mask employed by African Americans, reading their rag-time performance as "'the poetry of motion,'" while one of the club's black patrons cynically replies, "'Yes ... dancing in rag-time is the dialect poetry.'" In other words, the dancing is just another performance of the stereotypes by which whites judge blacks (Dunbar 116).

Skaggs's fumbling attempts to utilize the mask to get "in" with the blacks at the club, while being completely blind to the masking that the blacks themselves are doing, would be comical if the text did not also show the power he exerts over the representations of blacks. Governed by his ambitions, Skaggs is shown to be completely insensitive to the realities of black life; seeing the broken and disillusioned Berry Hamilton, Skaggs pronounces, "this is a very happy occasion." He gives Berry the address of his estranged wife, but fails to inform him that she is now remarried and his son has been sent to jail. Thus the text represents Skaggs as one who, regardless of his insensitivity to the realities of this black family, writes the story of the Hamiltons for the *Universe* and enables Berry's return to the South, where society is more or less falling apart around him. Thus the new perspective Skaggs offers is little more than another veiled exploitation of a pathetic image of blacks. He replaces the stereotype of blacks as thieving and untrustworthy with that of the helpless victim. His newspaper, the *Universe*, spreads its headlines across New York, "'A Burning Shame! A Poor And Innocent Negro Made To Suffer For A Rich Man's Crime. Great Expose by the *Universe*! A *Universe* Reporter To The Rescue!'" (Dunbar 137). The *Universe* takes the place of Southern paternalism in controlling the representations of blacks in the North. Thus, in the North, Skaggs, empowered by this mythical "Universe" recasts detrimental, confining, limited, and inaccurate fictions about blacks. Indeed, the white hegemony of the North is doubly sinister in its omnipresence, as well as in its attempts to remain invisible. However, only one as masterful at masking and unmasking as Dunbar could characterize Skaggs as the hero while unmasking him as the villain.

Like Dunbar, Hopkins incorporates black folklore as a way to mount a critique of contemporary discourse about African Americans, but, unlike Dunbar, she suggests that folklore does more than "critique." Black folklore can help recover an African American cultural lineage that inverts existing power structures. In her richly complex novel, *Of One Blood*, Pauline Hopkins incorporates various forms of folklore, including mysticism, spirituals, and conjuring to construct a vision of Africa that challenged the degraded constructions of Africa as the Dark Continent. In the late nineteenth-century ideology and rhetoric of evolution, Africa occupied a place firmly at the bottom of the evolutionary ladder. When it was recognized at all, Africa was evoked as an example of the primitive stage against which the progress of modern white Western civilization could be measured. *Of One Blood*, which was serialized between 1902 and 1903 in the *Colored American Magazine*, represents Hopkins's attempt to reorder this hierarchy, redefining and validating Ethiopia, and by extension Africa, as the site of a glorious past that African Americans could look to with pride. In the novel, the protagonist, Reuel Briggs, who has been passing as white to attend Harvard University and earn a medical degree, accepts an assignment to join an archeological expedition to the lost Ethiopian city of Telassar. Once there, Reuel learns that he is the long-awaited descendant of the city's ancient kings. The novel ends with Reuel assuming the throne of Telassar, with the hope that his reign will return the ancient city to its rightful place of glory.

Significantly, Reuel's recovery of his spiritual connections with Africa is mediated through African and African American folklore. While conjure and mysticism are treated as embarrassing relics of a superstitious past in Hopkins's earlier works, *Of One Blood* redefines black folklore, especially African spiritualism and conjure, as valuable cultural forms that carry the familial and cultural memories of a people. It is folklore that connects Reuel to his family, history, and culture, just as the various moments of conjure, mysticism, and visions propel the narrative forward to Reuel's inevitable return to Africa. Early in the novel, for instance, Reuel has a vision of Dianthe Lusk – a Fisk Jubilee singer and, unbeknownst to him, his estranged sister – before he sees her performing on the stage. His vision connects him to Dianthe and begins to reveal his hidden family past. Later, after Dianthe is seemingly fatally injured in a train derailment, he is able to bring her back to life through his powers of "reanimation" – powers, we are told, inherited from his mother: "From her he had inherited his mysticism and his occult powers. The nature of the mystic within him was, then, but a dreamlike devotion to the spirit that had swayed his ancestors; it was the shadow of Ethiopia's powers" (Hopkins 558). For Dianthe, too, folklore propels her self-discovery. At one point in the narrative, while Dianthe sings the spiritual, "Go Down Moses," a second voice, "a weird contralto," is heard "rising and falling" behind Dianthe's own voice. The voice that echoes her own is that of her deceased mother, Mira. Dianthe's Aunt Hannah, a well-known conjure woman, possesses the truth of Reuel and Dianthe's hidden and entwined genealogies, and relates to Dianthe that the voice she hears is that of her mother, Mira, who is also Reuel's mother.

Throughout the narrative, folklore serves as the vehicle of discovery, holding the hidden past that allows for a redefinition of individual, familial, and cultural identity. Propelled by his relationship with black folk traditions, Reuel is no longer the Harvard medical student passing for white, but assumes his rightful place as son of Mira, brother to Dianthe, and heir to the cultural and material wealth of the Ethiopian kingdom of Meroe. Here, black folklore helps revive a distinctive African civilization so technologically and scientifically advanced that it is on par with, and in many ways superior to, white Western civilization. While reordering the prevailing hierarchy of Hopkins's day that held white Western culture as the pinnacle of all civilization, her narrative ultimately remains confined to the hierarchy, because it nonetheless privileges material wealth and scientific and technological advancements as indicators of a society's worth. Unlike her contemporary, Anna Julia Cooper, who jettisoned the flawed ideology of civilization altogether, asking sardonically, "Whence came this apotheosis of greed and cruelty? Whence this sneaking admiration we all have for bullies and prize-fighters? Whence the self-congratulation of the 'dominant' races, as if 'dominant' meant 'righteous' and carried with it a title to inherit the earth," Hopkins never seems sufficiently to consider the dangers of ousting one dominant civilization by constructing another to take its place ("Higher Education of Women" 73).

In *The Conjure Woman*, Chesnutt's treatment of black folklore goes beyond critiquing the conventions of the plantation tradition or even inverting the racial hierarchies steeped in the contemporary discourses of civilization. It moves beyond minstrel realism or the discourse of civilization to point to an alternative way of constructing, perceiving, and responding to reality. In each story, Chesnutt employs black folklore to expose the many intertwined conventions that set the parameters of black representation. Not only does he expose the politics of cultural representation in his characterization of *The Conjure Woman*'s white narrator, he shows the limits of such an approach by employing conjure to present an alternative perspective on US racial realities.

In each of *The Conjure Woman*'s seven interconnected tales, Chesnutt creates a framed narrative in which the first narrator, John, a white Northern businessman and entrepreneur, recounts observations gathered during his foray into Southern land speculation. During the course of each of the stories, a second narrator, Uncle Julius, takes over the narrative to relate to John and John's wife, Annie, a conjure tale set in the antebellum South. Through the narrative frame, we learn that John's perspective is thoroughly circumscribed by the conventions of various fictions emerging from both the plantation tradition and the prominent folkloric and pseudo-scientific discourses of the day. Although John is presented as the outsider, he continually assumes responsibility for representing this Southern rural community. John perceives himself to be an astute observer of the human species, but as the text reveals, his observations are colored by popular myths about the "ole plantation." When he first encounters Julius, for instance, John explains Julius's continued occupancy on the plantation as a result of Julius's social conditioning, which has taught him to see himself as property. In another instance, John offers a well-stated explanation of the rabbit's foot, describing the black folk cultural artifact and the value it holds for slaves and free blacks. But again, his sense of having figured things out leaves him unable to grasp the deeper implications behind the folkloric item he analyzes. While Julius frequently manipulates the minstrel mask to reveal the distinction between the mask and the man, John continually misses the point. Julius's minstrel performances, however satirical, only further confirm John's preexisting ideas about African Americans. While Chesnutt's characterization of Julius works to expose the various conventions that defined the parameters of African American identity in the postbellum era, Chesnutt's text is more than an example of minstrel realism. Indeed, John's continual inability to recognize Julius's critiques suggests that *The Conjure Woman* can be read as a meditation on the inherent dangers of donning the minstrel mask to challenge the minstrel tradition. Instead, Chesnutt tests out a different literary strategy, incorporating conjure as a way to introduce an alternative worldview.

Culled from the principles of conjure, Chesnutt creates an aesthetic that recognized the value of symbolic representations in presenting to his audience an alternate perspective on US race relations. At the same time, conjure allowed Chesnutt to enact his foremost goal of initiating action and bringing about change. A highly symbolic ritual, conjure offered those who believed in its power a way to influence aspects of their daily lives that otherwise seemed beyond rational control. In black folk tradition, the conjure doctor was one skilled at reading the traditional signs. As he or she presided over the conjure rituals, his or her power to affect change was mirrored in his or her manipulation of symbolic icons. The methods of the conjure doctor varied from place to place, but more important than any formula or incantation was the degree to which the parties involved were willing to believe in the power of the conjure doctor: "Never mind what you mix," one observer states, "it will be powerful or feeble in proportion to the dauntless spirit infused by … the priest or priestess" (Owen 198). In one document published by the Hampton Folklore Society, for example, a patient reports seeking the services of a conjure doctor to find a cause and remedy for her chills. After receiving payment for his services, the conjurer prepares a "walking boy," a bottle that the doctor surreptitiously places a living creature in so that it will roll around on the floor, thereby directing the conjurer to the source of the young woman's illness. The patient explains that she knows the conjure doctor has animated the bottle and that the ceremony is done to impress her, but states, "as I had good faith in the 'doctor,' the chills vanished" ("Chills Cured"). As this example shows, conjure required a willingness to suspend disbelief and to accept the conjure ritual as constitutive of a symbolic, rather than mimetic approach to reality.

The Conjure Woman's second story, "Po' Sandy," demonstrates Chesnutt working his conjure aesthetic. In the story, Uncle Julius relates the heart-rending tale of a slave couple who try, against the wayward whims of the plantation owner, to stay together. Driven by the trauma of being "lent out" and the fear of being separated from his family, Sandy implores his wife Tenie, who is a conjure woman, to turn him into a tree so that he will not be sent away from her again. While the conjure works temporarily, eventually the very tree into which Sandy has been transformed is cut down when the slave master decides to use the wood to build a new kitchen. When Tenie discovers that even this desperate attempt to protect Sandy and to preserve their relationship has failed, she is so overcome with grief that she eventually dies of a broken heart. As we learn in the frame of the tale, the kitchen is eventually torn down and the wood from the kitchen is then used to build the very school house which John and Annie are considering tearing down to build their new kitchen.

When Julius concludes the story, John's wife Annie responds to the extreme actions that individuals were driven to take in an effort to preserve their families during slavery. She exclaims, "What a system it was … under which such things were possible … Poor Tenie!" Annie is receptive to the affective nature of the story, empathizing with Tenie as a woman, as a wife, and as a person. John, on the contrary, is stuck in the realm of the literal. He is unable to comprehend the deeper meaning of Sandy's transformation into a non-human object that becomes merely a resource for the material improvement of the master's house. In response to Julius's overtly allegorical story, John can only ask his wife, "in amazement," if she is "seriously considering the possibility of a man's being turned into a tree?" (23–4). As the frame of the story reveals, John's mode of understanding remains on the unemotional plane of reason. His literal belief system requires a verifiable and concrete representation of the past, and it inhibits him from sympathizing with the characters in the tale or from seeing how Julius's story might provide him with the "truth" of the plantation past and the reality of the present moment.

Annie, on the other hand, is willing to participate in Julius's conjure ritual. She accepts Julius's stories as symbols that point to a deeper reality – a reality that cannot be expressed mimetically, but that must be apprehended through the interpretation of symbols and metaphors. When John continues to press her, for example, half-asking, half-stating, "You would n't [*sic*] for a moment allow yourself … to be influenced by that absurdly impossible yarn which Julius was spinning to-day?" Annie responds, "I know the story is absurd … and I am not so silly as to believe it," but as she later explains, Julius's stories "bears the mark of truth if a story ever did … and might have happened half a hundred times … in those horrid days before the war" (61). At a more material level, Annie's participation in the conjure ritual not only influences her perspective, but also informs her actions. At the conclusion of "Po Sandy," for example, Annie decides that she no longer wants to use the wood from the school house to build her kitchen, thus leaving the school house intact, and, as we come to learn, allowing Julius to continue holding his church meetings there. John assumes Annie has been "duped," but, in fact, it is Annie's new understanding of the past that convinces her to adopt a different course of action in the present.

In *Chesnutt and Realism*, Ryan Simmons asserts that central to Chesnutt's literary work is "the conviction that understanding reality rightly requires action; no one who truly saw reality for what it was could stand by and do nothing" (Simmons 5). Thus Annie's decision to act completes Julius's conjure ritual and models for Chesnutt's readers the proper response to what he hopes will be their new understanding of US racial realities. In *The Conjure Woman*, Chesnutt demonstrates his acute awareness of the degree to which the conventions governing black representation had been co-opted by the various fictions emerging from the stage, the pseudo-scientific discourse and the various literary traditions. He is also deeply mindful of the material consequences of those representations for African Americans at the turn of the century. Chesnutt engages in narrative experimentation, creating a conjure aesthetic to explore how he might persuade his audience to understand and respond to the US racial situation differently.

For Dunbar, Hopkins, and Chesnutt, black folklore at the turn of the twentieth century constituted a contested space. Examining the varied ways each of the authors engages with black folklore reveals that African American writers did not "discover" black folklore as a source for their creative works during the 1920s. Instead, the relationship between folklore and African American literature extends back at least as far as the earliest written slave narratives. Post-Reconstruction writers faced their own set of unique challenges as they worked to legitimize a black folk tradition under assault in the various "learned" societies, on the stage, in the courts, and in the plantation tradition literatures. By locating their literary representations of black folklore firmly with this cultural, social, and political milieu, all three authors participated in redefining the meaning of black folklore in the African American literary tradition.

Bibliography

Baron, Robert and Nicholas Spitzer. *Public Folklore*. Washington, DC: Smithsonian Institution Press, 1992.

Ben-Amos, Dan. "Toward a Definition of Folklore in Context." *Journal of American Folklore* 84.331 (1971): 3–15.

Chesnutt, Charles. *Conjure Tales and Stories of the Color Line*, ed. William Andrews. New York: Penguin Classics, 2000.

"Chills Cured." *Southern Workman* 28.8 (1899): 314–15.

Cooper, Anna Julia. "The Higher Education of Women." 1890–91. In *The Voice of Anna Julia Cooper*. Ed. Charles Lemert and Esme Bhan. Lanham: Rowman and Littlefield, 1998. 72–87.

Cooper, Anna Julia. "The Negro's Dialect." 1930. In *The Voice of Anna Julia Cooper*. Ed. Charles Lemert and Esme Bhan. Lanham: Rowman and Littlefield, 1998. 238–47.

Dunbar, Paul Laurence. *The Sport of the Gods*. 1902. Rpt. New York: Penguin Putnam, 1999.

Ellison, Ralph. *Shadow and Act*. New York: Signet Books, 1966.

Harris, Trudier. *Fiction and Folklore: The Novels of Toni Morrison*. Knoxville: University of Tennessee Press, 1991.

Hopkins, Pauline. *The Magazine Novel of Pauline Hopkins*. Ed. Henry Louis Gates, Jr. New York: Oxford University Press, 1998.

Ives, Edward. *Joe Scott, the Woodsman-Songmaker*. Urbana: University of Illinois Press, 1978.

Ratliff v. Beale, 74 Miss. 247 (1896).

Owen, Mary. *Among the Voodoos*. 1881. Quoted in Newbell Niles Puckett, *Folk Beliefs of the Southern Negro*. Chapel Hill: University of North Carolina Press, 1926.

Newell, William Wells. "On the Field and Work of a *Journal of American Folk-Lore*." *Journal of American Folklore* 1.1 (1888): 6.

Plessy v. Ferguson, 163 US 537 (1896).

Simmons, Ryan. *Chesnutt and Realism: A Study of the Novels*. Tuscaloosa: University of Alabama, 2006.

Toll, Robert. *Blacking Up: The Minstrel Show in Nineteenth-Century America*. New York: Oxford University Press, 1974.

14

The Harlem Renaissance: The New Negro at Home and Abroad

Michelle Ann Stephens

Sometime between 1929 and 1930, Langston Hughes, probably the best-known African American poet at the time, lamented the end of the black artistic movement, the Harlem Renaissance. As he stated toward the end of his 1940 autobiography, *The Big Sea*, "That spring for me (and, I guess, all of us) was the end of the Harlem Renaissance. We were no longer in vogue, anyway, we Negroes" (Hughes, *The Big Sea* 334). Hughes's statement has come to define our sense that the Renaissance, a burst of black creative energy and literary output also known as the New Negro Movement, was over in the United States by the 1930s. And if we use the publication of key texts as our marker, Hughes would seem to have been correct.

By the beginning of the 1930s, most of the more famous novels of the Harlem Renaissance had been published, including Jean Toomer's experimental book of short stories and poems, *Cane* (1923), considered a literary masterpiece even by critics in the 1920s; *There Is Confusion* (1924), the first novel by writer and editor Jessie Fauset depicting middle-class life amongst black Americans from a woman's perspective; Claude McKay's *Home to Harlem* (1928), the Renaissance's most popular novel and one of the first bestsellers by a black author; and Nella Larsen's *Quicksand* (1928) and *Passing* (1929), works which together earned her the distinction of becoming the first black woman to receive a Guggenheim fellowship for creative writing. By 1930, much of the best-known poetry of the movement had also been published, including Hughes's first two collections, *The Weary Blues* (1926) and *Fine Clothes to the Jew* (1927). Perhaps most tellingly, the key anthologies and literary journals heralding the movement's emergence had come and gone, including the 1926 *Crisis* survey on "The Negro in art – how shall he be portrayed: A Symposium," and the March 1925 issue of the *Survey Graphic*, which Alain Locke edited and, later that year, expanded into the now canonical anthology, *The New Negro*. By 1930, the Renaissance had even matured enough to produce a younger, dissenting generation of artists, including Hughes, Zora Neale Hurston, Richard Bruce Nugent, and Aaron Douglas, all of whom contributed in 1926 to the first and only issue of *Fire!! a Quarterly Devoted to the Younger Negro Artists*.

The question of how long we should consider the span of the Harlem Renaissance has occupied many a scholar of the period, with some preferring to push the Renaissance back to the early appearance of a discourse of the "New Negro" in the 1890s, and others arguing that we can go forward as late as the 1940s. Regardless of the debates, most would agree that in the 10-year period between 1919 and 1929, black artists in the United States self-consciously set themselves the goal of defining a black presence in the arts, and by extension, a vibrant, black, cultural place in the nation as a whole. As Locke put it eloquently in his foreword to *The New Negro* anthology, "So far as he is culturally articulate, we shall let the Negro speak for himself … [The] New Negro must be seen in the perspective of a New World, and especially of a New America" (Locke xxv). The Harlem Renaissance would become a defining moment in the creation of a black cultural identity in the United States. Future generations of artists, including the members of the Black Arts Movement in the 1960s and 1970s and the cohort of black women writers who emerged in the 1980s, wrestled with the vision of the "Negro's" cultural contribution left behind in the creative legacies of figures such as Hughes, Hurston, and McKay.

Langston Hughes's comfort in closing the door on the Harlem Renaissance in 1930, however, may be important less for what it says about the movement's end than for what it reveals about the movement's capacious ability to influence a wider, black, literary and cultural world. If we study the New Negro's international influence, focusing less on *when* the movement occurred and more on *where* it had an impact, we find that it played a central role in shaping the racial formation of black writers in a number of locations outside of the United States at the beginning of the twentieth century. In the period between the World Wars, a broader, transnational idea of black consciousness took root, one more geographically neutral and befitting of the Harlem Renaissance's oldest name, a *Negro* renaissance or movement.

The New Negro and Black Internationalism

Henry Louis Gates, Jr. describes "the era of the myth of a New Negro" most broadly as the period from 1895 to 1925, when the idea of a "new Negro," who had moved beyond slavery, emancipation, and Reconstruction in the South, set out "in search of a Renaissance suitable to contain this culturally willed myth" (Gates, "The Trope of a New Negro" 132). This quest had two distinct phases. In early usage, at the turn into the twentieth century, the term "New Negro" had a more political focus. However, with the publication of Locke's anthology, the term took on a more cultural meaning focused on the arts. Gates traces the term's North American evolution as a political designation for a "new Negro" at the turn of the century, one who black leaders such as Booker T. Washington differentiated from the "Old Negro" of slavery. In the teens and the twenties a more artistic use of the term emerged in the context of the Harlem Renaissance. However, Gates's sense of the period leaves out the impact of black Caribbean artists and intellectuals also working in Harlem during the 1910s and 1920s, many of whom played an active role in creating a black internationalist consciousness that would also shape the Harlem Renaissance.

From 1915 to the mid-1920s, discussions of New Negro identity were fundamentally shaped by the geopolitical events of World War One and the Russian Revolution (Allen, Jr. 1991). In the early decades of the twentieth century, black migrants from both the American South and the Caribbean were traveling to Northern cities such as Harlem in unprecedented numbers. At the very same moment, the twentieth-century world was experiencing the upheaval and aftermath of World War One and the Russian Revolution. Black migrants and immigrants went North to escape poverty and racial discrimination in the US South and in the colonies, and to benefit from North America's wartime economic prosperity. They joined the war effort in significant numbers, with some 380,000 black soldiers serving in World War One (Allen). As the term "New Negro" moved further into the twentieth century as a way of identifying modern, black Americans, this already quite masculinist trope benefited from the new internationalism shaping global political discussion.

In the peace talks at Versailles after World War One, powerful nations advocated national self-determination and citizenship as a global and universal right for all. The Russian Revolution of 1917 offered an alternative idea of a political identity based on an internationalist class consciousness not limited or defined by nationality. War and revolution thus provided blacks in the New World, suffering from various forms of colonization and disenfranchisement, two suitable models of a free and self-determined political identity – one founded on the political model of the nation-state, and the other on the radical, revolutionary internationalism of the Bolshevik Revolution. National self-determination offered an empowering vision of freedom grounded in citizenship, while revolutionary internationalism suggested new ways of imagining black identity outside of the boundaries of the national.

The "New Negro," then, can be thought of as a black American social identity that traveled well beyond the confines of the United States, to serve as a metaphor for a rising, black, cultural and intellectual consciousness informed by international political events, which swept through the Americas and spilled over into metropolitan Europe. Thinking of the Harlem Renaissance through this lens, we find multiple groups of artists, in different locations, using the years between the wars to create an increasingly self-aware black world. A crucial set of institutions provided the political structure and internationalist framework for black diaspora artists to emerge. A constellation of black and radical journals, mass political movements and organizing efforts in the postwar era just prior to the Depression, and a host of international conferences and conventions such as W.E.B. Du Bois's Pan-African Congresses, solidified black intellectuals' awareness of their political context, a self-consciousness that would shape, directly and indirectly, the black poetry and literature of the Harlem Renaissance period.

To shift perspective from the domestic narrative to an international one, we must first follow the paths laid out by some of the movement's key political figures, W.E.B. Du Bois and Marcus Garvey. The African American intellectual, editor, and writer,

W.E.B. Du Bois, played a central role in creating the Pan-African Congress focused on the liberation of Africa. The Congress held its first meeting in Paris in 1919 to coincide with the postwar talks at the Versailles Peace conference. Du Bois and others hoped (unsuccessfully) for an opportunity to make the case that the principle of national self-determination should apply to colonial territories in Africa. After the second meeting in Brussels in 1923, both Du Bois and Jessie Fauset, another leading African American intellectual, editor, and writer, produced essays discussing their impressions of the Congress. Both authors mapped for their readers the political scope of the black world and the possibilities of its unification in first-person narratives that traveled through and across various black communities.

Du Bois and Fauset essentially created in these pieces a language for talking and thinking about "blackness" beyond a United States context, using new tropes and metaphors to describe an interwar world in which, "with nearly every great European empire today walks its dark colonial shadow" (Du Bois, "Worlds of Color" 386, 389). Fauset's message was one of diasporic solidarity, as she described the attendees at a preliminary meeting held in London: "We listened well. What can be more fascinating than learning at first hand that the stranger across the seas, however different in phrase or expression, yet knows no difference of heart? We were all one family in London … We felt our common blood with almost unbelievable unanimity" (Fauset, "Impressions" 76). Du Bois would go so far as to quantify the potential, combined, global force of these "worlds of color," these "distant world shadows," on the Western states' horizons (Du Bois, "Worlds of Color" 408, 386):

> Twenty-three millions of Negroes in British West Africa, eighteen millions in French Africa, eleven millions and more in the United States; between eight and nine millions each in the Belgian Congo and Portugese Africa; and a dozen other lands in Africa and America have groups ranging from two to five millions. This hundred and fifty millions of people are gaining slowly an intelligent thoughtful leadership. (411)

Two other political groups had access to print media that they also used to reach a transnational black audience. The Universal Negro Improvement Association (UNIA), Marcus Garvey's institutional base of his "Back to Africa" movement, distributed *The Negro World* throughout the United States, Europe, Africa, and the Caribbean. The African Blood Brotherhood (ABB), a radical underground organization espousing socialist and black nationalist principles, used *The Crusader*, edited by Cyril Briggs, to reach a wider black American readership. The leadership of all three of these groups – the Pan-African Congress, the UNIA, and the ABB – disagreed about specific strategies for the African American struggle for racial freedom. Garvey called for the return of all diaspora peoples to Africa, Du Bois advocated that black Americans fight for their rights as citizens, and the members of the ABB advocated more radical forms of protest and civil disobedience. However, all three articulated an emerging black consciousness that literally and figuratively connected different geographies and populations in the black world. Even the satirical black journalist

George Schuyler, who parodied the idea of a "black internationale" in his 1937 novel, *Black Empire: An Imaginative Story of a Great New Civilization in Modern Africa*, would proclaim as early as 1920: "The New Negro is here … aware that the balance of power is shifting in the world and so are his cousins in Africa, in India, in Malaysia, the Caribbean and China" (Schuyler 336).

Beyond the explicit political messages of the black internationalist writings of this period, we find writers and intellectuals thinking self-consciously about black interconnectivity, literally envisioning a "map of the world in colors before" them, as the African American character in McKay's *Home to Harlem* would exclaim after meeting and interacting with an Afro-Haitian for the very first time (McKay, *Home to Harlem* 134). Thus, the Harlem Renaissance occurred very much within the context of a broader, transnational discourse on the meaning of black self-determination. The "New World Negro" was not just a "cousin" to the New Negro, as George Schuyler once described, but an extension of New Negro consciousness beyond the nation, spreading out over the black and colonial world at large. While the New Negro's internationalist politics were more visible in the novels and essay collections of the period, a literary subgenre provided individual authors with the opportunity to reflect more personally on the significance of their travels. Hughes, McKay, and Zora Neale Hurston all produced travel narratives during this period – the first two written in the form of autobiographies, and the third published as an anthropological study. In the following sections of this essay, a closer look at the travelogues of McKay, Hughes, and Hurston can tell us as much about the New Negro abroad as at home, for all three authors encountered on their journeys alternative ways of thinking about modern blackness.

Claude McKay and the Making of a New, Transnational, Political Subject

In his autobiography *A Long Way from Home* (1937), McKay described the catalyst for his trip to Russia in 1922: "Go and see, was the command. Escape from the pit of sex and poverty, from domestic death, from the cul-de-sac of self-pity, from the hot, syncopated fascination of Harlem, from the suffocating ghetto of color consciousness" (McKay, *Long Way from Home* 150). Telling himself to "keep going," McKay describes Harlem as merely one stop, even if a significant one, on his journey "a long way from home" in the West Indian island of Jamaica. McKay had immigrated to the United States from Jamaica in 1912, leaving behind an English-speaking Caribbean just a few decades away from its own cultural revolution. In the 1930s, on the second largest Anglophone colony in the Caribbean, Jamaica's sister island of Trinidad, a group of men banded together to produce what Hazel Carby has called the "Trinidadian renaissance." Newspapers and newspaper editors also played a key role in this movement. Its members included Alfred Mendes and C.L.R. James, the co-editors of the *Trinidad* (of which only two issues were published), and Alfred Gomes, the editor of the *Beacon*.

Mendes described war and revolution as the two catalysts for the group's efforts to establish an "indigenous West Indian literary tradition," paralleling the black internationalist sensibility emerging in the United States a decade earlier.

Revolution was also the backdrop for McKay's trip to Russia in the early 1920s. In Part IV of his autobiography, "The Magic Pilgrimage," McKay describes how his "senses were stirred by the semi-oriental splendor and movement of Moscow even before my intellect was touched by the forces of the revolution" (McKay, *Long Way from Home* 158–9). He goes on to say that "it was all like a miracle, all that Byzantine conglomeration of form and color, shedding down its radiance upon the proletarian masses. It was like an *Arabian Nights* dream transforming the bleak white face of an Arctic waste." While in Russia, McKay attended the Fourth International Congress for the Communist International in November of 1922, a meeting at which an important debate took place concerning "the Negro question" in the United States and beyond. McKay became the representative black American radical at the meeting, providing an interpretation of the consequences of black participation in the war:

> The World War has fundamentally altered the status of Negroes in Europe. It brought thousands of them from America and the British and French colonies to participate in the struggle against the Central Powers. Since then serious clashes have come about in England between the blacks that later settled down in the seaport towns and the natives. (McKay, "Speech to the Fourth Congress" 97)

McKay drew the Comintern's attention to those black (and primarily male) communities remaining in Europe after the war, unattached to any official, nationally defined state. He also argued that, in the United States specifically, "the American capitalists" were aiming to pit blacks and workers against each other, lamenting further the American Communist Party's inability to see the roles that blacks and race more broadly were already playing in class warfare in the United States. Six years later, during the Sixth Congress of the Comintern in 1928, the Communists would identify "American Negroes" as constituting an oppressed nation within the nation, a "Black Belt" deserving national self-determination like other colonial territories.

Despite McKay's radicalism of the 1920s and his biographical connections with the stirrings of an Anglophone Renaissance in the Caribbean, it was the author's relationship to the Francophone world that would leave its most enduring aesthetic mark. In 1921, the Anglophone Caribbean writer Eric Walrond announced in the pages of an American newspaper an event significant for both his American and Caribbean audiences – the awarding of the French Prix Goncourt to the first black writer, René Maran, from the French-speaking Caribbean island of Martinique. Maran's novel, *Batouala: A True Black Novel* (1921), was translated into English by 1922 and influenced many of the leading figures of the Harlem Renaissance (Fabre). A close friend of Alain Locke, Maran tried to get *The New Negro* anthology translated into French, read and wrote pieces for key African American journals, and considered himself at the core of the movement rather than a passive observer of black American writers from France (Ikonné).

Claude McKay's 1929 novel, *Banjo*, would continue the circles of literary and artistic influence circulating between black America and black Paris in the 1920s and 1930s. After leaving Russia in 1923, McKay traveled to Europe, "The Cynical Continent," where in Paris he would "mix in among the cosmopolitan expatriates," the "lost generation" of American modernists, "lured to Europe because life was riper, culture mellower, and artistic things considered of higher worth than in America" (McKay, *Banjo* 243). McKay was not plagued by modernist angst, however. In his writings, he instead charted the efforts of New Negroes, whether African, Caribbean, or African American, to keep themselves afloat and in motion in a war-torn, racially divided Europe. A third black arts movement would draw from the discourse of New Negro writers such as McKay in the 1930s. Léopold Senghor and Aimé Césaire, two of the leading Négritude poets from Senegal and Martinique, respectively, described *Banjo* as a source of inspiration for their Francophone black poetics. Likewise, Hughes, in looking back at this period 30 years later, would use the French movement's name to describe Harlem in the 1920s, signaling the proximity of both movements' ideas (Hughes, "The Twenties Harlem and Its Negritude").

Langston Hughes's Wanderings and a New World Vernacular

With this international awareness in mind, it is easier to understand why Hughes described the Harlem Renaissance as over once we read the opening chapters of his second autobiography, *I Wonder as I Wander* (1956). Here he shifts his attention to the cultural and literary landscape of the black Americas, where he developed rich, cross-cultural relationships with other black poets such as Nicolás Guillén from Cuba and Jacques Roumain from Haiti. In the very first pages of *I Wonder as I Wander*, Hughes tells us that his response to the stock-market crash of 1929 (an event typically used to mark the end of the Harlem Renaissance) was to try to figure out how he could make a living as a black writer, but, specifically, one in touch with a black community. As he described,

> There was one other dilemma – how to make a living from *the kind of writing I wanted to do.* I did not want to write for the pulps, or turn out fake "true" stories to sell under anonymous names … I did not want to bat out slick non-Negro short stories in competition with a thousand other commercial writers trying to make *The Saturday Evening Post*. I wanted to write seriously and as well as I knew how about the Negro people, and make *that* kind of writing earn me a living. (Hughes, *I Wonder as I Wander* 5)

Hughes was experiencing a dilemma shared by the male writers of the Trinidadian Renaissance, namely, how to create relatively authentic black cultural forms for an indigenous black audience, without the resources of a publishing industry based in the First World and catering primarily to white readers. If the crash of 1929 marked the end of white publishers' interest in the Harlem Renaissance, it also positioned Hughes at the very heart of the cultural dilemma facing his Caribbean counterparts, who were eager to begin their own struggle for cultural autonomy from the old empires.

In 1931, on the advice of Mary McLeod Bethune, Hughes decided to give poetry readings at black venues throughout the South. Before putting this plan into action, he accompanied his friend Zell to spend the summer in Cuba. Since Hughes was already "wondering" about the relationship of his own writing to black audiences, it is not surprising that he was drawn to island artists and intellectuals who were intent on rooting their own forms of self-expression in an organic black community. Hughes's point of entry into local culture came with the help of a now recognizable figure, José Antonio, a newspaperman who would go on to become "an editor of *Orbe*, Cuba's weekly pictorial magazine" (Hughes, *I Wonder as I Wander* 7). José Antonio introduced Hughes to a range of artists, "best of all … Negro musicians," who then became central to the cementing of Guillén's and Hughes's ensuing friendship (Hughes, *I Wonder as I Wander* 7).

Hughes and Guillén found common ground precisely because Guillén wished to do for Cuban poetry what Hughes had done earlier with the blues: use the music of blacks to create a vernacular poetics. Like Hughes's efforts to create a jazz poetry, Guillén would draw from the sounds, rhythms, and lyrics of *són*, a popular Afro-Cuban musical form, to define an Afro-Cuban poetics in his collection *Motivos de son* (1930). Guillén and Hughes had met once before, in 1929, when Guillén interviewed the African American poet for a local newspaper. By 1931, Hughes's poems were already being published in Spanish in Cuban magazines, and he had given readings at various Havana cultural organizations including the "leading club of color." In *I Wonder as I Wander*, Hughes attempted to convey the power of these creolized, Afro-Cuban musical forms that so stirred the souls of these two poets:

> Rumbas and *sones* are essentially hip-shaking music – of Afro-Cuban folk derivation, which means a bit of Spain, therefore Arab-Moorish, mixed in. The tap of claves, the rattle of gourds, the dong of iron bells, the deep steady roll of drums speak of the earth, life bursting warm from the earth, and earth and sun moving in the steady rhythms of procreation and joy. (Hughes, *I Wonder as I Wander* 8)

Hughes's description mirrored almost word for word the kinds of values McKay would attribute in *Banjo* to African-derived musical forms that knitted together diverse communities of men.

As much as Hughes appreciated the shared sensibilities of diasporic cultures, he also observed important social and economic differences during his time in the Caribbean. In Cuba and again in Haiti, Hughes would comment on the sexual politics and gender relations of men and women on the islands. Circumspect throughout the autobiography about his own sexuality, Hughes observed in Cuba, as he had "in

Mexico and other Latin lands," the prevalence of "this custom of the mistress … where every man who was anybody at all had both a wife and a pretty mistress" (Hughes, *I Wonder as I Wander* 9). While Cuba's Afro-diasporic community had its own forms of patriarchy and gender oppression, nevertheless, as a predominantly black society, they were able to make visible the beauty of blackness in a way not possible in the United States: "all the love lyrics were about the charms of *mi negra*, my black girl, my chocolate sweetie or my mulatto beauty, plainly described as such in racial terms. These dusky nuances … are quite lost in the translations that Broadway makes of Cuban songs for American consumption" (Hughes, *I Wonder as I Wander* 10).

The "dusky nuances" of color – the ways in which complexion could determine social position on the island – led Hughes to coin a new term in his autobiography, "a sort of triple color line," to capture his sense of a "color scale" applicable across the Caribbean. With Du Bois's original metaphor of the color line in mind, Hughes's "triple color line" allowed him to think about race relations in the United States as they intersected with varying approaches to race and sexuality across the black New World. An equally cogent set of interpretations emerged from Hughes's observations on economic power in the islands. While in Cuba, he found himself the victim of exclusionary practices used to keep black locals out of popular hotels and beaches, a common dynamic of Caribbean tourism. Ironically, it was an American who had the job of policing Cuban beaches – "an old American boxer – white of course – with cauliflower ears and a flat nose" (Hughes, *I Wonder as I Wander* 12). This encounter revealed to Hughes the unequal relations between Caribbean locals and American tourists. By the end of the twentieth century, Hughes's experience would become the norm as the ex-colonies became the playgrounds for citizens from Europe and North America.

Affronted at being declined entrance to this beach, Hughes cried in astonishment: "Do you mean to tell me that you're drawing the color line on a *Cuban* beach against *American* citizens – and you're an American yourself?" (Hughes, *I Wonder as I Wander* 12). In this statement he expressed his frustration as a black American that the color line was transnational in reach, extending beyond the boundaries of North America to police New Negroes traveling abroad. Hughes also shared the opinions of a local policeman – "a Negro captain, an enormous, very dark, colored man" – on this extension of the North American state into the neighboring societies of the Caribbean: "This … is what happens to colored people in Cuba where white Americans are in control!" (Hughes, *I Wonder as I Wander* 14). Hughes was observing a dynamic in which the Caribbean tourist industry, catering primarily to white foreigners, repeated central features of colonial relations in the pre-independence Caribbean.

The beach incident occurs days before Hughes leaves Cuba for the island of Haiti, a romanticized site given its status as the home of the first and only revolution amongst black slaves in the Americas. His opening description demonstrates Haiti's centrality in Hughes's own revolutionary conception of blackness, as Moscow and Russia provided a similar sense of a heroic black identity for McKay:

> Haiti, land of blue sea and green hills, white fishing boats on the sea, and the hidden huts of peasants in the tall mountains. People strong, midnight black. Proud women whose heads bear burdens, whose backs are very straight. Children naked as nature … Port au Prince, city of squalid huts, unattractive sheds and shops near the water front, but charming villas on the slopes that rise behind the port. (Hughes, *I Wonder as I Wander* 15)

Hughes's images of a people in an organic relationship to the landscape, exposed but proud, glamour existing alongside squalor, echo the opening lines of the most famous poem of the Négritude movement, Aimé Césaire's "Notes on a Return to the Native Land" (1939): "This flat city shortly after dawn, exposed, stumbling commonsensically along, inert … And in this inert town the noisy crowd … some deep refuge of darkness and pride here, within this inert city, within this crowd that overlooks its cries of hunger, misery, revolt, hate" (Césaire). However, Césaire's nostalgia for Haiti's sister Francophone island of Martinique is in bitter contrast to the African American poet's sweeter tone, reflecting the fact that Hughes's impressions are based on history, Césaire's on living memory.

Yet, despite Hughes's own romantic investments in Haitian history, in *I Wonder as I Wander* he tried to offer a realistic portrayal of the differences that obtained in the island in the modern day. These differences were thrown into stark relief by the contrast between Hughes's status as an African American and the conditions of Afro-Haitians. Ignoring his letters of introduction to members of the cultural and political elite (due to his embarrassment at his own destitute circumstances), Hughes and Zell chose a nondescript hotel catering exclusively to locals, where Hughes finds himself struck by the impact of poverty in shaping the lives of the people. In a country where, at that time, owning a pair of shoes was a marker of one's more prosperous status, Hughes's observations about culture are necessarily inflected by the class context in which they are performed:

> Those who wear shoes and belong to the clerical classes, and who dance indoors to an orchestra with trumpets and strings, dance very much as people do in the United States. And the upper-class Haitians who have lived abroad know all the steps of Broadway and of Paris. But the black Haitians of the soil seem to remember Africa in their souls. (Hughes, *I Wonder as I Wander* 22)

In the Caribbean, class shapes the black subject's distance from or proximity to Africa, and the island peasant becomes a marker for authenticity as potent as the Old Negro of the South had been for the New Negro artists of the Renaissance.

While in Haiti, Hughes makes his own "magic pilgrimage" to the Citadel at Cap Haitien, the palace built by Haiti's revolutionary leaders, "this great relic of Negro pride … One of the most astonishing ruins in the New World" (Hughes, *I Wonder as I Wander* 16). Without diminishing the symbolic significance of the Citadel, Hughes places in counterpoint a description of Haiti's relationship to the United States, leaving it for his reader to decide how to put together the island's glorious revolutionary past with its present struggles against US occupation: "But in 1915 the American Marines came to Haiti to collect American loans, and were there when I came … All of the work that kept Haiti alive, paid the interest on American loans, and enriched foreign traders, was done by people without shoes" (Hughes, *I Wonder as I Wander* 27). As in Cuba, Haiti complicates Hughes's metaphor of the color-line for the complex forces shaping black life throughout the Americas: "It was in Haiti that I first realized how class lines may cut across color lines within a race, and how dark people of the same nationality may scorn those below them" (Hughes, *I Wonder as I Wander* 28). There was one member of the island's cultural elite, however, whom Hughes was willing "to dress up" for and have his "shoes shined": the poet Jacques Roumain, whom Hughes described as "one of the few cultured Haitians who appreciated native folklore, and who became a friend of the people without shoes" (Hughes, *I Wonder as I Wander* 29). As with Guillén, Hughes and Roumain cemented a relationship that would transcend their linguistic differences, leading Hughes to publish in 1947 his English translation of Roumain's classic Haitian novel, *Masters of the Dew* (1944).

Hughes's observations during his summer in Cuba and Haiti are an index of the types of relationship possible between First World and Third World black subjects in the early twentieth century, before the very notion of "three worlds" existed. Hughes enjoyed the cultural connections linking disparate black communities together, while appreciating the uniqueness of black, New World societies and their differences from each other. His associations with Guillén and Roumain are significant beyond the meeting of talented poets. Together, they discovered a shared sensibility emerging throughout the black New World, a poetic awakening to the vernacular languages and rhythms of blackness, as potent as the political awakening inspired by Du Bois's and Garvey's international movements.

Zora Neale Hurston: Anthropologist-Folklorist, and the Power of Black Speech

Hurston's career contradicts the story of the Harlem Renaissance's end with the stock-market crash of 1929. Although Hurston had already published short stories and plays in the 1920s, and was a prominent member of the group of artists responsible for *Fire!!*, most of her well-known works were published in the 1930s when the main energy of the Renaissance had diminished. These include *Jonah's Gourd Vine* (1934), her first novel; *Their Eyes Were Watching God* (1937), her second and even more popular novel; *Mules and Men* (1935), a collection of the folktales and hoodoo practices of poor Southern blacks; and *Tell My Horse* (1937), which combines ethnography, autobiography, and travelogue to offer a first-hand account of voodoo and other religious practices in Haiti and Jamaica. If Hughes, McKay, and Du Bois all extended the identity of the New Negro in the political realm, Hurston takes full credit for recording the diasporic affinities between black folk forms in the New World, charting even more thoroughly the path Hughes set out in his engagements with New World poets.

Between 1925 and 1927, when the Renaissance was at its peak, Hurston attended Barnard College and studied anthropology with Franz Boas. In her anthropological and ethnographic research throughout Jamaica, Haiti, and the US South, Hurston demonstrated the degree to which cultural affinities between Africa and diaspora peoples could be traced through black speech patterns and rhetorical forms. While Hughes's and McKay's travel narratives were written in the more conventional form of the autobiography, Hurston wrote *Tell My Horse* in the distinctive voice of both participant and observer, storyteller as well as documenter of social and political norms. Although primarily focused on exploring neo-African religious elements, Hurston's narrative includes lively accounts of political and economic life on the islands, interpreting from her (at times inaccurate) African American perspective, the intra- as well as interracial nuances of the color line in the Caribbean.

Unlike the more politically radical Hughes, Hurston's discussion of the color line includes idiosyncratic suggestions for African Americans. After first observing that in Jamaica, "[t]he color line … between the white Englishman and the blacks is not as sharply drawn as between the mulattoes and the blacks," Hurston goes on to state that "[p]erhaps the Jamaican mixed bloods are logical and right, perhaps the only question of what is to become of the negro in the Western world is that he must be absorbed by the whites" (Hurston, *Tell My Horse* 6–7). Such tongue-in-cheek comments often got Hurston in trouble with her mostly male colleagues in the Harlem Renaissance, who felt her strategy of cultural assimilation ran against the grain of the New Negro's privileging of black cultural self-expression and political self-determination.

However, embedded within Hurston's observations is a much less romanticized sense of the status and fate of black women within such mixed societies and sexual arrangements. As she observes further: "When a Jamaican is born of a black woman and some English or Scotsman, the black mother is literally and figuratively kept out of sight as far as possible" (Hurston, *Tell My Horse* 8). In one of the freshest passages in *Tell My Horse*, Hurston does more than observe the ways in which Caribbean societies enact patriarchy. She challenges her Caribbean male hosts to justify their sexist claims concerning not only the Caribbean woman's lack of self-knowledge and wisdom, but also the detrimental effects of "independence" on the American woman. Devoting a whole chapter to "Women in the Caribbean," Hurston translates some of the region's class and color hierarchies, along with the First- and Third World distinctions, into a critique of sexism amongst her diasporic, Caribbean brothers:

> Miss America, World's champion woman, you take your promenading self down into the cobalt blue waters of the Caribbean and see what happens. You meet a lot of darkish men who make vociferous love to you, but otherwise pay you no mind. If you try to talk sense, they look at you right pitifully … It is not that they try to put you in your place, no. They consider that you never had any. (Hurston, *Tell My Horse* 57–8)

While some find problematic Hurston's assumptions concerning the position of the American woman (black or white), nevertheless in one fell swoop she comments on three of the issues disturbing the possibilities for racial solidarity across the diaspora as they intersect with gendered and sexual economies. First, she calls Jamaican men to task for their misogyny; second, she points very early to tensions between Western feminists and women in colonial territories that continued to plague twentieth-century transnational feminist movements; and third, she points ahead to African Americans' future participation in the sexual economies of tourism in the Caribbean, the sexualized hierarchy of "First-" and "Third-"World black relations romanticized in the 1998 film, *How Stella Got Her Groove Back*.

Like Hughes, who preferred the culture of the Haitians "without shoes" to that of the island's elites, Hurston argued that where one did find a unifying sense of black consciousness in Jamaica was precisely in its folk culture. Whereas Hughes emphasized the musical contributions of diasporic black cultures, Hurston's real talent was in identifying the rhetorical register in autonomous black cultural forms, the creative elements of black speech that she documented from the everyday conversations and stories of islanders. For Hurston, these forms of "signifying" – a term used to describe the performative dimensions of black speech and the figurative capacities of black language – were as crucial to understanding a black New World poetics as the rhythms of the Haitian conga or Cuban *són* (Gates, *Signifying Monkey*). Hurston found Jamaican proverbs "rich in philosophy, irony and humor," representing a mindset, a sophisticated and wry approach to life, embedded within everyday black speech. She linked certain Caribbean folk figures to others found elsewhere in the diaspora and in the homeland, such as "Brother Anansi, the Spider, that great cultural hero of West Africa who is personated in Haiti by Ti Malice and in the United States by Brer Rabbit" (Hurston, *Tell My Horse* 25). Signifying forms of rhetoric may have had different features in Jamaica than in the US South, but both supported Hurston's idea that black language was a language with the "will to adorn" (Hurston, "Characteristics"). This attention to black languages was one of the primary contributions Hurston made to the diasporic conception of the New Negro developing in these years of the early twentieth century and beyond.

One of Hurston's sharpest political differences from figures such as Hughes and McKay, however, lay in her belief that the United States presence in Haiti was beneficial to the island. Whereas for McKay black people needed to carve out their own self-determined place in the glorious Revolution in Russia, and for Hughes Haiti represented proof of the black slave's Revolutionary possibilities, in Hurston's assessment the United States had to play the ultimate role in protecting the rights of the Haitians. In Hurston's version of Haitian history the struggle is for peace rather than freedom, a telling substitution of words that elided the revolution's impact on the island, and on colonialism and the politics of empire globally. Unlike Hughes, Hurston's introduction to Haiti focuses on the brutality of the island's internal political regimes, and her story begins not with the tragedy of black revolution, but rather with the utopia of American leadership:

> L'Ouverture had beaten back the outside enemies of Haiti, but the bloody stump of Sam's body [the deposed and beheaded President of Haiti] was to quell Haiti's internal foes, who had become more dangerous to Haiti than anyone else. The smoke from the funnels of the U.S.S. *Washington* was a black plume with a white hope … It was the end of the revolution and the beginning of peace. (Hurston, *Tell My Horse* 72)

Unlike Hughes's more nuanced depiction of the relationship between the peasants and the elites in contemporary Haitian society, Hurston infantilized both the Haitian peasants and the dictators: "The Haitian people are lovable except for their enormous and unconscious cruelty." This portrayal ultimately justified her sense of Haitians' need for paternal leadership from the United States (Hurston, *Tell My Horse* 82).

Hurston's travel narrative makes abundantly clear the ways in which the New Negro abroad was as much an American as an African American, the former identity coming more into relief against the backdrop of black worlds away from home. The period between the wars saw the emergence of an increasingly self-conscious New World Negro, who could use the language of revolutionary radicalism and national self-determination alike to shape a new sense of his own black political identity. Alongside political awareness came an artistic appreciation of the histories and cultural forms blacks in the New World potentially shared with each other, politics and culture combining to create the shadowy sense of a unified black, diasporic, imaginary. This black worldliness represented a shared set of beliefs and mindsets that provided the New Negro with counter-cultural tools to navigate the events of the early twentieth century. But the fractures and differences within New World blackness also came along for the ride, issues concerning color, gender, and sexuality adding nuance and complexity to the African American notion of a color line. Abroad, black double consciousness was tripled by the salient economic distinctions between blacks across the developed and underdeveloped worlds. Nevertheless, in his and her travels at the beginning of the twentieth century, the New Negro traced the contours of a globalizing black world whose variegated cultural, political, and social features still interact dynamically today.

Bibliography

Allen, Ernest, Jr. "The New Negro: Explorations in Identity and Social Consciousness, 1910–1922." In *1915, The Cultural Moment: The New Politics, the New Woman, the New Psychology, the New Art, and the New Theater in America*. Ed. Adele Heller and Lois Rudnick. New Brunswick, NJ: Rutgers University Press, 1991. 48–68.

Carby, Hazel V. "Proletarian or Revolutionary Literature: C.L.R. James and the Politics of the Trinidadian Renaissance." *South Atlantic Quarterly* 87 (1988): 39–52.

Césaire, Aimé. "Notes on a Return to the Native Land." In *The Negritude Poets*. Ed. Ellen Conroy Kennedy. New York: Thunder's Mouth Press, 1989. 66–79.

Du Bois, W.E.B. *The Souls of Black Folk*. New York: Oxford University Press, 2007.

Du Bois, W.E.B. "Worlds of Color: The Negro Mind Reaches Out." In *The New Negro: Voices of the Harlem Renaissance*. Ed. Alain Locke. New York: Macmillan, 1999. 383–414.

Fabre, Michel. *From Harlem to Paris: Black American Writers in France, 1840–1980*. Champagne, IL: University of Illinois Press, 1993.

Fauset, Jessie. "Impressions of the Second Pan-African Congress." In *Double-Take: A Revisionist Harlem Renaissance Anthology*. Ed. Venetria K. Patton and Maureen Honey. New Brunswick, NJ: Rutgers University Press, 2006. 75–82.

Fauset, Jessie. *There Is Confusion*. Boston, MA: Northeastern, 1989.

Gates, Henry Louis, Jr. *The Signifying Monkey: A Theory of African-American Literary Criticism*. New York: Oxford University Press, 1989.

Gates, Henry Louis, Jr. "The Trope of a New Negro and the Reconstruction of the Image of the Black." *Representations* 24 (1988): 129–55.

Guillén, Nicolás, Roberto Márquez, and David Arthur McMurray. *Man-Making Words: Selected Poems of Nicolás Guillén*. Amherst: University of Massachusetts Press, 2003.

Hughes, Langston. *The Big Sea*. New York: Hill and Wang, 1993.

Hughes, Langston. *I Wonder as I Wander*. New York: Hill and Wang, 1993.

Hughes, Langston. *Selected Poems of Langston Hughes*. New York: Vintage, 1990.

Hughes, Langston. "The Twenties Harlem and Its Negritude." *African Forum* 1 (1966): 11–20.

Hurston, Zora Neale. "Characteristics of Negro Expression." In *Double-Take: A Revisionist Harlem Renaissance Anthology*. Ed. Venetria K. Patton and Maureen Honey. New Brunswick, NJ: Rutgers University Press, 2006. 61–73.

Hurston, Zora Neale. *Jonah's Gourd Vine*. New York: Harper & Row, 1990.

Hurston, Zora Neale. *Mules and Men*. New York: Harper & Row, 2008.

Hurston, Zora Neale. *Tell My Horse*. New York: Harper & Row, 1990.

Hurston, Zora Neale. *Their Eyes Were Watching God*. New York: Harper & Row, 2006.

Ikonné, Chidi. "René Maran and the New Negro." In *Analysis and Assessment, 1940–1979 (The Harlem Renaissance, 1929–1940)*. Ed. Cary D. Wintz. New York: Routledge, 1996. 182–97.

Larsen, Nella. *Quicksand and Passing*. New Brunswick, NJ: Rutgers University Press, 1986.

Locke, Alain (ed.). *The New Negro: Voices of the Harlem Renaissance*. New York: Macmillan, 1999.

Maran, René. *Batouala*. New York: Albert and Charles Boni, 1930.

McKay, Claude. *Banjo: A Story without a Plot*. New York: Harcourt Brace & Company, 1970.

McKay, Claude. *Home to Harlem*. Boston, MA: Northeastern, 1987.

McKay, Claude. *A Long Way from Home*. New York: Harcourt Brace & Company, 1970.

McKay, Claude. "Speech to the Fourth Congress of the Third Communist International, Moscow." In *The Passion of Claude McKay*. Ed. Wayne Cooper. New York: Schocken, 1987. 92–7.

"The Negro in Art: How Shall He Be Portrayed." *The Crisis* (1926), 219–20.

Roumain, Jacques. *Masters of the Dew*. Portsmouth, NH: Heinemann, 1978.

Schuyler, George. *Black Empire*. Boston, MA: Northeastern, 1993.

Thurman, Wallace, ed. *Fire!! A Quarterly Devoted to the Younger Negro Artists*. Elizabeth, NJ: The Fire Press, 1985.

Toomer, Jean. *Cane*. New York: Liveright, 1993.

15

Transatlantic Collaborations: Visual Culture in African American Literature

Cherene Sherrard-Johnson

In "Un essai d'égo-histoire," renowned historian Nell Painter recounts an incident with a colleague following her receipt of a mentoring award. Painter writes: a colleague "came up to inform me that mentoring was my vocation as a historian. I reminded him that I also write books. He contradicted me: mentoring constitutes my 'real' vocation. Were I prone to violence, I would have socked him in his fat little jaw" (40). Painter's visceral reaction to what some might deem a complimentary observation illuminates a disturbing tendency in the critical consideration of black women's intellectual and artistic work. Obviously, mentorship is an important feature of academic life, but, as Painter painfully observes, it is often "too easy to reenvision a woman, a black woman, an older black woman as a nurturing figure" (40). Painter's essay inspired my approach to the collaborative work of female writers and visual artists between World Wars One and Two both in its call for a serious interrogation of black women's art and intellectual work, and her insistence on the necessity of living outside the United States as a way of understanding that "imperialism is so much more than race and color, even though a color line nearly always accompanied twentieth-century imperialism" (36).

During the Harlem Renaissance and beyond, black female artists and writers tended to take a backseat to the goliaths of visual art, like Romare Bearden and Jacob Lawrence, and emerging novelists, like Ralph Ellison and Richard Wright, who had taken up the New Negro's mantle with a vengeance. Art critics and biographers created lasting impressions of artists such as Lois Mailou Jones, Laura Wheeler Waring, and Augusta Savage as wonderful and inspiring teachers, privileging their influence on subsequent generations over their own art. This essay examines Jessie Redmon Fauset's two-part series "Dark Algiers the White," which was illustrated by Laura Wheeler Waring, and Lois Mailou Jones's paintings and illustrations (produced from 1937 to 1951) to show how the collaborative efforts of women artists and writers shaped black visual culture in the US and across the Atlantic. Keeping in mind Painter's observations, I position these collaborations as trailblazing artistic endeavors, rather than as acts of mentorship and midwifery – two terms that frequently obscure innovative experimentation in women's art. Examining these cross-genre collaborations expands our understanding of interwar social and artistic movements, like the Harlem Renaissance and Négritude, by broadening the boundaries imposed by chronology, geography, genre, and gender.

Understanding the Harlem Renaissance as a multidisciplinary era of collaboration is crucial. Artists from a variety of national and ethnic backgrounds, such as Aaron Douglas, Winold Reiss, and Miguel Covarrubias, worked with writers to create and/or illustrate period-defining texts like *The New Negro*, *Fy-Ah*, and *Survey Graphic*. Zora Neale Hurston developed a transnational relationship with Mexican muralist Miguel Covarrubias, who illustrated her book *Mules and Men*. The integration of visual arts also inspired new narrative forms, such as Jean Toomer's *Cane* (1923). Identifying points of intersections between visual and literary culture brings to light the interracial and internationalist aspects that propelled a presumably local phenomenon – the Harlem Renaissance – into a diasporic movement.

The Exhibit of American Negroes at the 1900 Paris Exposition is an early example of a collaborative effort that marked a profound moment of black visual modernity. Engineered by scholar-writer-activist W.E.B. Du Bois, the exhibit set the terms for how visual culture and literature would come to imagine the black subject in the early twentieth century. Antebellum nineteenth-century stereotypes of African Americans as servile, lazy, unintelligent, violent, and highly sexualized had persisted into the twentieth century. The photo albums and ephemera that comprised the Negro Exhibit challenged the social, legal, and economic barriers of the color line by telling a story of progress and transformation. The images selected by Du Bois presented a visual argument against the invisibility of the African American subject and a firm counter to the derogatory stereotypes proliferated through minstrel shows, commercial advertising, and generally racist images promulgated before and after emancipation. That the staging of the New Negro took place on the international scene is not accidental. The 1900 Paris exhibition was the largest to date, and a referendum on the status of Western culture at the dawn of the new century. The exhibit, which won an exposition grand prize, was a stark contrast to "the exoticized displays of African villages that reinforced white European estimations of their own 'civilized' superiority" (Smith, *American Archives* 161). Mainstream US papers ignored the exhibit, which was widely covered by black periodicals like *The Washington Bee*, *The Boston Guardian*, and *Negro World*. In Paris, the exhibit's presence amid cultural monuments to European superiority was a symbolic crack in the imperialist enterprise.

Du Bois assembled his albums with the help of black photographers like Thomas Askew. Together, they constructed a narrative of progress through industry and education that expressed the multifaceted diversity of black Americans. Photography played a critical role in shaping American visual culture at the turn into the twentieth century. As Deborah Willis argues, "[b]lack photographers created a new visual language for 'reading' black subjects" (52). The exhibit included several photographs of upper- and middle-class blacks. The clothing and backdrops were carefully chosen (by Du Bois and/or the photographers) to emphasize the subjects' modern and upwardly mobile status in both urban and rural settings. There is also a clear relationship between the subjects and the interior and exterior spaces they occupy. Children in fancy dresses sit in front of open books or at the piano, and students pose on the steps of their universities. There are also photographs of elaborately decorated parlors, living and music rooms. The offices of undertakers, newspapers, and even an ice truck function as testaments to education, industry, and progress. The exhibit was a precursor to the advancement of New Negro visual aesthetics, a sensibility and practice that would be refined, complicated, and taken in innovative new directions during the Harlem Renaissance.

Working closely with Du Bois as the literary editor of *The Crisis* from 1919 to 1926, Jessie Redmon Fauset was particularly attuned to the significance of visual culture and the symbiotic relationship between writing and visual art. She promoted and mentored painters and illustrators by featuring their work on the covers of *The Crisis* and in her short fiction. In some cases, the illustrations provided no more than a visual representation of the subject matter or events taking place; however, some collaborations were more complex. As Anne Elizabeth Carroll observes in her study of black periodicals, the interplay of visual art and writing can teach audiences about the "processes of representation." Such pairings can "suggest that a complete understanding of the topics at hand depends on an integrated reading of related texts" (106). Fauset saw this integration as essential to both the design of *The Crisis* and the structure of her fiction, poetry, and essays. One of her earliest published stories, "Emmy" (1912–1913), includes photographs of a dark-skinned heroine revealing the color conflicts at the heart of the romantic tragedy. If the albums comprising the Negro Exhibit represent Du Bois's defiant reinscription of a black masculine gaze, as Shawn Michelle Smith argues, then Fauset's travel narratives offer a subtle, cosmopolitan, black, female perspective on the black subject at home and abroad (363). A similar awareness of how interior and exterior spaces mark one's status and location in the world also permeates Jessie Fauset's travel essays. With her attentiveness to architecture and landscape, to how the physical and social geography of a place shapes its inhabitants and her characters, Fauset brings to life the flea markets of France and "The Court of Miracles" in French-occupied Algeria.

Beyond Marseille

Several critics have noted Claude McKay's double-edged description of Jessie Fauset as "prim and dainty as a primrose" and a writer of "fastidious and precious" novels (92). Despite the somewhat patronizing floral allusions, McKay does concede that in contrast to Anglo-authored novels about the black middle class, Fauset's novels were the "real meat." One of the most prolific writers of the Harlem Renaissance, she published four novels, several poems, short stories, biographical profiles, and essays. A few of her peers, Alain Locke, for one, notably misunderstood her satirical portraits of black bourgeois life and her critiques of internalized racism and sexism within the black community. What is striking about McKay's analogy is that the primroses he recalls grew "where I lived in Morocco, that lovely melancholy land of autumn and summer and mysterious veiled brown women" (92). He thinks of Fauset and her novels "[w]hen the primroses spread themselves across the barren hillsides before the sudden summer blazed over the hot land" (92). Why does McKay associate Fauset's novels with mysterious women, veils, and Morocco? Is it possible that McKay is thinking not of her novels, but of her 1925 travel essay, "Dark Algiers the White"?

Read collectively, Fauset's numerous travel narratives reveal what happens when the mantle of Western privilege is taken up (and occasionally cast off) by the black cosmopolitan traveler. Her firm nationalist longings always temper her commentary with a kind of anti-expatriatism, a sense of ambivalence with regard to her obvious Francophile predilections and love for travel. During the nineteenth century, black women made their first contributions to the travel-writing genre. African American diarist Charlotte Forten Grimké (1838–1914) wrote about her experiences educating former slaves in the South Carolina Sea Islands, and the heroic nurse Mary Seacole (1805–1881) recounts her adventures in Panama and the Crimean war in her autobiography. The primary purpose of Fauset's travel essays was to place black culture in a diasporic context and thus expose readers of *The Crisis* to cosmopolitan perspectives. Her impressionistic writing style both enhances and complicates the travel-writing tradition by drawing attention to the construction of persona and point of view. Aside from the published essays and a few overseas letters we do not know much about the logistics of her several trips across the Atlantic. Yet, from a much earlier piece, written when she was a Delta Sigma Theta Sorority delegate at the Second Pan-African Congress, we do know something of her mindset as she begins her voyage abroad. In "Impressions on the Second Pan-African Congress" (1921), she writes: "Between Brussels and the queen city of the world we saw blasted town, ravaged village and plain, ruined in a war whose basic motif had been the rape of Africa. What should we learn of the black man in France?" (79). Following the return of the black soldiers who fought in World War One, France acquired a fabled reputation for African Americans as a freer space. Such impressions were not completely unfounded, but the historical record tempers their romanticism. Indeed, while the French may have embraced black cultural expressions, their imperialist ventures in Africa and the Caribbean persisted. Fauset's question anticipates how she views those she encounters in her later travels in Southern Europe and French North Africa, where her gaze spotlights those who are marginalized, "other," or merely out of the ordinary.

"Dark Algiers the White" is a two-part travel essay published in *The Crisis* in April and May of 1925. Fauset departs from Marseilles, that diasporic port in France in which Claude McKay is relieved to find "Negroids from the United States, the West Indies, North Africa and West Africa, all herded together in a warm group" (213). Yet Fauset does not acknowledge the historical significance of Marseille (as an important port in the Atlantic slave trade) or any current multicultural presence. Instead, she writes: "Marseille, which from Paris seemed to beckon, proved on our arrival to be pointing the other way" (256). Fauset does not probe beneath the surface of the port city; however, this is her first reference to her unnamed traveling companion, Laura Wheeler Waring: the artist whose signature appears on the essay's dated illustrations.

To follow Fauset and Waring's voyage requires a bit of literary sleuthing. Laura Wheeler Waring first came to Paris in 1914 on a grand tour funded by a Cresson Traveling Scholarship from the Pennsylvania Academy for Fine Arts. Waring was one of many African American painters and sculptors, including Palmer Hayden, Meta Vaux Warrick Fuller, Nancy Elizabeth Prophet, Archibald J. Motley, Jr., and Augusta Savage, who came to Paris to study and pursue artistic careers in the 1920s and 1930s. As early as 1891, the renowned painter Henry Ossawa Tanner (1858–1937) arrived in Paris. After years of study at the Académie Julian, Tanner developed his own signature style and began to exhibit around the world. He decided to make Paris his permanent home and his international reputation drew African American artists to France with the hopes of following in his illustrious footsteps. In October of 1924, Waring is staying in Paris at the Hôtel Jeanne d'Arc at 57, rue Vaneau in Montparnasse. Perfectly poised to accompany Fauset on her visit to Algiers.

In the art world, Waring is known more for her portraiture than her illustrations. African American portraiture, though not particularly lucrative, was an important genre of New Negro visual art. Black artists like William Johnson and Archibald J. Motley, Jr. as well as German artist Winold Reiss, who painted the color plates for Alain Locke's *The New Negro: An Interpretation*, used this genre to give dignity and diversity to the African American subject. Waring's portrait of *Anne Washington Derry* (1927), winner of the first Harmon Foundation prize, exemplifies what art historian James Porter calls her "elegance of line, sensitive handling of dark and light, apt suggestion of the story in hand," and "truly graphic ability." Waring's most celebrated pieces are her portraits of women, especially the disturbingly lovely *Girl in a Red Dress* (1935) and the wistful *Susan Davis Lowery* (1937). Both paintings showcase her luminous use of color, and her striking ability to capture something of her subject's interior landscape. The incongruity of the subject's youth and mature ensemble in *Girl in a Red Dress* prompts the observer to search for a narrative that renders the image comprehensible. Waring's ability to tell a story through her painting and drawing made her an ideal illustrator for projects like *The Brownies Book*, an offshoot of *The Crisis* aimed at African American children, and edited and compiled by Du Bois and Fauset.

Most likely, Fauset first met Waring in Philadelphia. Both daughters of ministers, Fauset and Waring were both educated in Pennsylvania and France. From the time of their first published collaboration in 1912, through the publication of *The Brownies Book* and their trip to Algiers, Waring's illustrations had appeared in *The Crisis* upon Fauset's solicitation. One of the features of "female modernism" identified by Shari Benstock is that "women banded together, their writings often overtly demonstrating various modes of female bonding" (23). This aspect of female modernism may explain how Waring and Fauset's collaboration enhanced their mutual and individual artistic endeavors. Traveling together also provided a veneer of respectability for two women of color setting forth on their own. Safety concerns become paramount when Fauset enters the Arab quarter of Algiers, uncertain of how the region will interpret her ethnic and national identity.

A fascinating encounter at a flea market may have triggered Fauset's desire to visit North Africa. Fauset's "This Way to the Flea Market" (February 1925) describes her visit to the Marché aux Puces at Clignancourt: an expansive market on the outskirts of Paris. She is drawn to "the Kabyles," an ethnic group native to Algeria commonly referred to as "Berbers": "An easily detected group. They were all thin, all swarthy with a swarthiness different from that of the Italian, the American mulatto, or the Spaniard. They wore dull red fezzes, their hair was lank and oily, their faces grimed; yet even so one received an impression of pride and aloofness" (163). Possibly, Fauset's curiosity about this group, which she immediately racializes as "swarthy," with all its ominous and gothic connotations, prompts her Algeria trip. More than a precursor to "Dark Algiers," "This Way to the Flea Market" reveals the curiously detached persona Fauset often employs in her travel writings. One expects her to follow up her comments with an analysis or critique of empire and French colonialism, but she does not. Her reluctance to contextualize her impressions in critical ways compels scholars like Brent Hayes Edwards to disparage Fauset's reticence from providing a more assertive and sophisticated engagement of gender politics in her "portraits of women" (138).

To say that Fauset's travel narratives contain portraits of women, or visually evocative composites of her encounters, is quite accurate. Though not a visual artist herself, Fauset was acutely aware of how perception and ways of seeing informed her worldview. In her 1922 *Crisis* review of Négritude writer René Maran's novel published that year, *Batouala*, she singles out for praise a writing strategy she hopes to emulate: Maran's "almost cinema-like sharpness of picturization" (208). To achieve this quality Fauset has a tendency to consciously type individuals according to their specific racialized, ethnic, and/or national identity. This approach results in both the overturning of certain assumptions and the solidifying of others. She fixates her attention on subjects who are difficult to place in terms of ethnicity or phenotype, or whose identity can only be inferred by their surroundings. In "This Way to the Flea Market," for instance, she observes of her Alsatian guide: "had I seen him in America I should have taken him without further thought for a German. Thus constantly are shaken my preconceptions with regard to the appearance of the French; they run so persistently contrary to type, that is to the type which we are told in America they most resemble" (161). What Fauset does not share with her readers is that the Alsace-Lorraine changed hands between France and Germany countless times – another indication of the complex relationship of national and ethnic identity. Fauset's use of typing can be misleading; she frequently relies on shorthand assumptions to distinguish ethnic groups within the nations she visits. Other character sketches, like "Fabiola," question the wisdom of racial categorization based on phenotype: "[W]avy brown hair, rosy cheeks, and gray eyes make my Fabiola like one of those rare Italian girls born on the East Side from roots firmly planted about sunny Naples. You may call that Italian

Fabiola a jewel or a flower; but my Fabiola is a Negro. What must I call her?" (77–8).

Such typing results in a palpable tension surrounding the encounters in Fauset's travel writing that is similar to the experience of reading Zora Neale Hurston's *Mules and Men* (1935). In this illustrated collection of folktales, Hurston models a new ethnographic practice and reimagines the genre of autobiography. As Martha Jane Nadell observes, Hurston's book "employs image and text to question the viability of scientific anthropology for the representation of African American folk culture" (112). One of Hurston's most compelling strategies for gathering in-group data is to construct an appropriate persona for each particular cultural encounter (through dress, behavior, and speech). Albeit to a lesser extent, Fauset also cues the reader into the particular lens through which she views her subjects. She shifts between the perspectives of a dispassionate Westernized, modern woman and an eager tourist searching for "[a]ll the strangeness and difference of that life which, starting, far, far in the interior of Africa, yet breaks off so abruptly at the southern edge of the Mediterranean, rose instantly to meet us" ("Dark Algiers the White" 255). The metaphor in the next sentence exceeds the romantic flourish of the previous as Fauset writes: "Porters agile as monkeys swarmed up narrow ropeladders over the side of the ship" – a description that invokes the exoticist literature popularized by seventeenth- and eighteenth-century missionaries and explorers (256).

Frequent readers of *The Crisis* who may have been following Fauset's travels must have noted the fluidity with which she shifts from the Marché aux Puces to an Algerian bazaar. Her erudite cosmopolitan narrator reveals, but does not exactly interrogate, a world motivated by colonial and imperialist exchanges and barters. Instead, Fauset lets the juxtaposition of her descriptions do the work of contrasting what she calls the "anomaly" of French and Algerian culture co-existing: "Dark figures clad in European clothes but crowned with red fezzes bring East and West together. Down the Boulevard de la République shine the white minarets of an Arabian mosque. In the public square in the front rises the statue of the Duc d'Orléans, the shoulders and the head showing flat like card-board against the sky" (Fauset, "Dark Algiers the White" 256). There is a moment in "Dark Algiers the White" when she begins to reflect on "a curious phenomenon" in an East Indian merchant's shop: "the brothers are brown, we are brown, the Arabs are brown, but there is a difference in our brownness" (258). As is typical in her travel writings, Fauset does not articulate the nature of that difference, only that their shared Western apparel cannot hide it.

Unlike the charming ingénue figure that commonly appears in transatlantic travel writing as the naïve tourist who gains self-knowledge through a wider acquaintance with the world, Fauset's narrator seems aware that it is possible for black writers to slip into exoticist representation of the "other." If she views Algiers with "imperial eyes," to borrow a term from Mary Louise Pratt's concept of how the genre of travel writing shaped the relationship between the European metropole and those on the periphery, then her status as an African American woman adds another layer of complexity to transculturation, or the reciprocal but unequal process of exchange that happens at the moment of encounter (Pratt 6). This process may account for the misrecognition that often identifies Fauset as a woman of color yet renders her Americanness invisible. For instance, when she inquires into the safety of proceeding through the Arab quarter, a storeowner assures her: "you may go anywhere, anywhere Mademoiselle, and then besides one sees that you are from Martinique (Martiniquaise) and there is no danger here for a French woman!" (16). Fauset acknowledges neither the mistake nor its obvious complexity. Her response is simply: "Fortified I start again" (16). According to the storeowner Fauset's appearance enables her to pass as a French Antillean woman, but what protection does that guise truly offer? According to T. Denean Sharpley-Whiting's *Negritude Women*, the Antillean woman in Paris is "not a Frenchwoman like other Frenchwomen," but "a racialized Franco-Antillean Woman," uprooted and isolated from both her own countrymen and French culture at large. Fauset acknowledges that the "French drove [the Arabs] [to the hill tops] when they took the city a century or so ago," but the storeowner's assurance that there is no danger for a French woman seems to affirm the presumption that colonialists can go "anywhere, anywhere" the French flag is raised (16).

Waring's illustrations clarify some of the questions raised by the silences in "Dark Algiers," yet her presence as an unnamed character referred to only as "my artist friend" is peculiarly ephemeral. Waring's pictures work in concert with Fauset's evocative writing to visualize Algiers for their audience. The illustrations convey both their shared and disparate visions of the oxymoron that is "Dark Algiers the White." During their visit to the shop of an East Indian merchant that "by accident the artist of our group and I stumble" into, they apparently feel so at ease that Fauset tells us that "my friend voices her great longing to paint a Moorish woman" (258). This merchant, who reminds Fauset of Dr. Aziz in E.M. Forster's *Passage to India* (a 1924 novel about British colonialism), cleverly dissembles: "'if Madesmoiselle will look in tomorrow—.'" He promises that she might paint one of the girls who come in to embroider for the shop. But when they return the next day, the women are still not there. And the wily storeowner is apologetic to a fault.

Both Fauset and Waring oddly fetishize the veiled women they encounter (or hope to encounter) as inaccessible, aestheticized objects. The air of mystery provided by the veil is seductive to Fauset who describes even an elderly woman as "the very savor of the East" (256). The veils that will later play a central role in the Algerian war are traditionally worn to shield men from fitna – the chaos motivated by feminine seductiveness. The revolutionary psychiatrist Frantz Fanon's "Algeria Unveiled," the famous chapter from *Studies in a Dying Colonialism* published approximately 25 years *after* Fauset's article, portrays Algerian women simultaneously as revolutionary agents of decolonization and victims of Muslim orthodoxy. Fanon frankly recollects the predictable aspect of Fauset's response to these women when he notes: "the veil worn by women is at once noticed by the tourist" and "unifies the perception that one has of Algerian feminine society" (35–6). Though Fauset's voyeuristic gaze engages the senses and fetishizes her subject, she stops short of the sexualization Shari Benstock identifies as characteristic of expatriate, modernist women authors. What distinguishes Fauset from the typical tourist is that she immediately detects both the uniformity that the veil provides and how the women resist its anonymity: "Mystery shrouded her; her two eyes stared unseeingly before her; she was like an automaton beside her lord; there was no conversation. When they dismounted we saw that her robe was wonderfully soft and white; that the stockings encasing her dainty ankles were faintly pink; that her shoes were russet and delicate" (Fauset, "Dark Algiers the White" 256). Fauset's description highlights the individual, sensual choice of pink stockings and russet shoes, and Waring's drawings augment her descriptive prose. One page features paired illustrations of street scenes that reflect the gender-based social division of Algerian society. In the lower left picture, two women regard each other just outside a shop. Both wear the *häik*: a veil covering the face and the entire body. The eyes of the central woman are just visible; the other is completely hidden. The background accentuates their height in contrast to the narrow alleyway they occupy. Beneath voluminous robes, dainty, high-heeled shoes stand out against the cobblestone streets. An archway that appears in both scenes suggest that the opposite image reveals the conversation on the other side between two men holding walking sticks and traditionally attired in white burnouses and turbans. Waring uses ascending stairs to add depth to the shadowy arcade that forms the background for the men; it stands in contrast to the bright commercial avenue occupied by the women.

The multiple registers of the veil as image and metaphor allow Fauset to invoke the rhetoric of W.E.B. Du Bois's famous articulation of race relations in the United States in *The Souls of Black Folk* (1903): "After the Egyptian and Indian, the Greek and Roman, the Teuton and Mongolian, the Negro is a sort of seventh son, born with a veil, and gifted with second-sight in this American world, – a world which yields him no true self-consciousness, but only lets him see himself through the revelation of the other world" (3). Du Bois's veil is both a dividing line and a lens that provides "second-sight." Like the veil that lends the Algerian women "mystery and marvel," Du Bois's veil has almost supernatural qualities (Fauset, "Dark Algiers the White" 256). Black subjects must contend with the veil in their public lives, but it also suggests an impenetrable private life that the oppressors cannot access. According to Fanon, in the Algerian context, the veil is both a tool of resistance and a fetishized, sex object: he writes, the "rape of Algerian woman in the dream of a European is always preceded by a rending of the veil" (45). Fauset and Waring want to see through the mysterious veil that not only separates male from female, but also acts as an identifier of and barrier between the colonizer and colonized subject. However, as women of color, they can penetrate the veil only by figuratively putting it on themselves.

In Part I, Fauset is the observant tourist, but in Part II she masquerades as the "Martiniquaise" who can access the "Court of Miracles" where the women go "without face veils." (16). "Veiled" as a French colonial subject Fauset becomes privy to a private, female space in which the colorfully dressed women are very different from the white-cloaked "automatons" in Part I: "one of them passing directly before me wears a head-dress of scarlet, a green jacket with a purple collar, a cerise and yellow skirt. Another is dressed from head to foot in various shades of red. A woman carrying a copper water jug on her shoulder crowns her brown garment with a splendid turban of yellow and gold" (16). Part II gestures towards the instability that will lead to the French–Algerian war. At one point Fauset, standing alone and unveiled, strikes "an equally exotic figure in the middle of the sunlit road." She is unnerved by her conspicuousness and relaxes only when her guide, a French woman, returns with her husband who is a soldier stationed at the barracks nearby (17). Rather than offer an overt critique of ghettoization, she blandly relates: "Arab families live, I am told, as far as possible under one roof" (17). As Fauset descends through the quarter her tone changes and becomes more ominous. As her path narrows and darkens, she is unsure and unnerved by gazes of those she encounters as her guide leads her into a "dark oblong room five feet perhaps by eight" (17). It is here that she provides a searing portrait of life in the Casbah: "three figures of women sitting on the floor near a brazier of live coals … They sit thus, doing nothing, absolutely nothing; life slips by" (17).

Inexplicably, none of the encounters in the Casbah are illustrated. We are dependent on Fauset's extravagant description of her hostess Madame Kheira: "I stare at her in such complete absorption that her glorious eyes finally question me and I blurt out: 'You are so beautiful, Madame; I wish my artist friend could see you'" (18). Where is Waring during this exchange? While investigating the Arab quarters, Fauset disturbingly notes that the "unspeakably dirty and ragged" children "strike a picturesque note which makes [her] long for her artist friend" (16). She then disappoints her reader by saying "I cannot sufficiently describe the picture they made in their gay clothing …"; however, in the next sentence she proceeds to describe "the brilliant blue of the sky above, the strong gold of the sun above them, the black background of squalor and wretchedness behind" (16). She admits she does not have the words to convey the "palpable irony" of the scene, but that is precisely why Waring has accompanied her to Algiers (16). So it is confusing to find that instead of a series of sketches revealing the impoverished, yet "picturesque," quarter, Waring's last illustration depicts Fauset's exchange of money with her guide. This belated payment, solicited at the behest of the woman's husband, sullies the encounter. The illustration is titled "Once more we exchange adieux" (19). In the text, Fauset admits that the exchange is a "tarnished ending" to her "little idyll" beyond the veil. It reveals her not as a woman of color visiting those who share a similar relationship to the colonial power, but instead puts her in the place of the Western tourist who must pay for cultural experiences. Strangely, in the image Waring draws, Fauset has her hand outstretched as if she is receiving rather than bestowing the francs. The image is not of two women of color, but of a woman with shaded skin and cropped, textured hair wearing a modern short-sleeved dress (Fauset) opposite a pale French woman in a dark overcoat. One wonders if this last scene of Algiers, in which the dispossessed colonizer faces a woman of color in a position of power, foreshadows the troubles to come, and the vital role that Algerian women, and the veil, will come to play.

"Shackle Free Art"

In 1937, Lois Mailou Jones boards the SS *Normandie* on her way to Paris for a sabbatical from her teaching position in Howard University's Fine Arts department. The Parisian scene for black artists has become an increasingly vibrant, diasporic site of intellectual and artistic exchange. Just as the successes of early black painters prompt Waring's Parisian education, Jones specifically attributes her decision to embark on an artistic career to a formative conversation on Highland Beach in Martha's Vineyard with sculptor Meta Vaux Warrick Fuller – who had studied in Paris with Rodin – and with composer Henry Burleigh, who tells her "if you want to be successful in your career you're going to have to go abroad" (Jones and Rowell 358). Jones began her training in design and textiles, taking courses at the Boston Normal School, the Museum School and the Boston Designers Art School. Though Jones experienced some early exposure for her textiles and graphic design, she truly comes into her own in the liberating space of Paris. One of the Romare Bearden's critiques (in *A History of African-American Artists from 1792 to the Present*, under the category of "Art Departments in African-American Colleges") is that Jones never developed a unique, signature style. On the contrary, Jones is an influential and significant artist, because of her very ability to take on a variety of artistic and aesthetic styles and forms over a long career. That fluidity – or her openness to experimentation and her ability to transform her process and palette – is a valuable skill that can be traced from her early interest in graphic design and costume masks through her use of color. The design elements link her post-impressionist landscapes, her portraiture, and the geometric balance of African and Caribbean scenes.

Jones shared none of Fauset's ambivalence about Paris as a place to create and grow as an artist. In an interview with Charles Rowell, she says: "France gave me my stability, and it gave me the assurance that I was talented and that I should have a successful career" (Jones and Rowell 361). In Paris, Jones had the "studio of her dreams" with a view of the Eiffel Tower and the city she described as a "paradise." Paris was also a gateway to a specifically diasporic concept of African culture and aesthetics that governed her art for the next 50 years. Significantly, renowned historian Carter G. Woodson (founder of the *Journal of Negro History* and Black History month) and bibliophile Arthur Schomburg were there to see Jones off on September 1, 1937. She had worked as Woodson's illustrator for many years, contributing illustrations to *The Journal of Negro History* and other publications. Illustrating *African Heroes and Heroines* (1939) was to be her main project in Paris and she conducted the research for the illustrations between class sessions. As part of her research, Jones visited French galleries to study and sketch the masks she later would incorporate into her best-known painting: *Les Fétiches* (1938).

The innovative welding of African sculptural elements and graphic design in *Les Fétiches* make it a splendid example of Afro-modernist pastiche in which the question of the primitive as an aesthetic is given more than a superficial consideration. That

Jones had to go abroad to acquire both the technique and exposure to African art is both ironic and indicative of the fluidity of cultural exchange. No doubt the intellectual and artistic circle that propelled the so-called Négritude movement – René Maran, Aimé Césaire, and Léopold Senghor – influenced the sensibility and technique deployed in *Les Fétiches*. What's striking about the painting is how it forcefully engages Pablo Picasso's extrapolation of African sculpture in *Les Demoiselles d'Avignon* (1907): his iconic interpretation of the modern primitive. Jones's composition acknowledges that the Kongo headdress, and the Baule, Dan, and Yaure masks are themselves autonomous works of art. The symmetry of the central mask is balanced by the geometric stripes on the more abstract mask in the lower left of the painting. Jones's intuitive sense of design grounds the composition; yet, it also stands out during her exhibitions of impressionistic landscapes, portraits, and textile painting. It is emblematic of the "shackle free" art Jones produced in Paris (359).

While *Les Fétiches* is not exactly a collaborative project, it certainly evolved out of conversations with the Négritude writers and artists (as well as a group from Haiti known as the *Indigenists*) with whom Jones interacted in France. Jones's career trajectory, and her fusion of cubist shapes with Africanist subject matter, resembles the path of Aaron Douglas. One of the most famous visual artists of Harlem Renaissance, Douglas's technique and aesthetics were also influenced by conversations with artists and writers in salons – he frequently attended Georgia Douglas Johnson's "Saturday Nighters" in Washington DC. His murals and book illustrations appear in the most celebrated publications of the era. Also like Jones, Douglas successfully incorporated African and Egyptian elements into his work, answering Langston Hughes's call in his 1926 artistic manifesto, "The Negro Artist and the Racial Mountain," for an authentic black aesthetic free from the demands of white patrons, or the collective approval of the black community. When it came to the promotion of Jones's art, however, she was not above relying on white patronage. She circumvented the discriminatory practices of the American art establishment by asking white friends submit her paintings for prizes.

Jones's 29 black and white illustrations in Carter G. Woodson's *African Heroes and Heroines* provide a visual counter to images of Africa as primitive, comic, and bestial. Originally intended for high-school students, Woodson's goal was to show that "these leaders of a despised people measure up to the full stature of the heroic in the histories of other nations" (Preface). Given this directive, it is not surprising that many of the illustrations feature masculine figures engaged in acts of war. Woodson and Jones's mutual vision of the heroic African is one of resistance to European colonialism and/or intercontinental aggression. The strategy of counter-representation, of providing an array of images that emphasized the humanity, intelligence, and diversity of African people, is the method used to achieve the project's goals.

That both Jones and Waring illustrated books aimed at the young should neither surprise us nor diminish the artistic value of their art. Instead, we should look to such volumes as exemplars of the marriage of politics and aesthetics that characterized black artistic movements from the Harlem and Chicago Renaissances through the Black

Arts Movement of the 1960s and 1970s. Jessie Fauset and W.E.B. Du Bois's *The Brownies Book* was certainly a precursor to *African Heroines and Heroines*. The 20 issues of *The Brownies Book* (January 1920–1921) included folk tales, poetry, moral literature, photographs of children from around the world, and "As the Crow Flies," a column penned by Du Bois about current, international events. The title, as Fern Kory notes, illustrates a simultaneous borrowing and signification process (92). In the Irish and English tradition the "brownie" is a servile figure: a hardworking and industrious fairy that is also a trickster. Fauset's work with *Brownies* (as an editor and contributor) reflects her ambivalence about "blackening" European fairy tales. When Du Bois identifies African American children as "true brownies" he both inscribes them into a mythic literary tradition and draws on African oral traditions in which the trickster figure plays a primary role.

A different sort of signifying practice appears to be at work in the text of *African Heroes and Heroines*. Produced some 19 years after *The Brownies Book*, Woodson appears to have bypassed the assimilation project in favor of going directly to the continent for inspirational stories. Woodson offers an overt critique of imperialism: "all the European nations dominating Africa have their hands most shamefully stained." He cites the British discrimination against blacks as "worse than that in the United States" (214). Europe's colonial endeavors are evident from the text (Woodson includes a map showing the partition of Africa) and its illustrations. While the stories of the Songhay date back to the fourteenth century, many of the heroic tales chronicle courageous battles against invading Europeans from every part of the continent. In addition to correcting the official historical accounts slanted by the bias of European travelers – "what we know of the story of Africa has been all but a fairy tale spun out of the imagination of a few writers" (2) – Woodson hopes to counter monolithic perceptions of African languages, cultures, religions, and physical appearances. At the time of publication, historians were in the process of recovering the complex history of the so-called "Dark Continent." Woodson sets himself to the task of contradicting faulty Eurocentric understandings of Africa. Williston Lofton's review of *African Heroes and Heroines* singles out Woodson's treatment of the rise of Islam – called Mohammedanism – as a "great cultural force and bridge for outside contact" (477). At times the vastness of Woodson's subject, and the racist vocabulary at the center of imperialist histories, overwhelms his storytelling. As with Fauset, Woodson cannot completely rid himself of his "Western Eyes," as evidenced by the persistence of terms like "Negroland" and "Mohammedanized."

Those images that Jones includes of Mohammedanized heroes are some of the most striking to consider in conversation with paintings such as *La Mosquée*, which she painted in Paris. The illustrations of Muslim leaders Askia Mohammed and Ousman in the volume are more detailed versions of the white-turbaned and robed figures outside the mosque in her painting. The works that were exhibited in her solo exhibition in Paris, like *La Mosquée* and a portrait of a French Antillean woman entitled *Jeanne-Martiniquaise* (1938), show that Jones began to paint black diasporic subjects while in the unique social and intellectual atmosphere of late 1930s Paris.

Viewed collectively, Jones's illustrations portray the cultural diversity of the African continent; however, if the central theme of Du Bois's exhibit was progress, the theme of *African Heroes and Heroines* is resistance. Her portrait of the South African leader Khama in a suit wearing a serious, but kindly, expression is one of the few that relieves the images of war and armed struggle. And despite the inclusive title, the only heroine represented is the fearless Ginga, a brave sister of an Angolan chief who resists the Portuguese. Ginga holds a spear aloft and stands at the head of a band of warriors. She is elegantly dressed in a striped gown with a jeweled collar, bracelets, and a matching headband. Another significant illustration is a large, profile of Chaka, the chief of the Zulus; the image precedes another of him leading a charge. Finally, the image of the turbaned, Ethiopian Menelik on horseback with sword, shield, and flying cape could have served as the cover art for a text that concretizes an Afrocentric mythology as well as a counter-history to heroic tradition of the West.

In "Dark Algiers the White," Fauset recounts an image that resonates with Jones's illustration: "Men magnificently bronzed, lean and regal, a red cloak streaming behind them, thunder by on – obviously – Arabian steeds" (258). Fauset laments that Hollywood has spoiled the "integrity of this scene" by rendering it into a cliché. Viewed together in the context of the book, Jones's pictures evince a similar artificiality in that they ultimately enhance Woodson's vision of a primarily male-centered heroic tradition. Yet, the techniques that Jones learns while pursuing this project ultimately put her on the path towards developing a unique, diasporic style. As the Harlem Renaissance, already in full swing by the time Fauset and Waring visit Algiers, comes to a close, Jones's career makes a crucial leap enabled by the momentum of the fully realized Négritude movement. Recent scholars have unveiled a subtle, feminist presence in both the theorization and production of Négritude ideologies. This may account for Jones's welcoming experience in Paris. We can only speculate if, along the Left Bank, a conversation with essayist Suzanne Césaire on surrealism played a role in inspiring Jones's approach to *Les Fétiches*. The primacy of the African subject, however, continued to shape her aesthetics over her long career.

Examining collaborative works from the period between World War One and World War Two gives a sense of the significance of the black image in an international context. The visual images cannot stand alone, but must be read within the text that shapes and is shaped by them. In "Dark Algiers the White," Waring's illustrations help readers to envision Fauset's black cosmopolitan narrator and the complex perspective she offers on colonial North Africa. According to Susan Friedman, modernist women's expatriatism provided "freedom of mind and spirit … From convention, from the pressure to conform, to do the respectable, the proper, the expected. For women, the pressure to conform centered on the question of gender" (94–5). To gender we might add the intersections of race, class, and the not-so-subtle ways in which both influence national identity at home and abroad. Fauset remained invested in her American citizenship and her identity as a New Negro woman. Jones's life and work tells the story of a citizen of the African diaspora. Following her marriage to Haitian Louis Vergniaud Pierre-Noel, Jones later travels to Haiti, establishes a study, and paints several canvasses of Haiti and its people. Jones eventually returns to the US, but her work maintains the pan-Africanist worldview she first developed in Paris. Uncovering, and in some cases speculating on, the process and aesthetics of cross-genre collaboration prompts us to consider the genesis of presumably autonomous works of visual art and creative writing in an interwar era of transatlantic intellectual and artistic exchanges.

Bibliography

Bearden, Romare and Harry Henderson. *A History of African-American Artists: From 1792 to the Present*. New York: Pantheon, 1993.

Benjamin, Tritobia Hayes. *The Life and Art of Lois Mailou Jones*. San Francisco: Pomegranate Art Book, 1994.

Benstock, Shari. "Expatriate Modernism: Writing on the Cultural Rim." In *Women's Writing in Exile*. Ed. Mary Lynn Broe and Angela Ingram. Chapel Hill: University of North Carolina Press, 1989. 19–40.

Carroll, Anne Elizabeth. *Word, Image and the New Negro: Representation and Identity in the Harlem Renaissance*. Bloomington: Indiana University Press, 2007.

Du Bois, W.E.B. *The Souls of Black Folk*. Chicago: McClurg, 1903.

Edwards, Brent Hayes. *The Practice of Diaspora: Literature, Translation and the Rise of Black Internationalism*. Cambridge, MA: Harvard University Press, 2003.

Fanon, Frantz. *Studies in a Dying Colonialism*. 1959. Trans. Haakon Chevalier. London: Earthscan, 1989.

Farrington, Lisa E. *Creating Their Own Image: The History of African-American Women Artists*. New York: Oxford University Press, 2005.

Fauset, Jessie Redmon. "Dark Algiers, the White." *The Crisis* 29–30 (1925–6): 255–8; 16–22.

Fauset, Jessie Redmon. "Fabiola." *World Tomorrow* (March 5, 1922): 77–8.

Fauset, Jessie Redmon. "Impressions on the Second Pan-African Congress." *The Crisis* (November 1921): 12–18.

Fauset, Jessie Redmon. "This Way to the Flea Market." *The Crisis* (February 1925): 161–3.

Griffin, Erica. "The 'Invisible Woman': Abroad: Jessie Fauset's New Horizon." In *Recovered Writers/Recovered Texts: Race, Class and Gender in Black Women's Literature*. Ed. Dolan Hubbard. Knoxville: The University of Tennessee Press, 1997. 75–89.

Harris, Violet J. "African American Children's Literature: The First One Hundred Years," *The Journal of Negro Education* 59.4 (1990): 540–55.

Jones, Lois Mailou. *Peintures, 1937–1951*. Tourcoing: Presses Georges frères, 1952.

Jones, Lois Mailou and Charles Rowell. An Interview with Lois Mailou Jones. *Callaloo* 39 (1989): 357–8.

Kory, Fern. "Once Upon a Time in Aframerica: The 'Peculiar' Significance of Fairies in the *Brownies' Book*." *Children's Literature* 29 (2001): 91–112.

Leininger-Miller, Theresa. *New Negro Artists in Paris: African American Painters and Sculptors in the City of Light, 1922–1924*. New Brunswick, NJ: Rutgers University Press, 2001.

Lofton, Williston. Review of *African Heroes and Heroines*. *The Journal of Negro History* 24.4 (1939): 477–8.

McKay, Claude. *A Long Way from Home*. 1937. Ed. Gene Jarrett. New Brunswick, NJ: Rutgers University Press, 2007.

Nadell, Martha Jane. *Enter the New Negroes: Images of Race in American Culture*. Cambridge, MA: Harvard University Press, 2004.

Painter, Nell. "Un essai d'égo-histoire." In *Telling Histories: Black Women Historians in the Ivory Tower*. Ed. Deborah Gray White. Chapel Hill: University of North Carolina, 2008. 28–41.

Pratt, Mary Louise. *Imperial Eyes: Travel Writing and Transculturation*. New York: Routledge, 1992.

Sharpley-Whiting, T. Denean. *Negritude Women*. Minneapolis: University of Minnesota Press, 2002.

Smith, Shawn Michelle. *American Archives: Gender, Race and Class in Visual Culture*. Princeton: Princeton University Press, 1999.

Smith, Shawn Michelle. "Second-Sight: Du Bois and the Black Masculine Gaze." In *Next to the Color Line: Gender, Sexuality, and W.E.B. Du Bois*. Ed. Susan Gillman and Alys Even Weinbaum. Minneapolis: University of Minnesota Press, 2007. 350–77.

Waring, Laura Wheeler. *In Memoriam, Laura Wheeler Waring, 1887–1948: An Exhibition of Paintings, May and June 1949*. Washington, DC: Howard University Gallery of Art: Founders Library.

Willis, Deborah. "The Sociologist's Eye: W.E.B. Du Bois and the Paris Exposition." In *A Small Nation of People: W.E.B. Du Bois and African American Portraits of Progress*. New York: Amistad, 2003. 51–78.

Woodson, Carter G. *African Heroes and Heroines*. Washington, DC: Associated Publishers, 1939.

16

Aesthetic Hygiene: Marcus Garvey, W.E.B. Du Bois, and the Work of Art

Mark Christian Thompson

The antipathy Marcus Garvey and W.E.B. Du Bois felt for one another has been well documented (Grant 298–317; Lewis 37–84). This extreme dislike bordering on physical revulsion was both ideological and personal. The character of the conflict was of such a derogatory nature that we find Du Bois, in his 1923 *Century* article "Back to Africa," calling Garvey a "little fat black man, ugly but with intelligent eyes and a big head" (546–7). At first glance, it seems Du Bois at least gives Garvey credit for having "intelligent eyes," if not beauty. But even this is an insult. When taken with the total picture of Garvey's abject ugliness, his blackness, Garvey's intelligent eyes serve to transform him into a Caliban to Du Bois's Prospero.

Garvey responded to the Harvard master's comments in expected fashion. The "misleader" of the NAACP was described in the 1923 *The Negro World* rejoinder as "a little Dutch, a little French, and a dozen other things. Why, in fact, the man is a monstrosity" (*Universal Negro V* 223). Leaving aside for the moment the enigma of Du Bois's monstrosity, the far more interesting question posed by Garvey's article is: "Now, what does Du Bois mean by ugly?" (*Universal Negro V* 223). The question is one of aesthetic taste as well as of race and racism, and can be reformulated as such: "Now, what does Du Bois mean by the Beautiful?" The answer to this question was readily available to Garvey in Du Bois's published reflections on art. Garvey's own aesthetic guidelines remain far less clear.[1] Reading Du Bois's "The Criteria of Negro Art" (1926) in conjunction with scattered statements Garvey made regarding his aesthetic tastes serves in this essay as a means to understanding Garvey's conception of aesthetic "Beauty."

Having had little need for or recourse to art to mediate his opinions, the man Du Bois called "a lunatic or a traitor" was always clear about what he found to be beautiful. For Garvey, Black Is Beautiful. Garvey offered no systematic guidelines for the writing of Negro literature; and if we wish to find anything like an aesthetic in Garvey's work, it is inadvisable to begin by reading his poetry. There we find works of a staunchly traditional and stilted character which are of little interest to anyone but the historian, biographer, and rabid Garvey enthusiast. We gain a greater understanding of Garvey's relationship to "art" (intentionally conflated here with "Beauty") when we observe the way in which Garvey makes rhetorical use of the term in his speeches and writings. In Garvey's Emancipation Day speech of January 1, 1922, for example, he tells us that

> This race of ours gave civilization, gave art, gave science; gave literature to the world. But it has been the way with races and nations. The one race stands out prominently in the one century or in the one age; and in another century or age it passes off the stage of action, and another race takes its place. The Negro once occupied a high position in the world, scientifically, artistically and commercially, but in the balancing of the great scale of evolution, we lost our place and some one, other than ourselves occupies the stand we once held. (*Universal Negro IV* 324)

Art, like everything else, is essentially black. This race of ours gave it to the world. Every work of Western art stands on the shoulders of black giants. We have forgotten this undeniable fact. If there is a task of the Negro artist tacitly prescribed in Garvey's writings, it would have to entail nothing less than the recuperation of the origin of art, of art's essential blackness. Art will become black again, not to rejuvenate Western culture or integrate blacks therein, but to bring about the renaissance or new age of black cultural ascendency and help foster black political hegemony.

Although Garvey never described in any detail what this coming black art would look like, Du Bois would likely have found it as ugly as he did Marcus Garvey. Indeed, Du Bois's 1926 *Crisis* article "The Criteria of Negro Art," itself the text of Du Bois's address to the annual National Association for the Advancement of Colored People (NAACP) convention of that year, begins by caricaturing Garvey's position vis-à-vis art's impotence to effect political activism:

> I do not doubt but there are some in this audience who are a little disturbed at the subject of this meeting, and particularly at the subject I have chosen. Such people are thinking something like this: "How is it that an organization like this, a group of radicals trying to bring new things into the world, a fighting organization which has come up out of the blood and dust of battle, struggling for the right of black men to be ordinary human beings – how is it that an organization of this kind can turn aside to talk about Art? After all, what have we who are slaves and black to do with Art?" (Du Bois, "Criteria" 86)

Du Bois's rhetorical question mocks Garvey's criticism of the NAACP, which considered the useless contemplation of aesthetic matters to be the primary function of a worthless organization. Garvey writes:

> The difference between the Universal Negro Improvement Association and the other so-called Negro movements is this: That the U.N.I.A. is not afraid of work and its workers are not afraid of work. The difference between these organizations is that one

> is made up of a group of workers and the other is made up of a group of lazy men. They criticize Marcus Garvey and the U. N. I. A.; they criticize the African liberation program because they know it is a big job, and it is a man's job, and they are not prepared for a man's job. You cannot go about liberating a race – you cannot go about freeing a country and establishing a nation with silk stockings on. You talk about music and art and literature, as such men like Du Bois and Weldon Johnson take pride in doing. A nation was not founded first of all on literature or on writing books; it is first founded upon the effort of real workers, and that is where we differ from the N.A.A.C.P. (*Universal Negro V* 250)

For Garvey, the work of the NAACP is no work at all; it is the idle preoccupation of emasculated, effeminate men. The work of liberation is man's work. A man is not afraid to roll up his sleeves and work up a sweat. Men do not put on their silk stockings and discuss art and literature, which is apparently the preferred preoccupation of Du Bois and James Weldon Johnson. In strikingly and unexpectedly misogynist fashion, Garvey differentiates the UNIA and the NAACP along the lines of aesthetic preoccupation and manhood. The UNIA has better, more important, far manlier tasks to accomplish than does the perfumed, art-loving NAACP. Art is not a means of achieving racial liberation; it is a distraction of the sort caused by beautiful women. Real race men get their hands dirty (doing work) while Du Bois and Weldon Johnson sit at home reflecting upon poetry.

We need not forget or ignore the fact that Garvey wrote and read his fair share of verse; his target is not the reading of poetry or its creation. He attacks Du Bois and James Weldon Johnson for the "work" they ascribe to aesthetic production. For Garvey, writing a poem or a novel is tantamount neither to effecting political change nor to the cultivation of a shift in racial perception in preparation for universal Negro improvement. If undertaken in any sense with these expectations, art is a waste of time. Yet, with the right objectives, the cultivation of aesthetic taste and the creation of works of art hold, as we shall see, a place of honor in Garvey's ideal formulation of the Negro. The one thing that is certain in Garvey's consideration of the work of art is that considerations of the work of art as a direct political weapon are of no importance whatsoever.

Du Bois takes for granted the Garveyite position that the question of the work of art, in its import for the struggle for racial equality, will be seen by his audience to be at best of little importance and at worst an insult. Imagining his audience to be comprised of myriad Marcus Garveys, Du Bois admits, for the moment, that the fight of the NAACP transcends the mere trifle of art. Broaching his subject in Garvey-like fashion, it is incumbent on Du Bois to justify his approach. In response to the Marcus-Garvey-outrage Du Bois projects on his audience, he offers an apology for the work of art which hinges on the meaning of Beauty, or, rather, the problem of who is in the best position to define and realize the Beautiful. "After all," Du Bois asks:

> who shall describe Beauty? What is it? I remember tonight four beautiful things: the Cathedral at Cologne, a forest in stone, set in light and changing shadow, echoing with

> sunlight and solemn song; a village of the Veys in West Africa, a little thing of mauve and purple, quiet, lying content and shining in the sun; a black and velvet room where on a throne rests, in old and yellowing marble, the broken curves of the Venus de Milo; a single phrase of music in the Southern South – utter melody, haunting and appealing, suddenly arising out of night and eternity, beneath the moon. (Du Bois, "Criteria" 88)

In defining Beauty by example, Du Bois conjoins four separate, seemingly disparate aesthetic moments. He dilutes his conception of Beauty by comingling the apex of medieval Christian architecture; the summit of ancient Greek, or pagan, sculpture; an African village; and a Negro spiritual. Given that the use-value of the Venus de Milo was in all likelihood ritualistic, each example carefully chosen by Du Bois signifies a social intervention. Given his aesthetic tastes, art is for Du Bois intimately, definitively, bound to its social function. Beauty, therefore, does not exist for itself; it consists in the marriage between aesthetic form and social-political content. The perfect representation of the social-political life-world amounts to the instance, or instancing, of the aesthetic.

Also notable in Du Bois's short list of Beauty is the location of each work of art. Du Bois grounds his list in a travel narrative. Du Bois's aesthetic geography encompasses Europe, Africa, and African America. There is, then, no geographical-cum-racial separation, no nationalist-cum-racist divisions in the concept of Beauty. The African is as beautiful as the medieval German; the African American knows the same limits and excesses as the Greek. Indeed, Beauty is here unconditionally global, trans-historical, and trans-racial to the point of making race as constituent factor moot. The village of the Veys aside, one need not go back to Africa to begin the work of Negro art. A simple trip to a museum or a library will do.

In the totality of Garvey's thought, the return to Africa is never absent as cause and modus operandi of the black life-world, and thus of Negro art. Beauty does not stand alone, lending its essence to works of art of any racial origin. All aspects of existence, aesthetic or otherwise, are infiltrated, indeed ontologically dependent upon race. Shaped by an imperative of racial categorization, the art of the Negro can evince an a priori superiority to whites. Yet Garvey does not define Negro art in terms of formal aesthetics. Unlike Du Bois, Garvey is content to call Negro art any art created by the Negro which shows no attempt to curry favor with whites and which evinces an African origin. In insisting on "The promotion of an independent Negro literature and culture," and in demanding that "Negroes must produce their own literature," Garvey is convinced that "in Science and in Art, Africa [will claim] a position par excellence." These are extraordinary claims not because Garvey gives priority to the arts of Africa, but because he nowhere insists upon a recuperation of African art. Garvey does not impose strictures of style. The Negro artist is free to write in traditional Western verse, as Garvey himself once did. The defining characteristics of Negro art are its producer, its content, and its manner of dissemination, not its form. No matter how the Negro artist expresses his art, he must do so independent of the mainstream (or white) publishing industry and cultural apparatus, and always with the goal of promoting black liberation and the free black state.

There would seem to be a contradiction in Garvey's terms, given that the aesthetic register in which Garvey considers art is a Western construction. Would it not be a betrayal of the race to write in alexandrines even if the content of the poem is rabidly black nationalist? Garvey's response to this apparent incongruity in his own racial logic is both simple and brilliant. He reminds us:

> Scattered here and there among the pages of white history and literature you may find an accidental admission of Africa's past greatness, but not sufficient to be completely convincing. If you were to go to Homer's "Iliad" you will find that the Greek Poet that at one time in the history of the Greeks their only superiors were to be found among the gods of Ethiopia, the land of the blacks. (*Garvey Life and Lessons* 159)

The tacit belief here is that the poetry of Ethiopia, being prior to and better than that of ancient Greece, informs the art of Greek antiquity, the wellspring of Western art.

For Garvey, whatever has been produced under the guise of Western art, science, literature, etc., was always already African in origin. Not only is the art of Africa superior to that of whites (Homer knew this well), but it is also the origin of all Western aesthetic production. In other words, it is not an act race-betrayal if the Negro artist allows himself to be influenced by James Joyce; it is an act of racial recuperation. To wit, Joyce is always already a black writer. Thus "Beauty" is not a neutral term, open to anyone able to reach such great aesthetic heights. Beauty is black and black is the Beautiful. Because of this, for Garvey Beauty cannot be a means of gaining racial recognition and equality. Blacks cannot strive to achieve Beauty because they already possess the rights and copyrights to it. If anything, the white man must be made to recognize that Beauty belongs to the Negro, and that Beauty's theft is one of the white man's greatest crimes.

Indeed, Garvey recognizes modern history as a vast cover-up, an immense web of conspiracy designed to occlude the fact of the Negro's primacy in all areas of human existence. In the shape of a platonic dialogue (an essentially African form of exposition, we must understand) between a white man and a black man, Garvey asserts:

> BLACK MAN Your politics, your religion, your literature, your everything are a convenient lie.
>
> WHITE MAN Whether you call it lie or not it puts us on top. (*Garvey Life and Lessons* 173)

To accept this lie, even in the realm of the aesthetic, is to keep the white man on top. This is the ideological difference between the Universal Negro Improvement Association (UNIA) and the NAACP, between liberation and uplift, between life and art as Du Bois understands it. But the difference is not absolute. Garvey's notion of art is that all art is essentially, ontologically, African. Du Bois's great mistake is to accept the Western or classical history of art – the "lie" – as ontological truth. This is what blinds Du Bois to the genuine aesthetic claims of modern art. Such a polemic does not exist in Garvey's thought. Classical and modern art are not binary opposites; they are both part and parcel of a greater mystification, a more insidious deception. Thus Garvey could accept modern art as long as both its origin and its concomitant racial significations are acknowledged. To ignore these aspects of any Western art would be to disfigure the black self.

It is the care of the black self that concerns Garvey the most with regard to art. Because of this, Garvey, perhaps surprisingly, does not consider art to be propaganda. Certainly, Garvey believes that art has been used by whites as one of several means to propagate the lie of white superiority. But Garvey does not suppose to use art as a means of propagandist counterinsurgency. He does not propose to use art as a way to gain white recognition. His art does not speak to whites on any register. If art possesses any practical use for presenting oneself to the white world, it is the cultivation of a beautiful character. For, Garvey writes, "The world is attracted by beauty either in art or in expression. Therefore, try to read, think and speak beautiful things" (*Garvey Life and Lessons* 197). Aesthetic Beauty is a mode of expression used in order to improve the black self and attract the world, to become more persuasive in presenting one's arguments. Art is rhetoric, not propaganda. Thus, according to Du Bois,

> all Art is propaganda and ever must be, despite the wailing of the purists. I stand in utter shamelessness and say that whatever art I have for writing has been used always for propaganda for gaining the right of black folk to love and enjoy. I do not care a damn for any art that is not used for propaganda. (94)

Importantly, Du Bois does not claim that art that is not propaganda does not exist, but that it has been poorly executed. He is in essence speaking on two registers. There is art, and then there is Art. But what is Du Boisian Art; or, perhaps more importantly, what is Du Boisian art?

These questions can be answered only with recourse to Du Bois's understanding of art's reception. For Du Bois, the ability to perceive properly black Beauty is hindered by the racism inherent in Western historiography and by the instrumentality of everyday life (what would be for Garvey the racist conspiracy of white modernity). Although Beauty does not escape Du Bois's discerning gaze, it is not readily apparent to the untrained masses, blindfolded as they are by the ever and deeply invasive ratio of modernity. Thus Du Bois laments:

> Such is Beauty. Its variety is infinite, its possibility is endless. In normal life all may have it and have it yet again. The world is full of it; and yet today the mass of human beings are choked away from it, and their lives distorted and made ugly. This is not only wrong, it is silly. Who shall right this well-nigh universal failing? Who shall let this world be beautiful? Who shall restore to men the glory of sunsets and the peace of quiet sleep? (89)

Of course, there is but one subject or agent capable of implementing such corrective measures: "the Youth that is here today, the Negro Youth, [as] a different kind of Youth, because in some new way it bears this mighty prophecy on its breast, with a new realization of itself, with new determination for all mankind" (89). In terms of prophecy and salvation, the Negro youth enters the stage as a type of messiah not only of art but of nothing less than the entire world. He occupies a position located somewhere within the color-line itself and is thus able to mediate the monstrosities of modernity and modern art with an authentic, one could say primitive, being capable of shedding light upon the past and revealing a paradisiacal future.

The language and conceptual framework of Du Bois's aesthetic subjectivity is not wholly incompatible, at least on the surface, with the modern art he sees as frivolous, without political import, and in large part incomprehensible. This impression is not a wide leap from Du Bois's insistence on black subjectivity as somehow outside of modernity and thus capable, upon entering the field of modern cultural production in appropriated form, of altering, simplifying, and rejuvenating aesthetic, social, and political relations, to run-of-the-mill avant-garde primitivism. Furthermore, Du Bois's reliance on the idea of the "new," as in the "new man," mirrors the rhetoric of his aesthetic manifesto of the first half of the twentieth century. Of course, Du Bois had no love for modern art, writing in the 1924 essay, "The Younger Literary Movement": "The artist, of course, has a right deliberately to make his art a puzzle to the interpreter (the whole world is a puzzle) but on the other hand I am myself unduly irritated by this sort of thing" (Du Bois, "The Younger Literary Movement" 220).

Seeing that the art of Europe and America was committed to irritating him, Du Bois decides that

> It is the bounden duty of black America to begin this great work of the creation of Beauty, of the preservation of Beauty, of the realization of Beauty, and we must use in this work all the methods that men have used before. And what have been the tools of the artist in times gone by? First of all, he has used the Truth – not for the sake of truth, not as a scientist seeking truth, but as one upon whom Truth eternally thrusts itself as the highest handmaid of imagination, as the one great vehicle of universal understanding. Again artists have used Goodness – goodness in all its aspects of justice, honor and right – not for sake of an ethical sanction but as the one true method of gaining sympathy and human interest. (94)

Taking his cue from Keats, Du Bois voices what was even by this time the pedestrian statement that "Beauty is truth, truth beauty." Yet, for Du Bois, we need to know more than this. Although he adds "Goodness" to the equation, Du Bois is quick to dismiss the primacy of an ethical dimension to his poetics. The aesthetic triumvirate pertains here not to "sanction" but to the divination of the humanity of the Negro, thus gaining him "sympathy and human interest" in the white gaze. That is to say that the Negro work of art will eventually bring to the white gaze representations of the Negro that exist for themselves and are politically transformative. Art will (because for Du Bois it has not done this yet) allow the Negro to determine the nature of his own representation from behind the veil and within the white gaze, thus altering social-political relations and defeating American nationalism.

Momentarily trapped in the white gaze, the Negro and his work of art must represent themselves in the best light possible. The Negro finds himself uniquely positioned to create an art that would satisfy the conditions, or criteria, that Du Bois stringently, stridently demands of the aesthetic. Because of the Negro's newness, but also due to his archaic nature, he is able authentically to summon the forces of art's past epochs and render them modern. The Negro's archaic modernity commands Truth, Goodness, and Beauty, the unity of which defines the art of the past and future as art.

Thus Du Bois calls for a rejection of the lessons of modern art and a return to the glories of bygone eras. Here Du Bois is strictly anti-Hegelian, in that his teleology, at least in the aesthetic realm, moves backwards to go forward. Indeed, Du Bois finds himself in an odd temporal predicament, insisting that the future can be won solely through a return to the past. The Negro is the sole possible arbiter of a seemingly insurmountable and, given the ahistorical bent of Du Bois's and the Negro's thought, impossible challenge. As the modern man who is also primitive, the Negro can visit with past instances in the history of art and bring them to life exactly as they were in terms of their essential feature, namely, the representation of Truth, Beauty, and Goodness. For Du Bois, the revelation of Negro humanity is achieved not by the mere representation of Negroes suffering, laughing, loving, and hating, but by the technical, formal mastery of the Western tradition, which in turn has been given over to Negro themes. The recuperation of the work of art's ability to speak the truth means in no way here a return to classical themes, but rather a return to an older, still Eurocentric, way of writing, painting, and above all defining the work of art. The art of the past (and presumably the past ends with British Romanticism) has, inherent in its form, the essential ability to make present Truth, Goodness, and Beauty. These properties are in turn inherently communal because they are intertwined and instructive. Truth leads to Goodness, as does Beauty, which in turn leads to proper moral and ethical conduct, or Right. Beauty is Right, Right Beauty.

Du Bois says nothing of subject matter, of content; he is instead concerned with aesthetic form, the manner and quality of the work's execution. This means that Negro humanity makes itself known not merely through the events of the narrative, but, first and foremost, through the quality of the work's technical achievement. The consequences of this thought are rather grave. For, even though Du Bois names in his list of aesthetic wonders an African village and an African American spiritual, these works have worth to the Du Boisian critic only insofar as they are in some way recognizable, quantifiable, and comprehensible within the Western tradition – the Venus de Milo and the gothic cathedral. Du Bois's is not an aesthetic that embraces indigenous innovation or tribal art for themselves, but which seeks the Western-canonical element in black art and uses it as the starting point of aesthetic comparison and judgment. All art may be propaganda, but it is propaganda made legible to the white gaze, just as the Negro is human only if put in the language of Western humanism.

Alain Locke saw immediately and in unexpectedly Garveyite terms this danger in Du Boisian art as propaganda. Writing less than a year after the publication of Du Bois's "The Criteria of Negro Art," Locke went on the offensive in "Art or Propaganda?" (1928): "My chief objection to propaganda, apart from its betting sin of monotony and disproportion, is that it perpetuates the position of group inferiority even in crying out against it. For it lives and speaks under the shadow of a dominant majority whom it harangues, cajoles, threatens, or supplicates" (260). To create art as propaganda is not only to produce bad art, but to be in bed with the enemy. Propaganda propagates its own defeat, its own negative, more powerful propaganda. To follow Du Bois's aesthetic lead is to wage the battle from the wrong side. It would be to reinscribe the Negro artist in endlessly self-duplicating double consciousness – to redouble double consciousness, in a sense – rather than to assuage its effects. The burden Du Bois places on the shoulders of the Negro makes of the Negro artist, and perhaps Du Bois as well, a dupe, forcing him to follow a set of criteria designed to gain acceptance from the white gaze in terms of the Western aesthetic tradition, and all in the name of Negro spiritual strivings. This is the fruit of Du Bois's reactionary aesthetic position. Aesthetic integration under these terms is not integration but self-annihilation.

Recalling that Garvey insists on self-creation, or self-recuperation, and thus on a specifically Negro literature and culture, we see that his aesthetic, such that it is, finds its justification in praxis. The work of art is just that – work. The work of art is done in the present and for the present; it does not rely on the fulfillment of a promise. Art is produced and assimilated as an attempt to create the total man, the Negro, as an aesthetic object which nonetheless works and which never stops working. Indeed:

> One must never stop reading. Read everything that you can that is of standard knowledge. Don't waste time reading trashy literature. That is to say, don't pay any attention to the ten cents novels, Wild West stories and cheap sentimental books, but where there is a good plot and a good story in the form of a novel, read it. It is necessary to read it for the purpose of getting information on human nature. The idea is that personal experience is not enough for a human to get all the useful knowledge of life, because the individual life is too short, so we must feed on the experience of others. The literature we read should include the biography and autobiography of men and women who have accomplished greatness in their particular line. Whenever you can buy these books and own them and whilst you are reading them make pencil or pen notes of the striking sentences and paragraphs that you should like to remember, so that when you have to refer to the book for any thought that you would like to refresh your mind on, you will not have to read over the whole book. (*Garvey Life and Lessons* 184)

Art is a means to an end. It grants knowledge of human nature as it refines the character and self-presentation of its consumer. Garvey's aesthetic is one of self-fashioning and pertains not to the activity of the Negro artists, but to that of their audiences. In other words, Garvey offers us a reception theory of art which designates, in the case of literature, the reader as the object of art to be created, molded, and refined. Literary Garveyism is a form of aesthetic-racial hygiene brought into being in order to bring the Negro into being.[2] Art is not propaganda agitating for white recognition; it is a form of preparation for one's self-presentation and work in the world.

Garvey also sees art as inspiration to work. He makes clear that "You should also read the best poetry for inspiration. The standard poets have always been the most inspirational creators. From a good line of poetry, you may get the inspiration for the career of a life time. Many a great man and woman was first inspired by some attractive line or verse of poetry" (*Garvey Life and Lessons* 184–5). After all, Garvey continues, "There are good poets and bad poets just like there are good novels and bad novels. Always select the best poets for your inspirational urge" (*Garvey Life and Lessons* 185). There is here no consideration of the white audience. Negro literature is solely for the Negro, as is all Western literature. Garvey does not claim that the Negro must only read Negro authors. He can and must read anything that inspires him, or empowers him, to work toward the cause of black liberation, and that, in so doing, refines the character. Such a work of art is not propaganda; it is the long-hidden truth of black being contained in even the most canonical works of Western literature, works which are in any event a priori black. The consumption of these works engenders Beauty in the consumer. Beauty, then, is a project construed and executed as the means of aestheticizing the Negro as such. The true work of art in Garveyism is the man, not the book, not the painting. The Negro himself is the final aesthetic product, and he needs no form of recognition in the eyes of the white gaze. The Negro's humanity is this aesthetic-racial hygiene which requires no extraracial acknowledgment, no white certification of humanity, no propaganda. Following his own logic, then, Marcus Garvey was far more beautiful than W.E.B. Du Bois was able to admit. Indeed, Garvey was a work of art.

Notes

1 The influence of Garvey and Garveyism on the literature of the period has been well detailed by Tony Martin. What I am in search of here is not influence but rather a Garveyist aesthetic. See Martin, *Literary Garveyism*.

2 For the idea of racial hygiene in Marcus Garvey's political thought, see Gilroy; Thompson.

Bibliography

Du Bois, W.E.B. "Back to Africa." *Century* 105 (1923): 546–7.

Du Bois, W.E.B. "The Criteria of Negro Art." 1926. In *A W.E.B. Du Bois Reader*. Ed. Andrew G. Paschal. New York: Macmillan, 1971. 324–8.

Du Bois, W.E.B. "The Younger Literary Movement." 1924. In *The New Negro: Readings on*

Race, Representation, and African American Culture, 1892–1938. Ed. Henry Louis Gates and Gene Andrew Jarrett. Princeton: Princeton University Press, 2007. 219–20.

Garvey, Marcus. *Marcus Garvey Life and Lessons: A Centennial Companion to the Marcus Garvey and Universal Negro Improvement Association Papers*. Ed. Robert A. Hill and Barbara Blair. Berkeley: University of California Press, 1988.

Garvey, Marcus. *The Universal Negro Improvement Association Papers*. Volume IV. Ed. Robert A. Hill, Tevvy Ball, Erika Blum, and Barbara Blair. Berkeley: University of California Press, 1985.

Garvey, Marcus. *The Universal Negro Improvement Association Papers*. Volume V. Ed. Robert A. Hill, Tevvy Ball, Erika Blum, and Barbara Blair. Berkeley: University of California Press, 1987.

Gilroy, Paul. "Black Fascism." *Transition* 80.1 (2000): 70–91.

Grant, Colin. *Negro with a Hat: The Rise and Fall of Marcus Garvey*. New York: Oxford University Press, 2008.

Lewis, David L. *W.E.B. Du Bois: The Fight for Equality and the American Century, 1919–1963*. New York: Henry Holt, 2000.

Locke, Alain. "Art or Propaganda?" 1928. In *The New Negro: Readings on Race, Representation, and African American Culture, 1892–1938*. Ed. Henry Louis Gates and Gene Andrew Jarrett. Princeton: Princeton University Press, 2007. 260–1.

Martin, Tony. *Literary Garveyism: Garvey, Black Arts, and the Harlem Renaissance*. Dover, MA: Majority Press, 1983.

Thompson, Mark Christian. *Black Fascisms: African American Literature and Culture between the Wars*. Charlottesville: University of Virginia Press, 2007.

17
African American Modernism and State Surveillance

William J. Maxwell

Imagine a world in which a federal police force aims to decipher and revalue the best of African American writing; a world in which the repressive state apparatus moonlights as a racially expressive apparatus, not only monitoring African Americanist criticism, but also composing its own variety. For his part, Richard Wright could imagine such a world, since he trusted he was living in one beginning in 1942. In that hair-trigger year, Federal Bureau of Investigation (FBI) director J. Edgar Hoover, agitated by Wright's photo-history *12 Million Black Voices* (1941), ordered the Bureau's New York field office to review his collected works for signs of sedition. "If your inquiry develops information of an affirmative nature," Hoover directed, "you should of course cause an investigation to be undertaken as to the subject's background, inclinations, and current activities" (US, Wright file, December 8, 1942). Unsurprisingly, information of an affirmative nature was developed, and a thorough investigation undertaken, leaving Wright hyperconscious of the Bureau agents who seemed to track every twist of his literary and romantic lives. Wright's expatriation to *Paris Noir* and the wider black diaspora, launched in 1947 with encouragement from Hoover's spy-readers, delivered some of the analytical advantages of statelessness, but could not outrun the impression that FBI snoops lurked around each alien corner.

Consider Wright's voyage to Buenos Aires aboard the SS *Uruguay* in the fall of 1949. Snapshots taken on deck show him adopting the Ernest Hemingway brand of office casual, working bare-chested on a punching bag to slim down enough to play his most enduring character, the teenaged Bigger Thomas, in the Argentinean film version of his novel *Native Son* (Rowley 383). Yet Wright felt compelled to interrupt his rejuvenation in international waters long enough to complete a poem whose satirical take on state espionage incompletely masked its anxiety. In "The FB Eye Blues," Wright turned the tables on Bureau note-taking, filling classic blues stanzas with wry digs at the intimacy of spy-sight. Living under Bureau scrutiny, the poem joked, was uncomfortably close to sleeping – and co-writing – with the enemy:

That old FB eye
Tied a bell to my bed stall
Said old FB eye
Tied a bell to my bed stall
Each time I love my baby, gover'ment knows it all.

Woke up this morning
FB eye under my bed
Said I woke up this morning
FB eye under my bed
Told me all I dreamed last night, every word I said. (ll. 1–10)

Wright's compulsion to box with Hoover's shadow even while steaming toward foreign film stardom reveals his suspicion that the FB eye was just as able as he to board a chronotope of Black Atlantic mobility and sail beyond the limits of the nation-state. More important, however, this compulsion also unveils one of the most typical impulses in the African American literary modernism born with the Harlem Renaissance. Wright's unusually explicit wrestling with the long arm of the Bureau is representative of how this Afro-modernism was compelled to reckon with its image in the FBI's spyglass. To an extent that even Wright could not imagine, the Federal Bureau of Investigation, the best-publicized agent and symbol of the US national security state, shaped the leading edge of twentieth-century black American writing.

J. Edgar Hoover, the original fighting "G-Man," charismatic bureaucrat, and public-sector enemy of Dr. Martin Luther King, Jr., fostered an intimate relationship between state surveillance and African American literary experimentation from the birth of the Harlem Renaissance in 1919 to the height of the Black Arts Movement in 1972, the year Hoover died after five decades in the Bureau saddle. Targeting African American writers as exemplary as James Baldwin, Lorraine Hansberry, and Langston Hughes, Hoover's FBI acted as a concealed censor and border guard, distorting or deferring publications and forcing or sidetracking international travels. At the same time, Bureau spycraft could be received by its writer-targets as a stimulating new school for aesthetic research, inspiring the subgenre of the "counterfile" and an inventive modern poetics of double agency. And this spycraft spurred the FBI to become a pioneering archivist of black internationalism, tracing the intellectual connections of the "New Negro" across the Black Atlantic and into the Bolshevized Black Sea. Through both poles of its influence, the restrictive and the inspirational, the Bureau helped to mold a worldly but state-hunted, sometimes state-haunted, tradition of the new. As the entrenchment of post-9/11 security measures transforms the US into an "endemic surveillance society" ("UK and US Labelled"); and as the transnational vistas of cultural studies are tested by both the return of state Keynesianism and the raw divisions of global terror war, the time is now ripe to consider the nature and effects of the Bureau's many interactions with African American literary modernism.

1. The Growth of Hoover's National Police Agency Was Concurrent and Interconnected with the Growth of Afro-Modernist Writing

The FBI's 50-year campaign against African American protest is no longer a state secret. Armed with a Freedom of Information Act given teeth in 1986, New Left-leaning historians have confirmed that the Bureau's plot to shame Martin Luther King, Jr. into suicide was only the tip of the iceberg. Hoover's arrival at the FBI during the Red Summer of 1919 kicked off half a century of harassment of black political life, culminating in the bloody COINTELPRO (Counterintelligence Program) aimed at "Black Nationalist-Hate Groups" ranging from the Black Panthers to the non-nationalist, nonviolent Southern Christian Leadership Conference. Born the son of a Washington DC mapmaker in 1895, a child witness to the capital's belated segregation troubled by rumors of his own black ancestry, Hoover entered the Bureau convinced that New Negro discontent was triggered by the longings of African Americans for Marx and miscegenation. When not co-authoring the Palmer Raids, Hoover was poring over the *Negro World* and the Harlem *Messenger* and personally hatching a scheme to prosecute pioneering black nationalist Marcus Garvey for mail fraud. In a 1919 message to a Bureau underling, the G-Man complained that the provisions of the wartime Alien Act lagged behind his crusade to capsize the radicalizing traffic of the Black Atlantic. "Unfortunately," Hoover groused, Garvey "has not as yet violated any federal law whereby he could be proceeded against on the grounds of being an undesirable alien, from the point of view of deportation" (US, Garvey file, October 11, 1919). Hoover eventually got his man, succeeding in extraditing Garvey to his native Jamaica.

Yet relatively few scholars of African American literature have yet gotten the message that the Bureau's long offensive against black political leadership in fact began with Hoover's excited dread of black writing and climaxed in a ruthless imitation of it, a poison pen letter to King suggesting suicide while hijacking the voice of "us Negroes." From the late teens through the early 1970s, Hoover's hardline bureaucracy qualified as a rivalrous if inconspicuous consumer of African American texts, a half-buried interpretive empire with aboveground effects on the creation of Afro-modernism. Practically alone among publicly funded institutions of literary study, Hoover's FBI never treated African American writing as an ineffectual fad and never forgot its heavy traffic with the twentieth-century left. Classic Harlem Renaissance scholarship by Nathan Huggins and David Levering Lewis insinuates that the Bureau, acting in concert with Attorney General A. Mitchell Palmer, inadvertently nurtured the New Negro cultural awakening. The first American Red Scare, Huggins argues, sparked "a channeling of energy from political and social criticism into poetry … [and] fiction" (9), or what Lewis, adopting a psychoanalytical vocabulary, less sympathetically labels "the cultural sublimation of civil rights" (xxiv). Just as convincing as the proposition that New Negro militants went strategically artsy, however, is the case for the Bureau's own cultural turn under pressure from black renaissancism. Mounds of recently extracted paperwork plead that the FBI itself discerned the simultaneous emergence of Harlem's rebirth and the modern US security state. Documenting the radical byways of the Harlem movement in the wake of World War One, the Bureau rehearsed several of the techniques of literary meddling that Claire Culleton couches as Hoover's "manipulation of modernism" (17).

A year before Langston Hughes published his first book of poems, *The Weary Blues* (1925), his vernacular voice had already earned him the sort of personal file usually reserved for anarchist spokeswomen and socialist presidential candidates. Hughes's controversial proletarian poem "Goodbye Christ" (1932) did nothing to relieve this mistrust, tagging Hughes within the Bureau as a "Negro pornographic poet" (Robins 63). Even before it was looking for Langston, the FBI was tailing globetrotter Claude McKay, painstakingly reproducing his "violent sonnets" and directing customs officials to detain the poet and his literary effects at every US port of entry.

The line-up of African American authors who inherited the Harlem movement's bad reputation at Bureau headquarters is long and distinguished, and is not confined to close affiliates of the Communist Party such as Hughes and McKay. The loyalty of many veteran New Negroes was investigated during World War Two. Dossiers on Gwendolyn Bennett, Sterling Brown, Georgia Douglas Johnson, J.A. Rogers, George Schuyler, and Walter White all saw the light of the Justice Department between 1941 and 1945. Richard Wright, another wartime target, passed his FB eye blues down to defiant pupil James Baldwin, shadowed by a gang of confidential FBI sources that intercepted his mail and photographed his daily rounds, not just in Harlem and France, but also in Istanbul in 1964, where he began plotting retaliation through a never-completed anti-Bureau exposé (Campbell, "I Heard It Through the Grapevine" 153–67). The works and days of W.E.B. Du Bois clinched his high place on the Bureau's Security Index of imminently arrestable leftists from 1950 until his death in Ghana in 1963. Chester Himes did not make the Index, but his Harlem detective fiction was foreshadowed by FBI gumshoes who began investigating his prison time and anti-colonial outlook in 1944, with the results itemized in a file marked "Internal Security-Sedition" (Walters, "Policing the Borders of the Text"). Alice Childress's involvement with an alphabet soup of committees on the 1950s left attracted what her FBI file describes as "a discreet surveillance"; so did Lorraine Hansberry's early work as a labor journalist for Paul Robeson's paper *Freedom* (Washington 185–94). Paule Marshall and Ishmael Reed escaped with relatively slim files for the high crime of petition-signing, while Amiri Baraka's swath beyond the home base he rechristened "New Ark," New Jersey, was sufficient to generate over 2,000 pages of grapevine noise and reconnaissance beginning in 1960 (Robins 411, 349–52). Decades before Baraka helped to found the Black Arts Movement, a Bureau memo had wondered if fellow Jerseyite William Carlos Williams's "very queer or possibly mental" poetry concealed revolutionary cryptograms (quoted in Robins 293). Given the FBI's equally intense concern for the highlights of African American modernism, we may eventually discover that it judged Jean Toomer's *Cane* a work of both elusive Imagist fragments and secret Marxian code.

This drawn-out roll of literary suspects, stretching from the Harlem Renaissance to the Black Arts Movement's "Renaissance II," betrays an unshakable suspicion that authoring African American modernism and menacing national security were one and the same. In the elephant's memory of the FBI, black letters seemed to shatter the historical bonds of the slave narrative without breaking with the need to enter the literary under the sign of criminality. For this reason, among others, Hoover's ghostreaders never acknowledged the passing of the national emergency declared during World War One. The Treaty of Versailles officially sealed the conclusion of the global conflict philosopher Giorgio Agamben describes as a general laboratory for "testing … the functional mechanisms of the state of emergency," the executive's sovereign suspension of juridical order and legislative checks (7). Despite the war's end, the Sedition Act of 1918, formally rescinded by Congress in 1921, retained its unchecked authority at Bureau headquarters, still able to illegitimize the publication of what the Act dubbed "disloyal, profane, scurrilous, or abusive language about the form of government of the United States" (quoted in Agamben 21). Keeper of the Sedition Act's flame, the FBI doubled as the race-conscious protector of a state of counter-literary exception within the American state. From 1919 (the year of McKay's "If We Must Die") until 1972 (the year of Ishmael Reed's *Mumbo Jumbo*), the Bureau probed leading black writers for crimes against the American way of governance, and grew in institutional authority with aid from investigative procedures honed in collecting what it considered literary felonies.

2. The FBI Remains Perhaps the Most Dedicated and Powerful Forgotten Critic of Twentieth-Century African American Writing

Hoover's self-lacerating panic over unconcealed homosexuality once led him to ask an assistant "Isn't [James] Baldwin a well-known pervert?" and to assign the Bureau's General Crimes section to comb Baldwin's 1962 novel, *Another Country*, for traces of obscenity (Campbell, "I Heard It Through the Grapevine" 170). The director must have been disappointed with the book report that followed: an open-minded FBI reviewer discovered a novel of genuine "literary merit … [that] may be of value to students of psychology and social behavior" (quoted in Robins 347). Positive, blurb-worthy evaluations are not the norm in the FBI's many files on African American writers, but the gravity of the response, its tendency to overspill the immediate need to decode, discipline, and punish, is emblematic of the Bureau's generous appreciation of literature's sway. The publicity-savvy Hoover cultivated an inflated fear and respect for the power of authors to act as "thought-control relay stations" (quoted in Robins 50); he shared the modernist avant-garde's generous estimation of literature's ability to guide minds in a fallen world, though never the avant-garde's faith in its own virtuous novelty. Thick studies by Herbert Mitgang (1988), Natalie Robins (1992), and Claire Culleton (2004) document the repressive effects of the Bureau's alarm over literary dissidence. Dozens of American authors, they disclose, had their publications scanned by an FBI division actually named the Book Review Section. The most "anti-American" or "anti-FBI" among them had their phones tapped, their letters opened, and their lecture tours stalled. Publishers as influential as Bennett Cerf were pressed to become FBI informants. In-house sources supplied Bureau agents with notes from editorial board meetings at *Time* and *Life*, *Reader's Digest* and the *Daily Worker*. By the 1950s, when the Bureau's reputation for muscular rectitude reached its height, the school of Hoover had achieved something approaching total literary awareness.

For all the stress on *sub rosa*, pre-publication surveillance, however, Bureau files analyzing African American modernists did not always deny the pleasures of the dissident text. Chester Himes's file, for example, offers capsule interpretations of every early story he placed in *Esquire*. The direct object of these readings was to unearth treason, but their anonymous FBI author could not help from noting Himes's richly woven "descriptive material" (US, Himes file, August 1, 1945). Lorraine Hansberry's popular drama *A Raisin in the Sun* inspired heady asides on the nature of "self-expression and self-identification" in an anonymous agent of criticism sent to check a Philadelphia rehearsal for signs of the Communist line (US, Hansberry file, February 5, 1959). Amiri Baraka's dossier features a review of the iconic anthology *Black Fire* complaining of "ample servings of filth" and a "'far out' … method of presentation," but allowing that "the assembled works tend to have an energy that succeeds in impressing one with the violence and passion of the author's emotions" (US, Baraka file, April 29, 1969). It is not too much to propose that such readerly files should be considered as revealing works of literary criticism, as state-subsidized, collectively authored compilations of textual analysis bidding for interpretive dominance. The compatibility of the author and the spy has been remarked at least since the (pre-Harlem) English Renaissance of the sixteenth and seventeenth centuries. "A writer-spy like Marlowe," observes John Michael Archer, knew that his work on both sides of the hyphen depended on the "necessary lie" and the "observation of men and manners [that] made their manipulation through spectacle possible" (75). But what of the impact of the "critic-spy" or "ghostreader," a figure whose observation of authors and texts was enabled not only by decryption, identity theft, and hermeneutics of suspicion – techniques most every literary critic shares with the intelligence agent – but also by professionalized state surveillance?

The ingredients of the Langston Hughes file testify that more than a few Americans detected and trusted in the better knowledge of such ghostreading. They conceived of the Bureau as the ultimate critical arbiter of African American modernism, a sort of federal *Explicator* in trenchcoat and fedora. Dozens of letters from the likes of Arizona State College and the Springfield, Illinois, Urban League quiz Hoover about the meaning of Hughes's poems, in large part because of the director's public unveiling as a Hughes specialist in the widely seeded FBI pamphlet "Secularism – Breeder of Crime." A brave correspondent from the Methodist Church sought illumination on whether the intentional fallacy applies to black Bolsheviks, noting that Hughes himself had claimed that "Goodbye, Christ" was "not an expression of his own view but … a poetic mechanism describ[ing] what a Communist thinks" (US, Hughes file, March 3, 1948). The Bureau's reply failed to enlighten, but as late as 1970, then Congressman George H.W. Bush thought nothing of forwarding the FBI director a constituent's critical inquiry concerning both Hughes and the history of black theater. "I seem to remember," wrote a confused citizen from Bush's Houston district, that *A Raisin in the Sun* "was a highly controversial production … by a Leroi Jones and that Jones is something of a professional trouble maker and rabble rouser. If you cannot furnish information pertaining to this play and its author please advise where I might obtain such details" (US, Hughes file, 6 July 1970).

None of this correspondence goes to show, of course, that the FBI wisely fulfilled the office later assumed by this anthology or the *Oxford Companion to African American Literature*. The Bureau's readings and responses were abrupt, sometimes mistaken, and generally up to no good. It would take the emergence of the Central Intelligence Agency (CIA) and James Jesus Angleton – a 1941 graduate of Yale University, an admirer of literary critic I.A. Richards, a mentee of the poet Ezra Pound, a co-founder of the little magazine *Furioso*, later the chief CIA mole-hunter – to acquaint national intelligence with the intricacies of the intentional fallacy and other doctrines of the New Criticism, drawn upon in Angleton's theory of spycraft as "the practical criticism of ambiguity" (Epstein 84). Fully formalist spy-reading, devoted to wrestling with indeterminacies, might therefore be described as "CIA reading," the conquering method of the second Red Scare, when this intelligence agency surpassed the FBI in elite anti-Communist cachet, and when the New Criticism grew from Southern Agrarian dependent to national collegiate champion. "FBI reading," on the other hand, the master method born during the first Red Scare, reflects both the Bureau's place at the top of a federal intelligence hierarchy free from Ivy League intruders, and the theoretical grounding of the biographical-historical criticism of its own day of initiation.

McKay's file, for one, steadily exhibits not only the brusque, gossip-hungry diligence of such FBI reading, but also its infatuation with the independent literary artifact still imagined as an exotic confessional. Plucked from dozens of McKay poems, the sonnet "America" (1921) is found valuable enough for exacting transcription, but is stripped of most internal traction:

> Although she feeds me bread of bitterness,
> And sinks into my throat her tiger's tooth,
> Stealing my breath of life, I will confess
> I love this cultured hell that tests my youth! (ll. 1–4)

According to an FBI memorandum, a straightforward political moral for the poem – support your local America-hating alien – is thought clear as day: the sonnet directly precedes information that McKay "appeared … at Ellis Island, New York, as a witness in behalf of … a British Communist" within months of its publication (US, McKay file, January 26, 1924). The affected principle of FBI interpretive theory is proclaimed earlier in the same memo: "McKay's views, beliefs, principles, et cetera may properly be inferred from quotations from his writings" (ibid.). Avoidance of the "biographical fallacy" thus remains a task for the CIA's urbane tradecraft, and the only thing New Critically ambiguated by the Bureau's slant on McKay's poem is its author's patriotism.

The sheer volume of public trust in the FBI's critical authority is nonetheless instructive. An accurate impression of the Bureau's comprehensive attentiveness and backhanded admiration for African American literary intelligence escaped beyond the Beltway, as did word of Hoover's intent to outdo black criticism in public pronouncements as well as in his agents' secret files. The lawless appetite of FBI ghostreading could indeed create interpretive advantages, feeding paranoid insights into the transnational range of Afro-modernism. Authors of Bureau pulp criticism would have been happy to see McKay and company chucked into the nearest jail, but they also managed to perceive the far reaches of the Black Atlantic before their academic rivals.

3. The FBI Helped to Frame the Twentieth-Century Black Atlantic, both Criminalizing and Orienting Its Flows

Langston Hughes's FBI file repeatedly quotes his claim that "Negroes are growing in global consciousness" (US, Hughes file, June 3, 1947). His file and others, meanwhile, confirm that the Bureau concluded it should grow in the same way. Unlike Michel Foucault's famous eighteenth-century prisoners, prototypical citizens of his penitentiary modern state, Afro-modernists were known to see as widely as they were seen; FBI dossiers recognized them as subjects in communication with international movements even as they became objects of national police information. The Bureau thus often exceeded its traditional domestic jurisdiction when hunting for black literary offenders.

McKay's dossier, for instance, includes such artifacts of extranational surveillance as articles summarized from Soviet newspapers; reports on his Moscow speeches by American diplomats in Riga, Latvia, then a nest of anti-Communist espionage; and clipped schedules of Europe-bound shipping traffic. Like Hughes's *I Wonder as I Wander* (1956) and similar narratives of black transnational voyagers, McKay's file underscores political pilgrimage, economic immigration, and other passages typically absent from classic European travel writing. More pertinent here, this file also exposes blind spots within prevailing maps of modern black internationalism, including Paul Gilroy's *The Black Atlantic: Modernity and Double Consciousness* (1993), the high theoretical sea in which so many recent accounts of Afro-modernism have found their bearings. For Gilroy, the Black Atlantic world is not simply a spawning ground of liberating transethnic exchanges among dispersed black populations. His central chronotope of the sailing ship, chosen to "rethink … the African diaspora" via the history of the "western hemisphere," is intended to recall the racial violence of the Atlantic slave trade that built the Black Atlantic in the first brutal instance (17). Yet Gilroy joins a good deal of the work done in his wake by indicating that the transatlantic roaming of black moderns handily rewrites and redeems the coerced motion of the Middle Passage and its after-echoes. "What was initially felt to be a curse – the curse of homelessness or the curse of enforced exile," Gilroy writes, "becomes affirmed [and] reconstructed as the basis of a privileged standpoint from which certain useful and critical perceptions about the modern world become more likely" (111). The evidence buried within the FBI's alternative history of the Black Atlantic offers a markedly different reconstruction of the negative meanings of imperative movement, verifying that blocked and forced cosmopolitanisms were common among precisely those modern intellectuals most dedicated to the insights of Black Atlantic travel. The necessary mistranslations of intra-diaspora thinking, this is to suggest, were hardly the most pressing challenges to the articulation of twentieth-century black internationalisms.

For some of the diaspora-minded black moderns pursued by the Bureau, radical internationalisms led to US house arrest. The passport of W.E.B. Du Bois, a founder of Pan-Africanism, was withdrawn at the peak of the Cold War, and Hughes barely escaped the same fate. For other of these moderns, Atlantic crossings led to American banishments and the obligatory wandering of what I call "state-sponsored transnationalism": paradoxically, their rewritings and reversals of the Middle Passage brought unwilled returns. Think of the requisite Black Atlanticism of McKay, whose demigration from America in 1922, 10 years after his arrival from Jamaica, parallels both Marcus Garvey's Harlem-to-Kingston extradition and the ironic deportation of Trinidad-born C.L.R. James from the dock of Ellis Island. FBI vigilance ensured that McKay could not easily come home to Harlem and to its cultural rebirth before 1934, when New Negro elders finally intervened with contacts at the State Department (Maxwell 47–51). Wright's own decampment to France was partly motivated by Bureau prying, a fate he shared with Baldwin, whose flight to Turkey from Hoover's watch provoked an official FBI travel warning. Baldwin's political itinerary, like McKay's before him, was rewarded and fueled by a Bureau "Stop Notice" under which the Immigration and Naturalization Service (INS) was ordered to "immediately notify the FBI if [Baldwin] passes through the area" (quoted in Campbell, "I Heard It Through the Grapevine" 172).

No wonder that Wright considered an Atlantic cruise no place to forget the Bureau's roving eye. The State Department might send Louis Armstrong, Dizzy Gillespie, and fellow jazzmen on goodwill tours of Europe, Africa, and the Middle East, convinced that international news of racial discrimination was America's Achilles' heel in the global battle with Communism (Von Eschen 5). The CIA might fight the cultural Cold War by urging European roles for soprano Leontyne Price and other black opera divas, reasoning that the presence of African American artists abroad countered what one CIA surrogate called "the 'suppressed race' propaganda," forestalling "all criticisms to the effect that we … wouldn't let our own 'out'" (quoted in

Saunders 119). The FBI, by contrast, aspired to keep African American authors running scared when not down on the farm, reflecting those interests in the federal bureaucracy pleased with the Cold War state's hesitation to promote racial equality on the home front. Study of the FBI's patrolling of the Black Atlantic reveals a dialectic of Cold War recruitment of African American culture poised between Hoover's wary ghostreaders and the eager listeners of the Company and the diplomatic corps, between the strategic export of black music's putative abstraction and the managed travel of black literature's social text at home and abroad.

As Baldwin and his contemporaries knew intimately, to be trailed and propelled by the FBI was not to be entirely defined by it. Bureau files capture Hoover's spy-critics acting like G-Men Dr. Bledsoes, devising secret letters and scheming to keep black modernists running in tight circles. Their efforts met with disturbing successes, but never installed an intelligence network remotely sharp enough to discover, let alone dictate, all the routes within a vast oceanic territory. In the last analysis, however, the consequences of Hoover's early exposure to cartography cannot be ignored by Black Atlantic theory. His FBI strived to outmap a whole navy of black radical voyagers and succeeded in penetrating the time and space of the Black Atlantic system. The nonsynchronous present of this system, formed in the barbarous modernity of the slave trade, was punctuated by concrete echoes of a past of forced transportation courtesy of Bureau deportation orders. The sprawling diasporic geography of this system was striated internally not only by differences of class, gender, ethnicity, language, and so on, but also by the renationalizing atomization of Bureau Stop Notices and passport seizures. In both cases, a race-minded police bureaucracy influenced the making of a major black transnationalism, thus arguing that state powers inherently opposed to discourses of adversarial globalism may still do their part to inspire, translate, and drive them into action. The US national security apparatus itself reserved the right to think and feel beyond the nation, ensuring that the voluntary dispersal connoted by the term "diaspora" was tinged by the bitterness of *galut*. As Brent Hayes Edwards notes, *galut* is a rival synonym for exile in the Jewish Hellenistic tradition, signifying "forced homelessness" and the "eschatological dimension" of "things being not as they should be" ("Langston Hughes" 690).

4. Knowledge of and Opposition to FBI Ghostreading Informs a Surprisingly Deep Vein of Afro-Modernist Writing

To a historian jaundiced by the FB eye, the contentious milieu of black Paris during Wright's final expatriate years looks like the intended result of US covert operations. By the late 1950s, the *Rive noire* of the city Edwards classifies as the reigning symbol of black transnational "interaction, exchange, and dialogue" was rife with separation, information hoarding, and denunciation (*Practice of Diaspora* 5). "Everybody thought that everybody else was spying on someone or other for somebody," reported an eyewitness of the scene at the Café de Tournon, once a spot where black and white expatriates drank off their American racial masks, now a magnet for anxiety over American state sleuthing (quoted in Campbell, *Exiled in Paris* 196–7). Spy stories ricocheted off the café's walls and spattered everyone inside. Chester Himes wondered if William Gardner Smith received payments from the CIA, and vice versa; both charged cartoonist Ollie Harrington with spying; Wright had marked doubts about the loyalties of apprentice author Richard Gibson, and only slightly less concern about everyone else with whom he worked, spoke, or slept (Campbell, *Exiled in Paris* 196–7).

For his trouble, Wright himself was suspected of being a G-Man. "There is a story, a rumor about you that is going about," Kay Boyle warned in a letter all the way from Connecticut, "you are known to be working with the State Department, or the FBI" (quoted in Campbell, *Exiled in Paris* 197). This tangle of mutual suspicions rose to the surface of the expatriate community during the so-called Gibson Affair, a case of ghostwriting under Harrington's signature perhaps directed by the FBI. They exploded after Wright's sudden death in 1960, which Harrington was only the first to attribute, probably too creatively, to the Bureau. In the most benign rendition of the events, the FBI succeeded in persuading the literary intellectuals of *Paris noir* that their French harbor was as navigable by US intelligence as the Black Atlantic.

Hoover's bookish agents, capable of suggesting plots to the Tournon regulars, would not have the last word on overseas surveillance. The same FBI scrutiny that tested personal alliances inspired a notable family of *romans à clef*, each running changes on the theme of state reconnaissance and black counterintelligence. Wright's unpublished late novel, *Island of Hallucinations*, ships Fishbelly, the Mississippi-bred protagonist of *The Long Dream* (1958), to the City of Light, where he sifts intrigues among African American expatriates stoked by an American secret service. William Gardner Smith's fourth long fiction, *The Stone Face* (1963), plants a suspected G-Man among a crew of Tournon habitués whose Francophilic idyll is bruised by the Algerian revolution. Chester Himes's philosophical police procedural, *A Case of Rape* (1963), enters the mix with a would-be detective character that inherits Wright's habit of tracing the criminal jeopardy of black Parisians to government conspiracies. Common to all three novels is the task of out-investigating the FBI, of solving the mysteries of the black metropolis in public case records designed to pre-expose future Bureau informers. As Himes's surgical strike clarifies in particular, the books pioneer a novelistic subgenre of their own, that of the "counterfile," in which the tropes of the police dossier are aired and angled against their usual ghostreaders.

Minus many of the Parisian stage sets, the challenge of the counterfile is accepted in a deep pocket of real and imagined Black Arts-era literature. For nearly a decade, James Baldwin, the author of *The Evidence of Things Not Seen* (1985), threatened retaliation against the Bureau through a never-seen treatise titled *The Blood Counters*. Revenge against the national security state was taken more tangibly in the publications of Sam Greenlee's *The Spook Who Sat by the Door* (1969), Melvin Van Peebles's *A Bear for the FBI* (1968), and John A. Williams's *The Man Who Cried I Am* (1967) – this last book the great historical novel of the Tournon intrigue and a weighty brief for Wright as Hoover's document-hoarding, politically antithetical twin, thus the century's representative black intellectual. Ishmael Reed's esoteric litany *Mumbo Jumbo* (1972), published the same year that Hoover died in the Bureau saddle, casts the Wallflower Order, the military arm of the structurally unfunky Atonist Path, in the flatfoot mold of the FBI. In Reed's self-reflexive hands, the centuries-deep war between Africanized Osiris and Europeanized Set erupts in a decisive battle of detective bands beneath the monuments of the Harlem Renaissance. Freezing Western history with a citizen's arrest, his hoodoo private eyes outfox Bureau-style surveillance along with wittier blackface simulations.

Before any historical pastiche of the Harlem Renaissance was possible, however, Claude McKay had answered the Bureau's evident manhandling of his work with spiked, cunning sonnets including "America" (1921), among the Bureau's best-loved poems of the New Negro. "[A]s a rebel fronts a king in state," contends McKay's speaker at line eight, "I stand within her walls with not a shred / Of terror, malice, not a word of jeer" (ll. 8, 9–10). In the inverting camera obscura unwrapped at the poem's dramatic pivot, the inner seam of a half-Petrarchan, half-Shakespearian design, McKay reenvisions his protagonist as a covert renegade with unchallenged access to a head of government. Courtly political intrigue, rather than courtly love for a cruel-fair national incarnation, becomes the reigning enterprise. Like the knowing grandfather in Ralph Ellison's *Invisible Man* (1952), a kindred "spy in the enemy's country" made to "give up [the] gun back in the Reconstruction" (Ellison 16), McKay's speaker selects weapons of indirection, verbal cunning, and the silent collection of intelligence. All the same, through a mysterious channel of inside information, this secret agent knows of the violent future to be dealt by "Time's unerring hand" – through a whimper of fate, or perhaps a bang from a well-placed explosive, an accessible motor of history much in the postwar news. Not far outside the walls of McKay's sonnet, 38 US politicians and industrialists were in fact sent mail bombs for May Day in 1919, and Attorney General Palmer's front porch was blown apart soon after, leading Hoover to conclude that a radical putsch was a genuine peril. The poem's thick layers of allusion and anachronism would appear to disallow any reference to these local acts of sabotage, but McKay's revival of Elizabethan stratagems, at least, does not simply mask the possibility that his final lines exploit a vivid contemporary fear of radical terrorism. The Renaissance sonnets from which McKay draws were themselves aware of a court culture of rebellious surveillance, in which aristocratic author-soldiers propelled early modern intelligence and the rise and fall of great powers. When the noble lover of the first seven lines of "America" gazes darkly into the mirror of the second seven, he or she thus spies an apocalyptic but majestic reflection, a secret agent of political revenge who threatens presently – Palmer's house, or the White House? – yet speaks with historical dignity, in the cadence of Elizabeth's courtly spy-writers, as well as Petrarch, Shelley, and possibly Baudelaire, whose sonnets in self-mirroring "enclosed form" McKay learned to read in the original French.

There are many reasons why McKay's post-Creole verse of the mid-teens and 1920s sidestepped most aspects of the formal revolution of high modernism, from his early Jamaican training in the splendor of Keats, Milton, and the Elizabethan lyricists, to his conviction that the Poundian theater of modernist rebellion was nothing but stylistic, mere "bourgeois attitudinizing of the social revolutionary ferment" (McKay, Letter to Max Eastman). The least negotiable reason why his Standard English poems retained an uncolloquial, sometimes anachronistic diction was the need to elevate and obfuscate "anti-American" speech, therefore assuring that this speech would remain free. "America" and the like consciously excited Bureau attention with their whispered promises of direct action, but their backward-looking *anti*-Imagism, their *in*direct treatment of the mutinous thing, successfully thwarted Bureau-led censorship by observing the letter of sedition law. In this sense, FBI "counter-modernism," taking shape as an interdiction against profane or unreservedly critical political speech, wound up invigorating McKay's brightly torn brand of poetic modernism, in which expressive double agency, or speaking as a fervent rebel but without "a word of jeer," is the highest prize.

The ghostreaders partly responsible for McKay's sonnets prompt a final speculation on the readership that shaped the production of Afro-modernism. The Edgar Allan Poe critic Terence Whalen sensibly observes that "writers necessarily have some notion of audience which, above and beyond post-publication feedback, guides them in the production of texts" (Whalen 10). McKay and the impressive company of black modernists shadowed by state surveillance were badgered by what Whalen calls the "Capital Reader," the personification of the logic of literature as commodity who "pre-reads" any text produced for a capitalist marketplace (10). As discussed in much African American literary criticism, McKay and his peers were also pre-read by a racially divided general audience which carved out often distinct interpretive paths before the first page was printed. McKay was not alone among Afro-modernists in supposing that the next most powerful pre-reader of twentieth-century black letters was the "Capitol Reader" – accent on the letter "o" – the school of Hoover based in Washington's seat of government. In the case of McKay's work – and that of Wright, Baldwin, and many of the rest, keenly aware of the FBI's hot pursuit – the Capitol Reader provoked defining pre-revisions, not all regrettable, even when the manifest subject wandered far from the "FB Eye Blues."

Bibliography

Agamben, Giorgio. *State of Exception*. Trans. Kevin Attell. Chicago: University of Chicago Press, 2005.

Archer, John Michael. *Sovereignty and Intelligence: Spying and Court Culture in the English Renaissance*. Stanford: Stanford University Press, 1993.

Campbell, James. *Exiled in Paris: Richard Wright, James Baldwin, Samuel Beckett, and Others on the Left Bank*. Berkeley: University of California Press, 2003.

Campbell, James. "I Heard It Through the Grapevine." *Granta* 73 (2001): 151–82.

Culleton, Claire A. *Joyce and the G-Men: J. Edgar Hoover's Manipulation of Modernism*. New York: Palgrave Macmillan, 2004.

Edwards, Brent Hayes. "Langston Hughes and the Futures of Diaspora." *American Literary History* 19.3 (2007): 689–711.

Edwards, Brent Hayes. *The Practice of Diaspora: Literature, Translation, and the Rise of Black Inter-*

nationalism. Cambridge, MA: Harvard University Press, 2003.

Ellison, Ralph. *Invisible Man*. New York: Vintage, 1995.

Epstein, William H. "Counter-Intelligence: Cold-War Criticism and Eighteenth-Century Studies." *English Literary History* 57.1 (1990): 63–99.

Foucault, Michel. *Discipline and Punish: The Birth of the Prison*. Trans. Alan Sheridan. New York: Vintage, 1979.

Gilroy, Paul. *The Black Atlantic: Modernity and Double Consciousness*. Cambridge, MA: Harvard University Press, 1993.

Huggins, Nathan Irvin, ed. *Voices from the Harlem Renaissance*. New York: Oxford University Press, 1976.

Keen, Mike Forrest. *Stalking the Sociological Imagination: J. Edgar Hoover's FB Surveillance of American Sociology*. Westport, CT: Greenwood, 1999.

Lewis, David Levering, ed. *The Portable Harlem Renaissance Reader*. New York: Viking, 1994.

Maxwell, William J. "F.B. Eyes: The Bureau Reads Claude McKay." In *Left of the Color Line: Race, Radicalism, and Twentieth-Century Literature of the United States*. Ed. Bill V. Mullen and James Smethurst. Chapel Hill: University of North Carolina Press, 2003. 39–65.

McKay, Claude. "America." In *Complete Poems*. Ed. William J. Maxwell. Urbana: University of Illinois Press, 2004. 153.

McKay, Claude. Letter to Max Eastman. April 25, 1932. Claude McKay Manuscripts. Lily Library, Indiana University, Bloomington.

Mitgang, Herbert. *Dangerous Dossiers: Exposing the Secret War against America's Greatest Authors*. New York: Donald I. Fine, 1988.

Robins, Natalie. *Alien Ink: The FBI's War on Freedom of Expression*. New York: William Morrow, 1992.

Rowley, Hazel. *Richard Wright: The Life and Times*. New York: Henry Holt, 2001.

Saunders, Frances Stonor. *The Cultural Cold War: The CIA and the World of Arts and Letters*. New York: New Press, 2000.

United States [US]. Federal Bureau of Investigation. Amiri Baraka file self-deposited in the Amiri Baraka papers, Moorland-Spingarn Research Collection, Howard University Library, Washington, DC. Assorted documents dated 1957 to 1971. File no. 100–425307.

United States [US]. Federal Bureau of Investigation. Marcus Garvey file obtained under provisions of the Freedom of Information Act. File no. 198940.

United States [US]. Federal Bureau of Investigation. Lorraine Hansberry file obtained under provisions of the Freedom of Information Act. Assorted documents dated 1952 to 1965. File no. 100–393031.

United States [US]. Federal Bureau of Investigation. Chester Himes file obtained under provisions of the Freedom of Information Act. Assorted documents dated 1944 to 1964. File no. 105–2502.

United States [US]. Federal Bureau of Investigation. Langston Hughes file obtained under provisions of the Freedom of Information Act. Assorted documents dated 1925 to 1970. File no. 100–15139.

United States [US]. Federal Bureau of Investigation. Claude McKay file obtained under provisions of the Freedom of Information Act. Assorted documents dated 1921 to 1940. File no. 61–3497.

United States [US]. Federal Bureau of Investigation. Richard Wright file obtained under provisions of the Freedom of Information Act. Assorted documents dated 1942 to 1963. File no. 100–157464.

"UK and US Labelled 'Endemic Surveillance Societies'." *New Scientist*, January 12, 2008. www.newscientist.com/article/mg19726385.800-uk-and-us-labelled-endemic-surveillance-societies.html.

Von Eschen, Penny M. *Satchmo Blows Up the World: Jazz Ambassadors Play the Cold War*. Cambridge, MA: Harvard University Press, 2004.

Walters, Wendy W. "Policing the Borders of the Text and the Body of the Writer: Chester Himes and the FBI." Paper presented at the American Studies Association Conference, Washington, DC, November 2001.

Washington, Mary Helen. "Alice Childress, Lorraine Hansberry, and Claudia Jones: Black Women Write the Popular Front." In *Left of the Color Line: Race, Radicalism, and Twentieth-Century Literature of the United States*. Ed. Bill V. Mullen and James Smethurst. Chapel Hill:

University of North Carolina Press, 2003. 183–204.

Whalen, Terence. *Edgar Allan Poe and the Masses: The Political Economy of Literature in Antebellum America*. Princeton: Princeton University Press, 1999.

Wright, Richard. "The FB Eye Blues." In *Richard Wright Reader*. Ed. Ellen Wright and Michel Fabre. New York: Harper & Row, 1978. 249–50.

Part III

Reforming the Canon, Tradition, and Criticism of African American Literature: The Contemporary Period, c.1940–Present

18
The Chicago Renaissance

Michelle Yvonne Gordon

Anchored in Chicago's South Side "ghetto" that came to be known as "Bronzeville," the "Chicago Renaissance" describes a tremendous flowering of African American arts and letters between the mid-1930s and the mid-1950s. This black literary and cultural renaissance produced a wide range of visual arts, literature, and scholarship focused on many aspects of black life in America, in both the urban North and the more rural South. The writings and visual arts also cover a wide array of artistic forms, genres, and styles, including poetry, short fiction, the novel, drama, essay, creative nonfiction, sociology, historical fiction, cultural criticism, history, anthropology, and journalism, as well as photography, painting, sculpture, and dance. Much of the literature and art of the period bear deceptively simple documentary styles, and often aim to represent African American social conditions, history, and cultures in Chicago, the South, and throughout the United States. Renaissance artists frequently drew upon elements of black history and folk culture while engaging, and revising, European and Euro-American writing traditions and innovations, from the epic and sonnet to social realism, Gothic fiction, modernism, and the proletarian literature of the 1920s and 1930s. Chicago Renaissance writers also regularly took up African Americans' relationships to consumerism and American popular culture, which are often rendered as integral components of the cultural and psychological landscapes in their work. They regularly critiqued racial, class, and gendered oppression in their writing, and some participants intended that their work directly participate in and propel the era's mass movements for racial justice and social change. To accomplish the latter, the writers and editors sought to syncretize the dual impulses of black cultural nationalism and the integrationist politics advocated by the "Popular Front" and the Communist Party.

The Chicago Renaissance featured both major and minor black writers of the twentieth century. The key local organizations and institutions through which they worked include the National Negro Congress (NNC); the South Side Writers' Group (SSWG); the South Side Community Art Center (SSCAC); the George Cleveland Hall

Branch of the Chicago Public Library; the Communist Party; the Chicago School of Sociology; *New Challenge* and *Negro Story* magazines; and the federal government's relief projects for artists under the Works Progress Administration (WPA). Some of the movement's notable writings include: Richard Wright's critical literary manifesto, "Blueprint for Negro Writing" (1937), his short story "Almos' a Man" (1934), his first complete novel, *Lawd, Today!* (published posthumously in 1963), his first collection of short fiction, *Uncle Tom's Children* (1938, revised and expanded 1940), and *12 Million Black Voices* (1941); Gwendolyn Brooks's poetry collections, *A Street in Bronzeville* (1945) and the Pulitzer Prize-winning *Annie Allen* (1949), and her novel, *Maud Martha* (1953); Margaret Walker's award-winning first book of poetry, *For My People* (1942); Frank Marshall Davis's poetry collections, *Black Man's Verse* (1935), *I Am the American Negro* (1937), and *47th Street* (1948); the landmark sociological study of the South Side, *Black Metropolis: A Study of Negro Life in a Northern City* (1945), complied by anthropologist St. Clair Drake and sociologist Horace Cayton, with an introduction by Richard Wright; Theodore Ward's pro-Communist drama, *Big White Fog*, produced by the "Negro unit" of the Federal Theater Project in 1938; Arna Bontemps's historical novel about the Haitian Revolution, *Drums at Dusk* (1939), and his *They Seek a City* (1945), a documentary study about black migration in the United States, coauthored his WPA colleague, novelist and editor Jack Conroy; Willard Motley's novel of poverty, crime, and the immigrant experience, *Knock on Any Door* (1947), which became a motion picture starring Humphrey Bogart in 1949; and William Attaway's Great Migration novel, *Blood on the Forge* (1941), published after Attaway had moved to New York, but nonetheless shaped by his experiences as a writer, union organizer, and migrant in Chicago.

Like its writers, Chicago Renaissance visual artists emphasized an historical continuum of black experience and freedom struggle in the New World, depicting in myriad media black life in Bronzeville, as well as black labor, mythology, and cultural practices throughout the South and, more so than the writers, the Caribbean. Also, like Chicago Renaissance writers, the artists blended Afrocentric themes and aesthetics with Marxist perspectives and proletarian art styles. Notable work by visual artists of the period includes Archibald Motley, Jr.'s vibrant paintings of the South Side like "Nightlife" (1943) and "Bronzeville at Night" (1949); the African-inspired block print "Untitled-Metamorphosis" (1954) and linoleum cut portrait, "Bessie Smith" (1956) by Margaret Taylor Goss Burroughs; Marion Perkins's sculptures, "John Henry" (1943), "Ethiopia Awakening" (1948), and "Unknown Political Prisoner" (1953); the photography of Gordon Parks, which often starkly documented aspects of black life on Chicago's South Side; "Progress of the American Negro" (1939–40), "Frederick Douglass Lives Again (The Ghost of Frederick Douglass)" (1949), and "Woman Worker" by graphic artist Charles White; and "Southern Landscape (Southern Flood)" (1939–40), "In These Troubled Times" (1940), and "Peelin' Potatoes" (1945) by painter and sketch artist Eldzier Cortor.

Most of the poets, musicians, essayists, painters, social scientists, dramatists, journalists, editors, fiction writers, and cultural workers who generated this Renaissance were part of the Great Migration (1916–70) of African Americans from the largely rural South to the urban North. In part because of the campaigning of the black *Chicago Defender* newspaper and the number of industrial jobs the city offered once wartime immigration from Europe dwindled, at least 50,000 black Americans flocked to Chicago's South Side between 1916 and 1920, in search of jobs, the vote, education, and freedom from racial violence. By 1940, Chicago's black population had reached 278,000, and by 1960, over half a million more migrants arrived in the city's distinct "black metropolis." In short, Bronzeville was bustling with black-owned businesses, black educators, community-uplift institutions, a progressive black press that advocated racial pride, black politicians, a dynamic religious culture, black labor unions, a teeming nightlife, the nation's premier recording labels of the period's jazz and blues music, and a nationally prominent black publishing industry. Bronzeville had become a powerful symbol of the greater opportunity in the "Promised Land." Bordered by 22nd Street to the North, 63rd Street to the South, the Rock Island Railroad tacks and LaSalle Street to the West, and Cottage Grove Avenue to the East, Bronzeville's territory expanded little, despite its rapid population growth. This largely was due to the "race restrictive covenants" and anti-black violence surrounding the area, and resulted in tremendous housing shortages, high rents, elevated infant-mortality rates, and overcrowded schools.

Most of the literature, art, and cultural institutions produced during the Chicago Renaissance emerged from within Bronzeville's borders, and many writers engaged the transformative urbanization of black folk culture and life in response to mass migration and Northern segregation. In their quest to develop a modern black aesthetic, Renaissance writers and artists sought to represent the South Side's animated culture, but rarely did they overly romanticize this new kind of black life in urban America. A primary feature of Chicago Renaissance literature and visual art is its starkly realist portrayals of the poverty, racism, and exploitation shaping the lives of millions of black Americans, North and South. Renaissance writing also deals frankly with Bronzeville's intraracial class, cultural, gender, and political conflicts, challenging, and ultimately influencing, the dominant race politics and aesthetics of the black elite.

The art and writing of the Chicago Renaissance is an important part of black Chicago's organized mass protests and cultural responses to the Great Depression of the 1930s. The first organization of Chicago Renaissance writers – the South Side Writers' Group (SSWG) – grew directly out of black writers' participation in grassroots organizing along the city's "Negro People's Front," a far-reaching alliance of individuals and organizations committed to the labor movement, black freedom struggle, and racial "uplift" in the midst of the Depression. The Negro People's Front was understood to be part of an interracial, international "Popular Front," a constellation of activists and organizations formed in the 1930s to combat fascism and capitalist exploitation on economic, political, cultural "fronts." The Negro People's Front took its most broadly organized form in the National Negro Congress (NNC), first convened in Chicago in February 1935. There, young Communist Party member Richard

Wright had organized a panel entitled "The Role of the Negro Writer and Artist on the Social Stage," featuring himself, Harlem Renaissance writers Langston Hughes and recent Chicago transplant Arna Bontemps, and white Communist writer Morris Topchevsky. The session included a discussion about organizing Chicago's politicized black writers, and afterwards, Langston Hughes introduced a young Margaret Walker to Wright. This panel session led to the April 1936 formation of the SSWG, again organized and initially led by Wright.

The first known black writers' group of its kind, the SSWG met for about a year and a half, from 1936 to 1937. Consisting of approximately 20 aspiring black writers workshopping their works-in-progress with each other, the group was attempting to formulate a working theory of radical black writing and seeking to model themselves as the vanguard of a new literary movement. The SSWG included Margaret Walker, who worked for the Illinois Writers' Project, attended classes at the Workers' School, and led the SSWG after Wright left for Harlem in 1937. Other SSWG participants central to the Chicago Renaissance include poet, journalist, and early jazz critic Frank Marshall Davis, whose poetry collections largely disappeared from libraries and bookstores during the second anti-Communist "Red Scare"; playwright Theodore Ward, author of *Big White Fog* (1938), who migrated to Harlem in 1940 but returned to the South Side as a creative force of local Black Arts theater; Arna Bontemps, a former participant in the Harlem Renaissance whose historical novels about slave rebellions, *Black Thunder* (1936) and *Drums at Dusk* (1939), influenced younger SSWG members not only with his radical, realist treatments of black and proletarian history, but also with his concerns about the literary and social uses of black folk culture; Margaret Taylor Goss Burroughs, painter, teacher, activist, poet, public historian, and future founder of the Ebony Museum of Negro History and Art (now the DuSable Museum of African American History and still a cultural anchor of the black South Side); Marian Minus, literary critic and co-editor of *New Challenge* magazine; Fern Gayden, a social worker and future publisher of Chicago's *Negro Story* magazine (with educator Alice Browning); labor organizer and novelist William Attaway; poet and actor Bob Davis; elder Chicago poet, Fenton Johnson; Russell Marshall, Ed Bland and Alden Bland. While the group met at the Lincoln Center for only a year and a half, the writing, intellectual debates, and organizing of the participants determined the contours of the early Chicago Renaissance and continued to influence the literary production and activism of its writers for decades. Between 1936 and 1937, the SSWG functioned as the radical vanguard writers' group that shaped the early Chicago Renaissance. In the fall 1937 special issue of *New Challenge* magazine, Wright's "Blueprint for Negro Writing" declared the beginnings of a new black literary movement – a Chicago Renaissance – independent from the Harlem Renaissance.

Though it lasted for only the one issue and was published on the East Coast, *New Challenge* magazine was one of the two most important black little magazines of the Chicago Renaissance. The other crucial, and more successful, literary journal was *Negro Story* (1944–6), which was published in the South Side by Alice Browning and Fern Gayden and featured virtually every notable African American writer of the 1940s.

The publication of these magazines illustrates the influential vitality of black Chicago as a locus of black writing, institution building, and thought, and they reveal black women's centrality to leftist literary production and networking during the period. With the exception of Wright, all the editors of these magazines were women, and their publishing work did much to define the black leftist aesthetics of the period, and to address the social concerns and cultural interests of black women. The editorial policies of both publications placed an emphasis on realistic representations of everyday black life by black writers, but the politics of both journals were ultimately integrationist. In order to maintain editorial independence and divert the attentions of the American government, the editors officially declared their journals "nonpolitical." A majority of the literature published by both organs, however, offered explicit and implicit critiques of social struggle, racism, patriarchy, capitalism, and imperialism. Ultimately, both little magazines folded because of insufficient financial support, but together they document the literary trends, debates, and experiments at the heart of African American writing from the Depression to the end of World War Two.

New Challenge evolved from Dorothy West's Harlem-based *Challenge* magazine (1934–7). The new magazine featured a revised editorial policy – primarily authored by Wright – and showcased the movement-oriented poetry and prose of SSWG members Margaret Walker, Frank Marshall Davis, Bob Davis, and Marian Minus. With *Challenge*, West had desired to revitalize and politicize the flagging Harlem Renaissance, but the magazine met with sharp criticism from the SSWG for its lack of politically focused work. West insisted that this was due to the poor literary quality of magazine submissions dealing with black sociopolitical struggles, and she challenged the SSWG to do better. The result was *New Challenge*, which featured the poetry, theoretical work, editorial influence, and cultural criticism of the SSWG, including Wright's "Blueprint for Negro Writing," as well as pieces by Langston Hughes, Ralph Ellison, and Alain Locke. The evolution from *Challenge* to *New Challenge* documented key debates, continuities and shifts among key figures of the Harlem Renaissance and the mostly younger writers associated with the SSWG and early Chicago Renaissance. "Blueprint for Negro Writing" attempts to differentiate between the two movements:

> [T]he new role of the [black] writer is qualitatively different … [and] requires a greater discipline and consciousness than was necessary for the so-called Harlem school of expression … The Negro writers' new position demands a sharper definition of the status of his craft, and … [black writers] should seek through the medium of their craft to play as meaningful a role in the affairs of men as do other professionals. (63)

To achieve this, "Blueprint" insists that black writers should abandon Harlem Renaissance models of private white patronage. Wright further challenges black writers to fuse Marxist principles with black vernacular expression, but he warns against creating a "simple literary realism" that depicts black life as "devoid of wider social connotations … [or] the revolutionary significance of [black] nationalist tendencies." Such literary representations perform "a rank injustice to Negro people" and alienate "possible allies in the struggle for freedom" (59).

Between 1944 and 1946, *Negro Story* magazine very much modified and reworked the editorial policy of *New Challenge* by subverting the black radical literary politics outlined in "Blueprint," and by sharpening the focus on both black women's issues and American racism in the context of international politics. Edited by former SSWG member Fern Gayden and teacher Alice Browning, much of the fiction and poetry published in *Negro Story* offers radical critiques of racism, sexism, capitalism, and the war. First published in Browning's home with money borrowed from her husband, Browning sold *Negro Story* as a "product of Chicago," and in 1945, she insisted, "It looks as if Negro Chicago is trying to be the literary center of America. Look out New York!" ("Current Town Talk" 61; "Just to Mention That" 53–4). The little magazine first appeared on South Side newsstands in late spring 1944, and quickly developed a national circulation and began shipping to black military personnel abroad. In its nine issues, *Negro Story* published every significant black writer of the period, including Chicago Renaissance writers Wright, Brooks, Margaret Taylor Goss Burroughs, and Frank Marshall Davis, as well as Langston Hughes, Chester Himes, and Ralph Ellison. After three issues, Gayden left her position as editor to attend to her demanding duties as a social worker, and Browning continued as *Negro Story* editor. Responding to the government's attempts to subdue the black press's pointed criticism of American racism and participation in the war, and because of the rise in anti-Communism and anti-radicalism, *Negro Story*'s editorial policy claimed that, while primarily interested in publishing short fiction about contemporary black life, the journal was "non-political." The magazine primarily published short fiction, but featured some poetry as well. As editor, Browning maintained an emphasis on "plotless realism" – evocative of the documentary fiction of earlier radical proletarian writers – in selecting works that engage black feminist issues and perspectives, the experiences of black soldiers abroad, imperialism, and racial injustice at home.

Until the appearance of Robert Bone's 1986 essay, "Richard Wright and the Chicago Renaissance," most scholars of African American literature recognized only the Harlem Renaissance of the 1910s through the early 1930s and the Black Arts Movement of the 1960s and 1970s as the twentieth century's two periods of notable African American literary production. Bone's term, "Chicago Renaissance," explicitly suggests a black-centered literary movement comparable in scope and significance to the Harlem Renaissance. The Chicago Renaissance was in fact both a legacy of and response to the Harlem Renaissance. While literary scholars had failed to recognize the mid-century literary and cultural movement in Chicago, key figures of the Harlem Renaissance establishment did not. Not only did "Blueprint for Negro Writing" declare Chicago writers' independence from the Harlem school, prominent Harlem Renaissance participants like Alain Locke, Arna Bontemps, and Dorothy West publicly acknowledged Chicago as a new center of radical black literary influence in the 1930s and 1940s. In his *Negro Digest* essay about "Famous WPA Artists" (1950), for example, Bontemps insists that, "Chicago was definitely the center of the second phase of Negro literary awakening. Harlem got its renaissance in the middle 'twenties, centering around the *Opportunity* contests and the Fifth Avenue Award Dinners. Ten years later Chicago reenacted it on [the] WPA without finger bowls but with increased power" (46–7).

As Bontemps points out, Chicago Renaissance writers operated within very different economic contexts than had many Harlem-based African American writers in the Roaring Twenties, and these contexts markedly shaped the publishing politics, literary criticism, and artistic content of the two movements. The economic crises of the Great Depression not only diminished private white patronage for black arts that had been a hallmark of the Harlem Renaissance, but gave rise to the federal government's massive funding programs for the nation's writers and artists, called the Works Progress Administration's Federal Writers' Project, Federal Arts Project, and Federal Theater Project. The Illinois Federal Writers' Project in particular, overlapping with writers and artists organized along the left's "cultural front," extended the literary networks of black South Side writers far beyond those of the Harlem Renaissance. The Chicago Renaissance's expressed affinity with the Left is evident in its literature's emphasis on the black working-class and the poor. While important Harlem Renaissance writers like Hughes, McKay, and Zora Neale Hurston did focus on the black "masses," there was also an upper-class, "Talented Tenth" conservatism within the Harlem Renaissance – shaped by Alain Locke, W.E.B. Du Bois, and Jessie Redmon Fauset, among others – that informed much of the Harlem-based "New Negro" movement. Individual and organizational fellowships from the Julius Rosenwald Fund also helped liberate Chicago Renaissance writers from the restraints of private white patronage, and many movement participants themselves organized to secure financial support for black literary journals and community arts institutions independent from middle-class-oriented protest organizations like the National Association for the Advancement of Colored People or the Urban League, as well as from the WPA and the Communist Party.

The Harlem and Chicago Renaissances also share important, if sometimes overlooked, features. Like the writing of the Harlem movement, literature produced during the Chicago Renaissance focused heavily on racial themes, and elaborated upon elements of black folk and popular culture. While both movements were centered in the cities for which they were named, key contributors and institutions of both functioned outside Harlem and Chicago (such as in Washington, DC, and Detroit), and writers of both movements expressed various kinds of black radical and diasporic consciousness. This fact runs counter to the claims of Wright in "Blueprint for Negro Writing," and scholars should not regard Chicago as the earliest nexus of black Marxist literary influence. Arguably, the roots of a radical, folk-oriented, African American Marxist literary tradition originated not in the Chicago Renaissance but in the Harlem Renaissance, wherein the leftist artistic and political turns of African American writers predated those of their South Side-based contemporaries in the 1930s, 1940s, and 1950s. Wright's essay also fails to acknowledge the cultural and political activism of Harlem Renaissance writers like Hughes, McKay, and West, who, in the 1910s and 1920s, began to cultivate an "Afro-Marxist cosmopolitanism" that merged black aesthetic and cultural traditions with the Marxist perspective of proletarian art. The essay, finally, ignores the mentorship, literary models, publishing support, and networking that Harlem Renaissance "elders" like Hughes, West, Locke, and Bontemps provided to the mostly younger group of writers and artists that would lead the Chicago Renaissance.

Like Harlem Renaissance writers Hughes and McKay, SSWG writers understood black nationalism as a reality of segregated life, and they did not embrace it as the final solution to racism and poverty. Key SSWG members found themselves attracted to the Communist Party's explicitly anti-racist political and cultural platforms. Even more South Side writers were drawn to the Marxist theories of capitalism and class oppression, which offered a way to better understand – and therefore combat – the system of racism. Though Wright, Walker, Ward, and Frank Marshall Davis all joined and abandoned the Communist Party at different points of the 1930s and 1940s, such party membership alone does not accurately estimate the influence of the Communist Party on black cultural politics (and vice versa), the extent of black participation in the Popular Front, or the number of mid-century black writers that engaged black literary Marxism. Bontemps and Brooks, for example, never joined the Communist Party, yet their writings reflect party and Popular Front concerns with socially conscious representations of the black proletariat. As a group, the SSWG struggled to fuse Communist Party symbols and theories of revolution with signifiers, rhetoric, and idioms drawn from African American vernacular culture. As it critiqued the practicalities of achieving the party's interracial vision and international workers' revolution, the SSWG believed that, because of its emphasis on class as the basis for all oppression, Marxist theory and the Communist Party dealt inadequately with race and racism in American contexts. While the clarification in "Blueprint for Negro Writing" of the SSWG's criteria for a black Marxist literature did more than merely echo Communist Party dogma and aesthetic standards, Margaret Walker's *For My People* (1942) may be the group's most adroit embodiment of the "Afro-Marxist cosmopolitanism" outlined in Wright's essay.[1]

From the mid-1903s through the early 1950s, the black Chicago Renaissance may also be categorized as part of the third-wave of a larger Chicago Renaissance that included white writers like James T. Farrell, Nelson Algren, Jack Conroy, Studs Terkel, and Saul Bellow. Third-wave Chicago Renaissance writing grounded itself in, and responded to, the urban realism and naturalism already characteristic of so much Chicago writing. First- and second-wave Chicago Renaissance writers, such as Carl Sandburg, Theodore Dreiser, Sherwood Anderson, and Harriet Monroe, as well as important local institutions, such as the *Poetry* and *Story* magazines, influenced black and white third-wave writers. These earlier influences contributed to the third wave's convergence of realism, modernism, and proletarian literature to create socially relevant art of and for the working masses. Many third-wave writers helped comprise a strong and unusually integrated center of the literary Left associated with the Popular Front, WPA, Communist Party, and magazines like Jack Conroy's *New Anvil* and Browning's *Negro Story*. Such interracial cooperation shaped the integrationist politics and racial representations of both black and white renaissance writers, and their work contributed to interracial publishing ventures, grassroots cultural activism, and organizing, as well as longstanding literary friendships.

The relative absence of black Chicago Renaissance writers from accounts of the broader Chicago Literary Renaissance – with the occasional exceptions of Richard Wright and Gwendolyn Brooks – points to the traditional scholarly segregation of African American writing and figures from American literary and cultural history. This neglect also proves indicative of the characteristic scholarly exclusion of women, proletarian or "political" writing, and African American Communism from US literary, cultural, and social histories. The two most extensively studied writers of the Chicago Renaissance, Richard Wright (1908–60) and Gwendolyn Brooks (1917–2000), are not yet sufficiently understood as byproducts of their literary, cultural, and political milieu. In fact, scholars developed a "School of Wright" focused so heavily on Wright's work and politics that they have come to overshadow the diversity of black American writing from the 1930s through the 1950s. Wright is often understood as an isolated literary figure and one of the period's few black writers worthy of note, who was temporarily misguided by the Communist Party, and who was alienated from the black community. Understanding Wright as a member of the Chicago Renaissance complicates this narrative. In this period, Wright first developed his skills and commitment to black cultural activism, to grassroots organizing, and to a political literary aesthetic that shaped most of his writing career. Unlike Brooks, Wright neither grew up in Chicago nor remained there for much of the Renaissance, a fact that should not diminish his importance to the movement's emergence. Indeed, his experiences and literary networks in Chicago proved central to his development as one of the towering protest writers of the twentieth century.

One of the primary architects of its radical wing, Wright animated the literary experimentation, theorizing, publishing, and networking of the Chicago Renaissance. In Chicago, he not only began his writing career as a radical poet, he also completed his first novel, *Lawd, Today!*, wrote and workshopped "Blueprint for Negro Writing" and the short stories of his collection *Uncle Tom's Children*; he also collected much of his sociological research for his Great Migration study, *12 Million Black Voices*, written in consultation with a Bronzeville sociologist and the Parkway Community House director, Horace Cayton. He began experimenting with what would become his autobiography, *Black Boy* (1945), and he set *Native Son* (1940), the most acclaimed and widely read novel of his career, in the South Side. Wright recounted his relationship with and break from the Communist Party in Chicago in his essay, "I Tried to Be a Communist" (1944), as well as in the *American Hunger* portion of *Black Boy*, which publishers kept out of print until 1977. Wright's anti-Communist writings have colored scholarly understandings of his era's African American literary engagement with both Marxism and the Communist Party. After expatriating to Paris in 1946, Wright helped to extend the influence of Chicago Renaissance literature, publishing fiction, poetry, and sociological writing in the first issues of *Présence Africaine* (1947–present), the international quarterly of the Négritude movement, a largely Francophone diasporic movement that sought to generate an international anti-racist, anti-colonial black culture and political movement.[2]

A self-described "organic Chicagoan," Brooks remains the best-known poet of the Renaissance, and went on to be a vital elder and participant in the city's Black Arts Movement of the 1960s and 1970s. Encouraged by her mother to strive to become the "Lady Paul Laurence Dunbar," Brooks succeeded Carl Sandburg as Poet Laureate of Illinois in 1968. Her formal training as a poet included the early 1940s poetry workshops at the South Side Community Art Center (SSCAC), led by white socialite Inez Cunningham Stark. Brooks's affiliation with SSCAC brought her into critical contact with other black writers and visual artists of the renaissance. Her early collections of poetry, *A Street in Bronzeville* (1945) and the Pulitzer Prize-winning collection *Annie Allen* (1949), demonstrate the influence of these workshops, where Brooks engaged modernist poets such as e. e. cummings and began to cultivate her signature "Afro-modern" style that incorporated elements of "high" and "low" culture to treat black life and consciousness in the South Side. Brooks's Renaissance poetry and novel, *Maud Martha* (1953), consistently explore complex gender issues and black female consciousness – including black female labor, domestic abuse, sexual harassment, and intraracial discrimination – in ways not always comfortable or recognizable to her audience. For instance, reviewing her first manuscript for Harper and Row publishers, Wright declared the abortions discussed in her poem "the mother" as unfit subject matter for poetry. Other critics emphasized Brooks's "simplistic" renderings of "quaint" black life, meanwhile often missing her nuanced social and cultural critiques.

In the past two decades, a handful of literary critics have begun to dismantle prevailing notions of Brooks as a poet whose work can be divided into two major phases: the "apolitical" poetry of the Chicago Renaissance and her socially conscious Black Arts poetry, which had been transformed in terms of style and content by her black nationalist, political "conversion" inspired by young Black Arts Movement writers. Brooks herself discounted the disparagement of her early work as naïve and "apolitical," but she freely acknowledged a transformation in her poetic style during the Black Arts era in order to make her poetry and its messages more accessible to black audiences. She declared that never again would she write such difficult poetry as the kind that appears in *Annie Allen*. Still, important continuities exist between her Renaissance and Black Arts poetry, including her concern with the social and psychological conditions of life in the South Side, and her sharp critiques of racism, patriarchy, segregation, and consumer culture.

The relative absence of Fenton Johnson and Willard Motley from accounts of the Chicago Renaissance illuminates certain difficulties in defining literary movements. Johnson moved on the fringes of Chicago's literary circles during its Renaissance, in part because his poetry career began in the 1910s and ended in the 1930s, roughly the early years of the movement. His style was far more reflective of earlier imagistic poetry than it was of the democratic and vernacular styles of black poetry produced in 1930s and 1940s Chicago. Johnson did work for a period of time on the Illinois Federal Writers' Project (FWP). He produced a series of poems for the project, several essays on black education and history for the "Negro in Illinois" project; and, according to Bontemps, his literary executor, Johnson disappeared from the WPA without a word.

While Johnson complicates the chronology of the Renaissance, the fiction of Willard Motley further challenges its thematic and racial characterizations. Unlike his fellow writers, Motley emphasized the white immigrant experience in Chicago, and rarely dealt with African American characters. Drawing on his experiences in the interracial slums of Chicago in the 1930s and his work with the FWP, Motley began his first and best-known novel, *Knock on Any Door*, in 1940 and published it in 1947. The novel, made into a Columbia Picture film starring Humphrey Bogart in 1949, tells the sexually charged story of an Italian-American from Chicago's slums, following his transformation from an altar boy into an armed robber and killer. For some literary critics, the absence of black protagonists from Motley's work makes him a marginal writer of the Chicago Renaissance. For others, Motley's treatment of male sexuality and the homoerotic tension surrounding the novel's main character, Nick Romano, have deterred them. However, Motley did move in the same circles as other Chicago Renaissance figures, and his work challenges literary scholars to develop not only a more nuanced understanding of the period's literary treatments of male sexuality, but also, thematically and topically speaking, what constitutes "black" writing.

Johnson and Motley were just two of the Chicago Renaissance figures employed by the writing, art, and theater projects established by the Works Progress Administration (WPA), which provided work for thousands of artists during the Great Depression. Other Renaissance figures employed by the Illinois Federal Writers' Project (FWP), the "Negro unit" of the Federal Theater Project (FTP), and the local Federal Artists' Project (FAP) included Wright, Walker, Bontemps, and Ward, anthropologist and dancer Katherine Dunham, Shirley Graham (later Du Bois), young poet (and later novelist) Frank Yerby, and painters Archibald Motley, Jr. and Eldzier Cortor. Nationally, many of the WPA's arts projects advanced egalitarian politics and multiethnic aesthetics, and they sought to represent the daily lives and struggles of "ordinary" Americans. In shaping their art to represent "the people," WPA writers and artists believed their work could generate more labor-oriented and inclusive conceptions of American history, culture, and identity, while contributing to the development of a fully democratic national culture.

The FWP in Illinois proved to be one of the most successful of all the state writers' projects, and employed one of the highest numbers of black writers (nine). The FWP served as a major clearing-house for amassing information about African American life and culture in Chicago, and helped establish crucial local and national networks for South Side writers in the 1930s. Like most state writers' projects, the Illinois FWP collected vast materials for its state guidebook. The project also collected interviews and data about life in the Depression, African American history and migration, the black press, African American educational achievements, as well as black religious and popular cultures. Renaissance researchers and writers contributed to *The WPA Guide to Illinois: The Federal Writers' Project Guide to 1930s Illinois* (1939), as well as manuscripts related to the massive "The Negro in Illinois" project: "The Cavalcade of the American Negro: The Story of the Negro's Progress During Seventy-Five Years," "The Negro Press in Chicago," and "The Development of Negro Culture in Chicago." Additionally, the research and writing of the Cayton-Warner Project, underwritten with WPA funds, provided the primary data for Cayton and Drake's *Black Metropolis* (1945). After the FWP's dissolution, project supervisors Bontemps and Jack Conroy drew from unpublished project materials about black migration to collaborate on *They Seek a City* (1945), which appeared as a revised second edition, *Anyplace but Here*, in 1966. Recently, *African American Review* published Wright's "A Survey of Amusement Facilities of District # 35," and, reportedly, there are future plans to publish *The Negro in Illinois* and *The Negro Press in Chicago* in book form. The project's extensive research and writing about African American culture, struggles, history, and achievement remain a vital resource for researchers of black history and life.

While the WPA's Federal Arts Project and Negro unit of the Federal Theater Project employed fewer Chicago Renaissance figures, they too were important to the movement. In Chicago, both Archibald Motley, Jr. and Eldzier Cortor worked on the Federal Arts Project (FAP). The local Negro unit of the Federal Theater Project (FTP) employed Wright, Theodore Ward, and Shirley Graham (later Du Bois), as well as a number of black actors. Employed at the theater project, Wright left amidst conflicts with many of the project's actors over what constituted suitable black drama. In *American Hunger*, Wright explains that he suspected local members of the Communist Party, with whom he was in ideological conflict over his intellectual and artistic freedom, fueled the hostility he encountered there. Wright left the theater project, and joined the FWP.

In 1938, the FTP produced Ward's drama, *Big White Fog*, the most important and controversial play of the Chicago Renaissance. A pro-Communist drama about a black migrant family struggling to survive the Depression in Bronzeville, *Big White Fog* insists that interracial alliances of the Communist Party offered African Americans the only chance for achieving meaningful economic and social change. Concerned about the public's response to the play's pro-Communist agenda, FTP administrators assigned Shirley Graham to facilitate community dialogue about the play and gauge its reception within the African American community. Ultimately, the FTP staged the play at a theater in the Chicago Loop, but in the midst of a well-received run, project officials relocated *Fog* to a high school in the South Side ghetto, where the play closed in a matter of days. In October 1940, *Big White Fog* was the first play staged by the Harlem Playwrights' Company, which the newly relocated Ward and Wright formed with Langston Hughes and Paul Robeson.

The Cayton-Warner Project, which ran from 1936 to 1941, also supported the WPA's massive black research projects and the work of the SSWG, and even provided most of the data used in the landmark sociological study of the South Side, *Black Metropolis* (1945). Affiliated with the University of Chicago's School of Sociology, and influenced by the work of Robert E. Park, Bronzeville's black sociologists believed that social science could promote racial equality and social progress. *Black Metropolis*, in particular, focuses on a huge array of issues germane to black social life and culture, ranging from race leadership to black employment opportunities, from class conflicts to religious and secular life, from educational attainment and barriers to urban racial violence and the living conditions of the segregated South Side. Both the sociological theories and data provided by these scholars and researchers tremendously impacted the writings and social theories of Wright and the SSWG. Wright first encountered the Chicago School of Sociology through his family's social worker, and, in his written introduction to *Black Metropolis*, he acknowledged the Chicago School's influence on helping him to write about and interpret black life in America. Armed with the vast data collected by the Cayton-Warner Project and the University of Chicago, Wright and his literary peers sought to mold the hard sociological facts about life in the South Side into literature that illuminated the systems of black oppression and exploitation, while accurately representing African American social conditions and cultures.

Also growing out of the WPA was the South Side Community Art Center (SSCAC), a key South Side institution that linked the radical aesthetics and funding structures of the 1930s to black literary and artistic production of later renaissance years. Margaret Taylor Goss Burroughs, Frank Marshall Davis, and Ed Bland participated in both the SSWG and SSCAC, though chronologically the two organizations do not overlap. Established in 1939 on South Michigan Avenue, SSCAC initially derived part of its funding from the Federal Arts Project, but raised the bulk of its money from the local black community in order to pay for a building, utility bills, and art supplies – no small feat in difficult economic times. By 1943, all federal funds were withdrawn for the center. To this day, the local community's support of the SSCAC's development and survival indicates the import the South Side community placed upon artistic and self-expression, and providing access to instruction and exhibition space for black youth, artists, and writers. Early members included Margaret Taylor Goss Burroughs, Bernard Goss, Eldzier Cortor, Charles White, Archibald Motley, Jr., and William Carter; in addition to the FAP, early organizational supporters included the Urban League and the Arts Craft Guild, formerly the only organized group of black visual artists in Bronzeville in the 1930s.

As with the SSWG, many SSCAC artists were committed to achieving social relief and racial equality. Much of their work depicted black life in Bronzeville and engaged African ancestral and diasporic history, African American folk culture, and the sociopolitical movements of the day. In addition to the poetry workshops attended by Brooks, Goss Burroughs, and Davis, SSCAC offered courses in painting, photography, drawing, printmaking, sculpture, and crafts. The center also ran a Writers' Forum, which featured discussions with writers such as Brooks and Wright, and occasionally hosted the Nat "King" Cole trio on Saturday nights. SSCAC remained one of Chicago's few venues that exhibited African American visual artists, ranging from Goss Burroughs, Motley, Cortor, White, and Carter, to Henry Avery, Gordon Parks, Marion Perkins, and Joseph Kersey. SSCAC continues to operate as a vital creative community resource in the South Side today, and is the nation's only continual survivor of the more than 100 arts centers established through the WPA.

The vitality of the George Cleveland Hall Branch of the Chicago Public Library, also located on South Michigan Avenue, highlights the roles of intellectual community dialogues and research collection during the Chicago Renaissance. A Chicago native and the first African American to head up a public library in the city, head librarian Vivian Harsh developed the library into a central community institution. When the branch opened in 1932, the library quickly became a lively intellectual meeting place for Bronzeville's community activists, writers, and scholars. Aided by children's librarian Charlemae Hill Rollins, Harsh maintained an active programming agenda for the public, from its women's reading group to the lively Lecture Forum. Harsh also established a "Special Negro Collection," amassing books, periodicals, and other materials pertaining to African American history, life, and culture. The Lecture Forum hosted locally and nationally prominent writers and activists, including Horace Cayton, Gwendolyn Brooks, Langston Hughes, Richard Wright, Zora Neale Hurston, and Arna Bontemps. These forums helped writers respond to the period's calls for black literature intended for black audiences, and provided an exciting intellectual atmosphere and testing ground for developing a socially relevant black literature and community culture.

Harsh's Special Negro Collection is now the Vivian G. Harsh Research Collection of Afro-American History and Literature, and has been housed at the Carter G. Woodson Regional Library in Chicago since 1975. It is the oldest and most extensive collection of its kind in the Midwest, and its vast holdings contain highly valuable materials for researchers of the Chicago Renaissance, as well as of African American history, literature, and culture. The collection contains more than 70,000 books, over 5,000 microfilm reels, photographs, manuscript collections, and papers collections of many black Chicagoans. Holdings most pertinent to Chicago Renaissance study include 53 carefully indexed boxes of notes and drafts from the FWP's "Negro in Illinois" research project, including Kitty Chappelle's nearly-700-page manuscript, "Development of Negro Culture in Chicago," which describes and documents the production and performance of black literature, music, drama, film, dance, painting, and sculpture. Chappelle's manuscript also includes information about contemporary Renaissance writers Frank Marshall Davis, Fenton Johnson, Arna Bontemps, Robert Davis, and Katherine Dunham. The boxes also contain essay drafts, bibliographies, and notes produced for the project by Johnson, Bontemps, Wright, and Jack Conroy. Other notable Harsh collection holdings include manuscripts by Wright, Bontemps, and Langston Hughes, the Horace Cayton Papers, and the Alice Browning Collection.

With the exception of Brooks, Browning, and Goss Burroughs, most Chicago Renaissance writers and figures had left the city by 1950. But the movement's writers left their marks on Chicago's creative and activist black communities, and Chicago indelibly marks the century's African American writing and literary consciousness. Black writing and cultural activism in Chicago did much to define the artistic and political concerns of black writers of the period, and modeled modes of creative organizing, literary protest, publishing, and artistic innovation that shaped African American letters for decades to come. In particular, the literature and ideas of the Chicago Renaissance clearly anticipate and inform the Black Arts Movement of the 1960s and 1970s. Both Chicago's Renaissance and Black Arts writers perceived cultural production as an integral aspect of their freedom struggle, and they consistently engaged issues surrounding black migration and community formation, ghettoization, self-determination, and cultural independence.

Notes

1 Alan Wald first used the phrase "Afro-Marxist cosmopolitanism" to describe Claude McKay's attempts to unify Marxist perspective and politics with black vernacular and literary culture in his important study, *Exiles from a Future Time* (89).

2 In 1947, Senegalese intellectual Alioune Diop asked for Wright's support in launching what became the black cultural journal of the Négritude movement, *Présence Africaine*. Wright agreed to lend his name to the journal's list of sponsors, and he not only submitted his own story, "Bright and Morning Star," for publication, he also submitted Gwendolyn Brooks's poem, "Ballad of Pearl May Lee," and a sociological essay by Horace Cayton. All three appeared in the premiere issue of *Présence Africaine*. Their presence proves particularly important because of the limited number of English-speaking writers represented in the journal – Wright was the sole English-speaking and African American editorial sponsor – and also indicates that Wright understood the work of other Chicago Renaissance figures as valuable to Négritude's project of developing a diasporic, anti-racist, anti-colonial black culture. See Fabre, 193–5.

Bibliography

Bone, Robert. "Richard Wright and the Chicago Renaissance." *Callaloo: A Journal of African American and African Arts and Letters* 9.3 (1986): 446–68.

Bontemps, Arna. "Famous WPA Authors." *Negro Digest* (1950): 43–7.

Browning, Alice. "Current Town Talk." *Negro Story* 1 (1944–5): 61.

Browning, Alice. "Just to Mention That." *Negro Story* 2 (1945): 53–4.

Fabre, Michel. *The World of Richard Wright*. Jackson: University Press of Mississippi, 1985.

Langston Hughes Review 14.1–2 (1996), a Special Issue devoted to the Chicago Renaissance.

Mullen, Bill V. *Popular Fronts: Chicago and African-American Cultural Politics, 1935–46*. Urbana: University of Illinois Press, 1999.

Wald, Alan. *Exiles from a Future Time: The Forging of the Mid-Twentieth-Century Literary Left*. Chapel Hill: University of North Carolina Press, 2002.

Wright, Richard. "Blueprint for Negro Writing." *New Challenge* 2.2 (1937): 53–65.

19
Jazz and African American Literature

Keith D. Leonard

In fits and starts of creativity and political turmoil, African American writers and critics have used African American music in general and jazz in particular to create probably the most empowering sensibility of African American literature. It is a sensibility that Leroi Jones (now Amiri Baraka) characterizes well in all of its complexity and contradiction in his 1963 essay "The Myth of a Negro Literature." In it, Jones claims that "only in music, and most notably in blues, jazz, and spirituals, i.e., 'Negro Music,' has there been a significantly profound contribution [to American culture] by American Negroes." He goes on to say that "Negro music alone, because it drew its strengths and beauties out of the depth of the black man's soul, and because to a large extent its traditions could be carried on by the lowest classes of Negroes, has been able to survive the constant and willful dilutions of the black middle class." Offering a somewhat standard critique of bourgeois culture, Jones aptly identifies how the music was originally developed by untutored musicians and therefore came "out of the depth" of the soul rather than out of the Eurocentric artistic training that most African American writers had. He can thus allege, as many critics and artists have since, that "Negro music" is truer to a broader swath of African American emotional life and social interests than literature written in traditional styles. Thus, Jones captures what is now a central and sometimes troubling presumption in criticism: that black music reflects an identity that is pure, self-contained and poised in its authenticity against the diluted culture of the deluded black middle class. The music practically becomes blackness itself, as in Erskine Peters' claim that "black music *is* black history," so that only when it is similarly constituted from the soul could there be a genuine "Negro literature."

What makes this standard understanding of black music so empowering is that it celebrates how, despite racism and the temptation to assimilate completely, the African American artist has the tools and capacity to articulate black identity on its own terms. Ever since Langston Hughes initiated the consistent use of "Negro music" as a referent and model for literary style and form in the 1920s, the music has provided the terms for the best answer to the question that all African American artists confront: "how can the black subject posit a full and sufficient self in a language in which blackness is a sign of absence?" As Henry Louis Gates, Jr. implies in this framing of the issue, the English language and its literary conventions have imbedded in them a symbolic system in which "black" (as an abstract color) represents qualities of negation, absence and evil that get associated with "black" people, against which "white" (also as an abstraction) becomes value, presence and good, qualities which are then associated with "white" people. Worse, "white" culture also functions as a transparent norm rather than the imposed symbolic system that it is, making the judgments of such "white" people as literary critics seem objective rather than interested. Artists understandably found themselves potentially reinforcing this symbolic system by mastering European ("white") artistic conventions to earn the praise of putatively objective white critics. By contrast, the jazz musician and, later, the jazz writer adopted this new musical idiom predicated on African rhythms, ethnically specific practices of improvisation, black folk language, local urban themes, and the lives of ordinary black people as self-validating substitutes for the Eurocentric literary language, forms, subjects, and themes by which literary value has been determined. As Hughes's innovations were adapted and complicated by artists after World War Two, a new and ethnically distinctive tradition of literary expression did indeed emerge, as Jones suggests, one that, though sometimes politically discordant, was keyed to the cultural norms and distinctive perspectives of African American people.

However, since Jones's standard conception of music implies that music is blackness and that other forms of expression are not, it actually neglects probably the most powerful implication of the jazz idiom: its hybridity, namely, its complex ability to combine and remake different and sometimes competing cultural materials into ever-evolving improvisational assertions of black presence. In other words, it is a messy mixture of blackness, not the purity Jones and so many other writers prize, that allows the music to create a language through which a full and sufficient black self can be posited. If hybridity consists of the dynamics by which imperial and colonized cultures confront, blend with, and change one another, as Homi K. Bhabha has persuasively argued, then jazz's strength is in the fact that its rhythmic terms are rooted in African dissident cultures while parts of its harmonic and instrumental principles are rooted in imperial European culture. Through this combination, the music gave credence to the possibility that inherited Eurocentric literary language could be made to articulate a "black man's soul." For example, John Coltrane's remake of "My Favorite Things" from the film *The Sound of Music* into a black saxophone solo song, and Duke Ellington's use of European symphonic structures for some of his swing music both anticipate and inspire the effects such jazz writers as Hughes and Ralph Ellison achieve by similarly evoking and revising the literary techniques of European writers. Add to this hybrid blend the notion that improvisation could mean that each playing of a song could be different, and one gets the implication that, in jazz, black subjectivity – the social meaning of black consciousness as it is shaped and expressed by culture – consists of processes of becoming and expression.

Thus, the best way to understand jazz in African American literature is not to celebrate purity but to trace this improvisational and hybrid self-creation as it produced the distinctive literary forms that, as Jones declares, remade existing "white" cultural systems into an ever-changing, black cultural self, fully "sufficient," Gates might say, because it is no longer beholden to a language that presumes its absence.

Instead of proclaiming that more old-fashioned African American literature was a false myth, in other words, readers of jazz in African American literature must recognize that the remarkable distinctiveness the music inspired derived from the jazz artist's different, more assertive sense of ownership over inherited European culture. Not at all untrue to blackness, the earliest African American literary writers, both enslaved and recently freed, also understood literary value to inhere in "the black man's soul," so to speak, but they felt with great justification that the mastery (not the revision) of European traditions was the means to prove the existence of that soul. Educated to see the validity of European thought, these writers sought to inhabit that culture instead of remake it. They confronted René Descartes's Enlightenment premise of "I think, therefore I am," which a bevy of Western thinkers, from Georg William Friedrich Hegel to Thomas Jefferson, used as an ideal of rational selfhood to justify slavery and racism. For example, Jefferson argued in Query XIV of his *Notes on the State of Virginia* that "[slaves'] existence appears to participate more of sensation than reflection. To this must be ascribed their disposition to sleep when abstracted from their diversions, and unemployed in labour. An animal whose body is at rest, and who does not reflect, must be disposed to sleep" (146). Thus, though "[t]hey astonish you with strokes of the most sublime oratory; such as prove their reason and sentiment strong, their imagination glowing and elevated," Jefferson claims, "[b]ut never yet could I find that a black had uttered a thought above the level of plain narration" (146). In other words, self-contradictory as Jefferson's claim may be, without grand literature as written evidence of the capacity for reflection beyond "plain narration," African Americans could not, despite their "sublime oratory," prove they existed (or were a "presence") on the social scale of the human. The black soul needed to be a ready-made conjunction of rationality (such as the capacity to reason, reflect, and write) and sentiment (the ability to feel the noblest emotions and sympathies), a conjunction that could be best expressed through the formal language and rigorous conventional design that predominated literature throughout the eighteenth and nineteenth centuries. Black folk culture such as oratory was oddly the powerful exception that proved the rule of black incapacity for white observers such as Jefferson. Hence, the conventional autobiographies and bourgeois domestic fiction of African American writers were written in standard literary English and highlighted the rational interiority and self-narration of bourgeois African Americans. Critics like Jones have read this approach as a capitulation to an imperial cultural authority, and one certainly can make such critiques persuasive, but such writings were also instrumental in bringing about the abolition of slavery and the assertion of a kind of restrained, conventional black soul.

In these terms, the new idiom of jazz represented not the absolute break from a false or non-existent black literature that Jones and others since have made it out to be, but rather an adaptation of Enlightenment rational self-narration to the tradition of polyrhythmic communal expression and the improvisational modes of survival of the African and African American cultural traditions. Recognizing the limits of turning absence into presence within the existing symbolic system, in other words, African American writers embraced the "astonishing" oratory, if you will, of the black cultural tradition to confront the opportunities that modernity – the cultural upheavals in the West caused by capitalism, Darwinism, and military war, among other things – provided to remake Eurocentric cultural and social norms. The jazz age for African American literature began, in other words, because, in the 1920s during the famous Harlem Renaissance, African American writers, critics, visual artists, and musicians saw themselves as "New Negroes" who could liberate themselves through the modernist fractures in European cultural hegemony. They were demonstrating, as scholar and cultural critic Alain Locke put it in 1925, that the "vital inner grip of prejudice has been broken" as black people confronted the world "with renewed self-respect and self-dependence." For Locke, the great migration of hundreds of thousands of African Americans from the rural South to the urban North, the increased education and economic self-sufficiency of that mass, the growing fulfillment of democratic ideals in the United States, and the shrinking of European world empires, all indicated a modernity constituted by a great "race-welding" derived from an emergent "common consciousness," rather than a racial community derived merely from a common problem. While a large number of Harlem Renaissance writers continued to master so-called bourgeois artistic culture, critics like Locke, Jessie Redmon Fauset, W.E.B. Du Bois, and James Weldon Johnson identified and praised African American folk culture as the juxtaposition, renewal, and assertion of disparate cultural materials in the African American imagination.

The roots of Africanist practices of self-making in the New World enabled "Negro music" to challenge the models of rational individualism, formalized self-narration and transparent "white" culture that rendered Africans subhuman. Like its folk cultural predecessors – including the spirituals, work songs, ragtime, and the blues – jazz emerged in part from the unlettered folk. It gained from ragtime and the blues its syncopated rhythms, polyphonic ensemble playing, varying degrees of improvisation, often deliberate deviations of pitch, and the use of original timbres, all of which can be traced to certain West African musical forms and sensibilities. Indeed, jazz and the blues constitute a continuum, arguably deriving their formal functions and attitudes from an oft-cited historical moment in New Orleans: an 1819 ritual of West African drumming and dancing in a place called Congo Square. Characterized by numerous eyewitness accounts, this weekly slave dance ritual featured Africans playing percussion and stringed instruments identical to West African ones as well as a circular dance accompanied by a diverse harmony of ethnic songs, the ancestor of the African American spiritual practice called the "ring shout." This weekly event allegedly initiated the syncretism of African spirit practices, rhythmic sensibility and communal ritual with American individualism, European harmonics and Western instrumentation, along with a dose of what we would now call Latin American cultural elements contributed by migrant workers from the colonial Spanish Americas. The music was thus a central component of a fractured, attenuated, but nonetheless substantial community of ethnically distinctive colonized people. The music was also keyed to an emotionally sustaining practice through which these people endured their condition of servitude by expressing their rage and lament to sympathetic ears. A loud and open emotional defiance, this musical ritual corresponds aptly to the communal function of expression and affirmation which jazz and the blues eventually came to represent. Jazz literature particularly expanded on this communal function, justifying Stephen Henderson's claim that the music and the literature based on it are "saturated" with "black experiential energy."

Though few African American jazz writers knew the history of Congo Square, they nonetheless understood the model of open emotional defiance. They knew that a hybrid, multifaceted, improvised communal expressive practice and ritual affirmation can narrate black subjectivity as a flexible, self-created, and diversified improvisation. Both jazz and blues singers and writers could enact the existential self-assertion and communal validation of Congo Square, an impulse that Ralph Ellison describes as "finger[ing] the jagged grain" of a pained consciousness "to transcend [that pain], not by the consolation of philosophy but by squeezing from it a near-tragic, near-comic lyricism. As a form, the blues is an autobiographical chronicle of personal catastrophe expressed lyrically" (78–9). The jazz or blues musician can tell an individual story so that the music can confront and manage (not necessarily heal) the pain. And since the chronicle is to and for a community, it enacts what Houston Baker, Jr. has called a "blues matrix," the emotional and imaginative constructs through which "the blues … comprise a mediational site where familiar antinomies are resolved (or dissolved) in the office of adequate cultural understanding" (6). In these terms, the individual autobiographical chronicle of the blues, like the dances at Congo Square, mediated the anxieties and sadness of the participants. The chronicle also supported an understanding of not only the oppressive conditions responsible for that emotional experience, but also the importance of unifying and motivating others to archive the same mode of expressive self-narration. Contained within that self-narration is a multifaceted, multiethnic history appropriate for a multifaceted, multiethnic black self.

The ethos of existential emotional defiance of both racist psychology and material deprivation has generally been more directly attributed to a sensibility characteristic of the blues by critics who use music to theorize African American literature. Many writers, especially in the 1960s, however, found jazz, with its greater formal complexity and subtly affirmative ethos, to be more empowering than the blues. Conceptually, as novelist Gayl Jones suggests, jazz texts (both musical and literary) tend to be more complex than blues texts in terms of harmonies and rhythms, vocabulary and syntax, and in terms of a faster tempo, even as the jazz texts "shared with a blues text a sense of extemporaneity in its fluid rhythmical design and syncopated understructure, its sound and meaning systems, its rejection of duality" (200). Moreover, whereas blues saw lyricism as its primary thrust – a fingering of pain through expression, as Ellison would put it – jazz added to that momentary salve of expression the possibility of both personal and social transformation.

The raucous history of jazz includes several components: namely, ragtime, a piano-driven New Orleans musical form that, in Scott Joplin's hands, aggressively incorporated European elements. It also consists of the orchestral elements that contributed to the wild popularity of the swing bands of the 1920s and 1930s that would so powerfully inform Hughes's early jazz poetry. And, especially with swing, jazz tended to offer virtuosic piano playing at high speeds or horn stops when between 12 and 25 musicians sought constantly to make something new. Moreover, since swing was dance music, and since the cultural venues for these bands and their audiences accommodated illegal alcohol alongside the sexual commercialism of speakeasies, jazz involves joy, however tempered. (Note that this ethos evolves across musical history, from initial public joy to an expression of private angst and personal affirmation – an evolution that readers of jazz literature too often neglect or underestimate.) The formal complexity and improvisational multiplicity of the music thus contribute to the innovation, self-assertive sensibility, and distinction of African American literature.

Jazz was thus the alternative to the angst of the best-known European and (white) American modernist poets who confronted the modernity of the 1920s and 1930s by seeking to buttress edifices of culture they saw as crumbling. By contrast, African American jazz musicians and, eventually, jazz writers were riffing on these fractured cultural assumptions to create a new and messily empowering blackness. When Hughes originated the translation of jazz music and sensibility to literature, for example, he rooted his sense of its formal and thematic possibilities in his own experience of how the multiplicity and hybridity of blackness can validate his defiance of oppressive social norms. In his oft-cited 1926 essay, "The Negro Artist and the Racial Mountain," Hughes declared that jazz "is one of the inherent expressions of Negro life in America: the eternal tom-tom beating in the Negro soul – the tom-tom of revolt against weariness in a white world, a world of subway trains, and work, work, work; the tom-tom of joy and laughter, and pain swallowed in a smile" (694). Anticipating, via scholars such as Jones, Henderson, and Tony Bolden, that jazz was a kind of black essence, Hughes used the music to celebrate what he called, paradoxically enough, the "racial individuality" of the "low-down folks," as if there were an absolute communal cultural oneness of the folk, as opposed to the diluted individualism and deadening work ethic of a white majority – one from which a "black" individuality nonetheless emerged. And that individuality rejected the "white" Protestant work ethic, which, in conjunction with the angst of performing one's identity in front of empowered white Americans, created a weariness which this inherent music rewrote into a momentary and yet enduring vitality.

At the same time, though, in his 1940 autobiography, *The Big Sea*, Hughes declares early on: "You see, unfortunately, I am not black." He does so, of course, partly to confound the racists and the one-drop rule with the multiracial nature of his family history. But he also wants to acknowledge that the kinship he expected to find on his trip to Africa was likewise confounded when his light skin and Western ways pegged him to Africans as more American than African, thus contradicting his own racial essentialism. Moreover, though his one semester at Columbia University afforded him the opportunity to see jazz in Harlem, Hughes also had at least as significant an experience of jazz in Paris during his stay there in 1924. Also, throughout *The Big Sea*, Hughes chronicles his constant attendance at plays of all sorts in the United States and in Europe, his appreciation of the symphony and of European sculpture about which he learned from a tour of Italian museums with Locke, a cultural snob. Even Hughes's mobility, his rejecting his father's capitalist drive, and his jumping ship in Europe all bespeak a modern condition of possibility and alienation, of shifting social hierarchies and new cultural combinations. However inherent jazz may have seemed to "low-down" Negro life and soul for Hughes, in other words, he also implicitly and explicitly acknowledged and embraced non-black and upper-crust cultural elements in his conception of the music, literary artistry, and black subjectivity, making blackness an innovative, evolving modernist concept.

Thus, Hughes's early jazz verse exemplifies the ways in which jazz poets have always revised poetic form to assert a new, hybrid black subjectivity. In his first two volumes – *The Weary Blues* (1925) and *Fine Clothes to the Jew* (1926) – Hughes used refrains, adaptation of slang, phrases from French, traditional ballad stanzas, and innovative non-traditional stanza forms and imagery to enact the "a near-tragic, near-comic lyricism" of the blues and the improvisation of jazz. In jazz poems like "Jazzonia," for example, Hughes invites us to enter a new age and place in which the music was associated with rebellious sexuality. The poem remakes the image of the oversexed, primitive African American falsely conceived by bored and wealthy white bohemians into an empowering ideal of licentious, self-asserted freedom. In the poem, "In a Harlem cabaret, / Six long-headed jazzers play" for "a dancing girl" in a gold dress "whose eyes are bold." This moment of jazz joy, this emotional (rather than geographical) place that the title "Jazzonia" suggests, marks one historical endpoint in a long line of independence through sexual self-assertion:

Were Eve's eyes
In the first garden
Just a bit too bold?
Was Cleopatra gorgeous
in a gown of gold?

In a version of biblical typology, Hughes suggests that his contemporary dancing girl was as seductive as history's most infamous temptresses, attributing to all three women the agency to express sexuality. Moreover, each is associated with the black folk culture of the jazz cabaret (folks whom Jones would later and famously call "blues people"), making Cleopatra and Eve into racial ancestors of this bold new black jazz Eve. A version of carpe diem, this adaptation of jazz validated the possible richness of the individual life of pleasure within and against the heavy constraints of racism and poverty. Also, structurally, Hughes's poem has a refrain that validates this powerful joy. It starts with "Oh, silver tree! / Oh shining rivers of the soul!" and, like a good improvised melody, changes as it repeats: "Oh, singing tree! / Oh, shining rivers of the soul!" and then "Oh, shining tree! / Oh silver rivers of the soul." Repetition with a difference: this technique is a prime way to represent jazz improvisation in verse and, in this case, enhances the figurative implications of value, insight, beauty, and optimism associated with the adjectives "shining" and "silver." "Jazzonia" is a place of freedom from "work work work" indeed!

As is clear from celebrating a dancing girl as a historical temptress, jazz's remaking of social and cultural norms was fraught with complication. Poet Countee Cullen suggested that Hughes's jazz poems were not really poems at all. And W.E.B. Du Bois famously suggested that Claude McKay's 1928 novel, *Home to Harlem*, which depicted one of its characters in sexual exploits at jazz cabarets, made Du Bois claim, in a review of the novel, that he wanted to take a bath. Moreover, the music itself in the Roaring Twenties was potentially having its dissident edge co-opted by the aptly named Paul Whiteman and Benny Goodman, among others, white bandleaders who made the music popular and mainstream, fixing it as a saleable object. And the poets confronted this potential erasure, as in Hughes's poem "Harlem Night Club," celebrating the momentary space in which "White girls' eyes / Call black boys" and where "dark brown girls" are "in blond men's arms." Its hints of cynicism about the motivations of the white people "slumming" in Harlem reach a crescendo:

> Tomorrow … is darkness
> Joy today.

Carpe diem in blues-inflected jazz does not necessarily, as Ellison once asserted, provide consolation of philosophy or any kind of transcendence, since this version is about avoidance of pain rather than confrontation. And it is this avoidance that motivates blues poet Sterling Brown to write his one jazz poem, "Cabaret": as "rich, flashy, puffy-faced / Hebrew and Anglo-Saxon" "overlords" look on, "The jazz band unleashes its fury / *Now, now, / To it, Roger, that's a nice doggie, / Show your tricks to the gentleman*." The language of this passage evokes claims from Enlightenment thinkers like Jefferson that poets of African descent were like dogs who could do neat "tricks," a word also evoking clients of prostitution. In short, Brown's poem identifies how swing-era jazz and blues found popularity potentially at the expense of its innovative cultural self-affirmation.

Thus, as Helene Johnson, a magazine poet of the Harlem Renaissance, acknowledges in her poem "Song," exploiting eyes can potentially compromise the spirit of the music. On one hand, the speaker asserts that "I love" "your flashing hands" and "your shoulders jerking the jig-wa / And I love your teeth flashing," since the dancing means "I'm glad I'm a jig." Knowing that both the boy in the poem and the poet herself are being watched, Johnson draws on stereotypes – the flashing teeth, the term "jig" – in order to identify the joy and affirmation by which the dance is produced by someone who genuinely understands that such expression is not merely escapism or entertainment but self-validating self-narration. Nonetheless, the affirmation must constantly be asserted:

> Say, I think you're wonderful. You're
> All right with me,
> You are.

As historian Nathan Huggins would have suggested, the repeated affirmation betrays the doubt, as the jazz poem evokes and embodies the complex relation between the black subject and the oppressive culture, the ways in which this assertion of complex talent, when mixed with commodity and voyeurism, potentially transforms it into merely a marketable dog-and-pony show.

Here is why students of jazz in African American literature need to pay closer attention to the historical evolution of the music: the aggressive artistry of bebop rejected these compromises that sometimes marred popular swing music and gave an even greater number of African American writers a model for self-assertion that could resist commercial and racist exploitation. By the late 1930s, jazz musicians had tired of both the swing sound and the accommodationism it implied, including the fact that artists like Duke Ellington played at the segregated, whites-only Cotton Club, while artists like Louis Armstrong mugged for the cameras. Such perceived compromises of artistic and racial integrity, coupled with the post-Depression economic malaise, motivated bebop soloists, who were often also leaders of small bands, to step forward and shift the emphasis of the music from the audience to the artist, from carpe-diem dancing to the creativity and personal self-assertion of the honored, angst-ridden soloist. Bebop pioneer Miles Davis infamously turned his back to the audience, a gesture that at the time may have been innocent, but has since come to exemplify the defiance of the bebop era. Their more rapid, un-danceable songs and their conception of the music as "high art" led to a more aggressive engagement with hybridity as well as a more sardonic or even satiric relationship with Eurocentric culture. Reworkings of "white" music include Charlie Parker's use of Mendelssohn's "Wedding March" and Thelonious Monk's atonal, unmelodic piano-playing of a great swing standard like "It Don't Mean a Thing." Monk explicitly refused his audience by refusing to be recorded. In this way, bebop musicians may have justified Ellison's claim that the jazz combo constituted the grandest metaphor of democracy, as each member of the combo earned his or her solo in conversation with other solos and with the shared melody and harmony of the framing song. Instead of pleasure-seeking audiences and commodifying television spots, bebop required musically knowledgeable audiences that would be willing to seek the more difficult pleasure of attention to intricate music and existential self-reflection, practices somewhat more difficult to commodify.

Understandably, then, bebop led to some of the most formally innovative and politically rebellious verse in the African American jazz poetry tradition. In 1951 and

1961, respectively, Hughes published his two most challenging poems, *Montage of a Dream Deferred* and *Ask Your Mama*. Both poems explore the social and cultural consequences of "deferred" (or prevented) dreams, while *Ask Your Mama*, in particular, incorporates music of the African diaspora – the spread of African peoples and cultures from the sub-Sahara around the world – as part of its rebellious response. Section 7 of *Ask Your Mama*, entitled hybridly, "Gospel Cha-Cha," uses diasporic musical forms to suggest racial unity and power. It opens "IN THE QUARTER OF THE NEGROES / WHERE PALMS AND COCONUTS / CHA-CHA LIKE CASTANETS / IN THE WIND'S FRENETIC FISTS" and "ERZULIE PLAYS A TUNE / ON THE BONGO OF THE MOON" while "IN THE QUARTER OF THE NEGROES / MAMA MAMACITA PAPA PAPAMIENTO / DAMBALLA WEDO OGOUN AND THE HORSE / THAT LUGGED THE FIRST WHITE / TOURIST …" With its all-caps, its accusation of white exploitation and its affirmation of black cultural multiplicity (even as this multiplicity is used for entertainment), the poem takes its refusal of accommodation seriously, appropriating the folk culture practice of the dozens to insult any reader who questions its anti-swing mode. Telling the reader to ask his or her mama is declaring a circle of understanding that need not accommodate to the un-hip voyeur and that declares the speaker of the poem can lay claim to knowing (in every sense of that word) the mother of the ignorant. By taking such an attitude, the music – and the poem that celebrates it – can find in itself, despite its compromises, a kind of salvation: "WHEN I GOT TO CALVARY / UP THERE ON THAT HILL / ALREADY THERE WAS THREE – / AND ONE, YES, ONE / WAS BLACK LIKE ME./ *CHA-CHA . . . CHA-CHA / CHA. . .*" Reviewers were disappointed that Hughes had shifted to such a challenging approach to poetics. Apparently they did not ask the right person.

Such open defiance and such anti-commercial mining of African diasporic cultures anticipated and fulfilled the revolutionary ideals of the Black Arts Movement of the 1960s and 1970s. The movement rejected whatever could be called "white," from bourgeois individualism to Standard English syntax, from commercialism to other, more conservative black people. The result was a revocation of the dominant symbolic system that implied and validated in response the hermetic, pure blackness that Jones prizes. Michael Harper's magnificent "Brother John," from his volume *Dear John Dear Coltrane*, is a great example:

Miles, blue haze,
Miles high, another bird,
More Miles, mute,
Mute Miles, clean.
Bug-eyed, unspeakable,
Miles, sweet Mute,
Sweat Miles, black Miles;
I'm a black man;
I'm black; I am;
I'm a black man –

In the first seven lines of this stanza, there is no complete sentence, and not even a verb, unless we count "Sweat Miles" as a command rather than a description. Nonetheless, the poem's form transforms this list of Miles Davis's positive attributes into an explanation, with the help of an associative syntax, of his status as a fully sufficient black man. This poem's repetition with revision is meant to *sound* like a solo, not a speaking voice, with its repeated assonance, consonance, and alliteration being as significant as its syntax, and its five stanzas each celebrating a different musician evocative of a combo in democratic musical conversation. Though the stanza about Miles Davis is the best in this poem, Harper participates in the broad homage to Coltrane in African American verse in another stanza, a practice of homage so consistent that scholars Meta DuEwa Jones and Elizabeth Alexander saw fit to discuss the "Coltrane poem" as if it were a genre. All of the poems about Coltrane in the 1950s and 1960s share with this poem the idea in this poem's only consistent sentence: "I am."

In other words, the assertion of "I am" becomes more important than the external pleasure of gratification. The inward existential turn that Ellison discussed becomes the means by which musical and poetic pleasure avoids exploitation and validates a complex, hybrid self, even if that dual process means drawing boundaries. In the 1960s, Sonia Sanchez was among those poets who wrote poems or reviews suggesting that the existential ethos of the blues belonged to conservative, fearful, anti-revolutionary "negroes," while jazz more actively articulated the ideals of revolutionary "Blacks." Thus, on the printed page, the orthographic or visual reproduction of a jazz sound was meant to assert a distinctively black scream of rage, pain and "I am," as in Sanchez's "a / coltrane / poem":

> a/love/supreme, alovesupreme a lovesupreme.
> A LOVE SUPREME
> scrEEEccCHHHHH screeeeEEECHHHHHHHH.

While honoring Coltrane and trying to sound like him, Sanchez creates wonderful visual effects, as Meta Jones points out, as in the use of backslashes to signify both the pause of sentences and their unification into one long word, the lower and upper case words suggesting pitches of sound. Even though Sanchez probably meant to subordinate her poem to the music, as critics have usually done because of music's allegedly superior roots in blackness, the poem asserts itself most fully as a poem. What matters is what we "see" on the page, as a stimulus for what we "hear," especially since the first person at the beginning of the poem ("my favorite things / is u blowen / you/favorite things") first evokes the poetic speaker, *not* the musician. Since its visual layout matters, the poem is as much an assertion of its author's creativity as a musician's. Such orthographic practices belonged to a generation of such neglected poets as Russell Atkins, Ted Joans, Leroi Jones, and Bob Kaufman, who go even farther at times toward what might be called visual jazz. As the 2006 anthology, *Every Goodbye Ain't Gone,* shows by collecting the innovative work of these and other experimental black jazz poets, bebop opens up the possibilities of jazz poetry visually to offer the fullest empowerment of jazz sensibility.

Despite the 1960s poets' homage to what they saw as the pure blackness of jazz, then, their experiments in visual poetics and multifaceted self-narration actually made jazz's hybridity all the more apparent. Jazz broke boundaries between sound and logos as it riffed on making the individual voice the container of black history. In fact, this fractured, hybrid model for portraying the interrelation of individuality and African American history motivated the adaptations of the earliest jazz novelists. In her 1975 novel, *Corregidora*, Gayl Jones was one of the first authors to create jazz-inspired narrative form and she did so by foregrounding female sexuality rather than the traditional male self-assertion that dominated bebop. In previous examples, Ellison claimed that the episodic structure of his 1952 novel, *Invisible Man*, was influenced by jazz, because he listened to the music while he wrote the novel and he certainly improvises on his sources, ranging from phenomenologist thinkers to the greatest American novelists. And James Baldwin's 1957 short story, "Sonny's Blues," offers as eloquent a description of a bebop jazz combo's motivations and effect as is available in the literature, though within a fairly standard narrative arc. But Gayl Jones – in her version of the stream-of-consciousness narration pioneered by James Joyce, William Faulkner, and Virginia Woolf – was the first to structure her novel in ways that more accurately imitated both the formal patterning and anti-patterning of jazz and its ethos of existential self-narration. Using the perspective of the main character, Ursa, italicized passages narrate the historical memory that Ursa's mother and grandmother deemed as Ursa's life's purpose to articulate. That history was one of sexual exploitation, as the slave owner Corregidora was both Ursa's grandfather and her father, but this collective self-narration actually extended rather than resolved oppression. As she distinguishes herself – like any jazz soloist – from a heritage that she first had to make her own, Ursa finds sexual pleasure possible and the book becomes her tortured, affirming song. And she does so by accepting her foremothers' voices and the undeniable voice of the Portuguese slaveholder, accepting it all into herself so she could feel and sing again.

In fact, for contemporary African American novelists, this sympathetic acceptance of a material and discursive past enlivens the existential ethos of jazz to provide African American culture's answer to the nihilism associated with the standard epistemological stance of postmodern fiction. For example, John Edgar Wideman embraces the epistemology (or the philosophy of knowledge) of postmodernism – namely, that all knowledge is a narrative, an idea that detaches what we know from any absolute truth. In light of Jacques Derrida's deconstruction of philosophical truth and Michel Foucault's reminder that the writing of history is the practice of interpretive memory, not objective archiving, knowledge comprises stories told with greater or lesser social authority. Anglo-American postmodern poets like Charles Bernstein and novelists like Thomas Pynchon write in part to reflect this loss of possible meaning. They resort to the infinite play of words and characters that debunks all conventions of literary meaning and pleasure, and thereby implies that nothing can be known or at least that believing in knowledge is naïve and politically retrograde. But Wideman and Toni Morrison, to mention another author, use the communal ethos of jazz to counter this erasure of meaning. In Morrison's *Jazz* (1992), for example, the narrator experiences this insight as her gossipy understanding of her neighbor's love life soon confronts a history she does not know and motivations she cannot grasp. As she at first passes judgment based on a presumed absolute morality, she comes to see Joe Trace's affair with Dorcas *and* his relationship with his wife as a truer love than she had originally imagined. As the novel's structure of recursive, circular storytelling reflects the competing voices of history and memory, it validates, in postmodern fashion, the limits of one person's knowledge. Yet, the novel ends not in emotional disarray but in openness: "If I were able I'd say it. Say make me, remake me. You are free to do it and I am free to let you because look, look. Look where your hands are. Now" (229). By touching the book, the reader has both the freedom to make meaning and the connection to the material object of the book, with its interpretive archive and creation of identification with its characters, to authorize that meaning-making in ways that are respectful of difference, uncertainty and feeling. The freedom from false absolutes is also the freedom to sympathize and to make oneself through that sympathy.

In his celebrated 1998 novel *Sent for You Yesterday*, Wideman similarly evokes the sympathetic cacophony of Congo Square to imagine how one man's story incorporates not only different perspectives, but the stories of an entire community. Wideman entrusts his narrator, Doot (to the extent that there is a single narrator), to learn his personal story by hearing the stories of his father, mother, and neighbors, all of whose voices are interwoven. As the narratives of three generations of Pittsburgh's Homewood Avenue community slide seamlessly into one another, Doot acquires the belated knowledge of his family so he that he can come to know himself as a culmination and extension of that story. By the end of the novel, Doot, as an adult, is dancing simultaneously and figuratively with his child persona. Two narratives of Doot (whose name is, of course, a scat sound) meet and validate one another.

Instead of demonstrating the ironic play derived from the sense that signifier and signified (word and reference) have no natural connection, Wideman, like Morrison, also portrays an epistemology of shared historical knowledge and sympathetic imaginative projection that is an "autobiographical chronicle," which, to borrow again from Houston Baker, Jr., provides "a mediational site where familiar antinomies are resolved (or dissolved) in the office of adequate cultural understanding." A character named Lucy Tate, for example, leaves Doot and Carl, who were at first primary narrators, and takes over the narrative of the death of a child named Junebug. She starts by saying, "You had to be Samantha to understand" (127), and goes on to narrate her visits to Samantha in the asylum to hear Sam tell her dream where she inhabits the perspective of her dead child Junebug. Thus, at one point in the story, Lucy is projecting herself into the mind of Junebug's mother Samantha, who, in turn, imagines herself in Junebug's mind and describes the experience this way: "When I think *mama Sam's inside* [the house], she is inside. She's not me. In the dream there's no Samantha unless Junebug sees her or thinks about her. Then she's not me because I'm inside

Junebug's white skin." Knowing anything definitively is not possible and, because of that, paradoxically enough, knowing another person is possible because nothing (no artificial epistemological boundary) between self and other prevents one from being "inside" another through the dream of imaginative projection. Being free to "remake me" is not absolute freedom but it is a charge to be sympathetically inside, as each becomes part of one another, a call-and-response multiplicity that jazz most fully embodies. In this sense, there is love to believe in. The emotional defiance of Congo Square has come a long way.

By the late twentieth century, then, the conceptual and aesthetic breadth of jazz in literature has expanded to include anything from repeated refrains to stream-of-consciousness narration, from elegies and odes to jazz musicians to postmodern epistemological speculation, a breadth that is clearly the form's greatest possibility and greatest problem. On the one hand, as contemporary poet Yusef Komunyakaa put it, jazz poems "need not have an overt jazz theme as such," but need only "embrace the whole improvisational spirit of jazz" (Gotera 222). This improvisational spirit, associated with the "depth of the soul" of black musicians, means that Komunyakaa's own syllabic verses (poems organized by patterns of syllables rather than by meter or repetition or defined form) can function as jazz poems, whether they are about a Vietnam veteran's confrontation with the Vietnam War Memorial in Washington, DC in "Facing It," or about a validation of the healing power of the music in the face of loneliness and alienation in "February in Sydney":

> A loneliness
> lingers like a silver needle
> under my black skin,
> as I try top feel how it is
> to scream for help through a horn.

Jazz form is even open to satire and parody, as in Kevin Young's poem about shoes that did not arrive in the mail, or in Harryette Mullen's playfully serious critique of the objectification of women within blues music at the expense of their own self-narration:

> Sapphire's lyre styles
> plucked eyebrows
> bow lips and legs
> whose lives are lonely too. (*Muse & Drudge* 1)

Evoking Sapphire, the stereotype of a self-assured black woman with a bad attitude and a wicked tongue, Mullen plays with sound (internal rhyme, assonance and consonance) and free association (bow as what is tied on gifts and bow as a gesture of subordination) to suggest how an objectified black woman translates her attitude to cosmetics, reinforcing the loneliness that comes from refusing to be entirely subordinate. Here again is the infinite postmodern play evoked by jazz improvisation and the possibility of one's self-narration being commodified offered here with wit, sensitivity and an elaborated fierceness. All of this is jazz.

If indeed so, readers must avoid the exclusions of Leroi Jones and the inclusions of Komunyakaa in order to see more precisely the multifaceted continuity of sensibility and technique that definitively distinguishes the African American literary artist's practices in the jazz tradition. One need not draw such absolute boundaries that render jazz literature a pasture needed to be defended falsely from the wolves of innovation, as "Myth of a Negro Literature" does. But one should avoid the possible excess implied when Baker suggests that blues is the defining ethos and ideological function of all African American literature, or when Bolden suggests that though the spirituals preceded the blues in chronological time, that musical form was actually the blues in a preceding iteration. One should recognize three key lessons of the music, though: first, blackness is a hybrid mix always changing, always being made in confrontation and conjunction with oppressive European cultural norms; second, jazz as a form and ethos prizes the improvisational assertion of "I am" as a model evocation of "we are" on behalf of marginalized people; and, third, the ultimate epistemology of jazz focuses on a sympathetic assertion of self as a simultaneous imaginative projection inside an other to "remake" one another in a freedom bounded by the love of the sound. It pushes us to let go of entrenched binary notions of race politics – us versus them, black versus white – to a more complex ideal. Moreover, instead of erasing cultural differences in ways peculiar to the Enlightenment or postmodernism, jazz multiplies difference, ironically, to find its greater unity. No wonder it is one of the most empowering sensibilities in African American literature. Following the logic of the music and its powerful history in African American literature, we can all be like Wideman's narrator in *Sent for You Yesterday*: "I'm on my feet and Lucy says, *Go boy* and Carl says, *Get it on, Doot*. Everybody joining in now. All the voices. I'm reaching for them and letting them go. Lucy waves. I'm on my feet. Learning to stand, to walk, learning to dance" (208).

Bibliography

Alexander, Elizabeth. *The Black Interior*. St. Paul: Greywolf Press, 2004.

Anderson, T.J., III. *Notes to Make the Sound Come Right: Four Innovators of Jazz Poetry*. Fayetteville: University of Arkansas Press, 2003.

Baker, Houston, Jr. *Blues, Ideology and Afro-American Literature: A Vernacular Theory*. Chicago: University of Chicago Press, 1984.

Bhabha, Homi K. *The Location of Culture*. New York: Routledge, 1994.

Bolden, Tony. *Afro-Blue: Improvisations in African American Poetry and Culture*. Chicago: University of Illinois Press, 2004.

Gates, Henry Louis, Jr. *The Signifying Monkey: A Theory of African American Literary Criticism*. New York: Oxford University Press, 1988.

Gotera, Vicente. "'Lines of Tempered Steel': An Interview with Yusef Komunyakaa." *Callaloo* 13.2 (1990): 215–29.

Grandt, Jurgen E. *Kinds of Blue: The Jazz Aesthetic in African American Narrative*. Columbus: Ohio University Press, 2005.

Harper, Michael. *Dear John, Dear Coltrane*. Pittsburgh: University of Pittsburgh Press, 1970.

Henderson, Stephen. *Understanding the New Black Poetry: Black Speech and Black Music as Poetic References*. New York: William Morrow & Co., 1973.

Huggins, Nathan Irvin. *Harlem Renaissance*. New York: Oxford University Press, 1973.

Hughes, Langston. *Ask Your Mama: 12 Moods for Jazz*. New York: Knopf, 1961.

Hughes, Langston. *The Collected Poems of Langston Hughes*. Ed. Arnold Rampersad. New York: Vintage, 1995.

Hughes, Langston. "The Negro Artist and the Racial Mountain," *The Nation* 122 (1926): 692–4.

Jefferson, Thomas. *Notes on the State of Virginia*. Boston: Lilly and Wait, 1832.

Johnson, Helene. "Poem." Reprinted in *This Waiting for Love: Helene Johnson, Poet of the Harlem Renaissance*. Ed. Verner D. Mitchell. Amherst: University of Massachusetts Press. 38–9.

Jones, Leroi. *Home: Social Essays*. New York: William Morrow & Co., 1966.

Jones, Meta DuEwa. "Jazz Prosodies: Orality and Textuality." *Callaloo* 25.1 (2002): 66–91.

Komunyakaa, Yusef. "February in Sidney." *Neon Vernacular*. Hanover, NH: Wesleyan University Press, 1993. 178.

Morrison, Toni. *Jazz*. New York: Vintage International, 2004.

Mullen, Harryette. *Muse & Drudge*. Philadelphia: Singing Horse, 1995.

Nielsen, Aldon. *Black Chant: Languages of African American Postmodernism*. New York: Cambridge University Press, 1997.

Sanchez, Sonia. "a/coltrane/poem." *The Jazz Poetry Anthology*. Ed. Sascha Feinstein and Yusef Komunyakaa. Bloomington: Indiana University Press, 1991. 183–5.

Wideman, John Edgar. *Sent for You Yesterday*. Boston, MA: Houghton Mifflin, 1997.

20
The Black Arts Movement

James Edward Smethurst

There are a few basic questions that one inevitably asks about any cultural movement. What was it? When did begin? When did it end? What was its effect in both the short term and the long term? These questions are often quite vexed and closely tied together. Sometimes what is perceived as the basic stance or aesthetic of a successful movement lives on as a critical or even popular concept long after the supposed end of the movement, as in the cases, for example, of Romanticism and Surrealism. Sometimes artists refuse to accept what others see as the passing of the movement and continue to declare their adherence for decades. Again, artists still proclaim themselves members of a Surrealist movement three-quarters of a century after what is usually seen as the movement's heyday. Similarly, once a movement flourishes, there is also a tendency to read backward, to include earlier artists seen as kindred spirits even if they would not have understood themselves as Symbolists, Dadaists, members of the New Negro Renaissance, Beats, and so on.

All these vexations attend any attempt to understand the Black Arts Movement (BAM) of the 1960s and 1970s and its legacies. One of the major legacies of BAM and the political movement to which it was inextricably bound, Black Power, is that they have deeply inflected how African American literature, art, culture, politics, and identity have been understood, both inside and outside the African American community. One can see this clearly in the writings of the 44th President of the United States, Barack Obama, and in the political rhetoric surrounding his election campaign. In *Dreams from My Father* (1995), Obama describes his relationship with the radical black poet and journalist Frank Marshall Davis in Honolulu. Judging from Obama's account, it would be too much to call Davis a mentor, but Davis did provide the young Obama a living example of a serious black writer and intellectual. For the purposes of this essay, what is interesting about this account is the way Obama reads Davis through Black Arts and Black Power, describing Davis's "old Black Power, dashiki self" "living in the same sixties time warp" (96) as his mother. He does not portray Davis in the context of the leftwing black milieu of the 1930s and 1940s in which Davis came of age as an artist and an activist, even though Obama acknowledges that earlier milieu, calling Davis a contemporary of Langston Hughes and Richard Wright. Davis himself might have promoted such a recasting of his radicalism through his afro hairstyle, choice of clothing, and so on. The point is that Obama, perhaps encouraged by Davis, while coming of age after the apogee of the Black Power and Black Arts movements, could not but help read backward through those movements, just as he would read forward in his 2008 speech "A More Perfect Union," which describes his former pastor Jeremiah Wright as being basically imprisoned in the political imperatives of the 1960s. Of course, this speech was a response not only to the fragments of Wright's sermons circulated in the media and the internet (and repeated by the Clinton campaign to a certain extent), but also to the more general claims that Obama was a "black nationalist" and a "Marxist." Even assertions that he was a "Muslim" almost as frequently linked him to Malcolm X as to Osama Bin Laden. In other words, there was a persistent attempt to cast Obama in terms of the popular images of Black Arts and Black Power.

Of course, despite consciously distancing himself from "the sixties," in part for tactical reasons, Obama in many respects drew on the style of Black Arts and Black Power. While, at various times, he struck poses that were Rooseveltian, Kennedyesque, and Lincolnesque, his slogans, "Yes, We Can" and "We Are the Ones We've Been Waiting For," resonated with the black "we" of Black Arts and Black Power – as heard, for example, in Curtis Mayfield's 1967 soul classic, "We're a Winner," a song that many BAM activists saw as a popular anthem of black liberation and self-determination. While many have cited organizational acuity and mastery of new modes of communication in Obama's campaign as keys to his success, fewer commentators have noted the campaign's astute mixture of popular culture and politics, from the video "Yes, We Can," created by the Black Eyed Peas' will.i.am and Jesse Dylan, to Obama's own dismissal of attacks by the Clintons and their supporters by imitating Jay-Z's brushing off gesture in the video of the rapper's "Dirt Off Your Shoulder." While presidential campaigns have long employed popular songs and popular culture references, it is hard to think of any previous campaign in which such songs and references made any deep impression on the public memory. In fact, more often than not, candidates and office-holders attempted to define themselves against popular culture, especially black (or black-inflected) popular culture – as in Bill Clinton's famous (or infamous) encounter with rapper Sister Souljah. Obama's gestural quote of Jay-Z is practically unique in this regard. This sort of melding of visionary rhetoric, politics, and popular culture was standard operating procedure in much BAM artistic production.

That this sort of approach was successful also speaks to the way BAM has helped change the reception of art generally in the United States. The idea, now widely accepted, that popular culture can be artistically "serious" and socially engaged owes much to the success of BAM. This appeal beyond the African American community may seem somewhat ironic or counterintuitive. After all, though BAM contained many different and often conflicting tendencies, there was a widespread agreement that African Americans were an oppressed people or nationality with the right – or the obligation, really – to determine their own destiny outside of the polity of the United States as it was then constituted. Though there was some disagreement about how essentially "African" African Americans might be, there was a general consensus that their condition, psychology, culture, and political future had more in common with the peoples, independence struggles, and new nations of Africa, Asia, and Latin America than they did with the "mainstream" of North America and Europe. While, again, there was considerable debate about what African American culture was and should be, and even more dispute about the principles or deep structures underlying that culture, virtually all the participants in BAM and the BPM concurred that culture and the arts were essentially tools – or, perhaps more aptly, a crucial terrain – in the struggle for black liberation and self-determination.

One has to be careful not to simplify this relationship between art and politics in BAM. One could pose it in terms of the usual art and culture in the service of politics with that formulation's inevitable suggestion of vulgarization and ideological philistinism – at least in the United States. However, one could just as easily turn the formulation around and say it was politics in the service of culture and the arts. This is not to suggest, as is still too often asserted, that BAM and Black Power were all about symbolic politics rather than practical action. After all, BAM and Black Power activists played essential roles in the election of black officials (including the mayors of major US cities), the establishment and administration of important cultural institutions (many of which still exist today), the opening of historically white colleges and universities to large numbers of black students, the formation and governance of Black Studies programs and departments in the academy, and the great expansion of opportunities for people of color in many professions, to name but a few efforts with enormous practical consequences. Put another way, these activists saw the arts as practical, where the symbolic is intimately tied up with the political nitty gritty. The BAM commonplace that a defining characteristic of African and African American art is that it is "functional" revolves around this sense of art as part of the everyday life of the masses of black people rather than simply cordoned off in a museum or a theater, though BAM was certainly not opposed to museums and theaters as such. While the notion of functionality is vague in many respects, it basically prioritizes a process involving the community of artist and audience over the fetishization of product.

One thing that bound Black Arts and Black Power together was that their ideas and even organizational work moved through shared institutional spaces. On a very basic level, for example, frequently activists who were also artists would travel to various cities to participate in some political event or activity and would also find the time to do some cultural work (e.g., a poetry reading, the staging of a play, and so on). Conversely, artists who were also activists would come to cities and campuses for readings, performances, gallery openings, or arts festivals, but would also attend meetings, rallies, and planning sessions that were more strictly political in nature. Of course, very often, the cultural and political activity converged, as seen at the founding convention of an important Black Power political group, the Congress of African

People (CAP), in 1970. There the program chairman and chief organizer of the convention, Amiri Baraka, ended his main speech with a bravura performance of his poem, "It's Nation Time."

The core of BAM was made up of younger black artists, intellectuals, and activists, like Baraka, Larry Neal (who coined the term "Black Arts Movement"), Sonia Sanchez, Jayne Cortez, Haki Madhubuti, Nikki Giovanni, Edward Spriggs, Ed Bullins, Askia Touré, Ron Milner, and Woodie King, who were guided by a sort of do-it-yourself ethic that did not wait for the benediction of higher authorities, founding such journals as *Soulbook*, *Black Dialogue*, and *Journal of Black Poetry* – institutions that were concerned much more with promoting communication among mostly unknown young artists and activists than with seeking to publish established writers. At the same time, somewhat contradictorily, they were guided by an imperative toward charting out a black tradition, a sense of black political, social, and cultural ancestry. They were stirred by the anti-colonial revolutions of what became widely known as the Third World, especially after the 1955 Asian African Conference in Bandung, Indonesia. They were deeply affected by the Civil Rights Movement and were energized by the black student movement that erupted in sit-ins all across the South during 1960 and coalesced into the Student Non-Violent Coordinating Committee (SNCC). They were moved by the charismatic young leader of the Nation of Islam in Harlem, Malcolm X, who they felt spoke publicly and cogently to black anger, pride, and aspirations, and to white racism and hypocrisy in ways that others did only in private. And many were profoundly inspired by African American avant-garde or "free" jazz musicians, in the first place John Coltrane, who, following a trajectory from Charlie Parker, Thelonious Monk, and bebop, demonstrated a vanguard black art was not only possible, but in fact the most exciting art being created in the United States, if not the world.

This core of younger black radicals was joined to one degree or another by older black artists and intellectuals. Like Frank Marshall Davis, this group had been part of the black Left circles of the 1930s, 1940s, and 1950s. Some of these older radicals – such as Langston Hughes, the poet Margaret Walker, the novelist John O. Killens, the poet Sterling Brown, the visual artist Elizabeth Catlett, the activist and editor Esther Cooper Jackson, the editor Daniel Watts, the playwright Alice Childress, and the poet and visual artist Margaret Burroughs – provided crucial support for BAM, encouraging and promoting younger artists and activists when they thought those younger artists needed promotion and support and criticizing and educating as they thought necessary. For many of the older radicals who started or molded such institutions as the journals *Freedomways* and *Liberator* and the Ebony Museum (later the DuSable Museum) in Chicago, they saw the new black radicalism as a chance to renew their earlier commitments to social transformation and black liberation that had been ruptured by the Cold War in a mode that had a greater chance of success. At the same time much of their critique and education recalled that there was a long history of militant black struggle and radical black art in the United States. While the older radicals often stood a bit apart from BAM, their institutions helped nurture the new movement and they consciously encouraged the younger artists to emulate their institution-building ways. It was Margaret Burroughs, who, along with her husband Charles Burroughs, founded the Ebony Museum, and who first encouraged key Chicago BAM figure Haki Madhubuti (Don Lee) to publish his own poetry.

Other older artists and intellectuals, such as Dudley Randall, Hoyt Fuller, and Gwendolyn Brooks, identified themselves much more closely with the new movement. They not only served as presiding spirits of BAM, but, like others in their age cohort, built or reshaped much of the institutional infrastructure that supported the growth of BAM. Randall founded Detroit's Broadside Press in 1965. Broadside became the premier BAM press, publishing dozens of titles of poetry and poetry criticism and issuing hundreds of thousands of volumes between its first decade. Fuller edited *Negro Digest* (later *Black World*) for Johnson Publishing Company (the publisher of the popular magazines *Jet* and *Ebony*). He transformed the journal from a black version of *Reader's Digest* into a radical African American political and cultural journal with a circulation in the several tens of thousands. *Negro Digest/Black World* was a vehicle for BAM literature and visual art as well as the widest ranging chronicler of the movement as it spread across the United States in the middle and late 1960s. Fuller, sociologist Abdul Akalimat (Gerald McWhorter), and poet Conrad Kent Rivers founded the Organization for Black American Culture (OBAC), which anchored BAM in Chicago, especially in literature and the visual arts, during the 1960s and 1970s. Brooks's poetry workshop, along with OBAC's writers' workshop, was crucial in the development of such major BAM poets as Madhubuti, Johari Amini (Jewel Lattimore), and Carolyn Rodgers. Brooks's decision in the late 1960s to move from a "mainstream" publisher to a black-run press (Broadside) set a powerful example for other African American writers.

As noted earlier, determining the beginning date of movements is always a somewhat arbitrary business. In the early 1960s, black radicals and avant-garde artists established a flurry of new groups and institutions across the country. *Freedomways*, *Liberator*, the Umbra Poets Workshop (and its journal *Umbra*), and On Guard for Freedom emerged in New York; *Negro Digest*, the Ebony Museum, and the Association for the Advancement of Creative Musicians in Chicago; the Afro Folkloric Troupe in San Francisco; Arts Associates, the Watts Writers' Workshop, and the Watts Repertory Company in Los Angeles; the Muntu Group in Philadelphia; and the Free Southern Theater in Mississippi (later New Orleans). All these groups and institutions saw themselves as inspired by a political and cultural upsurge in the United States and around the world in the Civil Rights/Bandung/Malcolm X/Coltrane era. However, they did not see themselves as constituting a coherent movement – though some called for and envisioned such a movement.

The closest thing to a BAM declaration of independence took place with the founding of the Harlem-based Black Arts Repertory Theater and School (BARTS) in 1965. BARTS was the product of a union between black artists who had been living in downtown Manhattan, including Baraka, Neal, the poet Askia Touré (Rolland Snellings), and others already uptown in Harlem, such as Sanchez. The event that spurred

Baraka and many of the others was the murder of Malcolm X in 1965. BARTS was in many respects intended as the fulfillment of the call of Malcolm and the Organization of Afro-American Unity (OAU) for a black cultural center in Harlem. Perhaps more importantly, its founders wanted BARTS to inspire a nationwide radical black cultural movement. Significantly funded by federal anti-poverty money through the local community agency called Harlem Youth Opportunities Unlimited – Associated Community Teams (HARYOU–ACT), BARTS sponsored classes in the arts; held lectures on art, politics, philosophy, and history; and presented performances of poetry, music, and plays, often on the back of a flatbed truck in the streets of Harlem. The political leanings of the key participants varied widely, from Marxists to often anti-Communist nationalists to more traditional liberals. However, all supported black self-determination, community empowerment, and the development of black-run and black-oriented political and cultural institutions.

From the beginning, BARTS was plagued by extreme disagreements and personal conflicts, not to say dysfunctional and even pathological personalities. As a result of these conflicts, BARTS soon dissolved in threats and actual acts of violence that saw the departure of many of the group's most vibrant (and sane) members – including Baraka, Sanchez, and Touré – and the shooting of Neal. However, due in large part to the dynamic poetry and plays and charismatic personality of Baraka, as well as to the essays by Neal, Touré, Baraka, and others, especially in *Liberator* where Neal was Arts Editor, BARTS inspired the creation of new groups and institutions whose initiators did see themselves as part of a broader movement. This new sense of a national movement was demonstrated by the increasing circulation of the term "Black Arts" in the names of the new groups and institutions, as in Black Arts West in San Francisco, Black Arts West in Seattle, BLKARTSOUTH in New Orleans, and the 1966 and 1967 Black Arts conventions in Detroit. By the late 1960s, virtually every city and campus with an appreciable number of African Americans had some sort of theater, arts workshop or school, journal, newspaper, study group, music space, poetry reading series, bookstore, museum, and/or gallery linked to one degree or another in a burgeoning radical black nationalist network.

Again, as in the Black Power Movement (BPM), the ideologies and aesthetics of BAM were varied and not always mutually compatible – at least in theory. Some, especially those most influenced by the cultural nationalism of Maulana Karenga and his US organization, were deeply skeptical of popular culture, even black popular culture, and proposed a neo-African counterculture based on what they saw as traditional, pre-colonial African culture – as that of the jazz avant-garde, especially Coltrane. Others, such as Neal, Baraka, Sanchez, Touré, and poet Jayne Cortez, while deeply invested in both Africa and the new jazz, engaged far more with popular culture – including music, dance, film, and television – seeking to create an art that was simultaneously popular and vanguard. For the latter group, popular musicians like James Brown and Curtis Mayfield became models for BAM poets, especially the musician's ability to connect with audiences and articulate the deep emotions of blacks on a visceral level. "Listen to James Brown scream," Neal wrote in his essay, "And

Shine Swam On": "Ask yourself, then: Have you ever heard a Negro poet sing like that?" (Neal 20–1).

In practice, all the variations of these strains intersected. For example, Baraka for a considerable time was closely tied to Maulana Karenga and his neo-African Kawaida philosophy. Nonetheless, Baraka never agreed with Karenga on the character of black popular music, especially the blues, which Karenga considered reactionary and defeatist. Baraka's work continued to engage virtually every form of popular culture imaginable. In his poetry, the struggle often seems as much a contest between popular culture figures, say, film stars Ruby Dee and Elizabeth Taylor, as between more traditionally conceived political actors. At the same time, it was hard to find a black artist who was not influenced by some sort of countercultural vision of traditional African culture.

One thing that characterized BAM literature (and art generally), to the degree that generic distinctions are possible to make, was a new emphasis on performance, which often blended different artistic genres and media. At many BAM events it would often be hard to determine exactly what the audience was seeing and hearing in terms of the traditional understanding of the arts. When members of Chicago's OBAC Visual Arts Workshop created the renowned mural, *The Wall of Respect*, in 1967, they included the text of Baraka's poem "SOS," photographs, as well as more traditionally painted portraits of black political and cultural figures. As they worked on the mural, poets, actors, and musicians frequently performed. The site of the mural became a favorite spot for political and arts events on the South Side. In other words, not only did the mural combine media and genres, but frequently the spectators of the mural saw it in an even more dramatically mixed media context. The creation, content, and framing set a pattern for the BAM mural movement that spread to cities, towns, and campuses across the United States. Similarly, at a "concert" of Sun Ra and His Arkestra, one would hear a wide range of black musical styles as well as chanting and poetry and watch dancers and the movements of the band members whose appearance was simultaneously ancient and futuristic. Was this music, poetry, dance, or theater? Likewise, Baraka and Cortez often performed their poetry with a band. When Baraka performed a poem like "It's Nation Time" with a band and making wild James Brown-style vocalizations, was it poetry, music, or a political address? Even when declaiming without accompaniment, Baraka, Sanchez, Amus Mor, and Haki Madhubuti would interpolate songs, saxophone riffs, shouts, and moans, as well as drum on whatever was handy in order to merge poetry and music.

Even on the page, BAM poets gave a sense of this mixing of media and genre, especially an engagement with jazz and black popular music, as well as oral performance. BAM writers like Baraka, Sanchez, Askia Touré, and David Henderson also played with typography, lineation, space, and punctuation to approximate the form and feeling of R&B, soul, and the new jazz. This approach to textual arrangement was particularly evident in the many tributary poems to John Coltrane, such as Madhubuti's "Don't Cry Scream" and Sanchez's "a / coltrane / poem." Such strategies also serve as reminders of the continuing importance of texts in BAM despite its valuing of performance (with its intimate and immediate relationship between artist and audience) and performative ethic. After all, such journals as *Black World*, *Liberator*, *Black Dialogue*, *Soulbook*, and *The Journal of Black Poetry*, and such black-run publishers as Third World Press, Lotus Press, Jihad Productions, Journal of Black Poetry Press, and Broadside Press provided the main avenues of communication between the domestic and international outposts of the far-flung movement. This is not to underestimate the effect that a visit from Sanchez, Cortez, Baraka, Madhubuti, Nikki Giovanni, or the BLKARTSOUTH performance collective might have on a particular locale. The effects of such visits were often profoundly inspirational. Nonetheless, on a day-to-day basis, texts were the vital tool that gave BAM and its audience a sense of national (and even international) coherence.

Oddly enough, one of the great strengths (and long-term legacies) of BAM might also be seen as ultimately contributing to its demise. In large part due to the eruption of urban uprising in the black communities of cities, large and small, across the United States, large amounts of money and other material resources were made available to radical black artists and cultural institutions through anti-poverty programs funded by federal and local government as well as by private foundations. For example, the 1964 Harlem uprising spurred the movement of federal dollars to HARYOU–ACT, which in turn helped support the work of BARTS. The founding and growth of the Watts Writers Workshop in the aftermath of the Los Angeles uprising of 1965 owed much to direct and indirect public and private aid. The passage of the Comprehensive Employment and Training Act (CETA), essentially a public employment program akin to the WPA in the New Deal, by Congress in 1973 provided a means through which BAM institutions could hire and pay staff. Federal agencies like the National Endowment for the Humanities (NEH) and the National Endowment for the Arts (NEA) – especially the NEA's Expansion Arts Program, which was directed by poet and critic A.B. Spellman, a BAM activist in New York, Atlanta, and Washington, DC – provided important support to BAM and the creation of a public arts sphere.

The success of BAM in gaining financial and other sorts of material support from various levels of government and private foundations and agencies also contributed to its long-term decline. The use of tax dollars to support radical black art became something of a rallying point for the political Right in the United States. When the Reagan administration essentially abolished CETA in the early 1980s, the ability of many black arts centers, theaters, galleries, publications, and so on, to continue was severely challenged. Cutbacks at the NEH and NEA, along with increasing pressure at those agencies to curtail the support of socially engaged art (or at least nationalist and political Left, socially engaged art), either forced many groups and institutions to disappear or separated them from their BAM roots. Perhaps as important, or even more important, than direct coercion from increasingly conservative federal funding agencies were the more indirect efforts of federal agencies (and federal and state legislators) to lean on regional, state, and local arts agencies and programs, which in turn felt compelled to try to push black arts institutions and groups toward more depoliticized art.

Of course, not all the problems of BAM derived from these outside pressures. Like BPM, BAM was, on a national level and in many locales, wracked by disputes between Marxists, anti-Marxist nationalists, and others who were essentially liberal Democrats. Strangely, the successes of Black Arts and Black Power contributed to this conflict as well as the failures. For example, those movements played major parts in the election of black mayors, such as Coleman Young in Detroit, Maynard Jackson in Atlanta, and Kenneth Gibson in Newark. Gibson's campaign was basically spearheaded by Baraka and the political and cultural activists around him – and drew on the national BPM/BAM network. While these mayors were in some important respects far better for black people than the often racist white politicians who preceded them, they were unable, and sometimes unwilling to try, to change the fundamental problems of chronic unemployment, bad housing, poor schools, and so on, confronting poor black people in the urban United States. Some of these politicians became reabsorbed in the Democratic Party's political machines from which many of them came, or formed new versions of those old machines, despite their debt to the efforts of Black Power/Black Arts militants like Baraka.

As a result, many BAM/Black Power leaders and rank and file members, most prominently Baraka, embraced a more class-based politics, generally some variant of Maoism or "Third World Marxism," joining the already considerable Marxist strains in the movements. Others, such as Madhubuti, continued to advance a nationalist vision based far more on race or nation (in the sense that African Americans constituted a nation or nationality) that was skeptical about the viability of cross-racial class alliances and deeply suspicious of predominantly white Left organizations. Some, like Kwame Turé (previously named Stokely Carmichael) attempted to meld the two positions, advocating a Pan-Africanist Afrocentric Marxism. Despite efforts like those of Turé to find a middle ground, disputes between these tendencies undermined the effectiveness, and ultimately the viability, of many BAM and Black Power organizations and institutions, such as CAP and the African Liberation Support Committee. Not only did this conflict cause organizations and institutions to collapse, but it also limited the ability of BAM activists to rally an effective resistance to the closing of important BAM institutions, as when Johnson Publications shut down *Black World* in 1976, and the push to curtail the support of public agencies for radical, community-based black art.

Though it is tempting to date the ending of BAM with the closing of such iconic institutions as *Black World* and the demise of such crucial organizations as CAP, many important BAM institutions survived for years after the mid-1970s, often funded by public money. In some places, the apogee of community-based black art arrived after the mid-1970s, as was the case in Atlanta, where one might locate such an apogee in the 1980s with, among other things, the founding of the Fulton County Arts Council (1979), the creation of the National Black Arts Festival (1987), and the founding of Hammonds House Museum (1988). However, certainly by the early- to mid-1980s, there was a discernible decline of the movement and the radical, nationalist, community-based art and aesthetics associated with BAM. Such art did not disappear, but it became only one among several tendencies rather than the center of African American cultural production.

Yet, if BAM was no longer at the center of African American literature and art after the 1970s, the movement still continued to exert a powerful influence as black artists of all types long defined themselves and their artistic practice with and against BAM. For example, the late 1970s and early 1980s are often thought of as the moment in which such black women writers as Toni Morrison, Alice Walker, Sherley Anne Williams, Ntozake Shange, and Gloria Naylor found an unprecedented literary prominence inside and outside the African American community. In the United States generally and the movements for black liberation in particular, black women writers created a women-centered, if not always feminist, writing. While this body of work is obviously complex and multivalent, one way to read it is as a range of responses to BAM and Black Power that alternately seek to reject, reclaim, or revise those movements as vehicles for the empowering of black women. These women-centered responses fall into three somewhat fluid groups: those from within BAM who seek to remain within the somewhat nebulous and contested boundaries of the movement while responding to the feminist upsurge; those who posit a much more negative "outside" feminist reading of BAM in which the problems they raise are not resolvable within the Black Arts tradition or community; and those feminists who seek to honor a large part of the Black Arts tradition while extending the boundaries of the movement to include explicitly feminist interests and poetics.

One basic type of woman-centered literary response comes more or less out of this side of BAM. For example, Sonia Sanchez's prose poem "Just Don't Never Give Up on Love" from the 1984 collection *homegirls and handgrenades* travels a considerable distance from the 1974 *A Blues Book for Blue Black Magical Women*. In the earlier book, Sanchez quite straightforwardly argues that "contentment will never / be ours for this crackerized country has dealt / on us and colonized body and soul and / the job of the Black / wooomen is to deal with this / under the direction of Black men" (Sanchez, *Blues Book* 12). In the later work, a youngish black woman who is a parent (perhaps a single parent), a poet, an intellectual, a writer of book reviews, tired, harried, somewhat dissatisfied, and perhaps troubled in love, encounters an elderly black woman, Mrs. Rosalie Johnson. The ensuing bonding of the two women is closely related to the more feminist woman-centered responses, say, by Sherley Anne Williams or Alice Walker, in which there is a bonding of black women across generations, a sharing of African American women's experience and culture, and a reinvigoration of a troubled and dissatisfied female subject. Yet, in the final analysis, one finds a restatement of a certain Black Arts vision in which the fallen or degraded black man is paired against the vision of a "good" man. The narrator is reinvigorated by Mrs. Johnson's story of the redemptive powers of a good black man. In short, the poem-story stays largely within Black Arts boundaries while engaging feminism in a less directly antagonistic manner than Sanchez does in *A Blues Book for Blue Black Magical Women*.

Alice Walker, on the other hand, is one of the foremost artists linked to a more straightforwardly feminist critique of BAM during the late 1970s and 1980s, most notably and controversially in her 1982 novel *The Color Purple*. The term "feminist" must be used advisedly here, because Walker famously disassociated herself from much of what is sometimes referred to as "mainstream" feminism. Instead, Walker preferred the term "womanist," claiming a tradition of African American feminism often rooted in "folk" practices, say quilting, gardening, talk around a rural or small-town Southern kitchen table, and so on – though Walker remained engaged with "mainstream" feminism in various ways. *The Color Purple* is in many ways a polemic aimed at Black Arts activists, calling into question their basic integrity, principles, and judgment. What is challenged is the widespread Black Arts vision of a normative heterosexual and patriarchal relationship as the ideal of a liberated black nation, whether rooted in some vision of African American culture or some reconnection with traditional African values, arguing with many revolutionary nationalists, African American cultural nationalists, and neo-Africanists. At the same time, it is worth noting that the novel ends with a vision of a united and internationalist black community in which people of different class, educational background, gender, sexuality, and national origin come together in a sort of utopia that recalls BAM in spirit even if Walker's decentralization of normative heterosexuality and her placing of women in the lead of this community differ considerably from the vision of, say, Amiri Baraka in the poem "Black Art."

There was also a third category of black women artists and intellectuals who came to prominence in the late 1970s and 1980s. They saw themselves as writing from within BAM or the legacy of the movement while trying to extend the boundaries of the movement to include explicitly feminist concerns and subjectivities. An example of this third sort of stance can be found in the early work of Ntozake Shange. Like Walker's *The Color Purple*, Shange's poetry-play, *For Colored Girls* was the subject of fierce debate over its representation of black men and sexual politics within the African American community. However, unlike Walker, Shange did not (and does not) separate herself from the legacy of Black Arts, but instead proclaimed herself a daughter of BAM. At the same time, she was willing to criticize the movement for what she saw as a lack of space for black women writers – in the Northeast and the Midwest at least.

In short, as noted above with respect to how Barack Obama as candidate and writer was variously understood by himself and people of many different political persuasions, even now it remains almost impossible to talk about work by African American artists without reference to some of the criteria suggested by BAM and the BPM, especially with respect to notions of authenticity and the relation of the works to some idea of the black community.

BAM also did much to make broadly plausible the proposition that "high" art can (and should) reach a mass audience and that popular culture can do serious aesthetic and political work – a proposition that would not have seemed obvious in the early 1960s. This new attitude can be seen most clearly in hip hop, where the more consciously political artists publicly acknowledge Amiri Baraka, Askia Touré, Sonia Sanchez, the Last Poets, Gil Scott-Heron, and other BAM activists as their artistic ancestors in ways that one could not imagine large numbers of pop musicians doing before BAM. Even the least political hip hop artists feel the need to make some gesture toward affirming the social significance or reality of their work. And while so-called "conscious" rap might sell less than so-called "hardcore" or "gangsta" styles, virtually all the hip hop audience knows that the more political artists, such as Talib Kweli and the Roots, exist and accept them as an important part of hip hop. In fact, the Roots have reached such a level of acceptance they are now the house band for the *Late Night with Jimmy Fallon* show, which debuted on American television (NBC) in 2009.

BAM has been instrumental in the creation of a broad acceptance of governmental support of the arts to a degree unseen since the Great Depression. The support includes neighborhood mural programs, traveling theater groups, community-based museums, or, indeed, such large institutions as the NEA, the NEH, National Public Radio, and the Public Broadcasting System – institutions that BAM activists like Edward Spriggs, Jerry Ward, and A.B. Spellman played important roles in administering. BAM has also been at the heart of the discussion of what publicly supported art and cultural institutions should do – a debate that is still an important part of the political scene in the United States.

In the end, something of the power and the legacy of BAM can be seen in Elizabeth Alexander's poem, "Praise Song for the Day," that she read at Barack Obama's presidential inauguration in early 2009. Like much BAM literature, there is a certain optimism and an acknowledgment of ancestry and past history and a call for a rebirth or renewal. Of course, much the same could be said about Robert Frost's "Dedication," the poem he wrote for the Kennedy inaugural in 1961, or his "The Gift Outright," the poem he actually read. Yet, Alexander's poem – with its echoes of, among other things, the poetry of Margaret Walker and Gwendolyn Brooks (and of BAM), the sorrow songs, and the words of Malcolm X – speaks to a black experience as rendered through African American literature, oratory, and music. The poem's political argument is both particular to black people and ultimately plausible to a wide spectrum of people in the United States.

Bibliography

Baraka, Amiri. *The Autobiography of LeRoi Jones*. Chicago: Lawrence Hill, 1997.

Benston, Kimberly. *Performing Blackness: Enactments of African-American Modernism*. New York: Routledge, 2000.

Boyd, Melba Joyce. *Wrestling with the Muse: Dudley Randall and Broadside Press*. New York: Columbia University Press, 2003.

Clarke, Cheryl. *"After Mecca": Women Poets and the Black Arts Movement*. New Brunswick: Rutgers University Press, 2005.

Collins, Lisa Gail and Margo Natalie Crawford. *New Thoughts on the Black Arts Movement*. New Brunswick: Rutgers University Press, 2006.

Gayle, Addison, Jr., ed. *The Black Aesthetic*. New York: Doubleday, 1971.

Jones, Leroi and Larry Neal, ed. *Black Fire: An Anthology of Afro-American Writing*. New York: Morrow, 1968.

Neal, Larry. *Visions of a Liberated Future: Black Arts Movement Writings*. New York: Thunder's Mouth Press, 1989.

Nielsen, Aldon. *Black Chant: Languages of African-American Postmodernism*. New York: Cambridge University Press, 1997.

Obama, Barack. *Dreams from My Father: A Story of Race and Inheritance*. New York: Three Rivers Press, 2004.

Randall, Dudley, ed. *The Black Poets*. New York: Bantam, 1971.

Redmond, Eugene B. *Drumvoices: The Mission of Afro-American Poetry: A Critical History*. Garden City: Anchor, 1976.

Sanchez, Sonia. *A Blues Book for Blue Black Magical Women*. Detroit: Broadside Press, 1974.

Sanchez, Sonia. *homegirls and hand grenades*. New York: Thunder's Mouth Press, 1984.

Sell, Mike. *Avant-garde Performance and the Limits of Criticism*. Ann Arbor: University of Michigan Press, 2006.

Shange, Ntozake. *for colored girls who have considered suicide, when the rainbow is enuf; a choreopoem*. New York: Macmillan, 1977.

Smethurst, James Edward. *The Black Arts Movement*. Chapel Hill: University of North Carolina Press, 2005.

Snelling, Rolland. "Keep On Pushin': Rhythm & Blues as a Weapon." *Liberator* 5 (1965): 6–8.

Thomas, Lorenzo. *Extraordinary Measures: Afrocentric Modernism and Twentieth-Century American Poetry*. Tuscaloosa: University of Alabama Press, 2000.

Walker, Alice. *The Color Purple*. New York: Harcourt Brace Jovanovich, 1982.

21
Humor in African American Literature

*Glenda R. Carpio**

Humor has always been central to African American expressive forms. For centuries, in fact, African Americans have used various forms of humor – from satire, parody, tragicomedy, and burlesque to other forms more specific to African American culture, such as "signifying" – to face and critique the insidiousness and violence of racism. During slavery and the many subsequent decades of Jim Crow segregation, African American humor had to develop a Janus-face identity: on the one hand, it was a fairly nonthreatening form that catered to whites' belief in the inferiority of blacks, but one that usually masked aggression; on the other, it was a more assertive and acerbic humor that often targeted racial injustice, but one that was generally reserved for in-group interactions. For black Americans, humor has often functioned as a way of affirming their humanity in the face of its violent denial.

Yet the use of humor in African American letters has not always been encouraged or recognized. Racist assumptions regarding the purportedly innate relationship between blackness and buffoonery made it necessary for African American writers to avoid or disguise their use of humor. This behavior was especially true for African American writers of the antebellum period, since they wrote primarily for the abolition of slavery (and thus largely for white audiences for whom they needed to fashion "civilized" identities); and it was true for those after emancipation, when they were agitating against the violence of Jim Crow segregation, a cause considered too morally important and earnest to be treated through humor. Often, these writers chose irony, satire, and parody – more sophisticated vehicles for humor than the slapstick and buffoonery with which blackness was too often associated – to mock slavery and racism. Very often, they hid their critique in sheep's clothing in order not to chase away publishers or alienate readers. Yet, readers both past and present have not always seen beyond the clothing. Thus, critics still tend to emphasize the seriousness that Frederick Douglass maintains throughout his 1845 autobiography, *Narrative of the Life of Frederick Douglass*, without calling attention to the fact that he also employs a stinging satire towards the end. And for many, it still comes as a surprise that

Douglass, like Williams Wells Brown and other nineteenth-century black writers, was widely known for making his audiences laugh (see Ganter).

By contrast, contemporary African American writers, most notably Ishmael Reed, Charles Johnson, Suzan-Lori Parks, Colson Whitehead, and Paul Beatty, have fully embraced the rich tradition of African American humor. Why now and to what ends? Certainly, the social and political gains that African Americans have made since the Civil Rights Movement have made it possible for authors to express themselves more freely. And certainly, the fact that African American culture is no longer segregated from the mainstream, that it constitutes a great part of popular culture (at least in music), has facilitated the change. But the reason why contemporary African American writers have more fully embraced humor is also a creative response to the particular turn that race relations have taken in the America in the last 40 years. After playing a crucial role in the making of the American nation and throughout the nation's history, racial inequality has become, at least for some sectors of the country, a thing of the past (see Brown, Winant). The belief in a "post-race" America, despite overwhelming evidence to the contrary, reached a peak with the presidential election of Barack Obama in 2008. Meanwhile, African Americans, while fully conscious that institutional and overt forms of racism are not over, have also seen the need to question set notions of blackness that, while useful in achieving racial solidarity and political power, have also tended to erase diversity within African American communities. Against this background in which racial progress clashes against the residual impact of a long and violent history of racial conflict, African American writers have embraced various forms of humor, ranging from stinging satire to tragicomedy, to reflect on both the state of the country – its simultaneous movement towards and away from racial harmony – and the role of their craft in the creation of new forms of American racial consciousness.

Before examining the complexity of their strategies, it would be useful to consider what distinguishes the comedic and literary tradition of African American humor that these contemporary writers embrace as well as the main figures that paved their way. African American humor, like other kinds of humor that have arisen from oppression, has traditionally been understood as an expression of gallows humor, as a safety valve, as a conduit for community, as a release of aggression and tension. In this way, it has been linked to one of the three major theories on humor: the relief theory made popular by Sigmund Freud, which posits that we laugh as a way to release pent-up aggression. Much, but certainly not all, forms of African American humor fit this mold. African American humor has also been linked, although less often so, to the superiority theory, which posits that we laugh at other people's misfortunes. The tradition of signifyin', including the play of the dozens, of capping, of verbal battle, of boasting and toasting, belongs to this kind of humor, although the humor of "yo mama" jokes, and signifying in general, savors verbal wit over mean-spirited competition or insult. For centuries, African Americans had to keep the signifying tradition under guard, since, unlike the more innocuous forms of humor that they could share with white Americans, it was often used to criticize racial oppression. Known also as "mother wit," the signifying tradition remained largely segregated until the late 1960s, when Richard Pryor broke out of his original image as a slim, mild-mannered comedian who usually told charming jokes about his grandmother, and became an explosive, often profane and always provocative comedian who unabashedly used mother wit to expose racism in America. Although other comedians (for instance, Moms Mabley, Flip Wilson, Redd Foxx) had introduced aspects of African American humor to racially mixed audiences, Pryor made full use of the tradition, including some of its more controversial facets.

Unlike the Freudian model of humor, the signifying tradition does not depend on sublimation or the joke form but, rather, relishes exposure and finds expression through the telling of "lies" or stories. Pryor masterfully mined this stand of African American humor while producing a cross between performance art (see especially his 1971 filmed performance *Live and Smokin'*) and stand-up to expose how, for instance, police brutality against African Americans, the poverty of black ghettoes, the near invisibility of African Americans in films in the mid-twentieth century, the persistence of racial stereotyping, among other phenomena, could attest to the lasting effects of the ideologies that supported chattel slavery (see Carpio, Watkins).

African American humor also includes forms that are more directly connected to the incongruity theory of humor, which suggests that we laugh when our expectations are somehow disturbed. The humor of incongruity generally entails the playing of games, such as "what if" games that suspend normativity. At its best, the humor of incongruity allows us to see the world inverted, to consider transpositions of time and place, and to get us, especially when the humor is hot enough to push our buttons, to question the myopia and biases that can blind us when we are overcome by racial obsessions. This strand of African American humor does not find full expression until the twentieth and twenty-first centuries yet some of its characteristics, particularly its satiric undertones, can be found in early African American letters.

Lampooning the hypocrisy of slaveholders, for instance, is a constant in antebellum African American literature. In *Incidents in the Life a Slave Girl* (1861), Harriet Jacobs satirizes the "poverty, ignorance and moral degradation" of poor whites who, without "negroes of their own to scourge," take advantage of the repression following Nat Turner's rebellion to wreck violence against African Americans. She also pillories the moral degradation of wealthy whites, like her own master and mistress, who make a mockery of everything deemed sacred, ranging from marriage and family to religious faith. Other salient examples include David Walker's *Appeal* (1829), Harriet Wilson's *Out Nig* (1853), and Frederick Douglass's "What to the Slave is the Fourth of July?" (a speech delivered on July 5, 1852 at an event commemorating the signing of the Declaration of Independence).

The satire in these antebellum texts, however, is not conducive to laughter. Yet the performance work of William Wells Brown and Frederick Douglass in abolitionist circuits stands as a significant exception. Douglass and Brown were both gifted speakers on abolitionist podiums and were well known for using their skills as mimics to lampoon the moral deficiencies of the master class. Through their mimicry and campy burlesques of plantation life, Douglass and Brown mocked the false, scripted roles of slave society, making their audiences laugh while engaging them in a political cause. But Douglass ultimately rejected humor as a means to political protest, for he found it too risky a form to effect social change; he feared that his burlesques would affirm rather than rebuke racial stereotypes, and that they would merely entertain rather than incite his audiences. Brown, in contrast, believed that the risk was necessary, that humor could enhance activism by providing a different outlet than the overused forms of sentimentalism that were popular in abolitionist circles. He used humor not only on the abolitionist stage but also in his published works, including his play *The Escape; or, a Leap for Freedom* (1858) and, to a lesser extent, in certain passages of his novel *Clotel* (1853).

After the Civil War, Charles W. Chesnutt developed a brilliant form of tragicomedy that makes use of racist stereotypes to humorous, but also socially progressive ends. One of the first African American professional writers, and one with a tremendous command of his craft, Chesnutt appropriated and parodied the trickster animal tales featuring Brer Rabbit and Brer Fox, first popularized by Joel Chandler Harris in *Uncle Remus, His Songs and Sayings: The Folklore of the Old Plantation* (1880). Through his richly layered collection of stories, *The Conjure Woman* (1899), Chesnutt provided a crucial corrective to a popular trend, then established by Harris and others, of romanticizing plantation slavery and presenting life before the Civil War in nostalgic terms. Figures like Harris's Uncle Remus were key in the production of what came to be known as the local color tradition, which relied on dialect and stereotypes to give a sense of place, while creating a myth of the South as the background to a quaint, even picturesque, slavery. Chesnutt's Uncle Julius, a central character in *The Conjure Woman* tales, is a brilliant send-up of Uncle Remus, the docile, loyal retainer from the slave past who entertains the son of his masters with seemingly innocuous, comic tales in which weaker animals like the Rabbit often outsmart stronger ones such as the Fox through wit and cunning. Harris believed that the stories only depict the "roaring comedy" of animal life (Dundes 528). Yet critics have rightly argued that the stories allegorize the great imbalance of power between master and slave, and the ways that the enslaved, as represented by the Rabbit, found to sabotage it. Chesnutt highlights this aspect of the tales through Uncle Julius's stories, which operate at two levels of narration. Uncle Julius, an ex-slave living in the South, entertains John and his sickly wife Annie, two Northerners, with tales that are set in the antebellum years. The two levels of narration, the antebellum past of Julius's tales and that of the postbellum present of the story, inform one another in intricate ways, sometimes interlacing and sometimes putting in tension a number of dichotomies: North and South, literate and illiterate, textual and oral, antebellum and postbellum. The various contrasts and parallels through which the stories operate achieve high levels of irony and comment incisively on the stagnation and reactionary practices that characterized Reconstruction. But it is through the antebellum stories that Julius recounts that Chesnutt most dramatically focuses on what is paradoxically both a great source of comedy and a key principle underlying chattel slavery, namely, the inability to control one's body. All of Julius's stories involve forms of physical transformation in which the enslaved are turned into objects, animals, or spirits while echoing the marriage of violence and comedy found in the Brer Rabbit stories. The stories thus highlight the painful and tragic ends that the enslaved had to face given that they could not control their destinies or the integrity of their physical bodies. Through Uncle Julius, Chesnutt created a tragicomedy of slavery in which laughter is disassociated from gaiety and is, instead, a medium for representing the great violence of slavery against black bodies and psyches.

During the Harlem Renaissance Jessie Fauset, W.E.B. Du Bois, and James Weldon Johnson all wrote about the power of humor in African American culture. But it was George Schuyler, Zora Neale Hurston, and Langston Hughes who advanced its use in African American letters. Indeed, one of the most realized and earliest examples of the humor of inversion that I discussed earlier is Schuyler's *Black No More* (1931). The bitingly satirical novel narrates the events that unfold when a black scientist invents a machine that, by transforming black people's phenotypical features into those of white people, "solves" the race problem. It is thus that Max Disher, a roguish young black man, becomes Matthew Fisher, a white man who not only marries a white woman that spurned him when he was black but also becomes the leader of the Knights of Nordica, a white supremacist group that obviously parodies the Ku Klux Klan. Anticipating comedian Dave Chappelle's infamous black white supremacist skit on Comedy Central in 2003 the novel scathingly exposes white bigotry in the storylines of Max/Matthew Disher and that of Snobbcraft and Buggerie, two white members of The Knights of Nordica who turn out to be part black. When their secret is exposed, they run away but wind up in a particularly racist Southern town (Happy Hill, Mississippi) where, believing that they must hide their identities to protect their secret they decide to blacken their faces with cork. Nonetheless, they are summarily lynched not because their secret is exposed but because they *look* black. The novel also pillories groups like the National Association for the Advancement of Colored People, as well as historical figures such as W.E.B. Du Bois, James Weldon Johnson, and Marcus Garvey, among others. More generally, the novel exposes the ways that oppression can corrupt African Americans, making them, as Jeffrey Ferguson puts it, "want to imitate their oppressors, exploit their own people, invest in shallow materialism, revere fake symbols of exalted status," and "invest too heavily in an ideal of black peoplehood" (Ferguson 44). Schuyler's wit is eviscerating but also delightful, since through it he liberates his readers, both black and white, encouraging them to view race "complexly rather than dwell on it obsessively" (Ferguson 216).

In 1935, Hurston, a trained anthropologist, published *Mules and Men*, a groundbreaking collection of African American folktales and folklore, which includes the John and Master stories. Unlike the trickster animal stories that Joel Chandler Harris once collected, the John and Master stories drop the symbolic disguise of the Rabbit versus the Fox and depict a clever slave who often bests the Master in word and deed. John, writes Hurston, "was top superior to the whole mess of sorrow," for he could "beat it all, and what made it so cool, finish it off with a laugh." With his wit, John made "a way out of no-way. Hitting a straight lick with a crocked stick. Winning the jackpot with no other stake than a laugh" (Dundes 543). Hurston may have romanticized John, who does not always win his battle of wits against the Master, but she also helped preserve a rich source of African American humor, an archive she extended two years later, when she incorporated the humor of the folk, particularly the verbal pleasure of the dozens, in her 1937 novel, *Their Eyes Were Watching God*. But Hurston was lambasted by her peers, especially Richard Wright, for her use of African American dialect and humor. In his review of the novel, Wright chastises Hurston for "voluntarily" continuing the tradition of minstrelsy, and for keeping black characters "in that safe and narrow orbit in which America likes to see the Negro live: between laughter and tears." This kind of negative reception ultimately sent Hurston's work into public obscurity until 1975, when Alice Walker published "In Search of Zora Neale Hurston," an essay that revived contemporary interest in her work.

Hurston was not the first or singular African American author to suffer criticism and eventual obscurity as consequences of using humor. William Wells Brown and Charles W. Chesnutt both suffered similar fates after they manipulated and signified upon racist stereotypes, often using dialect to transform such stereotypes from vehicles of humor *against* African Americans to sources of humor *by* African Americans about and against racism. Hurston's approach was different, however; she incorporated a humor that was less obviously engaged with racial politics. In *Their Eyes Were Watching God*, the humor of the dozens operates more as a means to represent, in language, differences in class and gender within African American communities than as a means of intentional signifying on racial stereotypes. Yet sometimes her strategies backfired. Reviews of her novel stressed the fact that her use of dialect affirmed racist beliefs in the ignorance of black Americans. In 1930, she began collaborating with Langston Hughes on a comedy titled *Mule Bone*, based on her folktale "The Bone of Contention." Both the story and the play, like the porch scenes in *Their Eyes Were Watching God*, highlight the rich verbal rituals and forms of improvisation characteristic of African American folklore, including not only the play of the dozens, but also the rhythmically complex art of boasting and toasting. In all three works, the authors reject stock minstrel comic stereotypes (the lazy, overly sexualized, ignorant buffoons who would laugh at anything and speak nonsense) in favor of characters that enjoy manipulating language to comic, sometimes playfully competitive ends. However, quarrels between Hurston and Hughes prevented them from finishing the play, which was not performed on stage until 1991. Perhaps because Hughes and Hurston did not control the final form that the play took or, because adopting older forms of black vernacular, folklore and signifying practices for contemporary audiences has proven challenging, the 1991 performance of the play was not a success. In his *New York Times* review of the performance, Frank Rich argues as much, adding that the 1991 stage version of the play is not "a scrupulously authentic representation of what Hughes and Hurston wrote," but instead, a play so "watered down and bloated by various emendations" that it is hard to know if its producers were "conscientiously trying to complete and resuscitate a lost, unfinished work or merely picking its carcass." Rich does note, however, that on rare occasions the 1991 production of the play "does make clear what Hurston and Hughes had in mind," mainly the creation of a "startling, linguistically lush folk comedy that nonetheless reflects the tragic legacy of slavery."

Hughes's series of comic stories about a character named Jessie B. Simple, a kind of African American "Every Man," fared much better. The title character's last name (also known as Semple) signifies on a persistent racist stereotype, while the stories themselves feature humorous dialogues between Simple, who represents an outspoken and witty quintessential Harlem resident, and an overly reasonable middle-class African American, a rarely named character known as Ananias Boyd, who serves as comic foil. Simple's interchanges with Boyd are usually short pieces that include observations on a variety of topics – from love to national politics, race relations, world events, changes in African American communities, to people and events in Simple's life, among other subjects. The dialogues are provocative, since they present two often-opposing perspectives, but they are also full of a good natured humor through which Hughes exposes Simple's and Boyd's limitations, their biases and insights, especially with regard to the history and practice of racism in America. Boyd often pokes fun at Simple for being too sensitive, almost paranoid, about racial injustice or for being obsessed with racial difference. "White folks, white folks, white folks!" he tells him, "Everything you talk about is in terms of white folks … Don't you know this is a multiracial country, an interracial country made up of all kinds of people?" (Hughes, *Collected Works VIII* 100). But Simple exposes Boyd's sometimes naïve belief in racial progress through forms of mother wit that Boyd rejects in favor of a narrow rationalism and a passive acceptance of the status quo.

Hughes knew quite well the high stakes in using humor to comment on racial tensions. But he also knew the need for it. In the foreword to *Simple Stakes a Claim* (1957), the third of the five books he wrote about the character, Hughes notes:

> The race problem in America is serious business, I admit. But must it *always* be written about seriously? So many weighty volumes, cheerless novels, sad abstracts and violent books have been written on race relations, that I would like to see some writers of both races write about our problems with black tongue in white cheek, or vice versa. Sometimes I try. Simple helps me.

Hughes's Simple stories first appeared in the *Chicago Defender* between 1943 and 1949, but over Hughes's lifetime the character became popular nationwide. Reviewers recognized the risk Hughes took. Writing for *The New York Times*, Gilbert Millstein notes the courage a writer must have to deal with race in America through humor, "particularly if he is a Negro," because he "is apt to become the target of his own people" for not representing them in uncompromisingly heroic terms, and he "is equally open to the regretful tongue-clickings of humorless liberals." Finally, he might "do no more than confirm the rabid in their intransigence." Hughes, as did Brown, Chesnutt, Hurston, and Schuyler, each in their distinct forms, refused to render black Americans *only* in exemplary terms, thereby refusing to deny them their complex humanity. Instead, Hughes like other masters of African American humor, exposed how racial conflict, and the obsessive ways that it colonizes American minds, can divest *everyone*, albeit at different registers, of a sense of reality.

Chester Himes certainly continued the tradition these writers established. Himes is probably best known for his Harlem detective stories featuring Coffin Ed Johnson and Grave Digger Jones, two savvy and funny policemen who routinely outsmart their white police superiors while taking care of poor African Americans in the streets of New York City. While these novels, and the equally well known *If He Hollers Lets Him Go* (1945), feature Himes's quick wit, his 1961 novel *Pinktoes* is a comic tour de force so eviscerating that the novel had to be published first in Paris. *Pinktoes* is a wicked satire of the often close connection between racial and sexual obsessions and takes its title, Himes wryly noted, from "a term of indulgent affection applied to white women by Negro men, and sometimes conversely by Negro women to white men, but never adversely by either." In many ways a sexualized version of Schuyler's *Black No More*, Himes's novel treats the trials and tribulations of Mamie Mason, grand dame of Harlem, who organizes interracial sexual orgies to solve the race problem. But the orgies only perpetuate the problem, as people are much more interested in satisfying their sexual craving than promoting social progress. The novel is intended, Himes said, "as a satire on middle-class Negroes and their white sponsors who used the Negro problem to rid themselves of other social neuroses" (266).

The Civil Rights and Black Power eras produced more studies and edited collections of African American humor than humorous fiction per se. Some of the most prominent titles include Langston Hughes's and Arna Bontemps's *The Book of Negro Folklore* (1965), Philip Sterling's *Laughing on the Outside* (1965), Hughes's *The Book of Negro Humor* (1966), Richard Dorson's *American Negro Folktales* (1967), Roger D. Abrahams' 1964 *Deep Down in the Jungle*, a seminal study of African American folklore in the streets of Philadelphia (including a thoughtful study of the use of the dozens), and two seminal texts, Alan Dundes's *Mother Wit from the Laughing Barrel* (1973, with a second edition in 1990) and Lawrence Levine's *Black Culture and Black Consciousness* (1977), which includes the excellent chapter, "Black Laughter." Of course, the towering figure of Ishmael Reed, a brilliant satirist, stands as a significant exception. A prolific writer, Reed's most accomplished novels to embrace the full power of African American humor include *Yellow Back Radio Broke Down* (1969), a parody of myths, novels, and movies about the American West; *Mumbo Jumbo* (1972), a novel that simultaneously comments on the Harlem Renaissance and Black Arts Movement while parodying discourses that reduce the world to a dichotomy between the West and the Rest; and *Flight to Canada* (1976), a novel that transposes the Civil War and Civil Rights eras to similarly political but hilarious ends. Unlike some of his contemporaries – for instance, Addison Gayle, Jr., Amiri Baraka, Larry Neal and others connected to the Black Arts movement, the artistic sister to the Black Power movement – Reed refused to espouse a utilitarian and propagandistic view of black art, one that insisted on celebrating the African roots of African American identity and culture, and, more generally, on distinguishing these from Euro-American concepts of self and art. Reed has never been antagonistic to these views, but he has also rejected some of their more narrow incarnations in favor of a multicultural view of America and a view of black culture and identity that values both variety and individualism. Indeed, he has put his prodigious gifts as a satirist in the service of maintaining a fluid sense of national culture while working in opposition to "white supremacy and to the one-sided discussion of ethnicity and multiculturalism" projected "by the national media" (Reed, *MultiAmerica* xxiv).

In *Mumbo Jumbo*, for instance, Reed narrates the struggles of "The Wallflower Order," an international conspiracy obsessed with imposing monotheism and control, which is set against the culture germinating from "Jes Grew," a kind of virus associated with freedom, improvisation, spontaneity, and polytheism; it is a virus that renders life humorous and playful. The form of the novel embodies the spirit of Jes Grew, a name which signifies on Harriet Beecher Stowe's callous reference to African American natal alienation in *Uncle Tom's Cabin* when she describes Topsy, an orphaned and enslaved child, as someone who miraculously "just grew," like a weed. But the name also references James Weldon Johnson's appropriation of the term to describe the purportedly unstructured development of African American culture and its realization in ragtime and ultimately in jazz. *Mumbo Jumbo* is set in 1920s New York City, but it ranges freely in time and place, mixing historical, social, and political events with Reed's fictional inventions. The novel intertwines references to the American occupation of Haiti with ancient Greek and African mythology; with reflections on the Harlem Renaissance; and with satiric portraits of black militants, white liberals, and archconservatives.

No one is safe from Reed's satire. Like Schuyler, Reed pillories real and fictional characters with a sharp but ultimately liberating wit. At the core of the novel, as in his extensive oeuvre, is an earnest desire to champion artistic freedom, to question historical narratives that obscure more than illuminate, and, perhaps most urgently, to get us to think, as Schuyler did earlier, about race "complexly rather that dwell on it obsessively." In *Flight to Canada*, for instance, he turns our attention to the literature and historiography of slavery in order to question the legacy of the "peculiar institution" on the cultural landscape of 1970s America. Through an aesthetic that blends history and fantasy, political reality and parody, Reed parodies stereotypes of forbearance, most closely associated with Uncle Tom and the Mammy icon. He also parodies stereotypes of resistance and rebellion, of evil masters and benevolent abolitionists, to question the ways that these roles have ossified in the American imagination, and blocked access to a genuine engagement with the past. The novel maps the flight of three fugitive slaves within a fictional space that merges the past (antebellum and Civil War America) with the novel's present (the years after the Civil Rights Movement), two temporal frames that intersect with our moment of reading. By manipulating time in this fashion, Reed encourages us to consider the persistence of stereotypes across time. Significantly, in *Flight to Canada*, Reed also parodies ethnic stereotypes, including those of Jewish Americans and immigrants, as well as stereotypes about

Native Americans, thus urging his readers to consider the complexity of America's history and culture and to question the sometimes myopic focus that Americans place on racial struggles between black and white people.

In his more recent fiction, and in his numerous works of poetry and non-fiction, Reed continues to use his gifts as a satirist towards socially progressive ends. And his influence on the development of humor in African American letters is prodigious. Charles Johnson's novels, *The Oxherding Tale* (1982), and *Middle Passage* (1990), for instance, both explore antebellum American history in ways that recall *Flight to Canada*. Both novels blend established genres, such as the slave narrative, with philosophical explorations on the nature of freedom, including the use of Buddhist parables, while maintaining a comic perspective. *The Oxherding Tale,* for instance, begins when a slave owner and his slave, having stayed up drinking for too long and fearing the wrath of their wives, trade places in each other's bed. This preposterous set-up immediately reframes the reader's expectations and opens the way for Johnson's deep explorations into the nature of freedom. In both novels, Johnson presents highly educated protagonists who seek to liberate themselves from physical, emotional, and spiritual bondage. And in both, he uses humor to reflect on the nature of narrative and to expand traditional categories through which we think about the past. In *The Oxherding Tale*, he includes chapters such as "The Manumission of the First Person Viewpoint," which puns on the legal process of freeing a slave while meditating on the connection between writing and freedom. The novel includes a host of humorously drawn characters, a funny cameo by Karl Marx, and several instances of subtly poignant irony. "To some it might sound peculiar that I consulted with the Vet for a serious medical problem," writes Andrew Hawkins, the novel's protagonist, who is conceived the fateful night that his father trades places with his master and sleeps with the mistress, "In the South before Surrender, men of color were treated, if treated at all, by the local veterinarian" (Johnson, *Oxherding Tale* 67). Later, when Andrew is fleeing from Flo Hatfield, a mistress who delights in enslaving young men through their senses, he meets Reb, a coffin-maker and enlightened being who helps him escape from Soulcatcher, a kind of bounty hunter who catches slaves by penetrating through their strongest fears and desires. Johnson follows Andrew as he meets these characters through a satiric yet philosophical and comic style reminiscent of Miguel de Cervantes in *Don Quixote* (1605, 1615) and Laurence Sterne particularly in *The Life and Opinion of Tristram Shandy, Gentleman* (1759, 1767).

Like Reed and Johnson, playwright Suzan-Lori Parks has also advanced the development of humor in African American letters and turned to the antebellum period to meditate on contemporary discourses of race in America. Judging by subject and title alone, however, one might not see how humor figures in Parks's work. Her first major play, *Imperceptible Mutabilities in the Third Kingdom* (first produced in 1989), concerns some of the most painful aspects of chattel slavery. "Open House," the second section of this play, involves a dying slave whose teeth are extracted mercilessly as she recalls a life of dispossession. Parks's second play, *The Death of the Last Black Man in the Whole Entire World* (1990), by title alone suggests a dark topic. Its titular figure vividly recounts his own death from lynching and electrocution. Similarly, her third major work, *The America Play* (also produced in 1990), presents the repeated shooting of a black man. Yet in these early plays, as well as in her more recent work, Parks develops a brilliant tragicomedy reminiscent of Chesnutt's. Parks treats painful subjects in America's past, but she does so through a language that both grieves past injustices yet affirms the creativity of Black English and the cultural forms, like humor, that facilitated African American survival. She experiments with language, finally finding the means of bringing to the stage the language that fascinated Hurston and Hughes, without running the risk of having that language support racist stereotypes. She signifies on the varied layers on signification already inscribed in African American vernacular. In an interview she states,

> At one time in this country, the teaching of reading and writing to African Americans was a criminal offense. So how do I adequately represent not merely the speech patterns of a people oppressed by language (which is the simple question) but the patterns of a people whose language is so complex and varied and ephemeral that its daily use not only Signifies on the non-vernacular language forms, but on the construct of writing as well. If language is a construct and writing is a construct and Signifyin(g) on the double construct is the daily use, then I have chosen to Signify on the Signifyin(g). (Solomon 75–6)

The result is a "word-sound choreography" that, while evoking the creativity of Black English, "the spontaneity of jive, the ritual storytelling of the beauty parlor, juke joint, or barbershop," incorporates what Parks calls her '"foreign words & phrases," which are invented and improvised from spoken English (Bernard 692; Parks 17). Through her experiments with language, Parks not only extends the tradition of signifying that Richard Pryor so richly used, but also exposes the legacy of slavery in contemporary culture. In particular, she highlights how the demeaning images of blackness proliferated through the minstrel stage continue to haunt contemporary African American performance (not only in theaters but also in popular culture, as in, for instance, some commercial forms of hip hop). Rather than merely parodying the features of minstrelsy, however, Parks signifies on these features so expertly that she turns them into vehicles for mourning the violence that they have exerted. At the same time, Parks mocks the ghost of minstrelsy, providing cathartic relief from the hold that the past still has on the now.

If, as we have seen, contemporary African American writers turn to the antebellum period with frequency, they often do so through satiric or tragicomic modes expressive of a sensibility particular to what Nelson George and others have called "post-soul" black culture. In many ways, the generations belonging to this culture, those born roughly between the March on Washington in 1963 and the landmark case, *The Regents of the University of California v. Bakke* (1978), which imposed limitations on affirmative action, have experienced a deepening sense of cynicism due to the intense backlash against African Americans that occurred in the immediate post-Civil Rights years and that, in more subtle ways, continued through the presidential administration of Ronald Reagan. Aside from suffering the worst effects of economic recessions, black Americans in the post-Civil Rights era have also suffered an increase in police brutality. In 1975, they constituted "forty-six percent of people killed by police" (Kelly 574–5). African Americans also saw the reemergence of longstanding stereotypes regarding their character. A great reversal occurred almost as soon as the major Civil Rights acts passed: the focus was no longer on white racism – because segregation in public spaces, discrimination at the work, and disenfranchisement had been outlawed – but on the moral deficiencies of minorities. For African Americans, this meant the return of stereotypes of blacks as lazy, irresponsible, and in "violation of core American values" (Virtanen and Huddy 313). These stereotypes have been used to explain the undeniable inequalities in wages, access to healthcare, housing, and family income that have existed between black and white Americans in the last 40 years, and that, most recently, were dramatically exposed by Hurricane Katrina in 2005. As they face both the clear gains that African Americans have made since the Civil Rights movement and the backward shifts the nation has made as well, African American writers have developed a sensibility that Trey Ellis has defined succinctly. They are "not as shocked by the persistence of racism" as were the writers of the Harlem Renaissance, nor are "preoccupied with it, as were those of the Black Arts Movement." A novelist in his own right, Ellis speaks as a contemporary writer stating, "for us, racism is a hard and little-changing constant that neither surprises nor enrages" (Ellis 235). In their recognition that racial struggle is "little-changing," post-soul writers have reclaimed African American humor as a mode of meditating on the nation's simultaneous movement forward and backwards in its struggles with racial inequality.

The emphasis on the antebellum past and its connection to the present that we have been following is a significant part of this meditation, and figures early in Paul Beatty's hilarious novel, *The White Boy Shuffle* (1996). The novel takes place in the late twentieth century and follows Gunnar Kaufman, the "only cool black guy at Mestizo Mulatto Mongrel Elementary," the "all-white multicultural school," that he attends in Santa Monica (28). When his mother moves him and his family to a black and Latino ghetto in West Los Angeles, Gunnar undergoes a peculiar education: he must learn to transform from a slacker surfer, whose cultural associations are almost exclusively white, to a fast-talking street-smart ghetto kid who can hang with hardcore ball players and gangbangers. In other words, he must learn how to be "black." Early in the novel, Gunnar traces his bloodline through his male forebears, many of whom would make excellent Talking Androids, the name Ishmael Reed gives in *Mumbo Jumbo* to black people who are willing to peddle racists' agendas. With names like Euripides, Swen, Wolfgang, Ludwig, and Solveig, Gunnar's male ancestors are so "astoundingly servile" towards their oppressors that they are eager to fight for the Confederacy, collaborate in hanging "Whites Only" signs in the Jim Crow South, and sell out black vernacular forms. In doing so, Gunnar's ancestors make white men rich and famous, while keeping black people poor and even helping in the plot to assassinate Malcolm X (15).

Like Schuyler's and Reed's, Beatty's satire is wicked, eviscerating, but ultimately cathartic. Certainly the most colorful of Gunnar's ancestors is Swen Kaufman, who unintentionally becomes the "only person ever to run away into slavery" (12). Swen dreams of becoming a serious ballet dancer, but, "being persona non-anglo saxon," he is "unwelcome in serious dance circles and the local variety shows" cannot use his "'Frenchified royal court body syncopations' in their coony-coony minstrel productions. 'Take the crown off your head, jibaboo. Show some teeth,'" they say (12). Frustrated, Swen packs his ballet slippers and stows away on a merchant ship "bound for the Cotton Belt," where he finds a plantation that offers him "free room and board and plenty of rehearsal space." There, the "rise-and-fall rhythm of the hoes and pick-axes and the austere urgency of the work songs gave him an idea for a 'groundbreaking' dance opera":

> It would be a renegade piece that intertwined the stoic movement of forced labor with the casual assuredness of the aristocratic lyric. Entranced with the possibilities, Swen impetuously hopped the wooden fence that separated the slave from the free. Picking up a tool, he smiled at the bewildered nigger next to him and churned feudal earth until sundown, determined to learn the ways of the field slaves. (13)

Swen pays dearly for the artistic freedom he finds in slavery. Originally delighted to get a slave for free, the master of the plantation cannot tolerate Swen's dancing and whips him: "Demi-plié – five lashes. Second position – ten lashes. Pirouette over the cotton seedlings – fifteen lashes; rock salt and scotch in the wounds" (14). Beatty's preposterous story about a ballet-dancing slave prancing gracefully over cotton fields invokes comically yet poignantly the urgency and desire for artistic freedom, one often paid for at great cost, which has characterized the development of African American letters and culture. In brilliant short form, the story also signifies on the debate regarding the European and African roots of African American culture, while highlighting the class and educational differences that have existed in African American communities for centuries. The field slaves that see Swen prancing about the fields think he is a "fool," while Swen cannot understand their "pidgin drawl." Meanwhile, the master beats "the classic romanticism out of Swen's feet" leaving him crumpled and "broken on the ground, lips painted with blood, face powdered with red clay dust" (14). Clearly invoking the minstrel stage, and the violence it exerted over black expression, this last image also underscores Swen's persistence, which ultimately wins him the respect of other slaves and propels him to stage his groundbreaking opera even after the master beats him senseless. Beatty includes Swen's story at the beginning of Gunnar's, clearly framing the narrative of a culturally "white" black kid who must learn how to be "authentically" black in the context of a long history of racial strife that has reached violent but also absurd proportions. Beatty's novel marks and clearly satirizes two opposing arcs: that of Gunnar's ancestors who strive desperately to assimilate into white, European culture, and that of Gunnar, who, upon having moved to the ghetto, must drop his white ways and learn how to "keep it real."

Beatty's disarming wit probes the ironic countermovement of these arcs against the background of a multicultural America not always at ease with its diversity. "My early education consisted of two kinds of multiculturalism," Gunnar tells us, "classroom multiculturalism, which reduced race, sexual orientation, and gender to inconsequence, and schoolyard multiculturalism, where the kids who knew the most Polack, queer, and farmer daughter jokes ruled. The classroom cross-cultural teachings could not compete with the playground blacktop lessons, which were cruel but at least humorous" (28). In some ways, Beatty gives us his version of blacktop lessons, including characters like Psycho Loco, a Mexican American homeboy capable of murder but also of intense friendship, Mrs. Kim, daughter of a black GI and a Korean woman, who is adopted by a black family in her teens, and who later, while living in the ghetto, bombs her own grocery store in protest of the Rodney King verdict. The novel intertwines these parodies of ethnic stereotypes with those of the people Gunnar comes in contact with in his peculiar bildungsroman. During his first and only college class, for instance, he meets Negritude, a white woman who enjoys ululating and wearing braids because it makes her feel "Nubian." When a stunned Gunnar remarks on her name, she tells him, "My parents named me that so I could be a reminder of the hagiocratic innocence possessed by black people around the world" (179). Gunnar panics and quits college on the spot. If the novel satirizes various racial and ethnic groups for their obsessions and delusions, it does so as a way of suggesting crucial questions. Can America move towards a true post-racial future given its peculiar fixation on, rather than embrace of, racial and ethnic difference? And what shape should black political leadership take at a time in which African Americans and Americans, more generally, have come to see the necessity of questioning older and rigid conceptions of race and yet still suffer or support racist practices? (See Leader-Picone.) The novel stresses the urgency of these questions, showing how Gunnar is catapulted into a leadership position that he cannot control and that ultimately leads towards mass violence.

The White Boy Shuffle, then, is framed by references to the antebellum past but its focus is on contemporary issues. Other novels, particularly those by Colson Whitehead, drop the frame altogether but still explore, through an absurdist, subtle humor reminiscent of Franz Kafka's, the legacy of America's violent racial past. Whitehead's *The Intuitionist* (1999), for instance, recalls Reed's *Mumbo Jumbo* since it sets two groups, the Empiricists and the Intuitionists, in tension with one another, and plays on aspects of the noir detection genre. The time and place are not identified, although one surmises that the novel takes place in New York City, sometime in the early part of the twentieth century. The action revolves around the lives of elevator inspectors, a set up that Whitehead uses to comment wryly on discourses of racial uplift, while the novel focuses on Lila Mae Watson, the first black woman to join their ranks. The Empiricists are rational by-the-book inspectors while the Intuitionists rely on feeling to carry on their work. The two groups are loosely associated with white and black culture respectively, playing out, in understated ways, a contrast that Richard Pryor made popular in stand-up between white mechanicalness and black spontaneity. The contrast, as in Pryor's comedy, is meant to invoke but mock racial distinctions that have their roots in colonialist beliefs in the cultural supremacy of Europe and the primitivism of the rest of the world. The novel also highlights, through an absurdist but eviscerating humor, the disturbing racism of tokenism and the cost that people of color pay when they become the first to break social and professional barriers (surely a theme that resonates against the background of our first black presidency). As in his other novels, *John Henry Days* (2001), *Apex Hides the Hurt* (2006), and the more recent *Sag Harbor* (2009), Whitehead writes with a wit that not only probes the complexity of race in America but also expands the scope of African American literature.

The use of humor in African American letters has developed in rich ways since the nineteenth century and the titles we have examined thus far represent salient examples. Paul Beatty's excellent *Hokum: An Anthology of African American Humor* (2006) provides an insightful introduction as well as excerpts of many other rich texts in this tradition, while Mel Watkins's seminal *On the Real Side: African American Humor from Slavery to Chris Rock* (1994) has provided a much-needed corrective to the lack of sustained scholarship on African American humor that has persisted until recently. Ralph Ellison, whose *Invisible Man* (1952) surely incorporates the bounce and brio of African American humor, published a brilliant essay in 1986, in which he ventures far into the power of African American humor. Titled "An Extravagance of Laughter," the essay explores why comedy is "indispensible agency for dealing with the American experience" and its "rampant incongruities." The "stress imposed by the extreme dislocations of American society," writes Ellison, calls for comedy, because "the greater the stress within society, the stronger the comic antidote required."

Note

* Sections of this essay have been previously published in different forms in Glenda R. Carpio, *Laughing Fit to Kill: Black Humor in the Fictions of Slavery*.

Bibliography

Beatty, Paul. *The White Boy Shuffle*. New York: Picador, 1996.

Beatty, Paul, ed. *Hokum: An Anthology of African American Humor*. New York: Bloomsbury, 2006.

Bernard, Louise. "The Musicality of Language: Redefining History in Suzan-Lori Parks's *The Death of the Last Black Man in the Whole Entire World*." *African American Review* 31.4 (1997): 687–99.

Brown, William Wells. *The Escape; or, a Leap for Freedom: A Drama in Five Acts*. 1858. Ed. John Ernest. Knoxville: University of Tennessee Press, 2001.

Carpio, Glenda R. *Laughing Fit to Kill: Black Humor in the Fictions of Slavery*. New York: Oxford University Press, 2008.

Chesnutt, Charles W. *Stories, Novels and Essays*. Ed. Werner Sollors. New York: Library of America, 2002.

Dickinson-Carr, Daryl. *African American Satire: The Sacred and the Profane Novel*. Columbia: University of Missouri Press, 2001.

Dundes, Alan, ed. *Mother Wit from the Laughing Barrel: Readings in the Interpretation of African American Folklore*. Jackson: University Press of Mississippi, 1973–1990.

Ellis, Trey. "The New Black Aesthetic." *Callaloo* 12.1 (1989): 233–43.

Ellison, Ralph. "An Extravagance of Laughter." In *Going to the Territory*. New York: Random House, 1986. 145–97.

Ferguson, Jeffrey B. *The Sage of Sugar Hill: George Schuyler and the Harlem Renaissance*. New Haven: Yale University Press, 2005.

Ganter, Granville. "'He Made Us Laugh Some': Frederick Douglass's Humor." *African American Review* 27.4 (2003): 535–52.

George, Nelson. *Post-Soul Nation: The Explosive, Contradictory, Triumphant, and Tragic 1980s as Experienced by African Americans (Previously Known as Blacks and before that Negroes)*. New York: Penguin, 2004.

Haggins, Bambi. *Laughing Mad: The Black Comic Persona in Post-Soul America*. New Brunswick: Rutgers University Press, 2007.

Himes, Chester. *Pinktoes*. 1961. Jackson: University Press of Mississippi, 1996.

Hughes, Langston. *The Collected Works of Langston Hughes: The Early Simple Stories*. Volume VII. Ed. Arnold Rampersad. Columbia: University of Missouri Press, 2001.

Hughes, Langston. *The Collected Works of Langston Hughes: The Early Simple Stories*. Volume VIII. Ed. Arnold Rampersad. Columbia: University of Missouri Press, 2002.

Hughes, Langston. *Simple Stakes a Claim*. New York: Rinehart, 1957.

Hurston, Zora Neale. *Mules and Men*. 1935. New York: Harper Perennial, 2008.

Hurston, Zora Neale. *Their Eyes Were Watching God*. 1937. New York: Perennial Classics, 1998.

Johnson, Charles. *Middle Passage*. New York: Atheneum, 1990.

Johnson, Charles. *The Oxherding Tale*. New York: Scribner, 1982–2005.

Kelly, Robin D.G. "Into the Fire: 1970 to the Present." In *To Make Our World Anew: A History of African Americans*. Ed. Robin D.G. Kelly and Earl Lewis. New York: Oxford University Press, 2000. 543–613.

Leader-Picone, Cameron. "Rinehartism: Changing Representations of Race in Contemporary African American Literature." PhD diss. Harvard University, 2009.

Levine, Lawrence. *Black Culture and Black Consciousness*. New York: Oxford University Press, 1977.

Lowe, John. "African American Humor." In *Comedy: A Geographical and Historical Guide*. Ed. Maurice Charney. Westport: Greenwood, 2005. 34–47.

Lowe, John. "Theories of Ethnic Humor: How to Enter Laughing." *American Quarterly* 38.3 (1986): 439–59.

Millstein, Gilbert. "Negro Everyman." *New York Times*, September 29, 1957. *New York Times* online: www.nytimes.com/books/01/04/22/specials/hughes-claim.html.

Neal, Mark Anthony. *Soul Babies: Black Popular Culture and the Post-Soul Aesthetic*. New York: Routledge, 2002.

Parks, Suzan-Lori. *The America Play and Other Works*. New York: Theater Communications Group, 1995.

Reed, Ishmael. *Flight to Canada*. 1976. New York: Simon & Schuster, 1998.

Reed, Ishmael. *MultiAmerica: Essays on Cultural Wars and Cultural Peace*. New York: Viking, 1997.

Reed, Ishmael. *Mumbo Jumbo*. 1972. New York: Simon & Schuster, 1996.

Rich, Frank. "A Difficult Birth for 'Mule Bone.'" *New York Times*, February 15, 1991. *New York Times* online: http://theater2.nytimes.com/mem/theater/treview.html?res=9D0CE2DB1F31F936A25751C0A967958260.

Schuyler, George. *Black No More: Being an Account of the Strange and Wonderful Working of Science in the Land of the Free A.D. 1933–1940*. 1931. New York: Modern Library, 1999.

Solomon, Alisa. "Signifying on the Signifyin': The Plays of Suzan-Lori Parks," *Theater* 21.3 (1990): 73–80.

Virtanen, Simo V. and Leonie Huddy. "Old-Fashioned Racism and New Forms of Racial Prejudice." *Journal of Politics* 60.2 (1998): 311–32.

Watkins, Mel. *African-American Humor: The Best of Black Comedy from Slavery to Today*. Chicago: Lawrence Hill, 1994.

Watkins, Mel. *On the Real Side: A History of African American Humor from Slavery to*

Chris Rock. Chicago: Lawrence Hill, 1994.

Whitehead, Colson. *The Intuitionist*. New York: Anchor Books, 1999.

Winant, Howard. "Racial Dualism at Century's End." In *The House that Race Built: Black Americans, U.S. Terrain*. Ed. Wahneema Lubiano. New York: Pantheon Books, 1997. 87–115.

Wright, Richard. "Between Laughter and Tears." *New Masses*. October 5, 1937: 22–3.

22
Neo-Slave Narratives

Madhu Dubey

On July 26, 2008, in Sullivan's Island, South Carolina, the Toni Morrison Society inaugurated its "Bench on the Road" project of commemorating key sites of African American history. Morrison, along with some 300 people, participated in a memorial ceremony honoring the captured Africans who disembarked at Sullivan's Island, a major gateway of the transatlantic slave trade. This public gesture of remembrance initiated by a literary society attests to the vital significance of the past in contemporary African American literature. Since the 1970s, African American writers have insistently revisited earlier historical periods, in particular the era of slavery. This literary return to the past marks a break from the present-oriented impetus of African American literature from its origins up to the late 1960s. With very few exceptions (notably Arna Bontemps's *Black Thunder*, published in 1936), African American novelists steered clear of the topic of slavery through much of the twentieth century. The publication of Margaret Walker's *Jubilee* in 1966 initiated an outpouring of novels about slavery that continues unabated into the twenty-first century. These novels comprise an array of genres, including realist historical fiction, historiographic metafiction, ghost stories, fantasy, speculative and science fiction, and even vampire tales, and are generating a growing body of scholarship.

The most popular label used to describe fiction about slavery published since the 1970s is "neo-slave narratives," a term coined by Bernard Bell and defined as "modern narratives of escape from bondage to freedom" (289). In the first book-length study of the genre, Ashraf Rushdy employs the term "neo-slave narrative" in a more restricted sense, to refer to those "contemporary novels that assume the form, adopt the conventions, and take on the first-person voice of the antebellum slave narrative" (*Neo-Slave Narratives* 3). Rushdy's description applies to critically celebrated novels such as Ishmael Reed's *Flight to Canada* (1976), Sherley Anne Williams's *Dessa Rose* (1986), and Charles Johnson's *Middle Passage* (1991), among others, but several recent novels of slavery are not primarily situated in the antebellum period or narrated in the form of first-person testimony. Accordingly, Arlene Keizer proposes the term "contemporary narratives of slavery" to include a broader range of fiction that revisits slavery without necessarily rewriting the genre of the nineteenth-century fugitive slave narrative (3). Keizer also notes the diasporic scope of the resurgent literary interest in slavery since the 1970s: prominent Caribbean, African, and black British writers, including Caryl Phillips, Erna Brodber, Zakes Mda, and Fred D'Aguiar, have contributed to the stream of late twentieth-century novels about slavery, although the genre has proliferated most visibly in the US context.

Regardless of how they label the genre, scholars agree that its emergence in the 1970s marks a crucial juncture of historical reckoning that followed the racial upheaval of the previous two decades. Although it seems logical to assume that the genre of the neo-slave narrative emerged in response to historical amnesia about slavery, in fact it was preceded by a heightened public attention to slavery during the late 1960s. In the immediate aftermath of the Civil Rights and Black Power movements, slavery erupted onto the national scene as a matter of intense public interest and debate. Conflicts over how slavery should be represented in the realms of historiography, literature, and popular visual culture were clearly inflected by the militant black politics of the 1960s. The most important point of contention in the national discourse about slavery in this period was the issue of slave agency. By the end of the 1960s, historians had begun to challenge Stanley Elkins's influential account of the American slave as a "Sambo"-like figure whose personality was wholly shaped by the crushing victimage imposed by slavery. Notable historical studies of slavery that were published during the early 1970s, such as John Blassingame's *The Slave Community* or Eugene Genovese's *Roll, Jordan, Roll*, emphasized the resilience of the slave community as well as the sparks of rebellious agency that gave the lie to Elkins's Sambo thesis. Perhaps the most lasting contribution of what is now known as the revisionist historiography of slavery was its reassessment of prevailing standards of historical evidence. In an effort to incorporate the perspectives of slaves on their own experience, historians began to turn to folklore, oral tradition, antebellum fugitive slave narratives, and Works Progress Administration interviews with former slaves, and for the first time in the academic study of slavery the first-person testimony of slaves was accepted as legitimate historical evidence. The official archive of slavery was radically expanded by the beginning of the 1970s, with the reissue of numerous antebellum fugitive slave narratives.

The question of how best to recover the perspective of the enslaved was also being hotly contested in the realms of literary and visual culture from the late-1960s through the 1970s. Concerns about who can and should speak for the slave surfaced in response to the spate of movies and television shows that were released during this period, including a film version of John Oliver Killens's *Slaves* (1969), a TV adaptation of Ernest Gaines's novel *The Autobiography of Miss Jane Pittman* (1974), and a historical dramatization of the life of Harriet Tubman, *A Woman Called Moses*, that aired on NBC in 1978. Notwithstanding their heroic treatments of slave agency and resistance, these shows drew sharp rebuke from black commentators for their common use of white narrators to filter the experience of slavery to the American viewing public. In the literary sphere, the publication of a fictionalized slave narrative by a white writer, William Styron's *The Confessions of Nat Turner* (1967), provoked the most acrimonious debates about authentic representations of slavery. In *William Styron's Nat Turner: Ten Black Writers Respond* (1968), historians, intellectuals, and public figures associated with the Black Power movement took issue not only with Styron's caricature of Turner as a hypersexual fanatic, but also with his assumption of the first-person voice of the slave. As Ashraf Rushdy points out in his carefully researched account of the controversy sparked by Styron's novel, concerns about white appropriation of the slave's voice were crucially entwined with issues of historical accuracy (*Neo-Slave Narratives* 54–95).

Emerging out of this broader cultural context, the earliest novels of slavery took on the task of recovering the authentic perspectives of slaves on their own experiences. In keeping with the aims and methods of the 1960s revisionist historiography of slavery, novelists such as Margaret Walker and Ernest Gaines turned to oral testimony as the most effective means of correcting and supplementing the historical record. In *Jubilee* (1966), Walker adapted her great-grandmother's oral stories of slavery, and further reinforced the importance of oral tradition as a conduit of slave culture by using excerpts from spirituals as chapter epigraphs. The narrator of Gaines's *The Autobiography of Miss Jane Pittman* (1971) is a history teacher who ostensibly tape-records, edits, and transcribes the oral testimony of Miss Jane Pittman, who was born a slave. When asked about his motives ("What's wrong with them books you already got?"), he replies simply, "Miss Jane is not in them" (vi). The main impetus of realist historical novels of slavery is to fill such gaps in the official historical archive. Barbara Chase-Riboud's *Sally Hemings* (1979), which narrates the long suppressed story of Thomas Jefferson's slave mistress, opens with an epigraph from John Adams that begins, "Records are destroyed. Histories are annihilated, or interpolated, or prohibited" (n.p.), signaling the novel's ambition to rectify the historical record, to offer a more full and accurate account of slavery.

Some later novels of slavery remain committed to this realist project of historical reclamation; notable examples include Sherley Anne Williams's *Dessa Rose* (1986), Lorene Cary's *The Price of a Child* (1995), and Jewell Parker Rhodes's *Douglass' Women* (2002). Like *Sally Hemings*, these novels are inspired by the life stories of actual women who were enslaved, and explicitly set out to correct the blind spots and misrepresentations of dominant historical texts and narratives. Cary and Rhodes reinvent the stories of women (black as well as white, slave as well as free) who were crucial in various ways to the anti-slavery struggle, but who appear only in passing references or footnotes in historical documents about the abolitionist movement. *The Price of a Child* recounts the story of Jane Johnson, a runaway slave who eventually became an abolitionist lecturer, while Rhodes's novel alternates between the stories of Frederick Douglass's first wife, Anna Murray, who was instrumental to his escape from slavery, and his long-term white mistress Ottilie Assing, who offered behind-the-scenes support for Douglass's anti-slavery agenda.

Whether narrated in the first or third person, all these novels are centrally concerned with the question of *voice* as a measure of authentic historical recovery. Cary traces ex-slave Mercer Gray's struggle to modulate her speaking voice to suit the priorities of the anti-slavery movement, and is careful to include those memories of slavery that could not be expressed within the framework of the abolitionist lecture circuit. In an interview, Jewell Parker Rhodes asserts that her novel celebrates two women "who have been reclaimed from history. Ottilie and Anna are no longer lost, historical figures. They are no longer silent … I want readers always to remember that Ottilie and Anna had their *own* voices" (Rhodes n.p.). Of course, it is not coincidental or surprising that women novelists of slavery are the ones most fervently engaged in the enterprise of historical recovery or that this enterprise continues into the twenty-first century. As Rhodes remarks, history still all too often gets written as the story of great men, erasing or veiling the contributions of women.

Among the realist novels of slavery, Williams's *Dessa Rose* contains the most pointed critique of the ways in which traditional historiography has muffled the voices of slave women. In common with many other novels of slavery published since the 1970s, the cast of characters in *Dessa Rose* prominently features a historian, in this case Adam Nehemiah, author of a book on slave management techniques, *The Master's Complete Guide to Dealing with Slaves and Other Dependents*. The first third of the novel is narrated predominantly from Nehemiah's point of view, in the form of notes that he hopes will lead to the publication of a second book on the roots of slave rebellion. This section of the novel may be seen as a "master text," or a document about slavery written from a position of dominance, with its very title, "The Darky," alluding to one such authoritative discourse, the plantation tradition of the late nineteenth and early twentieth centuries, in which slaves were represented as simple-minded creatures driven by physical appetites and incapable of reason. Like Margaret Walker and Ernest Gaines, Williams relies on oral tradition (especially song) to counter Nehemiah's master text and to convey the experience of slavery from a first-person perspective. In an Author's Note to the novel, Williams writes that "Afro-Americans, having survived by word of mouth – and made of that process a high art – remain at the mercy of literature and writing; often, these have betrayed us" (ix). Williams's suspicion of written texts of slavery is directed specifically at William Styron's *Confessions of Nat Turner*, which, as noted earlier, was the most visible literary account of slavery published in the 1960s. Denouncing Styron's novel as a travesty of "the as-told-to memoir of slave revolt leader Nat Turner" (ix), Williams is clearly extending the literary project of corrective counter-representation that African American writers initiated during the 1970s. While acknowledging her alienation from traditional history – "there was no place in the American past I could go and be free" – Williams draws inspiration from a work of revisionist historiography, Angela Davis's influential essay, "Reflections on the Black Woman's Role in the Community of Slaves." The character of Dessa Rose is based on an actual enslaved woman, briefly mentioned in Davis's essay, who led an uprising and escaped from a coffle while pregnant. Williams remarks that Davis's article "marked a turning point in [her] efforts to apprehend that other history" (x) – the history of slave agency that falsifies a master text such as Nehemiah's journal, with its dehumanizing portrait of Dessa Rose as a primitive "darky" incapable of master-minding a slave rebellion.

Lorene Cary and Jewell Parker Rhodes similarly take pains to cite the historical sources that went into the making of their fictional texts, demonstrating their investment in the truth-telling claims typical of realist historical fiction. In addition to the teleological assumptions implicit in any task of historical correction, realist novels of slavery chart progressive plot trajectories from slavery to freedom, equating freedom with the power of authentic representation. For example, *Dessa Rose* tracks a liberatory movement beginning with a racist text that defines the slave woman as "The Darky" and culminating in the final section, "The Negress," which is largely narrated in Dessa's oralized first-person voice. In most realist fictions of slavery, the incorporation of oral voices and sources into the written medium of the novel functions as an analogue for the integration of subjective testimonies into the official historical archive of slavery. In this respect, such novels are fully consonant with the revisionist historiography of slavery: while keenly attentive to the unequal power relations that frame the writing of history, they remain committed to the progressive historical enterprise of more inclusive representation.

Although realist historical novels of slavery continue to appear sporadically even into the twenty-first century, much more common are novels that depart from narrative realism to varying degrees, with the ultimate aim of challenging narratives of African American history as a process of racial advancement. In counterpoint to the linear historical vision of realist fictions of slavery, formally experimental novels such as Gayl Jones's *Corregidora* (1975) and Leon Forrest's *Two Wings to Veil My Face* (1983) fracture narrative time in order to reveal the lingering grip of slavery on the present. Like virtually all fiction about slavery published since the 1970s, these novels take as their point of departure the gaps in the official historical archive that generate the need for stories, whether oral or literary. Because written records of slavery have long since been burned by the masters in *Corregidora*, the foremothers of Ursa, the protagonist, compulsively repeat their stories about the past, in order to ensure that their historical version of slavery is transmitted to future generations. Likewise, in Forrest's novel, Sweetie Reed commands Nathaniel, her adopted grandson, to write down her stories about her enslaved ancestors because "too much has been erased in time" (7). Oral storytelling sustains a specific kind of historical memory in these novels, testifying to a systematic element of slavery – the rape of women by their masters – not likely to appear in official documents of the institution.

The familial narratives of slavery that are at the forefront of Forrest's and Jones's novels carry disquieting implications for the post-Civil Rights and Black Power generation, as becomes immediately clear by comparing these novels to the most popular story of slavery to emerge during the 1970s, Alex Haley's genealogical saga, *Roots* (1976). The spectacular cross-racial success of the TV mini-series based on Haley's book was partly due to its smooth reconciliation of the demands of black cultural nationalism and US patriotism. While affirming African ancestral origins as the foundation of contemporary black identity, Haley's "up from slavery" narrative also confirms the promise of the American dream. Leon Forrest and Gayl Jones do not offer either kind of reassurance. With rape and miscegenation at the center of their "family genesis" stories (Forrest 90), *Corregidora* and *Two Wings* obviously cannot deliver a secure or racially pure conception of black identity. Oral traditions in these novels, whether familial lore or blues music, only confound notions of racial or cultural authenticity, for they are revealed to be shot through with contradictions, complicit as much as oppositional in their relation to the "master's text." In *Corregidora*, it is not just the history of rape but also the ancestral imperative to keep reproducing this history that proves to be stifling to Ursa, as her story about her own sexuality is repeatedly interrupted by the stories of her enslaved ancestors. Both novels follow a pattern of recurrence to the "backwater time" of slavery (Forrest 13), fostering an impression of temporal stasis and simultaneity. While calling for an unflinching confrontation with the painful history of slavery, *Corregidora* and *Two Wings* multiply rather than resolve questions about the proper way of remembering this history in the post-Civil Rights period.

Corregidora and *Two Wings* belong to a subset of post-1970s fiction about slavery that Ashraf Rushdy calls "palimpsest narratives," novels that explore the impact of the past on the present by adopting a "bi-temporal perspective" (*Remembering Generations* 5), inscribing two different historical periods on the same textual plane (8). On the plot level, palimpsest narratives deal with contemporary individuals who are haunted by family secrets that can be uncovered only by delving into the unofficial history of slavery (5). The shameful family secret usually has to do with the rape of a female slave ancestor by her master, as we have already seen to be the case in Forrest's and Jones's novels. In addition to *Corregidora*, Rushdy includes two other novels written during the 1970s within his rubric of palimpsest narratives, Octavia Butler's *Kindred* (1979) and David Bradley's *The Chaneysville Incident* (1981). Although *Kindred* is often classified as science fiction because it uses the time-travel device to return its twentieth-century protagonist to antebellum slavery, its similarities with *Corregidora* and *Two Wings* are easily apparent. Like Ursa and Nathaniel, Dana is pulled back to the past by an ancestral imperative, and she discovers the family secret that her own genesis is entangled in a violent history of rape and miscegenation. A white slave-owning ancestor, Rufus Weylin, keeps involuntarily summoning Dana back to the past whenever his life is endangered. During her visits to the plantation, Dana makes it her mission not only to save Weylin's life, but also to ensure her own future birth by abetting Weylin's rape of Alice, her enslaved foremother. Dana's complicity in the rape of a slave ancestor raises disturbing questions about the self-interested motives that guide her recovery of her familial history. Like Forrest and Jones, Butler denies Dana as well as her readers the genealogical solace offered by a text such as *Roots*. Dana, Ursa, and Nathaniel are all forced to acknowledge white slave-owners and black female slaves as kin. Such impure racial origins imply that return to the history of slavery will not yield easy answers to questions of black identity in the post-Civil Rights period.

The palimpsest form of all these novels not only reveals the ways in which the history of rape and miscegenation informs the sexual and racial sensibilities of late twentieth-century individuals, but also belies widespread conceptions of US racial history as an emancipatory movement commencing with the abolition of slavery and culminating in the Civil Rights movement. In *Kindred*, assumptions of racial progress are challenged at the levels of public and personal history. At the beginning of the novel, Dana proudly proclaims herself to be "free, born free, intending to stay free" (Butler 38) – a statement immediately undermined as she is literally remanded to slavery, stripped of all the rights and privileges she takes for granted, and consequently forced to confront the limits of her modern notions of choice, consent, and free will. Dana's final trip back to slavery significantly takes place on July 4, 1976, the bicentennial anniversary of US Independence, in what Butler describes as "some kind of reverse symbolism" (243). This regressive movement, common to the plots of all the palimpsest narratives, foreshortens the temporal distance between the antebellum slave and the post-Civil-Rights-era black subject. *Kindred* most radically breaches this distance, thanks to its time-travel mechanism, which provides Dana a first-hand experience of slavery. Exhibiting the suspicion of historical knowledge found in so many neo-slave narratives, *Kindred* presents Dana's deepening immersion into slavery to be contingent on her increasing distance from the history textbooks she brings with her from the late twentieth century. Although these books do provide Dana with some valuable information, only after burning them does she gain an affective and immediate experience of slavery – an experience that permanently mutilates her body, as she loses an arm in her final attempt to escape back from slavery into the twentieth century.

David Bradley's *The Chaneysville Incident* launches a similar although more sustained assault on conventional historical knowledge. Bradley's protagonist, John Washington, is a professional historian trying to discover the cause of his father's death, a quest for knowledge that ultimately leads him to the graves of 12 fugitive slaves who chose to kill themselves when threatened by recapture. John is not able to reconstruct this buried story of slavery until he disavows the methods of traditional historiography. During the early part of the novel, John tries to learn what happened to his father by conducting historical research: he catalogs every fact that may be relevant to his father's story on color-coded index cards which he orders into a strictly chronological sequence. But when this system fails to yield any valuable insights, John begins to develop a scathing critique of his disciplinary training. The modern study of history, as John now sees it, is outmoded insofar as it is still guided by the principles of seventeenth-century Newtonian science, such as mechanistic laws of cause and effect, which have long been revaluated in the study of the natural sciences. Another fallacy that John must unlearn is the presumption that historians are detached and objective observers who remain "unaffected, unchanged, unharmed" by the process of researching the past (Bradley 140). This neutral stance is especially untenable for a historian such as John who "specialize[s] in the study of atrocities" (186) and whose research focuses on his own ancestors. John begins to discern the truth of what happened in the past by thinking like a novelist rather than a historian – in other words, by turning away from the "cold facts" (146) and instead drawing on the faculties of emotion and imagination. Not surprisingly, the novel ends with John burning his pens and pencils, pads and papers – the "tools of [his] trade" as a historian (431).

John Washington's dismissive remark that the historian is nothing but a "frustrated novelist" (Bradley 49) is echoed by the narrator of Ishmael Reed's *Flight to Canada* (1976), who declares that Edgar Allan Poe "says more in a few stories than all of the volumes by historians" (10). Reed's novel, along with Charles Johnson's *Oxherding Tale* (1982), can be characterized as historiographic metafiction, Linda Hutcheon's influential label for postmodern novels that playfully parody established forms of historical writing in order to identify and question the artifice involved in the construction of historical truth (105–23). As the two most irreverently humorous novelists of slavery, Reed and Johnson employ parody to expose the unreliability of the official historical record of slavery. *Flight to Canada* is full of anachronisms (such as a fugitive slave escaping to freedom on a jumbo jet or President Abraham Lincoln's assassination being shown on television) that disrupt linear chronology as well as realism, two of the most common conventions in the writing of history. Johnson, too, violates the cardinal principle of historical realism in *Oxherding Tale* by inventing extravagantly fictive scenarios in which, for example, a slave-owner hires a tutor to give his slave an education in philosophy, Karl Marx pays a visit to the plantation, and, most outrageously, a male slave is sexually apprenticed to a white female slave-owner. By casting actual historical figures in blatantly implausible roles, such as President Lincoln dancing a waltz with a slave woman named Mammy Barracuda or Karl Marx showing more interest in what is being served for dinner than in labor relations on the plantation, Reed and Johnson mock the "great men" model of history. Instead, both novelists focus on "subhistoric" matters (Johnson, *Oxherding Tale* 43), such as the sexuality of black male slaves, which are missing from official archives of slavery.

While critique of traditional historiography is a common feature of contemporary narratives of slavery, what may initially seem surprising is that Reed and Johnson also parody the genre of the fugitive slave narrative, which had recently been legitimized as evidence thanks to the efforts of revisionist historians of the 1960s. *Flight to Canada* and *Oxherding Tale* assume the form of fugitive slave narratives, but only to highlight the restrictive features of the genre, which was heavily edited to suit the priorities of the abolitionist movement. Reed's novel shows how easily the slave's story could be exploited by abolitionists, through his merciless portrayal of Harriet Beecher Stowe stealing and making a hefty profit from the slave narrative of Josiah Henson. This emphasis on abolitionist manipulation of slave narratives suggests the difficulties implicit in the project of historical recovery, as even the first-person documents of ex-slaves were written under severe constraints and therefore cannot be fully trusted to reveal the authenticity of slave experience. Johnson takes this skepticism about the reliability of fugitive slave narratives to a hilarious (yet utterly serious) extreme, including in his novel a chapter titled "The Manumission of First-Person Viewpoint."

In this chapter, the first-person voice of the primary narrator of the novel, the fugitive slave Andrew Hawkins, is abruptly interrupted by an omniscient narrator's reflections on what may be the "only invariant feature" of the antebellum slave narrative: its reliance on first-person voice. This convention was crucial to the credibility of slave narratives, as is clear from the clause, "written by him (or her) self," that was often appended to the titles of these texts. But Johnson's omniscient narrator takes a very different approach to the point of view that helped validate slave narratives as historical evidence: "What we value most highly in this viewpoint are precisely the *limitations* imposed upon the narrator-perceiver, who cannot, for example, know what transpires in another mind … or in a scene that excludes him; what we lack in authority, we gain in immediacy: a premise (or prejudice) of Positivist Science" (152). This metafictive commentary on the first-person voice of fugitive slave narratives parallels David Bradley's critique of modern historiography: both forms of writing depend on truth claims that are grounded in the premises of positivist science.

The fact that fugitive slave narratives were implicated in modern conceptions of knowledge and being helps explain why so many late twentieth-century novelists began to expose the limitations of the genre not long after it was finally admitted into the official historical archive. In her essay, "The Site of Memory," Toni Morrison observes that the slave narratives were written during the "Age of Enlightenment," which was also the "Age of Scientific Racism" (301), closely echoing the omniscient narrator's assertion in *Oxherding Tale* that "the Age of Reason overlaps the age of slavery" (152). As Paul Gilroy argues in *The Black Atlantic*, slavery formed a constitutive rather than aberrant part of Enlightenment modernity. Pseudo-scientific claims about the biological inferiority of peoples of African descent served to disqualify them from human status and thereby to sanction their enslavement. Writing during an era when slaves were relegated to subhuman status because they were believed to be innately incapable of reason, the authors of antebellum slave narratives displayed their possession of rationality to gain access to modern definitions of the "human." When Frederick Douglass, in his 1845 fugitive slave narrative, took pains to add a footnote discrediting the root-work practiced by a fellow slave as ignorant superstition, his own commitment to reason helped to demonstrate the fitness of slaves for freedom and citizenship.

While appreciating the urgent political work performed by fugitive slave authors in the historical context of scientific racism, Toni Morrison remarks in "The Site of Memory" that the exercise of writing is necessarily "very different" for African American authors in the late twentieth century (302). In the historical context of the post-Civil Rights period, once African Americans were finally granted legal access to the modern human rights sought by Frederick Douglass and other fugitive slave authors, contemporary novelists of slavery became more interested in exposing the racial abuses that had been perpetrated in the name of humanism and reason. Morrison's most recent novel, *A Mercy* (2008), traces the process of racialization that was just beginning to take root in late-eighteenth-century America as a means of rationalizing slavery. The early chapters of the novel present a society in which the buying and selling of enslaved Africans coexist with the indentured servitude and debt bondage of white and Native American labor. Over the course of the novel, these racially fluid relations of labor exploitation are restructured into a rigidly dualistic distinction between "Europes" and "Africs" (46). The institutionalization of chattel slavery is shown to require a reclassification of the captured African from "person" to "black" (165), from human being to "a thing apart" (115). Morrison indicts this dehumanizing racial logic not by demonstrating the slave's possession of reason but through the simple and powerful observation of an African when she is first inducted into slavery: "Unreason rules here" (164).

Charles Johnson's *Middle Passage* (1991) reveals this binary racial logic of slavery to be a crucial component of Enlightenment notions of humanity. The novel probes the "wound" of dualism inherent to modern conceptions of human being: the modern subject requires an object, a non-self in order to gain coherence, and slavery, according to Johnson, racialized this "bloody structure of dualism" (98). Johnson suggests that the racialized structure of modern being may be transcended only by disavowing the positions of both subject and object. In *Middle Passage*, a counter-modern way of being is embodied in the fictive African tribe of the Allmuseri, who are characterized as the pure others of the modern West: they are a "tribe of sorcerers" who lack a tradition of positivist science and whose language is attuned to intuitive rather than analytical modes of thought. Their god possesses "a hundred ways to relieve men of their reason" (102), and insofar as "it can't be an object of knowledge for itself" (101), this god epitomizes a unity of being that is unavailable to modern Western subjects including the narrator of the novel, the ex-slave author Rutherford Calhoun. But even as Johnson builds up a logic of polar opposition between rational Western subjects and their African others, he deconstructs this logic as itself a product of modern dualism. For Rutherford Calhoun, the Allmuseri god holds out the promise of the end of history, or of the violent process by which Africans were inducted into Western modernity. But Rutherford eventually recognizes the "stupidity" of his own desire to see the Allmuseri tribe as "pure essence, outside history" (124). Rutherford himself is inescapably enmeshed in modern history, as is clear from the fact that his first-person narrative of the Middle Passage is written at the behest of the Captain of the slave ship and takes the form of a master's text, in this case a captain's log.

Whereas Frederick Douglass in his 1845 narrative affirmed literacy as his gateway to freedom, authors of neo-slave narratives express deep ambivalence about the emancipatory potential of print literacy by citing and resignifying various sorts of master texts in their novels, including Adam Nehemiah's guide to slave management in Williams's *Dessa Rose*, Master Swille's will in *Flight to Canada*, or the captain's log in *Middle Passage.* The most notable such master text is Schoolteacher's Notebook in Toni Morrison's *Beloved* (1987). With its columns listing the animal and human characteristics of the slaves, the notebook starkly clarifies the ways in which writing was embroiled in the ideologies of racial difference that were used to rationalize slavery. People of African descent were categorized as subhuman because of their alleged deficiency in print literacy, deemed to be the preeminent marker of rational culture. Yet, in a contradictory twist, once enslaved they were legally prohibited from learning how to read and write. In *Beloved*, Morrison presents the unlikely scenario of slaves encouraged to acquire literacy by their master, only to realize, in stark contrast to Frederick Douglass, that writing is too deeply complicit in the master's ideology to be a vehicle of freedom. Not surprisingly, Sethe defines freedom as "no notebook for my babies" (198) and the novel as a whole counters the dehumanizing master text of Schoolteacher's Notebook through the oral traditions of song, sermon, and storytelling.

Morrison has described *Beloved* as an effort to "fill in the blanks that the slave narratives left" ("The Site of Memory" 303), an effort that involves a critical revaluation not only of the liberatory possibilities that ex-slave authors often invested in literacy, but also of the rational and realist imperatives of the fugitive slave narratives. Phenomena that defy narrative realism and rational understanding abound in late twentieth-century novels of slavery. One of the most bizarre examples is the Allmuseri god, in Johnson's *Middle Passage*, who has been captured and is being taken to the New World in the hold of a slave ship. Just as Johnson refuses to offer a plausible explanation for the god's presence, Morrison too deliberately confounds reason through the "miraculous resurrection" of a murdered infant daughter in *Beloved* (105). While Sethe's killing of her daughter is shown to be perfectly understandable within the bounds of reason (she wants to prevent her from being captured back to slavery), the character of Beloved is not amenable to clear or exclusively rational interpretation. Beloved can be seen as symbolic of Sethe's repressed past as well as of the "disremembered and unaccounted for" spirits of the "sixty million and more" who died during the Middle Passage and to whom the novel is dedicated (274). But a symbolic reading of Beloved's character does not exhaust all the interpretive possibilities entertained in the novel, some of which demand that readers believe that Beloved is not a ghost or a hallucination or a symbolic projection, but a flesh and blood reincarnation of Sethe's dead daughter. In order to accept that Beloved has actually returned from the dead, readers must suspend rational notions of mundane reality. Exceeding the conventions of narrative realism, Beloved's return evokes the dark underside of Enlightenment rationality; through its powerful critique of the unreason of slavery, Morrison's novel contributes to what Paul Gilroy has famously called a "black counter-culture of modernity" (36).

In addition to undermining Enlightenment rationality, many late twentieth-century novelists of slavery develop a counter-culture of modernity by reclaiming alternative forms of belief suppressed by the modern legacy. These other ways of knowing are often specifically identified as African. For example, in Octavia Butler's *Wild Seed* (1980), Anyanwu, a conjure woman who is captured from Africa and transported to the New World, draws on her magical shape-shifting abilities to elude reproductive slavery. Frank Yerby's neo-slave narrative, *A Darkness at Ingraham's Crest* (1979), recounts the story of a slave who exerts considerable control over his masters by practicing vodun. The Dahomean, as Yerby repeatedly calls him, channels the power of the "Tau Vudun," or ancestral gods, a power that white people on the plantation can grasp only through the mocking vocabulary of "ghosts" or "ha'nts" (55). In *The Chaneysville Incident*, David Bradley's narrator explains that what is at stake in the distinction between ghost and ancestor is two utterly disparate conceptions of the meaning of death, which signifies the end of life in European culture but a passing on of spirit in Africanist belief systems (428). The term "ghost" makes sense only to those who expect finality from death, whereas the word "ancestor" reflects the belief that dead forebears continue to inhabit the same dimension as the living. The crucial point elaborated in Bradley's novel is that the distinction between ghosts and ancestors is not a matter of reason versus superstition but a difference between two incommensurate but equally coherent belief systems. Once the historian-narrator of *The Chaneysville Incident* opens his mind to the worldview of the fugitive slaves whose story he is trying to recreate, he begins to hear them running, singing, and breathing, a form of material evidence from which he concludes that "the dead really are there" on the same level of reality as the living (389).

Whereas Bradley's novel explores the legitimacy of this alternate belief system from within the bounds of narrative realism, other novelists have increasingly turned to the genres of fantastic and speculative fiction to elaborate a black counter-culture of modernity. Numerous recent narratives about slavery deploy paranormal, supernatural, or magical devices to dislocate linear time and to bring about the uneasy coexistence of distinct historical periods on the same narrative plane. The best-known example is Toni Morrison's concept of rememory, which suggests that traumatic histories can outlast the consciousness of those who directly experienced them and can be apprehended as memories by future generations. A remarkably similar sense of the material presence of the past permeates Steven Barnes's *Blood Brothers* (1996), a hybrid of cyberfiction and neo-slave narrative, and Phyllis Alesia Perry's *Stigmata* (1998), both of which feature late twentieth-century protagonists who are possessed by slave ancestors, to the point that they directly experience the brutality of slavery on their own bodies. The entire story of J. California Cooper's *Family* (1991) is narrated in the first-person voice of an ancestor who has died but lives on in a state of limbo as long as her descendants are still subject to slavery. In Jewelle Gomez's *The Gilda Stories* (1991), a young fugitive slave girl becomes a vampire and time-travels through various periods stretching from the antebellum era to the mid-twenty-first century. Any progressive possibilities that may be implicit in Gilda's movement forward through time are undercut by her perception of human history as marked by the recurrent return of slavery.

While the persistence of the past in the present is the most common form of temporal disjunction found in fantastic fictions of slavery, several recent novelists take the apparently opposite approach of flashing-forward to the future. In James McBride's *Song Yet Sung* (2008), an enslaved woman, Liz Spocott, can look into the post-Civil Rights era – a paranormal ability that does not feel like much of a gift to Liz because it reveals images of future black people living in various states of unfreedom. Edward P. Jones's critically acclaimed novel, *The Known World* (2003), at first glance seems to be the very epitome of realist fiction, an impression reinforced by lengthy pseudo-historical passages about slavery narrated in the past tense. While these passages foster a view of slavery as a finished and remote period of history, the novel also contains disorienting flash-forwards that inform readers of events that will occur decades beyond the narrative present. For example, the story of a character who is a slave, Stamford Crow Blueberry, suddenly leaps forward from the antebellum period to 1987, when the city of Richmond in Virginia officially renames a street after him at the urging of his step-great-granddaughters. Disrupting the notion of self-contained time periods typical of realist historical fiction, such temporal interruptions suggest that slavery should not be seen as a closed chapter of US history.

The conviction that slavery is not yet a matter of history lies behind the various time-rupturing devices found in post-1970s novels of slavery, including rememory, time travel, flashbacks, flash-forwards, and possession. In his preface to *A Darkness at Ingraham's Crest*, Frank Yerby asserts: "American slavery lasted from 1619 to 1865, two hundred forty-six years. It was further extended under various shabby subterfuges until well into the 1960's, that is, if one concedes that it has even ended yet" (9). Some variant of this pessimistic view of US racial history impels most novels of slavery published since the 1970s, especially those that break from narrative realism. When the hero of Bradley's *The Chaneysville Incident* disavows the realist and rational principles guiding modern historiography and, as a consequence, begins to sense the lingering presence of long-dead fugitive slaves, he takes this as an indication that slavery "is still going on" (213–14). In her essay, "The Time of Slavery," Saidiya Hartman asks, "to what end is the ghost of slavery conjured up" so persistently in late twentieth-century black culture (763)? In response, Hartman suggests that the contemporary preoccupation with slavery is primarily "a way of lamenting current circumstance" (771), of debunking the idea that the Civil Rights Movement brought a decisive end to the long history of racial oppression that originated in slavery.

While most African American novelists since the 1970s have revisited slavery in order to apprehend "history as an injury that has yet to cease happening" (Hartman 772), a few authors of speculative and science fiction have taken the unusual approach of writing novels about enslavement that are not centrally concerned with the history of antebellum US slavery. For example, Steven Barnes's novel *Lion's Blood* (2002) imagines an alternative history in which Africans have colonized the Americas and enslaved people of European descent, and Octavia Butler's *Wild Seed* focuses on a vampirical African male, Doro, who subjects New World peoples of different races to reproductive slavery. Whereas both these novels are set in the distant past and are intended to defamiliarize the dualistic concept of racial difference instituted by antebellum US slavery, two futuristic science-fictional texts, Samuel Delany's *Stars in My Pocket like Grains of Sand* (1984) and Butler's *Parable of the Sower* (1993), deal with systems of enslavement that are not primarily organized by race. The slaves in *Parable* belong to all races and the predominant forms of slavery in Butler's twenty-first-century dystopia are sexual trafficking and debt servitude to multinational corporations. Butler selectively reanimates the conventions of the fugitive slave narratives, such as the flight from slavery in the South to freedom in the North, in order to render the harrowing labor conditions confronting Latino, Asian-American, and white, not only African American, workers. Delany's novel takes a similar approach, adapting the familiar motif of the slave's illicit quest for literacy to a racially unmarked system of slavery founded on unequal global exchange of information. Although these novels may seem ahistorical (in dissociating the term "slavery" from its most familiar historical referent), they promote a historicizing approach that can register breaks as well as continuities between the past and the present. By transposing the conventions of the fugitive slave narratives on to unfamiliar and ambiguously racialized forms of inequality, *Parable* and *Stars in My Pocket* explore the ways in which the meanings and workings of race are being reconfigured at the turn of the twenty-first century. Taken together, science-fictional neo-slave narratives by Barnes, Butler, and Delany provoke readers to imagine a future in which the racial legacy of antebellum US slavery may finally be consigned to the realm of history.

Bibliography

Beaulieu, Elizabeth Ann. *Black Women Writers and the American Neo-slave Narrative*. Westport, CT: Greenwood, 1999.

Bell, Bernard. *The Afro-American Novel and Its Tradition*. Amherst: University of Massachusetts Press, 1987.

Bradley, David. *The Chaneysville Incident*. New York: Harper and Row, 1981.

Butler, Octavia. *Kindred*. Boston, MA: Beacon, 1979.

Chase-Riboud, Barbara. *Sally Hemings*. New York: Avon, 1979.

Forrest, Leon. *Two Wings to Veil My Face*. Chicago: Another Chicago Press, 1983.

Gaines, Ernest. *The Autobiography of Miss Jane Pittman*. New York: Bantam, 1971.

Gilroy, Paul. *The Black Atlantic: Modernity and Double Consciousness*. Cambridge, MA: Harvard University Press, 1993.

Hartman, Saidiya. "The Time of Slavery." *South Atlantic Quarterly* 101.4 (2002): 757–77.

Hutcheon, Linda. *A Poetics of Postmodernism: History, Theory, Fiction*. New York: Routledge, 1988.

Johnson, Charles. *Middle Passage*. New York: Plume, 1991.

Johnson, Charles. *Oxherding Tale*. New York: Plume, 1982.

Jones, Gayl. *Corregidora*. Boston, MA: Beacon, 1975.

Keizer, Arlene. *Black Subjects: Identity Formation in the Contemporary Narrative of Slavery*. Ithaca, NY: Cornell University Press, 2004.

McDowell, Deborah and Arnold Rampersad, ed. *Slavery and the Literary Imagination*. Baltimore: Johns Hopkins University Press, 1989.

Mitchell, Angelyn. *The Freedom to Remember: Narrative, Slavery, and Gender in Contemporary Black Women's Fiction*. New Brunswick, NJ: Rutgers University Press, 2002.

Morrison, Toni. *Beloved*. New York: Plume, 1987.

Morrison, Toni. *A Mercy*. New York: Knopf, 2008.

Morrison, Toni. "The Site of Memory." In *Out There: Marginalization and Contemporary Cultures*. Ed. Russell Ferguson, Martha Gever, Trinh T. Minh-Ha, and Cornel West. Cambridge, MA: MIT Press, 1990. 299–305.

Reed, Ishmael. *Flight to Canada*. New York: Random House, 1976.

Rhodes, Jewell Parker. *Douglass' Women*. New York: Washington Square Press, 2002.

Rody, Caroline. *The Daughter's Return: African-American and Caribbean Women's Fictions of History*. New York: Oxford University Press, 2001.

Rushdy, Ashraf H.A. *Neo-Slave Narratives: Studies in the Social Logic of a Literary Form*. New York: Oxford University Press, 1999.

Rushdy, Ashraf H.A. *Remembering Generations*. Chapel Hill: University of North Carolina Press, 2001.

Smith, Valerie. "Neo-slave Narratives." In *The Cambridge Companion to the African American Slave Narrative*. Ed. Audrey Fisch. Cambridge: Cambridge University Press, 2007. 168–85.

Spaulding, Timothy. *Re-Forming the Past: History, the Fantastic, and the Postmodern Slave Narrative*. Columbus: Ohio State University Press, 2005.

Van Deburg, William. *Slavery and Race in American Culture*. Madison: University of Wisconsin Press, 1984.

Williams, Sherley Anne. *Dessa Rose*. New York: Berkley, 1986.

Yerby, Frank. *A Darkness at Ingraham's Crest*. New York: Dell, 1979.

23
Popular Black Women's Fiction and the Novels of Terry McMillan

Robin V. Smiles

In a 1994 interview in *The New York Times*, Toni Morrison expressed excitement over recent changes in the publishing industry, where books by black women authors were making the bestseller list and being chosen as book-of-the-month club selections. "There is now such a thing as *popular black women's literature*. Popular!" said Morrison in the interview (quoted in Dreifus 74). As one of a small group of black women writers who struggled to find an audience and publisher for their fiction in the late 1960s and early 1970s, Morrison could barely imagine at the time a literary marketplace with more than one "popular" black woman writer. In 1992, however, when Morrison's *Jazz*, Alice Walker's *Possessing the Secret of Joy*, and Terry McMillan's *Waiting to Exhale* appeared on *The New York Times* bestseller list simultaneously, the milestone marked a shift in the marketplace for fiction by black women authors. The three authors spent several weeks on the list together, but McMillan lasted the longest, further expanding what literary critics have identified as a writing and reading renaissance led by black women writers and reinforcing the emergence of *popular* black women's literature.

Since the early 1990s, McMillan and a number of newer black male and female writers, such as Connie Briscoe, Tina McElroy Ansa, Bebe Moore Campbell, and E. Lynn Harris, continued publishing what I am defining as popular black women's fiction: bestselling books that both address the contemporary concerns of black females and target black female readers. Much like the fiction of established black women writers such as Morrison and Walker, the newer writers focus on the portrayal of black women. Yet, their fiction exhibits a number of other defining characteristics, including post-integration, urban settings; upwardly mobile, or middle-class, college-educated protagonists; and, importantly, conflict that centers on romantic relationships. More specifically, Morrison and Walker primarily favor post-slavery settings to support a historical emphasis, tales of Northern migration to illuminate the effects of overt racism, abusive and loveless marriages with black men to emphasize black female independence, and tight-knit, monolithic black communities to emphasize a distinction from the white mainstream. In contrast, the newer writers are more likely to imagine contemporary settings; stories of women moving away from their communities to the suburbs or to the West Coast who are thus isolated and separated from family; unsatisfying and disappointing relationships with black men; an exploration of the possibilities and problems of being single; and elements of intraracial strife perpetuated by economic and class distinctions.

McMillan remains one of the most recognized and most commercially successful authors of this group. *Waiting to Exhale*, her third novel, stayed on *The New York Times* bestseller list for 43 weeks, selling over 650,000 hard copies the first year. Pocket Books paid a record $2.64 million for reprint rights to the book (the second highest at that time), which brought in over $1.75 million in hardcover and paperback sales. *Publisher's Weekly* listed it as one of the year's top 10 bestsellers. McMillan's subsequent novels continued this trend, recording long stints on the bestseller lists and significant hardcover and paperback sales figures. Her fourth novel, *How Stella Got Her Groove Back*, reached the top of the *Publisher's Weekly* bestseller list in the first week of its release and stayed in the top five for over 20 weeks (Richards).

Although McMillan's novels offer the perfect lens through which to evaluate the significance of popular black women's fiction, most discussions of McMillan's works and her bestselling contemporaries are limited to conversations about commercial success. Many credit McMillan with igniting or forecasting new interest among publishers in popular black fiction. Critics also recognize that McMillan has helped to create what some have deemed a new subgenre of fiction called "sistah fiction," or "sista girl" and "brotherman" novels, colloquialisms that aptly characterize the ostensible appeal of those works to an "everyday" African American reading audience and its central focus: portraying the intimate relationships and friendships between and among African American males and females. Yet, while commercial success and the new subgenre of fiction are noteworthy, neither is a sufficient basis to evaluate the literary values of McMillan's fiction and popular black women's fiction in general. What exactly are the conditions that allowed these novels to flourish? How do they adhere to or challenge canonical protocols? How do they build on or expand the category of black women's fiction? How do they revise portrayals of black females? How do they engage new audiences and/or satisfy new purposes? Investigating such questions is essential to assessing the value of this fiction, not just in the commercial marketplace, but in the field of literary studies.

A number of factors, both literary and extra-literary, combined to create the conditions for popular black women's fiction to flourish in the 1990s. In the 1970s and early 1980s, Morrison, Walker, and other black women writers, such as Toni Cade Bambara, Gayl Jones, and Gloria Naylor, published works that helped feature the black female in the literary and cultural marketplace. While the Black Arts Movement had created a viable market for its literary and cultural production, it was dominated by the voices of black men. Black female writers, along with black feminist critics, converged to create a literary identity for black women's fiction that McMillan and others have been able to exploit. Books such as Morrison's *Sula* (1974), which was nominated for a National Book Award, and *Song of Solomon* (1977), which was named a book-of-the-month club selection and winner of the National Book Critics Circle Award, enabled black women writers to craft original literary heroines as well as those that revised representations of black women emerging from the Black Arts Movement. As a former editor at Random House, Morrison played an important role in this movement, editing and publishing works by Jones and Bambara, in particular, that countered existing representations of black women and revealed the particular experiences of black women in the world, specifically the challenges posed by racism and sexism.

The early works of Morrison anticipated the interest of a reading audience in the stories of black women. In the 1990s, this audience emerged more fully. The increase in book clubs and community reading groups, particularly in the African American community and among black female readers, was evidence of a viable black readership and a growing demand for books to meet this readership's needs. As Elizabeth McHenry argues, while the phenomenon of African Americans coming together in intimate group settings to discuss literature dates back to the nineteenth century, such gatherings garnered newfound interest in the 1990s. The emergence of black popular romance novels in the early 1990s also validated for publishers a commercial interest in stories of intimate relationships between black men and black women, a defining characteristic of popular black women's fiction. While popular romance novels had dominated the mass-market paperback industry in the United States since the late 1970s, black popular romance novels did not enter the market in a sustained manner until 1994, when Kensington Publishing launched Arabesque, the first imprint devoted to black romance novels.

The expansion of the paperback romance industry, at times the largest fiction category in terms of sales generated and titles released, highlights another circumstance that allowed popular black women's fiction to flourish in the 1990s: corporate consolidations within the publishing industry that focused on such bottom-line issues as profits and entertainment. As publisher Andre Schiffrin details in *The Business of Books*, the buyout of small, independent publishing houses by large media conglomerates in the 1980s changed the infrastructure of the publishing industry. With new corporate owners – many of which owned a variety of entertainment venues – publishers faced greater pressure to meet the economic standards of the entertainment industry, where bestsellers and celebrity authors were more the norm than the exception. Industry consolidation meant that media companies were looking for ways to maximize their products and their profits. For instance, Disney, as owner of Hyperion Books, or Viacom, as owner of Simon and Schuster, would be more likely to publish those books that could be transferrable to other entertainment media (such as movies and television) and thus more profitable for the corporate owners. Two of McMillan's novels, for example, were made into feature films, and both became box-office successes. Twentieth Century Fox paid $1 million for the film rights to *Waiting to Exhale*, and, just several years later, $2 million for *How Stella Got Her Groove Back* (Richards). Another novel, *Disappearing Acts*, was made into a cable television movie by Home Box Office. Indeed, McMillan's novels were particularly fit for the new book economy.

Recognizing the conditions that helped create popular black women's fiction highlights the substantial relationship between this fiction and changes in the broader marketplace. It is also important to understand how the relationship between the broader marketplace and the academic arena influenced the rise of popular black women's fiction. The shift in the literary marketplace toward popularity, celebrity, and entertainment, for instance, brought more attention to the field of African American literature, increasing readership and the reach of black authors and their works. It also helped to perpetuate a long-held divide in literary studies between the "scholarly" and the "popular," where books that appeal overwhelmingly to a popular audience and receive widespread commercial success are often assumed to have little literary value.

Within the field of African American literature in the 1990s, the increase in popular fiction written by black authors heightened this divide. On one hand, black authors were writing more fiction, expanding popular genres, moving black literature to the "popular" mainstream, and reaching widespread audiences. (In addition to the emergence of popular black women's fiction and black romance novels, African American authors published more fiction in other popular literary genres. For example, Walter Mosley, Valerie Wilson Wesley, and Octavia Butler helped popularize black detective and science-fiction novels.) On the other hand, scholars of African American literature were working to define an African American literary tradition and establish its canons. Consider the publication of the *Norton Anthology of African American Literature* in 1997. In discussing the Norton anthology before its publication, series editor Henry Louis Gates, Jr. defined the task of the editors as "bring[ing] together the 'essential' texts of the canon, the 'crucially central' authors, those whom we feel to be indispensable to an understanding of the shape, and the shaping, of the tradition" (Gates 102). And although the Norton was not the first anthology of African American literature, it is first to carry the mark of W.W. Norton, a name that has come to represent the epitome of canonization in the field of literary studies.

The publication of the Norton anthology represents the culmination of a large project among scholars of African American literature, one that began with efforts in the late 1960s and early 1970s to establish the field of African American literary studies. By the late 1980s, the increase in African American literature courses on college campuses could document success in this endeavor. By the late 1980s and early 1990s, then, the focus shifted from ensuring the canonical inclusion of black authors in literary studies to managing the political implications of that inclusion. Hence, Gates and the other Norton editors set out to determine which authors to include by identifying a set of criteria that best represented the African American literary tradition. At the center of the Norton editors' tradition is Gates's own theory of signifying, which posits that texts in the African American literary tradition respond to earlier texts, thus reproducing certain narrative elements and themes. The result is an intertextuality that links all the "essential" texts and "crucially central" authors to one another. In the current study of African American literature, such narrative elements as the use of the vernacular and a focus on themes of racial uplift and social protest allegedly represent the best of African American literature.

The rise in the 1990s of "popular" fiction, along with the culmination of the "scholarly" endeavor to create an African American literary tradition and its representative canon, created a dilemma for critics of African American literature, who were faced with commenting on the emergence of new fiction by black authors that often defied what they had determined to be of "canonical" quality. McMillan's fiction and the popular black women's fiction it represented did not readily meet these criteria. The stories of confronting overt racism and sexism, uplifting the black community, and honoring familial ties and tradition, as well as traditional uses of the vernacular, the folk, and the blues, are either present in new ways in or absent entirely from these new novels. Literary scholars who reviewed this fiction emphasized these absences in their analyses. In discussing the emergence of these new "90s writers" (McMillan included), Thulani Davis, for instance, laments the absence of the "shared yearnings based on race, gender, generation, or family so common to black fiction" (Davis 26). Similarly, in a review of McMillan's first novel for the journal *Callaloo*, Michael Awkward writes, not necessarily negatively, that "unlike the tradition's most representative texts, *Mama* offers no journeys back to blackness, no empowering black female communities, no sustained condemnation of American materialism or male hegemony" (Awkward 650).

The presence of McMillan in the Norton perhaps best illustrates the dilemma scholars of African American literature faced with managing these two pivotal moments in African American literary production. Though one of the most commercially successful and popular authors in the latter half of the twentieth century, with several bestselling novels by the time, McMillan is not represented in the Norton by any of her popular novels, but by an obscure short story, "Quilting on the Rebound." The editors presumably chose "Quilting" to link McMillan to the literary tradition represented in the Norton. The story is about a 38-year-old single black woman who turns to quilting to heal her heartache after being stood up at the altar by her much younger 26-year-old boyfriend. An esteemed practice in African American culture, quilting is often associated with acts of resistance and protest during slavery. By choosing the quilting narrative to represent McMillan, the Norton editors attempt to show McMillan's fiction representing a particular social and cultural act of resistance in African American history. Yet, the Norton editors also misrepresent McMillan's canon, which does not typically rely on historical and traditional markers as symbols of resistance. In fact, the presence of quilting in McMillan's canon is more the exception than the norm.

By including McMillan in the Norton, the editors rightly suggest that her works are integral to African American literary studies; however, they provide little context for a serious critical analysis of her works. Instead, the Norton editors limit their discussion of McMillan's literary significance to her commercial success. The introduction to the "Literature since 1970" section mentions McMillan only to say that she appeared on *The New York Times* bestseller list along with Morrison and Walker, and that her novels "made black romance stories a central part of U.S. publishing success." Similarly, in the brief text that introduces McMillan's short story, the emphasis again is on her commercial success, with descriptions of McMillan moving "farther on her way to literary celebrityhood," being "truly a force to be reckoned with," and her novels as having "upped the ante for those writing after her" (Gates and McKay 2572).

A serious analysis of McMillan's fiction, and other popular black women's fiction, must acknowledge the ways in which this fiction extends and updates existing critical paradigms. By limiting their discussion of McMillan to her commercial success, and simultaneously forcing her into traditional critical paradigms, the Norton editors miss an opportunity to illuminate the ways in which McMillan's fiction updates and extends such paradigms. As Gene Andrew Jarrett argues, anthologies often resort to "problematic essentialist paradigms of canon and tradition that prioritize the authenticity of African American literature without recognizing the various and frequent ways in which African American writers themselves were working *beyond* this paradigm" (Jarrett 6).

McMillan's fiction, as well as the popular black women's fiction that her novels have come to represent, work beyond existing critical paradigms in modern African American literary studies in a number of ways. As popular fiction, these works are successful precisely because they deliberately address the concerns of a commercial audience rather than satisfy the purposes of an academic one. McMillan's books, for instance, are full of references to popular culture and consumer goods, such as movies, television shows, magazines and name-brand fashions. These references work to attract an audience (such as those who recognize these references and their significance) to her fiction. As Susanne Dietzel argues, "for popular fiction to work, to be successful and to attract and maintain a body of devoted readers, it has to embody elements of recognition and identification" (Dietzel 159). In the case of McMillan's fiction, this audience comprises the same demographic she portrays in her works: young, urban, upwardly mobile or middle-class black females. For this audience, as well as for her characters, possession of (or the desire for) these material goods serves as an outward or tangible marker of economic status and class.

Moreover, by portraying relationships of romantic love as the most important issue facing African American characters, McMillan's fiction defies modern critics' expectation that African American literature must privilege racial conflict. Romantic relationships between black women and black men lie at the center of McMillan's most popular novels. *Disappearing Acts* is devoted entirely to the relationship between Zora and Franklin; *Waiting to Exhale* is propelled by the characters' experiences and escapades with black male lovers; and *How Stella Got Her Groove Back* revolves around the courtship between Stella and Winston and the problems they face because of their age difference. Yet, romance is often seen as a theme antithetical to the critical agenda advanced by modern African American literary studies. Ann duCille argues, for instance, that "until recently, love and marriage were all but dismissed as female, or, at least feminized themes little worthy of study when juxtaposed to the masculinized racial and freedom discourse assumed to characterize the African American novel" (duCille 3). We must work to change this accepted viewpoint.

Just as popular romantic fiction pushes the bounds of existing genres, popular black women's fiction stands outside existing critical paradigms in modern African American literary studies. It does not follow, however, that in defying specific critical paradigms, these works also defy the broad goals and functions that critics have identified as characteristic of African American literature, particularly that of providing a means of racial uplift and a platform for social protest. In McMillan's novels, in particular, racial uplift and social protest are filtered through a different lens, specifically through her portrayals of young, urban, upwardly mobile, or middle-class black females and their quest for "domestic success."

While this quest for domestic success – that is, for having a promising or thriving professional career and a happy or satisfying marriage or romantic relationship – is not new in fiction by African American female writers, it is redefined in the post-Civil Rights, post-feminist, late twentieth-century setting in which McMillan's novels take place. The Civil Rights and feminist movements both created new professional opportunities for black women as well as expanded society's perceptions of womanhood. McMillan's characters embody these advances as their quest for educational and professional opportunities move them away from their communities and homes and from traditional notions of domesticity. Their search for fulfilling heterosexual unions takes them beyond idealized notions of love and marriage. At the same time, on this new journey – to new geographic spaces, new economic wealth, and new social relationships – McMillan's characters encounter new obstacles. They respond by creating new paradigms of contemporary domesticity and redefining gender roles within heterosexual unions.

Like most contemporary black women authors, McMillan uses her novels to challenge conventional notions of women as homebound, immobile, and static. In most of these conventional works, the narrative centers on female protagonists who must return home and negotiate the surrounding community. Often, the success or failure of such native returns is used as a measure of her respect for history or her commitment to the ideals of the past. In contrast, McMillan's focus is on how her characters operate in their new settings: the friendships and new communities they create; the challenges they face with new careers; and how they maintain their closeness to family and friends despite the physical distance. While most authors use the return home to evaluate their characters' perceptions of history, family, and/or community, it is on the "quest" for domestic success where McMillan's characters are forced to reevaluate home and community, especially their relationships with the female relatives they have left behind, and thereby their perceptions of womanhood and traditional notions of domesticity.

In each of her first three novels, for instance, McMillan presents protagonists who journey away from their families and communities to unfamiliar areas, trading small-town boredom and familiarity for career and/or educational opportunities. Freda, one of the main characters in McMillan's first novel *Mama*, leaves Point Haven, Michigan, for Los Angeles right after high school, immediately landing a job as a secretary at an insurance company, making $90 a week, a figure unheard of in the economically depressed Point Haven. She also enrolls in a nearby community college where she "had an ocean of knowledge at her disposal … all within walking distance" (142). Zora, the female protagonist in *Disappearing Acts*, leaves Toledo, Ohio, with plans to launch her singing career in the entertainment haven of New York, increasing her prospects of a successful singing and songwriting career. Similarly, in *Waiting to Exhale*, the novel begins with Savannah packing her bags for Phoenix, the fourth city in 15 years she has lived in. Savannah is moving to Arizona, via Denver, Boston, and Pittsburgh, to begin a new job at a TV station. Although the job comes with a $12,000 pay cut, the job comes with "plenty of opportunities to advance" and a chance for Savannah to diversify her publicity skills (3).

Freda's, Zora's, and Savannah's movements are emblematic of African Americans in the post-Civil Rights and post-integrationist era, encouraging us to describe *Waiting to Exhale* in terms of the broader literary and cultural history of African American migration. Indeed, McMillan's novels can be read along with what Farah Jasmine Griffin has identified in her pioneering study *Who Set You Flowin'?* as "one of the twentieth century's dominant forms of African American cultural production": the migration narrative (3). Migration narratives "portray the movement of a major character or the text itself from a provincial (not necessarily rural) Southern or Midwestern site (home of the ancestor) to a more cosmopolitan, metropolitan area" (Griffin 3). This narrative is also characterized by distinct "pivotal moments," one of which is the "event that propels the move Northward." This event is often the threat or the act of violence: lynchings, mobs, beatings, sexual abuse, and rape. While the catalyst for the move might vary in migration narratives, in all cases the South is portrayed as "an immediate, identifiable, and oppressive power," which is "unsophisticated in nature" (Griffin 4–5).

McMillan replaces the migration narrative's Southern power with that of a domestic power in her fiction. Indeed, her characters are "set flowin'" for much less dramatic reasons than in the typical migration narrative: to escape the dreary Point Haven, to launch a singing career, to hone publicity skills. Yet, beneath each character's expressed intention for leaving is the suggestion of something more pernicious. The "immediate, identifiable, and oppressive power" that serves as the catalyst for McMillan's characters' migration is not the threat of racial or sexual violence that their ancestors faced, but the threat of stifling domesticity and economic stagnation. For example, the lack of jobs and professional opportunities for the people of Point Haven creates an atmosphere of deprivation that imprisons Freda's family and friends. Her brother, Money, goes to jail. Her high-school girlfriends are "living in the projects with one or two babies" (149). And the guys from high school are spending "all of their waking hours in front of the pool hall, drinking wine or nodding over cigarettes" (149). These scenarios suggest that if Freda chooses to stay at home or return permanently to her native community, she would also succumb to such circumstances.

In *Disappearing Acts*, when Zora moves into her new brownstone in New York, she is leaving behind more than a "safe, little, cozy" life in Toledo. She is also abandoning a history of placing herself in potentially abusive relationships and, thus, the threat of domestic violence (20). In the novel's first pages, Zora recounts her history of making poor decisions in the relationship arena: "I've got a history of jumping right into the fire, mistaking desire for love, lust for love, and, the records show, on occasion, a good lay for love" (15). As a result, Zora has had a number of bad breakups; one prompted her move to New York, another led her to change her phone number to an unlisted one, and another "goodbye," she says, was "so ugly that when I missed my period again, there was no way I could bring myself to tell him. So I did it again, but swore I would never hop up on one of those tables and count backward from a hundred unless whatever came out was going home with me and my husband" (21). While Zora's bad luck with relationships might appear benign, her "addiction" to men, naïveté, indiscriminate choices, and self-esteem issues with her weight make her vulnerable to abusive relationships. Although she does not express the presence of physical or verbal abuse, there is evidence of controlling partners and volatile partners – in particular, a cocaine addict whom Zora assumed was "sniffling all the time" because of sinus problems (21). In *Waiting to Exhale*, Savannah's moves are not just the manifestation of her seeking career advancements, but also the evidence of her need to avoid the type of unsatisfying and unfulfilling relationships and marriages that her mother and sister have experienced. The possibility of ending up like her mother or sister or inheriting their willingness to settle down and settle for less threatens Savannah, who is critical of her mother's and sister's contentment throughout the novel.

For these protagonists, the ability to go somewhere – or, more specifically, to flee the "domestic" threat – is essential. Mobility allows McMillan's characters to expand their knowledge and their experiences and to create a different future for themselves and their families. Therefore, it is on the journey to a new place, as opposed to their return home, that McMillan's characters realize alternative "domestic" situations. As a result, her novels forge new perceptions of black women as no longer tethered to their old communities, but pioneering new ones. Once free of their original communities, many of McMillan's characters thrive. The financial success they experience as a result of their decisions to pursue educational and career opportunities allows for new "domestic" arrangements as well. They can provide their parents with financial support, move their sisters and brothers away from economically depressed environments, provide an alternative for their relatives and potentially alter the future of their families for generations to come.

These new domestic considerations also manifest in the protagonists' relationships of romantic love. In both *Disappearing Acts* and *Waiting to Exhale*, we see signs of resistance in the protagonists' refusal to adhere to proscribed gender roles within heterosexual unions. The clear opposition between "mobility" and "settling down," or marriage, in McMillan's novels signals that her characters will not marry. In the absence of marriage, engagement, or any such relationship for her female characters, McMillan's novels are more concerned with defining the social stability and status of the contemporary *single* black woman. As such, she redefines gender roles within heterosexual unions in her novels, primarily by reversing these roles. For one, it is more likely that the *men* in McMillan's novels are "trapped" in unhappy marriages, and, in several cases, the reader is encouraged to empathize with them.

In *Disappearing Acts*, for example, Franklin complains that his wife, Pam, stopped wanting to make love, or take care of herself, and that the only things that interested her were soap operas and food. Both Franklin and Zora characterize their fathers as victims in their respective marriages. Zora complains that her stepmother takes advantage of her father, demanding that he work overtime, taking his paycheck, and denying him affection. Franklin blames his poor relationship with his father on his father's inability to stand up to his controlling and overbearing wife. In *Waiting to Exhale*, several of the male characters purport to be in unsatisfying marriages. Russell and Kenneth complain of wives who do not understand them, and characterize their marriages as mistakes, having married, at least in Kenneth's case, because the women were pregnant. But it is James whom the character Bernadine meets the night her divorce is final, who is most likely to garner the empathy from the reader usually given to women characters. James and his wife are planning to divorce, but before the divorce can be finalized, James's wife is diagnosed with a rare form of breast cancer, and he is compelled to stay with her.

A similar role reversal occurs over issues of financial stability. In traditional stories of love and romance, for instance, male marriageability is equated with financial wealth. Male suitors are measured by their ability to provide financially for their wives and families, and a man with substantial means is deemed a "good catch." In several of McMillan's novels, these economic roles are reversed: the female character brings wealth and economic status to the union. The question of "worth" is at the center of the conflict between Zora and Franklin in *Disappearing Acts*. On several occasions, Zora tries to convince herself of Franklin's "worth" despite his inability to keep a steady job:

> For some stupid reason, I started thinking about the yardstick friends like Portia and women's magazines used to measure a man's worth. They measure wrong. I mean, standing right here in front of me was a man, and a man who loves me, who just opened himself up and took a chance by telling me the truth … How many of them have told me the truth? And when was the last time I met a man this smart, this sexy, this gentle, this strong? (96)

Because of Franklin's financial instability, Zora looks to such qualities as his intelligence, honesty, sense of humor, and strength to determine his value. Yet, both Zora and Franklin express discomfort with their reversed economic roles. Zora comments that it "just felt so lopsided" (342). And Franklin, unable to be the "provider," struggles with defining his own worth. While he is proud of the success Zora is finding as a singer and songwriter, he is also ashamed of his inability to fulfill traditional characteristics of male identity: "I looked at her hard and pictured her onstage with people screaming and shit 'cause she had just tore the roof off the place. Then I started wondering. Where would that leave me? Her man, the construction worker who couldn't even be sure if he was gon' get paid every week or not" (101). In a further reversal of domestic roles, it is Franklin, who in recognizing that Zora is a "good catch," wants to "trap" Zora with a baby, a stereotypical role usually reserved for females: "Ain't no sense in my lying – I didn't really plan on having no more kids, but I love Zora and I wanna keep her. I guess this was one way of guaranteeing it" (277).

McMillan's novels again reverse the roles of men and women in courtship and engagement. While traditional notions of bachelorhood have been reserved for men, McMillan bestows this "privilege" on her single, black, female protagonists. Her characters count the proposals they have turned down as marks of achievement, of evidence of their ability to move on. For instance, when Freda informs her mother that she is moving yet again, this time to New York for graduate school, Mildred typically diminishes her accomplishments and encourages her to settle down: "What you need to be doing is looking for a damn husband. Writing for newspapers and thangs sound glamorous and everythang, but when you gon' slow your ass down?" (224). Freda responds: "You just don't seem to understand what it means to be black and female and be accepted to these schools, do you, Mama? They don't let just anybody in! I can have a baby any time … I could've been married at least three times by now, if you want to know the truth" (224). Similarly, when we meet Zora in the first few pages of *Disappearing Acts*, she recounts the several proposals she has turned down. Savannah, as well, is happy that she did not marry the three men she lived with because "they were all mistakes." Qualities typically associated with the eligible bachelor – unattached, free to move, no responsibilities – now all belong to McMillan's protagonists. Single black womanhood is privileged in these novels. Instead of settling for the possibility of an unhappy marriage, McMillan's characters choose to remain single. And the way these novels represent heterosexual unions and marriage as unsatisfying and rare appears to endorse decisions to bypass marriage altogether.

Finally, McMillan's characters exercise the sexual autonomy and freedom usually reserved for male characters and, in so doing, redefine notions of black female sexuality. Zora's friend Portia encourages her to go ahead and sleep with Franklin, but not to share any information with him about her past relationships or to fall in love. "We need to be more like them," Portia tells Zora (83). Portia imagines that these actions will empower Zora in the relationship, suggesting that a woman's emotional investment in a relationship, often triggered by sexual intimacy, is a sign of weakness. In *Waiting to Exhale*, Bernadine likewise follows Portia's counsel as she pursues a sexual relationship after her husband leaves her for his secretary, admitting that the only thing she wanted from her new lover was "between his legs" (293). Similar to Portia,

Bernadine rejects the stereotype of women associating sexual intimacy with love, and thus places herself in a position of power usually reserved for men.

By reversing the traditional gender roles in heterosexual unions and by validating a number of new paradigms of contemporary domesticity, McMillan's fiction, and those fictions like hers, help to redefine contemporary perceptions of black female identity and sexuality. These new perceptions, filtered through the lens of young, urban, college-educated, middle-class, and contemporary black females concerned with family, career, friends, and romantic relationships, are characteristic of both McMillan's fiction and the popular black women's fiction of the 1990s. Although these works are not the only ones to portray this perspective in African American literature, not until the 1990s does this perspective become widely explored in the literary marketplace. Thus, for the readers who identify with these perspectives, popular black women's fiction helps to validate their own social experiences, anxieties and concerns, pointing to the "racial uplift" function of popular black women's fiction.

The emergence of a viable book-buying audience interested in the stories of black women was an important factor in creating an environment for popular black women's fiction to flourish. Contemporary book clubs, for instance, assign reading a role more profound than formal analysis. Particularly those among black female readers, the clubs "are about far more than the communal analysis of a good book," argues Elizabeth McHenry (303). "Although reading literature provides the catalyst for their coming together," McHenry says, "the impact of black women's associations with a reading group is usually felt on both an intellectual and an emotional or spiritual level" (303). These reading groups fill a void in their members' lives, providing them with a support network and an outlet to discuss everyday challenges, such as feeling isolated as the only African American in the workplace and balancing a demanding career and family responsibilities. Popular black women's fiction, with its emphasis on characters' everyday concerns, lend themselves to the type of communal analysis common to the book-club setting, as well as to the ability of fiction to perhaps improve its readers' lives.

In analyzing the literary significance of popular black women's fiction, critics must move beyond existing critical paradigms and toward those that encourage evaluation of this fiction on more substantial grounds than its commercial success. These new paradigms challenge traditional canonical protocols of racial uplift and social protest, break down binaries between the scholarly and the popular, and allow for discussions of communal processes of reading and other extra-literary factors that also determine the "contingencies of value" in literary texts.

Bibliography

Awkward, Michael. "Chronicling Everyday Travails and Triumphs." *Callaloo* 36 (1988): 649–50.

Davis, Thulani. "Don't Worry, Be Buppie: Black Novelists Head for the Mainstream." *Village Voice Literary Supplement*, May 1990: 26–9.

Dietzel, Susanne B. "The African American Novel and Popular Culture." In *The Cambridge Companion to The African American Novel*. Ed. Maryemma Graham. Cambridge: Cambridge University Press, 2004. 156–70.

Dreifus, Claudia. "Chloe Wofford Talks about Toni Morrison." *New York Times Magazine*, September 11, 1994: 72–5.

duCille, Ann. *The Coupling Convention: Sex, Text, and Tradition in Black Women's Fiction*. New York: Oxford University Press, 1993.

Gates, Henry Louis, Jr. "The Master's Pieces: On Canon Formation and the African American Tradition." *South Atlantic Quarterly* 89.1 (1990): 89–111.

Gates, Henry Louis, Jr. and Nellie Y. McKay, ed. *The Norton Anthology of African American Literature*. New York: W.W. Norton and Company, 1997.

Griffin, Farah Jasmine. *Who Set You Flowin': The African-American Migration Narrative*. New York: Oxford University Press, 1996.

Jarrett, Gene Andrew. "Introduction: 'Not Necessarily Race Matter.'" In *African American Literature Beyond Race: An Alternative Reader*. Ed. Gene Andrew Jarrett. New York: New York University Press, 2006. 1–22.

McHenry, Elizabeth. *Forgotten Readers: Recovering the Lost History of African American Literary Societies*. 2002.

McMillan, Terry. *Disappearing Acts*. New York: Washington Square Press, 1989.

McMillan, Terry. *How Stella Got Her Groove Back*. New York: Viking Penguin, 1996.

McMillan, Terry. *Mama*. New York: Pocket Books, 1987.

McMillan, Terry. *Waiting to Exhale*. New York: Signet, 1992. (Citations are from the Signet 2005 paperback edition.)

Richards, Paulette. *Terry McMillan: A Critical Companion*. Westport, CT: Greenwood Press, 1999.

Schiffrin, Andre. *The Business of Books: How the International Conglomerates Took over Publishing and Changed the Way We Read*. London: Verso, 2000.

Smith, Barbara Herrnstein. *Contingencies of Value: Alternative Perspectives for Critical Theory*. Cambridge, MA: Harvard University Press, 1988.

Thurston, Carol. *The Romance Revolution: Erotic Novels for Women and the Quest for a New Sexual Identity*. Chicago: University of Illinois Press, 1987.

24
African American Science Fiction

Jeffrey Allen Tucker

Images of the Future, or Why "African American Science Fiction" Is Not an Oxymoron

"The Digital Divide" is a formulation that has experienced considerable circulation in late twentieth- and early twenty-first-century popular discourse. This phrase speaks to the very real fact that not everyone in the world has working knowledge of or even access to the dizzying array of emergent electronic technologies. In the context of the United States, the "divide" draws attention to how economic disadvantage and structural racism limit the contact of some groups, including a disproportionate amount of people of color, to personal computers and "New" (digital) media; it also identifies how those groups' relationships to such technologies and media are primarily as consumers or objects of representation, as opposed to producers or interpreters/mediators. However, Alondra Nelson suggests that such language can be as prescriptive as it is descriptive, and it runs the risk of becoming a self-fulfilling prophecy that defines certain racial and/or class identities as something other than tech-savvy, or as always already alienated from technological culture (Nelson, "Future Texts"). A counterpoint to such representations has emerged in contemporary African American culture in the form of "Afrofuturism." In "Black to the Future" (1994), Mark Dery uses this term to refer to "speculative fiction that treats African-American themes and addresses African-American concerns in the context of 20th-century technoculture – and, more generally, African-American signification that appropriates images of technology and a prosthetically enhanced future" (Dery 180). In "Future Texts," Alondra Nelson describes Afrofuturism as "African American voices with other stories to tell about culture, technology, and things to come" (Nelson, "Future Texts" 9). Whatever its signifieds, "Afrofuturism" certainly has a different story to tell about the relationship between people of African descent and technological culture, one in which writing in the genre associated with technological culture, science fiction (SF), plays an important role.

The tension between "Afrofuturism" and "the Digital Divide" as discourses, as languages that shape understanding, was evident in conversations I had during the 1990s. Mentioning the topic of SF writers of African descent in polite conversation often triggered confused expressions, giggles, and/or stunned silence among white and black discussants alike. After I identified African American science fiction as an interest of mine, whites asked me, in tones expressing incredulity, genuine curiosity, or a combination of the two: "*Is* there such a thing?" And I heard African Americans say, in stern approbation, confident rebuke, or both: "Oh no; *we* don't do that. We leave that sort of thing to white folks."

Such attitudes were not completely baseless, however; there are reasons for why SF has been seen as "a white thing." In "Why Blacks Don't Read Science Fiction" (1980), black Canadian fantasy writer Charles R. Saunders – author of the *Imaro* series, with its distinctly black titular action-hero – explained that for much of its modern history, from its emergence in the pulp periodicals of the early twentieth century to the development of cyberpunk in the 1980s and beyond, the genre has been dominated by white (and male) writers, readers, editors, and characters: "A black man or woman in a space-suit was an image beyond the limits of early science fiction writers' imaginations." According to Saunders, for much of its history in North America, SF has been "akin to the proverbial driven snow [or] as white as a Ku Klux Klan rally" (Saunders, "Why Blacks Don't Read Science Fiction" 160). This has been due in large part to the active and passive exclusions of people of color from the genre. For example, the legendary writer and editor John W. Campbell, Jr. refused to publish Samuel R. Delany's *Nova* (1968) in *Analog* magazine. Campbell told Delany's agent, "For heaven's sakes, he's got a Negro for a protagonist! It's a good book, but our readers aren't going to be able to identify with that" (quoted in Peplow and Bravard 32). There is also the long-held assumption that SF is implicitly "post-racial." According to this line of thinking, in the far-off future in which many such stories are set, humanity will have evolved away from such provincial concerns, and encounters with extraterrestrial beings will render moot the racial divisions with which we are familiar. Mark Bould notes how scholars once lauded the genre's assumption "that America's major problem in this area – black/white relations – would improve or even wither away" as evidence of SF's progressive politics and intellectual heft. As reasonable or desirable as post-racial scenarios may have been, however, their assumptions had the practical effect of impeding the publication of SF by African American creators and SF featuring black characters.

"Far beyond the Stars," a 1998 episode of the television series *Star Trek: Deep Space Nine* written by Marc Scott Zicree, dramatized this problem. African American Starfleet Capt. Benjamin Sisko experiences visions of himself as a writer for a SF magazine in the 1950s. After he submits a story that meets with universal admiration from his peers, "Benny" is shocked by his editor's instructions to "make the captain white," which are accompanied by concerns that publishing the original story "could start a race riot" as well as comparisons to the work of a lesser writer who "doesn't care about Negroes or whites; he writes about robots." Such comments demonstrate how, as Bould states, SF's "color-blind future … excluded people of color as full subjects" (Bould 177). They also suggest how publishers have occasionally engaged in some fancy footwork to make sure that SF that did feature people of color was successfully marketed to its target demographic. For example, even though the protagonists of Delany's *Return to Nevèrÿon* series (1979–87) and Octavia E. Butler's *Dawn* (1987) are explicitly described as black, the covers of the first editions of these books featured representations of these characters as white. The title of a 1983 essay by Thulani Davis summed up the situation neatly: "The Future May Be Bleak, But It's Not Black."

However, there is another component to the equation: African American attitudes toward SF. Saunders observes that the emergence of new black SF writers depends on the exposure of black readers to the genre. Yet he also notes that black readers have preferred the works of writers who have been more readily recognized as participants of an African American literary tradition, including Paul Laurence Dunbar, Ralph Ellison, and Toni Morrison. He also considers the notion that black readers generally prefer literature perceived to be speaking either to their own lived experiences as an African diaspora in America, or to the earlier experiences of African generations. What Saunders is getting at here is the degree to which social realism has monopolized the preferable – the *authentic* – literary mode in black writing for much of the twentieth century. In contrast, SF has been seen as escapist fantasy that fails to represent the history of people of African descent or speak to their experiences. In "Far beyond the Stars," a fellow Harlemite tells Benny, "White folks on the moon – Man, who cares about that?!" perhaps in an allusion to Gil Scott-Heron's famous poetic performance, "Whitey's on the Moon" (1970). Moreover, the discursive association of technological culture, which includes SF, with white or other non-black identities, as in the numerous representations of technophilic Asians and Asian Americans on television and in contemporary film, has shaped such responses, as has black skepticism toward the special kinds of intellectualism represented by "nerds" or "geeks" and regarded as insufficiently masculine or racially inauthentic. (Booker T. Washington's characterization of a black scholar in chapter 8 of his 1901 autobiography, *Up from Slavery*, comes to mind.)

For every possible reason for African Americans' disinterest in SF, there are counterexamples. The most conspicuous can be found in popular music. Black artists as popular and diverse as John Coltrane, Sun Ra, Jimi Hendrix, Earth, Wind & Fire, Parliament/Funkadelic, Afrika Bambaataa, DJ Spooky, and more have created extraordinary music that incorporates SF-related themes. SF also has a particular relevance to the history and present experiences of African Americans, who are "in a very real sense," Dery writes, "alien abductees" (Dery 180). Indeed, the narrative of Africans' capture and enslavement, the Middle Passage, and the emancipation of slaves upon the near apocalypse called the Civil War do not sound too far off from something George Lucas might have written. The "escapist" tag also assumes that there is something wrong with escapism itself, and ignores the fact that most literature is escapist to some extent. Like all fiction, SF invites its readers to fantasize; and, like any kind of writing, it is a byproduct of the historical moment during which it is composed.

Contrary to most characterizations of the genre, Delany reminds readers that "science fiction is not 'about the future.'" Rather, it is "a significant distortion of the present that sets up a rich and complex dialogue with the reader's here and now" (Delany, *Starboard Wine* 176).

Consider, for example, how the conflict between the Morlocks and the Eloi in *The Time Machine* (1895) captures H.G. Wells's own fears about class warfare during the Industrial Revolution, or how the Martian invasion of England in Wells's *The War of the Worlds* (1898) turns British imperialism on its head. And for anyone with an investment in working toward a more just society, SF provides the tools and methods for envisioning alternatives to the social, political, cultural, and economic structures of the world. Delany explains: "Even the most passing mention by an SF writer of, say, 'the monopole magnet mining operations in the outer asteroid belt of Delta Cygni,' begins as a simple way of saying that, while the concept of mines may persist, their object, their organization, their technology, their locations, and their very form can change" (Delany, *Starboard Wine* 188). More simply put, the settings of many works of SF are places where things are different. Such visionary exercises represent the first step in any "real" political work, such as correcting the unfair inequalities based on racial difference with which we are all too familiar. "We need images of tomorrow," Delany stated in his 1978 address at the Studio Museum of Harlem, "and our people need them more than most" (Delany, *Starboard Wine* 35). The efforts and examples of Saunders, Delany, and others have contributed to an increase in black SF readers and writers in recent years. In 2000, Charles Saunders published "Why Blacks Should Read (and Write) Science Fiction," a rejoinder to his earlier essay. Indeed, in the twenty-first century, it is impossible to discuss contemporary African American literature without some consideration of SF.

Definitions and How to Avoid Them

In *The Metamorphoses of Science Fiction* (1979), Darko Suvin states that it is necessary to define science fiction before serious scholarship on it can commence or before the genre can be taken seriously in the academy. He then defines SF as "a literary genre whose necessary and sufficient conditions are the presence and interaction of estrangement and cognition" (Suvin 16). This definition has been used by many scholars and is as good as any other that a reader may encounter. Indeed, one may encounter *many* definitions of SF. Among the more notable of these are those composed by inventor and publisher Hugo Gernsback ("a charming romance intermingled with scientific fact and prophetic vision"), SF icon Isaac Asimov ("that branch of literature which is concerned with the impact of scientific advance upon human beings"), and Brian Aldiss ("the search for definition of man and his status in the universe which will stand in our advanced but confused state of knowledge (science), and is characteristically cast in the Gothic or post-Gothic mould"). But perhaps the famous non-definition in Damon Knight's *In Search of Wonder* (1967) is the most accurate: "Science fiction is what we mean when we point to something and say 'That's Science Fiction!'" (quoted in Jakubowski and Edwards 256). This is to say that any definition of SF is bound to be partial and incomplete. As I will argue in the following pages, what makes a text "science fiction" is not necessarily the presence of spaceships, rayguns, AIs (artificial intelligences), or BEMs (bug-eyed monsters). Rather, it is the text's ability to allegorize familiar situations from the reader's world and to take the reader to where, as Capt. Lorq Von Ray states in Delany's *Nova*, "all law has broken down." When a crewman asks Lorq, "Which law do you mean? Man's, or the natural laws of physics, psychics, and chemistry?" Lorq replies, "All of them" (Delany, *Nova* 24).

Moreover, Delany has convincingly argued that the project of defining the genre actually works against its growth and general acceptance. SF is exemplary as "paraliterature," a term coined by Suvin to identify "the popular, 'low,' or plebeian literary production of various times, particularly since the Industrial Revolution" (Suvin vii). Delany explains that paraliterature is the generic Other against which literature defines itself: "Just as (discursively) homosexuality exists largely to delimit heterosexuality and to lend it a false sense of definition, paraliterature exists to delimit literature and provide it with an equally false sense of itself" (Delany "The *Para•doxa* interview" 205). In the twentieth century alone, SF has gone through a number of names and styles: pulp fiction, "hard" SF, "soft" SF, cyberpunk, and more. The diversity of the genre has not stopped anyone from trying to define it, of course. Yet the notion that whatever SF is, its meaning is containable, fixable to a single spot, actually serves as evidence, to the many who are (unfortunately) inclined to believe it, that the genre is hopelessly bound to the realm of lowbrow juvenilia. Literary critics, Delany points out, gave up trying to define "literature" decades ago. The quest for the first work of SF – which has yielded a diverse range of candidates including Cyrano de Bergerac's "A Voyage to the Moon," Jules Verne's *Five Weeks in a Balloon*, Mary Shelley's *Frankenstein*, Sir Thomas More's *Utopia*, and Lucian of Samosata's *True History*, among many others – is similarly futile and wrong-headed, according to Delany. Moreover, it usually fails to acknowledge the pivotal role played by early twentieth-century American pulp magazine pioneer Hugo Gernsback, the namesake of the World Science Fiction Society's prestigious Hugo Award. Although SF has integrated elements from traditions such as Romance, the Gothic, travel narratives, and more, any putative "origin" of the genre is, according to Delany, more "political construct" than "objective reality" (Delany "The *Para•doxa* interview" 239, 246).

Delany's characterization of the discursive uses to which the paraliterary genres are put should ring a bell with scholars of African American Studies. It is congruent with the structure of disidentification through which whiteness defines itself against blackness. James Baldwin explained the centrality of a debased notion of blackness to white identity in a manner compatible with Delany's words about supposedly easy-to-define paraliterary genres: "the black man has functioned in the white man's world as a fixed star, as an immovable pillar" (Baldwin 20). Such a structure operates not only between races, but also within African American culture, to borrow Gene Andrew Jarrett's formulation, one cannot have "deans" of the tradition of African American literature, writers understood to "embody" this tradition, without "truants," those located at – and who are thereby defining – its limits and boundaries. SF has served as an irreconcilable category of black writing that gives the rest of the tradition its coherence, even though both categories of writing have experienced marginalization in the academy. Consider the fact that there is only one work of SF, Octavia E. Butler's "Bloodchild," in *The Norton Anthology of African American Literature* (1997, 2004), and that the text by Delany that was selected for inclusion in that canonizing volume is an excerpt from his novella *Atlantis: Model 1924* (1995), an experimental ode to the jazz era and a variation on the African American migration narrative, but hardly representative of the genre with which this author is most frequently associated.

Note, however, that SF is relevant to African American Studies beyond the similarity of structures of disidentification. The respective emergence of the most prominent black voices in SF – Delany and Butler – occurred in the mid-1960s and 1970s, when the Black Power, women's, and gay liberation movements were asserting alternative social structures and transforming America's vision of itself. As John Pfeiffer puts it, "radical change in imaginative mode and radical change in the social order" were emerging simultaneously (Pfeiffer 35).

Conscientious Sorcerers

In 1975, Pfeiffer published "Black American Speculative Literature: A Checklist" in the scholarly SF journal *Extrapolation*. The list featured many works by recognized writers of the African American tradition, including W.E.B. Du Bois, George Samuel Schuyler, Leroi Jones/Amiri Baraka, Douglas Turner Ward, and John A. Williams among others. The recent *Dark Matter* volumes – *Dark Matter: A Century of Speculative Fiction from the African Diaspora* (2000) and *Dark Matter: Reading the Bones* (2004) – cast similarly wide nets, drawing in writers such as Charles W. Chesnutt, Ishmael Reed, Derrick Bell, and Charles Johnson. As such, the volumes provide an excellent gateway for SF-curious scholars familiar with more traditional literary forms. As their titles suggest, Pfeiffer's checklist and the *Dark Matter* volumes are, appropriately and productively, organized around "speculative fiction" (or "spec-fic"), an inclusive term that embraces, links, and perhaps domesticates a variety of fantastic genres: fantasy, sword and sorcery, horror, magical realism, as well as SF. Indeed, it could be argued that "speculative fiction" deconstructs the frequently invoked opposition between SF and "fantasy" (for example, *Conan the Barbarian* or *The Lord of the Rings*), a genre that has often served as SF's discursive Other.

At the risk of contradicting the critiques of definitions and authenticity above, however, many of the writers featured in these collections have not identified their work as SF. Nor would most readers, for that matter, recognize the majority of their work as such. One possible exception would be George Samuel Schuyler, author of *Black No More* (1931), a satire of America's obsession with race and color that imagines a technological process that turns blacks into whites. Schuyler also wrote for the *Pittsburgh Courier* an episodic adventure titled *The Black Internationale* (c.1936–8), which bears evidence of his familiarity with the pulp fiction published by Gernsback and others at the time. These stories have been collected in a volume entitled *Black Empire* and feature the megalomaniacal Dr. Henry Belsidus, a black genius accurately described as "Du Bois, Booker T. Washington, George Washington Carver, and Marcus Garvey rolled into one fascist superman" (Gates 42). The narrative is full of pulp elements: Belsidus eliminates his foes by dissolving them in vats of acid; he attacks Europe by having airplanes fly over its cities, dropping disease-infested vermin; and he fends off attacks on his African headquarters with his very own death ray. (No self-respecting world conqueror should be without one.) *Black Empire* also features more feasible futurisms, such as hydroponic agriculture and underground airplane hangars, in a manner comparable to Hugo Gernsback's quintessential space opera *Ralph 124C 41+: A Romance of the Year 2660* (1912). That said, it is likely that Schuyler – the author of "The Negro Art-Hokum" (1926), an essay which argued that any assertion of black cultural specificity was an assertion of unbridgeable difference that could serve white supremacist thought – intended to offer these tropes in a satirical manner, just as his Dr. Belsidus was intended to satirize both black nationalism and pan-Africanism.

Any discussion of African American SF must include (as this one already has) Samuel R. Delany. He is the first major black voice in the genre, one of the first gay writers in the genre to feature explicitly queer content in his writing, and a literary and cultural critic of remarkable breadth and insight. "Chip" Delany was born and raised in Harlem, into one of the more famous families in African American history. Delany's father, also named Sam, ran a funeral home and had moved to Harlem from North Carolina in 1924. Samuel Ray Delany Sr. and his siblings were the children of not only the first black archbishop in North Carolina, but also an administrator at St. Augustine's College (now University), one of the oldest historically black schools in the country. Chip's paternal aunts, educator Sarah Elizabeth and dentist A. Elizabeth Delany (a.k.a. Sadie and Bessie), earned fame for writing the memoir *Having Our Say* (1993). His uncle was Hubert T. Delany, a judge with the Court of Domestic Relations in New York, and a major figure in the National Association for the Advancement of Colored People. Chip's mother introduced him to a variety of cultural sources and literary figures, including those from the Harlem Renaissance, some of whom knew the Delany family. He discovered SF as a teenager in the 1950s; early influences included Theodore Sturgeon, Alfred Bester, and Robert A. Heinlein. Delany also trained at the Breadloaf Writers Conference in Vermont. He published his first novel, an otherworldly adventure tale entitled *The Jewels of Aptor*, in 1962 at age 20, and has since published over 30 volumes. He is a multiple recipient of both the World Science Fiction Society's Hugo Award and the Science Fiction and Fantasy Writers of America's Nebula Award, the highest honors associated with the genre. Blacklisted in the 1980s by a major retail bookseller for the gay content of his *Return to Nevèrÿon* series, he has since received the William T. Whitehead Memorial Award for Lifetime

Achievement in Gay and Lesbian Literature. In 2002, Delany was inducted into the Science Fiction Hall of Fame.

Delany has stated that his earliest published works "yearned to be at – (were) suffused with the yearning for – the center of the most traditional SF enterprise" (quoted in Dery 190). Although those early works feature few conspicuous markers of Delany's identity as an African American, they heralded the emergence of a figure who expanded the range of what readers can expect, in terms of prose quality as much as content, from SF. Representative of this fact was Harlan Ellison's claim that he was saving the best for last when he included Delany's short story "... Aye, and Gomorrah" as the concluding tale in the famous short-fiction collection *Dangerous Visions* (1967). Envisioning the sexualization of "spacers," humans desexed by the government-sponsored surgery that enables their interplanetary jaunts, the story represents a level of narrative craft, the skillful construction of language and story, at the most elemental levels. It comes from the pen of a writer as familiar with W.H. Auden and Hart Crane as with Isaac Asimov and Robert Heinlein. Implicitly, the story states what Delany would explicitly argue in his essay "About 5,750 Words" (1977): that despite its paraliterary status, SF can be as rich an aesthetic experience as any other mode of writing. A recent collection of Delany's short fiction entitled *... Aye, and Gomorrah* (2003) is an excellent introduction to this important writer.

Other "early Delany" texts include The Fall of the Towers trilogy – *Out of the Dead City* (1963), *The Towers of Toron* (1964), and *City of a Thousand Suns* (1965) – which counters the militaristic antagonisms that characterize many SF adventures with antiwar themes. *The Ballad of Beta-2* (1965) introduces a common Delanean topic, the interpretation of a text. More specifically, it details an Archaeology graduate student's attempts to discern the fate of the diasporic "Star Folk" by analyzing the remnants of a song. *Empire Star* (1966) is notable for its Möbius-strip-shaped narrative structure, a device Delany develops in subsequent works. The same year as that novel, Delany published *Babel-17*, which represented a shift in the meaning of the kind of "science" in which science fiction could engage – from the natural sciences to the social sciences (in this case, linguistics) – as Earth enlists a poet to assist in countering the invasion by an alien race wielding a devastatingly effective linguistic weapon. Many Delany novels similarly feature writers or artists as protagonists or major characters. *The Einstein Intersection* (1967) figures social identity and difference, as well as the Great Migration, in a futuristic Earth society in which a mutant protagonist named Lo Lobey – whose flute doubles as a weapon – faces off against a powerful psionic killer known as Kid Death. *Nova* (1968) alludes to everything from *Moby-Dick* to the Tarot as it charts the quest for fire of a disfigured black starship captain who races through the galaxy with a crew that includes a budding novelist and the Mouse, the master of the sensory-syrynx, which, like Lobey's flute, can either create or kill.

The "early Delany," therefore, seems "traditional" only when compared to the radically innovative material that emerged post-1968, when, the author states, "I sat back and decided to figure out what I was really doing here" (quoted in Dery 1994: 190). It was at this time that Delany started writing *Dhalgren* (1975), which conspicuously demonstrates the influence of the black, gay, and women's liberation movements on his writing. This behemoth of a novel, clocking in at over 800 pages, is set in the American city of Bellona, which has endured an unspecified apocalyptic event, perhaps an uprising by the city's black inhabitants, leaving the survivors – which include a preacher, an astronaut, a musician, a newspaper publisher, hippies, leather queens, an "ordinary" American family, and gangs of youths called "scorpions" – to create new social, cultural, political, economic, and sexual structures. The novel's protagonist – an ambidextrous, bisexual, Native American called the Kid – wanders through the city looking for clues to what happened to the city, questioning his own sanity, and writing a book a poetry. The novel's final chapter is a transcript of the Kid's journal, complete with marginalia and an editor's comments. A reading experience like no other, *Dhalgren* immerses its reader in a world where laws have broken down and are created anew.

"Return to Nevèrÿon" is the name of Delany's four-volume foray into the genre of "Sword-and-Sorcery" or "Fantasy," which often shares writers, publishers, and readers with SF, despite the efforts of one side or the other to emphasize the genres' differences. This series is distinguished by its detailed representations of slavery and society, its unabashed representations of queer sexuality, and its demonstrations of the author's familiarity with critical theory. Epigraphs from figures such as Michel Foucault, Barbara Johnson, and Homi Bhabha punctuate the chapters of volumes that could conceivably be used as textbooks in a graduate seminar on post-structuralism. The series implicitly critiques the Eurocentrism of typical fantasy and sword-and-sorcery tales, set usually in some variation of Medieval England, by locating its stories in Nevèrÿon, the location of which is ambiguous, but which nonetheless signifies as Asian or African, Mesopotamian or Mediterranean. The series is loosely organized around Gorgik the Liberator's simultaneous quests: to abolish slavery in the Empire of Nevèrÿon and to satisfy his sexual desires, which involve slave collars. The series includes "The Tale of Plagues and Carnivals," the first full-length work of fantastic fiction to address the AIDS crisis. Delany's purposeful engagement with gender and sexuality continues in such texts as *Trouble on Triton* (1976), subtitled "an ambiguous heterotopia," and *Stars in My Pocket like Grains of Sand* (1984), a galaxy-spanning gay love story about slavery, cultural difference, and competing systems of knowledge that anticipates the World Wide Web.

Delany is also the author of pornographic texts such as *Equinox* (1973), *Hogg* (1988, rev. 1995), and *The Mad Man* (1995). Over the last 15 years, Delany has moved away from SF. His most recent works of fiction, such as *Phallos* (2004), *Dark Reflections* (2008), and the graphic novel *Bread and Wine* (1999), address sex and sexuality, whereas his criticism addresses a range of literary and paraliterary topics, including the changing sexual landscape of New York City in *Times Square Red, Times Square Blue* (1999). Ursula LeGuin called Delany SF's "finest in-house critic" (LeGuin 27), a reputation based on essays that appear in collections such as *The Jewel-Hinged Jaw* (1977), *The American Shore* (1978), *Starboard Wine* (1984), *The Straits of Messina* (1989), and recent volumes of interviews and essays such as *Silent Interviews* (1994), *Longer Views* (1996), *Shorter Views* (1999), and *About Writing* (2005). Delany is also the author of the Nebula Award-winning autobiography *The Motion of Light in Water* (1988) and other memoirs: *Heavenly Breakfast* (1979), which details the author's days as a self-described "flower child" in the titular commune/rock band, and *1984* (2000), a personal history of the AIDS crisis in epistolary form. Delany has created an immense body of work characterized not only by explicit representations of diverse sexual behaviors, but also by an intellectual sophistication of the highest order and, above all, by way of superbly crafted fictional elements that refute ill-informed evaluations of SF as sub-literary. Highlighting the intersections of African American Studies, Gay and Lesbian Studies, and critical theory, Delany's writing provides a diverse and adventurous readership with unparalleled imaginative experiences.

Octavia E. Butler produced a body of work that similarly refutes assumptions about SF's aesthetic impoverishment and the mutual exclusivity of SF and African American literature. A storyteller of the highest order, Butler wrote works of fiction that have found receptive audiences across races and genders as well as beyond the traditional SF readership. The honors she has received – including multiple Nebulas and Hugos, the Langston Hughes Medal, and a 1995 McArthur Foundation "Genius" grant – attest to both the popularity and the exceptional quality of her storytelling. It is hard to identify another writer, of any genre, whose writing can consistently transform the reader's understandings of themselves and their world while being so gripping as to be, quite literally, hard to put down.

Born in 1947 in Pasadena, California, Butler was raised in a strict Baptist household by her mother and grandmother. As a child and teenager, she was not allowed to leave the house and socialize with other young people; therefore, she said, she always felt like an outsider, noting that SF tends to be attractive to outsiders, herself included. In the late 1960s and early 1970s, she met and workshopped with some of SF's best writers, including Harlan Ellison and Joanna Russ. Her story, "Speech Sounds" (1983), a bleak tale of the dissolution of social order that follows the loss of language in a major American city, won the Hugo Award. "Speech Sounds" and Butler's other award-winning short fiction can be found in a collection entitled *Bloodchild*, the title story of which (1984) conveys a youth's loss of innocence as he faces the imminent implantation of alien eggs into his body as part of a pact between human refugees and the alien beings who shelter them. "Bloodchild" is perhaps the most representative of Butler's works, not only for its high-resolution representations of violence and viscera, but also for its themes and for how those themes are often (mis)read. There are textual examples that could suggest that the relationship between the story's humans and the alien race known as the Tlic allegorizes antebellum slavery: the humans are kept on a "preserve," they are fed narcotic substances that keep them content, and they are not allowed to drive or possess firearms. However, one could also contend that "Bloodchild" presents a different set of themes that runs through much of Butler's work: the *symbiotic* relationship between a species and its environment or another species, as well as the changes that humanity must – or more hopefully put, is able to – endure in order to survive.

The "slavery" reading of "Bloodchild" can be seen as the result of an over-reading of the significance of its author's racial identity, but it may also be an effect of the prominence of Butler's most explicit engagement with the history of American slavery, *Kindred* (1979). This Harriet Jacobs-meets-H.G. Wells novel finds Dana Franklin, an African American writer, inexplicably transported through time and space from Los Angeles in 1976 to antebellum Maryland, where she saves the life of a white child named Rufus. Dana reasons that she is being pulled into the nineteenth century periodically for exactly that purpose and realizes that Rufus is her ancestor. To ensure her own existence, therefore, she must not only repeatedly save the danger-prone boy's life, but also enable him to rape the black woman who is also her ancestor. Like much of Butler's other work, *Kindred* places its protagonist in numerous impossible situations.

Scholars of African American literature have interpreted *Kindred* as a neo-slave narrative, a first-person post-Civil Rights-era novel that grapples with the history and twentieth-century legacies of race-based slavery in America. Butler steadfastly denied that "science fiction" was an accurate descriptor for *Kindred*. Since the mechanics of time travel are unexplained, she explained, there is no "science" in the novel. However, the novel does feature numerous representations of the effects on human lives produced by changes in technology. Therefore, *Kindred* responds to the calls sent out by its two kinds of antecedents: the time-travel tales in the tradition of SF and the slave narratives that are at the root of the tradition of African American literature. It is a hybrid text that contributes to a deconstruction of the literature/paraliterature binary.

Most of Butler's novels belong to one of three series. The first, The Patternist Saga, includes *Patternmaster* (1976), *Mind of My Mind* (1977), *Wild Seed* (1980), and *Clay's Ark* (1984). (These books have recently been collected in a 2007 volume entitled *Seed to Harvest*.) This series involves a network of psionic and telepathically linked beings belonging to "the Pattern." The racial, class, and gender hierarchies familiar to Butler's readers are figured in the divisions between "Clayarks," "mutes," "outsiders," and "Housemasters" of the Pattern. Set in the far-off future, *Patternmaster* features a deadly conflict between two powerful Patternist brothers that involves Amber, a black woman with healing powers. The prequel *Mind of My Mind* goes back in time to the twentieth century and presents Doro, a powerful and ruthless being of African origin, who has lived for several millennia by inhabiting his victims' bodies. Doro engages in a power struggle with his telepathic daughter Mary over the Pattern, the psionic connection amongst the family/army of telepaths that Doro has created. *Wild Seed* goes from the seventeenth to the nineteenth century and pairs Doro with his lover-antagonist Anyanwu, a defiant African woman with an extended lifespan and the ability to metamorphose into various human and animal forms. With a diverse array of female characters, some of whom counter violence and hierarchy through nurturing and instruction, this series demonstrates how Butler's writing provides useful source material for Gender and Women's Studies scholars.

Butler's Xenogenesis series – *Dawn* (1987), *Adulthood Rites* (1988), and *Imago* (1989) – has been recently collected in one volume entitled *Lilith's Brood* (2000). In this second of three series, set after a nuclear war that has nearly eliminated all life on Earth, the remnants of humanity are rescued by an alien race known as the Oankali. These traders in genetic information seek to interbreed with human beings so as to continue the genetic expansion of their own species, repopulate Earth, and remove "the human contradiction," humanity's genetic inclination toward hierarchical thinking, the basis for our species' (self-)destructive behavior. The first human that the Oankali awaken, a woman of African descent named Lilith Iyapo, must confront not only the skepticism of other human survivors, but also her own ambivalences toward the Oankali and their gifts. At the heart of these stories are questions about how much human behavior is determined by biological "nature," and about what possibilities exist for revising that nature and behavior. The Oankali aspire to a symbiosis with the humans they have rescued, but as with the Tlic in "Bloodchild," it is tempting to characterize this relationship as a recasting of antebellum slavery in a futuristic setting. Xenophobic groups of human beings known as Resisters indeed see it that way, and oppose the Oankali at every opportunity in the name of genetic purity. The Resisters demonstrate that the closing of ranks among humans in response to a close encounter with sentient alien life, an assumption invoked to fence off SF from racial issues and people of color, would not necessarily be a healthy or progressive development. Unlike some traditional SF narratives, the series does not pit two races against each other in interstellar combat. Rather, it represents the inevitable changes – sociological as well as genetic – produced by their contact. The series consistently values hybridity and serves as useful raw material for discussions of cyborg feminism and the post-human.

Butler's Parable books make up her third series. *Parable of the Sower* (1993) is set in a bleak near-future version of Southern California, where lethal gangs addicted to a drug that makes watching fires feel orgasmic roam at night, where multinational corporations keep employees in a form of wage slavery, and where citizens are forced into walled communes in order to survive. The novel's protagonist, Lauren Olamina, is "hyperempathic," born with the ability to feel others' pleasure and pain, which is a net liability in such a dangerous environment. *Sower* traces her efforts to establish a religion that sustains herself and others spiritually and provides a practical knowledge-base for survival in a menacing world: "A unifying, purposeful life here on Earth, and the hope of heaven for (oneself and one's) children. A real heaven, not mythology or philosophy. A heaven that will be (its members') to shape." Lauren names her religion Earthseed, the central tenets of which are that "God is Change" and that the "Destiny of Earthseed is to take root among / the stars" (Butler 234, 220, 68). *Sower*'s Nebula Award-winning sequel, *Parable of the Talents* (1999) is told from the viewpoints of both Lauren and her daughter, Asha Vere, who comments on the contents of her mother's journals. The novel depicts an American society transformed further by nationalism, corporate values, and Christian fundamentalism, where Earthseed becomes the target of a vicious crusade. The novel is quintessential Butler in its representation of ordinary people placed in extraordinary circumstances and facing a seemingly unstoppable opposition.

Published posthumously, *Fledgling* (2006) is Butler's own version of a vampire story, a mode associated with other contemporary black women writers of speculative fiction, such as Jewelle Gomez, author of *The Gilda Stories* (1991), and Tananarive Due, who is known for horror or "dark fantasy" novels such as *The Between* (1995), *My Soul to Keep* (1997), *The Living Blood* (2001), *Blood Colony* (2008), and more. Butler's tale is told by Shori Matthews, a member of a vampiric race called the Ina, who has lost her memory following a murderous attack on her family. Butler extends themes addressed in earlier texts in that her vampires have symbiotic relationships with groups of humans of both genders, forming complex emotional and sexual relationships. It is no accident that Butler and Delany, the most accomplished black voices in SF, have written texts that are characterized not by addressing race alone, but by investigating the intersections of race and gender as well as of species and their environments. Butler's passing leaves a hole that her many devoted readers may feel will never be filled. However, it is important to value not only the legacy that her body of work represents but also her influence and nurturing relationships with younger black SF writers.

Nalo Hopkinson represents one of the finest black writers to emerge in the last 10 to 15 years. A recipient of the Campbell Award for Best New SF Writer and a resident of Toronto who grew up in Jamaica, Guyana, and Trinidad, Hopkinson frequently draws on Afro-Caribbean cultural sources for characters, settings, situations, and most notably, language: "Oho. Like it starting, oui? Don't be frightened, sweetness; is for the best. I go be with you the whole time. Trust me and let me distract you little bit with one anasi story" (Hopkinson, *Midnight Robber* 1). This opening from Hopkinson's second novel, *Midnight Robber* (2000), is not only a surefire way to hook the reader, it also represents the Creolized linguistic style that both figures and is featured in her fusions of Afro-Caribbean culture and cyberculture. Nelson describes Hopkinson's *Brown Girl in the Ring* (1998), which won the *Locus* Award for Best First Novel, as "mix(ing) Caribbean dialects, references to Derek Walcott's play *Ti-Jeanne and His Brothers*, and quotations from a popular Caribbean children's ring game … with more familiar science fiction conventions such as biotechnology and a postindustrial dystopic urban setting" (Nelson, "Making the Impossible Possible" 98). *Midnight Robber* (2000), as Jillana Enteen suggests, could be called a postcolonial cyberpunk story; it is set on the planet Toussaint, where an Artificial Intelligence named Granny Nanny "manages her society through an electronic web that incorporates ideologies and myths from traditional African, Caribbean, and both North and South American cultures" (Enteen 264). Hopkinson has penned a number of stories that bring legends from these cultures to life, such as "Greedy Choke Puppy," which is about a *soucouyant*, a fiery being that drains life from infants. The story can be found in *Dark Matter* and in *Skin Folk* (2001), a collection of Hopkinson's variations on Caribbean folklore. "Throughout the Caribbean," she explains, "under different names you'll find stories about people who aren't what they seem. Skin gives these skin folk their human shape"

(Hopkinson, *Skin Folk* 1). Hopkinson is also the editor of the collections *Whispers from the Cotton Tree Root: Caribbean Fabulist Fiction* (2000) and *Mojo: Conjure Stories* (2003), and she has taken advantage of the traditional SF conceit of encounters with "new worlds and new civilizations" to co-edit with Uppinder Mehan a collection of Post-colonial Science Fiction and Fantasy entitled *So Long Been Dreaming* (2004). Other works include the novel *The Salt Roads* (2005), a pan-Africanist womanist parable, linking the stories of black women across centuries and continents. Hopkinson's most recent novel is *The New Moon's Arms* (2007), and she shows no signs of slowing down, for which numerous readers are grateful.

Steven Barnes is another writer who has benefited from the example and support of Butler. An accomplished screenwriter and prolific author of works both within and outside of SF, his first works of note were collaborations with SF grandmasters Larry Niven and Jerry Pournelle. His early solo SF novels, *Street Lethal* (1983), *Gorgon Child* (1989), and *Firedance* (1993), feature a black protagonist named Aubrey Knight, and provide somewhat ordinary action-hero fare; however, those texts in no way represent the limits of this author's ambitions or talents. Barnes wrote *Far beyond the Stars* (1998), a novel based on the *Star Trek: Deep Space Nine* episode, and, in 2002, Barnes published *Lion's Blood*, aptly subtitled "A Novel of Slavery and Freedom in an Alternate America," which imagines the colonization of the New World by Islamic Africans who enslave whites captured from Ireland. The story opens in "15 Shawwal 1279 Higira" or "April 4, 1863 *Anno Domini*" (Barnes 3), and most of the events are set in "Bilalistan," that is, North America. Although it features plenty of action and adventure, much of the story addresses the relationship between Kai, the son of the Wakil of the Dar Kush estate, and Aidan, Kai's servant, specifically pursuing the issue of whether something like friendship is even a remote possibility within a system in which the liberties certain groups enjoy are predicated on the bondage of others and violence routinely enforces the social order. Some readers may speculate that Barnes's novel could be co-opted by parties invested in downplaying the legacy of slavery in the twenty-first century and who often invoke black African participation in the slave trade to support their claims. However, rather than lending ammunition to such arguments, *Lion's Blood* disarticulates domination from whiteness and submission from blackness, denaturalizing characteristics that racist discourse seeks to fix to racial signifieds. Barnes has published a sequel to *Lion's Blood* entitled *Zulu Heart* (2003), and has most recently published works of speculative fiction set in pre-historic Africa that address spiritual themes: *Great Sky Woman* (2006) and *Shadow Valley* (2009).

The Shape of Things to Come

In 1998, Walter Mosley, famous for his detective fiction, published the essay "Black to the Future." The author of several SF novels – including *Blue Light* (1998), *Futureland* (2001), *47* (2006), and *The Wave* (2007) – Mosley predicted that "there will be an explosion of science fiction from the black community" (Mosley 34). This emergence of new writers may be less an explosion than a continual, ongoing process; however, the conditions for it have never been better. The popularity of writers such as Butler and Hopkinson and of the *Dark Matter* volumes contributes to the development of a black SF readership, from which new writers can be cultivated. The *Dark Matter* volumes present newer writers such as Nisi Shawl and Kalamu Ya Salaam, as well as a diverse range of SF texts that demonstrate that the genre is not limited to technobabble-laden expositions, space operas, wagon trains to the stars, or adolescent power fantasies (enjoyable though these may be), and they do the valuable work of showcasing recent writers and placing their work in SF in relation to traditions of black literary and cultural production. Writing that puts people of African descent, their histories, and their cultures at the center of visions of not only future (or past or present) technologies but also the alternatives they enable serves us all. And despite the recent language about "post-racialism," the color-line persists as a problem to be confronted as often in the twenty-first century as it had in the twentieth. We live in an "Information Age" in which technology is changing at an ever-increasing pace, thus it is necessary to pause and to theorize the effects of such changes on human beings and the structures of the world that we have created. This is a project to which the voices of people of African descent will continue to have much to contribute. If cyberpunk "helped to revitalize interest in SF among academic as well as popular audiences" in the 1980s (Enteen 262), then Afrofuturism may do the same for both SF and African American literature in the twenty-first century.

Bibliography

"Afrofuturist Literature." *Afrofuturism*. www.afrofuturism.net/text/lit.html.

Baldwin, James. *The Fire Next Time*. New York: Dell, 1963.

Barnes. Steven. *Lion's Blood*. New York: Warner/Aspect, 2002.

Barr, Marleen S., ed. *Afro-Future Females: Black Writers Chart Science Fiction's Newest New-Wave Trajectory*. Columbus: Ohio State UP, 2008.

Bould, Mark. "The Ships Landed Long Ago: Afrofuturism and Black SF." *Science Fiction Studies* 34.2 (2007): 177–86.

Butler, Octavia E. *Parable of the Sower*. New York: Warner/Aspect, 1993.

Davis, Thulani. "The Future May Be Bleak, But It's Not Black." *The Village Voice*, February 1, 1983: 17–19.

Delany, Samuel R. *Starboard Wine: More Notes on the Language of Science Fiction*. Pleasantville, NY: Dragon Press, 1984.

Delany, Samuel R. *Nova*. New York: Vintage, 1968–2002.

Delany, Samuel R. "The *Para•doxa* interview." 1995. In *Shorter Views*. Hanover, NH: Wesleyan University Press, 1999. 186–217.

Dery, Mark. "Black to the Future: Interviews with Samuel R. Delany, Greg Tate, and Tricia Rose." In *Flame Wars: The Discourse of Cyberculture*. Durham, NC: Duke University Press, 1994. 179–222.

Eglash, Ron. "Race, Sex, and Nerds: From Black Geeks to Asian-American Hipsters." *Social Text* 20.2 (2002): 49–64.

Enteen, Jillana. "On the Receiving End of Colonization: Nalo Hopkinson's 'Nansi Web." *Science Fiction Studies* 34.2 (2007): 262–82.

Fox, Robert Elliot. *Conscientious Sorcerers: The Black Postmodernist Fiction of LeRoi Jones/Amiri Baraka, Ishmael Reed, and Samuel R. Delany*. New York: Greenwood Press, 1987.

Gates, Henry Louis, Jr. "A Fragmented Man: George Schuyler and the Claims of Race." *New York Times Book Review*, September 20, 1992: 31, 42–3.

Hopkinson, Nalo. *Midnight Robber*. New York: Warner/Aspect, 2000.

Hopkinson, Nalo. *Skin Folk*. New York: Warner/Aspect, 2001.

Jakubowski, Maxim and Malcolm Edwards, ed. *The SF Book of Lists*. New York: Berkley, 1983.

Jarrett, Gene Andrew. *Deans and Truants: Race and Realism in African American Literature*. Philadelphia: University of Pennsylvania Press, 2006.

Kilgore, DeWitt Douglas. *Astrofuturism: Science, Race, and Visions of Utopia in Space*. Philadelphia: University of Pennsylvania Press, 2003.

LeGuin, Ursula K. "Introduction." In *The Norton Book of Science Fiction*. Ed. Ursula K. LeGuin and Brian Attebery. New York: Norton, 1993. 15–42.

Mosley, Walter. "Black to the Future." *The New York Times Magazine*, November 1, 1998: 32, 34.

Nelson, Alondra. "Introduction: Future Texts." *Social Text* 20.2 (2002): 1–15.

Nelson, Alondra. "Making the Impossible Possible: An Interview with Nalo Hopkinson. *Social Text* 20.2 (2002): 97–113.

Peplow, Michael W. and Robert S. Bravard. Introduction. In *Samuel R. Delany: A Primary and Secondary Bibliography: 1962–1972*. Boston, MA: G.K. Hall, 1980. 1–61.

Pfeiffer, John. "Black American Speculative Literature: A Checklist." *Extrapolation* 17.1 (1975): 35–43.

Sallis, James, ed. *Ash of Stars: On the Writing of Samuel R. Delany*. Jackson: University Press of Mississippi, 1996.

Saunders, Charles R. "Why Blacks Don't Read Science Fiction." In *Brave New Universe: Testing the Values of Science in Society*. Ed. Tom Henighan. Ottawa: Tecumseh, 1980. 160–8.

Saunders, Charles. "Why Blacks Should Read (and Write) Science Fiction." In *Dark Matter*. Ed. Sheree Thomas. New York: Warner/Aspect, 2000. 398–404.

Scholes, Robert and Eric S. Rabkin. *Science Fiction: History, Science, Vision*. New York: Oxford University Press, 1977.

Suvin, Darko. *The Metamophoses of Science Fiction*. New Haven: Yale University Press, 1979.

Tucker, Jeffrey Allen. *A Sense of Wonder: Samuel R. Delany, Race, Identity & Difference*. Middletown, CT: Wesleyan University Press, 2004.

25
Latino/a Literature and the African Diaspora

Theresa Delgadillo

> *It is generally believed that the first black man came to the Americas as a member of the second expedition of Christopher Columbus in 1493. He was apparently a free person. African slavery, however, was not introduced into the New World until 1501.*
>
> Palmer 7

In the United States, research on the African diaspora of the Americas has been primarily devoted to the history, cultures, arts, and experiences of diasporan descendants in what is now the United States of America. Although much of this research is concentrated on African Americans in the Southern, Eastern, and Midwestern regions of the country, there has also been considerable work, both historical and contemporary, on African Americans in the Southwest, California in particular, and in the Pacific Northwest. However, in recent decades interest in the African diaspora throughout the Americas has grown. There has also been a more intense interest in comparative approaches to hemispheric research on the arts, cultures, histories, and societies of the Americas – work that includes comparisons among US, Latin American, and Caribbean diasporas but also addresses contrasts between dominant societies. This work has illuminated the conditions and cultural exchanges through which contemporary literatures, arts, and societies were formed and continue to evolve. A principal goal of the study of African diasporas throughout the Americas thus has been to develop more profound understandings of diasporan peoples, cultures, experiences, and histories.[1] These concerns are not entirely new; in fact, interest in the African diaspora throughout the Americas has long been a part of African American, Latin American, and Latino/a Studies scholarship, even if not always at the center of these distinct areas of study. However, as the above quote suggests, African diasporan peoples are as constitutive of continental and national histories and cultures in the Americas as Native, Spanish, or English peoples.

While there has long been scholarly interest in this area, the questions and direction of research have been varied. For example, scholar and performer Katherine

Dunham, working in the mid-twentieth century, pursued the collection, preservation, and dissemination of black arts and performances in the Americas, while Cuban scholar Fernando Ortiz, working earlier in the century, explored how African, Spanish, and Native societies and cultures intermixed to create new cultural and uniquely American phenomena.[2] Paul Gilroy's work examines the cross-cultural formation of Caribbean and English colonial and postcolonial cultures, while Frances Aparicio analyzes diasporan and European influences in the development of salsa, an important Puerto Rican form of popular music. Literary critics José David Saldívar and Vera Kutzinksi in contemporary comparative analyses of twentieth-century literatures, explore common but also differing conceptions of race, ethnicity, and citizenship in the Americas. In this essay, I will examine a representative sample of the numerous studies that have enriched our knowledge of the African diaspora in Latin American and Latino/a cultures and offer readings of a few Latino/a texts that address African diaspora.

At the outset, it will be useful for my readers to make a distinction between, on the one hand, work on the African diaspora in Latin America, and, on the other hand, work that focuses on the African diaspora among Latino/as, that is, US populations of Latin American heritage. Examples of the first case include *Café con Leche: Race, Class, and National Image in Venezuela* (1993) by Winthrop Wright; George Reid Andrews' *Afro-Latin America, 1800–2000*; Robin D. Moore's *Nationalizing Blackness: Afrocubanismo and Artistic Revolution in Havan, 1920–1940* (1997) and Ben Vinson III's *Bearing Arms for His Majesty: The Free-Colored Militia in Colonial Mexico* (2001), not to mention the scholarly work of Latin Americans in this area. Examples of the second case include Frances Aparicio's *Listening to Salsa: Gender, Latin Popular Music, and Puerto Rican Cultures* (1998); Suzanne Bost's *Mulattas and Mestizas: Representing Mixed Identities in the Americas, 1850–2000*; and Susan D. Greenbaum's *More Than Black: Afro-Cubans in Tampa* (2002). In the first part of this brief essay, I will address the relationship between Latino/a cultural productions and the African diaspora, particularly the ways that Latino/a literatures and arts incorporate, claim, or represent the African diaspora as a Latino/a phenomenon. In the second part of this piece I will discuss Willie Colón's instrumental album *El Baquiné de Angelitos Negros*, an important Latino/a version of an Afro-Venezuelan poem about diaspora previously adapted by both Mexican and African American artists.[3]

Is a Latino/a African American?

> *"Let's walk," I said. I didn't feel so much angry as I did sick, like throwing-up sick. Later, when I told this story to my buddy, a colored cat, he said, "Hell, Piri, Ah know stuff like that can sure burn a cat up, but a Negro faces that all the time."*
>
> *"I know that," I said, "but I wasn't a Negro then. I was still only a Puerto Rican."*
>
> Thomas 104

One of the first Puerto Rican texts to receive widespread attention and acclaim in the latter half of the twentieth century deals head-on with the issues of racial formation in terms of African diaspora and *Latinidad*. Piri Thomas in the 1967 memoir *Down These Mean Streets*, excerpted above, understands and identifies himself as Puerto Rican, that is, by an ethnicity and nationality, until he confronts the fact of his interpellation as a black man in the United States. However, Thomas does not merely acquiesce to an identity foisted upon him by whites unable to perceive the world in anything other than two colors or races, but instead undergoes a transformation in both his ethnic and racial identities. The constant of his race in the US forces him, and his family and friends, to consider their glossed-over yet implicit racial identity. Written in 1967, Thomas's memoir describes his growing sense of affiliation with African American friends with whom he shares the bane of discrimination and marginalization, and through whom he learns about "race," skin color, and the differences these make. Yet, he also arrives at a different understanding of himself – one he conveys to family and friends around him – as a Puerto Rican black man.

Thomas's memoir chronicles his mid-twentieth-century youth in New York City. His family takes up residence in neighborhoods with or near African American inhabitants, as had others arriving in New York from Puerto Rico during this period of significant migration from the island to the mainland. Considered *trigueño* on the island, Thomas is among those Puerto Ricans who by virtue of phenotype are read as African Americans in the US. Thomas initially objects to this label, asserting his ethnic and national pride, but soon realizes the consequences of that negation in the US, a situation that prompts him to peer beneath the veneer of Puerto Rican ethnic unity, where lay racial prejudices. His ability to come to terms with this dilemma is a central issue in his memoir, a realization that he underscores when he tells his father, who is also dark-skinned and has spent a lifetime cleaving to a Spanish and Indian identity, that he cannot accept his family's insistence that a white identity is preferable: "I can't fool me any more. I can't dig another color and make it mine just 'cause it's some kind of worth. It's not my worth. My own is what I want, nothing more" (152). Thomas's exposure to racial formation in the US underscores a different racial formation in Puerto Rico, where black/white paradigms do not necessarily apply, yet where racial prejudice persists.

Thomas's meditations and experiences with respect to race revolve around the questions of racial privilege and citizenship, issues key in US racial hierarchies determined by phenotypes. Thomas is repeatedly challenged by black friends and acquaintances to acknowledge his blackness, and eventually he does, identifying the shared fate of Puerto Ricans and African Americans in struggling against discrimination. However, Thomas is not an activist; his racial awareness does not immediately allow him success or noble pursuits, but eventually does lead him to develop greater self and social understanding and eschew racial privilege. The complexity of racial, ethnic and national identities in *Down These Mean Streets* has been addressed by scholars such as Marta Caminero-Santa, Lisa Sanchez Gonzales, and Marta Sanchez.

Thomas's recognition of Puerto Rican blackness is also an acknowledgment and acceptance of the African diaspora as constitutive of Puerto Rican identity, revealing an underemphasized aspect of Puerto Rican ethnicity and nationality but one that would soon receive more widespread attention and study. As Thomas's memoir demonstrates, how Latino/as fit into US racial categories, and how black Latino/as, in particular, are read into US racial categories, surface as important issues in Puerto Rican, Cuban American, Dominican American, and Mexican American literatures, both historically and contemporarily, though the issue is more significant in the former three than in the latter. This confrontation between different systems of racial formation and the implications for the recognition and acceptance of African diaspora as constitutive of Latino/a identities is one of the principal ways in which Latino/a literatures addresses its African diasporan heritage.

It is interesting to consider that in 1967, the year that Thomas's memoir appears, the three top box-office hits at the cinema were movies starring Sidney Poitier, including *In the Heat of the Night*; *To Sir, With Love*; and *Guess Who's Coming to Dinner* (see Grant). In these three films Poitier plays a black man who is an educated, accomplished, and assertive professional – alternately a detective, teacher/engineer, and doctor – who gains the respect, trust, and equal acceptance of the white characters with whom he works and lives. Although these films explore the black/white problematic, and thereby further inscribe it as the predominant racial paradigm of the US, the multifaceted characters Poitier portrays in these films suggest the necessity of reconfiguring and amplifying "black." In this way, the films parallel Piri Thomas's attempts to negotiate race, ethnicity, and national culture – for just as Poitier's characters aim to escape the reductionism and homogeneity of "black" as read in dominant society, so, too, does Thomas strive to escape that reductionism. However, while Poitier's characters achieve that recognition in the film, it is not clear that Piri Thomas, and by extension Afro-Latino/as, achieve similar success. His interpellation as "black" continues, even at the end of his narrative, when referred to as "black bastard" by a plainclothes police officer. He responds: "If you don't mind, I'm a Puerto Rican black bastard," a declaration that insists on a more complex identity that the one, still, allowed him under predominant racial paradigms (235).

Puerto Rican literature and popular culture in the US since the Piri Thomas memoir have been more inclusive of the legacy of African diaspora and have more forcefully addressed the issue of racial discrimination on the island and among Puerto Ricans. Judith Ortiz Cofer's *Silent Dancing: A Partial Remembrance of a Puerto Rican Childhood* (1990) locates the contradiction between the African diasporan roots of Puerto Ricans and forms of race prejudice that circulated in the stories from her childhood. These understated tales manage to highlight these contradictions in telling ways. In one recollection, Cofer contrasts her grandfather's disapproval, for racial reasons, of her aunt's suitor with her grandmother's devotion to the Black Virgin of Montserrat. In another remembrance, Cofer describes an overheard conversation between teachers at elementary schools expressing racial prejudice. The irony of the story is that this takes place at La Escuela Segundo Ruiz Belvis, Belvis being a nineteenth-century Puerto Rican abolitionist and revolutionary political figure. Changes in the discourse about blackness and the African roots of Puerto Rican identity have led to greater appreciation for the Afro-Antillean roots of Puerto Ricans in recent decades, and transnational exchange has strengthened Afro-Caribbean culture, but neither has yet definitively done away with a discourse of "blanqueamiento" or whitening (Torres).

The difficulty of Thomas's project in the US is akin to that of Dominicans and Dominican American cultural productions. Silvio Torres-Saillant cautions against the temptation to view the African American influence on Latino/as or Afro-Latino/as as one of educating or modeling acceptance of African diasporic identities, and instead urges us to recognize both the historic significance of blackness in the formation of the Dominican Republic and its citizens as well as the impact of US discourses of race on the inhabitants of the island nation. He notes that the first arrival of blacks in the Western Hemisphere occurred at Hispaniola, also the site of the first black maroon rebellion in 1503 and the first black slave insurrection in 1522. Slavery was first abolished there in 1801, he notes, and today the population is 90 percent black and mulatto. While elite and official culture in the Dominican Republic has traditionally demonstrated negrophobic and Eurocentric views, according to Torres-Saillant, working people as well as artists and writers have long affirmed the centrality of African American cultural practices and ethnic and racial fusion as key to Dominican identity. Racial identity of Dominicans has been, in part, impacted by US racial paradigms. For example, the fear of Dominican blackness was certainly a factor in nineteenth-century US considerations of whether to annex the island, just as more contemporary Civil Rights movements and traditions have contributed to furthering a discourse of black pride. However, racial and ethnic identities remain uniquely intermeshed in Dominican cultural productions that address African diasporan roots (Torres-Saillant 274–88).

In Dominican American writer Julia Alvarez's historical novel about the life of famed Dominican poet Salomé Henríquez Ureña, *In the Name of Salomé* (2000), the recognition accorded African diaspora within the independence movement later gives way to the insidious logic of whitening in government policy and perception of citizenship. The young and gifted Salomé recognizes the precarious position of the African diaspora in the independence movement and newly forming Republic. Even her suitor was not exempt, as she describes in this passage:

> I felt my face burning, and looked away. Had I talked too much? I wondered. Or was he hinting that he felt attraction toward my person and conversation? I glanced up, catching his eye again. But the look I saw there was the glazed one of an admirer. He was seeing the famous poetisa who had agreed to read *The Hebrew Girl* and whom he hoped would write a poem in the paper in praise of it. He was not seeing me, Salomé, of the funny nose and big ears with hunger in her eyes and Africa in her skin and hair. (94)

Salomé's desire to be seen, truly seen by her lover – who later becomes her husband – and embraced for her difference remains an unrequited desire throughout her life.

The novel pays tribute to a poet of national renown in the Dominican Republic, yet one who it figures as a forgotten or misremembered luminary of both political struggle and literature due to her gender and race, this despite the conscious efforts of independence leaders to create a multiracial society wherein all were free, abolishing slavery almost immediately, as Silvio Torres-Saillant. Restoring Henríquez Ureña to the national and hemispheric imagination is also a restoration of a Dominican identity that embraces its African diasporic roots and a contestation of the policy of "blanqueamiento" or whitening that surfaced in the Caribbean in the 1920s, and took hold in several nations. This policy is reflected in the novel's dialogue between Camila, daughter of Salomé and Pedro, and a student who, in helping her to pack her belongings for a move from the US back to the Caribbean, discovers a posthumous portrait of Salomé created by Pedro:

> "Actually that pretty lady is my father's creation. I have the actual photograph somewhere."
>
> The young woman looks at her, waiting for further explanation, as if she does not understand.
>
> "He wanted my mother to look like the legend *he* was creating," Camila adds. "He wanted her to be prettier, whiter ..."
>
> Something shifts in the young woman's eyes. She looks at Camila closely, "You mean, your mother was a ... a negro?"
>
> "We call it mulatto. She was a mixture," Camila explains.
>
> "That's amazing," the girl says finally, as if that is the safest thing to say. (44)

This exchange, in the small US college town where Camila teaches Spanish, highlights the differing sensibilities about race between the two women. In this scene, the student helping Camila to pack expresses a US logic – the so-called one drop rule – in describing Salomé as black, while Camila expresses a Latin American sensibility about degrees of difference. Indeed, the significance of nicknames that refer to one's coloring or phenotype, or the description of characters with a wide variety of phenotypes, circulates within Latino/a literature as a marker of an affiliation to African diaspora – a marker that is at times pronounced, at others muted. Torres-Saillant notes that Dominicans have a rich vocabulary for describing the skin colors they share, and tend to define themselves not by skin color, as in the US, but by nationality, that is, culture, language, and shared experience (Torres-Saillant 280).

The paradigm of *mestizaje* in which racial mixture is foundational to Latin American subjectivity and national culture, the acceptance of a populace with variegated phenotypes and skin colors, as well as indications of social mobility available to citizens of all colors in Latin American countries, attracted many African Americans seeking relief from the segregated US in the early and mid-twentieth century. The influx included African American artists, performers, writers, and athletes – contacts that undoubtedly influenced conceptions of race and diaspora for all involved. Among these was James Hughes, the father of Langston Hughes, who relocated to Mexico in 1903, where he built a life as a successful businessman and where his young son visited him in 1919. Sixteen years later, by the time he returned to Mexico upon his father's death, Langston Hughes had become a celebrated African American poet and writer widely recognized in Mexican literary and artistic circles (Rampersad).

Another African American migrant to Mexico was Virgil Richardson, a Tuskegee airman who relocated to Mexico City in the post-World War Two period and stayed for nearly five decades. Richardson describes his life in Mexico as one that allowed him and many other African Americans a freedom hitherto unavailable in the segregated and discriminatory United States (Vinson). However, African American interest in Latin America was not uniform. Indeed, historian Gerald Horne contrasts the experiences of two famous early twentieth century African Americans with respect to Mexico and Mexican Americans: boxer Jack Johnson, who advertised his ability to live free of discrimination in Mexico; and Henry O. Flipper, who, as a spy and "Indian fighter" for the US Government informed on Mexicans, African Americans, and Mexican Americans (Horne 2, 45). It is important to acknowledge the significant shortcomings of the prevailing racial paradigm of *mestizaje* – such as its lean toward "whitening" in some eras or its privileging of a mestizo subject while rendering Indian and black subjects invisible – yet it contributed to a Latin American race context different enough from that of the US to open the road to the further national incorporation of African diasporic peoples and cultures, and to attract US African Americans in search of less discriminatory climes. Scholar Winthrop Wright cites this difference as a reason for his interest in traveling to Venezuela in the 1980s and studying its attitudes toward blacks and black culture. His work, *Café con Leche: Race, Class, and National Image in Venezuela*, explores the rise of the 1920s political and cultural movement in Venezuela that values African diasporan roots – one in which poet Andrés Eloy Blanco figured prominently – but, ultimately, does not succeed in eliminating racial discrimination.

In Latino/a literature, the incorporation of African folklore or religious ritual and belief, the use of popular or vernacular idioms of Spanish, as well as the tensions of skin color and race, often suggest African diasporan subjectivities as well as their enduring influence on Latino/a subjectivity in general. We might read these representations in accord with Edward Kamau Brathwaite's view of the four modes in which African influence appears in Caribbean literature: they include rhetorical allusions to Africa, depictions of practices or beliefs that are survivals of African culture, literature that uniquely expresses an African-influenced language or worldview, and literature that reconnects to Africa (Brathwaite). Following this rubric, Cuban American writer Cristina Garcia employs three of these modes in her fiction about Cuban and Cuban American characters. The storylines of her 1992 novel, *Dreaming in Cuban*, and her 2003 novel, *Monkey Hunting*, include the influence of African diaspora in Cuban culture, representations of African practices, the history of slavery on the island, the discursive confluence of race and nation, as well as the narrative events and elements that draw on African worldviews.

Dominican American writer Junot Diaz assumes Latino/a African diaspora in the opening pages of his novel, *The Brief Wondrous Life of Oscar Wao* (2007):

> They say it came first from Africa, carried in the screams of the enslaved; that it was the death bane of the Tainos, uttered just as one world perished and another began; that it was a demon drawn into Creation through the nightmare door that was cracked open in the Antilles. *Fukú americanus*, or more colloquially, fukú – generally a curse or a doom of some kind; specifically the Curse and the Doom of the New World. (1)

The narrator of this novel repeatedly attributes the several misfortunes, setbacks, and disasters afflicting the de Leon family and particularly Oscar de Leon to the mysterious *fukú*, making it almost a central character in the novel. The narrator combines the tough and tongue-in-cheek in creating this name to convey the seriousness of the curse without creating a disabling knowledge. Situating his story squarely in the history of the Middle Passage at the outset of his narrative – in fact, making this the founding moment of the Americas rather than "discovery" – the narrator asserts African diaspora and Native peoples and cultures as foundational to the Americas. Historically a major site for the importation of enslaved Africans, the Antilles emerges in this excerpt as a site of actions that reverberate throughout the hemisphere. The *fukú* appears to be born of historical events rather than the directed curse of slaves or natives. Not a power exerted through the agency or religious practices of these groups, the *fukú* exists as a force born of awful events that cannot be undone, the place where resistance meets oppression and is crushed. The meeting and mixing of cultures in this novel is a given, a fact of life, but one that also has tragic consequences. This is not a novel primarily about race, yet race is a factor that manages to cripple lives and politics in strange ways. The narrator of Diaz's novel, in contrast to the Piri Thomas memoir of almost 40 years earlier, does not hesitate to assert an African diasporic identity or to claim the African diaspora as constitutive of Dominican identity, culture, and nation.

While Chicano/a literature frequently references a situation of shared discrimination with African Americans – as, for example, when Mary Helen Ponce describes segregated movie theaters in mid-twentieth-century Pacoima, California, in her 1993 autobiography *Hoyt Street* – in general this literature emphasizes the more predominant Native American roots of Chicano/a cultures. However, awareness and research on African diaspora in Mexican and Chicano/a cultures have been evident in histories of Mexico, particularly during the colonial era and among Californio society; the discourse of the "cosmic race" in Mexico; the history and arts of bolero, *danzón* and racially themed films of Mexico; and more recently the recognition in Chicano/a studies of the need for further research on African diaspora, expressed by Gloria Anzaldúa in *Borderlands/La Frontera* (1987) as follows:

> Before the Chicano and the undocumented worker and the Mexican from the other side can come together, before the Chicano can have unity with Native Americans and other groups, we need to know the history of their struggle and they need to know ours. Our mothers, our sisters and brothers, the guys who hang out on street corners, the children in the playgrounds, each one of us must know our Indian lineage, our afro-*mestisaje*, our history of resistance. (86)[4]

In this passage Anzaldúa asserts African diaspora as an element of Chicano/a and Mexicano/a identity and culture, reversing the well known and influential formulation of Mexican racial identity offered by José Vasconcelos in the early twentieth century of the "cosmic race," or mixing of multiple races with the "superior" European race. Instead, Indian and African culture and history must be studied and known rather than subsumed under any other experience.

These, in short, are some of the ways that Latino/a literatures have addressed African diaspora in the Americas – namely, the recollection of history and racial formation in the Americas, the recognition of African American culture as an aspect of Latino/a life, the incorporation of African American expressions and forms of expressions in Latino/a literature, the representation of skin color and phenotype in ethnic and national subjectivities, the exploration of the shared conditions of discrimination and marginalization between African Americans and Latino/as, and the discussion of the contrasts between experiences of racial formation for Latino/as and African Americans.

Black Angels in Latin American and Latino/a Cultural Productions: The Depth of Diasporan Practice and Identity

In the 1940s, Venezuelan poet Andrés Eloy Blanco wrote "Píntame angelitos negros," a poem in which a black woman's lament over the death of her baby opens a critique of racial discrimination and Eurocentrism that decries the absence of blacks in representations of heaven. With this poem, Blanco, who had long been a part of popular political movements to establish greater representation for blacks in Venezuela's political system and to recognize Afro-Venezuelan contributions to national culture, directly engages in the work of incorporating the African diaspora in the national culture and critiques its marginalization – the absence of black angels in popular portrayals of heaven metaphorically represents the absence of blacks and diasporan culture from national political and arts arenas.

I discuss this poem and some of its other versions in earlier essays (see Delgadillo). Here, I would like to take up another context for the circulation of this poem that sheds further light on the significance of African diaspora in Latino/a cultural production. Blanco's poem, however, also works on two other levels to incorporate diasporic influence and engage Latin American racial paradigms. The first speaker in the poem, La Negra Juana, laments the death of her child and declares that God must have already assigned him his place as an angel in heaven. Diasporic influence on language is represented in the use of vernacular "colocao":

Se me murió mi negrito;
Dios lo tendría dispuesto;
ya lo tendrá colocao
como angelito del Cielo.

[My little black one died
God would already have him
will seat him
as an angle of heaven.][5]

Juana is soon disabused of her belief by the second speaker who reminds her that a discriminatory regime reigns as this second speaker enumerates the many skin shades that are missing from depictions of heaven that always represent angels as white-skinned. The speaker lists *morenos* [brown], *perla fina* [fine pearl], *medio pelo* [mixed race with reference to hair], *catires* [blond], *indios* [Indian], *zamuritos* [Indian and black], *torditos* [coastal blacks], *trigueños* [tawny skin with brown hair], finally asking the painter to remember his people:

y al lado del angel rubio
y junto al angel trigueño,
aunque la Virgen sea Blanca
píntame angelitos negros.

[and by the blond angel's side,
and near the tawny angel
even though the Virgin is white
paint me black angels.]

Blanco's poem proclaims a Venezuelan and Latin American experience of multiplicity in skin color and race within an ethnic or national subjectivity that is also a Latino/a experience – one expressed in Latino/a literature, music and arts.

The movement in which Blanco participated was one of hemispheric significance. Across the Americas writers and artists took pride in blackness, as in the 1954 poem by Nelson Estupiñán Bass. Bass, an Afro-Ecuadorian poet and important figure in Afro-Latin American literature, in this brief excerpt writes:

Algunos creen insultarme
gritándome mi color,
más yo mismo lo pregono
con orgullo frente al sol:

> Negro he sido, negro soy,
> negro vengo, negro voy,
> negro bien negro nací
> negro negro he de vivir
> y como negro morir.[6]

As the example of Bass's poem suggests, movements of diasporic peoples and cultures flourished in Latin America and the US. There was also significant interplay and exchange among these movements, whether it was via the travel of performers and politicians or the circulation of arts and culture.

In the three decades following the publication of Blanco's poem, "Píntame angelitos negros" traveled from Mexico to the United States and abroad via its performance as a ballad sung by Mexican film and recording star Pedro Infante in 1948 and US singers Eartha Kitt in 1953 and Roberta Flack in 1969. The ballad, first performed by Pedro Infante in the 1948 Mexican film directed by Joselito Rodriguez, *Angelitos Negros*, incorporates the lines of the second speaker in the Blanco poem in critiquing the painter who omits black angels from depictions of heaven and calling upon that painter to include blacks in heavenly portrayals.[7] The Mexican film, based on Fannie Hurst's novel and the subsequent US film *Imitation of Life*, released in 1934 and directed by John M. Stahl, offers a perspective on race different from that of the US novel and film.

Both the US novel and 1934 film version of *Imitation of Life* feature Annie, a black nanny who gives herself completely to the service of her white mistress. Although her employment is figured as essential to her ability to provide for her daughter, Annie's devotion to her white mistress supercedes the necessity of providing for her daughter and she becomes the stereotypic figure of black subservience and cheer. In the Mexican *Angelitos Negros*, Merce, the black maid and nanny, is secretly the mother of the blond and light-skinned Ana Luisa to whom she happily tends. Both films insist on particular paradigms of gender that enshrine women in a motherhood complicated by race: the American film links Annie's devotion to motherhood with subservience to her employer, while the Mexican film links Ana Luisa's racist rejection of her own daughter with both her refusal to submit to the authority of her husband and the rejection of traditional motherhood.

While both films depict blackness as a misfortune, only in the US film is it an insurmountable bar to social mobility – Peola must accept her fate and join her mother, Annie, as subordinate to that of her white patrons. Ana Luisa, in contrast, faces a situation of racial prejudice but one that does not end her social mobility or her upper middle class status. She remains the wife of famous and wealthy singer, José Carlos, played by Pedro Infante in the film, who married her with the full knowledge of her "real race." The film ends with the restoration of the authority of the Mexican mestizo patriarch, José Carlos, who presides over the newly reestablished family, one that broadens the definition of Mexican family with an ambivalent acknowledgment of African diaspora as constitutive of Mexican national identity.

The later performances by both Kitt, in 1953, and Flack, in 1969, of this poem/ballad as a protest against racial discrimination in the case of Kitt, and an assertion of black pride, in the case of Flack, pick up on the different racial meaning of "Angelitos Negros" and *Angelitos Negros*. These instances of this text's circulation demonstrate the kinds of cultural and political exchanges among diasporic peoples and about African diaspora in the Americas that are worthy of much more study and exploration, for they reveal a hemispheric consciousness of diaspora and inequalities and a context for racial formation and movements of racial equality that extend beyond national borders. In making this song part of their repertoires, Kitt and Flack situate themselves in a continental diasporic movement that extends beyond the borders of the US. Their versions of the song also differ radically from Infante's performance, a difference that challenges predominant paradigms of gender and sexuality.

The image of the mulatta or mestiza in Latin American, Caribbean and Latino/a literatures is one fraught with notions of betrayal or ascriptions of subjection and violence. Indeed, these notions are also present in the films discussed above. To borrow from Vera Kutzinski's work, problematic constructions of "racially mixed femininity" frequently underwrite the creation of "interracial masculinity" (16). It is useful to recall that the portion of Blanco's poem that becomes a ballad is not that of La Negra Juana, but of an interlocutor correcting her misapprehension yet also protesting this state of affairs. In performing this ballad, Pedro Infante establishes the mestizo male subject as that interlocutor, which the film *Angelitos Negros* further supports. Kitt's and Flack's performances, in contrast, perform a restoration of the mulatta, mestiza and black woman's voice, who is no longer the subject whose condition prompts sympathy and facilitates male interracial solidarity, but is instead the speaker of her own truth. In Kitt's performance, a playful instrumental assertion of varied cultural influences gives way to her strong challenge to discrimination, while Flack's performance unfolds as an energetic assertion of black pride. In this way, both performers remake the poem and ballad to address the intersections of race, ethnicity, gender, and sexuality, returning the mulatta, mestiza, and black woman subject to the positions of speaker and active agent.

However, the significance of this poem and ballad goes beyond the expressions I have been discussing, and beyond its emergence in a particular movement of African diasporic consciousness or use in an antidiscrimination context. At varied periods in the history of the Americas, dominant colonial, criollo, mestizo, or white societies have looked upon the rituals and celebrations through which African diasporic peoples performed community and created meaning as threats. Examples of this abound: the prohibition against African dance and music under slavery, the decision by Brazil in 1890 to make capoeira illegal, limitations on African diasporic religious practices in both Latin America and the US in the twentieth and even twenty-first century (Andrews 122–6). The pressure that these conditions exerted on diasporic peoples to alter, cloak, or abandon cultural practices has often been commented upon in the scholarship. It was not uncommon, for example, for cultural syncretisms to emerge or for hybrid practices and beliefs to take shape. The synthesis of African spirituality and Catholicism in particular was pronounced in nineteenth-century Latin American centers of black population and is reflected in the Blanco poem with its emphasis on representations of angels in churches. Of course, syncretism and hybridity are not solely the product of efforts to hide or cloak, but also often the result of cultural encounter itself. Among the diasporan practices that flourished throughout the Americas is the wake and funeral for infants and children, a common practice due to the high infant mortality rate among diasporan communities. Known as the *baquiné* in some parts of Latin America, these funeral events involved the entire community, and it is this practice and the correspondent belief that is referenced in the Blanco poem and then in subsequent versions in song. The poem, therefore, not only rhetorically invokes Africa and expresses African influence on language, it melds a continuing diasporan practice with a contemporary demand for equality. Kitt's and Flack's versions of the song go further in effecting a reconnection to Africa through the arrangement and use of African percussive instrumentation.

George Reid Andrews notes that the funeral ceremony for infants was organized by women who enjoyed a spiritual authority among diasporan communities not available to them in traditional religious organizations. Andrews describes the ritual as follows:

> Women had primary responsibility as well for another all too frequent ritual observance in the black villages: the funerals of babies and newborns. Under freedom, both black birth rates and the size of black families seem to have increased during the first half of the 1800s. But infant mortality remained extremely high, and burials of *angelitos* (little angels) were a common occurrence of village life … in Ecuador, for example, it was local custom for mothers to rest for 44 days after giving birth … Yet despite such precautions to protect the mother's and infant's health, many children died during their first year of life … Child funerals were so common in the Esmeraldas rainforest of Ecuador that to this day *rezanderas* (prayer women) hold an annual service on December 24 in which the dead Baby Jesus is sung into heaven in memory of all the other angelitos who have joined him there. (105)

Andrews continues on the significance of this custom:

> The funerals of the angelitos were exemplary of the changes wrought by freedom. Unlike on the colonial plantations, where the deaths of slave infants seem to have gone largely unmarked, libertos and peasants were now at liberty to leave work in collective remembrance of a deceased child and to celebrate the angelito's entry into paradise with festive eating and drinking. They were at liberty as well to construct the networks of family, friends, and villagers within which the death of a child was not just an isolated event but an occasion for the communal expression of joy and sorrow. (105)

From this description it is evident that the *baquiné* was an expression of self-love, family, community, and protest denied to blacks under slavery, hence its combination of both celebration and mourning.

There is some suggestion that the *baquiné* is an African-origin practice rather than an American phenomenon of liberated black communities. As Andrews's discussion above illustrates, descriptions of *baquiné* ceremonies have been attached to discussions of African diaspora peoples in several Latin America nations, including a 1612 description of black funeral ceremonies in colonial Mexico that included "singing, shouting and dancing, they smothered the corpse with oil and wine and did the same to the grave … and having thrown dirt into it they raised one arm in a menacing manner" (Appiah and Gates 168).

In 1977, Puerto Rican salsa star Willie Colón wrote and produced an album-length instrumental soundtrack titled *El Baquine de Angelitos Negros*. The album appeared under the Fania Records label, the very successful salsa music label, and included 28 musicians employing all variety of strings, horns, and percussive instruments. The foundations for this instrumental opera are twin: the Blanco poem turned into song by Manuel Alvarez Maciste, "Angelitos Negros," and the rich and contemporary transcultural sound of salsa that Colón pioneered. This instrumental opera is divided in two sections that follow the pattern of the historic African diasporan ceremony, one that musically renders the mourning and protest of Juana and the community and one that suggests celebration. *El Baquiné de Angelitos Negros* includes 12 musical compositions in this order, with my translation in brackets:

1. Angustia Maternal [maternal anguish]
2. Camino al Barrio [walk/march to the neighborhood]
3. Son Guajira del Encuentro [poem/song of the encounter]
4. Angelitos Negros, Part I
5. Cuatro por Tres (El Sueño de Juana) [four for three, Juana's dream]
6. Acuerdate [remember]
7. Angelitos Negros, Part II
8. Para Los Viejitos [for the old folks]
9. Apartamento 21 [apartment 21]
10. 8th Avenue (in the Park)
11. El Baquiné [the wake]
12. 8th Avenue (El Fin) [the end].

The first section runs from Track 1 to Track 6, taking listeners through the mother's mourning and the community gathering to join her in mourning. In this first half of the album, "Angelitos Negros I" is played with acoustic guitar, slowly, suggestive of lamentation. The second section runs from Track 7 to Track 12 and presents a musical portrayal of the celebration of life, with vibrant and fast-paced salsa tempo predominating. "Angelitos Negros II" in this section begins with up-tempo bongos, loud and vibrant horns, and fast-paced piano. Track 11 slows down into a softer, final funeral commemoration, followed by Track 12, which closes the instrumental opera with a quick-tempo salsa rhythm, and establishes a marching beat through whistles and drums suggestive of a communal movement forward.

Colón's instrumental opera begins where Blanco's poem also begins, with the black mother Juana and her anguish over the death of her infant. It continues, taking us through each stage of the ceremony wherein Juana is joined by the collective in her mourning, and through which the infant is fixed in the heavens and remembered. Part II of Angelitos Negros signals the celebration of life, perhaps of the longevity of the old folks and the survival of the community as well as the celebration of the infant's life and place in heaven. Although it is speculative, the celebration of spiritual afterlife might also be a celebration of reunion with African ancestors. Even without this latter element, Colón's *baquiné* takes listeners back to the complete ceremony, the complete practice – which had only been referenced in the poem and even more obscurely alluded to in both song and film, creating a work that reconnects to Africa and African diaspora in content (the complete ceremony rendered musically) and form (the extensive use of African-origin percussive instruments). Colón brings all of his salsa innovation to the creation of this brilliant work of music. *El Baquiné de Angelitos Negros* is a vibrant contemporary reclamation of African diaspora as constitutive of Puerto Rican and Latino/a subjectivities and cultures.

When Willie Colón created this instrumental opera, he was already a widely recognized salsa musician, well known for his contributions to remaking salsa for contemporary urban audiences, though, as many have noted, not well known outside of Latino/a music circles for the early part of his career. For Colón to create *Baquiné* in the midst of a very successful career as a salsero suggests both a tribute to salsa's roots in African rhythms and musical forms as well as a desire to lend his success to furthering consciousness of African diaspora and perhaps Latino/a and African American solidarity. In adopting the earlier poem, "Píntame angelitos negros" by Andrés Eloy Blanco and music "Angelitos Negros" by Manuel Alvarez Maciste, Colón joins in a hemispheric effort to recognize, embrace, and honor African diaspora in Latino/a, Latin American and African American cultural productions.

In conclusion, this discussion provides a small introduction to the many Latino/a texts – novels, memoirs, dramas, poems, short fiction, as well as music and film that represent African diaspora in Latino/a communities and cultures. Although these are works that frequently grapple with articulating the historical difference in the formation of Afro-Latino/a cultures and subjectivities in contrast to African American cultures and subjectivities, and, therefore, appear to focus on "race," this is only one aspect of Latino/a representations of blackness. As this essay has explored, there is a strong consciousness of African diaspora in Latino/a literature, music, and art.

Notes

1 Some important comparative work on hemispheric literature and art that is attentive to African diaspora and/or the contingencies of race and blackness includes but is not limited to work of José David Saldívar, Vera Kutzinski, Kirsten Silva Gruesz, Sonia Saldivar-Hull. Important work that examines African diaspora in the formation of Latin American and

Latino/a histories and cultures includes Fernando Ortiz, Frances Aparacio, Silvio Silvant-Torres, and Ben Vinson. See also Gilroy.

2 My use of "American" departs from the colloquial usage of it denoting US citizenship or affiliation to the US. Instead, I use it here as an adjective that refers to all of the Americas.

3 At the outset I advise my readers that this is by no means a comprehensive study, particularly since I do not take up any discussion of African diaspora in Latino/a literature prior to 1940.

4 Readers might also consult Menchaca.

5 Translation is my own.

6 Whitten and Quiroga provide the following translation for the verses cited in their footnotes: "Some believe they insult me / mocking my colour, / but I myself proclaim it / with pride in the face of the sun: / black I have been, black I am, / black I come, black I go."

7 "Angelitos Negros," words by Andrés Eloy Blanco, music by Manuel Alvarez Maciste (1946), in *Sing Out! The Folk Song Magazine*, January 1967: 2–3. © 1946 Editorial Mexicana de Musica Internacional, SA.

Bibliography

Alvarez, Julia. *In the Name of Salomé*. New York: Plume, 2001.

Andrews, George Reid. *Afro-Latin America, 1800–2000*. New York: Oxford University Press, 2004.

Anzaldúa, Gloria. *Borderlands/La Frontera: The New Mestiza*. San Francisco: Aunt Lute, 1987.

Appiah, Kwame Anthony and Henry Louis Gates, Jr. *Africana: The Encyclopedia of the African and African American Experience*. 2nd edn., Volume II. New York: Oxford University Press, 2005.

Benítez-Rojo, Antonio. *The Repeating Island: The Caribbean and the Postmodern Perspective*. 2nd edn. Durham, NC: Duke University Press, 1996.

Blanco, Andrés Eloy. "Píntame angelitos negros." In *Apreciación de Andrés Eloy Blanco con apendice de textos del poeta*. Ed. Romulo Gallegos. Los Teques, Venezuela: Ediciones del Gobierno del Estado Miranda, 1985. 67–9.

Brathwaite, Edward Kamau. "The African Presence in Caribbean Literature." In *Africa in Latin America: Essays on History, Culture, and Socialization*. Ed. Manuel Moreno Fraginals. New York: Holmes and Meier Publishers, 1984.

Caminero-Santangelo, Marta. *On Latinidad: U.S. Latino Literature and the Construction of Identity*. Gainesville: University Press of Florida, 2007.

Colón, Willie. *El Baquiné de Angelitos Negros*. Fania Records, 1977.

Delgadillo, Theresa. "'Angelitos Negros' and Transnational Racial Identifications." In *Rebellious Reading: The Dynamics of Chicana/o Cultural Literacy*. Ed. Carl Gutiérrez-Jones. Santa Barbara: UCSB Center for Chicano Studies, 2004. 129–43.

Delgadillo, Theresa. "Singing 'Angelitos Negros': African Diaspora Meets *Mestizaje* in the Americas." *American Quarterly* 58.2 (2006): 407–30.

Diaz, Junot. *The Brief Wondrous Life of Oscar Wao*. New York: Riverhead/Penguin, 2007.

Garcia, Christina. *Dreaming in Cuban*. New York: One World, 1992.

Garcia, Christina. *Monkey Hunting*. New York: Knopf, 2003.

Gilroy, Paul. *The Black Atlantic: Modernity and Double Consciousness*. Cambridge, MA: Harvard University Press, 1993.

González, Lisa Sánchez. *Boricua Literature: A Literary History of the Puerto Rican Diaspora*. New York: New York University Press, 2001.

Grant, Lee, dir. *Sidney Poitier, One Bright Light: His Life, Films and Contributions*. An American Masters Production, 1999.

Greenbaum, Susan D. *More Than Black: Afro-Cubans in Tampa*. Gainesville: University Press of Florida, 2002.

Horne, Gerald. *Black and Brown: African Americans and the Mexican Revolution, 1910–1920*. New York: New York University Press, 2005.

Kutzinksi, Vera M. *Sugar's Secrets: Race and the Erotics of Cuban Nationalism*. Charlottesville: University of Virginia Press, 1993.

Menchaca, Martha. *Recovering History, Constructing Race*. Austin: University of Texas Press, 2001.

Moore, Robin D. *Nationalizing Blackness, Afrocubanismo and Artistic Revolution in Havana, 1920–1940*. Pittsburgh: University of Pittsburgh Press, 1997.

Palmer, Colin A. *Slaves of the White God: Blacks in Mexico, 1570–1650*. Cambridge, MA: Harvard University Press, 1976.

Ponce, Mary Ellen. *Hoyt Street: Memories of a Chicana Childhood*. New York: Anchor Books, 1995.

Rampersad, Arnold. *The Life of Langston Hughes*. Volume I: *1902–1941, I, Too, Sing America*. New York: Oxford University Press, 1986.

Saldívar, José David. *The Dialectics of Our America: Genealogy, Cultural Critique, and Literary History*. Durham: Duke University Press, 1991.

Sánchez, Marta E. *"Shakin' Up" Race and Gender*. Austin: University of Texas Press, 2005.

Thomas, Piri. *Down These Mean Streets*. 1967. New York: Vintage/Random House, 1997.

Torres, Arlene. "La Gran Familia Puertorriqueña 'Ej Prieta de Beldá' " (The Great Puerto Rican Family is Really Really Black). In *Blackness in Latin America and the Caribbean*, Volume II. Ed. Arlene Torres and Norman E. Whitten, Jr. Bloomington: Indiana University Press, 1998. 285–306.

Torres-Saillant, Silvio. "Dominican Blackness and the Modern World." In *Perspectives on Las Américas: A Reader in Culture, History, and Representation*. Malden: Blackwell, 2003. 274–88.

Vinson, Ben III. *Bearing Arms for His Majesty: The Free-Colored Militia in Colonial Mexico*. Stanford: Stanford University Press, 2001.

Vinson, Ben, III. *Flight: The Story of Virgil Richardson, A Tuskegee Airman in Mexico*. New York: Palgrave, 2004.

Whitten, Norman E., Jr. and Diego Quiroga. " 'To Rescue National Dignity': Blackness as a Quality of Nationalist Creativity in Ecuador." In *Blackness in Latin America and the Caribbean*, Volume I. Ed. Norman E. Whitten, Jr. and Arlene Torres. Bloomington: Indiana University Press, 1998. 75–99.

Wright, Winthrop. *Café con Leche: Race, Class, and National Image in Venezuela*. Austin: University of Texas Press, 1990.

26
African American Literature and Queer Studies: The Conundrum of James Baldwin

Guy Mark Foster

Consider the following short passage lifted from the African American writer James Baldwin's 1962 novel, *Another Country*: "He wondered who had been with her before him; how many, how often, how long; what he, or they before him, had meant to her; and he wondered if her lover, or lovers, had been white or black. What difference does it make? he asked himself. What difference does any of it make?" (172). What "difference" indeed. The passage records, in part, the troubled interior monologue of a 20-something-year-old white American male as he muses on the sexual history of his black female paramour, a woman with whom he has fallen in love. Not only are these questions interesting for what they reveal to readers about this particular young man's concerns, but the questions are also interesting for what they do *not* reveal as concerns necessarily. That is, while this young man appears to have a strong curiosity as to the racial identities of his girl's previous sexual partners (especially if they were black or white), he is curiously silent, or else indifferent, on the issue of gender – that is, as to whether any of those partners were male or female. This is a startling discovery. For it flies in the face of Michel Foucault's well known insight that, starting at the end of the nineteenth century, sexual definition in the West underwent a radical transformation. Foucault writes famously that at this time the "homosexual became a personage, [someone with] a past, a case history, and a childhood, in addition to being a type of life, a life form, and a morphology," one distinct from the heterosexual (Foucault 43). From that moment on, according to some notable scholars, people in the West began to exhibit a near obsession with uncovering the truth of their own and their neighbor's sexuality, and that such "truth" was characterized chiefly in gendered terms only – in other words, everyone was believed to be either a heterosexual or a homosexual based on their affinity for either males or females. If so, why then does Baldwin's young white American refer to a second organization of desire upon pondering his twentieth-century future with his girl, one that subordinates gender to another category of difference, namely, "race"?

As evidenced by the coining by two Northern political foes of President Lincoln's in 1864 of the Civil War term "miscegenation," commonly known as "the sexual mingling of the races," throughout much of American history an intense, even obsessive, preoccupation with race has long distinguished both scientific and popular discourses on human sexuality (Hodes, *Sex, Love, Race*; *White Women, Black Men*; Lemire). However, starting around the end of World War Two, official national interest abruptly began to decline in this form of desire, to the extent that gender systematically displaced "race" from these discourses. The reason for this displacement is widely linked to the US government's efforts to distance the country from the heinous crimes inflicted on European Jews by the racist regime of Adolf Hitler and by the Nazi party in particular (Lubin; Romano). Underpinning this drive to relegate what had formerly been a highly valued taxonomical category to the cultural margins was the belief, and fear, on the part of many postwar white Americans in the apparent disturbing similarities between the debased status of the Jew throughout much of Europe and the debased status of the black within the US. Certainly one reason for this disturbance was the fact that the first comparison inferred a second – namely, that between white Americans and the Nazis. This implicit comparison between blacks and Jews, on the one hand, and between Nazi Germans and white Americans, on the other, prompted the US to adopt the practice of race-blindness as a corrective to centuries-long race-consciousness in order to distance its racially dominant citizens from such discomforting associations (see Sollors). With race, both blackness and whiteness, effectively sidelined, gender would then emerge as the sole and exclusive analytical category in scientific and medical theories of human sexuality made popular by such thinkers in the US as Alfred Kinsey in the 1940s and 1950s, and Masters and Johnson, among others, from the 1960s to the early 1980s (Robinson). Since the mid-1980s, the interdisciplinary fields of lesbian and gay/queer scholarship have been the unlikely inheritors of this deracinated postwar discourse on human sexuality. And indeed, much of this work is deeply indebted to Foucault's periodization of homosexuality as an identity category. Due in part to how this institutionalization of sex research coincided so neatly with the rise of the modern lesbian and gay movement (symbolized for many by the Stonewall rebellion of June 1969), a heterosexual–homosexual binary model of desire, with its singular focus on gender of object-choice, would quickly supplant the earlier race-centered model (characterized by a "same-race"/"different-race" opposition) that had previously obsessed much of US popular and critical discourse up to this period.

While the black–Jewish, white American–Nazi German analogy will serve as an important backdrop to the subsequent analysis, the specific purpose of the present essay is to determine the impact this systematic suppression of "race" from US critical discourse on human sexuality has had in the academic field of Queer Studies. To assess this impact I selectively evaluate scholarly responses to a writer whose literary output has perhaps maintained the most vigilance in contesting our nation's sustained efforts to conceal the always already intersecting nature of "race" and sexuality: James Baldwin. As both an African American and sexually different (and, as I hope to show, the identity labels "homosexual" and "gay" are simply too reductive to use when referring to this author and his writings), Baldwin has presented something of a conundrum to both mainstream and non-mainstream literary scholarship within the US. While the dominant (white) literary establishment prior to the 1970s had condescended to view Baldwin through the lens of his Civil Rights activism rather than his literary production, later scholars – most notably those within African American literary studies and Queer Studies – have tended to subdivide Baldwin (and, alternately, his novels) into component parts. For some scholars within African Americanist discourse, for instance, Baldwin (or his novels) is perceived as more African American-identified than queer – that is, homosexual; and here, the two terms function as synonyms for sexual deviance and are therefore interchangeable. In contrast, for some critics within lesbian and gay/queer discourse, Baldwin's trenchant critiques of heteronormative gender and sexual norms, at least where men are concerned, allows these writers to perceive him as more queer-identified than African American. The unfortunate consequence of such critical practices is that "race" and sexuality are often placed in direct opposition to one another. As Kevin Ohi has observed, "rarely, though more often with [Queer Studies] than with [African American scholarship], do the poles of either of these oppositions come together" (Ohi 261). Even scholars who situate their critical practice at the intersection of these two fields often place "race" and sexuality in opposition to some extent. As we will see, many of these scholars within Queer Studies produce this opposition by limiting what they mean by the term "sexuality" to same-sex identities and desires almost exclusively, with little or no attention to other mediating factors, such as "race" or ethnicity, class, nationality, to name but a few. This is exactly the point linguist Don Kulick makes when he asks:

> What does "queer" mean? What is special or unique about queer? And most importantly: if queer is *not* the same as lesbian, gay, bisexual or transgender – as all queer theorists insist that it is not – why, then, is the only language ever investigated to say anything about queer language the language of people who self-identify, or who researchers believe to be, lesbian, gay, bisexual or transgendered? (Kulick 65–6)

Kulick's insight becomes especially useful when applied to Baldwin. As evidenced by the earlier passage from *Another Country*, Baldwin rarely privileges racially neutral depictions of opposite-sex or same-sex identities and desires, the latter the ostensible proper object of much queer scholarship, even as he attempts to engage these concerns. Rather, the bulk of Baldwin's writing always incorporates a complex matrix of desire that consistently takes into account the racialized dimensions of gendered desire. As reductive forms of intimacy, homosexuality and heterosexuality are simply not relevant categories of desire in the Baldwinian representational landscape. Indeed, Baldwin once stated famously, "Those terms, homosexual, bisexual, heterosexual, are twentieth-century terms which, for me, have very little meaning. I've never, myself, in watching myself and other people, watching life, been able to discern exactly where the barriers were" (quoted in Mossman 54). With this single comment, Baldwin expertly directs our attention back not to gender alone but to that *pre*-twentieth-century term for understanding human sexuality – indeed, "miscegenation" – which privileges *racial* distinctions. And while depictions of same-gender identities and desires recur throughout the author's oeuvre, these depictions, I would argue, often serve a utilitarian function in that they assist Baldwin in making visible cross-racial group dynamics as a form of erotic practice that psychologically and politically influences their central characters. Moreover, these effects may often exceed their presumed racial meanings. Baldwin's depictions of racialized sexual scenarios in his fiction and nonfiction, whether same-gender or opposite-gender, are not to be analyzed in terms of gender identity alone, but rather – to borrow Shane Vogel's useful formulation – in terms that acknowledge "subjective possibilit[ies] that could include but always excee[d] the closures of 'sexual identity' as such" (Vogel 403).

More recently, in an effort to stabilize and fix the meaning of "queer" to demarcate same-gender identities and forms of desire solely, much of contemporary gay and queer scholarship – especially the version practiced by many white gay male scholars – has failed to comprehend that Baldwin's literary preoccupations are not narrowly focused on the relatively small group of sexual minorities known as gay men, a term and a community from which the author often felt himself personally estranged. I am well aware that my use of the appellation "white gay male" may strike some as essentializing the views of a relatively small group of critics based on their personal identities. After all, such men certainly have no control over their racial affiliation. Moreover, it is simply a truism that not all white gay male scholars exhibit in their work this same racial self-interestedness I am describing in these pages. But the fact of the matter is that, as I will address shortly, some of the most influential of these scholars do. In his important essay "The Responsibility of and to Differences: Theorizing Race and Ethnicity in Lesbian and Gay Studies," queer theorist Earl Jackson, Jr., himself a white gay man, writes that because gay men like himself "have had a purchase on power and privilege unique to otherwise disenfranchised individuals," they have "specific responsibilities" to contest traditional power relations within the academy and the culture at large. "These power relations are central to the historical configurations of white gay male identities and their modes of articulation, which cannot be assumed to be applicable to gay men of color or other marginalized groups." Jackson goes on to explain that, consequently, "[a]ny consideration of gay male studies as a critical endeavor, and of the homosexual/gay male cultural practices that form some of its objects, entails confronting the ways in which both are inscribed in dominant traditions, reflecting the paradoxical relations between male homosexuality and racist, classist, and sexist hegemonies" (Jackson 136). To paraphrase Devon Carbado's timely insight about the privileges accorded to black men in anti-racist discourse, "even when discussions about [homophobia] are focused on [white gay men], those discussions are not always understood to be gendered or [race-based] discussions; they are understood to be discussions about the plight of the crisis of [gay] America" (quoted in Carbado 9). It was perhaps out of his own innate sense of the way that blackness tends to "compete" with other forms of difference in minority discourses, such as gendered and sexual, that Baldwin refrained from centering a black lesbian or gay male character in his fiction until his final novel, *Just above My Head* (1979). After all, "[a] black gay person," Baldwin once offered, "who is a sexual conundrum to society is already, long before the question of sexuality comes into it, menaced and marked because he's black or she's black. The sexual question comes after the question of color; it's simply one more aspect of the danger in which all black people live" (quoted in Goldstein 180). Indeed, a guiding assumption of the present inquiry is that white homosexuals have not been the original queers, in the sense that in its etymological root "queer" means different, unusual, abnormal. That mantle fell to Americans of African descent, whether heterosexually oriented or not, long before white lesbians and gay men took it up. For the latter, homosexuality serves as the sole marker of stigma, while their membership in the dominant racial group is downplayed. In contrast, "[t]he construction of African American sexuality as wild, unstable, and undomesticated," as Roderick Ferguson usefully notes in *Aberrations in Black: Toward a Queer of Color Critique*, "locates African American sexuality within the irrational, and therefore outside the bounds of the citizenship machinery. Though African American homosexuality, unlike its heterosexual counterpart, symbolized a rejection of heterosexuality, neither could claim heteronormativity. The racialized eroticization of black heterosexuals and homosexuals outside the rationalized (i.e. heteronormative) household symbolically aligned black straight and gay persons" (87). Because of the inextricability of white queers from the array of benefits and privileges accorded all whites in anti-black societies, and the inextricability of blacks *tout court* from having to endure the object-effects of embodying blackness in those very societies, the same claim could *not* be made about the relation between white straight and gay persons. This insight is an important one to keep in mind throughout what follows. As Robert Reid-Pharr points out, "discourses of blackness are overdetermined by discourses of queer sexuality" (*Once You Go Black* 63). In much of what follows, this essay will demonstrate that nowhere is this conflict over racial or sexual interpretation more on display than in scholarly engagements with Baldwin's 1962 novel, *Another Country.*

(White) Queer Studies and *Another Country*

Set predominantly in New York City's Greenwich Village in the period separating the early Civil Rights movement from the tumultuous events that would tear the nation apart in the 1960s, *Another Country* recounts the often stormy interpersonal relationships among a group of 20-to-30-something-year-old Americans that in many respects come to anticipate and even mirror these larger, more public events. At the center of these relationships is the black jazz musician, Rufus Scott. Each of the other characters in the novel shares a personal, and in some cases a sexual, history with Rufus that serves as the catalyst for the narrative events that proceed from his untimely suicide, a tragic moment which occurs quite early in the novel. Not all these other characters are women; some are men, and though most of these interpersonal relationships are heterosexual in nature, some are homosexual, and many are in fact homo*erotic* in their psychosexual underpinnings. Moreover, at least one of these characters, Rufus's younger sister Ida, is black, while the rest are white, including Ida's white American beau, Vivaldo Moore, with whose interior musings I began this essay. The overtly racialized dimensions of these relationships transforms them from, on the one hand, the types of human entanglements that can be analyzed simply by relying upon terms and concepts that privilege gender as the most significant variable in making sexual desire legible to, on the other, those that require terms and concepts that consider both categories at once. The novel's inclusion of a range of sexual dissidents, *including* cross-racial heterosexual couplings, recontextualizes the exclusions that form the core of much of contemporary Queer Studies scholarship.

First, let us begin by sketching out the historical relation between Queer Studies and African American literature, and to do so via Baldwin. This tendency to approach Baldwin as a queer rather than a black writer – and to place the two categories in opposition – began with the emergence in the mid-1980s of critical research tools calibrated to challenge heterosexism and homophobia in contemporary literary scholarship. Emmanuel Nelson's "The Novels of James Baldwin: Struggles of Self Acceptance" (1985) is an early, but notable, example of this type of critical engagement. Yet, rather than impose on Baldwin's literary texts a recognizable political context that would anchor his primary investment in same-sex desire, Nelson appeals to the black writer's reputation as "one of the most important and influential *homosexual* writers of the twentieth century" (11; emphasis mine). As Nelson claims, "to grasp the full literary and cultural significance of Baldwin's works, one has to bear in mind that central to Baldwin's life and art is his confrontation with and acceptance of his sexuality" (11). With this statement, Nelson offers a reading of Baldwin's view on sexuality that nowhere acknowledges the author's keen awareness of the structuring influence of socially derived understandings of "race" on that process. "Baldwin," Nelson writes, perhaps too confidently, "views human sexuality in terms of a *homosexual–heterosexual continuum*: while some may be exclusively homosexual and some others exclusively heterosexual, many possess varying degrees of bisexual potential" (13–14; emphasis mine). On its face, such a statement overlooks Baldwin's many published statements on the subject of human sexuality – one of which I have already cited. In answer to a question as to what he thinks gay people will be like in the future, Baldwin offers what we now recognize as a characteristic response: "No one will have to call themselves gay," he says, when that time arrives. "Maybe that's at the bottom of my impatience with the term. It answers a false argument, a false accusation … Which is that you have no right to be here, that you have to prove your right to be here. I'm saying that I have nothing to prove. The world also belongs to me" (quoted in Goldstein 184). To discount these statements by the author, as Nelson does, is to fail to confront a fundamental paradox anti-homophobic critics face when they write about African American literature and its preoccupations: How does such a critic engage the work of a black writer, whether that writer is straight, gay, or otherwise, with the sole purpose of excavating sexual content without also trying to understand how that content is shaped, in profound ways, by the history of racial hierarchy?

I want to suggest that Nelson's steadfast refusal to acknowledge that human sexuality – for Baldwin in general, and for all Americans in particular – is not *merely* determined by gender identity alone, which a "homosexual–heterosexual continuum" unproblematically assumes, but also by "racial" identity, is typical of how many contemporary Queer Studies scholars writing throughout the 1980s and 1990s have taken up the author's work. However, similar critical engagements with Baldwin's most controversial novel by scholars affiliated with Queer Studies have continued up to the present day. While more sophisticated than Nelson's analysis, James Dievler's "Sexual Exiles: James Baldwin and *Another Country*" (1999) replicates Nelson's tendency to overdetermine same-sex desire by narrowly linking it to the author's sexual autobiography. Dievler does this by turning to a well known essay Baldwin published two years before his death, in 1987, "Freaks and the American Ideal of Manhood," and later retitled "Here Be Dragons," in which the author famously discusses his early sexual experiences. Although he does not completely overlook the racialized sexual dynamics of the novel, or of Baldwin's life, as Nelson does, Dievler fails to integrate this aspect fully into his analysis. One reason for this oversight is that Dievler only refers to those passages in "Freaks and the American Ideal of Manhood" that support the homosexual–heterosexual binary framework in which his argument operates. Hence, Dievler does not mention those passages in the essay that might complicate this emphasis, such as Baldwin's numerous *heterosexual* relationships with *white* women, or, for that matter, the episodes in which the racist "speculations" of some white gay men concerning "the size of [Baldwin's sex] organ" proved menacing to him – a reference to which I will return later (*Collected Essays* 823–9).

To consider either of these passages in Baldwin's essay would, I suspect, radically undercut any effort to fix the author's own sexual orientation as a gay man. It would also reduce Baldwin's understanding of human sexuality to a homosexual–heterosexual framework, especially one unmediated by historically and culturally changing racialized distinctions. Dievler refers to this particular essay in order to contend that, in *Another Country*, Baldwin "portrays the devastation wrought in a country dominated by a categorically limited sexual culture and offers both a view of and the means of transport to 'another country', beyond the confines of the narrow identity categories that imprisoned Americans in the immediate postwar period and still do so today" (162–3). On the surface, such a project would need to be preoccupied as much with the racialized sexual dimensions of the postwar period as with its gendered sexual dimensions. After all, Americans during this period witnessed the formal dismantling of nearly four centuries of state-sponsored racial oppression, including the 1948 California Supreme Court ruling in *Perez v. Sharp* that struck down the state's laws against racial intermarriage. Nineteen years later, the US Supreme Court would follow this decision with its own landmark ruling in *Loving v. Virginia*. However, Dievler's narrow interpretation of Baldwin's essay, if not also his life, employs the phrase "sexual culture" as a synonym for gay subculture only. But as the racial and gender identities of the plaintiffs in these court cases make clear, (white) gay men and lesbians were not the only "sexual culture" struggling for recognition in postwar America; black- and white-identified heterosexual couples were also constituted in these terms as well.

Any revisionist look back at the postwar, pre-Civil Rights era – the same period in which Baldwin's novel is set – would need to include black- and white-identified men and women who dared to cross the color line for love and marriage in this category as well. This last point cannot be overstated, given postwar American culture's intense preoccupation during this era with the hotly debated subjects of black–white intermarriage and racial equality, subjects that were frequently rhetorically linked in political and popular commentary at the time (see Pascoe; Romano). As the present essay contends, such couple relationships, to borrow Dievler's terms, were "dominated [no less] by a categorically limited sexual culture" that "imprisoned" the desires of millions of black and white *heterosexual* Americans than by the "narrow identity categories" that had likewise oppressed millions of lesbians and gay men of the postwar era, whatever their racial or ethnic identities. The relatively recent experiences of the latter has simply tended to overshadow those of the former in terms of academic research – that is, until contemporary social scientists and historians, among others, began challenging this systematic erasure of interracial heterosexual-couple dynamics (see Childs; Dalmage; Hodes, *Sex, Love, Race*).

In contrast to Dievler's analysis, William Cohen's engaging essay, "Liberalism, Libido, Liberation: Baldwin's *Another Country*" (2000), provides a detailed and rigorous analysis of the novel, while being careful to keep in the foreground the author's emphasis on racial oppression. Although frequently persuasive, the force of Cohen's insights is nonetheless marred by his surprising adherence to a narrowly conceived homosexual–heterosexual binary framework to structure his analysis as well. This framework makes it difficult for Cohen to recognize the limitations of this model and the need, therefore, for a more nuanced approach – one that acknowledges racialized desire *as desire* – for making legible the novel's complex preoccupations. The following passage offers a telling example of the type of interpretive limitation I am describing: "It is now clear," Cohen writes,

> just how closeted the pre-Stonewall setting of Baldwin's novel is: There is no coming out of the closet because there is nowhere to come out to. Sexuality was, therefore, "perfectly" private – it had not yet found a public voice – and it is for this reason that Baldwin's fantasy of *racial* mixing and equality (which had, by this period, certainly gone public) was everywhere deflected onto sexual dynamics. (Cohen 218)

Cohen's use here of metaphoric language linked to gay and lesbian/queer definition, i.e. "coming out" and "the closet," reveal in stark terms the degree to which his interpretive framework relies heavily on same-sex desire and identities, rather than on racialized dynamics, to make sexuality legible as a category of analysis. His assertion, for instance, that the novel's racial concerns are "deflected" onto concerns about sexuality – as if sexuality and "race" were completely separate phenomena – expose how the two remain, in his analysis, mutually exclusive rather than mediating categories. *Racial* difference, then, between sexually intimate partners, can only register within Cohen's framework as a form of social conflict between differently opposed racial groups, and *never* as a historically changing form of desire that structures interpersonal relations that cross the color line. Unfortunately, textual depictions of heterosexually and homosexually intimate interracial bonds can become legible only as commentary on "racial" concerns, not as commentary on the "sexual" concerns that have *racialized* dimensions.

This critical tendency within Queer Studies scholarship to polarize "race" and sexuality in analyses of Baldwin's literary texts, especially *Another Country,* reached its apotheosis in the early 1990s, when the interdisciplinary field gained institutional legitimacy, however qualified, with the emergence of what has come to be known as "queer theory" (de Lauretis). In his close look at Baldwin's first novel, *Go Tell It on the Mountain* (1953), Bryan Washington's analysis recalls my earlier point as to the definitional conundrum that Baldwin presents to academic scholarship when he reaches this conclusion about the nature of some of the critical research produced early in the decade on the author's work: "As a black critic presented with the challenge of responding to recent readings of Baldwin," writes Washington, "I have been unable to avoid the unhappy conclusion that white gay theory is disturbingly self-interested, that it looks to Baldwin for absolution and disciplines him when he refuses to give it" (85). Washington is referring here to several prominent "contributions to gay theory," as he calls this sophisticated body of literary criticism, including Claude Summers's *Gay Fictions, Wilde to Stonewall* (1990), David Bergman's *Gaiety Transfigured* (1991), and Lee Edelman's *Homographesis: Essays in Gay Literary and Cultural Theory* (1994). For Washington, these critics exhibit an apparent "irritation and frustration" with Baldwin's portrayals of and remarks on homosexuality, even as they also celebrate him for daring to produce such representations at all. While Summers accepts *Giovanni's Room* (1956) as " 'a central text … in the American literature of homosexuality'," he apparently finds *Go Tell It on the Mountain* (1953), according to Washington, "questionable because race, rather than sexuality, is allegedly its primary preoccupation" – this is the case even though same-sex desire is integral to the novel's plot (Washington 78). On the other hand, Bergman is critical of the African American author's "refusal to accept the classification of 'gay writer'," reading into Baldwin's reticence the possibility of a latent internalized homophobia. Thus, for Washington, these critics view "blackness and homosexuality [as] 'polarized' " (79). Such a critical stance leads Bergman to side at least partially with the famous homophobic critique in Eldridge Cleaver's *Souls on Ice* (1968), which likewise rebukes Baldwin for his fictional portrayals of homosexuality, but for reasons far different from Bergman's.

Moreover, Washington takes particular exception to Edelman's essay, which he calls "frequently disturbing" (79). Edelman sets out on a provocative project in his attempt to disentangle from the cultural category gay men the notion of African American writers who figure white-male-on-black-male sexual abuse as an instance of emasculating these men, therefore reducing black men to putative homosexuals.

For Edelman, given that our society's "dominant optic … registers any act of male–male sex as 'homosexuality'," black writers' textual critique of this violence can only "acquir[e] visibility through the demonization of male–male sexual relations" (quoted in Edelman 54–5). By the latter, Edelman no doubt means contemporary gay male identity formations. His primary contention is that such identities are, or should be anyway, viewed as conceptually distinct from the identity formation of the straight white male racist. If such a distinction is not somehow made evident in a black writer's text, then that representation, as well as that writer, risks the charge of homophobia. As Edelman himself puts it:

> The complexities generated by these figures in which the racist persecution of African-American men is imaged through the violence of male-male sexual (which is always construed as male *homo*sexual) aggression, prevent the passages [from black writers] from being dismissed as simple demonstrations of an authorial inclination to draw upon the homophobia that seems to be America's one endlessly renewable, though by no means "natural," resource. The figures themselves, after all, *as* figures produce a confusion of trope and referent that has everything to do with the confounding and dismantling of the active/passive distinction. While it is clear, in other words, that these textual moments put the fear and hatred of homosexuality strategically into play, only the particularity of a reading can determine if the passages are to be interpreted as homophobic themselves or, conversely, as subjecting homophobia to a much-needed analysis. (57–8)

While Edelman's comments here refer to Baldwin's *Tell Me How Long the Train Has Been Gone* (1968) and *Just above My Head* (1979), and not to *Go Tell It* or to *Giovanni's Room*, his second and, for some critics, his much "gayer" novel, Washington considers Edelman's reading to be closely related to the readings by Summers and Bergman. Washington's basic point is that these scholars are unhappy with Baldwin's portrayal of homosexuality and homosexuals. The portrayals avoid unequivocally positive depictions of gay men who have triumphed over society's homophobic condemnation of them, and offer instead a vision of homosexuality that is, to these gay male critics, narrowly specific to African American experience. The fact that Baldwin, as a black writer who was primarily, though not exclusively, attracted to other men, may have had different experiences of homosexuals – and particularly *white American* homosexuals, who, after all, as white Americans living in the postwar era, were liable to hold anti-black beliefs the same as their heterosexual counterparts – does not seem to be of interest to these critics. Simply, these writers chastise Baldwin for not privileging his allegiance to white queers like themselves over his apparent, to them, "marginal" allegiance to blacks in general, whom these writers curiously appear to assume to be exclusively heterosexual.

In this vein, Edelman criticizes Baldwin for conflating (white) homosexuals with white racism rather than viewing, as he apparently should, as a gay man himself (albeit a black one), (white) homosexuals as similarly oppressed victims caught within the same ideological structures of domination as people of color. As Washington puts it:

> To chide Baldwin and other black writers [as Edelman does] … for the moments in their work when homosexuality is associated with white racism is to suggest that whites have been misrepresented, that they are not the oppressors. If whiteness in American culture is not the emblem of power and aggression, what is it? Why, in short, would black writers conceive whites differently? (79)

Washington goes on to rebuke Edelman in turn for the latter's claim that Baldwin's representation of white homosexuals in a passage in "Freaks and the American Ideal of Manhood" evinces homophobia. As Washington argues, "it is important to read [Baldwin's remarks] with its context in mind." In other words,

> Baldwin refers to his early experience with the New York "gay world," a world he describes as alienating because of the racial and sexual stereotypes operating within it. "The very last thing this black boy needed," [Baldwin] writes, "were clouds of imitation white women and speculations concerning the size of his organ." Arguing that he was exploited "by people who truly meant … [him] no harm," [Baldwin] quickly points out that "they could *not* have meant him any harm because they did not see … [him]." (83)

For Washington, Baldwin's supposed discomfort with homosexuality in general and with homosexuals in particular is best understood by considering how the author's various references were conditioned by the collision between stereotypes about black embodiment with the social hierarchy characteristic of the largely white gay male community. The latter is a point that many contemporary scholars of Queer Studies often fail to consider in their assessments of Baldwin, perhaps because of what I have referred to as their overinvestment in recuperating affirming portraits of (white) homosexual identity and desire to offset those that are demeaning and pathologized.

My goal has been to use Washington's commentary as a valuable lens through which to understand how some white-identified scholars operating within a Queer Studies hermeneutic have tended to approach *Another Country*, a novel that does not privilege same-sex desire but in fact privileges *black–white* desire, both heterosexual and homosexual. Washington's point is that Summers, Bergman, Edelman, and other "gay theorists" who minimize or disregard racialized concerns altogether have not analyzed Baldwin's novels on their own terms. Rather, such theorists have used these texts opportunistically to center almost exclusively their depictions of same-sex desiring scenarios and identities at the expense of a particular text's overall narrative design. Washington would argue that the design may center not those particular scenarios and identities, but those filtered through concerns germane to African American experiences as an historically subjugated racial minority group. Moreover, these critics fault Baldwin for failing to provide them with representations that satisfy late twentieth-century politicized expectations, organized chiefly around promoting depictions of (white) queer psychological wholeness and self-empowerment. However, Baldwin himself, in 1984, may just have anticipated this criticism from select white gay male scholars:

> I think white gay people feel cheated because they were born, in principle, into a society in which they were supposed to be safe. The anomaly of their sexuality puts them in danger, unexpectedly. Their reaction seems to me in direct proportion to the sense of feeling cheated of the advantages which accrue to white people in a white society. There's an element, it has always seemed to me, of bewilderment and complaint. Now that may sound harsh, but the gay world as such is no more prepared to accept black people than anywhere else in society. It's a very hermetically sealed world with very unattractive features, including racism. (quoted in Goldstein 180)

In recent years, several critics have noted this seemingly resurgent white gay male identity politics that has come to characterize Queer Studies overall, and view it as a significant limitation of the field, as Baldwin no doubt would have. In their jointly authored essay, "What's Queer about Queer Studies Now," David Eng, Judith Halberstam, and José Estéban Muñoz (an Asian gay man, a white Jewish transgender woman, and a Latino gay man) warn that "Much of queer theory nowadays sounds like a metanarrative about the domestic affairs of white homosexuals" (12). Indeed, in her own essay, "Shame and White Gay Masculinity" (2005), Halberstam predicts an apocalyptic end to the field if such narrow concerns are not ultimately displaced: "The future of queer studies … depends absolutely on moving away from white gay male identity politics and learning from the radical critiques offered by a younger generation of queer scholars who draw their intellectual inspiration from feminism and ethnic studies rather than white queer studies" (220).

Queer Studies (of the Future) and *Another Country*

I would like to conclude by taking a moment to gesture towards some of the work produced by those scholars whom Halberstam suggests can help ensure that the "future" of Queer Studies as an academic field of research is not so narrowly focused on a small minority who are both gay men and white. Without exception, the critical preoccupations of these scholars operate self-consciously at the crossroads of racial *and* sexual discourses. In contrast to the critics I have discussed throughout much of this essay, most of these critics combine a focus on African American and queer discourse to explore Baldwin's depictions of same-gender desire in his fiction and late essays. Because of how these critics are situated methodologically, their work takes aim at both forms of scholarship that have tended to marginalize their own doubled concerns. Hence, not only does much of this research challenge the normative racial assumptions of (white) mainstream Queer Studies scholarship, but much of it also challenges the normative sexual assumptions of mainstream African American literary critical discourse as well, which is overwhelmingly heterosexist. If Bryan Washington's critique of Edelman, Bergman, and Summers can be said to be focused on contesting the racial assumptions of what he calls "white gay theory," then many of these other writers take critical aim at what one scholar has dubbed "black straight studies" (McBride 35).

Moreover, many of the current scholars who work at these intersections often do so with the express aim of challenging heterosexist and homophobic biases that pervade the African American literary tradition. Thus, in "'Ain't Nothin' like the Real Thing': Black Masculinity, Gay Sexuality, and the Jargon of Authenticity" (1996), Kendall Thomas challenges the routine homophobia that critics of color have perhaps inadvertently exhibited with respect to Baldwin's work. In addressing one of these writers, in particular, Thomas states:

> [This critic's] awkward answer to those who would "deracinate" Baldwin and reduce the writer to his sexuality is to "desexualize" Baldwin and reduce him to his race. To be sure, these two equally misguided moves are impelled by very different purposes: where Baldwin's detractors magnify his sexuality in order to renounce him, [this critic] minimizes Baldwin's sexuality in order to redeem him. (59)

Likewise, in "White Fantasies of Desire: Baldwin and the Racial Identities of Sexuality" (1999), Marlon Ross continues Thomas's critique by indicting black intellectuals such as Houston Baker for their unwillingness to integrate Baldwin's focus on sexual concerns with his focus on racial matters. In addition, Ross discusses at least two of Baldwin's early literary works, including *Another Country*, in relation to the critical commentary that has been generated on the novel. Ross's main point (which intersects with Bryan Washington's critique of white gay scholars) concerns the fact that because Baldwin often chose "the apparently curious option of treating male homosexuality through the fictional experiences of white characters, if not from a white point of view," critics of his early novels often tended to place race and sexuality in opposition to one another (19–20).

However, Robert Reid-Pharr, who is also dually invested in African American and queer critical discourses, offers a reading of *Another Country* that both implicitly critiques his other like-minded counterparts working within what has recently become known as "black queer studies" (see Henderson and Johnson 2005), as well as explicitly takes to task scholarly work within (white) Queer Studies that persists in downplaying questions of race. In his iconoclastic collection of essays entitled *Black Gay Man* (2001), Reid-Pharr argues that scholars whose work has been organized chiefly around producing sophisticated theoretical concepts and insights about non-normative sexual identities and practices have steadfastly avoided interrogating some of the most basic questions about subjectivity in the act of enacting our sexual selves. Reid-Pharr is especially concerned with highlighting the sexual formation of cross-racial desire as a crucial site for anchoring such explorations, a form of desire that only a handful of other black queer studies scholars have taken on (see Scott; Williams). He contends that "nearly two decades of writing and film by people of color, and in particular that by Black gay men, has spoken to the experience of sex with whites, painting it at once as liberatory and repressive" (Reid-Pharr, *Black Gay Man* 86). The same, however, has not been the case with white writers. Reid-Pharr poses the question: "Why is it that we often find such sustained discussions of cross-racial desire among people of color while whites remain largely silent?" (88).

To answer this question, Reid-Pharr turns to the emerging work by scholars whose research focuses on whiteness as an ideological construct. He concludes with a provocative insight: "that, in fact, the tendency to insist upon the innocence of our sex, the transparency of desire at the moment of penetration, is itself a part of the complex ideological process by which whiteness is rendered invisible, unremarkable except in the presence of a spectacularized Blackness" (*Black Gay Man* 77–8). In other words, Reid-Pharr discovers that the injunction not to speak (or think) about race when we engage in sexual acts with others – on the part of blacks as well as on the part of whites – is to collude in the ideological process of rendering whiteness invisible and blackness overdetermined. The potential antidote to such collusion, Reid-Pharr suggests, is for Americans to not only speak race when we "fuck," but also to think it, even in the face of powerful institutional and cultural powers that insist otherwise (76). In his own tour de force rereading of *Another Country*, Reid-Pharr uses these critical insights into whiteness to argue that Baldwin recognized this tendency of liberal white Americans especially to avoid the topic of race as it pertained to their sexualities. For Baldwin, this silence was one that had the unfortunate effect of reinscribing, even as it actively repudiated, the workings of a white supremacist culture by insisting on the invisibility of one racial category (whiteness) while insisting on the hypervisibility of another (blackness). The entire process was organized through an elaborately produced denial on the part of liberal whites of what was in fact seen, i.e. "black" and "white" bodies. "[T]he tragedy, the horror that both the white and the Black subject must confront in Baldwin's universe," Reid-Pharr contends, "is the racial fantasy that denies access to the body, that denies access to the beloved, and instead seals each partner into a bizarre competition in which mutual invisibility is the inevitable outcome. Indeed, the 'lovemaking' in *Another Country* is as much an act of rage as of adoration and devotion" (81). For Reid-Pharr, as perhaps too for Baldwin, the solution to such a dilemma is simply to speak the unspeakable, or at least to dare thinking it as a prelude to speaking out eventually.

Conclusion

I have argued in this essay that some critics have performed opportunistic readings of Baldwin's controversial third novel, *Another Country*. In so doing, these critics have exhibited an unwillingness to engage the novel's own preoccupations with interracial figurations by imposing onto their readings political contexts and arguments that recenter the struggles of gay men. As such, these critics conveniently displace the novel's ongoing preoccupation with the theme of post-World War Two racial struggle and the central role that sexual relationships across the color line played historically during that period. This sociopolitical context has been systematically overlooked in much of contemporary Queer Studies in favor of the privileging of (white) same-sex identities and desires. And while the emergence of black queer studies has recently sought to remedy this oversight, sadly much of this work, with some notable exceptions, too often operates within its own homosexual–heterosexual binary framework, albeit one configured differently from its mainstream counterpart. In short, the former merely reproduces a new binary opposition within the old model – namely, *black* heterosexuality / *black* homosexuality that is then placed alongside, or *within*, the (white) heterosexuality / (white) homosexuality framework that is common to (white) queer theoretical and political activist discourse. However, as Cathy Cohen has pointed out, such a binary "narrowly posits a dichotomy of heterosexual privilege and queer oppression," one that I suggest is merely doubled by race. Not only does this *re*-racialized opposition produce "monolithic understandings" of these two categories, heterosexuality and homosexuality, but it also fails to recognize the varying relations to power that exist among members of both groups, "in which identities of race, class, and/or gender either enhance or mute the marginalization of queers, on the one hand, and the power of heterosexuals, on the other" (210, 215).

My point here has been to argue that *Another Country*, but also many other texts within the African American literary tradition, offers these and other scholars potentially rich literary narratives for analyzing racial and sexual content that resist overly conventional analyses. In other words, if we are to take seriously what the authors of "What's Queer about Queer Studies Now?" claim when they write that "the 'subjectless' critique of queer studies [ideally] disallows any positing of a proper subject *of* or object *for* the field by insisting that queer has no fixed political referent" (Eng, Halberstam and Muñoz 3), then I would say that, in the twenty-*first* century, the literature by people of color, whether homosexual or otherwise, and the intersectional nature of our concerns, ought to serve as a more elucidating object of study for such critical practices than would texts that cater primarily to the monolithic identity concerns of white lesbians and gay men. Earl Jackson, Jr. reminds us that "[a] marginal sexual identity does not warrant reductive identifications across other differences" (Jackson 151). And as my brief look at the critical literature within Queer Studies of Baldwin's *Another Country* has tried to demonstrate (a work, after all, in which "different-race" sexuality is privileged over "same-gender"), this marginality should extend to the difference, and even in some cases to the sameness, of race as well.

Bibliography

Baldwin, James. *Another Country*. 1962. New York: Vintage International, 1993.

Baldwin, James. *Collected Essays*. New York: The Library of America, 1998.

Carbado, Devon, W., ed. *Black Men on Race, Gender, and Sexuality: A Critical Reader*. New York: New York University Press, 1999.

Childs, Erica Chito. *Navigating Interracial Borders: Black-White Couples and Their Social Worlds*. New Brunswick, NJ: Rutgers University Press, 2005.

Cohen, Cathy. "Punks, Bulldaggers, and Welfare Queens: The Radical Potential of Queer Politics." In *Sexual Identities, Queer Politics*. Ed. Mark Blasius. Princeton: Princeton University Press, 2001. 200–27.

Cohen, William A. "Liberalism, Libido, Liberation: Baldwin's *Another Country*." In *The Queer Sixties*. Ed. Patricia Juliana Smith. New York: Routledge, 2000. 201–22.

Dalmage, Heather. *Tripping on the Color Line: Black–White Multiracial Families in a Racially*

Divided World. New Brunswick, NJ: Rutgers University Press, 2000.

de Lauretis, Teresa. "Queer Theory: Lesbian and Gay Sexualities – an Introduction." *Differences: A Journal of Feminist Cultural Studies* 3.2 (1991): iii–xviii.

Dievler, James. "Sexual Exiles: James Baldwin and *Another Country*." In *James Baldwin Now*. Ed. Dwight A. McBride. New York: New York University Press, 1999. 161–83.

Edelman, Lee. *Homographesis: Essays in Gay Literary and Cultural Theory*. New York: Routledge, 1994.

Eng, David, Judith Halberstam and José Esteban Muñoz. "What's Queer about Queer Studies Now?" *Social Text* 23.3–4, 84–5 (2005): 1–17.

Ferguson, Roderick. *Aberrations in Black: Toward a Queer of Color Critique*. Minneapolis: University of Minnesota Press, 2004.

Foucault, Michel. *History of Sexuality*, Volume I: An Introduction. New York: Vintage, 1990.

Goldstein, Richard. "'Go the Way Your Blood Beats': An Interview with James Baldwin." In *James Baldwin: The Legacy*. Ed. Quincy Troupe. New York: Simon & Schuster, 1989. 173–85.

Halberstam, Judith. "Shame and White Gay Masculinity." *Social Text* 23.3–4, 84–5 (2005): 219–33.

Henderson, Mae G. and E. Patrick Johnson, ed. *Black Queer Studies: A Critical Anthology*. Durham, NC: Duke University Press, 2005.

Hodes, Martha. *Sex, Love, Race: Crossing Boundaries in North American History*. New York: New York University Press, 1999.

Hodes, Martha. *White Women, Black Men: Illicit Sex in the Nineteenth-Century South*. New Haven: Yale University Press, 1997.

Jackson, Earl, Jr. "The Responsibility of and to Differences: Theorizing Race and Ethnicity in Lesbian and Gay Studies." In *Beyond a Dream Deferred: Multicultural Education and the Politics of Excellence*. Ed. Becky Thompson and Sargeeta Tyagi. Minneapolis: Minnesota University Press, 1993. 131–61.

Kulick, Don. "Queer Linguistics?" In *Language and Sexuality: Contesting Meaning in Theory and Practice*. Ed. Kathryn Campbell-Kibler, Robert J. Podesva, Sarah J. Roberts, and Andrew Wong. Stanford: Center for the Study of Language and Information, 2002. 65–8.

Lemire, Elise. *"Miscegenation": Making Race in America*. Philadelphia: University of Pennsylvania Press, 2002.

Lubin, Alex. *Romance and Rights: The Politics of Interracial Intimacy, 1945–1954*. Jackson: University Press of Mississippi, 2005.

McBride, Dwight A. *Why I Hate Abercrombie & Fitch: Essays on Race and Sexuality*. New York: New York University Press, 2005.

Mossman, James. "Race, Hate, Sex, and Colour: A Conversation with James Baldwin." In *Conversations with James Baldwin*. Ed. Fred L. Standley and Louis H. Pratt. Jackson & London: University of Mississippi Press, 1989. 46–58.

Nelson, Emmanuel. "The Novels of James Baldwin: Struggles of Self-Acceptance." *Journal of American Culture* 8.4 (1985): 11–16.

Ohi, Kevin. "'I'm not the boy you want': Sexuality, 'Race', and Thwarted Revelation in Baldwin's *Another Country*." *African American Review* 33.2 (1999): 261–81.

Pascoe, Peggy. *What Comes Naturally: Miscegenation Law and the Making of Race in America*. Oxford: Oxford University Press, 2009.

Reid-Pharr, Robert. *Black Gay Man: Essays*. New York: New York University Press, 2001.

Reid-Pharr, Robert. *Once You Go Black: Choice, Desire, and the Black American Intellectual*. New York: New York University Press, 2007.

Robinson, Paul. *The Modernization of Sex: Havelock Ellis, Alfred Kinsey, William Masters and Virginia Johnson*. Ithaca, NY: Cornell University Press, 1989.

Romano, Renee. *Race-mixing: Black-White Marriage in Postwar America*. Cambridge, MA: Harvard University Press, 2003.

Ross, Marlon. "White Fantasies of Desire: Baldwin and the Racial Identities of Sexuality." In *James Baldwin Now*. Ed. Dwight A. McBride. New York: New York University Press, 1999. 13–55.

Scott, Darieck. "Jungle Fever? Black Gay Identity Politics, White Dick, and the Utopian Bedroom." *GLQ: A Journal of Lesbian and Gay Studies* 1.3 (1994): 299–321.

Sollors, Werner, ed. *Interracialism: Black–White Intermarriage in American History, Literature, and Law*. New York: Oxford University Press, 2000.

Thomas, Kendall. "'Ain't Nothin' like the Real Thing': Black Masculinity, Gay Sexuality, and the Jargon of Authenticity." In *Representing Black Men*. Ed. M. Blount and G. Cunningham. New York: Routledge, 1996. 55–69.

Vogel, Shane. "Closing Time: Langston Hughes and the Queer Poetics of Harlem Nightlife." *Criticism: A Quarterly for Literature and the Arts* 48.3 (2006): 397–425.

Washington, Bryan R. "Wrestling with 'The Love that Dare Not Speak Its Name': John, Elisha, and the Master." In *New Essays on "Go Tell It on the Mountain."* Ed. Trudier Harris. Cambridge: Cambridge University Press, 1996. 77–95.

Williams, Rhonda M. "Living at the Crossroads: Explorations in Race, Nationality, Sexuality, and Gender." In *The House that Race Built: Black Americans, US Terrain*. Ed. Wahneema Lubiano. New York: Pantheon Books, 1997. 136–56.

27
African American Literature and Psychoanalysis

Arlene R. Keizer

The prevailing narrative in American literary and cultural studies is that, until quite recently, African American writers and critics refused to engage with or outright rejected psychoanalysis, one of the most influential theoretical trends in twentieth-century thought. In this essay, I show how new archival research and new attention to materials long available to critics reveal an extended history of African American involvement with psychoanalytic theory and practice that has rarely been acknowledged or studied. From the 1920s to the present, African American writers, psychologists, and other cultural commentators have engaged with psychoanalysis and considered its utility as a method of healing for "the souls of black folk," as W.E.B. Du Bois put it in 1903. In so doing, these intellectuals have highlighted the limits of psychoanalysis that derive from its presupposition of white European/European American subjects as the prototypical analysts and analysands. At the same time, this group of black intellectuals has also suggested what psychoanalysis might bring to the understanding of racialized subjectivities and what a thoroughgoing consideration of race might bring to psychoanalysis.

More and more frequently, psychoanalytic theory is being deployed to analyze the literature of racialized ethnic minorities in the United States. From the path-breaking work of Hortense Spillers on the applicability of Freudian and Lacanian models to African American literature, to Claudia Tate's exploration of desire in forgotten African American novels, to more recent work by Anne Cheng, David Eng, Sara Clarke Kaplan, and others on "racial melancholia" and "diasporic melancholia" in African American, Asian American, and other American ethnic literatures, psychoanalysis has been enjoying increasing popularity in ethnic studies. This essay establishes a new frame for this work, placing the theoretical projects that began in the 1980s in the context of a longer tradition of black engagement with psychoanalytic theory. At least since Nella Larsen's playful invocation of Freudian concepts in her personal correspondence in the 1930s, and since Richard Wright's and Ralph Ellison's essays on the founding of the Lafargue Psychiatric Clinic in Harlem in the mid-1940s, African American literature and culture have been in open dialogue with psychoanalysis.

The forms of engagement between black intellectuals and this body of theory fall into two broad and occasionally overlapping categories: the speculative and the applied. A speculative approach to psychoanalysis characterizes the work, published and unpublished, of African American writers and intellectuals from the 1920s through the 1950s. As psychoanalytic ideas became widely disseminated and increased in popularity during these years, many black intellectuals were as taken with these concepts as their white counterparts were. Wright's body of work illustrates this fascination better than that of any other African American writer. About Wright's *Black Boy* (1945), Ellison writes, "Imagine Bigger Thomas projecting his own life in lucid prose, guided, say, by the insights of Marx and Freud, and you have an idea of this autobiography" ("Wright's Blues" 77). Many conversations between the two writers on these theorists informed Ellison's comments on Wright's autobiography. Ellison was not simply guessing about his mentor and friend's concerns – he already had firsthand knowledge of Wright's psychoanalytic preoccupations. Wright's long-time friend Horace Cayton underwent analysis for several years. In fact, Margaret Walker, in her salacious and often scathing biography of Wright, claims that "the two men [Cayton and Wright] did share an obsession with psychoanalysis, sex, and race" (M. Walker 169). Wright himself participated in a free-association experiment with another good friend and collaborator, the analyst Frederic Wertham, who published the results of this experiment, "An Unconscious Determinant in *Native Son*," in 1944. In the early 1940s, Wright also corresponded with the psychoanalyst Benjamin Karpman. The subjects about which they exchanged letters – "psychopathology, criminality, black homosexuality, and female alcoholism and promiscuity" – were major elements in Wright's psychic life (Tate 206n6). Though his connections to psychoanalytic works and practitioners have been noted by most biographers and many critics addressing his oeuvre, the extent of Wright's conscious engagement with psychoanalytic theory and practice has never been fully documented or explicated in relation to his literary works. On the one hand, Wright's most deliberately psychoanalytic text, *Savage Holiday*, was dismissed as "schoolbook Freud" (Tate 87); on the other hand, the critic who does the most detailed psychoanalytic reading of this novel, Claudia Tate, recognizes Wright as a self-conscious intellectual using a body of theory in his fiction yet primarily analyzes the writer and his novels as analysands. (Tate's subtle and powerful readings of Wright's biography and *Savage Holiday* are, it must be said, a substantial improvement over Walker's summary condemnation of the novel as "a Freudian nightmare.") A detailed exploration of Wright's use of free association in his writing and his application and transformation of Freudian theory in his work would fundamentally alter the way readers and critics of American literature perceive the relationship between black writers and psychoanalytic theory. Similar archival and theoretical reconsiderations of Ellison, Larsen, Zora Neale Hurston, and others would round out this new vision that has, in a sense, been hiding in plain view in the available materials on twentieth-century African American writers.

Ellison's novel *Invisible Man* (1952), for example, can be read as an African American exploration of the problems and possibilities of Freudian psychoanalytic theory. At least four major allusions to psychoanalysis appear in the novel: in the Trueblood episode, in the nameless narrator's meeting with Mr. Emerson, Jr., in the character Brother Tarp, whose limp is an hysterical symptom, and in the depiction of the Invisible Man's repressed sexuality. In the Trueblood episode, the novel signifies heavily on *Totem and Taboo* (1913), in which Freud most clearly expresses his pervasive view that the psychic lives of "savages" provide a window into the psychological past of the modern, Western subject. (If readers miss this first allusion, the book itself turns up on the young Emerson's side table pages later in Ellison's novel.) The novel's playful and ironic treatment of the white Western belief in the greater sexual licentiousness of people of African descent reflects Ellison's recognition that blacks were relegated to second-class status in psychoanalytic theory as much as in any other Western tenet. For example, Norton sees his own fantasies of sexual involvement with his daughter played out in Trueblood's tale of accidentally having intercourse with his daughter Mattie Lou. But *Invisible Man* goes further in its commentary on Freudian psychoanalysis. The Norton–Trueblood exchange names the father's desire for the female child in ways that Freud himself refused to acknowledge in his development of the theory of the Oedipus complex and the "family romance" more generally. In this and other as-yet-unexplored ways, Ellison's novel functions as a critique of aspects of Freud's theory, and demonstrates yet again how comfortable this African American writer was in manipulating the great ideas of his time.

Recent biographies of Larsen and Hurston also suggest their familiarity with the psychoanalytic theory available in the US in the 1920s, 30s, and 40s. Psychoanalytic readings of their work would be richer and more accurate if they incorporated a recognition of these writers' deliberate evocations of Freud's concepts. All of these writers were considering the appropriateness and utility of psychoanalytic theory for black self-understanding, healing, and self-making. Their speculation about psychoanalytic theory was a critical part of the project of comprehending black modernity and making black modernist literary art.

Due to the political imperatives under which all African American writers have crafted their fiction, the extended exploration of ideas unrelated to racial struggle and survival has been discouraged in both blatant and subtle ways. As the work of critics such as Tate and Gene Andrew Jarrett has recently made clear, when African American writers turned away from explicit explorations of racial problems, their audiences proved unwilling to follow them into new territory. The terrain of psychoanalysis appears to have been especially daunting. Margaret Walker's sharp critique of psychoanalysis in *Richard Wright: Daemonic Genius* is emblematic of the responses of many educated African Americans in the mid-twentieth century and shows why black intellectuals would downplay or keep secret their psychoanalytic forays. In her censure of Cayton, Walker equates his investment in psychoanalysis with his alcohol and drug abuse, as if his search for mental health were a symptom rather than an attempt at a cure. She writes: "Cayton was strongly self-destructive and not only hit the skids but hit the pits with alcohol, prescription drugs, and the results of four years of psychoanalysis … He was a classic example of how the psychiatrist can pick a man to pieces but, unlike the god-maker, cannot put him together again. Humpty-Dumpty" (M. Walker 168–9). Walker's comments on Cayton denigrate his choice to step outside of an African American cultural milieu in search of psychic healing. She implies that he would have been far better off in church. Black and white readers alike expected black writers to represent the African American condition as it was generally understood – as primarily a struggle for human dignity in the face of anti-black racism. There was little or no cultural space available for these writers to explore publicly their engagement with the project of psychoanalysis.

In the 1960s, the Black Power and Black Arts Movements enjoined black artists, writers, and other intellectuals to work toward African American cultural liberation while eschewing European and Euro-American artistic and theoretical models. This black nationalist moment was a critical, if sometimes problematic, step in the development of African American literature. Indeed, the work of such luminaries as Toni Morrison, Charles Johnson, Alice Walker, and Ishmael Reed would have been literally unimaginable without the Black Arts Movement. Despite its phallocentrism and some of the exclusionary notions of blackness it fostered, this movement fulfilled the promise and many of the goals of the Harlem Renaissance, facilitating black writers' creation of literary forms that spoke directly to black American audiences and mining the brilliance of African American spoken-word and musical traditions for literary art. While the works of the Martinican psychoanalyst Frantz Fanon, *The Wretched of the Earth* especially, were celebrated as handbooks for the revolution against imperialism and white supremacy at home and abroad, the specifically psychoanalytic aspects of his books were left by the wayside. Ironically, Fanon had been influenced to a certain degree by Wright's work; the novelist's representations of black psychic and material suffering provided the analyst a window into the African American experience of racial oppression.[1]

The 1960s also saw one of the most egregious examples of psychoanalytically derived theory being used to stigmatize African Americans. In 1965, Daniel Patrick Moynihan released *The Negro Family – The Case for National Action*, a report commissioned by the federal government. In this now-infamous report, a major building block of neo-conservative political ideology, the black family, deprived of male leadership through the institution of slavery, was seen as pathologically deviating from the patriarchal norm. Despite the institutional pressures represented as producing this crisis, Moynihan's report nevertheless blamed what he saw as the "matriarchal" structure of African American families on black mothers. In *Feminism and Its Discontents*, a remarkable, combined study of psychoanalysis and feminism in the twentieth century, the historian Mari Jo Buhle shows how Moynihan's report was a policy paper based on the work of Abram Kardiner from the early 1950s. Kardiner's *The Mark of Oppression: A Psychosocial Study of the American Negro* (1951) was an instance of "Momism," the strain of popular psychoanalysis that laid social ills at the door of inadequate, domineering, or otherwise problematic mothers. If African American intellectuals had not been inclined to reject psychoanalysis in the 1960s in favor of a different critical agenda, the stigmatizing uses to which psychoanalytic interpretation was being put would have been reason enough.

The current engagement of theorists of race and racialization with psychoanalysis followed the battles of the 1980s and 1990s within African American Studies over the appropriate sources of theories for analyzing African American literary texts and the institutionalization of African American Studies within historically white universities. While there are still a number of African Americanist scholars who look with disfavor upon the use of European and Euro-American structuralist and poststructuralist theories, they do not dominate the field. Of the myriad critical strands that developed within African American literary studies in the 1970s and early 1980s, black feminist theory is the one that led most directly to contemporary African Americanist psychoanalytic investigations.

The work of Hortense Spillers, a black feminist literary critic, therefore forms a bridge between, on the one hand, the black intellectuals of the 1920s through the 1950s and, on the other, the burst of interest in African American literature and psychoanalysis that began in the late twentieth century. Representing the apotheosis of the speculative position, Spillers always frames her deep knowledge of psychoanalytic theory within the context of her equally extensive knowledge of African American literary and cultural traditions. In a group of influential essays that began appearing in the late 1980s, she has consistently tried to establish when, how, and whether psychoanalytic concepts are applicable to black expressive culture. "'All the Things You Could Be by Now, If Sigmund Freud's Wife Was Your Mother': Psychoanalysis and Race," originally published in 1996, manages to critique both African Americanist literary criticism and the oeuvres of Freud and Lacan for their mutual lack of engagement with the key concepts in the other body of work. The title and last segment of the essay allude to the knowledge about psychoanalysis in the black artistic community sketched above; Spillers' title was coined by the jazz bassist Charles Mingus. Though Mingus refused to elaborate upon the meaning of his song title, Spillers treats it as a complex and cryptic "your mama" joke, registering an as-yet-unnamed engagement with Freudian theory. Her essay examines the work of Fanon and social scientists studying black psychology in sub-Saharan Africa[2] in search of models that might assist psychoanalytic projects on African American literature and culture. The challenge Spillers issues in this article – "I think it is safe to say … that the psychoanalytic object, subject, subjectivity now constitute the missing layer of *hermeneutic/interpretive* projects of an entire generation of black intellectuals now at work" (Spillers 377, original emphasis) – was soon answered by a flood of critical essays and books using psychoanalytic theory to read African American literature. Thus 1996, in retrospect, turns out to be a watershed year. Claudia Tate, whose *Psychoanalysis and Black Novels* (1998) would be the first full-length psychoanalytic study of African American literature, published a speculative essay in the first issue of *JPCS:*

Journal for the Psychoanalysis of Culture and Society entitled "Freud and His 'Negro': Psychoanalysis as Ally and Enemy of African Americans." Tate's article explores the anxieties about ethnicity and race in Freudian theory, using as her signal example a joke Freud told for many years, beginning in the 1880s, in which his patients were to him as "Negro" slaves to their masters.[3]

In addition to Spillers's catalytic essays, a number of other literary/critical events ushered in psychoanalytic interpretations of African American texts.[4] The 1987 publication of *Beloved*, Toni Morrison's Pulitzer Prize-winning novel, for example, generated an outpouring of responses from across the spectrum of American literary studies. In the 1991 anthology *Contemporary American Identities*, Spillers published Mae Henderson's "*Beloved*: Re-Membering the Body as Historical Text," one of the earliest and best psychoanalytic readings of Morrison's novel. A 1992 conference, "Psychoanalysis in African American Contexts: Feminist Reconfigurations," revolved around the contrasting readings of this novel by two conference organizers, Barbara Christian and Helene Moglen.[5]

Moreover, from the 1990s to the present, numerous critical projects have been published that utilize either psychoanalytically derived trauma theory or theories of melancholia extrapolated from Freud's 1917 essay "Mourning and Melancholia," in order to examine literary representations of the African American psyche. In the growing critical literature on slavery in late-twentieth-century fiction, drama, and poetry, for example, the "peculiar institution" has come to be understood by many as a cultural trauma equivalent to the Holocaust. Trauma theory is also being engaged to analyze representations of the forms of racial terrorism employed against blacks in the post-slavery era: lynching, sexual assault, police violence, and mass incarceration.[6]

Since the early 1990s, the concept of melancholia, interpreted in strikingly different ways by different critics, has come to inform new work on race and subjectivity. A small sampling includes Anne Cheng's *The Melancholy of Race*, José Esteban Muñoz's *Disidentifications: Queers of Color and the Performance of Politics*, David Eng and Shinhee Han's "A Dialogue on Racial Melancholia," Sarita See's "*An Open Wound*: Colonial Melancholia and Contemporary Filipino/American Texts," Sara Clarke Kaplan's "Souls at the Crossroads, Africans on the Water: The Politics of Diasporic Melancholia," David Kyuman Kim's *Melancholic Freedom: Agency and the Spirit of Politics*, Ranjana Khanna's *Dark Continents: Psychoanalysis and Race*, Paul Gilroy's *Postcolonial Melancholia*, as well as many of the essays collected in Eng and David Kazanjian's anthology *Loss*. Surprisingly, no two critics revive and engage the concept of melancholia the same way. Even more striking is the fact that some critics, like Eng and Han, See, and Muñoz, use melancholia to refer to the affect experienced by the racialized or colonized (or formerly colonized); others, like Gilroy, use it to refer to the affect of the former colonizers; and still others, like Cheng, argue that both dominant and subordinated groups experience race melancholically.

Melancholia has become an attractive theoretical concept in critical race and ethnic studies for four major reasons. First, despite its near-eclipse in American academic psychology, Freud's work still has substantial influence in the literary humanities and in cultural studies. Thus critics engaged with race, racialization, and imperialism have lately found engagement with psychoanalytic theory to be a way to secure a larger scholarly audience for their concern with the grief of the subaltern. Of course, the question of why melancholia has been selected out of the extremely rich and varied body of Freud's work remains still to be answered. The second reason, then, for melancholia's popularity is that it bespeaks the epidemic of depression in late-capitalist society. Putting a name to this pervasive sorrow – some of it turned against the self – and linking this affect to the political realm is a task that each of these theorist-critics has undertaken. Locating a political dimension to melancholia is a way of thinking hopefully about an otherwise paralyzing problem, one not often addressed in political terms. What all of these re-articulations of melancholia share is the idea that identifying this condition within a group can lead to collective action. Freud beckons because Prozac is clearly not enough. Third, Freud's incomplete and tentative theorizations of melancholia are especially available to contemporary re-articulation. In "Mourning and Melancholia," Freud's vacillation between a somatic explanation for melancholia and a psychogenic one and his varied statements about whether and when melancholic symptoms might subside belie the authority with which commentators have often imbued his words.

Fourth, and most significantly, melancholia provides a tool for examining the psychology of the subjugated without recourse to the concept of victimhood. More active than the victim, the melancholic does things, albeit unconsciously, with the "lost object," whatever that object may be. In this regard, many of the critics referenced here depart from Freud's original concept of melancholia to try to imagine positive uses of this psychological state and envision collective action against racial injustice arising from this affective state. Melancholia has begun to dominate analyses of psychic pain and damage within literary and cultural criticism, especially in ethnic and postcolonial studies, because it avoids the language of victimization that has recently come under fire from scholars and from the culture at large.[7]

Studies of racial or postcolonial melancholia (particularly those conducted by Cheng, Eng and Han, Gilroy, Muñoz, and See) invite us to examine a range of questions: How does the concept of melancholia advance an inquiry? In each re-articulation of Freud's concept, what is the lost object? What other terminology or concepts might melancholia be obscuring? What is the epistemic status of a social or cultural diagnosis such as racial/colonial/postcolonial melancholia? What treatment or "cure" might such a diagnosis entail? Overall, in the present scholarly discourse on melancholia, the status of psychoanalysis as a hermeneutics for understanding literary and cultural texts and its status as a means of diagnosing and attempting to cure psychic illnesses are coming into contact in potentially fruitful but also deeply problematic ways. This strand of criticism – one of the major applications of Freudian theory to African American literature and culture – has not resolved its most significant internal contradictions.

A major aspect of melancholia's value, for Muñoz, Kaplan, and Eng and Han, is that this psychic state provides a space of contemplation, that the failure to surrender the object until one has worked through one's ambivalence toward it is a useful psychological position for the disenfranchised. These critics take up Judith Butler's contention that the melancholic's unwillingness to relinquish the object can serve as a form of resistance. Yet, in Freud's articulation of melancholia, the melancholic doesn't precisely know *what* he or she has lost. For melancholia to serve as the basis for resistance, those who have suffered losses would, at a bare minimum, have to come to understand the exact nature of those losses. Once fully acknowledged, do these losses still produce melancholia? Is the melancholic not then free to mourn and to turn to new objects? Why melancholia and *not* mourning? Why not mourn, if, as Freud acknowledged in his later work, mourning performs some of the same work of identification that is inherent within melancholia? The last powerful trace that remains to separate melancholia from mourning is thus the subject's self-denigration, enacted upon the image of the object installed within the ego. It is precisely this self-denigration, coupled with the other painful, debilitating effects of melancholia, that makes the argument that melancholia might lead to political action a difficult one to accept fully. For what would it mean to agitate for change melancholically? The melancholic would be the least likely person to create social change. To turn briefly to another strand of theory, Antonio Gramsci suggested that what was necessary for social activism was "pessimism of the intellect and optimism of the will." This "optimism of the will" is precisely what the melancholic lacks. Whether its causes are racial injury, familial dysfunction, discrimination based on gender or sexual orientation, or some combination of these forms of damage, melancholia is not a position from which to mount effective action for the transformation of society.[8]

Perhaps melancholia has become an appealing concept only recently in African American Studies because there are deep, long-standing resources within African American culture for dealing with the depredations of racism. These intragroup strategies of healing have not been primarily melancholic; instead, African Americans have employed them to mourn clearly identified losses: the many loved ones who have died prematurely through racist violence or exclusion and the ideal of equal treatment and recognition as human beings.

In the context of a brief genealogy of the relation between psychoanalysis and African American literary culture, racial/colonial/diasporic/postcolonial melancholia can most productively be viewed as a provisional name for an emotional and social complex that has not yet been properly identified and theorized. Rather than critiquing the new theorists of melancholia through a re-instantiation of the original Freudian dichotomy between mourning and its dysfunctional counterpart, here I argue for an understanding of melancholia, in the context of racialization and imperialism, as a placeholder for a more accurate and politically useful designation that is currently in formation.[9] Treating the use of melancholia as a functional misnaming analogous to Gayatri Spivak's "strategic essentialism" – an intellectual and political move on the way to another position – I champion Spillers's stance of speculation (what one might also call her deeply engaged skepticism) as a principle of investigation. To be more explicit: formulating an ever wider and more radical set of questions about the interactions and intersections between black expressive culture and psychoanalytic theories and practices must remain at the heart of this enterprise. We are still at the very beginning, and none of the apparent answers or critical formulations has proven to be more than a potentially useful fiction for considering the losses that persist, in spite of significant gains and the rhetoric suggesting the end of racism.[10] Learning to love the questions themselves seems to be a necessary critical strategy if the goals are conceptual clarity and social utility. A final strand of inquiry vis-à-vis African American culture and psychoanalysis is underdeveloped and must be built up: the realm of the historical and archival. Further investigating black writers' links to psychoanalysis, connecting the work of black psychoanalysts to the knowledge gleaned from literary history, and showing how black artists, musicians, and performers – the dancer Katherine Dunham, for example, as well as numerous others – engaged psychoanalytic concepts: these tasks must be pursued in tandem with theoretical inquiries. The more we know about the history of African American involvement with psychoanalytic theory, the more accurate our literary and cultural interpretations will be and the more powerful our theories linking these two bodies of knowledge.

Notes

1 Michel Fabre, *The Unfinished Quest of Richard Wright*, trans. Isabel Barzun (1973). Urbana and Chicago: University of Illinois Press, 1993, pp. 383 & 436.

2 Spillers analyzes *Les Structures anthropologiques de la folie en Afrique noire* (*Anthropological Structures of Madness in Black Africa*) by Dr. Ibrahim Sow and *Oedipe africain* (*African Oedipus*) by Marie-Cécile and Edmond Ortigues alongside Fanon's *Wretched of the Earth* and *Black Skin, White Masks*.

3 Given Tate's alertness to the possibilities *and* problems of Freudian psychoanalysis and its theoretical descendants, one might have expected *Psychoanalysis and Black Novels* to critique psychoanalytic theory to a certain degree, yet the book is free of such criticism.

4 Because Tate's "Freud and His 'Negro'" is rarely cited, it would be difficult to argue that it helped to spark the explosion of psychoanalytic readings of African American literary texts that followed.

5 The conference essays appear in the volume *Female Subjects in Black and White: Race, Psychoanalysis Feminism.* I had the enormous good fortune to be present at this conference, which took place during my graduate education at UC Berkeley.

6 See Jacqueline Goldsby's discussion of James Weldon Johnson's brush with lynching in *A Spectacular Secret: Lynching in American Life and Literature*. Chicago: University of Chicago Press, 2006, pp. 164–213; and Bruce Simon's article "Traumatic Repetition: Gayl Jones's *Corregidora*," in *Race Consciousness: African-American Studies for the New Century*, ed. Judith Jackson Fossett and Jeffrey A. Tucker. New York: NYU Press, 1997, pp. 93–112.

7 Wendy Brown's *States of Injury* is the most influential of these critiques of identity putatively based on psychic damage. Carolyn Dean's book *The Fragility of Empathy after the Holocaust* is an attempt to document and critique the growing impatience with Holocaust remembrance and testimony in contemporary Europe, France in particular.

8 See the work of Butler, Douglas Crimp, and Jeffrey Prager for other perspectives on melancholia, mourning, and identity formation among the marginalized.

9 This essay seeks to spur discussion of new concepts that might contest or succeed racial melancholia: Racialization fatigue? Sorrow of

color? Fred Moten's "black mo'nin'"? (*Loss* 72) Sharon Holland's "tragic empowerment"? (*Raising the Dead* 7).

10 I thank the LOUD Collective for their help in refining this analysis of contemporary theories of melancholia.

Bibliography

Abel, Elizabeth, Barbara Christian, and Helene Moglen, ed. *Female Subjects in Black and White: Race, Psychoanalysis, Feminism*. Berkeley: University of California Press, 1997.

Buhle, Mari Jo. *Feminism and Its Discontents: A Century of Struggle with Psychoanalysis*. Cambridge, MA: Harvard University Press, 1998.

Butler, Judith. "Afterword: After Loss, What Then?" In *Loss: The Politics of Mourning*. Ed. David L. Eng and David Kazanjian. Berkeley: University of California Press, 2003. 467–73.

Butler, Judith. *The Psychic Life of Power: Theories in Subjection*. Stanford: Stanford University Press, 1997.

Cheng, Anne Anlin. *The Melancholy of Race: Psychoanalysis, Assimilation, and Hidden Grief*. Oxford: Oxford University Press, 2001.

Crimp, Douglas. "Mourning and Militancy." In *Melancholia and Moralism: Essays on AIDS and Queer Politics*. Cambridge, MA: MIT Press, 2002. 129–49.

Ellison, Ralph. *Invisible Man*. 1952. New York: Modern Library, 1994.

Ellison, Ralph. "Richard Wright's Blues." *Shadow and Act*. New York: Random House, 1964. 77–94.

Eng, David L. and Shinhee Han. "A Dialogue on Racial Melancholia." In *Loss: The Politics of Mourning*. Ed. David L. Eng and David Kazanjian. Berkeley: University of California Press, 2003. 343–71.

Fanon, Frantz. *Black Skin, White Masks*. 1967. Trans. Charles Lam Markmann. New York: Grove, 1982.

Fanon, Frantz. *The Wretched of the Earth*. Trans. Constance Farrington. New York: Grove, 1963.

Freud, Sigmund. *The Standard Edition of the Complete Works of Sigmund Freud*. Trans. James Strachey. London: Hogarth Press and the Institute of Psycho-Analysis, 1953–73.

Gilroy, Paul. *Postcolonial Melancholia*. New York: Columbia University Press, 2005.

Henderson, Mae G. "Toni Morrison's *Beloved*: Re-Membering the Body as Historical Text." In *Comparative American Identities: Race, Sex, and Nationality in the Modern Text*. Ed. Hortense J. Spillers. New York: Rouledge, 1991. 62–86.

Holland, Sharon Patricia. *Raising the Dead: Death and (Black) Subjectivity*. Durham, NC: Duke University Press, 2000.

Johnson, Barbara. *The Feminist Difference: Literature, Psychoanalysis, Race and Gender*. Cambridge, MA: Harvard University Press, 1998.

Kaplan, Sara Clarke. "Souls at the Crossroads, Africans on the Water: The Politics of Diasporic Melancholia." *Callaloo* 30.2 (2007): 511–26.

Khanna, Ranjana. *Dark Continents: Psychoanalysis and Colonialism*. Durham, NC: Duke University Press, 2003.

Kim, David Kyuman. *Melancholic Freedom: Agency and the Spirit of Politics*. Oxford: Oxford University Press, 2007.

Morrison, Toni. *Beloved*. New York: Knopf, 1987.

Moten, Fred. "Black Mo'nin'." In *Loss: The Politics of Mourning*. Ed. David L. Eng and David Kazanjian. Berkeley: University of California Press, 2003. 59–76.

Muñoz, José Esteban. *Disidentifications: Queers of Color and the Performance of Politics*. Minneapolis: University of Minnesota Press, 1999.

Prager, Jeffrey. "Melancholic Identities: Post-traumatic Loss, Memory and Identity Formation." In *Identity in Question*. Ed. Anthony Elliott and Paul du Gay. Los Angeles: Sage, 2009.

See, Sarita. "*An Open Wound*: Colonial Melancholia and Contemporary Filipino/American Texts." In *Vestiges of War 1899–1999: The Philippine-American War and the Aftermath of an Imperial Dream*. Ed. Angel Shaw and Luis Francia. New York: New York University Press, 2002. 376–400.

Spillers, Hortense J. *Black, White, and in Color: Essays on American Literature and Culture*. Chicago: University of Chicago Press, 2003.

Tate, Claudia. "Freud and His 'Negro': Psychoanalysis as Ally and Enemy of African Americans." *Journal for the Psychoanalysis of Culture and Society* 1, no. 1 (Spring 1996): 53–62.

Tate, Claudia. *Psychoanalysis and Black Novels: Desire and the Protocols of Race*. New York: Oxford University Press, 1998.

Walker, Margaret. *Daemonic Genius, Richard Wright*. New York: Warner Books, 1988.

Wertham, Fredric. "An Unconscious Determinant in Native Son." *Journal of Clinical Psychopathology* 6, no. 1 (July 1944): 111–15.

Name Index

Subject Index